근대한국외교문서 편찬위원회 편

近代韓國外交文書

조영수호통상조약

제5권

2013년도
대한민국학술원 선정
우수학술도서
이 도서는 교육부의 지원으로
대한민국학술원에서 선정한
"2013년도 우수학술도서"임

동북아역사재단

근대한국외교문서 편찬위원회 편

近代韓國外交文書

조영수호통상조약

제5권

동북아역사재단

간행사

저희 동북아역사재단에서는 2009년에 발행한 두 권의 외교문서(제1권: 『제너럴 셔먼호 사건 · 병인양요』, 제2권: 『오페르트 사건 · 신미양요』)에 이어 이번에 세 권의 외교문서(제3권: 『조일수호조규』, 제4권: 『조미수호통상조약』, 제5권: 『조영수호통상조약』)를 추가로 출간하게 되었습니다.

한국의 외교문서 편찬은 정조 때의 『同文彙考』에서 그 연원을 찾을 수 있습니다. 『동문휘고』는 사대교린의 예(禮)규범과 관련된 문서를 엮은 것으로, 정조의 명으로 1788년에 초편 60책이 발간되었고, 순조 · 헌종 · 철종을 거쳐 1881(고종 18)년까지 증보를 거듭하였습니다. 이 『동문휘고』는 중화질서 권역에 속했던 중국이나 일본에서도 그 유례가 없는 선구적인 외교문서집이었지만, 개항 이후 공식 외교문서집 편찬은 불행히도 단절되고 말았습니다. 그렇기에 본 『근대한국외교문서』 편찬 사업은 정조가 이룩한 『동문휘고』의 역사적 위업을 계승하는 민족사적 의의를 갖는 일이라 할 수 있겠습니다.

외교문서집을 간행하는 목적이 이곳저곳에 흩어져 있는 사료를 단순히 한 곳으로 모아 엮어놓는 데에만 있는 것이 아님은 주지의 사실입니다. 외교문서는 정부 간 상호작용과 외교행위démarche의 기록물인 동시에 국가 구성원의 대외인식의 정신구조를 담고 있는 과거의 역사적 자료입니다. 또한 그것이 한 국가의 현재와 미래의 외교 구상과 외교정책 수행능력을 보여주는 지표가 되는 이상, 외교문서집 간행의 목적은 상당히 다양해질 수밖에 없습니다.

그간 근대한국 외교문서집의 부재로 말미암아 역사 연구, 그중에서도 특히 관계사나 외교사 연구 등에서 외국의 외교문서집에 주로 의존함으로써 근대한국 대외관계의 객관적 사실이라든지 대외인식의 실체를 바르게 파악 · 포착하지 못하는 등 문제가 적지 않았습니다. 『근대한국외교문서』 편찬의 주된 목적은 근대한국이 행했던 외교행위에 대한 주체적 관점에서의 분석은 물론 주요 열강들의 대(對)한국 정책을 다각도로 분석할 수 있는 외교문서를 집록하는 것에 있습니다. 한국이 주체가 되어 주요 외교적 사건의 시말(始末)을 파악할 수 있도록 관련 외교문서를 기사본말체(紀事本末體) 형식에 의거하여 배열한 것도 그 목적의 일환입니다.

이번에 발간하는 세 권의 외교문서집은 근대한국이 동아시아의 전통적 외교질서체제였던 '조공·책봉체제'로부터 서구의 '조약체제'로 이행하는 시기를 다룬 것으로, 근대 한중일 3국이 신구(新舊)의 국제질서체제 속에서 각기 어떠한 위치에서 어떻게 대응했으며, 또 그 대응방식에 의해 3국의 명운이 어떻게 갈라져 나아갔는가를 파악할 수 있게 해준다는 점에서 상당히 중요한 외교자료·사료가 될 것으로 확신합니다.

『근대한국외교문서』는 앞으로도 계속 간행돼 총 30여 권으로 편찬, 끝마무리되는 것으로 알고 있습니다. 하지만 저희 동북아역사재단의 여러 사정 상 이번에 간행되는 외교문서집 3권을 포함해 총 5권의 발행으로 부득이 중간마무리를 하게 돼서, 그 애틋한 마음은 이루다 표현하지 못할 정도입니다. 그러나 다행히도 이『근대한국외교문서』편찬사업이 2010년 하반기부터 한국연구재단 토대기초연구사업으로 선정되어 그 편찬을 지속할 수 있게 되어 한편으로 크게 안도하고 있습니다.

그간 어려운 형편 속에서도 『근대한국외교문서』 편찬사업을 묵묵히 수행해 주신 근대한국외교문서편찬위원 여러분들과 김용구 편찬위원장께 심심한 감사의 말씀을 드립니다. 앞서 간행된 두 권과 함께 이번에 새로이 간행되는 세 권의 『근대한국외교문서』 역시, 외교사 연구자뿐만이 아니라 일반 독자들에게도 한국근대사에 대한 이해와 인식의 폭을 넓히는 데에 작은 도움이 되었으면 하는 바람입니다.

2012년 12월

동북아역사재단 이사장 김 학 준

서문

　수호조약의 체결로 사대질서를 규정하는 회전(會典, 1690~1882)과 교린질서를 뒷받침하는 약조(約條, 15세기~1875)의 시대는 종언을 고한다. 이제 한국외교사의 흐름은 조약의 시대로 접어들게 되었다. 편무적(片務的)인 영사재판제도, 비유럽세계의 불완전한 법 주체성, 5% 전후의 저율 관세 제도, 그리고 아시아·아프리카 지역을 유럽 세계에 예속시킨 차관제도를 특징으로 하는 19세기적인 세계화 과정이 시작된 것이다. 조선(1876~1910), 중국(1842~1949), 그리고 일본(1856~1911)의 조약 시대는 모두 이런 특징으로 점철되었으나 조선의 경우는 장정(章程, 1882~1895)의 시대와 겹쳐 형극(荊棘)의 길을 걷게 된다. 유길준이 말하는 양절체제(兩截體制)가 이것이다.

　용어 문제를 잠시 살펴보기로 한다. 본 편찬위원회에서는 이번에 출간되는 문서집 3책의 부제를 "개국조약"이 아닌 "수호조약"이라고 명명하였다. '개국(開國)'이란 낱말은 19세기 중엽 일본 정부가 자신들의 대외관계를 선전하려는 정치적 표어였다. 이를 서양 학자들이 한반도에 빗대어 'Opening of Korea'라고 즐겨 사용하였으며, 1950년대 이후 국내 학계 일각에서 무심코 이를 답습하여 "개국조약"이라고 불러왔던 것이다. 그러나 Opening은 야만단계의 지역이 서양 세계와 조약을 체결하면서 문화의 단계로 나아가게 되었다는 어감을 함축하고 있다는 데 유념해야 한다. 그리고 서양 공법에서 말하는 "조약"이란 용어는 병인·신미양요 시기 조선의 관찬사서(官撰史書)에 등장하기 시작해 1876년 이후로는 보편화되었다.

　조일조약은 메이지유신 일본 정부의 새로운 조선 정책으로부터 그 체결 문제가 대두되었다. 이는 "만국공법에 입각해 조선과의 관계를 다시 수립해야" 서양 열강이 납득할 수 있다는 명분에 근거한 것이었다. 이로 인해 교린과 공법의 두 질서가 8년 동안이나 충돌한다. 개념으로서는 자주(自主)와 독립(獨立)의 대립이었다. 강화도 조약

제1조의 '조선은 자주지방(自主之邦)'이라는 규정이 이를 상징적으로 말해 준다. 그런데 자주는 사대교린 질서의 개념이었던 바, 이것이 조선이 제1조의 구절을 아무런 반대 없이 수락한 배경이 되었다. 메이지 정부는 만국공법의 명분 이외에 "조선을 일등하(一等下)"의 국가로 간주한다는 정책을 명백히 하였다. 19세기에 들어오면서 나타나기 시작한 그들 특유의 조선관(朝鮮觀)이 현실 정책으로 구체화된 것이다.

조미조약은 1880년을 기점으로 획기적으로 변화한 중국의 조선 정책의 산물이었다. 『조선책략』, 「주지조선외교의(主持朝鮮外交議)」, 「삼책(三策)」, 그리고 조선의 양무(洋務)를 북양대신과 도쿄의 중국 공관이 관장하는 제도 개편이 뒤따랐다. 사대질서의 '조공국'을 공법질서의 '속국'으로 전환하려는 정책이 채택되었던 것이다. 중국은 이 정책을 수행하기 위해 미국을 이용하였다. 한편, 미국 정부는 한반도 문제에 무관심하였기 때문에 몇 명의 정치인과 해군제독의 정치적 입장을 손쉽게 수락하였다. 예컨대 10%의 관세율, 아편 금지, 자동 조정(調停)의 규정을 흔쾌히 삽입했던 것이다. 그러나 이윽고 미국 정부는 곧 서울 정부에 등을 돌리고 말았으며, 이러한 대(對) 조선 태도는 1905년까지 계속되었다.

조영조약은 어떤 열강도 한반도 문제에 개입하지 않는 한 영국과 러시아 두 세계 국가는 조선 문제에 간여하지 않는다는 침묵의 균형이 깨짐과 동시에 성립하였다. 강화도에서 일본의 운요 호 침략이 자행되자, 영국 정부 일각에서는 거문도 점령을 거론했다. 또 '아마추어'적인 미국 정부가 조선과 관대한 성격의 조약을 체결하자 영국 정부는 이러한 사태변화를 좌시할 수 없었다. 이러한 배경 속에서 외교 전문가가 아닌 해군 제독을 파견해 조미조약의 내용을 모방한 제1차 조영조약을 체결했으나, 영국 정부가 이를 비준할 리 없었다. 반면에 조선에서는 개화파 인사들을 중심으로 도

교의 영국 공관을 통해 제1차 조영조약의 조속한 비준을 촉구했는데, 결국 영국 정부는 이를 빌미로 제2차 조영조약을 새로 체결함으로써 아편 및 관세 문제 등에 관한 그들 본래의 목적을 달성했던 것이다.

한 가지 애석한 점은 여러 행정적 이유로 말미암아 지난 수년간 작업해 온 조독(朝獨), 조불(朝佛), 조러(朝露)조약의 문서집이 이번에 함께 발간되지 못했다는 점이다. 이들 문서집은 추후에 별도로 발간할 예정이다.

우리의 『외교문서집』이 없다는 것은 세계 학계의 수준에서 보자면 실로 수치스러운 일이었다. 2007년 동북아역사재단 이사장 김용덕 교수의 지원은 이러한 난맥상을 바로잡는데 결정적 계기가 되었다. 동북아역사재단의 지속적 후원 하에서 본 편찬위원회에서는 지난 2009년에 『근대한국외교문서』 1, 2권(병인·신미양요)을 세상에 내어 놓은 바 있으며, 금년에 다시 『근대한국외교문서』 3, 4, 5권(수호조약) 3책을 발간하게 되었다. 김용덕 이사장의 퇴임 이후에도 본 편찬사업에 대한 동북아역사재단의 지원은 계속되었다. 정재정 전 이사장, 그리고 김학준 현 이사장의 아낌없는 지원과 본 편찬사업에 대해 보여준 학문적 관심에 감사하는 바이다. 오랜 기간 번다한 실무를 맡아준 역사연구실 연구위원 김민규 박사의 노고 또한 잊을 수 없다. 끝으로 매 격주 토요일마다 한림대학교 국제대학원대학교와 서울대학교 규장각에 모여 토론과 연구를 계속해 온 20여 명의 교수 및 석·박사 연구원들의 열정에 더 없는 고마움을 전한다.

2012년 12월

『近代韓國外交文書』 편찬위원장 김 용 구

편집방침

1. 본 문서집은 한반도의 역사적 현주소를 밝히는 데 중요하다고 판단한 좁은 의미와 넓은 의미의 국내외 외교문서를 망라해 수록하였다. 좁은 의미의 외교문서는 정부의 토의 문서와 훈령, 외무 담당자들의 교섭과정 문서 documents préaratoires, 그들의 왕복 문서, 본국정부에 발송한 보고문, 그리고 국제조약을 가리킨다. 그리고 넓은 의미의 외교문서는 이 밖에 교섭 담당자들의 회고록이나 문집을 비롯한 개인 문서를 포함한다.

2. 본 문서집의 편집은 주요 열강의 외교문서집 편찬 방식에 따랐다. 주요 국가들은 외교문서를 보관하는 특별 기관을 보유하고 있어서 이 기관의 문서들 중 대외관계에 중요하다고 판단되는 문서들을 기사본말체로 편집하고 있다.

3. '중요하다고 판단'하는 편집자들의 '인식'이 외교문서집 발간의 국제정치적 성격을 나타내 주고 있다. 대외관계 문서집의 효시인 19세기 각국의 칼라 북스 Color Books, 미국의 Foreign Relations of the United States를 비롯하여 제1차 세계대전 이후 발간되기 시작한 독일의 Grosse Politik der europäschen Kabinette 1871-1914, 소련의 Vneshnaya politika Rossii: XIX i nachala XX beka, 그리고 Dokumenty vneshnei politiki SSSR, 영국의 British Documents on the Origins of the War, 1898-1914(G. P. Gooch & H. Temperley eds.), Documents on British Foreign Policy, 1919-1939(R. Butler & E. L. Woodward eds.), British Documents on Foreign Affairs(K. Bourne & D. C. Watt, eds.), 프랑스의 Documents diplomatiques français 1871~1914, 일본의 『日本外交文書』들이 모두 이런 방식을 취하고 있다.

4. 이들 외교문서집은 자국의 문서보관소의 문서들을 선별하여 편집하고 있다. 이들 선별된 문서들과 이를 채록한 원문서와의 관계를 검증하는 작업은 특수 분야를 연구하는 전문 연구자들이 담당하고 있다. 외교문서 편집과는 차원이 다른 연구 분야이다. 그러나 본 문서집은 '한국'의 '문서'집이기에 조선 문서의 경우, 채록 문서와의 관계를 가능한 한 규명토록 노력하였다.

범례

1. 조선에서 사대질서의 '外交' 개념과 전혀 다른 diplomacy의 번역어로 '외교'란 낱말이 사용되기 시작한 것은 1880년 이후의 일이다. 따라서 1866년 병인양요와 1871년 신미양요의 대외문서를 '외교문서'라고 지칭하는 데에는 비역사적인 측면이 있다. 그러나 본 문서집은 1910년까지의 문서를 편집하는 사업으로 1880년 이전의 자료를 편의상 외교문서로 분류하였다.

2. 조선은 1895년에, 중국은 1912년에, 그리고 일본은 1872년에 양력을 채택하였으나 본 문서집에서는 그 이전의 음력을 모두 양력으로 환산해 적었다. 1917년 소련혁명 이전의 제정 러시아력(曆)도 양력으로 환산하였다. 19세기 제정 러시아력은 양력보다 12일이 앞서 있다. 이들 날짜를 모두 양력으로 환산시킨 것은 특히 아편전쟁 이후 한반도 문제를 포함한 세계의 모든 문제들이 세계외교사의 흐름과 연결되어 있기 때문이다. 다만 독자들이 동양 자료를 검색하는 데 도움을 주기 위해 중요한 날짜인 경우 음력을 병기하되 한자로 표기함으로써 양력 날짜와 구분하였다.

3. 중국과 일본의 인명, 지명은 모두 원음으로 표기하였다. 러시아어의 영문 알파벳 전자(轉字)는 *The Current Digest of Post-Soviet Press* 방법에 의거하였다. 한글 표기는 한국 교육인적자원부 편수자료를 따랐다.

4. 본 문서집은 연구자들에게 검색상의 편의를 제공하기 위해 문건 별로 문서의 내용에 관하여 간략한 정보를 표시하였다.

예

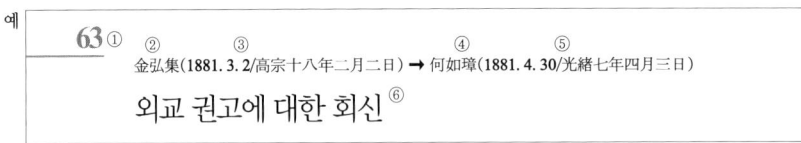

① 본 문서집이 부여한 고유의 문서번호이다.
② 문서의 발신인(기관)을 가리킨다. 문서의 수/발신인(기관)은 직함 등을 생략하고 인명만을 원어로 적는 것을 원칙으로 하였다. 인명을 특정하기 어려운 경우엔 문서에 나타나는 관직명만을 표기했다. 한편, 일본과 같이 일부 동일 인물의 성명 및 동일부서의 명칭이 시기별로 달라지는 경우에는 아래와 같은 원칙에 따라 표기하였다.
  • 대마번(對馬藩)의 경우 폐번치현(廢藩置縣)과 관련하여 공식적인 명칭이 수차례 변

경되었다. 관례적인 의미로 '對馬藩'으로 통일해 표기하였다.
- 宗義達과 같이 인명이 변경되었을 경우, 고친 이름[改名]을 기준으로 표기하되 기존의 이름을 괄호 내에 병기하였다.
  예) 宗重正(宗義達)
- 동일한 부서가 여러 가지 다른 이름으로 원문에 나타나는 경우 독자의 혼란을 피하기 위해서 단일한 명칭으로 통일하였다.
  예) 朝鮮事務辨理中, 朝鮮事務辨理御中, 朝鮮事務 → 朝鮮事務掛
③ 문서의 발신일을 가리킨다.
④ 문서의 수신인(기관)을 가리킨다.
⑤ 문서의 수신일을 가리킨다.
⑥ 본 문서집이 작성한 문서의 제목이다.

5. 문서의 수/발신일을 특정하기 어려운 교섭 담당자들의 회고록, 수기, 메모, 일기와 같은 사문서의 경우는 수/발신인 대신에 문서작성자의 이름을 표시했으며, 회담의 경우는 해당 회담의 기록자 이름을 표시하고, 제목에 회담 참석자를 나타냈다.

예)
238
趙寅熙(1876. 8. 5/高宗十三年六月十八日)
趙寅熙·宮本小一 회담(1)

6. 문건의 배열은 발신일을 기준으로 하였으나, 발신일을 확인할 수 없는 문건의 경우는 수신일에 의거하여 배열하였다. 어떤 문건의 발신일과 또 다른 문건의 수신일이 동일한 날짜에 겹치는 경우는 수신된 문서를 먼저 배열하였다. 문서에 발/수신일이 나타나지 않고 월(月)만이 표시된 경우는 그 내용을 분석한 후, 문맥상 다른 외교문서와의 전후 관계를 고려하여 발송되었다고 추정되는 날짜에 의거하여 배열하였다. 내용으로 선후관계를 추정하기 어려운 문서는 해당 월의 말미에 배열하였다.

7. 중요한 외교문서의 경우, 각 국가의 외교관들이 이를 자국 언어로 번역해서 본국에 보고하는 것이 일반적인 관례이다. 이와 같이 특정한 문서에 대해 여러 언어로 작성된 번역문이 존재할 경우, 본서에서는 이를 [英譯文], [漢譯文], [日譯文], [佛譯文]이라고 표시하여 해당 문서 다음에 첨부하였다. 특정한 외교 교섭에 관해 참석

자들이 서로 다른 언어로 기록한 문건 역시 번역문의 범주에 포함된다. 번역은 단순히 문자 기호 사이의 등가적 교환이 아니고 번역자의 특정한 정치적 의도나 작위가 개재되는 실천적 행위이다. 특히 외교문서와 같이 정치적 성격을 띠는 문서에 있어서는 번역 과정에서의 특정한 언어의 선택, 미묘한 어감의 차이, 오역의 발생 여부 등을 더욱 면밀하게 살펴볼 필요가 있다. 본서에서는 원문서와 번역문을 병행 수록함으로써 연구자들로 하여금 사건의 시말을 보다 다각적으로 파악하는데 도움을 주고자 하였다.

8. 독립된 외교문서로 간주하기에는 형식적, 내용적 측면에서 부족한 면이 있으나 특정한 외교문서의 작성과정이나 사후처리 과정을 이해하는데 도움이 되는 문서는 [관련문서]라고 표기하여 해당 외교문서의 뒤에 첨부하였다. 또한 회고록이나 수기, 대화기록, 광범위한 보고서 등 근대한국 외교사에서 중요한 사료적 가치를 가지는 자료들은 [관계자료]로 분류하여 각 권의 말미에 별도로 수록하였다.

9. 동일한 외교문서인 경우에도 이를 기록하고, 전달하고, 재수록하는 과정에서 일부 자형이 변경되거나 오탈자가 발생하는 경우가 있다. 이 경우 본 문서집에서는 각 국가의 공식 외교문서집에 수록된 문서를 기준으로 수록하였으며, 오탈자가 있다고 의심되는 경우에는 (Sic.)라고 표시하였다. 원문의 오탈자가 문맥상 다른 글자로 추정되는 경우, [ ] 안에 별도로 표시하였다. 각 국가의 공식 외교문서집 에 수록되지 않은 미간문서 가운데는 문서 자체의 훼손이 심하여 특정 글자나 단어를 판독하기 어려운 문서들이 존재한다. 이와 같은 미식별 문자의 경우 로마자는 [_____], 한자와 일본어는 O의 기호로 표시하였다.

영국 국립문서보관소(TNA) 문서군 목록

FO: Records created or inherited by the Foreign Office

FO 17: Foreign Office: Political and Other Departments: General Correspondence before 1906, China - FO 17/702, 720, 831, 857, 859, 900, 915

FO 27: Foreign Office and predecessor: Political and Other Departments: General Correspondence before 1906, France - FO 27/2162, 2163, 2164

FO 46: Foreign Office: Political and Other Departments: General Correspondence before 1906, Japan - FO 46/191, 195, 201, 202, 206, 207, 208, 231, 246, 256, 257, 258, 284, 285, 288, 290, 297

FO 64: Foreign Office and predecessor: Political and Other Departments: General Correspondence before 1906, Prussia (later German Empire) - FO 64/851

FO 94: Foreign Office and Foreign and Commonwealth Office: Ratifications of Treaties - FO 94/697

FO 363: Tenterden Papers - FO 363/1

FO 405: Foreign Office: China and Taiwan Confidential Print - FO 405/33, 34

FO 410: Foreign Office: Confidential Print Japan - FO 410/15

FO 881: Foreign Office: Confidential Print (Numerical Series) - FO 881/2700, 4521, 4595, 4695, 4718

FO 1080: Foreign Office: Chinese Secretary's Office, Embassy and Legation, Peking, China: Miscellanea - FO 1080/6, 190, 191

ADM: Records of the Admiralty, Naval Forces, Royal Marines, Coastguard, and related bodies

ADM 125: Admiralty: China Station: Correspondence - ADM 125/142

약어표

* 한글로 표기된 것은 한국 자료, 한자는 중국과 일본 자료, 로마자는 구미(歐美) 자료를 의미함.
* 자료의 나열은 한글 음 차례에 따름.

가오: 『嘉梧藁略』李裕元, 서울대학교 규장각한국학연구원 소장
고환당: 『古歡堂收艸』姜瑋, 서울대학교 규장각한국학연구원 소장
공거: 『公車文』편자 미상, 서울대학교 규장각한국학연구원 소장
구한국: 『舊韓國外交文書』고려대학교 아세아문제연구소 편, 22책(서울: 고려대학교 출판부, 1965~1973)
나암: 『羅巖隨錄』朴周大, 국사편찬위원회 편(서울: 국사편찬위원회, 1980)
대청: 『大淸欽使筆談錄』金宏集, 한국학중앙연구원 장서각 소장
동래계: 『東萊府啓錄』서울대학교 규장각한국학연구원, 한국학중앙연구원 장서각 소장
동문: 『同文彙考』국사편찬위원회 편, 4책(서울: 국사편찬위원회, 1970)
면암: 『勉菴集』崔益鉉(서울: 민족문화추진회, 1982)
미통: 『通商美國實記』서울대학교 규장각한국학연구원 소장
부록: 『修好條規附錄』서울대학교 규장각한국학연구원 소장
비변사: 『備邊司謄錄』국사편찬위원회 편, 251-265책(서울: 국사편찬위원회, 2010)
서계록: 『書契所報關錄』3책, 서울대학교 한국학연구원 소장
수신사: 『修信使記錄』국사편찬위원회 편(서울: 국사편찬위원회, 1958)
수호: 『修好條規』서울대학교 규장각한국학연구원 소장
실록: 『高宗實錄』3책(서울: 探究堂, 1970)
심행: 『沁行日記』申櫶, 2책, 고려대학교 한적자료실(상권)·국립중앙도서관(하권) 소장
영통: 『朝英通商條約』서울대학교 규장각한국학연구원 소장
왜사: 『倭使日記』서울대학교 규장각한국학연구원, 한국학중앙연구원 장서각 소장
용호: 『龍湖閒錄』宋近洙, 국사편찬위원회 편, 4책(서울: 국사편찬위원회, 1979)
운양: 『雲養集』金允植, 서울대학교 규장각한국학연구원 소장
윤치호: 『尹致昊日記』尹致昊, 국사편찬위원회 편, 6책(서울: 국사편찬위원회, 1973~76)
음청: 『陰晴史』金允植(『從政年表/陰晴史』, 국사편찬위원회 편, 서울: 국사편찬위원회, 1955)
일기: 『承政院日記(高宗朝)』국사편찬위원회 편, 15책(서울: 국사편찬위원회, 1967~1968)
일동: 『日東記游』金綺秀, 서울대학교 규장각한국학연구원 소장

일록: 『日省錄(高宗朝)』서울대학교 고전간행회 편(서울: 서울대학교 고전간행회, 1972)
자문: 『啓下咨文册』統理機務衙門, 서울대학교 규장각한국학연구원 소장
조미: 『朝美條約』서울대학교 규장각한국학연구원 소장
주연: 『珠淵集』한국학중앙연구원 장서각 소장
통상실기: 『美國通商實記』申櫶, 서울대학교 규장각한국학연구원 소장
환재: 『瓛齋集』朴珪壽, 서울대학교 중앙도서관 고문헌자료실 소장

東華: 『光緒朝東華錄』朱壽朋 編, 五冊(『東華錄·東華續錄』王先謙·朱壽朋 編, 上海: 上海古籍出版社, 2008)
李文: 『李文忠公全集』吳汝綸 編, 七冊(臺北: 文海出版社, 1962)
庸盦外: 『庸盦文外編』薛福成, 四卷四冊(1893) 서울대학교 중앙도서관 고문헌자료실 소장
輶軒: 『輶軒尪議』余乾耀(『近代中國史料叢刊續編』第百輯, 臺北: 文海出版社, 1983)
夷務始末: 『籌辦夷務始末』李書源 整理, 十冊(北京: 中華書局, 2008-11) [지금까지 학계에서 일반적으로 이용한 판본은 國風出版社 影印本, 七冊(臺北: 1963)으로, 본 문서집에서 인용한 판본은 영인본의 누락문서를 보완하고 문서 제목을 새로 추가한 것임.]
李鴻章: 『李鴻章全集』顧廷龍·戴逸 主編, 三十九冊(合肥: 安徽教育出版社, 2007)
中日: 『淸光緒中日交涉史料』故宮博物院文獻館 編, 二冊(臺北: 文海出版社, 1963)
中日戰: 『中日戰爭』中國史學會 主編, 七冊(新知識出版社, 1956) [『中日戰爭』戚其章 主編, 十二冊(臺北: 中華書局, 1889~1996)은 1956년 본에서 누락된 문서를 보완한 것임.]
中日韓: 『淸季中日韓關係史料』中央研究院近代史研究所 編, 十一冊(臺北: 近代史研究所, 1972)
中朝續編: 『淸代中朝關係檔案續編』中國第一歷史檔案館 編, 二冊(中國檔案出版社, 1998)
中朝滙編: 『淸代中朝關係檔案史料滙編』中國第一歷史檔案館 編, 二冊(北京: 國際文化出判公司, 1996/1998)
淸外: 『淸季外交史料』王彦威·王亮 輯編, 九冊(臺北: 文海出版社, 1964)
何如璋: 『何如璋集』吳振淸·吳裕賢 編校(天津: 天津人民出版社, 2010)
黃遵憲: 『黃遵憲全集』陳錚 編, 二冊(北京: 中華書局, 2005)

公文: 『公文錄』日本國立公文書館 所藏
陸奧文: 『陸奧宗光關係文書』陸奧宗光, 日本國會圖書館憲政資料室 所藏
別錄: 『公文別錄』日本國立公文書館 所藏
事務: 『朝鮮事務書』日本外務省外交史料館 所藏
森: 『森有禮文書』日本國會圖書館憲政資料室 所藏
三條家: 『三條家文書』日本國會圖書館憲政資料室 所藏
續通信: 『續通信全覽』通信全覽編集委員會 編, 五十四冊(東京: 雄松堂出版, 1983~1988)
雲揚記事: 『明八孟春・雲揚朝鮮廻航記事』日本防衛省防衛研究所 所藏
伊藤: 『伊藤博文文書』伊藤博文文書刊行會 編, 百二十七冊(ゆまに書房, 東京: 2007) [舊『秘書類纂』]
日外: 『日本外交文書(明治年間)』外務省, 七十三冊(東京: 外務省, 1933~1963)
日韓資料: 『日韓資料集成』金正明 編, 十冊(東京: 巖南堂書店, 1966)
雜纂: 『對韓政策關係雜纂』日本外務省外交史料館 所藏
朝鮮御用控: 『王政復古以來朝鮮御用筋相關ル候書付類控』국사편찬위원회 소장
條約類纂: 『韓國條約類纂』朝鮮統監府(東京: 統監府, 1908)
黑田: 『黑田清隆關係文書』黑田清隆, 日本國會圖書館憲政資料室 所藏

AADM: *Anglo-American Diplomatic Materials Relating to Korea, 1866~1886*, Park Il-Keun ed. (Seoul: Shinmundang, 1982)

ADPP: *American Diplomatic and Public Papers ; The United States and China*, Series II, *The United States, China, and Imperial Rivalries, 1861~1893*, Vol. 9~11, Davids, Jules, ed. 3 vols. (Wilmington, DE:Scholary Resources, 1979)

BDFA: *British Documents on Foreign Affairs*, K. Bourne & D. C. Watt, eds. Part I Series E Vol. 2; *Korea, Ryukyu Islands, and North-East Asia, 1875~1888* (Bethesda, MA: University Publication of America, 1989)

BFSA: *British and Foreign Papers*, Foreign Office/ Foreign and Commonwealth Office (London: H.M.S.O., 1814-1977)

FRUS: *Foreign Relations of the United States*, 1866~1882.

NARA I and II: National Archives and Records Administration Micro Films

RWS(국편): *Robert Wilson Shufeldt Papers*, 국사편찬위원회 소장

RWS: *Robert Wilson Shufeldt Papers*, Library of Congress, Washington DC

TNA: The National Archive(舊 Public Record Office)

편찬위원회 명단

편찬위원장 : 김용구 (한림대학교 한림과학원장)

편찬위원 :
김형종(서울대학교 동양사학과 교수)
김흥수(공군사관학교 인문철학부 교수)
신욱희(서울대학교 정치외교학부 교수)
우철구(영남대학교 정치외교학과 명예교수)
이근욱(서강대학교 정치외교학과 교수)
이상찬(서울대학교 국사학과 교수)
장인성(서울대학교 정치외교학부 교수)
최덕수(고려대학교 한국사학과 교수)
최희재(단국대학교 사학과 교수)

연구원 :
김종학(서울대학교 정치외교학부 박사과정 수료)
민회수(서울대학교 국사학과 박사과정 수료)
배민재(국사편찬위원회 사료연구위원)
이경미(서울대학교 정치외교학부 박사과정 수료)
이지영(서울대학교 동양사학과 박사과정 수료)
조병식(서울대학교 동양사학과 박사과정)
한보람(서울대학교 국사학과 박사과정 수료)
한승훈(고려대학교 한국사학과 박사과정 수료)
홍문기(서울대학교 국사학과 박사과정 수료)

연구조교 :
노진국(서강대학교 정치외교학과 석사과정)
송지예(서울대학교 정치외교학부 박사과정)
정민경(서강대학교 정치외교학부 석사)
정신혁(토론토대학교 역사학과 박사과정)
정연(서울대학교 정치외교학부 석사과정 수료)
조국(와세다대학교 대학원 문학연구과 박사과정)
조덕현(서울대학교 정치외교학부 석사과정 수료)
황수경(서울대학교 동양사학과 석사과정 수료)

차례

(1) 조약 체결 이전 영국의 조선 관련 보고

1. 조선에 파견할 일본군함의 동정 보고 2
2. 玄昔運・森山茂 교섭 결렬 보고 4
3. 조일 갈등과 러시아 개입 가능성 보고 6
4. 영국 선박의 난파 조선인 구출 보고 9
5. 木戸孝允의 조선정책 각서 보고 12
6. 조일 교섭 가능성과 黑田淸隆 조선 파견 계획 보고 15
7. 일본의 조선교섭 준비 보고 18
8. 黑田淸隆의 강화도 파견 및 러시아 개입 가능성 보고 23
9. 黑田淸隆 파견 관련 森山茂의 내방 및 회견 보고 35
10. 조일 교섭에 대한 주변국 반응 보고 39
11. 조일수호조규 체결을 알리는 鮫島尙信 등 메모 보고 40
12. 조일수호조규 영역본 보고 44
13. 강화도 협상 관련 森山茂와 회담 보고 49
14. 조일수호조규 분석 55
15. 프랑스의 협조 의사 보고 58
16. 독일의 협조 의사 보고 59
17. 조선 교섭 방식에 관한 전보 60
18. 조선의 배외정책 보고 및 교섭시 무력 동원 건의 61
19. 청국에 중개 요청 건의 63
20. 조선 교섭시 영·불·독의 연합함대 파견 건의 64
21. Parkes의 보고에 대한 프랑스 정부 입장 보고 68
22. 일본의 중개에 관한 寺島宗則와 회담 보고 70
23. 수신사 金綺秀의 동정 및 森山茂 회견 보고 72
24. 宮本小一의 조선 교섭 및 *Sylvia*의 조선 해안 탐사에 관한 보고 ... 78
25. 조선 연해 탐사에 대한 조선 정부의 태도 변화 보고 81
26. 일본의 중개에 관한 岩倉具視와 회견 보고 84
27. 서양선박 보호에 관한 宮本小一의 제안 보고 86
28. 조선의 배외주의와 수교 가능성에 관한 嚴倉와 회견 보고 92
29. 조선 교섭 연기 지령 95

30. *Barbara Taylor* 조난시 조선 정부의 원조 보고 97
31. E. Satow의 제주도 파견 보고 100
32. 관세 협상을 위한 花房義質의 조선 파견 보고 109
33. Satow가 지참한 감사 서한의 접수 거절 보고 114
34. Satow의 제주도 방문시 조선인의 우호적 태도 보고 116
35. 일본 정부 중개의 한계 보고 119
36. 개항장 추가를 위한 花房義質의 조선 파견 보고 122
37. Shufeldt의 조선행 관련 花房義質와 면담 내용 보고 125
38. Satow의 제주도 파견 경과 보고 126

(2) 제1차 조약 체결 과정

39. 조선과 서구 열강의 수교를 總署에 건의한 사실 보고 130
40. 井上馨와 회견 보고 (1) 133
41. 청-러 개전 가능성 및 일본, 조선의 동향 보고 135
42. 井上馨와 회견 보고 (2) 137
43. 청-러 개전 가능성 및 조선과 조약 체결 필요 상신 140
44. 李裕元-李鴻章 왕복 서한 및 조선관련 정보 보고 143
45. 조선의 개국 가능성 보고 156
46. 何如璋의 조약 체결 권고 보고 159
47. 러시아의 조선 영토 일부 점령가능성 보고 161
48. 조영조약 체결을 위한 청국의 중재 가능성 확인 지령 162
49. 조영조약 체결 시기에 관한 Memorandum 163
50. 러시아 동향 보고 166
51. 조약 체결에 대한 청국의 입장 확인 지시 167
52. 청국의 중개를 통한 교섭 추진 보고 168
53. Wade의 기밀보고서에 관한 Memorandum 170
54. Spence의 부산, 원산, 영흥만 조사 보고서 171
55. 러시아 함대의 원산항 점령 가능성 보고 203
56. 조사시찰단(朝士視察團) 일본 파견 및 何如璋 문서 보고 205

57. 조영조약 체결 관련 업무의 잠정 중단 보고 208
58. 러시아의 조선 점령 가능성 및 미국의 조선 교섭 계획 보고 210
59. Shufeldt의 교섭 시도 보고 211
60. 최혜국대우 균점(均霑)을 위한 교섭 권한 부여 214
61. Willes의 조선행을 지시한 외무부 전신 수령 215
62. 조선의 수입관세율 전망 보고 216
63. 조미조약 체결 이후 일본의 조선정책 전망 보고 218
64. 조선에 제시할 소개 서한 요청 220
65. 李鴻章의 일시 사직 보고 222
66. 조선 문제 관련 李鴻章 및 總署와 교섭 보고 224
67. Shufeldt의 청국 해군 임용 실패와 조미조약에 대한 청국 태도 보고 231
68. 조미수호통상조약안 분석 보고 233
69. 조미조약안의 조선 속방론 규정에 관한 보고 236
70. 베트남, 조선 문제에 관한 李鴻章과 회견 보고 238
71. 조미조약초안의 한문본 전달 및 馬建忠 접촉 지시 242
72. Willes 통역 지시 245
73. Willes에 앞서 조선에 갈 것을 지시 246
74. 조미 교섭에 관한 李鴻章, 總署 王大臣과 면담 보고 247
75. Willes의 芝罘 출항 보고 249
76. Maude의 조선행 보고 250
77. 조영조약에 조미조약 원용 건의 251
78. 馬建忠 · Willes 회담 252
79. 영국과 조약 체결 권고 253
80. 趙寧夏 · 金弘集 협상 전권 부여 254
81. 馬建忠 · 韓文奎 · 高永周 회담 255
82. 속방조회문(屬邦照會文) 257
83. 馬建忠 · 趙寧夏 회담 258
84. Dillon 영사 내방과 조불조약에 관한 의견 보고 260
85. Hughes 영사의 Shufeldt 면담 보고 266
86. 조영조약안 결정 경위 보고 269
87. 조영조약 외 추가 3개조의 성명을 요구하는 조회 270

88. 조영수호통상조약 체결 보고 272
89. 조선주재 외교관 임명에 관한 상신 280
90. 조미조약 한문 초안의 번역문 보고 281
91. Willes의 통역으로 Aston 파견 보고 289

(3) 제1차 조약 이후 청조(淸朝)의 대응

92. 조영조약의 체결을 알리는 자문(咨文) 292
93. 조영조약 체결 통보 293
94. 조영, 조독 조약 체결 전말 상주 294

(4) 제2차 조약 체결 과정

95. 1차 조영조약에 대한 비판 및 조선 영사관 설치 건의 298
96. 아산, 인천 등 서해안 개항장 후보지 조사 보고 302
97. 1차 조영조약 체결 과정에 관한 Maude Report 323
98. 1차 조영조약에 따른 일본의 조약개정 요구 보고 334
99. 조선의 개항과 수출입 현황에 관한 Spence Report 337
100. 영국 군함의 조선 해안 측량 보고 349
101. 조선의 국제적 지위에 관한 井上馨와 회견 보고 350
102. 조영조약 비준 요청에 대한 회신 353
103. Aston의 조선 개항장 조사 보고 354
104. 수신사 朴泳孝 일행 임무 보고 370
105. 金玉均과 면담 보고 371
106. 수신사 朴泳孝 일행의 내방 및 조선 정세 보고 374
107. Möllendorff의 외교고문 초빙 보고 375
108. 조청상민수륙무역장정 영역문 보고 379
109. 조러 육로교섭 보고 385
110. 조청상민수륙무역장정 체결에 따른 1차 조영조약 개정 건의 ... 386

111. 朴泳孝와 1차 조영조약 개정 협상 보고 391
112. 朴泳孝의 전권 소지여부에 관한 회신 398
113. 1차 조영조약에 대한 橫濱 상공회의소 의견 상신 399
114. 조일 관세율 협정에 관한 朴泳孝·井上馨의 회담 보고 404
115. 조약 개정에 관한 金玉均과 회담 보고 406
116. 1차 조영조약에 대한 上海 상공회의소 의견 상신 409
117. 1차 조영조약에 대한 香港 상공회의소 의견 상신 413
118. 조청상민수륙무역장정과 1차 조영조약 비교 424
119. 조영조약의 개정을 위해 독일과 공조 필요 상신 430
120. 조청상민수륙무역장정에 대한 미국의 견해 확인 431
121. 1차 조영조약에 대한 London 상공회의소 의견 상신 432
122. Aston의 조선행 보고 434
123. 김옥균 및 井上馨와 회담 보고 435
124. Aston의 조선행 승인 438
125. 조청상민수륙무역장정 이후 조선의 국제적 지위에 관한 보고 439
126. Aston의 조선행 및 지시내용 보고 441
127. Parkes 조회에 대한 회신 454
128. 조선 관세율에 관한 井上馨와 회견내용 통보 455
129. 1차 조영조약에 대한 香港 상공회의소 의견 상신 457
130. Willes의 지시에 따른 Moorhen과 Darling의 임무 교대 보고 469
131. 조선 광산 탐측 결과 보고 472
132. 조독조약 비준 연기를 알리는 Bismarck의 통지 보고 484
133. 공관부지 선정 및 공법 준수요청에 대한 회신 488
134. Darling 함장 Eliott의 해임 경위 보고 489
135. 조선의 조약 개정 의도와 정세에 관한 Aston 전보 보고 500
136. Aston의 조선행 및 지시내용에 관한 추가 보고 503
137. 독일과 영국의 조약 비준 연기 통보 506
138. Aston의 재파견을 알리는 조회 508
139. 1차 조영조약의 비준서 교환 연기를 통보하는 조회 509
140. 조선에서의 협상에 관한 Aston의 despatch 발송 510
141. 조선 정세에 관한 Aston의 Memorandum 발송 520

142. Aston의 영국공관, 영사관 부지 선정 보고 …………………………… 528
143. 조영, 조독조약 비준서 교환 연기 통보를 위한 Aston의 재파견 보고 ……… 536
144. Foote의 일본 도착 보고 ……………………………………………… 544
145. 상업 특권 양여에 대한 미국의 반대 보고 …………………………… 545
146. Foote와 회견 및 Foote의 조선행 보고 ……………………………… 546
147. 비준서 교환 연기 요청 수락 ………………………………………… 548
148. Aston과 협의한 3개조 조약안의 시행여부를 문의하는 조회 ………… 549
149. 조약 개정에 관한 李鴻章과 회견 내용 보고 ………………………… 551
150. 李鴻章 · Willes 회담 보고 …………………………………………… 554
151. 비준서 교환 연기협정 보고 (1) ……………………………………… 556
152. 비준서 교환 연기협정 보고 (2) ……………………………………… 560
153. 비준서 교환 연기협정 보고 (3) ……………………………………… 562
154. 비준서 교환 연기협정 보고 (4) ……………………………………… 563
155. 조선의 정세에 관한 Aston의 Memorandum 발송 ………………… 568
156. 조일무역규칙 초안 및 3개조 조약에 관한 Aston의 Memorandum 발송 … 574
157. 1차 조영조약 개정에 관한 의견 ……………………………………… 585
158. Parkes 서신에 대한 洪禹昌과 閔泳穆의 회신 보고 ………………… 593
159. 조약 개정 교섭시 해군 파견에 관한 훈령 …………………………… 596
160. 2차 조영조약 초안, 무역규칙안, 관세율안 보고 …………………… 597
161. 金玉均과 면담 보고 …………………………………………………… 625
162. Parkes에게 조약개정 전권 부여 후 조선 파견 예정 통보 …………… 629
163. Parkes 전권위임장 …………………………………………………… 631
164. 조선 개항장 현황 보고 ………………………………………………… 632
165. 아편 수입금지 조항에 대한 Granville경의 견해 문의 ………………… 633
166. Zappe의 조선 파견 통보 ……………………………………………… 635
167. 조선에 부임하는 Zappe 독일 공사와의 협조 지시 ………………… 636
168. 아편 수입금지 조항에 대한 Kimberley경의 견해 전달 ……………… 637
169. 아편 수입금지 조항 및 수정 조약안에 관한 훈령 …………………… 639
170. 조약 개정 협상을 위한 사전준비 및 전권 임명을 청하는 조회 ……… 641
171. 조약 개정 협상을 위한 조선행 보고 ………………………………… 644
172. 天津 조약에 준하는 전교, 내지여행권 명문화 요구 ………………… 649

173. 李鴻章 · Parkes 회담 650
174. 아편 수입금지 명문화를 촉구하는 청원 651
175. 조선 입국 보고 653
176. 조선 입국 직전 李鴻章과 회견 보고 656
177. 조선 입국 후 교섭경과 보고 661
178. 선교사들의 전교, 내지여행권 명문화 청원 665
179. 閔泳穆 전권위임장 667
180. Parkes와 협상에 관한 Foote의 자문 668
181. 관세협상 결과 671
182. Parkes와 협상 결렬 기록 672
183. 영사재판권 조항의 재고를 청하는 자문 673
184. 세칙(稅則) 관련 문제발생시 재협상을 확인하는 조회 674
185. 비준서 교환시 高宗의 조회에 대한 국서 교부를 청하는 조회 675
186. 보호선척장정(保護船隻章程) 발송 조회 676
187. 2차 조영조약 체결 보고 678
188. 2차 조영조약 관련 청국 · 일본 상공회의소에 보낼 서신 발송 679
189. 2차 조영조약 협상 전말 보고 682
190. 속방조회문에 대한 회답 국서 요청 보고 698
191. 조청무역에 비해 상대적 불이익 발생시 재협상 약속 보고 701

(5) 후속 조치 및 비준

192. 李鴻章과 회담 보고 704
193. Parkes와 회담 및 조영조약 관련 보고 711
194. 영사재판권의 조속한 시행 건의 712
195. 조선 총영사직 설치 건의 714
196. 高宗 알현시 교지(敎旨)와 답사(答辭) 보고 719
197. 2차 조영조약의 조항별 분석 보고 722
198. 청국의 종주권에 관한 陳樹棠 포고문 보고 738
199. 2차 조영조약문에 속방 관계조항 누락 보고 741

200. 조영조약문 내 속방 관계 명문화에 관한 조회 742
201. 회답 국서의 의장(意匠)에 관한 건의 744
202. 여왕의 비준서 및 국서 발송 예정 통보 745
203. 조청무역에서 관세율 특혜가 있을 경우 독일 정부의 방침 전달 746
204. Parkes의 비준서 교환 전권위임장 749
205. 영국 비준서 750
206. 조선 총영사 임명장 751
207. 조선 부영사 임명장 752
208. 2차 조영조약의 비준을 알리는 조회 753
209. 대원군 귀국설 및 조선의 비준서 교환 거부설 보고 754
210. 2차 조영조약의 비준 의사를 확인하는 조회 759
211. 조선의 비준 의지 보고 760
212. 영접관 파견을 알리는 조회 767
213. 내지여행권 조항에 관한 高宗과 Foote의 대화 768
214. Aston 일행 파견 통보 769
215. 비준 완료 보고 770
216. 2차 조영조약 비준서 교환 보고 771
217. 高宗 알현시 수행원 명단 773
218. 高宗 알현 일시 통보 774
219. 비준서 교환시 축사 775
220. 2차 조영조약 비준서 교환 통보 776

〖關係資料〗
1. 1차 조영수호통상조약 778
2. 2차 조영수호통상조약 789
3. Hertslet Memorandum(1882. 12. 19) 820

부록 문서 목록 845

(1) 조약 체결 이전 영국의 조선 관련 보고

1

H.S. Parkes (1875. 5. 25) ➜ Derby

조선에 파견할 일본군함의 동정 보고

No. 65

Yedo,
May 25, 1875

My Lord,

I have the honour to forward copy of a dispatch I addressed to Mr. Wade on the 22nd instant relative to the affairs of Corea, and in particular to the reported despatch of two Japanese gunboats to Corean waters.

I am assured by the Foreign Minister that this report is incorrect, and that the gunboats in question are only being sent to Tsushima for surveying purposes. Nothing definite appears to have yet resulted from the mission of Moriyama to Corea which I reported in my despatches No. 24 and 33 of February last, but the Government expect that he will shortly return and report his proceedings.

I have the honor to be, with the highest respect,
My Lord,
Your Lordship's most Obedient,
Humble Servant,
Harry S. Parkes

Inclosure 1

Yedo, May 22, 1875

Sir,

I have the honor to acknowledge the receipt of your despatch of the 17th ultimo enclosing two highly interesting Memoranda by Mr. Mayers relative to the political condition of Corea. It is owing to my absence from Yedo that I have not been able to tender you sooner my best thanks for these valuable papers.

The Envoy of the Japanese Government referred to in one of these papers returned to the Japanese settlement in Corea last February, and the Japanese Government entertain the hope that the deposition of the Regent will lead to the establishment of more favourable relations than those which have hitherto obtained between the two countries. The Japanese Ministers assure me that they have no idea of coercing Corea into more intimate relations and will be content if these should improve only very gradually; they also are that Japan assumes no position of superiority in her negotiations with Corea, and is quite prepared to treat with the latter as an equal.

At the same time I observe it stated in the local press that two Japanese gun vessels have recently been ordered to proceed to Corea, and report says that they are to go to the West Coast and to survey the approaches to the Capital. The Japanese Foreign Minister has stated to me that this report is incorrect, that the vessels in questions are being sent to cruize for surveying practice only, that they will confine their operations to the Island of Tsushima (which is in sight of Corea), and that they have not been authorized to cross to the Corean Coast. The event will show how far this plan of proceeding will be adhered to.

I leave &c,
(signed) Harry S. Parkes

玄昔運·森山茂 교섭 결렬 보고

Sir H.S. Parkes to the Earl of Derby (Received August 24)

(No. 91)

Yedo, July 17, 1875

My Lord,

I should inform your Lordship that it was reported, apparently upon good authority, on the 11th instant, that official intercourse between Japan and Corea had been broken off, and that the Japanese Envoy or Agent Moriyama and all the Government officials had left Corea on the 5th instant. The Japanese traders, it was added, remained at the Japanese settlement of Corea, but trade as well as foreign intercourse had been stopped.

I endeavoured to obtain some information from the Foreign Minister relative to this report on the 12th instant. He admitted that a difficulty had arisen between Moriyama and the Corean authorities on a point of dress, owing to the latter having refused to receive Moriyama in European costume. But it was not true, he said, that Moriyama had broken off relations or had left Corea; he had only dispatched Hirotsu, one of his officers, to Yedo with his report, and that officer had not yet arrived.

The Prime Minister, Sanjô Daijôdaijin, also stated to me on the 13th instant that Moriyama had not left Corea. The Foreign Minister repeated this to me on the 15th, and mentioned that Hirotsu had arrived in Yedo; but, he added, that he had not yet seen him, nor had he heard the character of his intelligence.

In the meantime the report referred to above found circulation in the native press in the form of a letter said to have been received from an officer of a Japanese ship-of-war, which was reported to have arrived at Nagasaki from Corea. The Government were much annoyed at the publication of this letter, and are said to have threatened the editors of three papers with prosecution for having published it. I inclose a translation of the letter in question, accompanied by the remarks of one of the offending papers after it had been warned by the

Government.

It is curious to note in the said letter a circumstantial account of the surveying operations said to have been carried on by a Japanese ship-of-war on the Corean coast. If this account be true, the said ship examined nearly the whole eastern coast line of Corea, together with the important northern harbour of Port Lazaret(*Sic*.). It also mentions the arrival of a second ship-of-war at Fusankai (Corea), and that she also had been engaged in surveying.

It will occur to your Lordship that I reported in my despatch No. 65 of the 25th May that I had asked the Foreign Minister whether it was the case that two Japanese ships-of-war were then being dispatched to Corea, and that he had assured me that this report was not true, and that the vessels in question were only being sent to the Japanese island of Tsusima in order to give the officers some practice in surveying. I also observed in my letter to Mr. Wade, which I inclosed in my despatch to your Lordship, that the Foreign Minister had added that these vessels had not been authorized to cross the Corean coast, but that the event would show whether these injunctions, if given, would be observed.

It is not impossible that the appearance of these ships in Corean waters, and their proceedings there, if these be of the kind named in the printed letter, may have had as much to do with bringing about the difference now reported as the question of dress. It is only as events gradually transpire that we shall probably learn the true bearings and extent of this difference; but the true belief among Japanese at present is that the course of negotiations between their country and Corea has been disturbed.

I have, &c

3

H.S. Parkes (1875. 7. 24) ➜ Derby (1875. 9. 5)

조일 갈등과 러시아 개입 가능성 보고

Sir H.S. Parkes to the Earl of Derby (Received September 5)

(No. 94 Confidential)

Yedo, July 24, 1875

My Lord,

In continuation of my despatches Nos. 91 and 92 (the latter of which was forwarded by English mail on the 21st instant), I should now add that I have ascertained from another conversation with the Japanese Foreign Minister, Terashima, that the Mission of Moriyama to Corea has been entirely unsuccessful. It was thought that he would gain access to higher authorities than those he had previously met, and that negotiations which would advance relations between Japan and Corea would be entered on. To promote this object, he was provided with a friendly letter from the Foreign Minister of Japan to the Government of Corea, and the delivery of this letter was to form the preliminary step in his proceedings.

After several months' detention, however, at the Japanese Settlement in Corea (Sorio), he has failed to effect even this primary object, in consequence of the Corean authorities having refused to meet him, or to receive the letter from his hands, if he visited them in European costume. The action of the Corean Government amounted, Terashima observed, to the rejection of intercourse with Japan. He could not yet say, however, what might be the consequence of such behaviour. Moriyama had not yet been withdrawn, and it was understood that the local Corean authorities of Fusankai had made further references to the capital (Seoul). But he admitted that Japanese gun-vessels were in the meantime employed in surveying the Corean coast, and he dropped the observation that their surveying operations had been very successful.

Another Japanese Minister observed to me, on the 22nd instant, that he considered the Corean question had assumed a serious appearance. He believed that Moriyama would shortly return to Japan, and that it would be difficult to avoid war with Corea.

I have heard other Japanese officers in high position make similar remarks, and one observed to me that, in determining upon the measures to be adopted against Corea, Japan must take into account the probable action of China and Russia. The position of the latter Power, however, did not appear to occasion the speaker any anxiety.

In reporting on this subject to Lord Granville, in my despatch No. 91 of the 3rd of November, 1873, I mentioned that Soyéshima, who had just resigned the portfolio of Foreign Affairs, had stated to me in positive language that Russia would be neutral in a war between Japan and Corea. In reply to the inquiry put by myself as to how this neutrality would be secured, Soyéshima replied, "By giving them Saghalin;" and, in answer to a further question whether such an offer had been made, he observed, "No, but I am sure it would be accepted."

Since then, the Japanese portion of Saghalin has been offered to and accepted by Russia, and it remains to be seen whether the chain of Kurile rocks, beset during the greater part of the year by ice, form the only consideration which Japan has received for this transfer. It may be supposed that the understanding upon which Soyéshima placed so much reliance in the autumn of 1873 admitted of confirmation or renewal in the spring of 1875.

It is unnecessary for me to observe that war between Japan and Corea would furnish Russia with an opportunity of prosecuting her own aims either on the Corean or the Chinese frontier, which it would be idle to suppose she would not take advantage of. The value to Russia of Port Lazaret (*Sic.*), in Broughton Bay (east coast of Corea, latitude 39′ 20″), which is free throughout the year from ice, and to which I referred in my despatch No. 92, is one of those points which naturally occur to the mind in this connection. When Vice-Admiral Shadwell visited the Russian Settlements of Possiette, Vladivostok, and Aniwa, in the autumn of 1873, he estimated the force then in garrison at those three places at 4,000 men, and the acquisition of the whole of Saghalin will naturally lead to the increase of this force.

In Japan I believe that public opinion will be in favour of a war with Corea, and it remains to be seen whether the Government will care to endeavour to stem this feeling. The affair of Formosa has given increased confidence to the country, and in particular to the soldiery, who do not trouble themselves about the cost of wars. Being assured probably of the neutrality or the support of Russia, and believing also that Corea cannot expect active aid from China, the Government of Japan may count upon encountering no interference from other Powers in a quarrel with Corea, and feel that they are able to cope with her alone.

Under these circumstances, I venture to submit that the attention of Her Majesty's Government should be directed to Corea, and that measures should be taken to prevent the possible operations of Japan or other Powers in these seas having the effect of securing to them exclusive advantages or acting prejudicially to British interests.

I have, &c.
(Signed) HARRY S. PARKES

H.S. Parkes (1875. 12. 6) ➜ Derby (1876. 1. 21)

영국 선박의 난파 조선인 구출 보고

No. 164

Nagasaki,
December 6, 1875

My Lord,

In a Despatch dated the 10th ultimo Mr. Consul Eusden has reported to me that the master of the British Barque "Ocean Vidal" when on a voyage from Shanghai to Hakodaté had picked up a Corean from a raft fifty-five miles off Quelpart Island, and on his arrival at Hakodaté had delivered him into Mr. Eusden's charge. As the man spoke only his own language it was difficult to obtain from him a clear account of his misfortunes, but as far as his story could be understood it appeared that he was driven out to sea while fishing off the Corean Coast, and when saved by the "Ocean Vidal" he had been ten days without food, and had eaten part of his clothes to satisfy the cravings of hunger. Having some knowledge of Chinese characters he was able to explain to a Chinese at Hakodaté that he is thirty-four years of age and has a wife and two children, but his interrogator could not understand to what part of Corea he belongs.

When the man was given over to Mr. Eusden he took him to the Japanese Authorities who were also unable to elicit any information from him beyond the obvious fact that he was a Corean. They declined to take charge of him, and begged that Mr. Eusden would do so because he had been brought to Hakodaté in a British vessel. Mr. Eusden, therefore, complied with this request, and he asked me to instruct him as to the course he should now take.

I have accordingly authorized Mr. Eusden to send the man to the Legation. His presence there may in the first instance prove of some service to Mr. Aston who is giving attention to the study of the Corean Language, and his restoration to his native country may be better arranged at Yedo than at any other place.

This, it appears to me, may be managed in two ways either by requesting the Japanese Government to return him to Corea through their agent at Sôriô (the Japanese settlement in Corea), or by ourselves taking measures for sending him to his country. The former is certainly the easier course of the two, but the latter would furnish an opportunity for making a friendly communication to the Corean Government in case Her Majesty's Government should deem it desirable to attempt to do so.

I am disposed, therefore, to retain the man at the Legation, if he should be willing to remain there for a few months, until I receive Your Lordship's instructions on the subject. If Your Lordship thinks it desirable that we should endeavour to restore the man ourselves, Admiral Ryder would probably not find it convenient to undertake this service before the return of fine weather in April or May.

In the event of it being decided that the latter course should be followed, it would probably not be difficult to give notice to the Corean Government through that of Japan of the object of the visit, and thus prevent that object being misunderstood. A similar communication might be also be made with advantage through the Government of China. We must not, however, shut our eyes to the fact that the character of the reception which would be given to the Coreans to any of our vessels visiting them even for this humane purpose is at least doubtful, and that if the reception should prove to be hostile, serious consequences, for which we should be prepared, would probably ensue.

If we attempt to return the man ourselves, I should think the proper point of delivery would be near the Capital where we are more likely to meet with responsible officers than anywhere on the coast. In case communications could be opened at that point, I would then suggest that the Corean Government should be informed that the survey of the channel between Fuelpart and the South Coast of Corea has become a necessity to foreign navigation, and that they should extend friendly treatment to, or at least should refrain from opposing, or obstructing, any vessels that may be employed on that service.

Judging from the experience gained by the recent visit of Her Majesty's surveying vessel "Sylvia", which I reported in my Dispatch No. 140 of October 11th, there are no grounds for hope that this survey could now be prosecuted without incurring collision with the Coreans. There in no doubt that the latter intended to attack the "Sylvia" as Corean officers have openly boasted to the Japanese Agent at Sôriô that they would have destroyed her if she had not retired, and that the force, which prematurely attacked the boats of that vessel had been collected for that purpose. It is noteworthy, as showing the treacherous character of the Coreans, that while these preparations for attacking the "Sylvia" were being made, the principal Corean authority of the locality visited Captain St. John on two successive days, spent several hours on board the "Sylvia" on each occasion, and partook freely of the hospitality which was offered him.

I would also submit that the same occasion should be taken advantage of to point out to the Corean Government the responsibility which devolves upon them of treating shipwrecked foreigners with due humanity. The Japanese have an understanding with the Coreans on this subject, under which the shipwrecked people of either nation are taken care of and restored by the Government of the country upon whose shores they may be thrown, and it would be as barbarous as it would be unreasonable for the Corean Government to refuse to make similar arrangements with other foreign governments.

I beg again to observe to your lordship that the considerable and increasing foreign traffic, which, as noticed in my Despatch No. 140, now passes the Corean Coast on its way between Japan and China, renders it necessary that some arrangements of this nature should, sooner or later, be arrive at with the Corean Government. I have therefore thought it my duty to report to Your Lordship the circumstances of this shipwrecked Corean having fallen into our hands in order that Your Lordship may judge whether it affords a suitable opportunity for attempting to open friendly communications with that country, although I am by no means sanguine that any well-meant effort on our part will be favourably responded to by the Corean Government.

I have the honor to be,
with the highest respect,
My Lord, Your Lordship's most Obedient,
Humble Servant,
Harry S Parkes

5

H.S. Parkes (1875. 12. 6) ➡ Derby (1876. 1. 21)

木戸孝允의 조선정책 각서 보고

Confidential
No. 165

Nagasaki,
December 6, 1875

I have the honor to forward translations of a memorial by the Councillor Kido Takayoshi on the subject of the relations of Japan with Corea, as I believe that this memorial has had weight with the Government, and that they are shaping their policy in accordance with its suggestions.

Kido thinks that the attack on the "Unyôkan" cannot be passed over, that Japanese forbearance in respect to Corea has reached its limits, and that it is useless for Japan to continue her long-protracted endeavours to bring the Coreans to reason by friendly persuasion. That which using this language, in deference perhaps to a feeling of resentment which is doubtless widely entertained in Japan against Corea, he counsels caution in the course to be adopted. China is first to be communicated with, and the nature of her relations with Corea to be ascertained beyond doubt. If Corea is claimed by China as a dependency, then satisfaction for the attack on the "Unyôkan" is to be asked from China, but if the latter admits that the Japanese are free to deal with Corea themselves, then a further attempt to adjust relations by means of direct negotiation with Corea should precede recourse to coercive measures, and even if war should be ultimately decided on, it need not be engaged in on the spur of the moment but only after the expense and the proposed operations have been well considered, and a favorable opportunity secured.

I notice that this policy is partially re-echoed in the enclosed article from the "Akebono Shimbun," a native newspaper which has hitherto been the loudest in its advocacy of war with Corea. This article observes that the lesson taught Japan by the Formosa affair should not be forgotten, and that a distinct understanding should be arrived at, in writing with China as to her relations with Corea before hostilities are engaged in.

With a view probably to obtain the desired explanations from China Mr.

Arinori Mori, the late Representative of Japan in the United States, has been appointed Envoy Extraordinary and Minister Plenipotentiary to China. He left Yedo for Peking at the close of last month, but I observed, when at Hiôgo on the 29th ultimo that the despatch-vessel in which he is travelling had been disabled by an accident, and his arrival at his destination may therefore be delayed.

Before leaving Yedo on the 12th ultimo I had an opportunity of conversing on the subject of Corea with Mr. Moriyama, the Japanese Agent, who had just returned. He considers that the Japanese Gov't have grave cause for complaint against Corea, not only for the attack on the "Unyôkan", but for the breach of the agreement made with him last year. Corea then undertook to enter into regular communication with Japan, and chose the first of the following three courses which had been proposed by Japan. 1stly to receive a letter from the foreign minister. 2ndly to receive a letter from the ex-prince of Tsushima, who is attached to the foreign office. 3rdly to send a Corean Mission to Japan. But when Moriyama presented himself in Corea last spring as bearer of the despatch from the Foreign Minister, the Corean authorities refused to receive it, because he would have appeared at the interview in a uniform of foreign fashion. This question of dress, he observed to me, was of course used as a mere pretext for not taking delivery of the despatch, and for avoiding fulfillment of the agreement as to the mode of conducting official communications in future.

Mr. Moriyama has been engaged for about seven years in fruitless endeavours to persuade the Coreans to adopt improved relations with Japan, and it is perhaps not surprising after the annoyance to which he has been subjected, that he should now urge his Government to adopt a more strenuous policy. He says that no one in Corea dare openly advocate the establishment of intercourse with the outer world. When it is forced upon them they will accept it—perhaps without much difficulty—but they will never grant it as a voluntary concession. He describes the government of the country as most despotic, and the condition of the people generally as very miserable and poor. Foreign Commerce, Mr. Moriyama observed, is essential not only to the improvement of Corea, but also to the maintenance of her integrity, and he assured me that the aim of his government was the establishment of commercial relations, not conquest, and that the maintenance of the interdependence of Corea was considered of the first importance to Japan. I have already reported to Your Lordship that the Vice Prime Minister, Iwakura, has made similar observations to me as to the desire of Japan to see Corea maintain her position as an independent state.

The present condition of affairs as between Japan and Corea suggests the ensuing whether the Powers who have large interests in China and Japan might not unite in an endeavour to persuade Corea to accept foreign intercourse. Her present anomalous position is one that cannot long be maintained, and she might be more inclined to listen to the advice, or remonstrances, of several powers, than to the demands of one alone. If left to herself, a collision with Japan, or possibly with some other foreign power to whom she may offer insult, or wrong, is only a question of time. The favorable opportunity for hostilities to which the Councillor Kido refers, may be brought about by the internal condition of Japan, or by any other accident. If the recent discussions between Her Majesty's Government and China had resulted in war, I do not doubt that Japan would have taken advantage of the opportunity to attack Corea, and the Russian Commandant at Possiette made to Captain Church, (whose report I forwarded to Your Lordship in my confidential despatch No. 147 of October 18th), the following observation: "what keeps us from going to Port Lazareff (in Corea) is our emperor's desire not to become bad friends with England." The reports both of Captain Coloumb and Captain Church show that the Russian settlements on the Manchurian coast are by no means permanently formed, and that removal to other points might at time be undertaken.

I have the honor to be,
with the highest respect, My Lord,
Your Lordship's most Obedient, Humble Servant,
Harry S Parkes

F. R. Plunkett (1875. 12. 9) ➡ Derby (1876. 1. 17)

조일 교섭 가능성과 黑田淸隆 조선 파견 계획 보고

Mr. Plunkett to the Earl of Derby.—(Received January 17, 1876)

(No. 167)

Yedo, December 9, 1875

My Lord,

I HAVE the honour to inform your Lordship that, having received a private note from Mr. Terashima stating that he wished to see me about some current business, I called at the Foreign Department at 2 o'clock this afternoon, accompanied by Mr. McClatchie.

Instead of entering on the business he had mentioned in his note, his Excellency at once began the conversation by stating that he wished to speak to me on a subject which he had frequently discussed with Sir Harry Parkes.

I was doubtless aware of the peculiar relations which have existed for the last three hundred years between Japan and Corea, and he need not allude to the accusations made by the public papers against Her Majesty's Minister of having encouraged the warlike aspirations of Japan in that quarter. These accusations were totally false, and the Government had at once published a formal denial of the charge. He merely now alluded to them as a preface to what he was going to say.

The position of the Japanese Settlement at Sorio was becoming untenable, the Coreans would not act up to the Convention concluded with Mr. Moriyama, and finally, the attack on the Imperial gun-boat "Unyokan" had exhausted the patience of the Japanese Government, and they felt the time was come when they must take steps to place their intercourse with Corea on a more satisfactory footing.

He, therefore, now wished to take the first opportunity of informing me, as Sir Harry Parkes was not within reach, that the Government had decided on sending a special High Commissioner to the capital of Corea, to propose the negotiation of a preliminary Treaty of Commerce and Navigation.

The person selected for this mission is Mr. Kuroda, one of the Cabinet Ministers and head of the Ministry of Colonization. He will set out in about ten days, and will be accompanied by several secretaries, and also by two or three men-of-war and a very small body of troops. This small force is in no way intended to act aggressively, but is only for his protection in case the Coreans should attack the Mission.

If the Corean Government receive Mr. Kuroda and accept his proposals, there need be no difficulty in the matter; but, should he meet with a hostile reception, it will be his duty simply to return and await the further instructions which may be given to him.

No special military arrangements are being made in view of this Mission, and the Government hope it will be found unnecessary to have recourse to strong measures.

I allowed Mr. Terashima to give me all the above details without once interrupting him; but, when he stopped, I told him that I had listened to all he said with the greatest interest, and thanked him for having given me such full details. That I was acting temporarily in the absence of Her Majesty's Minister, and that he must consider what I might say as having only an unofficial character; but, as he had been so frank with me, I begged leave to ask one or two questions. I begged him to inform me whether the Government had decided what should be done in case the Mission should meet with the hostile reception, which in point of fact it is quite sure to encounter, and, secondly, whether Japan had inquired how the two neighbouring Powers, China and Russia, would look upon a Japanese expedition to Corea.

In reply to the first question, Mr. Terashima declined to say more than that he trusted the Coreans would receive the Mission in a proper way. He continued at some length to argue that letters had at various times passed between the Corean Government and the Japanese; that their Mission was quite different from that of any other nation, for it only went to claim the fulfillment of promises already made. There ought, therefore, to be no reason why a Japanese Mission should not be admitted to King-hi-tao.

I saw there was no use asking anything more on this point, so I again inquired as to the attitude he expected would be assumed by Russia or China.

His Excellency disposed of China very briefly, maintaining that she had no right whatever to interfere as she had acknowledged a couple of years ago to Mr. Soyeshima at Peking that she had no desire to shield the Coreans.

Moreover, as a matter of fact, China had not interfered in any way when the French or Americans had made expeditions to Corea. He, therefore, considered that Japan had nothing to fear in that quarter.

With reference to Russia, his Excellency said that although no positive promise had passed, yet he had been informed by the Russian Minister here that Russia would not interfere in the matter.

I thought it right to press somewhat on this point, and finally, Mr. Terashima said: "if the Mission meet with opposition and war ensues, Russia would think it well."

Having seen in Mr. Doria's despatch No. 287 inclosed in your Lordship's despatch No. 99 of the 15th of October, that the Japanese had asked permission to land troops inside the Russian frontier for an attack on Corea, I inquired casually whether, in case hostilities should unfortunately break out, the Japanese troops would attack the capital itself, or go from Sorio, or from some of the harbours on the Russian frontier. He answered briefly, "to the capital direct, certainly not from the Russian frontier."

I had previously learnt that Mr. Kuro-ôka, an employé of the Japanese Naval Department, had lately proceeded to Vladivostock; I, therefore, took an opportunity to inquire what business had taken him there at this inclement season of the year. Mr. Terashima assured me that he was only charged with some naval matters of no interest.

I think it my duty to lose no time in bringing the above to your Lordship's notice, but as I have only a couple of hours to catch the first steamer leaving today for San Francisco, I trust you will be pleased favourably to excuse the hurried manner in which I have been obliged to recount the interview.

I think it right to add that I abstained throughout from expressing anything like approval, and confined myself to reminding his Excellency twice of the serious warnings which Sir Harry Parkes had already given in this matter to the Japanese Government.

I have, &c.
(In the absence of Sir H. Parkes),
(Signed) F. R. PLUNKETT

7

F.R. Plunkett (1875. 12. 13) ➡ Derby (1876. 1. 30)

일본의 조선교섭 준비 보고

Mr. Plunkett to the Earl of Derby.—(Received January 30 1876)

(No. 171)

Yedo, December 13, 1875

My Lord,

WITH reference to my despatch No. 167 of the 9th instant, I have the honour to lay before your Lordship a brief statement of the various events which have occurred in this capital during the last fortnight in connection with the Corean question.

Sir Harry Parkes has kept your Lordship fully informed of all the phases through which this question has passed since the year 1873. I need, therefore, only refer to his last despatch, No. 150 of the 26th of October, in which he reported that, in spite of the attack upon the gun vessel "Unyokan," the prevalence of Japanese opinion appeared then to be in favour of a peaceful policy; but that, whether it would so continue or not, would probably depend upon the news which might be subsequently received from Mr. Moriyama. He had also frequently informed your Lordship that the exigencies of their internal policy might, at any moment, force the Japanese Government to yield to a war cry.

Mr. Moriyama arrived in Yedo early in November.

The question whether an apology should be demanded for the attack on the "Unyokan" continued to be frequently discussed In the Japanese newspapers, but generally in a peaceful spirit; and there was nothing to indicate that a hostile expedition to Corea was imminent. On the contrary, the general impression was that the leaders, at least, of the Government and the majority of the people were adverse to extreme measures.

I inclose, as a fair example of the then prevailing tone, a translation of an interesting article taken from the "Nichi Nichi Shimbun" of November 24.

Sir Harry Parkes has explained, in his despatch No. 159 of the 23rd ultimo, the causes which were supposed to have led to the retirement of the Sa Daijin Shimadzu Saburô. It subsequently, however, appeared that, although obliged to succumb to his opponents in the Cabinet, his influence was still so great that it was deemed necessary not to break with him entirely, for, on the 25th ultimo, he was appointed to a high, but purely honorary post in the Emperor's household.

Since the date of the withdrawal of Shimadzu from the Cabinet, there have been a succession of disquieting rumours; whether by design or accident is not very certain, but the number of two-sworded men in the streets suddenly increased to a very remarkable extent; extra guards were placed round the residences of the Ministers; and a general apprehension existed, although scarcely avowed, that riots might at any moment be expected.

On the 27th ultimo, Mr. Moriyama paid me a friendly visit, and remained for a considerable time, during which the conversation naturally turned almost exclusively upon Corea. He spoke in enthusiastic terms of what could be done; of the riches of certain portions of Corea in rice, Indian corn, and minerals; of the facility with which a small body of troops could produce great results; and, finally, how, having devoted his life to the subject, he trusted yet to be the Perry of the Corean Peninsula. His tone was that of an enthusiast, and he declared openly his conviction that, except by force, nothing could be obtained. He added also, as his opinion, that the sooner force was employed the better it would be for Japan.

These, however, were only his own views; the Government, he said, was more inclined to temporize, and desired to avoid war as long as possible. He assured me that nothing was yet decided, and he laughed at the report then current in the Japanese papers that General Saigo was about to be despatched on a mission to Corea.

On the 2nd instant I had occasion to meet Mr. Sameshima, the Assistant Vice-Minister of Foreign Affairs, and inquired of him what news there was from Corea, and whether there was any truth in the report of disturbances having taken race, or being apprehended, in consequence of the late change in the Cabinet? He denied emphatically that there was any reason for fearing a disturbance of the public peace, and, with reference to Corea, said that there was nothing new.

Next day there appeared a paragraph in the "Choya Shimbun" giving as a rumour that one of the less prominent of the Cabinet Ministers had been selected to proceed on a special mission to the capital of Corea; and the "Nisshin Shinjishi" of the same date announced that Mr. Kuro-ôka, an official of the Marine Department, had been sent to Vladivostok on Government business.

On the 4th instant the "Nichi Nichi Shimbun" announced the approaching departure of Mr. Hirotsu, who had served for some years at Sorio as second in rank to Mr. Moriyama, and that about the 15th instant a certain personage would proceed to Corea, accompanied by some troops.

On the 6th the "Stochi Shimbun" announced that Mr. Kuroda was the Cabinet Minister who had been selected for the mission, and that Mr. Hirotsu had left Yedo already.

It is believed that the latter gentleman has been sent to prepare the way for Mr. Kuroda, by requesting the officials of Fusankai to inform the Central Government that a Japanese Special Envoy will shortly appear in the capital. It is hoped that this may conciliate them, and induce them to receive the mission properly.

In view of these reports, I thought it my duty, on the 6th instant, to endeavour to ascertain whether what had often been predicted by Her Majesty's Minister had already come to pass, viz., that the Government, finding themselves threatened with internal troubles, had accepted a foreign war as an outlet for the unruly passions of their Southern subjects.

I accordingly called on Mr. Sameshima, and sent Mr. M'Clatchie to Mr. Moriyama, but, unfortunately, neither of these gentlemen were at home; and one of the foreign Representatives on whom I called expressed his decided opinion that there was no cause for apprehension, as the Government were strong enough to resist the pressure put upon them by the war party. He had seen Mr. Sameshima and the Minister of Marine that very morning, and had been told there was nothing new.

On the 7th instant, Mr. Mori Arinori, the new Japanese Minister at Peking, who had left Yedo for China on the 24th ultimo, and then suddenly returned to this capital on the excuse of his steamer having broken down in the Inland Sea, left equally suddenly for the South in a small steamer belonging to the Yokohama Custom-house.

His proceedings have been much commented on, for it was generally believed that he had only accepted the appointment to Peking in view of the negotiations which would ensue with China on the Corean question.

On the same afternoon I received a private note from Mr. Terashima, asking me to call at the Foreign Department, as he wished to speak about procedure in Courts of Appeal, a question which Sir Harry Parkes had desired me to attend to during his temporary absence from Yedo.

I accordingly called on his Excellency at the appointed hour, when he made me the communication I had the honour to report to your Lordship in my despatch No. 167 of the 9th instant.

Mr. Moriyama was on this day promoted to be a Shôjô of Foreign Affairs.

Next morning (the 10th) I received, quite unexpectedly, a visit from Mr. Soyeshima (Mr. TerashiMa's predecessor in office), with whom I was not acquainted, and who, finding Her Majesty's Minister was away, requested to see me.

After a very few complimentary phrases, the conversation turned on the approaching mission of Mr. Kuroda.

Mr. SoyeshiMa's proclivities in favour of a Corean war are well known, and have been more especially reported in Sir H. Parkes's No. 91 of the 3rd November, 1873.

It was at that period that the present Cabinet was consolidated, and Mr. Soyeshima and the rest of the war party had to yield to the more peaceful policy of Messrs. Sanjo and Iwakura.

On this occasion Mr. Soyeshima went almost word for word over the same ground, and used the same arguments as he did to Her Majesty's Minister in 1873. Two year's reflection would not appear to have moderated his views to any appreciable extent.

He maintained that Japan was now well prepared for an attack on Corea, as she had about 40,000 men drilled and armed on the latest European principles, and behind this force were all the Samurai class, accustomed to arms, and thirsting only for the fray. He himself, he said, had begged to be allowed to join the expedition, and there were thousands of others ready to proceed at a moment's notice.

I ventured to inquire whether ha had not somewhat exaggerated the number of drilled troops at the disposal of the Government, and also asked whether he considered it would be quite wise to send all those troops, on which the Government is supposed to be able to count, out of the country at a moment when there was said to be a considerable fermentation going on within it.

Mr. Soyeshima would not for a moment allow that any inconvenience possibly could arise. The nation wanted war, and if it got it in Corea the whole population would be satisfied. Money which was now hoarded would flow in from all sides, and the Government need have no fear whatever of internal disturbances.

As to Russia she would secretly approve and would watch events, ready to take advantage of any opportunity which might arise. He did not think Japan had much to fear from Russia, even if she did, perhaps, secure some harbour for herself further south than Possiette. Mr. Soyeshima went on to explain that, in his opinion, the best thing for Japan would be to occupy and annex the large Island of Quelpart, and also to land troops on the Island of Kôkwa, at the mouth of the Seoul River. Any force on this island would effectually blockade the Corean capital, and by preventing the approach of junks stop the supply of rice for its inhabitants.

The capital being surrounded by mountains is usually provisioned entirely by the river, and any lengthy stoppage of the traffic on it must, according to him, infallibly bring the Corean Government to reason.

As I had already done in my interview with Mr. Terashima, I carefully abstained from expressing any approval, and I allowed Mr. Soyeshima to talk on as long as he was inclined.

On the 12th instant a Proclamation was published announcing that Mr. Kuroda was about to be despatched to Corea as Special and Plenipotentiary High Commissioner, and the "Stochi Shimbun" announced that the mission will sail about the 18th or 19th instant.

I have the honour to inclose, for your Lordship's information, translations of the various articles to which I have made reference.

Since the Mission has been decided on, the Japanese papers have not ventured to express any very decided opinion; but it would seem from the two extracts of the papers of the 12th that the public qutie see the gravity of the position, and understand that, whatever hopes the Government may profess to entertain of a peaceful solution, the despatch of a High Commissioner, with three men-of-war and a considerable body of troops, to a country where they are sure not to be received, can only be prelude to actual hostilities.

I have, &c.
(In the absence of Sir H. Parkes),
(Signed) F. R. PLUNKETT

H.S. Parkes (1875. 12. 31) ➜ Derby (1876. 2. 12)

黑田淸隆의 강화도 파견 및 러시아 개입 가능성 보고

Sir H.S. Parkes to The Earl of Derby.—(Received February 12, 1876)

(No. 182 Confidential)

Yedo, December 31, 1875

My Lord,

MR. PLUNKETT'S despatches Nos. 167 and 171 of the 9th and 13th instant will have informed your Lordship of the determination taken by the Japanese Government to deal with the Corean question by dispatching to that country a High Commissioner and Special Envoy charged with the negotiation of a Treaty of Commerce, and supported by considerable naval and military force.

In my last despatch to your Lordship on this subject (No. 165 of the 6th instant) I observed that action of this nature had been advocated in the Cabinet; that I believed the Japanese Government contemplated the possibility of having Soon to engage in hostilities with Corea, and that such an issue might, at any time, be occasioned either by the internal condition of Japan or by the casual occurrence of circumstances which might seem to favour such a movement.

It can scarcely be doubted that the resolution to send a High Commissioner to Corea, which appears to have been taken about the time I wrote that despatch, is eminently calculated to bring about such an issue, and, therefore, unless the Coreans should act towards this Mission in a manner very different to that which may be expected of them, I look upon a collision between the two countries as imminent.

Since my return to Yedo on the 22nd instant I have endeavoured to learn why the Japanese Government adopted this step at the present time, and how far the execution of their plans had advanced.

The Foreign Minister stated to me on the 24th instant that, having once taken the determination to send a High Commissioner to Corea, the Government thought it desirable to carry it out promptly. Such a mission was judged necessary because events had shown how hopeless it was to attempt to treat with the local Corean officials at Fusankai, and the relations of Japan with Corea could no longer remain on their present unsatisfactory footing. In order to effect the necessary changes, certain essential conditions would be required at once, while others might be obtained gradually. Those which would at once be demanded from the Coreans were:—

Firstly, the opening of one or more Corean ports, to which the Japanese should be admitted to trade freely.

Secondly, proper provision for the treatment of shipwrecked Japanese, and for the relief of Japanese vessels requiring shelter from stress of weather.

Thirdly, a satisfactory explanation of the attack upon the "Unyokan," and an assurance that the Japanese flag should not again be exposed to similar outrage.

The Japanese Government had, at one time, supposed that the first and second conditions might have been obtained by means of the arrangement made by the Japanese Agent Moriyama with the local Corean officials last year. The Coreans then agreed to receive a letter from the Japanese Government, and to dispatch an Envoy in return to Yedo. But when Moriyama returned with the letter this year they refused to receive him. The trifling traffic now carried on bu the Japanese at Sôriô could not be called trade. The Japanese admitted to that settlement were supposed to belong to the Island of Tsushima only, and they could only buy and sell such commodities as the Corean officer in the settlement chose to permit.

Shipwrecked Japanese were not properly treated by the Coreans, nor were Corean cast-a-ways received from the Japanese in a becoming manner; and the firing on the "Unyokan" proved that Japanese vessels might be attacked if they approached the Corean shores. If the Corean Government refused to concede these three points when demanded by the High Commissioner, the refusal would be regarded as a rupture of relations. In that event, or if the High Commissioner were not received, or encountered insult or attack, he would have to return and leave it to the Government to take the course they would then be compelled to adopt. But, considering the moderate nature of the Japanese demands, he (Terashima) did not see why negotiations should not be successful. Every allowance would be made for the prejudices of the Coreans, and only such an amount of intercourse, whether official or commercial would be asked for as the Coreans in their present condition could grant. The Japanese

Government were quite willing to reserve for a later period the question of whether a resident Minister should be sent to Corea. The force sent with the High Commissioner was only intended for his protection.

In reply to my inquiry as to when Kuroda, the High Commissioner, would be despatched, Mr. Terashima stated that the precise time was uncertain. It had been suggested that the navigation of the river leading to the Corean capital might be impeded at this season by ice. That contingency had not been thought of when it was proposed that he should leave on the 25th instant.

In discussing the subject the same day with another Japanese Minister, he observed that the Coreans would be fully informed of the approach of Kuroda, and of the objects of his mission. Mr. Hirotsu, the officer who had been sent to Sôriô to give them notice, had already arrived there. The announcement which he would make to the local Corean officials at Fusankai could be forwarded by them to the Government at the capital by the 25th instant. Mr. Kuroda would not arrive off the river leading to the capital before the 20th of January, and thus the Corean Government would receive nearly a month's notice of his arrival. He would endeavour to obtain, by friendly negotiation, the right of trade, protection to navigation, and an explanation of the attack on the flag. The latter point would be easily adjusted if the two former were conceded, but, if they were refused, then Japan would be at liberty to treat the firing on the "Unyôkan" as a hostile act, and to exact signal reparation. The possibility of the Coreans refusing to treat was more readily allowed by this Minister than by Mr. Terashima; and, in order to meet the contingencies of war, the Government, he said, were preparing a force of 12,000 men. The consequences might be serious, but, if the Government had not taken up the question at this time, naive agitators would have made much of the subject, and, at a later date, might have forced the hand of the Government, and obliged them to act with less caution and moderation.

The Government were trying to control and guide the popular feeling on the subject, and, in taking it up at this time, were not actuated solely by a desire to divert attention from home topics, such as the much agitated question of the pensions of the Samurai, or taxation and popular representation.

I afterwards saw the Prime Minister, who observed to me that the Government had resolved to close with the Corean question, because they thought that it could not longer be deferred. Some arrangement of the long-standing differences between the two countries had become necessary. This arrangement might be effected by peaceable means, but he was alive to the consideration that the Japanese overtures might be rejected by the Coreans; and, in that case, collision would prove unavoidable.

From the Vice-Prime Minister I obtained more important information than that supplied me by the previous informants. He visited me on the 25th instant, and commenced his observations on the subject by impressing on me the peaceable objects of the Government.

In order, however, to satisfy their own people, it was necessary, he said, that something should now be done to secure for Japan an improved condition in Corea. Sôriô, their present settlement, was little better than a prison, and they, therefore, wanted to obtain a port where trade might be conducted in a reasonable manner. Considering what the state of Japan was twenty years ago, he could not loudly complain of Corea being now in a similar condition. He was also mindful of the opinion which I had frequently expressed, and in which he entirely concurred, that the independence of corea was of the first importance to Japan. He considered it essential to the security of Japan that Corea should remain interposed between Japan and Russia. Being impressed with this feeling, the Government would do all in their power to compose their differences with Corea without coming to an open breach with that country.

I observed that I did not for a moment question the peaceable objects of the Government, but felt, as he probably did, that the measures they were now taking entailed the risk of hostilities. He had, doubtless, therefore, well weighed all the contingencies that would arise from war, and among these the danger to the independence of Corea, upon which he set so jest a value. No one, I was, aware, had given greater attention to the subject than his Excellency, and he had, of course, considered the steps which Russia was likely to take in the event of war; probably he had already fully discussed the question with the Russian Minister.

He replied that he had not done so, though, as the conversation proceeded, I elicited from his Excellency that discussion had taken place between the Russian Minister and the Japanese Foreign Office, and that the result arrived at was that Russia approved of Japan engaging in war with Corea, and had promised to come to the assistance of Japan if she needed help. In giving me this information his Excellency urged me to treat it with the strictest confidence.

I observed that he was, of course, prepared to find that Russia would help herself at the same time that she helped Japan. This he admitted was a natural consequence, but he hoped that danger might be avoided by the understanding that Russia was not to intervene until desired to do so by Japan.

His Excellency had thus in the same breath dwelt upon the importance to Japan of the independence of Corea, and had then admitted that his Government had become a party to a scheme which is eminently calculated to destroy that independence.

The disclosure is so important that I cannot altogether attribute it to an unintentional admission made in the course of conversation, or to the confidence resulting from our long acquaintance, or the many and intimate conversations we have held with each other on the Corean subject. I therefore think that it may have occurred to him that the best way of preventing Russia deriving more advantage than is desirable from her proposed co-operation with Japan would be to endeavour to impose a check upon her action through the medium of another Power.

The danger of a combination in which Russia would be the only Power allied with Japan against Corea is too great to be overrated. It would afford her an opportunity of repeating the policy which she played so successfully when the Allied Powers were before Peking in 1860. She then extended her coast line on the Pacific from latitude 52° to latitude 42°; but the southernmost ports which she thus acquired—Vladivostok and Possiette—are obstructed by ice in several of the winter months, and it is significant how little she has done to construct at either of those ports establishments or defences of a permanent character. The two principal ports on the eastern coast of Corea are Port Lazareff, in latitude 39° 20′, and Fusankai (Chosan Harbour of our charts), in latitude 35°. I am not aware whether the former port is free from ice throughout the year, although I may mention that a Russian officer lately stated at Yokohama that the Russian Government are in the habit of sending a vessel of war to winter there. The Harbour of Fusankai is, however, of far higher importance than Port Lazareff; it is very safe and capacious, may be easily defended, and commands the China, Japan, and Yellow Seas, It is within sight of Tsushima, from which island, as your Lordship is aware, the Russians were dislodged by Admiral Sir James Hope in 1861. It is within two days' sail of Shanghae and the Yangtse River, and within twelve hours sail of the western entrance of the inland sea of Japan, through which all traffic between China and Japan passes. If Russia, therefore, were to obtain possession of Fusankai, or any other equally commanding position in the south of Corea, she would be able to control, whenever she wished to do so, the whole foreign trade of China and Japan. Both port Lazareff and Fusankai could be occupied and held with the utmost ease, as against the Coreans, by the force which Russia now has in Eastern Siberia and Saghalin. This occupation might be effected before any other European nation became aware of the fact, as our men-of-war seldom cruise on the Corean coast.

Although these considerations naturally occurred to me when the Vice Prime Minister informed me of the secret understanding arrved at between Japan and Russia, I had no opportunity of observing how far they were present to his mind, as, after making the above disclosure, he seemed anxious to avoid further conversation on the subject, and took his leave. But at a second interview which I had with him on the 29th instant, he allowed me to return to the topic, and on my observing that I thought it very undesirable that a third Power should become mixed up in the questions now arising between Japan and Corea, his Excellency volunteered the remark that he was aware that Russia wished to take part in those questions, and that he also knew that she was not satisfied with Possiette and Vladibostok, and would like to acquire some other better situated port.

It is evident, therefore, that his Excellency is aware that Russian aid is not to be obtained without compensation. That the Japanese have considered this point is evident from the remark made by Mr. Soyejima to Mr. Plunkett, as reported by the latter to your Lordship in his despatch No. 171. Russia, he said, would watch events, ready to take advantage of any opportunities which might arise, but he did not think that Japan had much to fear from Russia, even if she did secure some harbour for herself further south than Possiette.

As far as is yet known, Port Lazareff and Fusankai are the only good harbours on the east coast of Corea, and perhaps Mr. Soyeshima, or the Japanese Government, may think that the former of these would satisfy the Russians. It is so freatly inferior, however, in point of position to Fusankai, that I question whether they would be content with it.

In this second conversation the Vice Prime Minister observed that if hostilities should break out with Corea Japan must guard against complications with Russia, should break out with Corea Japan must guard against complications with Russia, by taking care that the war should prove short and decisive. But, looking to the stubborn character of the Coreans, I doubt very much whether the Japanese will find it easy to make a short and decisive war.

Russia, on the other hand, will certainly know how to play her game as well as Japan, and is not likely to lose an opportunity which she has been looking forward to for years, of completing the advance which she made in 1860 by acquiring a position whence she could control, in the event of war, the foreign trade of China and Japan.

I think it is now easy to see, my Lord, that the understanding which has been effected between Russia and Japan on the Corean question has not been suddenly formed. My despatches Nos. 92, 94, and 105 will have shown that I strongly suspected the existence of such an understanding as early as last July. If I did not now know from Vice Prime Minister that it is an accomplished fact, the information contained in Mr. Doria's despatch of September the 22nd to your Lordship, which you forwarded to me in despatch No. 99, would go far to confirm that suspicion.

A great deal must have been said at St. Petersburgh on the subject before the Japanese would think of proposing to land troops in a Russian port to attack Corea. I venture to doubt whether they ever made such a proposal, for no movement could be less profitable in a military point of view. It would be like attempting to attack Berlin by way of Archangel. A Japanese force operating from Possiette would first have to make a sea voyage of upwards of 1,000 miles, presuming Yedo to be the point of departure, and would then have to undertake a difficult march of more than 200 miles through a mountainous part of Corea before it could reach a point where it could strike an effective blow; whereas the same force might be thrown directly, and with far greater ease, upon several vulnerable and important points on the Corean coast, say, for instance, Fusankai, which is within forty-five miles fo Tsushima, or it might be sent round to Kôkwa on the west coast, and landed in the immediate neighbourhood of the capital.

The mention, however, of such a proposal as that of landing troops in one of Russian Siberian ports shows that the Corean question was discussed at St. Petersburgh, and in connection, as I think, with the transfer of Saghalin and the Kuriles. The Japanese would have made bot an indifferent bargain if they only obtained a chain of rocks in a frozen sea in exchange for the more valuable territory which they surrendered in Saghalin; and it is now evident that they secured, in addition, the approval of Russia to a war with Corea, and the promise of assistance in that war if help were needed.

Russia, it may be concluded, will take care that her shall be needed.

If hostilities occur, the Japanese will probably endeavour to capture Kôkwa (or Kwang-Kwa in Chinese), the city which the French took in 1866. It is situated on capital, which is about twenty miles distant. But I doubt whether this movement and the blockade of the capital would have the effect, as Mr. Soyeshima told Mr. Plunkett it would, of bringing the Corean Government to reason. I learn from an Englishman, who once took a British ship up to Kôkwa, that the capital is not dependant on the sea for supplies, and that the junk trade on the river is not large. From Kôkwa, as their base, the Japanese could attack the capital, Séoul; but, even if they succeeded in capturing it, that success might not prove conclusive if the King and the Court were to escape into the interior. I find that well-informed Japanese are of opinion that the Coreans, if driven out of Séoul, would probably retire upon Ping-Yang, a city to the north of the capital, and from that again to a third city in the same direction. The tide of the struggle would, therefore, set towards the north, and this, if it became protracted, would cause commotion in the direction of the Russian frontier. Russia would then have as good a reason for occupying the eastern provinces of Corea as she now has for occupying the Chinese Province of Ili, and might, therefore, take such a step on this ground independently of her promise to assist Japan.

The latter would, doubtless, be deeply chagrined to see Russia's assistance take the form of the occupation of Fusankai, or any other point of similar importance in Corea. Her chief inducement in seeking that assistance, if indeed, it were sought by her in the first instance, and not offered by Russia, was, I believe, to use the latter Power as a shield against China. Resenting, as China does, the part taken by Japan in the Formosa question, it is not likely that she should entertain at the present moment any good will for Japan, and, in the event of war, her sympathies would naturally be with Corea, which still pays her some of the outward homage of a tributary State. It would not be strange if China should give Corea more than moral support, or that the history of the last Japanese invasion should be repeated. China then sent a considerable army to the assistance of Corea, and by means of this assistance the Japanese invaders were driven from the country. If Russia should prevent China from giving active support to Corea in the present instance, she would certainly render Japan material service, and would establish a claim to the territorial compensation which, if she be allowed to shape her own course, she will scarcely fail to secure.

The necessity of furnishing China with an explanation of their proceedings in Corea has naturally occurred to the Japanese Government, and hence the mission of Mr. Arinori Mori, which was referred to in my despatch No. 165 of the 6th instant. He is to explain the peaceable objects of Japan, that she seeks to make no conquest in Corea, but only to establish friendly and commercial intercourse; and that she is not sending there a miliary expedition, but only a diplomatic mission. Japan would be well pleased if China would advice Corea to treat with Japan, but, as the Vice-Prime Minister observed to me, Japan cannot ask China to do this. Japan has done little to improve her relations with China since the Formosan affair, for as soon as that was concluded the Japanese Minister left Peking, and has not since returned. The Chinese Government will, therefore, connect the reappearance of a Japanese Minister at Peking with some unpleasant associations, and Mr. Arinori Mori will probably endeavour to effect his objects through the foreign Representatives, and may try to move them to urge China to dissuade Corea from resistance.

The Vice-Prime Minister observed to me that Mr. Mori counted upon receiving great assistance from Sir Thomas Wade.

The notice of the Japanese Mission to Corea which Mr. Mori conveys to Peking will be too brief, however, to admit of anything being done by China before it is known whether the Mission is received or opposed, and probably this is part of the Japanese plan. Mr. Mori was dispatched at too late a date to allow of his arriving off the Peiho before the river was frozen, and he was accordingly landed at Chefoo. The journey from that port to Peking overland will take time, and then, if the present arrangements be adhered to, he will arrive at his destination about a fort night befor the High Commissioner Kuroda reaches Kôkwa. China will, therefore, be able to exercise no influence over the reception of Mr. Kuroda, which is probably what Japan desires. Nor could China, in midwinter, render Corea any direct assistance, even if she were disposed to do so.

A Report has reached the Japanese Government that the Coreans, alarmed at the possible consequences of their having fired upon the Japanese vessel "Unyôkan," sent to Peking to ask for assistance, and that the Chinese Government are divided in opinion as to whether this should be granted. They have also heard that the Chinese have been told by some foreign Minister that if China assists Corea against Japan she will become liable to claims for indemnity from the French and United States' Governments for the repulse of their respective expeditions by the Coreans. Perhaps this diplomatic pressure may mark the commencement of the assistance that Japan has contracted for with Russia.

The conclusion I have formed is that Japan has entered into the Corean question deliberately and in conjunction with Russia, the understanding arrived at having been effected at St. Petersburgh. With such an alliance Japan hopes that she can insure success either in negotiation or in war; and that while raising her reputation as a spirited nation and a champion of progress in the East, the Government will succeed in gaining the good opinion of the Samurai, and in diverting attention from troublesome home questions. The programme required that the transfer of Saghalin should first be effected. This has accordingly been done; the principal Agent employed on the side of the Japanese Government to make the transfer being Mr. Kuroda, the present High Commissioner to Corea, whose intercourse with the Russian authorities for some time past has been of an intimate character. I also believe that the despatch of the two Japanese gun-vessels to Corea in May last, nominally to survey, but really to reconnoitre the coast, formed also a feature of the plan. The Japanese Foreign Minister was careful to deny, as I reported to your Lordship in my despatches Nos. 65 and 91, that these vessels were being sent to Corea at all. They did, however, reconnoitre the whole of the east coast of Corea, from Possiette to Fusankai; they then visited the south coast, and also Port Hamilton, and it was in pushing their reconnaissance on the west coast as far as the river leading to the capital, that the fire of the Coreans, which was probably anticipated, was eventually encountered. This incident, which occurred on the 20th September, was not immediately taken up by the Japanese Government, and their Agent, Mr. Moriyama, remained in Corea until the end of October without demanding any explanation from the Corean Government. By that time all the Commissioners, Japanese and Russian, had returned from Saghalin and the Kuriles, and by the end of November the despatch of Kuroda to Corea had been determined on.

The 18th of December was first named as the date of his departure, and then the 25th, but when that time came a fresh delay occurred. It was explained that information was needed by the Government as to whether Kôkwa could be reached in winter, and whether the navigation of the river would be impeded by ice. The Russian Minister asked me whether I was acquainted with the cause of the delay, which he appeared to think unnecessary, and whether I thought that trouble would be caused to foreign interests by the expedition.

With regard to the latter point, I replied that I thought not, if the Coreans and Japanese were allowed to settle their differences by themselves; and he then observed that trouble might occur to the present Government if the Japanese sustained any reverse in Corea, or found their undertaking more serious than they had at first anticipated. The 6th of January is now named for the departure of the expedition, the object of the Government in despatching it at this inclement season of the year being doubtless to have the spring available for military operations, in case these should become necessary. Ten military officers of carious grades, from that of General downwards, have been added to Mr. Kuroda's staff, and Mr. Inouye Bunda has been appointed Second Commissioner.

This appointment is significant, as it shows that the Government think it worth their while to recover the adherence of Mr. Inouye and his friends, as a compensation, perhaps, for the recent defection of Shimadzu Saburô and Itagaki, which I reported in despatch No. 159. Mr. Inouye Bunda, or Kaoru, had charge of the finances, as Vice-Minister, during the absence in Europe, as Ambassador, of Mr. Okubo, the Minister of Finance. While in this position Mr. Inouye thought it necessary to resign office, and, in doing so, he wrote and published a Memorial, in which he denounced the policy of the Government, and made some very damaging statements relative to the finances of the country. I reported this occurrence in my despatch No. 20 of 1873. For this indiscretion he was prosecuted and fined, but though he has not since been employed in office, it is known that, in his private capacity, he has obtained many of the Government contracts for cloth or war material. He was made a member of the inchoate Senate, called the Geuroin, on the 27th instant, as a preliminary to his present appointment.

It is curious to note that the dispatch of kuroda's mission to Corea awakens no enthusiasm on the part of the native press. I inclose translations of two articles which almost predict failure and misfortune, and declare that the chances are greatly on the side of a war in which China is very likely to come to the assistance of Corea. I also add two translations of two other articles, the contents of which have probably been derived from official sources, in order to satisfy the popular cry for information as to the intentions of the Government. A statement purporting to be instructions issued to Mr. Mori is given in the first of these. The second (the Hioron), after supplying the explanation of the pacific policy of the Government, and the course they propose to take to guard against collision, states Plainly, on its own part, that, if the Government really do not want war, they should allow the Corean question go drop; but that to send an Envoy to Corea in the present state of affairs, trusting only to the turn of events for the result, is a policy that will defeat itself, and will surely involve war.

In conclusion, I may mention that it is no part of the plan of Japan to negotiate with Corea in the interest of other foreign Powers. Her objects may be legitimate enough, bit whether the gain will repay the cost and risk which she incurs is a point that she can only determine for herself. It is solely in her own interest, however, that she undertakes this expedition, and it is natural to suppose that the Power with whom she has allied herself will also only be actuated by the same motives. I ventured to inquire in my despatch no. 165 of the 6th instant, whether the Corean question was of sufficient interest to those Powers who have large material interests in China and Japan, to induce them to take some steps to persuade Corea to accept foreign intercourse on terms which would be beneficial alike to all nations, and which, by preserving the independence of Corea, would at the same time prove most conducive to her own interests. It appears to me that this is a question which, in view of the circumstances related in this despatch, increases in importance, and that I may be excused for again submitting it to your Lordship's notice.

I have, &c.

(Signed)　　HARRY S. PARKES

H.S. Parkes (1876. 1. 10) ➡ Derby (1876. 2. 21)

黑田淸隆 파견 관련 森山茂의 내방 및 회견 보고

Sir H. Parkes to the Earl of Derby.-(Received February 21)

(No. 5 Confidential)

Yedo, January 10, 1876

My Lord,

IN continuation of my despatch, Confidential, No. 182, of the 31st ultimo, I have now to add that the High Commissioner Kuroda left Yedo on his Corean Mission on the 6th instant. The squadron consisted of two vessels of war and three transports, and the military force embarked appears to have been limited to the three companies previously spoken of, or 750 men.

The day before the, departure of the expedition, I was visited by Mr. Moriyama, who has so long represented his Government at the Japanese Settlement of Sorio at Fusankai, and who is one of the members of the Mission.

As no one is more able than he is to form an opinion as to the manner in which the Coreans are likely to receive the Mission, I endeavoured to ascertain his views on this point. He told me plainly that he could not say how they would be received. He did not think the Coreans would fire upon the ships, as they would have received ample notice of their arrival, and the ships would do all they could to avoid the Corean forts. What he apprehended was that the Coreans might not send officers to meet and treat with them at Kôkwa. The High Commissioner might, in that case, find it necessary to send him (Moriyama) on to the capital, and the Coreans might fire upon him on his way there. What the High Commissioner would do in the event of encountering either open attack' or negative opposition in the form of refusal to treat, it was impossible to say. He (Mr. Moriyama) was disposed to expect some good result from the excitement which the approach of the Japanese expedition would create at the Corean capital. They knew that Mr. Hirotsu, who had been sent on beforehand to give notice of the despatch of the Mission, had landed at Sorio on the 17th December, and was to be met by a Corean officer on the 19th.

The announcement made by Mr. Hirotsu would, therefore, be known at Seoul by the 25th, and would probably give rise to considerable commotion there. If this were directed against the party in power who are opposed to foreign intercourse, the objects of the Mission might be materially facilitated. It was part of the Japanese plan, therefore, that the Mission should arrive before this excitement could calm down.

Whatever might be the event, he did not look for an early settlement, and thought that the proceedings of the Japanese must take time. In one sense, their difficulties had been increased and, in another sense, lessened by the action of the French and Americans in Corea. Both those nations had committed, the error of retiring too precipitately, and had thus given the Coreans room to boast that they had driven them away. On the other hand, their expeditions had contributed to the discussions and divisions which now exist in Corea on the general question of foreign intercourse.

At the time of the American expedition, the opponents of foreigners advocated resistance and the removal of the capital inland, while the other party held that the American demands were perfectly reasonable, and clamoured for the degradation and execution of the old Regent.

Similar excitement would probably again occur on the arrival of the Japanese expedition. The Japanese, however, if obliged to use force, must be prepared to follow it up, and to hold their ground until a final settlement was arrived at. With the means they possessed of making war, he did not think that hostilities would be long protracted, and he believed that the capture of the capital, if it had to be undertaken, would prove a decisive blow.

On the practical question of whether the Séoul or Hankong River could be entered at this season of the year I found that Mr. Moriyama, rightly or wrongly, anticipates no difficulty. The Government, he says, are satisfied from information derived from Corean informants, that the ice will not be thick enough to impede navigation. He also told me, as an ascertained fact, that ships can go in and out of Port Lazareff (on the east coast of Corea) all the year round, and, further, that only a month ago the Tumen River, which forms the frontier between the Russian .and Corean territory, was still open.

The question of peace or war would depend greatly, he admitted, on the nature of the Japanese demands, and I gathered from him that in presenting these, the High Commissioner would be greatly influenced by the course of events. The Japanese Government have to determine whether they shall be satisfied with concessions which will preserve appearances only, or whether they shall insist upon others of a substantial character, Demands made with the former object might be met by the fulfilment of the agreement concluded last year by the Coreans with Mr. Moriyama, by which formal communication between the two Governments was , to be established, and by obtaining some apology for the attack on the "Unyokan," and some improvement in the very objectionable manner in which intercourse and trade are at present conducted between the Goreans and Japanese at Sorio. But the Japanese Government are not likely to be content, or to satisfy those whom they have to please with such a moderate result. The feeling is no doubt widely ,entertained that it is the Mission of Japan to open Corea effectively, at least to their own people, and that the latter should obtain similar rights in Corea to those which foreigners have acquired in Japan. Judging the Coreans by themselves, they also believe that the former will yield to demands which are supported by force, provided they are not encouraged to hold out by China. The probable action, however, of the latter Power causes them some perplexity, and I think there is little doubt that it is with the view of depriving the Coreans of Chinese support and advice that they send forward their Mission in mid-winter when speedy communication between Corea and China will be impracticable. Mention, however, was recently made in Chinese newspapers of the despatch of two Chinese Envoys to Corea in November last for the assigned object of investing the son of the young King with the title of heir aparent. It is possible1 therefore, that these Envoys may be at Seoul at the time that Kuroda's Mission arrives at Kokwa, and that Chinese influence may, therefore, not be wanting in the proceedings which will ensue.

    The Japanese Government wish to open three Corean ports to Japanese trade—Kokwa, or some port on the west coast, Fusankai, and Port Lazareff—and these are the places which it is highly desirable to see open in the interest of foreigners generally. Unless this resnlt be soon attained, there is, I think, much room to fear that the two latter ports are destined to pass into the hands of Russia. I append two articles from the Japanese press which have appeared since the date of my despatch of the 31st ultimo, and which, like those formerly forwarded, do not speak approvingly of the Government policy. It is possible, however, that the Government would probably have encountered popular censure if they had not determined' to close with the Corean question. They have done so, however, suddenly, and from motives of policy, and are greatly influenced, as I believe, by the help promised them by Russia, which they probably regard as a counterpoise to any opposition they may meet with from China. I can only repeat, however, that this one-sided alliance, as far as I am able to judge, is attended with danger, not only to Japan and Corea, but also to our own interests in these regions, and to those of other European Powers, and it is this feeling which prompts me again to submit to your Lordship's consideration the desirability of our being prepared to take some part in measures having the object of opening Corea to the world before a position is secured there by Russia, which, in the event of war, would place at her feet our commerce in China and Japan. I have only to add that, in view of probable eventualities, the Japanese Government have already called out the reserves of the year, a step which under usual circumstances would not be taken before the spring.

I have, &c.
(Signed) HARRY S. PARKES

T.F. Wade (1876. 2. 16) ➡ Derby

조일 교섭에 대한 주변국 반응 보고

(No. 58)

Peking

16th February 1876

My Lord,

 I had this day the honor to forward to Your Lordship, via Shanghai, the following Telegram in cypher:

 "Regarding Japan and Corea, the Chinese are greatly alarmed, but can do nothing. The Coreans reject their advice to make terms.

 I doubt that Russia has promised more than landing for Japanese troops.

 French Charge' d'Affairs is moving French government to send powers to come one to treat with Corea if Japan opens country.

 No hurry, but should Your Lordship approve similar measure, powers had better be sent to JJ. M Lyation in Japan, rather than to me. My hands will be full here, and China would put constructions on the proceeding that Japan will not."

 I have the honor to be with highest respect, My Lord,

 Your Lordship's most obedient humble servant,

Thomas Francis Wade

11

F.R. Plunkett (1876. 3. 3) ➔ Derby (1876. 4. 4)

조일수호조규 체결을 알리는 鮫島尙信 등 메모 보고

Mr. Plunkett to The Earl of Derby.—(Received April 24)

(No. 40)

Yedo, March 3, 1876

My Lord,

About 9 o'clock on the afternoon of the last instant I received a private note from Mr. Iwakura, translation of which is herewith inclosed, informing me that negotiations with Corea were concluded, and that a Treaty had been signed on the 27th of February.

I have the honour to inclose copy of the reply I wrote unofficially to Mr. Iwakura on receipt of his Excellency's note, as well as of a private letter which I received next morning from the Vice-Minister for Foreign Affairs, and of the note which I sent to him in acknowledgment of his communication.

No particulars having yet been published, I called this afternoon on Mr. Terashima, and after congratulating his Excellency on having so quickly obtained a pacific solution of the Corean question, I inquired whether he could tell me what were the conditions of the Treaty.

His Excellency, who were evidently overjoyed at the success of Mr. Kuroda's mission, replied that he could tell me nothing more than what I had heard from Mr. Sameshima.

Mr. Kuroda had merely telegraphed one single line from Shimonoseki, and was coming on directly to Yedo, where he ought to arrive on the 5th. After the Commissioner's arrival only would the Cabinet itself know the conditions; but Mr. Terashima added laughingly, "when the news is good, one line is sufficient."

The substance of Mr. Kuroda's telegram was published yesterday in the Proclamation, of which a translation is herewith inclosed.

Nothing whatever had been heard from Mr. Kuroda since the end of January, and nothing had transpired as to how he had been received on his arrival at Kokwa. The intelligence, therefore, has taken everybody by surprise, and has been, as far as I can yet judge, received with pleasure, and more especially with relief, by the public, both foreign and Japanese.

I have, &c.
(Signed)   F. R. PLUNKETT

Inclosure 1
Mr. Iwakura to Mr. Plunkett.

(Translation)

Yedo, March 1, 1876.

According to the promise which I made to you when you were so kind as to visit me and have friendly conversation a few days since, I beg to inform you that a telegram was received at 2 o'clock this afternoon from Kuroda, our High Commissioner Plenipotentiary, now residing at the Island of Kokwa, in the country of Corea, to the effect that his negotiations with that country have been completed, and that the seals of both parties were attached to a Treaty on the 27th ultimo.

In haste,
(Signed)   IWAKURA TOMOMI

Inclosure 2
Mr. Plunkett to Mr. Iwakura.

Sir,

I beg to thank your Excellency for your kind note on yesterday, and for having so promptly informed me of the happy conclusion of the negotiations with Corea. I hasten to offer you my best congratulations on an event which will mark an epoch in the history of this Empire.

I avail, &c.
(Signed)   F. R. PLUNKETT

Inclosure 3
Mr. Sameshima to Mr. Plunkett.

My dear Mr. Plunkett,

It gives me much pleasure to inform you that Mr. Kuroda arrived yesterday at Shimonoseki, whence he has telegraphed the satisfactory news that he has concluded a Treaty with Corea. Knowing you are interested to hear about Corea, I take the earliest opportunity to inform you of the above facts.

Sincerely yours,
(Signed)   SAMESHIMA

Inclosure 4
Mr. Plunkett to Mr. Sameshima.

My dear Mr. Sameshima,

I hasten to thank you for the friendly note you sent me this morning, and beg at the same time to congratulate you on the excellent news you have received from Corea.

Believe me, &c.
(Signed)   F.R. PLUNKETT

Inclosure 5
Notification No. 25

(Translation)
To In, Shô, Shi, Chô, Fu, and Ken.

It is hereby notified that a telegram has been this day received, to the effect that our High Commissioner Plenipotentiary, Kuroda Kiyotaka, has concluded his negotiations with the Corean Government, and that a Treaty was exchanged with the said Government on the 27th ultimo.

March 2, 1876
(Signed)   SANJO SANEYOSHI, Daijo-Daijin

II.S. Parkes (1876. 3. 25) → Derby (1876. 5. 7)

조일수호조규 영역본 보고

Sir H. Parkes to the Earl of Derby.—(Received May 7)

(No. 55)

Yedo, March 25, 1876

My Lord,

I HAVE the honour to report .that the Japanese Government published yesterday the Treaty. concluded with Corea, and that they have also communicated it to the foreign Representatives.

I now beg to forward a copy by the American mail, which leaves to-morrow; but I think it desirable, especially as the opportunity is not a fast one, to reserve the observations I have to offer to your Lordship on this Treaty for the French mail, which closes on the 27th instant.

I have, &c.
(Signed) HARRY S. PARKES.

Inclosure in No. 20

Treaty of Peace and Friendship between Japan and Corea.

(Translation)

THE Governments of Japan and Chōsen, being desirous to resume the amicable relations that of yore existed between them and to promote the friendly feelings of both nations to a still firmer basis, have for this purpose appointed their Plenipotentiaries, that is to say, the Government of Japan, Kuroda Kujotaka, High Commissioner Extraordinary to Chōsen, Lieutenant-General and Member of the Privy Council, Minister of the Colonization Department, and Inouye Ka-o-ru, Associate High Commissioner Extraordinary to Chōsen, Member of the Genrō-in; and the Government of Chōsen, Shinken

Han-choo-soo Fu Ji, and Injishō, To-so-Fu, Fuku-sō-Kwan: who, according to the powers received from their respective

Governments, have agreed upon and concluded the following Articles: -

ARTICLE I

Chōsen, being an independent State, enjoys the same sovereign rights as does Japan.

In order to prove the sincerity of the friendship existing between the two nations, their intercourse shall henceforward be carried on in terms of equality and courtesy, each avoiding the giving of offence by arrogation or manifestations of suspicion.

In the first instance all rules and precedents that are apt to obstruct friendly intercourse, shall be totally abrogated, and in their stead rules liberal and in general usage fit to secure a firm and perpetual peace shall be established.

ARTICLE II

The Government of Japan at any time fifteen months from the date of the signature of this Treaty, shall have the right to send an Envoy to the capital of Chōsen, where he shall be admitted to confer with the Rei-so-han-sho, on matters of a diplomatic nature. He may either reside at the Capital or return to his country on the completion of his mission.

The Government of Chōsen in like manner shall have the right to send an Envoy to Tokio, Japan, where he shall be admitted to confer with the Minister of Foreign Affairs on matters of a diplomatic nature. He may either reside at Tokio, or return. home on the completion of his mission.

ARTICLE III

All official communications addressed by the Government of Japan to that of Chōsen shall be written in the Japanese language, and for a period of ten years from the present date they shall be accompanied by a Chinese translation. The Government of Chōsen will use the Chinese language.

ARTICLE IV

Sōrio in Fusan, Chōsen, where an official establishment of Japan is situated, is a place originally opened for commercial intercourse with Japan, and trade shall hence forward be carried on at that place in accordance with the provisions of this Treaty, whereby are abolished all former usages; such as the practice of saikensen (junks annually sent to Chōsen by the late Prince of Tsusima to exchange a certain quantity of articles between each other).

In addition to the above place, the Ooverriment, of Chōsen agrees to open two ports, as mentioned in Article V of this Treaty, for commercial intercourse with Japanese subjects.

In the foregoing places Japanese subjects shall be free to lease land and to erect buildings thereon, and to rent buildings, the property of subjects of Chōsen.

ARTICLE V

On the coast of five provinces, viz., Keikin, Chiusei, Zenra, Keishō, and Kankiō, two ports, suitable for commercial purposes, shall be selected, and the time for opening these two ports shall be in the twentieth month from the second month of the ninth year of Meiji, corresponding with the date of Chōsen, the first moon of the year Heishi.

ARTICLE VI

Whenever Japanese vessels, either by stress of weather or by want of fuel and provisions, cannot reach one or the other of the open ports in Chōsen, they may enter any port or harbour either to take refuge therein, or to get supplies of wood, coal, and other necessities, or to make repairs; the expenses incurred thereby are to be defrayed by the ship's master. In such events both the officers and the people of the locality shall display their sympathy by rendering full assistance, and their liberality in supplying the necessities required.

If any vessel of either country be at any time wrecked or stranded on the coasts of Japan or of Chōsen, the people. of the vicinity shall. immediately use every exertion to rescue her crew, and shall inform the local authorities of the disaster, who will either send the wrecked persons to their native country or hand them over to the officer of their country residing at the nearest port.

ARTICLE VII

The coasts of Chōsen having hitherto been left unsurveyed are very dangerous for vessels approaching them, and in order to prepare charts showing the positions of islands, rocks, and reefs, as well as the depth of the water, whereby all navigators may be enabled safely to pass between the two countries, any Japanese mariner may freely survey said coasts.

ARTICLE VIII

There shall be appointed by the Government of Japan an officer to reside at the open ports in Chōsen for the protection of Japanese merchants resorting there providing that such arrangement be deemed necessary. Should any question interesting both nations arise the said officer shall confer with the local authorities of Chōsen and settle it.

ARTICLE IX

Friendly relations having been established between the two contracting parties their respective subjects may freely carry on their business without any interference from the officers of either Government, and neither limitation nor prohibition shall be made on trade.

In case any fraud be committed or payment of debt be refused by any merchant of either country, the officers of either one or of the other Government shall do their utmost to bring the delinquent to justice, and to enforce recovery of the debt.

Neither the Japanese nor the Chōsen Government shall be held responsible for the payment of such debt.

ARTICLE X

Should a Japanese subject residing at either of the open ports of Chōsen commit any offence against a subject of Chōsen, he shall be tried by the Japanese authorities.

Should a subject of Chōsen commit offence against a Japanese subject, he shall be tried by the authorities of Chōsen.

The offenders shall be punished according to the laws of their respective countries.

Justice shall be equitably and impartially administered on both sides.

ARTICLE XI

Friendly relations having been established between the two contracting parties it is necessary to prescribe trade regulations for the benefit of the merchants of the respective countries.

Such trade regulations, together with detailed provisions, robe added to the Articles of the present Treaty, to develop its meaning and facilitate its observance, shall be agreed upon at the Capital of Chōsen or at the Kok'wa-fu, In the said country, within six months from the present date by Special Commissioners appointed by the two countries.

ARTICLE XII

The foregoing eleven Articles are binding from the date of the signing hereof and shall be observed by the two Contracting Parties, faithfully and invariably, whereby perpetual friendships shall be secured to the two countries.

The present Treaty is executed in duplicate, and copies will be exchanged between the two Contracting Parties.

In faith whereof, we, the respective Plenipotentiaries of Japan and Chōsen, have affixed our seals hereunto this twenty-sixth day of the second month of the ninth year of Meiji, and the two thousand five hundred and thirty-sixth since the' accession of Zimmu Tenno, and in the era of Chōsen, the second day of the second moon of the year Heishi, and of the founding of Chōsen, the four hundred and eighty-fifth.

  (L.S.) KURODA KIYOTAKA, High Commissioner Extraordinary to Chōsen, Lieutenant-General and Member of the Privy Council, Minister of the Colonization Department.
  (L.S.) INOUYE KAORU, Associate High Commissioner Extraordinary to Chōsen, Member of the Genroin.
  (L.S.) SHIN KEN, Dai-Kwan, Han-Choo-Soo-Fuji of Chōsen.
  (L.S.) IN-JI-SHIO, Fuku-Kwan, Tosofu, Fuku-Sokwan of Chōsen.

H.S. Parkes (1876. 3. 27) ➜ Derby (1876. 5. 11)

강화도 협상 관련 森山茂와 회담 보고

Sir H.S. Parkes to The Earl of Derby.—(Recieved May 11)

(No. 57)
Confidential

Yedo, March 27, 1876

My Lord,

  Mr. Moriyama, who is already well known to your Lordship as the Agent of the Japanese Government in Corea since 1868, and who formed one of the leading members of the recent Mission, called on me yesterday, upon my invitation, and gave me the following interesting account of the manner in which the Japanese negotiations in Corea were conducted.

  Your Lordship may remember that when the Japanese Government decided to send Kuroda's mission to Corea, they despatched an officer, Mr. Hirotsu, in advance to Fusan, in order to announce this intention to the Corean Government. Mr. Moriyama told me that the despatch which Mr. Hirotsu was instructed to deliver plainly told the Corean Government that the High Commissioner would proceed to the capital or its vicinity, and would demand satisfaction for the breach of the agreement concluded with Moriyama in 1874, and for the attack on the Japanese gun-boat. When the Mission reached Tsushima, Mr. Hirotsu reported that the despatch had been delivered at Fusan, but that the Corean local authorities earnestly deprecated the visit of the Mission to the capital. Mr. Kuroda, therefore, determined to proceed to Fusan, in order to make it plainly understood to the Corean authorities that he would carry out his instructions to the latter, and proceed with his ships to Kôk'wa. His stay of a week at Fusan enabled the Corean officers to see the number of his ships, and gave Mr. Moriyama opportunity to intimate to them in plain language that the Japanese Government would not accept anything less than the satisfaction they demanded.

  The Japanese Commissioners being satisfied, from what they heard at Fusan, that the display of sufficient force would insure the success of the Mission, applied to their Government from Fusan for additional troops; but this application, as I reported to your Lordship at the time, was not entertained by the Government at Yedo.

When the ships assembled at the rendezvous off Isle Fournier, they were boarded by local officers, who offered presents, and said that the Government had instructed them to supply their wants. Nothing was accepted from them; and, in order to afford time for the authorities at the capital to know of the arrival of the fleet, they were told that in four or five days the ships would move up to the nearest convenient anchorage to Kôk'wa which proved to be Chôsan-to.

On arriving at Chôsan-to they were again visited by Corean officers, including several of the local authorities of Fusan, with whom Mr. Moriyama was well acquainted, and who now seemed anxious to propitiate him, and to induce him to give a friendly turn to the expected negotiations. Mr. Moriyama was instructed to inform them that the Japanese High Commissioners were willing to discuss the business of their mission with high functionaries of similar rank to themselves at Kôk'wa, but unless they were immediately met there by such Commissioners on the part of the Corean government, they would proceed on to the capital.

Shortly afterwards the were informed that Corean Commissioners would be sent to Kôk'wa and on the 5th February Mr. Moriyama and a Secretary were sent to that city to arrange for the reception of the Japanese Commissioners.

They landed at a point about three miles distant from Kôk'wa, and Mr. Moriyama was then again urged by the subordinate Corean officers, and even by the people of the place, to do his utmost to promote a friendly settlement. The authorities of Kôk'wa, however, made certain tentative efforts to treat him with less courtesy than he considered due to him, but these he immediately overruled. He insisted on the main gate of the reception hall being opened to him, and on the seat of honour being conceded to him. After securing a proper reception he said that he required accommodation for the Japanese High Commissioners and their guard of 1,500 men. The local authorities, who had made a display of ill-armed troops of about that number, or, as Moriyama believed, of men accoutred for the nonce as soldiers, protested their inability to provide such extensive accommodation, and urged the alarm which the landing of such a large Japanese force would occasion.

Mr. Moriyama then said that out of consideration for their feelings, the High Commissioners' guard should be limited in the first instance to 500 men (being really the whole strength of their escort), but that another thousand men would be landed if they were needed. He also insisted on seeing the Corean Commissioners, and carried this point also after some evasions and excuses. The local officers at first said that the Commissioners were a long way off, but they eventually proved to be close at hand, and Mr. Moriyama was conducted to them in sedan chairs, befitting his rank.

On seeing the Corean Commissioners, Mr. Moriyama informed them that he could tell them nothing as to the business of the Japanese Commissioners, and that his duty was then confined to seeing that proper arrangements were made for their reception.

These arrangements were concluded without delay, and on the following day, the 6th February, he returned to the ships. On the 8th February, the guard of about 400 men were landed, together, as Moriyama said, with eight or nine field pieces, four of which were Gatling guns. The High Commissioners followed on the 10th.

These arrangements took some time to complete, as the anchorage of the fleet was about twelve miles below Kôk'wa. (Mr. James, the English pilot, has informed me that the Japanese selected that anchorage in preference to a nearer one, which could have been reached by the Northern channel, in order that the Coreans might not be able to ascertain by close observation the actual strength of the ships, which, with the exception of one corvette, consisted only of light vessels).

The Japanese Commissioners landed and proceeded to Kôk'wa in considerable state, and on the 11th they had their first interview with the Corean commissioners. They said they had been sent by their Government to learn, firstly, why the Coreans had broken the Agreement of 1874, which they had made with Moriyama; and, secondly, why they had fired in September last upon the Japanese gunboat "Unyôkan." The Corean Commissioners pleaded that the local officers of Fusan were to blame for the Agreement not having been carried out, as they had not reported what had occurred to the Government at the capital; and that the firing on the "Unyôkan" was a mistake, as the Coreans did not know that she was a Japanese vessel.

The Japanese Commissioners observed that the two charges having thus been fully admitted, the question of reparation remained to be considered, and, breaking off the interview suddenly, they said they would inform the Corean Commissioners the next day of the satisfaction they had to demand.

The interval was employed in working upon the fears of the Corean Commissioners, who indirectly were led to apprehend that the Japanese would follow a similar course to that which they had adopted in the Formosan affair, that they would demand from Corea a large indemnity, which the latter would be wholly unable to pay, and that it would then be open to the Japanese to make other onerous demands. They seemed, therefore, somewhat relieved when, at the interview next day, the Japanese Commissioners placed in their hands the draft of a Treaty which the latter said they would accept as satisfactory redress, provided it were at once agreed to. They were willing to allow the Corean Commissioners four or five days, but not more, to consider it.

The Corean Commissioners asked for ten days, as they had to submit the Japanese demands to the Government at the capital. The Japanese Commissioners replied that they would allow that time, provided that within the ten days the negotiations were completed, and the Treaty signed and exchanged.

The Corean Commissioners appeared to acquiesce, but on the ninth day they began to urge objections, and firstly on point of form. The draft Treaty gave the Mikado the title of "Kôtei" (Chinese, "Hwang-te," or Emperor), and the King of Corea, "ô" (Chinese, "Wang," or King). This did not denote equality between the two nations, which was professed in the 1st Article of the Treaty. As the Coreans could not adopt the title of Kôtei, they wished the Agreement to run in the names of the respective Commissioners only. This could not be acceded to by the Japanese Commissioners, who, however, expressed themselves willing to use the names of the two nations Kôtei—Dai Trippon and Dai Chôsen (Great Japan and Great Corea)—instead of the titles of the Sovereigns. The Corean Commissioners then began to raise other difficulties, which were met by the Japanese Commissioners threatening to break off negotiations. On the tenth day (22nd February) they did return to their ships, saying that they would give the Corean Commissioners two or three days to consider whether they would sign the Treaty as it stood, with no other alteration than the one above-named, as they (the Japanese Commissioners) would agree to no further modifications. On the 25th the assent of the Coreans reached the Japanese Commissioners, who proceded again to Kôkwa on the 26th, signed the Treaty at 9 A.M. on the 27th, re-embarked the same day, and on the 28th the fleet weighed and left Corea.

Mr. Moriyama, in remarking on the above successful result, observed that it was attributable entirely to the firm and straightforward tone adopted by the Japanese Commissioners.

Following the rules of Western diplomacy instead of those of the East, they asked, he said, for nothing which they did not intend to obtain. On the other hand, as they did not wish to make difficulties for Corea, they demanded nothing which she could not easily grant. But, he added, she only yielded to us, and will only yield to others what she feels compelled to grant.

The possibility of other nations coming to Corea and making similar demands to those made by Japan is fully foreseen by them, and they are in some measure prepared for it. They have copies of all the Treaties concluded between China and foreign Powers, and possess the Peking translation of Wheaton's International Law. One of the officers met by Moriyama had been a constant visitor at Peking for twenty years, and had also been to Hong Kong, so that they are not uninformed as to the different nationalities of Europe and America. They express great aversion to foreigners, and give as the reason the French and American attacks, and the fear that foreigners wish to take their country. They are chiefly afraid of Russia, and see that the contiguity of that Power is the chief source of their danger. Mr. Moriyama took pains, he said, to point out to those Corean officers with whom he came in contact, that weak Powers could not stand by their own strength, but only by cultivation friendly relations with other Powers, and he cited to them, as an instance of this, the case of Turkey, which had been supported by other Powers against the neighbour whom Corea so greatly dreaded.

Mr. Moriyama expressed anxiety that the independence of Corea should be a reality and not a name. The Treaty with Japan may do something, he observed, to promote that independence, but it will not alone suffice. Similar Treaties with other Powers are also needed.

I observed that the conduct of the Coreans had hitherto been such as not to attract much sympathy on the part of Western Powers, who had hitherto felt that to visit Corea was to risk insult or attack, and that the object to be gained was held by some to be scarcely worth the trouble that collision would involve.

He replied that he did not think the Coreans would not attack a foreign vessel, but that they would doubtless make no concessions to any foreign visitors unless they believed that it would be more dangerous for them to reject them than to listen to their proposals. The young King and his present Ministers were certainly more intelligent and more liberally disposed than the old Regent and his party, but it would not do for them to appear to depart from a long time-honoured policy of their own free will. At the same time, he added, they are utterly unable to engage in a quarrel with any foreign Power. They have no army worthy of the name, and no navy. The permanent army consists probably of only a few thousand men, and their arms and artillery are similar to the obsolete weapons of China. A couple of Japanese regiments (1,200 men each) would suffice, he said, to take and hold the capital.

He did not advocate, however, that this weakness of the Coreans should be taken undue advantage of. On the contrary, he hoped that their long exclusion would be taking into consideration, and that while some dictation in dealing with them was doubtless necessary, he thought every endeavour would be made to dispel their mistrust, and give them more generous ideas. The illiberality and ignorance of the Corean Government entailed much misery on the people, who were oppressively taxed, whose industry had no scope, and who could therefore accumulate no wealth. Most of them only managed to gain a miserable livelihood, and wide tracts of country were left uncultivated. For these reasons he did not expect much from the trade which was now to be opened with Japan, but this, he believed, would gradually increase if it were only allowed natural development.

I have thought it well to report this conversation to your Lordship, which appears to me specially interesting as coming from a Japanese in Mr. MoriyaMa's position. He begged, however, that the information he had given me might be treated as strictly confidential, and that his name should not be quoted as the authority for these remarks.

It may not be out of place for me to inclose in this despatch a description of Corea, which has appeared in print, and which has been written by one of the leading secretaries of Kuroda's Mission, as it furnishes some further information confirmatory of the above remarks respecting the capacity of Corea for trade, and the condition of the Corean people.

I have, &c.

(Signed)   HARRY S. PARKES

P.S.—With reference to Mr. MoriyaMa's account of the negotiations, I should mention that the Foreign Minister took pains to assure me, on the 25th instant, that the Treaty had been obtained by Mr. Kuroda without the employment of menace of any kind.

H.S. Parkes (1876. 3. 27) ➡ Derby (1876. 5. 11)

조일수호조규 분석

Sir H. Parkes to the Earl of Derby.-(Received May 11)

(No. 58)

Yedo, March 27, 1876

My Lord,

IN continuation of my despatch No, 55 of the 25th instant, which was sent via America, and in which I forwarded without comment a copy of the Treaty recently concluded between Japan and Corea, as. communicated to me by the Japanese Foreign Minister, I have now the honour to inclose a duplicate copy, and to offer .the following observations.

In my despatch No. 57 of this date, I explain why this Treaty runs in the name of the' Governments of Japan and Chosen (Corea) instead of in the names of the respective Sovereigns of those countries.

Article I acknowledges the independence of Corea, and the equality of the two Contracting Powers. I learn that this Article, which was naturally acceptable to the Coreans, is also valued by the Japanese (by whom it was suggested) as denoting that Corea is independent of China.

Article II gives to each Power the right of establishing a Legation at the capital of the other, a right which it is believed the Coreans will not be eager to avail themselves of.

Articles IV and V open three ports to Japanese trade. One of these, namely Sorio or Fusan, where the Japanese have hitherto had their settlement, is to be opened at once, and the two other ports, which have yet to be chosen, in twenty months' time. By this arrangement the Japanese are relieved of the highly vexatious and derogatory restrictions under which they have hitherto traded at Sorio.

Article VI opens all Corean ports to Japanese vessels in want of supplies or repairs, or needing shelter from stress of weather, and makes special provision for the careful and hospitable treatment of ship-wrecked crews.

Article VII provides, in view of the highly dangerous character of the Corean coasts, that "any Japanese mariner" may take soundings and make charts and surveys of those coasts. This task, however, will naturally devolve upon the Japanese Government.

Article VIII gives Japan the right to appoint officers (or Consuls) to protect Japanese trade and interests at the open ports.

Article IX provides that trade shall be carried on between Japanese and Coreans without interference on the part of the officers of either Government, who are not to place any limitation or prohibition upon trade. The respective Governments are to do their best to enforce payment of debts, but are not to be held responsible for the recovery of them.

Article X is specially noteworthy as showing that the Japanese Government, who have lately complained of the extra-territorial clauses of the foreign Treaties with Japan, have been careful to stipulate for the right of jurisdiction over their own people in Corea. They have also imitated those Treaties in not making this right reciprocal, as the foreign Minister has explained to me that this Article does not give the Coreans jurisdiction over their people in Japan. It is, in short, almost a repetition of Articles IV and V of the British Treaty of 1858 with Japan.

Article XI stipulates that all rules necessary for the regulation of trade, and any other provisions that may be required either to explain the meaning of the present Treaty or to facilitate its observance shall be negotiated by special Commissioners appointed by both countries, who shall meet for this purpose within six months, either at the capital of Corea or at Kok'wa.

Article XII provides for the Treaty coming into immediate operation.

The resemblance between this Treaty and the British Treaty of 1858 with Japan is remarkable. The omissions or differences are almost entirely confined to those. Articles in the last-named Treaty, which relate to the exchange of coin, Custom-house control, and similar subjects. It has been explained to me that the Japanese Commissioners omitted mention of these matters on finding that the Corean Commissioners were wholly uninformed about them, and unable to discuss them intelligently, and they therefore inserted instead the XIth Article, which secures the due consideration and the management of all such details within six months.

No allusion is made in the Treaty to any other nation.

As a criticism on this Treaty, which may be regarded as coming from the Japanese side, I beg to inclose an article from the "Japan Gazette" of the 25th instant. It states that, as the Corean Treaty contains extra-territorial clause which the Japanese Government have been trying to expunge from the foreign Treaties with Japan, they delayed its publication until they saw they could not gain the latter object. It congratulates Japan on having avoided a war, with its contingent conquest, which Russia might not have allowed her to enjoy, enlarges on the great concessions she has obtained for herself, and observes that other foreign nations seeking relations with Corea must, as Japan has had to do, make their own terms, and that they cannot do better than imitate, although they may not hope to equal, the firmness and power of persuasion shown by Kuroda, the Japanese High Commissioner.

I have, &c.
(Signed) HARRY S. PARKES

15

Adams (1876. 4. 15) → Derby

프랑스의 협조 의사 보고

The Earl of Derby
No. 260

Paris
April 15, 1876

My Lord,

Up to today, the French Government had received no official intelligence of the Treaty concluded between Japan and Corea. I have therefore communicated to the Duc Decazes its chief stipulations as contained in the telegram from Sir H.S. Parkes, a copy of which was inclosed in Your Lordship's No. 332 of the 11th instant.

His Excellency states that when the French Government is in possession of the requisite information, it will be quite disposed to form with Her Majesty's Government in concerting any measure which may seem desirable in the direction of commercial negotiations with Corea.

I have the honour to be,
With the highest respect,
My Lord,
Your Lordship's most obedient, humble servant,

Adams

B.O. Russell (1876. 4. 22) ➜ Derby

독일의 협조 의사 보고

The Earl of Derby

Berlin
April 22 1876

My Lord,

I have communicated the contents of Your Lordship's dispatch No. 236 of the 11th instant, respecting the publication of the Commercial Treaty between Japan and Corea to Herr von Bülow, and have asked him whether the German Government propose to take any action at present in the direction of commercial negotiations with Corea. His Excellency says that the question will be taken into consideration when the Government is in possession of more detailed information than has hitherto been received, but that he would be glad of an exchange of views on the subject, so as to act in common with Her Majesty's Government, if it should be thought advisable to enter upon commercial negotiations with Corea, as suggested by Sir Harry Parkes in his telegram of the 28th ultimo.

I have the honour to be, with great truth and respect,
My Lord,
Your Lordship's most obedient, humble servant,

B. O. Russell

17

H.S. Parkes (1876. 5. 12) ➡ Derby

조선 교섭 방식에 관한 전보

(No. 82)
The Earl of Derby

Yedo
May 12, 1876

My Lord,

　I had the honour this day to address to Your Lordship the following telegram in cypher dated May 12, 3:45 PM.

　"I have received the telegram of 5th instant. Am assured by competent Japanese authority that nothing will be effected in Corea by any foreign power unsupported by force, but that presence of adequate force would ensure success and prevent collision. It would be better not to attempt negotiation unless we are prepared to insist on our demands.

　The Envoy should be supported by seven or eight ships including four or five gunboats and should endeavor to reach the Capital. Japan, if invited, would probably render friendly assistance by informing Corea of pacific objects of Mission. Both Chinese and Japanese Interpreters would be required.

　The sooner such a Mission is sent the better, as the recent Japanese success is not likely to [yield substantial] results and if not followed up by other powers some reaction may occur in Corea. A Corean Envoy is expected to arrive in Yedo on 24th Instant but the objects of his Mission are not known.

　The three Governments might act collectively, or as we have force sufficient on the spot the best plan might be to proceed to Corea at once and allow later Expeditions by France and Germany to keep the question open and prevent reaction."

　　I have, &c.

Harry S. Parkes

Adams (1876. 5. 12) → Derby

조선의 배외정책 보고 및 교섭시 무력 동원 건의

No. 319

Paris May 12, 1876

My Lord,

　　With reference to Sir Harry Parkes' dispatch No. 54 of the 20th of March, inclosed in copy in Your Lordship's dispatch No. 474 of the 10th instant, I have the honor to state that I have received trustworthy information, in strictest confidence, that not only did the Corean Government wish to stipulate that the Japanese should bring no foreigners to Corea, but that they told the Japanese Commissioners that though they were ready to negotiate a Treaty with Japan, they did not at all wish to have dealings with any European nation; that, in fact, they considered that there were only three real nations in the world, the Chinese, the Japanese, and the Corean, and that all the rest of the world were "outer barbarians" and inferior people.

　　I mention this because, if Her Majesty's Government decide to open negotiations with Corea, it is well that they should know (if my information be correct) that in all probability Great Britain will only be able to conclude a Treaty by an imposing display of force, and in any case, against the will of Corea. The Coreans, there can hardly be a doubt, still in the main consider that they worsted both the French and the Americans who invaded their country.

　　There appears too, as I learn, to be a peace party in Corea, and that it was due to that party, and not as has been published in the press, to the fear of the approach of some 12,000 Russians, that the Japanese Commissioners obtained their great success.

　　I have the honour to be with the highest respect,
　　My Lord,
　　Your Lordship's most obedient, humble servant,

Adams

Mr. Adam and Korseg [_____]

    I think it would be better not to send this dispatch to Sir H.S. Parkes. Mr. Adams had marked it "strictly confidential" and the informant is (I believe) an Englishman in the employment of the Japanese [Delegation] in Paris.

    P.S. Perhaps it would be as well not to send it—though there is not much in it [_____] I see no—particular objection to its being sent, but if there is a [truth] better keep it back.

D. May 19

Adams (1876. 5. 12) ➜ Derby
청국에 중개 요청 건의

Paris May 12, 1876

No. 320

My Lord,

    Since writing my preceding dispatch, I have seen the Due Decazes and His Excellency threw out the following suggestion, viz whether it would not be well to attempt to get at Corea through China, and to try and persuade the Chinese Government to influence that of Corea to extend the Treaty with Japan to other nations.

    I have the honor to be, with the highest Respect,
My Lord,
Your Lordship's Most obedient humble servant,

Adams

H.S. Parkes (18/6. 5. 23) → Derby

조선 교섭시 영·불·독의 연합함대 파견 건의

(No. 86)
Confidential

Yedo
May 23, 1876

My Lord,

    Shortly after I received Your Lordship's telegram of the 5th instant informing me that Her Majesty's government were in communications with the French and German Governments on the subject of Corea and directing me to report my opinion as to the precise measures which should be adopted if it were thought desirable to open relations with that country, I endeavored to indicate within the narrow compass of a telegram, which I sent to your Lordship on the 12th instant, the course which I thought should be pursued in order to attain that object. I then stated that the Japanese Authorities, who are most competent to judge, are confident that nothing will be gained from the Coreans without a display of force, which is necessary not only to ensure the success of any negotiations, but also to prevent hostility on the part of the Coreans, that the sooner negotiations were undertaken the better as the Japanese Treaty alone was not likely to produce any material change in the disposition of the Coreans, and that some reaction might be looked for in Corea if the initiative action of the Japanese is not followed up by endeavors on the part of other Powers to establish intercourse with that country.

    I now beg to support this opinion with a few further remarks.

    My despatch No. 57, of the 27th March, will have shown Your Lordship how the Japanese Envoy obtained his treaty, that it was not voluntarily conceded by Corea, but was accepted only in satisfaction of the demands of Japan, which Corea believed the latter was prepared to enforce. I also stated that the informant, from whom I received this intelligence, had distinctly assured me that he believed the Coreans would make no concessions to any foreign visitors, unless they believed it would be more dangerous for them to reject than to listen to the proposals made to them. The same high Authority on Corean subjects has since stated to me that he believes nothing can be effected in Corea by any negotiator who may proceed there unsupported by an adequate force, that, with such support, success may be relied on, but that without it a foreign envoy would not only gain nothing, but would probably not be treated with due respect.

I certainly think that any force which may be sent to Corea for the protection of the representative of a Western power should be of a kind which could ensure his safety at the capital, in case he found it desirable to conduct his negotiations at that place. It should, therefore, comprise at least, four or five vessels of light draught which would be able to ascend the River to Se'oul. Concerted action on the part of such Powers as Great Britain, France, and Germany could not fail to have an impressive effect upon the Coreans, but if those powers are not prepared to act promptly I think valuable time would be lost. So little is known of the political condition of Corea that it is impossible to calculate how long the old Regent may remain out of power, but all accounts agree in stating that, if he were to recover his position, no hope could be entertained of opening relations with the Corean Government by amicable means. The present advisers of the King are believed to be more liberal and intelligent than those whom they have displaced, but even if they were disposed to do so, they could not appear to agree willingly to such an innovation as the admission of foreigners, and they would probably, therefore, derive support from the presence of a foreign force, as indicting a pressure which they could assign as a reason for concession.

The present Government appear to expect that the Treaty they have concluded with Japan will prompt Western Powers to advance similar demands, and it would be well that this anticipation should be realized before they have had time to consider how such demands may best be met with refusal. I have heard confidentially that the departure of the Japanese Envoys from Corea was followed by some unfavorable demonstration at Se'oul, and it remains to be seen what object the Corean Government have in sending so soon to Japan the Envoy, who, as reported in my Despatch No. 44 is shortly expected to arrive at Yedo. The Japanese Government do not fail to call to mind how, in their own case, when they concluded Treaties with several Foreign Powers in 1858, their first thought after the departure of the ships which brought the Foreign Envoys to their shores was how they might free themselves from the obligations they had contracted. But, whatever may be the object of the Envoy's visit, some of the members of the Japanese Government see that only slight political or commercial gain will accrue from their Treaty with Corea unless it be followed up by similar agreements with other Powers, that the trade between Japan and Corea will be trifling unless stimulated and developed by means of simultaneous traffic with other countries, and that it is only by entering into relations with Western Powers that Corea can hope to derive political support against Russia.

I am inclined to believe therefore, that, in the event of Her Majesty's Government wishing to open relations with Corea, some assistance might be derived from the Japanese Government, so far, at least, that, if invited to do so, they would probably be willing to give notice of the approach of a Mission to the Corean Government, to assure them of its pacific objects, and to recommend them to conclude with Great Britain, and other foreign Powers a treaty similar to that which they have concluded with Japan. The Corean Government, if they received such notice, would have no excuse for treating a Foreign Mission in a hostile manner. It would scarcely be less than an act of hostility on their part to refuse to treat shipwrecked seamen with humanity, or to afford relief to foreign ships entering their posts in distress, and it would be unreasonable to deny to other Foreign Powers intercourse of the same nature as that which they have now agreed to hold with Japan.

I mentioned in my telegram of the 10th instant that both Chinese and Japanese interpreters would be required in conducting negotiations with Corea. The necessity of such interpretation is obvious when it is seen that all official communications between the Japanese and Corean Governments are to be conducted in Chinese. By the 3rd Article of their Treaty, the Japanese Government, although stipulating for the right of addressing the Corean Government in Japanese, agree to send for a period of ten years a Chinese translation with all their communications, and the Corean Government, on the other hand, are to use the Chinese language in addressing the Japanese.

In connection with this subject, it affords me much pleasure to mention to Your Lordship that I have incidentally learned that in the negotiation of their Treaty with Corea, the Japanese Envoys derived considerable assistance from a Corean officer who has repeatedly visited Peking and made the acquaintance there of [NW. Mayers.] They found that, owing to the information and advice which that officer had received from [NW. Mayers] he was the most intelligent agent with whom they had to deal, and that, although holding no high rank his arguments with reference to foreign questions had weight with his superiors. I believed this to be the same officer whose conversations with [NW. Mayers] have been reported to Your Lordship from time to time by Thomas Wade, and it is gratifying to think that a British officer should have been able to exercise such a beneficial influence over a Corean mind. The circumstance encourages the hope that the ears of the Coreans are not wholly closed against reason, and that the intelligence thus awakened will prove as serviceable in the course of British interests as in those of Japan.

The visit of the Corean Envoy, who is expected to arrive in Yedo in a few days, may afford me an opportunity of learning more of the feelings of his Government towards foreigners. The shipwrecked Corean whom I handed over to the Japanese Government, as I reported in my despatch No. 70 of the 10th Ultimo, has been detained here in order that he may be delivered to the Envoy, and it will be curious to notice whether the rescue of this man by a British Ship, and his subsequent treatment in our hands will elicit any acknowledgment from this functionary.

I have, etc.

(signed) Harry S. Parkes

21

Adams (1876. 6. 2) → Derby

Parkes의 보고에 대한 프랑스 정부 입장 보고

Paris
June 2 1876

No. 388

My Lord,

On receipt yesterday of Your Lordship's Despatch No. 542 of the 29th instant and of its enclosure. I draw up a paraphrase of the telegram sent to Your Lordship on the 12th ultimo by Sir H.S. Parkes stating the measures which he considered it would be desirable to adopt for opening negotiations with Corea.

This I communicated to the Duc Decazes and I told His Excellency that before coming to any decision on the subject Her Majesty's Government would be glad to learn the opinion of it entertained by the French Government.

I have the honour to enclose herewith a copy of the paraphrase.

That Duke told me this morning that he had consulted with the Minister of Marine on the subject and that they were both of opinion that it would be a great imprudence on the part of the French Government to send an expedition to the Corea, where the difficulties of navigation were so considerable.

I have the honour to be,
With the highest respect, My Lord,
Your Lordship's most obedient, humble servant,

Adams

Copy

H.M.G. received on the 20th instant, a telegram from Sir H.S. Parkes stating in substance that he had learnt from a competent Japanese Authority that, unless supported by force, nothing will be effected in Corea by any Foreign Power, but that the presence of an adequate force would prevent collision to ensure success.

Sir H.S. Parkes considers that it would be better not to attempt to negotiate at all, unless we are ready to insist upon our demands, and his opinion is that if an Envoy is sent to Corea, the latter should be accompanied by seven or eight ships, amongst which there should be four or five gunboats, in that an endeavour should be made to reach the Capital. He thinks, that if Japan were invited, she would be inclined to afford friendly assistance by informing the Government of Corea that the Mission had pacific objects. He says that both Chinese and Japanese interpreters would be required. He thinks that the sooner the mission is sent the better, because the success of the Japanese will probably not produce substantial results and if other Powers do not follow it up there may be a reaction.

He reports the expected arrival in Japan of a Corean Envoy on May 24 and that the object of his Mission is not known.

British Embassy
Paris June 1 1876

H.S. Parkes (1876. 6. 9) ➡ Derby (1876. 7. 16)

일본의 중개에 관한 寺島宗則와 회담 보고

(No. 102)
Confidential
The Earl of Derby

Yedo
June 9, 1876

My Lord,

    I informed Your Lordship in my telegram of the 6th instant that the Foreign Minister hesitated to give any pointed advice to the Corean Envoy now in Yedo as to the desirability of his country entering into relations with Western nations because he had no grounds for taking up the subject, and I added that I had strong reason to believe that, if Foreign Powers contemplated sending Missions to Corea, Japan would, in that case, recommend the latter to make treaties similar to that which she has concluded with Japan.

    I formed this opinion from a conversation I held with the Foreign Minister on the 5th instant. I observed to him that I believed the views of his Government and my own were identical as to the desirability of Corea maintaining her independence, the 1st Article of the Japanese Treaty with Corea proved this to be the wish of Japan, and as he must be aware that it was essential to the realization of that wish that Corea should enter into relations with Western Powers. I enquired whether he did not think it expedient to profit by the presence of the Corean Envoy to press this view on his attention.

    He observed to me that he found it difficult to approach a subject which he felt would be distasteful to the Envoy, and which he had no particular reason for bringing forward. If he did so spontaneously the Coreans would probably suspect Japan of some complicity with foreigners but if a question arose between the latter and the Coreans in consequence of foreign ships visiting Corea he thought Japan would in that case be ready to give Corea proper advice, and there would then be some chance of that advice being listened to. At present, he feared, Corea was inclined to regard all foreign nations as her natural enemies.

    Japan, I replied, should endeavor to disabuse Corea of such an unreasonable idea, and to convince her that if she accepted relations with Western Powers, they would become interested in seeing her independence preserved. Japan could now speak to Corea as a friend, and the experience she had gained in foreign matters entitled her advice to attention. Siam might be cited as an instance of a small country having protected herself by foreign intercourse whilst Annam afforded an example of the danger of avoiding it. The risk to which Corea was exposed by exclusion was doubtless as well understood by him as by me. The difficulty of foreigners coming to any understanding with Corea lay with the latter. They might, at least, be advised not to attack visitors who went to them with a friendly object, as if they adhered to this disposition they might, at any time, bring trouble upon themselves. Foreigners would sooner or later have to treat with Corea if only on such subjects as navigation, and the treatment of shipwrecked people, and when the necessity arose Corea should be prepared to act in a reasonable manner.

Mr. Terashima observed that, although the Envoy carefully avoided discussion on any subject beyond his immediate business he believed that some of his suite held the view that Corea would no longer think of attacking any foreign ship that might visit her shores. He greatly regretted that Gokeshiyaku, the Corean Officer who has so often seen Mr. Mayers at Peking—had not come with the Mission as he well understands the importance of foreign relations to Corea.

I think it may be concluded from the above remarks that if I were in a position to inform Mr. Terashima that a foreign Mission is really about to visit Corea for the purpose of negotiation the Japanese Government would not then hesitate to counsel the Coreans to receive it in a friendly way. Mr. Moriyama has told me that he feels confident that the Coreans would not now attack such a mission, and his sympathies are so strong in favour of Corea concluding Treaties with Foreign Powers that I feel satisfied he would do all in his power to bring about such a result.

If a mission were contemplated it would be well that the Envoy should convey the news to Corea on his return, but if not, then I think, as I mentioned in my telegram, he should receive notice of the Survey of the "Sylvia" if this is to be proceeded with.

I have, &c.

Harry S. Parkes

23

H.S. Parkes (1876. 6. 9) → Derby

수신사 金綺秀의 동정 및 森山茂 회견 보고

(No. 100)
The Earl of Derby

Yedo
June 9, 1876

My Lord,

In my dispatch No. 97 of the 6th instant I reported the arrival of the Corean Mission which I informed Your Lordship in my dispatch No. 77 was being sent from Corea to Yedo.

The Japanese Government are gratified to find that the object of the Mission is entirely friendly and intended by the Corean Government to confirm the new relations established by the recent Treaty.

The Envoy is a functionary of the third rank, and he is accompanied by two Assistants who are believed to be of even higher rank than their Chief. His suite is composed partly of officers who have been stationed at Fusan and who are, therefore, familiar with the past relations of Japan at that Port, and partly of officers who were employed in the negotiation of the Treaty at Kokwa. The Japanese Government seem to have expected that some of the members of the Mission would have been authorized to study and report upon the new institutions of Japan, but the Envoy has explained that this part of the plan has been deferred until a later period, and that his visit is intended as one of ceremony only, having for its chief object to express the hope of his Government that the friendly relations now established between Corea and Japan should be strengthened and maintained.

The Japanese Government naturally wish to show the Envoy all the principal objects of interest in Yedo, but I have been informed that he has responded to their invitations with great reserve, and that he considers that it would be unbecoming of him to indulge in amusement, or to evince curiosity in the novel scene which surrounds. It appears that he will only accept arrangements made for his entertainment, or edification when assured that it is the express wish of the Mikado that he should do so, and he then complies because he considers that his duty requires him to respect the commands of the sovereign to whom he has been sent. Another peculiarity, real or professed, is his alleged aversion to foreigners, and in showing him over the public departments the Japanese Government assign this as the reason for desiring the absence of their foreign employees.

He also appears to avoid as far as possible incurring obligations towards the Japanese Government, and two or three days after his arrival he declined their offer to supply his table, and the wants of his suite during his stay, and insisted on using his own inferior provisions which he had brought with him from Corea. He also thinks it necessary to move about only in his own conveyance, which is a clumsy kind of chair carried on the shoulders of twelve men; he is always accompanied by his band which plays most discordant music, and by a numerous retinue equipped in very fantastic dresses, and carrying halberts and other strange ensigns of rank. The contrast between the appearance of the Corean and that of the Japanese is very striking, and is, I need scarcely add, very favourable to the latter.

It is aborous, however, that the forced, and unnatural rigidity of the Coreans must relax when it comes in contact even with such solvents as the Japanese are able to apply, and Mr. Moriyama, the well known Japanese agent at Fusan for many years, has observed to me that he considers that great advances have already been made in persuading the Coreans to modify their prejudices. Last year, he remarked, the Corean Authorities would not receive me at Fusan, because I went there in a foreign built ship and wore clothes of foreign fashion. Now a Corean Envoy has traveled to Japan in a foreign built ship, and has prostrated himself before our Sovereign who wore a foreign costume, when entertained by us at table they have always been served in foreign form, with foreign food and wines, of both of which they partook freely; they have listened to foreign music, some of them have been driven in foreign carriages, and at the military shows which they have witnessed they have seen nothing but foreign uniforms, arms, accoutrements, artillery and drill, and cannot but be sensible of the superiority of these, and of the greater comforts enjoyed by the Japanese as compared to those of their own country. The railway by which they traveled from Yokohama to Yedo caused them great surprise which they were entirely unable to conceal.

Mr. Moriyama also mentioned to me a satisfactory instance of their being ready to profit by scientific knowledge. The Japanese surgeon of one of the ships lately sent to Fusan was freely allowed to dispense gratuitous medical aid to sick Coreans who came to him in large numbers, and he profited by the opportunity to introduce vaccination among them to a considerable extent.

I enclose a translation of an interesting article from a Japanese newspaper which compares the present condition of Japan and Corea, and argues that although Japan has suffered some inconvenience from having been forced into relations with the outer world, she has been more than compensated by the superior knowledge she has there acquired. The writer contrasts the reception which Japan is now able to give to the Corean Envoy with the feebler course they would have followed if they had remained in their old condition, and he congratulates his country on being able to assume towards Corea an attitude similar to that of Commodore Perry when he appeared with his squadron in Japanese waters in 1853.

I have, &c.

Harry S. Parkes

Inclosure

"*Hochi Shimbun*"—*(May 31, 1876)*

Newspaper article upon the advantages gained by Japan and her relations with foreign countries.

(Translation)

Upon consideration of the first commencement of our relations with foreign lands, we find that since that time more than twenty years have elapsed. Now what was the actual nature of the stage of advancement to which Japan had attained twenty odd years ago? If we cast a backward glance over this period, there crowd across our vision, swarming like caterpillars, events, some of them worthy of laughter, others, of grief, and others again, of indignation. Two hundred years of profound peace had sapped the energies of the whole nation, and the policy of exclusion had become in their eyes a law as precious as gold or jewels, when some black vessels suddenly forced their way into the Shinagawa sea, and aroused us from our spring-tide dream of peace and tranquility. The fishermen who angled for profits left us, but again returned, and with a cast of their net caught and entangled the minds of the officials and Shogunate, alarming them with a display of their power. Their specious baits deceived the latter, who were approached both by persuasion and by threats, and even the settlement of those Treaties, by which an inch was granted but ten feet taken, was quietly agreed to by us, in our ignorance of the hardships those Treaties might in after time entail upon us. Our sole object was merely to avoid present troubles. How could we foresee that the peach blossoms of our tranquil state would fall scattered hither and thither, leaving no fragrance behind, and that when the spring time had passed and the summer had gone by, our former joys would eventually give place to present regrets; or that we should ever reach a day like the present, when the autumn winds blow shrill upon us!

Upon reflection, how could our countrymen, at the date of the first arrival of the Americans, possibly have known how to deal with them diplomatically? Even had we at the time resented and refused the Treaties, this would not have arisen from our calculations of future advantage. Intimate relations with foreigners being the matter of all others most distasteful to the Japanese people, the only anxiety of the Shogunate would have been the question of whether the people would create disturbances or would remain quiet. How should the Shogunate have felt the desire of extending, by means of these Treaties, its benefits down to the present day? For this reason, then, even though we may at the present time, when we look at the Treaties granted by the Shogunate, feel anger thereat, still, how can we exclusively ascribe them to the fault of the Shogunate. It was owing to an unavoidable tendency of affairs.

If, however, we consider how matters stood more than twenty years ago, and enquire into the state of progress then existing, and if we then make a comparison with the present time, we shall find that the period of over twenty years has certainly not merely passed by uselessly. For even though we cannot but feel regret that our wealth and possessions should have been driven forth beyond the seas, we must nevertheless feel pleased that we have acquired knowledge from foreigners, which we have developed amongst ourselves. Supposing that we had caused the spring-breeze of former days to blow warm even up to the present moment, had preserved our peach blossoms and our happy dreams, and had never at any time unfastened the lock on the entrance to our cavern, how could we at the present time be able to view the state of affairs we now behold? If we fix our attention on this, we must cease to chatter about the troubles that have arisen from our foreign relations, and consider for awhile the advantages accruing therefrom. When we reflect that we have by means of the wealth and treasure of our land acquired the knowledge and arts of foreigners, we ought not, even though the price be an exceedingly high one—to feel the slightest regret for this.

We will proceed in the same spirit to make some remarks on the nature of the circumstances which led to the recent arrival of a Corean embassy and the re-establishment of friendly relations with that country. Just consider what was the source of our ancient literature. It came originally from China. Thus, then, its real home was China, but still its introduction direct from China was a matter of much later date. In the first instance it must have been through the medium of Corea, a branch-establishment as it were of China, that we received it, second-hand. There is, therefore, no necessity for arguing the fact that one half of our literature in olden times was obtained from Corea. And at the present time, seeing that there are clear proofs of our literature having been imported from Corea, it is only necessary to give a glance at this evidence of her having, in olden times, rendered aid to that literature. The intercourse between Corea and ourselves was, however, all but wholly broken off after the expedition of the Toyotomi Taiko, and the single link connecting us with her was that still maintained by the merchants of Tsushima. But the Coreans looked upon the people of Tsushima solely with glances of hatred and suspicion, and their demonstrations of friendliness were of course for form approaching cordiality. Owing to these circumstances we had no means of ascertaining accurately the condition of the interior of the territory of Corea, or the extent to which her state of wealth and literature had advanced. But from the recent visit of our High Commissioner to that country we have at last acquired a knowledge of the natural condition of their internal affairs, and that condition has raised in our mind some quite unexpected impressions.

Supposing that the old condition of our country had been maintained up till the present time, consider what would have been presented to our view on the occasion of the recent arrival of the Corean embassy. Would we have seen those officials arrive on board ship,* and, landing at Yokohama, at once proceed by rail to the Shimbashi station? They would have braved the waves in a single-sailed vessel and so come to Nagasaki. Next, they would have to come overland to Yedo. The persons appointed to look after them, again, would not

---

*[원주] Meaning that the Coreans have now come in a large foreign-built ship direct to Yokohama, instead of proceeding, as in olden times, to Nagasaki in a small vessel with but a single sail.

only have been beings of a different stamp to the Coreans, but would on the contrary, as regards such matters as literature &c., have been actually inferior to them. At that period, even though they had ridiculed the Coreans, their laugher would merely have been excited by the difference apparent in their style of dress, and this would have been just the same as their laughter as they first saw the Americans. But still, when we now look at the Coreans and examine their condition, the ideas that spontaneously arrive in our minds do not, it is very clear, come from similar considerations to those which caused us in former days to laugh when we saw the Americans.

We have obtained an article recently published in the "Gazette" newspaper treating of the relations between Japan and Corea. It says: "At the present time the Japanese have dealt with the Coreans in the same manner as that in which they themselves were in former times being treated by others (meaning, by foreigners). Upon a consideration of the Treaty drawn up between the two nations, it will be found that they have already rejected the objectionable spirit of the East, and have adopted the usages of the West. Japan is the fore-runner of civilization in regard to the East…&c..." Now, although we cannot give full credit to this article, still there may not be wanting some reason for Western people to hold ideas of the above nature.

By the treaty which we have now concluded with Corea, we have not only dried up the source that has for many years given rise to internal disturbances in Japan, but we have also the satisfaction of observing that our present mode of dealing with Corea is unlike that existing twenty years ago, and is similar to that adopted by the Americans towards us at the time in question. Thus, if we now judge the Coreans by the standard of their appearance to our eyes, we can easily conjecture the degree of advancement to which we have attained during the period of twenty years and can also ascertain the extent of our advancement prior to the said twenty years. These reflections will assist us to forget the losses we have sustained for the past twenty years, and will afford us some slight degree of consolation.

24

H.S. Parkes (1876. 8. 11) ➜ Derby

宮本小一의 조선 교섭 및 *Sylvia*의 조선 해안 탐사에 관한 보고

Confidential
(No. 133)
The Earl of Derby

Yedo

August 11, 1876

My Lord,

  My despatch No. 102 of June 9th will have informed Your Lordship that I took advantage of the presence of the Corean Envoy at Yedo to advise the Foreign Minister to press on his attention the desirability of Corea entering into relations with Foreign Powers. He then informed me that, although the subordinate Japanese Officers who were in communication with the Corean Mission neglected no opportunity of supplying them with information on foreign subjects, and suggesting that Corea should lay aside her seclusion, and unfriendliness to other countries, he himself had no opportunity of using such arguments to the Envoy, although willing to do so if an occasion offered. I suggested that, as the visit of Foreign vessels to Corea, for the purposes of negotiation, was probably only a question of time, it would be well for Japan to prepare Corea for such a contingency, and to persuade her, whenever it should occur, to act in a reasonable manner.

  On the 6th of June I telegraphed to Your Lordship that, if I were in a position to intimate that Foreign Powers contemplated opening relations with Corea, I had strong reasons to believe that the Japanese Government would recommend Corea to make Treaties similar to that concluded with Japan. As Your Lordship, however, did not authorize me to make such an intimation I had no opportunity of recurring to the subject during the stay of the Envoy at Yedo.

  The despatch of Her Majesty's Ship "Sylvia" to Corea which I heard of just as the Japanese Commissioner Miyamoto was leaving for that country, in the beginning of last month, enabled me, as I reported in my despatch No. 117, to convey notice to the Corean Government of the object with which the "Sylvia" is being sent, and to request that she might be properly treated. The tone of the letter of the Corean Envoy, written in acknowledgment of the kindness shown by us to the ship wrecked Corean Li Yuen Chun (translation of which was forwarded in my despatch No. 113) led me, I observed, to hope for such a result. I also suggested that Mr. Miyamoto might impress upon the Corean Government that it would now be sound policy for them to accept relations with foreign powers, and that he might possibly obtain from them some assurance that, if a Foreign Mission were sent there, for the purpose of friendly negotiation, it would be well received.

Although the Foreign Minister willingly undertook to inform the Corean Government of the "Sylvia"'s Survey, and to request, as I suggested, that she should be properly treated, he avoided making any promise as to the latter part of my proposal. The Vice Prime Minister Iwakura being absent, at that time, from Yedo I could not engage his influence in favour of my suggestions, but, on his return, which occurred lately, I took an opportunity of conversing with him on the subject. He then told me that if Mr. Miyamoto brought back a favourable report from Corea the Japanese Government might then be disposed to act in the manner I wished. Until his return they did not feel quite sure as to their own footing in Corea, but if the visit of the Envoy to Yedo had produced a good effect by showing the Coreans, among other things, the advantages of foreign intercourse, and how it should be conducted, and if there was reason to hope that the unreasonable hostility and dislike hitherto shown by the Coreans to foreigners was abating, the Japanese Government might then exert their influence to persuade the Corean Government to conclude Treaties with other Powers. His Excellency reminded me that the Coreans entertain a special aversion for the French, chiefly because they charge them with having desecrated and plundered the mausolea of some of the old Kings, and this aversion, he said, it will be very difficult to correct.

Mr. Miyamoto's return is looked for at the close of this month.

I have now received from Your Lordship Mr. Adams' despatches Nos. 360, 388, and 389 of the 25th May and 2nd June from which I learn that the Duc Decazes will endeavor to obtain a Treaty with Corea through the good offices either of the Chinese or Japanese Government, and that he considers that it would be a great imprudence on the part of the French Government to send an expedition to Corea where the difficulties of navigation are so considerable.

It would certainly be well if the anti French feeling in Corea, which appears to tell against other nations, could be allayed by any friendly intervention, but when we have seen a Japanese squadron of eight or nine vessels navigate the Corean Waters in mid winter, without sustaining loss or casualty, it may be hoped that foreign nautical skill would not be found less capable whenever it may be judged desirable to employ it.

The Corean interpreter referred to in Mr. Adams' despatch No. 389 as having been so serviceable to Kuroda is doubtless GokeShiyaku—the man mentioned in my despatch No. 102—who acquired his information and liberal views as to foreign politics from Mr. Mayers at Peking.

I have, &c.

Harry S. Parkes

H.S. Parkes (1876. 8. 11) → Derby

조선 연해 탐사에 대한 조선 정부의 태도 변화 보고

(No. 132)
The Earl of Derby

Yedo
August 11, 1876

My Lord,

    I have to thank Your Lordship for having been so good as to communicate to me in your despatch No. 72 the views of the Admiralty relative to the Survey of the outlying Islands on the Corean Coast by H.M.S. "Sylvia."

    That my action in this matter may not appear inconsistent I trust it will be borne in mind that, when I suggested, in my despatch No. 61, of April last, that this Survey should be delayed the circumstances were different to those which existed in July 1875 when I recommended that it should be undertaken.

    At the latter date there seemed no prospect, whatever, of Corea being brought into amicable relations with any power, and the feeling which prevailed in that country at that date may be judged of by the attack which was shortly afterwards made on the Japanese Ean vessel "Unyokan," and also on the boats of H.M.S. "Sylvia." In advising the survey, in the first instance, I certainly was of opinion that we could not be expected to wait for that feeling to change before we took measures to protect our ships from the risk to which they are now exposed whenever they pass the Corean coast; but there appeared reason to suppose that a favourable change was occurring when we learned that the Corean Government had conceded to the Japanese Mission sent early this year full rights of navigation and commerce as soon as they were demanded, and had also given Japan permission to make a Survey of the whole Corean Coast. It then occurred to me as possible that our own Government, on becoming acquainted with the Treaty concluded by Japan with Corea, would perhaps be disposed to send a Mission there to negotiate for similar advantages. In that case, I think it would have been better, even in the interest of the Survey alone, that it should have been postponed until the Corean Government had been communicated with, as it is obvious that much more can be accomplished when the Authorities of the country are willing to afford assistance to surveyors than when they meet them with obstruction or opposition. It may occur to Your Lordship that my views on this subject were epitomized in my telegram of the 6th of June in which I observed "I am of opinion that it is undesirable to proceed with "Sylvia"'s Survey if a mission be contemplated, but, if not, then that Corean Envoy should receive notice of the Survey."

As no mission, however, is apparently, at present contemplated, I have no longer any objections to offer to the Survey being resumed, and indeed I think it is desirable that this should now be done for the reasons I gave in July last year. My despatch No. 110 will have informed Your Lordship that, as soon as I heard through Admiral Ryder, on the 25th of June, that the survey was to be prosecuted I took advantage of the despatch of the Japanese Commissioner Mr. Miyamoto to Corea to request the Japanese Foreign Minister to urge the Government of Corea to give directions that H.M.S. "Sylvia" and "Swinger" should be properly treated, and I lately had the satisfaction of hearing from the Vice Prime Minister, whose opinion is probably the best obtainable on Corean Subjects, that if Mr. Miyamoto's representations are made in time he believes they will have the effect of preventing opposition being offered by the Coreans to the surveying operations of those ships.

The Lords Commissioners of the Admiralty naturally attach importance to the experience gained by our surveying vessels on the Coast of Corea in 1861-63, but it should be remembered that various events have occurred since that period which have affected the policy and self esteem of the Corean Government. In the interval they have burnt the American vessel "General Sherman," and murdered all on board, and they have repulsed, in their opinion, the squadrons of France and the United States. They have also issued orders that whenever a foreign vessel appears on their coast she is to be driven away. We have seen that they applied this rule to the Japanese last year, and also to the "Sylvia." We have also seen, however, that they apologized to the Japanese Government, and promised to behave differently in the future, as soon as the latter sent an expedition, composed, it may be observed, of very indifferent ships, to demand redress, and it may now be hoped that through the influence of the Japanese Government the above named orders may be abrogated, and that the "Sylvia" may be treated differently on her present cruize.

I have the honour to be with the highest respect,

My Lord,
Your Lordship's most Obedient, humble Servant,

                                    Harry S. Parkes

26

H.S. Parkes (1876. 8. 15) ➜ Derby

일본의 중개에 관한 嚴倉具視와 회견 보고

(No. 137)
Confidential
The Earl of Derby

Yedo
August 15, 1876

My Lord,

  I have the honour to report, in explanation of the telegram which I forwarded to Your Lordship on the 13th instant, that on the previous day I visited the Vice Prime Minister by invitation, and that His Excellency referred at once to the conversation relative to Corea which passed between us at our last interview, and which I reported to Your Lordship in my Despatch No. 133.

  His Excellency informed me that he had submitted to the Cabinet my suggestions that Japan should endeavor to persuade the Corean Government to enter into relations with Foreign Powers, that the Japanese Government were now of opinion that it was desirable that they should act in accordance with those suggestions, and that, on the return of Mr. Miyamoto, they would take up the question and use all their influence for that purpose.

  It affords me much pleasure to make this announcement to Your Lordship, as from the moment that I found that the visit of the Corean Envoy to Yedo denoted the establishment of a friendly understanding between the two countries, I have urged the Japanese Government to take a resolution of this nature. For the reasons stated in my Despatch No. 102 the Foreign Minister hesitated to give me any assurance on the subject; he was afraid to awaken suspicion on the part of the Coreans by spontaneously advising them to accept intercourse with foreign countries, but if a foreign government had taken any step, or had proposed to take any step, for the purpose of opening relations with that country Japan could then have acted as the adviser of the Coreans without exciting their distrust, and with some prospect of being listened to.

  The present resolution of the Government is perhaps attributable in some measure to favorable accounts received from Mr. Miyamoto, and partly perhaps to a desire that Japan should not be behind China in the counsels of Corea. Another object is also discernable in a remark made to me by the Vice Prime Minister that he believed that some of the Coreans were satisfied that in order to hold their country against Russia they must make friends among other Powers.

The Government do not appear to have yet heard of Mr. Miyamoto's arrival at the capital, but a letter from one of his suite reporting his visit to Fusan while en route to his destination has been published, and shows that the Coreans received him at that place with much more cordiality than they have ever before shown. He appears to have been willingly entertained in Dorai, the city to which Moriyama had vainly striven for years to gain admission, and the Governor or Prefect of that city returned his visit on board his ship at Gorio, this being I believe the first time that Corean Authorities have paid an official visit to a Japanese ship. I enclose a translation of this account.

I have the honour to be with the highest respect,
My Lord,
Your Lordship's most obedient humble servant

Harry S. Parkes

27

H.S. Parkes (1876. 9. 26) → Derby

서양선박 보호에 관한 宮本小一의 제안 보고

No. 153
Confidential
The Earl of Derby

Yedo
September 26, 1876

My Lord,

    In my despatch No. 149 of the 12th instant, I reported that Mr. Miyamoto had returned to Yedo the previous evening. This, although announced in print, proved to be a mistake as he did not arrive until the 20th instant.

    It soon became known that this mission had proved satisfactory, and that he had succeeded in negotiating all the supplementary arrangements contemplated by the XIth Article of the Treaty of February last. As Mr. Miyamoto had kindly promised to visit me, I had hoped to have been able to furnish Your Lordship with some particulars of his negotiations, but illness has unfortunately prevented the fulfillment of his promise. In common with several of his suite he appears to have suffered from the climate of Corea.

    The Vice Prime Minister, however, called on me yesterday and supplied me with the following interesting information.

    Mr. Miyamoto, he said, had been exceedingly well received. On arriving at Kokwa, he was at once invited to the Capital, and to an audience with the King. The ceremony of his reception at Court was as honourable as could be desired, the best conveyances were placed at his disposal, and he was escorted by officers of the highest rank, and by a large retinue of musicians and mounted men. His negotiations proceeded rapidly and satisfactorily, and on the 21st or 22nd of August he concluded a supplementary treaty. The readiness shown by the Coreans to negotiate on this occasion contrasted strongly with the difficulties they had made when the first Treaty was being discussed. The visit of the Corean Envoy to Japan had evidently created a marked effect, and had induced the Corean Government to abandon their former reserve.

The supplementary Treaty, the Vice Prime Minister went on to observe, relates only to Japanese Affairs, with the exception, however, of one article which concerns foreigners and which is to the following effect:

"Hitherto Corea has had no relations with foreign countries, but Japan for some years past has been in friendly alliance with all nations. In future, therefore, whenever ships belonging to any of those nations happen to be shipwrecked on the Coast of Corea, their crews will be treated, as justice requires, with the utmost kindness and consideration, and in case they should wish to return to their country, they shall be handed over to the Japanese Consul, resident at one of the open Ports, who will take charge of them."

I observed to the Vice Prime Minister that the insertion of such an Article in the new Treaty was very creditable to Japan, and the Envoy who had negotiated it.

His Excellency then remarked that Mr. Miyamoto had intended to wait until he had concluded his Treaty before entering on the subject of the Surveying operations of the British Ships, respecting which he had been charged by the Foreign Minister, at my request, to make an announcement to the Corean Government, as I reported to Your Lordship in my despatch No. 117 of the 10th July. But the Corean Ministers, themselves, brought up the question by enquiring if he knew that the English ships were off the coast.

Mr. Miyamoto replied that he intended to speak to them on that subject, that, before he left Yedo, the British Minister had asked the Japanese Minister for Foreign Affairs to inform the Corean Government—as foreign Governments had no means of communicating with Corea direct—that these ships were proceeding to Corea for surveying purposes, but with no unfriendly object, and only in order to provide for the present necessities of navigation. He assured them that they might fully rely on the truth of this announcement in support of which he proceeded to explain that although the dangers of the Corean Coast did not formerly concern foreigners, this was no longer the case, as their ships are now continually passing that coast on voyages from Shanghai and the three Northern Ports of China to the ports of Japan and the Russian settlements to the North of Corea. The survey of the numerous islands and rocks which stud the Corean Coast had, therefore, become indispensable. He therefore strongly advised the Corean Ministers, in the interests of their own country, to offer no discourtesy to these Surveying vessels, but to treat them well, and he urged that it was erroneous of them to suppose that their country could be protected by the height of its mountains or the shallowness of its seas.

The Corean Ministers replied that they were quite disposed to act as he desired, and that orders to treat these ships well should be issued by the local Authorities. The latter before Mr. Miyamoto left had reported that they had supplied the "Sylvia" and "Swinger" with wood, water, and rice.

The Vice Prime Minister then proceeded to give some account of Mr. Miyamoto's communications with the Corean Government respecting foreign countries. After the Supplementary Treaty had been signed he was entertained by all the Ministers of State. Maps and globes were produced, and Mr. Miyamoto pointed out the relative positions of the various countries, and particularly of the "six great powers." "You have one of these," he observed, "as your immediate neighbour, and another of them—England—is as good as your neighbour, while they can all approach you with their ships whenever they please. Hitherto your view of the outer world has been limited to China on one side, and Japan on the other, and while your intercourse with those two nations has been guided by the maxim that China should be treated with Li (courtesy) and Japan with Sin (good Faith) your uniform policy towards other powers is described by the phrase, 'Close the country and repel the barbarians'. This policy you cannot longer maintain. You should endeavor to treat all nations equally with Li and Sin, as it is hopeless for you to think of opposing them with arms. If you have any doubt as to the truth of what I tell you, choose some men, and send them to Europe and America, and let them see and judge for themselves. Japan will supply them with interpreters and guides."

The Corean Ministers heard all that Mr. Miyamoto said without offering any observations. In the evening, however, two members of the Council went to Mr. Miyamoto's residence, and made some apology for the silence with which his remarks had been received. The acknowledged the justice of his arguments, and regretted that he had not been asked for the fuller information which they— the visitors—would be glad to learn. This gave Mr. Miyamoto an opportunity of going over the same ground again in greater detail. After hearing all that he urged in favor of friendly relations with foreign countries, they told him that unfortunately their laws did not admit of change, and even if they should come to an understanding with foreigners, the innovations which foreign intercourse would introduce into the country would occasion internal difficulties of the gravest nature. The Government had pledged itself to the people to resist all intercourse with foreigners, and this resolution had been recorded on pillars of stone, which had been erected in every district, and stood in every highway. These pillars bore the inscription "Should foreigners invade our land he who does not attack them, but counsels peace, is a traitor to his country." Under these circumstances they thought it impossible to open relations with foreign countries, and they asked Miyamoto to communicate to the latter a message to that effect.

Miyamoto replied that Japan was on friendly terms with all foreign powers as well as with Corea, and was willing to use her good offices between them whenever she should be invited to do so, but that she could lend no support to a policy of exclusion, and could not be the medium of communicating to foreign countries such a message as the above.

At this point, said the Vice Prime Minister, the discussion closed. Mr. Miyamoto could not prevail upon the Corean government to say that they would accept foreign intercourse, but he is satisfied that he has convinced them of the futility of attacking any foreign ships that may happen to visit them, and acts of open hostility, he believes will not again be repeated.

I thanked the Vice Prime Minister warmly for this interesting communication, and then enquired what steps the Japanese Government proposed to take in order to carry out the assurance he had given me (as reported in my despatch No. 137 of the 15th ultimo) that on the return of Miyamoto they would use all their influence to persuade the Corean government to enter into relations with foreign Powers.

He replied that I had asked him a difficult question, and one which he was not then prepared to answer. It would be necessary, he said, to find out some plan by which the Corean Government could get over the pledge they had give their people as to resisting foreigners, without having to submit to too grave a compromise. A great change had to be effected without it being called a change, as that was a word to which the Coreans entertained the strongest aversion, and it was not easy to see how such a revolution of opinion was to be brought about. His Excellency observed that Japan was, at one time, in the same difficulty, but the restoration of the Mikado to power gave the new Government an opportunity of reforming their position towards foreigners, and, since that time, everything had gone on well. Unfortunately, the antecedents of the foreign question in Corea carried with them some unhappy associations, and foreigners were regarded as national enemies. The French expedition, and the spoliation of the Royal tombs which took place on that occasion rankles deeply,

His Excellency remarked, in the Corean mind, and has left a very unfavourable impression.

The Corean Government might save appearances towards their own people, I suggested, by allowing themselves to be satisfied that foreigners had now become their friends. We, the English, had lately given them a proof of friendship in our treatment of the shipwrecked Corean Li Yuen-Chun, and on the other hand our thanks would be due to the Coreans for the Attention which His Excellency informed me they had shown to our surveying ships. Might not a visit from a friendly nation which has never had any trouble with Corea—a visit designed, if it were thought advisable, for the exchange of courtesies only—enable the Corean Government to take fresh ground, and announce to the people that the condition of affairs was changed, and that they had no longer anything to apprehend from foreigners. The mere fact that two or three English ships going to Corea, and being well received by the Government would surely have a good effect.

The Vice Prime Minister agreed with me that such a visit might have a very good effect, and he began to put questions to me as to the proceedings of the surveying vessels and their intercourse with the Coreans. On this point, however, I could give him no information, which surprised His Excellency, as Her Majesty's Ship "Sylvia," he reminded me, had lately visited Nagasaki. I am sorry that Captain St. John, who has since returned to his Surveying ground, did not give me an opportunity of profiting on that occasion by the experience he has gained.

His Excellency then terminated the interview, which was rather a hurried one, by observing that he would again consider the subject with me at a later date. He added that, as the Foreign Minister Mr. Terashima, had that day returned to Yedo, I should obtain official information from him respecting Miyamoto's proceedings in Corea, and should treat as confidential the particulars he had given me.

I congratulated His Excellency on the result of Mr. Miyamoto's negotiations observing that Japan had achieved the success of placing her own relations with Corea on a satisfactory footing, and she would also gain much additional credit if she was instrumental in bringing Corea into friendly intercourse with the world.

His Excellency remarked upon the change that had already taken place in Corea as affording some hope that more might be accomplished. This time last year, he observed, our representative (Moriyama), was refused an interview with the Prefect of Torai, an officer of comparatively low rank, and now the King of Corea had himself invited another of our Envoys (Miyamoto) to an audience and had shown him every possible attention. Last year the Coreans would look at nothing of foreign make or shape, but on the occasion of Miyamoto's visit, his ship was filled from morning to night with persons of various ranks, officers, draftsmen, artizans and others, who made the closest examination, and took drawings of everything in the ship. The Corean Authorities also showed the utmost interest in maps and books on foreign subjects, and the old Regent himself—the greatest opponent of foreigners—wrote to ask Miyamoto to give him any maps he could spare.

I need not observe to Your Lordship that this change for the better is not limited to the Japanese. We have now a distinct guarantee based on the faith of a Treaty stipulation that shipwrecked foreigners shall be humanely treated and restored to their countries, our own surveying vessels, it appears, are being well treated and allowed to carry out their surveying work, and we have also a reliable assurance that foreign vessels visiting Corea are no longer exposed to the risk of attack. I believe, therefore, that English ships might now proceed there without fear of collision, thought it is evident that it would be of no advantage to them, but the reverse to go there on the first occasion in the company of French ships.

I have, &c.

Harry S. Parkes

28

H.S. Parkes (1876. 10. 11) ➜ Derby

조선의 배외주의와 수교 가능성에 관한 嚴倉와 회견 보고

No. 163
very Confidential
The Earl of Derby

Yedo
October 11, 1876

My Lord,

    With reference to my Despatch No. 153 of the 26th ultimo, I should inform Your Lordship that on the 5th Instant I had another conversation with the Vice Prime Minister on the subject of how relations might be brought about between Corea and foreign powers.

    His Excellency dwelt a good deal upon the difficulties with which the Corean Government would have to contend in departing from their old policy of exclusion. They had committed themselves to that policy towards the nation, and would find it very hard to turn round and sanction an opposite course. The stone-pillars referred to in the above-mentioned despatch as denouncing all foreigners as national enemies, had been set up by the Government themselves, and would be a standing record against them. He could appreciate their embarrassment as Japan was at one time in a similar position.

    I replied that I thought the difficulty of Corea was not so great as that which Japan had so successfully encountered. Corea had no feudal system to contend with; the Government was not divided against itself as was the case with Japan under the Shogunate; and the will of the rulers of Corea was law to the nation. They had chosen at one time to call upon their people to treat foreigners as their enemies; and if they were satisfied, as they should be, that no case existed for maintaining that enmity any longer, and that it was now impolitic to do so, they might find a way of establishing friendly feeling in its stead. A reasonable Government would be glad to have an opportunity of announcing to their people that they were on good terms with the world; and in taking such a step the Corean Government would not have to contend with popular opposition, but probably only with diverse opinion among themselves.

Their chief difficulty appeared to me to be one of amour propre, which I thought they might get over by assigning a change of circumstances as a ground for a change of policy. At one time they regarded foreigners as their enemies; now they had reason to look upon them as their friends. Their action should therefore be suited to this change of position.

His Excellency remarked that it was doubtful whether the Coreans were yet satisfied that foreigners are their friends, and they had no particular facts to point to as a reason to be given to their people for a change of policy.

I asked His Excellency what effect a foreign visit might have if paid purely for friendly purposes. Suppose, I said, that England should wish to thank Corea for her friendly reception of our surveying ships, or to acknowledge the good feeling shown by Corea in engaging, in the Supplementary Treaty recently concluded by Mr. Miyamoto, to treat shipwrecked foreigners with kindness, might not the Corean Government be able to point to a visit paid to them for such objects, as a proof that foreigners were no longer enemies, but friends?

His Excellency replied that he thought such a visit might have a very happy effect, if undertaken for the objects named, and not for the purpose of obtaining a Treaty. If good feeling were once established, Treaties would probably follow.

His Excellency then added, with some earnestness, that he was satisfied that relations between Corea and Foreign Powers, if they could be brought about in a friendly way, were essential to the independence of that country. A baby, he observed, could see that Russia wants to possess Corea, and the former, therefore, would not be pleased to see Corea concluding Treaties with western Powers. He was anxious to know what Powers were disposed to make Treaties with Corea, and what Russia would think or do, if she saw that Corea was willing to negotiate such Treaties.

I replied that although Russia might not care to see Corea entering into relations with Foreign Powers, she could not possibly object to her doing so. She would have to accept the situation, whatever that might be—preferring probably the absence of Treaties, but accommodating herself to their existence if they were made. The action of other countries in regard to negotiations with Corea would depend mainly upon that of Great Britain. If the latter thought it worthwhile to treat with Corea, and succeeded in doing so, several of the other leading nations, as France, Germany, and the United States, would doubtless follow her example.

I may here refer to a remark made me by Mr. Miyamoto, the Japanese

Envoy who has just returned from Corea. In speaking of the difficulty of persuading the Coreans to accept relations with foreign countries, he observed that less opposition would probably be offered to England, if she were the first to make the attempt, than to other countries. The French, he said, are hated by the Coreans, and they do not think favourably of the Americans.

To return to my conversation with the Vice Prime Minister, I should add that His Excellency observed that he did not think China would make any endeavour to bring Corea into communication with foreign countries. Japan, on the other hand, he said, was quite disposed to make an earnest effort in that direction, as he could see that the interest of Japan in the independence of Corea, was second only to that of Corea herself. The work of persuasion, however, was one which it was very difficult for Japan to execute singlehanded; and he hinted to me that if England desired relations with Corea, she should do something herself to bring them about.

It occurs to me to suggest to your Lordship that perhaps a friendly visit of the kind above mentioned might serve to pave the way for ulterior negotiations. A vessel of war of some size, with one or two gun vessels in company—probably those employed upon the survey would be well suited—might proceed to Kokiva in the spring, and endeavour to open friendly communications with the Government at the capital. Subject to the opinion of Her Majesty's Minister at Peking, I may venture to remark that the Chinese Secretary of that Legation would perhaps be the most fitting officer to be entrusted with this preliminary negotiation; but it would also, I think, be highly desirable that he should be accompanied by an officer from this Legation proficient in the Japanese language, and familiar with Japanese relations with Corea.

The possibility of England and other countries seeking the assistance of Japan in establishing relations with Corea, has already struck the attention of the native press and I enclose a translation of a leading article containing an interesting argument on this subject; and professing to disapprove of Japan interfering for such an object. The writer considers that it would be impossible for Japan to please both Corean and western Powers, and observes that England will probably be able to accomplish her own work in Corea, without coming to Japan for help.

I have, &c.

H.S. Parkes

FO (1876. 11. 30) → H.S. Parkes

조선 교섭 연기 지령

F.O. Nov. 30, 1876

Sir H.S. Parkes
No. 126 Conf.

Copy to Admiralty
Sir,

I have had under my consideration your Despatch No. 163 the 11th Oct., marked "Very Confidential" reporting a conversation which you had held with the Japanese Vice Prime Minister upon the subject of Corea.

With reference to the suggestions which you make for establishing intercourse between Corea and this country, I have to state to you, that before making any overtures with this object, H.M.'s Gov't are disposed to await the result of the Treaty recently concluded with Corea by Japan, and they do not therefore consider it desirable, for the present at any rate, to send an expedition such as you propose.

Inclosure

Sir H.S. Parkes No. 163 very Conf:

The conclusion of a Treaty with Corea or even the establishment of relations of any kind seems a doubtful advantage. As far as we can learn there is no trade in that country worth speaking of, and any expedition such as Sir H.S. Parkes suggests would run the risk of coming into collision with the Corean Govt. or of being treated in a manner which would compel us to resort to force. We can always make use of the Japanese should occasion arise for holding communications with Corea.

W.E.C.

Inclosure

F.O. Nov. 27, 1876

I am inclined to think that we had better wait till we see how the Treaty between Japan & Corea works before making any overtures of our own. The expedition might be hazardous & there is no particular hurry about Treaty making with Corea.

It looks as if the Japanese were trying to get us to do something to help them to secure the execution of their own Treaty.

Tell Sir H.S. Parkes that Ministers are disposed to await the results of the Treaty between Corea & Japan before making any overtures and that they do not therefore consider it desirable to send any expedition at all events for the present.

I quite agree.
D
N. 28

H.S. Parkes (1878. 11. 11) ➜ Salisbury

Barbara Taylor 조난시 조선 정부의 원조 보고

The Most Noble
The Marquis of Salisbury, K.G.
No. 113

Yedo
November 11, 1878

My Lord,

I have the honor to report that a British merchant schooner, the "Barbara Taylor" of Greenock, Official Number 67,922, was wrecked on the Corean island of Quelpart on the 21st September, and that the crew were treated in a very hospitable manner by the Corean Authorities, who enabled the master to salve and bring away from the island a great part of the cargo of the wrecked vessel.

I first heard of this occurrence on the 15th October from Mr. Consul Troup, who communicated it to me in the following cypher telegram:

"Is there any objection to man-of-war visiting Quelpart Island to take off shipwrecked crew of British vessel."

To which I at once replied by telegraph in cypher:

"No objection. Telegraph particulars of shipwreck and which man-of-war goes to take off crew. Take care not to offend natives."

On the 20th October, Mr. Troup again telegraphed to me in cypher:

"Norwegian steamer goes to Quelpart tomorrow for crew and cargo. Japanese-Corean interpreter accompanies. Is there any objection to Paul going."

To this I replied by wire, in cypher:

"I entirely approve of Paul going. He should hold as much friendly intercourse as possible with the Corean Authorities."

I should mention that Mr. Paul is the Assistant at present attached to the Nagasaki Consulate.

Subsequently, I received from Mr. Troup a despatch dated the 17th October, in which he reported to me the particulars of the wreck, and the measures which were then being considered by the master and his agents, and also by Mr. Troup and the Senior Naval Officer at Nagasaki, for bringing away from Quelpart the salved cargo of the "Barbara Taylor," as well as the shipwrecked crew. I enclose a copy of this despatch (from Mr. Troup, October 17, 1878) and its three enclosures (Affidavit—October 10, 1878; Mr. Taylor to Mr. Troup—Oct. 15, 1878; Mr. Troup to Mr. Taylor—Oct. 17, 1878), one being the Affidavit of the Master, Mr. John Taylor, in which he describes the way in which his vessel was wrecked and the kind treatment he received from the Corean Authorities.

Although the Senior Naval Officer was quite prepared to proceed to Quelpart, on Mr. Troup's request, to bring away the shipwrecked crew, the latter considered that the salving of the cargo was a service which Her Majesty's Ships could not be expected to render under such circumstances; and indeed it would have been impossible for vessels of the size of the two gun-vessels then at Nagasaki to have taken the salved cargo on board. Eventually the agents of the wrecked ship succeeded in chartering a private steamer—the "Hakon Adelstein," under the Norwegian flag--for this purpose, and Mr. Troup then concluded that it would be unnecessary to send in addition one of Her Majesty's Ships. He determined, however, to give the master and his agents the assistance of Mr. Paul, on hearing from me, as mentioned above, that I approved of his being despatched on this service. In the enclosed despatch (Oct. 23, 1878) Mr. Troup reported to me the departure of the "Hakon Adelstein," and the instructions he had given to Mr. Paul (Oct. 31, 1878).

I have now received from Mr. Troup a further despatch (Nov. 1, 1878), reporting the return of the "Hakon Adelstein," and enclosing a very interesting report by Mr. Paul (Oct. 31, 1878) of his communications with the Corean Authorities. The principal authority of the island sent twice to invite Mr. Paul to visit him at the Capital, and I regret that Mr. Paul was unable to accept this invitation. The time of his stay at the scene of the wreck depended on the movements on the "Hakon Adelstein" and she being a private vessel, chartered at the expense of the agents of the master or the underwriters, he could not request her detention for such a purpose.

His report shows that the Corean Authorities treated both himself and the shipwrecked men with great kindness, that they would accept no remuneration for all of the cost they had incurred in salving the cargo of the "Barbara Taylor," and in reshipping it on board the "Hakon Adelstein," and that the latter brought away everything that could be saved from the wreck. It is curious to notice that the Corean Authorities insisted on burning the hull of the wreck; but as it was of no value, and could not be removed, this act entailed no loss on the insurers. It is undesirable, however, that the Corean Authorities should follow on all occasions a similar course.

Mr. Troup mentions the assistance he received from the Kenreior Prefect of Nagasaki, who lent him the services of an Interpreter in Corean. I intend to thank the Japanese Foreign Minister for this assistance, and to confer with His Excellency as to the best way of conveying to the Corean Authorities some expression of my sense of the kindness they have shown to those shipwrecked British subjects, and, if possible, of dissuading them from burning on all occasions foreign ships that may unfortunately be stranded on their coast. I should also wish the Chief Authority of the island to understand the cause of Mr. Paul's inability to visit him, and that he should not take umbrage at the latter having omitted to do so.

It is very gratifying to me to be able to report to Your Lordship such friendly action on the part of the Corean Authorities, as it denotes a material mitigation of the hostile feeling they have hitherto evinced towards foreigners, and a disposition to give full effect to that Article of their Supplementary Treaty with Japan of 1876, by which they engaged to treat shipwrecked foreigners with kindness, and to restore them to their homes through the agency of the Japanese Authorities. Their humanity in this instance has been extended to an Italian subject—the sole survivor of the Italian barque "Bianca Pertica," who, as shown by Mr. Paul's report, was also brought away from Quelpart by the "Hakon Adelstein."

Mr. Troup's proceedings in this matter, and also those of Mr. Paul, have afforded me much satisfaction, and I beg to recommend them to your Lordship's approval.

I have &c.

Harry S. Parkes

31

H.S. Parkes (1878. 11. 25) → Salisbury

E. Satow의 제주도 파견 보고

No. 117
The Marquis of Salisbury. KG

Yedo
November 25, 1878

My Lord,

    In my Despatch No. 113 of the 11th instant reporting the wreck of the British schooner "Barbara Taylor" on the Island of Quelpart and the hospitable behavior of the Corean Authorities and people, I mentioned that I should confer with the Japanese Foreign Minister as to the best way of conveying to those Authorities my thanks for the great kindness they had thus shown to our distressed countrymen.

    Having mentioned to His Excellency that I thought it desirable to send a Secretary of this Legation to Quelpart for the above purpose in one of Her Majesty's ships, His Excellency concurred in this course, and willingly consented to give me the assistance of the Japanese Interpreter in Corean who accompanied Mr. Paul. He also concurred with me in thinking it desirable that the Officer selected for the service, after visiting Quelpart, should proceed to the Port of Fusan on the mainland, which is now open to Japanese trade in order that the Corean Authorities there might be accurately informed of the object of the visit, and thus be able to make a correct report of the same to the Central Government at Seoul.

    Having then observed to the Foreign Minister that I would send Mr. Satow to Quelpart, he at once furnished him with a letter to the Prefect of Nagasaki instructing him to place the services of the Interpreter in Corean at his disposal, and also with a letter to the Japanese Consul at Sorio (Fusan) directing him to assist Mr. Satow with his good offices in case he should require them.

    I also thought it well to seek the cooperation of the Chinese Minister at this Court on account of the influence which I believe China maintains in Corea, and also because no less than nine out of the twelve men who were saved from the "Barbara Taylor" were Chinese. His Excellency approved of the propriety of the course I was taking and spontaneously offered to give Mr. Satow a Note to the Chief Authority of Quelpart (the "Taionshiu") in order to assure him of the real object of the visit and to request him to give Mr. Satow a friendly reception.

I then applied to Captain Poland, the Senior Naval Officer in Japan, for the services of Her Majesty's Ship stationed at Nagasaki, and I instructed Mr. Satow to proceed to that port by the Mail Steamer of the 13th instant. I have heard from Mr. Consul Troup that Mr. Satow arrived at Nagasaki on the night of the 17th, and that he was to leave for Quelpart in H.M.S "Egeria" on the morning of the 19th.

I now beg to enclose a copy of the instructions I furnished to Mr. Satow. I carefully thought over the course I directed him to take, and I do not think it possible that any risk of misunderstanding with the Corean Authorities can thereby be incurred, or that it can expose us to any slight at their hands. It appears to me to be clearly incumbent upon us to acknowledge the great kindness shown to our shipwrecked people by the Corean Authorities, and I have desired Mr. Satow to do this in the manner that shall be most acceptable to those Authorities. I cannot suppose that they will not be willing to receive him with the same friendly feeling as they showed towards the master of the "Barbara Taylor," and subsequently to the party of foreigners who visited them in the Norwegian steamer "Hakon Adelstein," but if this anticipation shall not be realized, I shall feel that we have at least done our duty in the matter, and Mr. Satow may still be able with the assistance of the Japanese Consulat Sorio (Fusan) to satisfy the Corean Government that the visit was well meant, and was prompted by a legitimate and praiseworthy object.

I add an English version of my letter to the Chief Authority of Quelpart (the Taionshiu) which was written in Chinese, as I believe that the written character of that language is understood by all Corean officials. I was also able to send with Mr. Satow the Chinese writer Liu Shegan, whose employment at this Legation I had previously recommended to your Lordship, and who can assist Mr. Satow in communicating with the Corean Authorities in written Chinese, in case the spoken language should be unintelligible to them.

I also enclose a translation of the Note of the Chinese Minister to the Taionshiu, and beg to recommend to Your Lordship notice the good feeling he has shown in writing in such favorable and appropriate terms.

It remains for me to add a copy of my letter to Captain Poland, requesting the services of H.M.S. "Egeria," and in which I pointed out the necessity of the utmost care being taken to guard against any offence being offered to the Coreans—I feel satisfied from my knowledge of Commander Douglas, who is an officer of great experience, and was selected by the Admiralty in 1873 as the Director of the Naval College in Japan, that no endeavour will be wanting on his part to give effect to this request, or to assist Mr. Satow in his mission.

Your Lordship will observe that both the Chinese Minister and myself, in our Notes to the Chief Authority of Quelpost, have impressed upon him the impropriety of the Corean officers insisting upon burning all foreign vessels thrown upon their coast, in which practice, as they stated to Mr. Paul, they were guided by the existing Corean law. I trust that these representations, which will be supported by Mr. Satow in his communications with the Corean Authorities, will lead to the abandonment of such an undesirable rule.

In addition to the report of his visit to Quelpart which I forwarded to Your Lordship in my Despatch No. 113, Mr. Paul has now furnished some Notes on Quelpart, of which I enclose a copy. It contains some interesting particulars respecting the productions, government, and the people of that island and some acceptable evidence of the earnestness of the friendly demonstrations of the latter towards their recent foreign visitors.

In concluding this Despatch I beg to express the hope that my proceedings in this matter may be approved by Your Lordship. I trust I shall not be disappointed in the expectation I have formed that it will serve to promote friendly impressions towards us on the part of the Coreans, while it will at least afford us an opportunity of judging the extent of the improvement in their disposition towards foreigners which is now attributed to them.

I have, &c.

Harry S. Parkes

Inclosure

Mr. Satow's visit to Corea. Sir H.S. Parkes' Instructions.

Yedo
November 13, 1878

As I am of opinion that the humane and friendly conduct of the Corean Authorities of Quelpart Island, in the matter of the wreck of the "Barbara Taylor," should be officially acknowledged, I wish you to proceed to that island in order to convey to them my thanks for their kind treatment of the shipwrecked crew and for the generous assistance which they rendered to the master of that vessel in salving the cargo.

You will accordingly proceed to Nagasaki in the Mitsu Bishi mail steamer leaving from Yokohama today, and on passing Kobe you will communicate personally with Captain Poland, the senior naval officer in Japan, and deliver to him the accompanying despatch. He will instruct Commander Douglas, of Her Majesty's Ship "Egeria," at present at Nagasaki, to convey you to Quelpart and he will give you his instructions to Commander Douglas.

It is desirable that you should be accompanied by Mr. Paul of H.M.'s consulate at Nagasaki, who has lately visited Quelpart, and I have therefore requested Mr. Consul Troup to place that officer under your orders. As arranged between the Foreign Minister and myself, you will apply to the Prefect of Nagasaki for the services of Mr. Takeda the Interpreter in Corean, who lately accompanied Mr. Paul to Quelpart, and in order that you may be able to communicate in China, I also attach to you Mr. Lew Shegan.

I have requested Captain Poland to instruct Commander Douglas to proceed at first to the spot where the "Barbara Taylor" was wrecked, and on arriving there you should endeavour to communicate with the officer, called by Mr. Paul in his report of the 31st October, the "Pu-on-shin." You will inform him that you have been sent by me to thank him and the chief Authority of the Island—called by Mr. Paul the "Tai-on-shin"—for the kindness they showed to the Master and Crew of the "Barbara Taylor." You will explain to him why Mr. Paul was unable to accept the invitation of the Tai-on-shin to visit him at his residence at "Che-ju-pu," and you will state that I wish you to proceed to that city to deliver my thanks to the "Tai-on-shin," and the letters which I and the Chinese Minister at Yedo have addressed to that Functionary. Should the Pu-on-shin object to your proceeding to Che-ju-pu, you will not insist upon doing so, although you will endeavor by friendly persuasion to induce him to consent. He may perhaps wish to take the instructions of the Tai-on-shin on the point. If, in the end, you find that you cannot communicate directly with the latter, you will then hand the two letters to the Pu-on-shin, and request him to forward them to the Tai-on-shin and to give you a receipt for them.

You will inform him of the character of the contents of these letters, and you will mention that I have requested that on any future occasion of a British ship being wrecked at Quelpart, the Corean Authorities will not burn the stranded hull unless it shall have been abandoned by the master or owners as worthless and irremovable. You will at the same time state that I do not complain of their having burned the hull of the "Barbara Taylor," as it was of no value, but you will explain that in other cases it might be possible to float a stranded hull, or to break up and bring away the materials which may sometimes be of value to the owners. If you succeed in seeing the Tai-on-shin, you will also draw his attention to this subject, and you should explain to him or the Pu-on-shin that although appreciating the gratuitous assistance they rendered in salving the cargo of the "Barbara Taylor," we neither expect nor desire that the cost of such assistance should in future be borne by the Corean Authorities.

After visiting Quelpart, I think it is desirable, as I have stated to Captain Poland, that Her Majesty's Ship "Egeria" should proceed to Fusan, as [_____] have had more experience of Foreign questions than those of Quelpart, and are in more immediate communication with the Government at the Capital. It is important that the latter should receive a correct account of this case of wreck, and of the object of the visit of Her Majesty's Ship "Egeria" to Quelpart.

On anchoring off the Japanese settlement at Sorio, you will ascertain whether it is possible to communicate with the Corean Authorities of Fusan, and, if you succeed in doing so, you will express your readiness to wait upon the Prefect of Sorio, if he is willing to receive you. You will inform him, or such of the Corean Authorities of Fusan as you may be able to see, of all of the particulars of the wreck of the "Barbara Taylor," of the highly satisfactory action of the Quelpart Authorities, and of my wish that my thanks for their kindness should be conveyed to the Government at Seoul. You will furnish copies of my letter and that of the Chinese Minister to the Tai-on-shin, and will also draw their attention to my request that stranded British ships should not be burned or destroyed until they have been abandoned as possessing no longer any value to the owner.

If you find the Corean Authorities at Fusan unwilling to hold any communication with you, you will then request the Japanese Consul at Sorio to be so good as to explain to them the object of your visit, and to deliver to them the copies of the letters to the Tai-on-shin. The Foreign Minister has been so good as to furnish you with a letter to the Consul at Sorio, instructing him to render you his good offices in this matter.

As the main object of your expedition is to impart favorable impressions to the Corean Authorities, and to induce them to perceive that we only entertain friendly feelings towards them, you will be careful not to take any step to which they object, or which you find would cause them annoyance. It is of course desirable that you should hold as much communication with them, and acquire as much information as possible on commercial or other subjects, but in doing so you will carefully avoid exciting their suspicion or distrust, and will chiefly endeavor to make your visit an opportunity for improving their feelings towards ourselves. I have no doubt that Commander Douglas, to whom you will show these instructions, will cordially cooperate with you in this important object. I feel that I can add no advice as to the time of your stay at Quelpart or at Fusan, as he and you must naturally be guided in this respect by the circumstances of the position, and the manner of your reception by the Corean authorities.

(signed) Harry S. Parkes

Inclosure

Sir H.S. Parkes to the Chief Authority of the Island of Quelpart, Corea

Yedo. November 12, 1878

Mr. Satow deputed to convey thanks of H.M.'s Minister to Authorities of Quelpart for kindness shown to shipwrecked crew of British merchant ship.

Translation
Sir Harry Parkes, Her Britannic Majesty's Minister in Japan, addresses this communication to the Chief Authority (Taionshin) of the Island of Quelpart in Corea.

The British Consul at Nagasaki has reported to the Undersigned that on the 21st September a British merchant vessel bound from Shanghai to the Russian Settlements on the Amoor with a cargo of tea encountered a heavy storm and was thrown upon the coast of the district of Tsuigi (Chegui) within your honorable jurisdiction when she became a wreck. The Master and the crew escaped to the shore where they at once received friendly succour from your Officers and people, who housed them, supplied them with food, and exerted themselves to the utmost to save and store in safety the cargo of the ship. The honorable Sai-on-shin was then so good as to arrange that the Master should proceed to Nagasaki in a Japanese junk, for the purpose of engaging a vessel to remove the crew and cargo, and when he returned to Tsuigi (Chegui) in another ship accompanied by an officer of the Consulate, they again experienced the same kind treatment from your officers who gave over to them the crew and cargo, and would not allow the master to make them any compensation for the expenses incurred either in the entertainment of the shipwrecked men or in salving the freight.

The Consul concluded his report by recommending to my notice the humane feeling and generous disposition towards foreigners which had thus been shown by the Corean Officers and people.

The Undersigned could not fail to be deeply impressed by this report, and he at once felt that it was incumbent upon him to endeavour to convey to the honorable Tai-on-shin a suitable acknowledgment of his high appreciation of the exceedingly kind services which had [_____] distressed countrymen. But being sensible that he cannot adequately express his thanks in writing he has deputed Mr Satow, a Secretary of Her Majesty's Legation (who is accompanied by a literary Chinese in the Minister's service named Liu Shegan) to proceed to Quelpart on one of Her Majesty's ships in order that he may personally deliver to the honorable Tai-on-shin the thanks of the Undersigned. The latter hopes by this means to increase the friendly feeling which already exists, and he feels assured that that feeling may be relied on to promote hereafter a good understanding between the two countries.

H.M.'s Minister has been informed that the wreck of the vessel was burned by the Corean Authorities, and as it possessed no value he does not take objection to that course having been followed in this instance. But he requests that whenever a shipwreck again occurs the Corean Authorities will allow the Master or the persons interested in the vessel, either to repair or to break up the hull, as they may desire. In the event however of their determining to abandon the wreck as worthless, the Corean Authorities will then be at liberty to deal with it as they may see fit.

As nine of the sailors of this vessel were Chinese, and as they received the same kind treatment as the rest of the crew, the Undersigned has informed the Chinese Minister in Japan of this circumstance and the latter has also written a letter of thanks which he has entrusted to the Undersigned for delivery to the honorable Tai on shin.

The Undersigned begs to conclude this communication by wishing the friend whom he addresses the attainment of the highest prosperity.

(signed) Harry S. Parkes

Inclosure

Chinese Minister in Japan to the Authorities of Quelpart Island

Translation.

To the Chief Authority of Tse-chow (Quelpart)

The Undersigned having been accredited as Minister of China to Japan, has resided here for a year, and is therefore in relation with the various resident foreign Ministers of other countries. His intercourse with the Envoy and Plenipotentiary of Great Britain is of particularly friendly character. From him he has learned that in the course of the last ninth months a British ship laden with tea fell in with a heavy storm at sea, which drove her on the coast of the district of Tsuig-i (Chegui) belonging to your honorable country; that the Corean officers and people promptly succoured the shipwrecked men and salved the cargo; and, in addition to this, they also housed and fed the crew, carefully supplied all their wants, and declined to accept from the Master any remuneration for these generous services.

Thus, by a single act, a twofold good was performed. Good feeling was shown towards a foreign nation, and distress was treated with benevolent consideration. The Englishmen belonging to the wrecked vessel were exceedingly grateful for the kindness they received, and the Master on his return to Nagasaki spoke of his treatment with unbounded admiration. The British Minister is now sending a Secretary of his Legation in a ship to Quelpart, for the special purpose of expressing to you his grateful thanks; and in view of the dependent connection which exists between your honorable country and the high Court I represent, he has requested me to assist him in making his sentiments known by adding a note to the communication which he himself is addressing you.

To this invitation I cordially respond, as I have experience of the sense of right and the regard for courtesy which actuate the great European States, and can appreciate the desire of the British Minister to prove to you his estimation of the kindness you have shown his countrymen. As the natural feelings of courtesy and right draw you towards each other, the rules of friendly intercourse will not fail to be observed (between you). I therefore particularly request that you will receive the British officers now visiting you as guests who merit your confidence, and I sincerely trust that you will inform all the people within your jurisdiction that they come for the purpose of offering you thanks, and that their visit need not be regarded with any apprehension or distrust.

As it appears that eight Chinese were among the crew of the wrecked British ship, and as they also participated in your kindness, I feel that I should add my own thanks to those of the British Minister.

I thank the opportunity afforded me by this communication to express my wishes for your happiness.

(signed) Ho Ju Chang
Kwang-su, 4th year, 10th month, 18th day-(November 12, 1878)

Postscript.

I am informed that the wreck in this case was burned (by the Corean Authorities). I should therefore point out that on any similar occasion you should render the disabled vessel all the assistance in your power, and if you are not successful (in saving the ship) you should then leave it to the Master or the owners to take what steps they please, but you should not burn or destroy the wreck.

H.S. Parkes (1878. 12. 2) ➜ Salisbury

관세 협상을 위한 花房義質의 조선 파견 보고

Confidential
No. 125
The Marquis of Salisbury KG

Yedo
December 2, 1878

My Lord,

    I reported in my Despatch No. 118 of the 25th ultimo that the Japanese Government had sent Mr. Hanabusa, one of the First Secretaries of the Foreign Department, to Corea in order to endeavour to adjust a difference which had arisen at Fusan in consequence of the Corean Authorities having lately imposed duties on Japanese Trade amounting apparently to about fifteen or twenty per cent, and which were considered by the Japanese to be prohibitory.

    In a conversation which I have since had with Mr. Terashima, the Minister for Foreign Affairs, His Excellency observed that, although it was understood when Japan made her treaty with Corea that Customs duties should not be levied by either government on the trade between the two Countries, still he could not deny that Corea had the right to impose such duties, provided they were of moderate amount, if she wished to do so, as Japan also had the right to impose duties on Corean imports. But that it had been distinctly stipulated in an Agreement, which had not been made public, that no charges of the character of inland duties should be levied by the Corean Authorities, and the charges now complained of were of that description. He believed however that Mr. Hanabusa would be able to persuade the Corean Authorities to agree to a rational arrangement. This issue was a narrow one as the Corean Authorities alone desired to impose these charges; the Corean people were opposed to them and were on the side of the Japanese in the matter.

    On my suggesting a doubt as to whether Mr. Hanabusa would find that the local Corean Authorities were able to discuss and settle a question which could probably be only competently treated by the Central Government, His

Excellency remarked that Mr. Hanabusa would be guided by circumstances. In the absence of functionaries empowered to treat with him direct he could convey his representations to the local Corean Authorities through the Japanese Consular officer at Fusan, and he would not attempt to proceed to the Corean capital without receiving further instructions from Yedo.

His Excellency added that the accounts which had found their way into the Japanese press of the collision which had occurred between the Japanese residents of Fusan and the Coreans were derived from private letters, and were, he believed, exaggerated. It was true that a party of Japanese had proceeded to the city of Sorio to present a protest against the levy of charges complained of, that they had been stoned by the Coreans, and had used staves of wood with some effect in self-defence, but the number of the party was by no means as great as had been stated—he believed it was less that fourteen—and that no serious wounds had been inflicted on either side.

I enclose a statement from a local paper which describes this demonstration. It says that the Japanese residents at Fusan, being dissatisfied with the mild action of their Consular Officer, had resolved to take the matter into their own hands, and overawe the Corean Authorities by delivering their own protest against the charges imposed upon their trade. That a body of about a hundred and sixty had proceeded to Sorio and for this purpose, and that in the disturbance which ensued, about thirty Coreans were wounded and six Japanese. It is also stated elsewhere that in consequence of this demonstration the Corean Authorities agreed to allow the delivery, free of the new charges, of such goods as had been purchased by Japanese before those charges were imposed.

I believe it is the intention of the Japanese Government to proceed deliberately and cautiously with the discussion of this affair, but in dealing with it they will probably find it difficult to avoid that consideration of other questions, such as that of the two other ports which according to the Treaty should have been opened in October 1877. I believe that the Japanese wish to obtain one Port on the East Coast, and one on the West. As the former, they have named the fine harbour of Yun-san well known to the Russians as Port Lazareff, while they appear to have not yet made up their minds as to the Port on the West coast. I heard from a Japanese Minister that the Corean Government had refused to open Yun-san, and that they do nothing to facilitate the choice of either one or the other of the tow Ports.

It is not impossible therefore that the current of these negotiations may not run as smoothly as could be desired. War with Corea has long had many advocates in this country, and although I believe the Government continue to be opposed to such views, they may yet find it difficult in case of anything unforeseen occurring, such as the failure of Mr. Hanabusa's mission, or a fresh collision between the Japanese and Coreans at Fusan, to control the agitation which might thereby be created either among their political opponents or their excitable troops. It may also be concluded I think that under such circumstances Russian arguments would not be wanting to encourage them to engage in hostilities with Corea, which have already been freely talked of in the Japanese press.

In this connection I beg to invite the special attention of Your Lordship to the enclosed Article from a native journal which has a semi-official character. It seems to be intended to allay excitement by showing that the object of Mr. Hanabusa's mission is to persuade the Corean Government by friendly negotiation to agree to a fair tariff and such other commercial arrangements as are required in the mutual interest of both countries, and it argues that full allowance should be made for the ignorance of the Coreans on the subject of trade, and for their repugnance to foreign intercourse, which is similar to that which at no remote date was entertained by the Japanese themselves. The writer then proceeds to dwell with considerable force on the important political position of Corea. It may be a poor country, but Japan cannot allow it to be annexed or occupied by any other power. The great Eastern question which has so long agitated Europe has now he observes reached the centre of Asia, and will soon extend to Corea, for "Corea is the Turkey of the East of Asia, and Fusan is Constantinople. If it falls into the hands of Russia, and if she can combine both land and naval forces at Fusan she will then have no difficulty in advancing towards Japan on one side while she can also threaten China on the other." He remarks that the present want by Russia of a good harbour on the Pacific border of her dominons naturally attracts her insatiable greed for territory in that direction, but he adds "if Russia be suffered to take possession of Corea in the East of Asia, this would be like furnishing a tiger with wings or supplying a thief with a key." He refers to Tsushima as showing that as early as 1862 Russia had designs on that important island, although he fails to describe correctly the part taken by Admiral Sir James Hope in obliging the Russian vessel which had remained there for months, and had put up buildings on shore, to retire from the position she had assumed. As China, he believes, has no power to do anything in the East, it rests with Japan to maintain the balance of power in that quarter by securing the independence of Corea. To effect this object friendly relations should be preserved between the two countries and Japan should seek to lead Corean gradually onward in the path of civilization, and endeavor to induce her to enter into treaties with England, France, and other countries. He concludes by observing that preparations should be made in anticipation of possible and indeed probable events.

Judging from conversations which I have had with the Chinese Minister at this Court I have reason to think that his Government, or certain members of it, are as deeply impressed as this Japanese writer is with the danger of Russian aggression in Corea. He is evidently sensible that China is far more vulnerable in that direction and in Manchuria than in Kashgar, or on the confines of Ili, and he is convinced that the only way by which Corea may be preserved as a nation is for her to open her Ports to the Commerce of European Powers. He has also mentioned to me in strict confidence that Li Hungchang has very lately written to the Chief Minister of the Corean Government to the following effect—"The time has come for you to relinquish your old policy of foreign exclusion, and to show that you comprehend the true situation of your country as regards Russia whose frontier joins yours, and who has now formed large military establishments on that frontier. Japan is friendly to you; she wishes you to open your Ports and has asked for Yun-san. Russia is opposed to the opening of Yun-san, or any of your ports, but you should not fail to understand her real object in desiring to see you maintain your present exclusion. In order to defeat that object you should keep on good terms with Japan, but more than this you should enter into friendly relations with other countries, and that without loss of time."

I have thought it desirable to report these particulars to Your Lordship as either the proceedings of Japan in Corea, or the course of events in Central Asia may at any moment bring Corea into a degree of prominence, well deserving of the attention of Her Majesty's Government, who may not think it expedient that Russia should acquire the commanding position in these seas which the possession of one or more good ports in Corea would give her. I am not prepared to place much confidence in the endeavours either of Japan or of China to induce that country to place itself in relations with the world, as efforts would not be wanting to divert Japan from steadily pursuing such a policy by holding out the temptations of a Russian alliance, while the slowness of Chinese action does not give promise of the counsel above-mentioned being earnestly impressed upon Corea, unless a lively sense of her own danger should induce China to do so. But it appears to me that such endeavours either on the part of Japan or China are deserving of encouragement, and that the preservation of the integrity of Corea affects Great Britain almost as largely as it does those two countries.

 I have, &c.

Harry S. Parkes

33

H.S. Parkes (1878. 12. 2) ➡ Salisbury

Satow가 지참한 감사 서한의 접수 거절 보고

No. 127
The Most Noble
The Marquis of Salisbury KG

Yedo
December 2, 1878

My Lord,

　　In continuation of my Despatch No. 117 of the 25th ultimo I have the honor to report that on the 28th ultimo, I received the enclosed telegram from Mr. Satow in cipher reporting his return to Nagasaki. He therein informs me that the Chief Authority at Quelpart and also the Corean Authorities at Fusan had declined to receive visitors or letters, but that good effects had been produced by the visit, the people at both places being friendly and the Corean functionaries polite.

　　As I look for Mr. Satow's return on the 5th instant I shall soon be in a position to furnish Your Lordship with full particulars of his proceedings and probably with the reasons of the Chief Authority of Quelpart for declining to receive Mr. Satow while he had twice pressed Mr. Paul to visit him at his residence in the capital of the island. It is possible that he may have been influenced by instructions received in the meantime from the mainland.

　　I take this opportunity to forward to Your Lordship an account of the visit of the "Hakon Adelstein" to Quelpart which has been published by one of the private persons who accompanied that vessel, as the writer gives some additional information to that contained in Mr. Paul's reports, while he entirely confirms the impressions of the latter as to the openhearted kindness shown by the Corean Authorities and people both to the shipwrecked crew of the "Barbara Taylor," and to those who subsequently visited them in the "Hakon Adelstein."

　　I have, &c.

Harry S. Parkes

Inclosure

Copy
(Telegram)
To Sir H.S. Parkes,

　　Returned today. Island chief Funcionary refused (to) receive letters (or) visitors. Showed copies to his messengers. Continent functionary refused likewise. Handed copies (to) Japanese Consul. Good effects produced nevertheless. People (of) both places friendly, functionaries polite. Return (in) steamer tomorrow.

　　　　　　　　　　　　　Received at 6:20 p.m., November 28, 1878

34

H.S. Parkes (1878. 12. 18) ➔ Salisbury

Satow의 제주도 방문시 조선인의 우호적 태도 보고

No. 141
The Most Noble
The Marquis of Salisbury KG

Yedo
December 18, 1878

My Lord,

In continuation of my Despatch No. 136 of the 12th instant I beg to offer the few following remarks relative to Mr. Satow's visit to Corea.

I think it may be gathered from the reception of Mr. Satow and also that of Mr. Paul that neither the Corean officials nor the Corean people entertain any positive antipathy towards foreigners. Mr. Satow observes in his report that at Quelpart "not a single hostile look appeared on the faces of either officials or common people, on the contrary, they were all courteous and friendly in their bearing." And at Fusan he remarked that "as on all previous occasions the Coreans abounded in courteous phrases, and I detected no signs of personal unfriendliness to foreigners. They alleged in reply to every proposition that the 'law of the country' was the obstacle which lay in the way of official relations. A large crowd of the ordinary people accompanied us down to the boat, smiling, courteous, and good-humoured." Mr. Paul also observes in the Memorandum attached to Mr. Satow's Report "The natives of Quelpart are of a friendly and polite disposition. That they have received orders from the Capital to reject all intercourse with foreigners I have no doubt, but I am confident that the people themselves have not only no antipathy to foreigners, but would gladly welcome them did no such orders exist." Similar evidence of the friendly disposition of the people of Quelpart is also given in the account by a private visitor to Quelpart which I forwarded to Your Lordship in my Despatch No. 127.

The Corean Authorities are of course under the influence of the traditional policy of seclusion, and it is not surprising that the local officers who met Mr. Satow should have hesitated in the face of a long standing law or order to the contrary to incur the responsibility of initiating communications of an official character. Any change of that law or practice must naturally proceed from the Government which established it. Whether the arguments addressed to the Corean Government by that of China and Japan to which I referred in my Despatch Confidential No. 125 of the 2nd instant will have a favorable effect remains to be seen, but the following passage in a letter from Newchwang addressed to the "Shanghai Courier" under date the 16th ultimo and recently republished at Yokohama seems to indicate that the subject is under the consideration of the Corean Government.

"We learn from Corea that the foreign Missionaries are quite safe there now, and that the Government will soon be prepared to place all nations on the favored clause footing occupied by the Japanese."

The above observation appears to me worthy of notice because this Newchwang correspondent, who is unknown to me, appears to possess means of information as to what is going on in Corea. A letter from I believe the same hand which was published in Shanghai in March last gave a detailed account of what occurred at the Corean Capital when a Japanese Mission visited it last year, and Mr. Hanabusa who was charged with that Mission has observed to me that he was struck with the correctness of many of the particulars, which had evidently not reached the writer from a Japanese source.

I think therefore from the experience gained by the wreck of the "Barbara Taylor" and from the above-mentioned circumstances that a favourable change of opinion is slowly influencing the Corean mind on the subject of intercourse with foreigners and that Mr. Satow's visit is calculated, though it may be only in a small degree to stimulate such favorable impressions. He was well received by local officers both at Quelpart and Fusan; at the former place they also visited the "Egeria," and at the latter a call was paid with unusual promptness by the Pansaikwan to the Japanese Agent in order to excuse himself for not visiting Mr. Satow and to thank the latter for having come to Corea with such a friendly object. Although my letter and that of the Chinese Minister to the Chief Authorities of Quelpart were not received, their contents were carefully studied and warmly approved, and at Fusan copies were taken by the Pansaikwan. I have little doubt that these will be communicated to the Central Government at Seoul, as that officer stated to the Japanese Agent at Fusan that he would report full particulars of Mr. Satow's visit to his Government and would bring to their notice my objections to the Corean practice of burning wrecks in order that fresh orders might be issued on the subject.

Mr. Satow's observations as to the relations of the Coreans and Japanese at Fusan are also instructive. The show that Japanese influence in Corea is still exceedingly limited, and that the result of the Treaty made between Japan and Corea three years ago have not come up to Japanese anticipations. The remarks of the Agent as to the futility of Japan endeavouring to force Corea to adopt a more liberal policy are doubtless just, and reflect I believe the opinion of the Government. Corea has little to fear from Japan, and she knows she has nothing to fear from China, but it is to be hoped that she may soon be prevailed on to perceive that her safety from her northern neighbour depends upon her acceptance of relations with Western nations.

I have, &c.

Harry S. Parkes

H.S. Parkes (1878. 12. 30) → Salisbury

일본 정부 중개의 한계 보고

Confidential
No. 147
The Marquis of Salisbury KG

Yedo
December 30, 1878

My Lord,

    In the course of a call which I made on the vice Prime Minister Iwakura on the 27th instant, His Excellency introduced the subject of Corea. He referred to the conversations he held with me in September and October 1876, which I reported in my Despatches Nos. 153 and 163 of the same year, and seemed anxious to learn whether Her Majesty's Government or any European State were disposed to make any endeavor to induce the Corean Government to open their country to Western Powers.

    I observed that although I entirely concurred with His Excellency that it was highly desirable in the interests of Corea and also, I might add, of those of Japan and China that Corea should be brought into friendly relations with Western Powers, he had himself indicated in the conversations to which he referred, the difficulties which stood in the way of Her Majesty's Government making any overtures to that of Corea. I was not aware that the latter government were more willing at this date, than they were in 1876 to receive such overtures in a becoming manner, and as Her Majesty's Government did not wish to expose themselves to any slight from the Corean Government, which might have to be resented, he preferred to see whether the Treaty concluded between Japan and Corea would have the beneficial effect of modifying the prejudices of the Coreans against foreign intercourse. I enquired whether anything had been done by his Government in reference to a resolution which, I understood, had been presented to the Senate of the United States by an American Senator of April last, by which it was proposed that a Commissioner should be appointed to represent the United States in an effort to arrange, by peaceful means and with the aid of the friendly offices of Japan, a Treaty of Peace and Commerce between the United States and Corea.

His Excellency replied that he knew nothing of this proposal, and I may add that the Foreign Minister gave me a similar answer when I put the same question to him sometime ago. I beg to inclose a copy of the resolution above referred to, which appeared in a local newspaper of last July.

His Excellency Iwakura then observed to me that he did not think Corea would be guided by Japanese advice in respect to the opening of the country. He believed that the influence of China was much more potent in Corea than that of Japan, and he thought it very desirable that Her Majesty's Minister at Peking should urge the Chinese Government to endeavour to persuade that of Corea to enter into relations with Western Powers without loss of time. The fugitive emigration of Coreans across their frontier into the adjoining Russian territory was, he remarked, a very serious matter as being eminently calculated to promote Russian designs and facilitate future aggression. He believed that more than twenty thousand Coreans had thus fled from their own Government, and had been domiciled under that of Russia.

I observed to His Excellency that I believed this emigration was known in China, and that I had some reason to think that the Chinese Government were becoming sensible that the continued seclusion of Corea might soon prove fatal to the independence of the latter state. Also that they perceived that the maintenance of Corean independence was of great importance to the interests of China, as it was to those of Japan.

For the grounds of this opinion I beg to refer your Lordship to the statements made to me by the Chinese Minister at Yedo, which I reported in my Despatch, Confidential, No. 125 of the 2nd instant.

I have little doubt that the interest in the opening of Corea to Western Powers, which was thus evinced by His Excellency Iwakura, is attributable in some degree to the questions which have lately arisen between Japan and Corea, and which I brought to Your Lordship's notice in the above-mentioned Despatch.

I have observed for some time past that the Japanese Government do not expect to be able to effect much in inducing the Corean Government to abandon their policy of seclusion, and that the former believe that they would derive support from the presence of other Powers in Corea, and secure by that means the better fulfillment of their own Treaty. The Japanese position in Corea is shown by Mr. Satow's report (inclosed in my Despatch No. 136 and referred to in my Despatch No. 141, both of this month) to be far from satisfactory or influential. When I called at the Foreign Office, on the 28th instant, the Vice Minister for Foreign Affairs seemed as desirous as His Excellency Iwakura to learn whether England or France was inclined to give attention to Corean affairs, and on the same occasion Mr. Yoshida, the Japanese Minister at Washington, observed to me that the resolution of Senator Sargent, above referred to, had fallen to the ground.

    I have, &c.

Harry S. Parkes

36

H.S. Parkes (1879. 5. 15) ➔ Salisbury (1879. 6. 21)

개항장 추가를 위한 花房義質의 조선 파견 보고

No. 105

Yedo, May 15, 1879

My lord,

  I had the honour to report to your lordship in my despatches No. 118, 125, and 139 of November and December last and in No. 5 of 11th January the occurrence of a difficulty in the relations of Japan with Corea, and its temporary adjustment. The difficulty was caused by the latter country having levied duties, which the Japanese called inland or transit duties on Japanese goods, in opposition, as the Japanese Government maintain, to an unpublished Agreement which provides that such duties shall not be levied; and the question was adjusted by the Corean Government having consented to suspend the levy of the so called inland duties pending the consideration at a later date of a Customs Tariff, which the Japanese Government admitted they had a right to make. I mentioned in my dispatch No. 5 that Mr. Hanabusa who had been sent to Corea to adjust this difficulty would probably have to visit the Corean capital in the Spring for the purpose of negotiating an import and export tariff.

  I should now inform Your Lordship that Mr. Hanabusa process to Corea last month as Charge di Affaires. This is the third occasion on which that offer has been sent for a short internal to Corea in that capacity since the conclusion of the Treaty of February 26. 1876, the Japanese Government considering that by means of these visits they maintain their right under the second Article of that Treaty to send either a temporary or a permanent Diplomatic Mission to that country.

  In this instance Mr. Hanabusa is chargéd with the negotiation of the question of the two new Ports, the opening of which under the 5th article of the same treaty could have been claimed by Japan at the end of October 1877. I observed in one of the above mentioned Despatches (Confidential No. 125) that this was a question which would soon demand consideration. He is not to suggest to the Corean Government that they should establish a Customs Tariff on imports and exports, but if they wish to take this measure a novel one in a country which prior to the Treaty of February 1876 with japan had no maritime commerce with any State—he is to receive their proposals and submit them to the consideration of his government. He informed me before having that his government would only consent to a moderate tariff, and would object to any tariff being so suddenly imposed as to affect prejudicially the existing trade.

This remark confirms the observations I mentioned to make in one of the above mentioned Despatches (No. 118) as to the different course pursued by the Japanese Government in treating tariff questions with the Corean Government to that which they propose to adopt in revising their Treaties with Foreign Powers.

The analogy which may be traced between the relations of Japan with Corea, and those of foreign relations with Japan is shown in the enclosed memorial presented to their government by the Japanese merchants trading to Corea. They are that the heavy duties proposed by the Corean Government would "deal a death blow to their trade," and that this result is the object of the proposal. They pray their government to protect them against this design, and to claim the opening of the additional ports agreed to by treaty, as their trade cannot expand while it is confined to the poor district in which the single open port of Fusan is situated. They demand facilities as to currency such as it was found necessary to provide for in this Foreign Treaties with Japan—that the Coreans should be induced to open their mines which the Japanese have so long been urged to do; that the Japanese Minister should take up his residence at the Corean Capital in order that Japanese commercial interest may be adequately protected, and the Corean Government convinced by his representations of the importance of encouraging commerce; and that the Coreans should be required to make payment of the debts due by them to the Japanese traders.

I add copies of two letters which were published at the time the petition appeared for the purpose of pointing out how closely the position of foreigners in Japan is reflected by the position of the Japanese as foreigners in Corea.

Both the Foreign Minister and Mr. Hanabusa informed me that the Japanese government intend to demand the opening of the Port of Yunsan on the East Coast.

There has not been time for Mr. Hanabusa to report progress since his departure. In the meantime a collision has occurred between the Japanese and the Coreans in consequence of the Commander of a Japanese man of war having marched a body of his men to the city of Torai near to Pusan. The Japanese having been stoned by the Coreans, the commander landed a larger force the following day and proceeded, accompanied by the Japanese Consul to Torai. They appear to have endeavoured to carry off the Corean governor, and serious disturbance ensued in which the governor was wounded by the sword of the Japanese Consul. I enclose extracts from two Japanese newspapers giving the details of the collision and an article from a third newspaper strongly condemning the conduct of the Japanese officers. It remarks that the latter could not have expected to seize the governor without resistance and that the consul even in a moment of confusion should not have taken upon himself to run his sword into an officer of a treaty power.

I have the honour to be with the highest respect
My Lord,
Your Lordship's most obedient and humble servant,
Harry S. Parkes

H.S. Parkes (1879. 5. 15) ➡ Salisbury (1879. 6. 21)

Shufeldt의 조선행 관련 花房義質와 면담 내용 보고

No. 106

Yedo, May 15, 1879

My Lord,

I have the honor to acknowledge the receipt of your lordship's Despatch No. 85 of December 28th communicating to me a copy of Sir Edward Thornton's Despatch, commercial No. 51 on the subject of the mission of Commodore Shufeldt, which has for its principal object the extension of the commercial relations of the United States with various remote countries – including Corea.

I observed that Mr. Hanabusa was anxious to get information Respecting Commodore Shufeldt's mission before he proceeded to Corea last month as reported in the dispatch No. 105 of this date. He remarked to me that he hoped the Commodore would go to Corea, and that the Japanese Government would do what they could to help him. Mr. Hanabusa convinced the same desire to see Foreign Powers taking an interest in Corea as had been shown by the Vice Prince in the conversation which I reported to your lordship in my despatch confidential No. 147 of the 30th of December last, and doubtless for the same reason—the support which Japan hopes to derive from the presence of other powers in that country. He remarked that nearly all the import trade of the Japanese merchants in Corea consisted of British manufactures, and he thought that circumstances should induce Her Majesty's Government to regard Corea with the same interest as is shown by the United States.

I replied to Mr. Hanabusa in the same terms as those which I used with the Vice Prime Minister, and which I reported in the above-mentioned despatch, but I could see that Mr. Hanabusa entertained similar views to those of the Vice Prime Minister as to the limited influence of Japan in Corea.

I have the honor to be, with the highest respect,
My Lord,
Your Lordship's most obedient, Humble Servant,
Harry S Parkes

38

H.S. Parkes (1879. 5. 15) ➡ Salisbury (1879. 6. 21)

Satow의 제주도 파견 경과 보고

No. 107

Yedo, May 15, 1879

My lord,

    I have the honour to acknowledge the script of your lordship's Despatches No. 17, 18, and 29 relative to Mr. Satow's mission to Quelpart in November last.

    Your lordship disapproves of my having sent this mission but it is gratifying to me to observe that the conduct of the officers to whom the service was entrusted is appreciated by your lordship.

    Your lordship regards the mission as a failure, and considers that the occasion did not justify the expense of a special mission in one of Her Majesty's ships, especially as your lordship is of opinion that Mr. Paul had already represented Her Majesty's legation in the matter.

    One of my principal reasons for sending Mr. Satow was that Mr. Paul had been unable to represent the legation and I fear I may not have made this point clear to your lordship. Owing to his having gone to Quelpart in a private ship he was unable to see the Chief Authority of the island, although the latter invited him to do so. I was guided by precedent in sending on of Her Majesty's ships, as I could mention several instances in which those ships have been sent to greater distances in those seas in order simply to deliver presents in acknowledgment of services rendered to our shipwrecked people. In this case of I incurred no expense on account of presents, knowing that the Corean officers would in all probability refuse to accept them, but I know of no instance in which they would been better deserved. They kept the crew of the wrecked ship for more than a month, housed them, fed them, and clothed them, salved the cargo, and stored and reshipped it – all without fee or reward of any kind. I thought that such services coming for the first time from the Authorities and people of a nation which numbers about eight millions, and on whom I presume it is desirable to create a friendly impression was at least deserving of thanks.

When such acknowledgements can alone be offered the mode of conveying them may add greatly to their value, and I thought that it would be more complimentary to that Coreans and more dignified on the part of Her Majesty's government to deliver their thanks by one of their own officers sent in one of Her Majesty's ships instead of through the intervention of the Japanese Authorities, who are not held in high repute in Corea.

The cost of the mission amounted to $352.87 £66.33, being a much smaller sum than I have experienced by the authority of Her Majesty's government on many occasions in presents to Japanese who have rendered smaller services in other cases of shipwreck. It may be said that the cost of the coal consumed by Her Majesty's ship should be taken into account, but the same amount of coal would have been expended in one ordinary cruize between port and port such as the same vessel would have taken if she had not gone on this mission.

I had hoped that Your Lordship would not have regarded the mission as a failure if only for the reason that I trust it will it have the effect of dissuading the Corean Authorities from banning foreign vessels in future when stranded on their coasts. The local Corean Authorities at Fusan promised to bring my representations on this subject to the notice of their government at the capital in order that they might rescued the existing decrees which require the destruction of all foreign wrecks – If such new orders should be issued, the advantage to our shipping which may accrue from them will, I respectfully submit, have been cheaply gained by an expenditure of sixty six pounds.

I have the honor to be, with the highest respect,
My Lord,
Your Lordship's most obedient, Humble Servant,
Harry S Parkes

(2) 제1차 조약 체결 과정

39

Braus (1879. 7. 3) ➡ H.S. Parkes

조선과 서구 열강의 수교를 總署에 건의한 사실 보고

Peking
July 3, 1879

My dear Sir Harry.

  Many thanks for your long and interesting note of April 28. If I have not answered it before this, pressure of business and the poor state of my health were the only causes of my apparent neglect and I need hardly tell you that I shall be most happy to renew our correspondence. The memory of the times when we used to fight back to back is a too pleasant one not to make me gladly welcome any direct news from my old companion in arms.

  From what I heard at London and Berlin and from what I read in the papers I can fully understand the difficulties you have to contend against in the revision of your treaty or rather of most of the treaties now pending. The way in which the Japanese government went about it, the little estimable allies it found in de Gendre & co. and the native press, the proceedings of the United States Govt. in concluding a separate treaty, which gives nothing to Japan that would cost the United States a shilling but throws all the compensation for the advantages they obtain upon your and our shoulders all unite to make your and our position in Japan a very difficult one, but I have no doubt that common sense will come out first in the long run. Jwan-ura & company are evidently bent upon driving the foreigner from Japan; what assassinations and the court at Kioto could not accomplish is now to be tried under pretence of the offended dignity of the nation and the sovereignty of the Micado. But I should like to know what Japan would be worth to the world at large if the right of trading between the open ports (what the Japanese and Americans call the coasting trade of Japan) were taken from the foreigners and their manufacturers excluded from the Jap. Markets by a prohibitory tariff. We might just as well return to Desima at once. Our revision in China does not proceed much more favourably than yours in Japan. We contend in vain against the stolid power of resistance, the *vis inertiae* you know so well, and if we do not yet encounter the same phrases about abolition of extraterritoriality, submission to Chinese jurisdiction and sovereign rights, which you do in Japan, it is simply because the hostile elements are not yet educated enough to take to that claptrap; they are however not wanting European teachers who will very soon bring them up to that point.

The great question here is for the moment the annexation of the Liu Kiu Islands by Japan. The Chinese are very much enraged about it and talk very openly that it must lead to war between the two countries; so openly that I rather believe them to intend on the one hand to try to intimidate the Japanese and on the other to exercise a certain pressure upon the foreign Representatives in order to make them look more favourably upon a demand for mediation. The Yamen is at this moment waiting for the results the endeavors of General Grant may have; when they have failed as I have not doubt they will as far at least as I know the Japanese, the Yamen will then try foreign mediation either through the representatives here or in Japan, I rather suppose in Japan as they are likely to be met here with rather unpleasant remarks about non-fulfillment of treaty obligations. But were if everything should fail how Chinese could act on the offensive against Japan, they are utterly unfit to lead an expedition to the Liu Kiu islands and not much more capable of defending themselves against Japanese invaders, as long as the invaders would not attempt to gain a permanent footing on the mainland. A little war between China and any foreign Power would do it an immense deal of good and would make it progress more in six months' time that it would do otherwise in twenty years. The great fear of the Chinese however is that the same thing which has happened with regard to the Liu Kiu islands may repeat itself with regard to Corea, and they are certainly not very far from the truth in supposing that relations between Japan and Corea must end sooner or later in an armed conflict. I have told them twenty times that the best means of preventing an attempt by Japan to secure Corea would be to throw that country open to foreign intercourse, they and especially Li Hung Shang fully agree with me, but they do not take to council and work a course to the Coreans, who appear to act the part of "le enfant terrible" towards China, bullying her and reviling her for her convenience towards foreigners.

Taken all together the situation is not without interest and may have rather far reaching consequences.

Sir Thomas Wade has returned to the delightful place a few days ago hale and hearty, after adventures enough to finish three ordinary mortals. He had the good luck to get wrecked with the Shaulu at some part of the coast where a German ship had suffered the same fate in December last and had been plundered unmercifully. At our demand a general bambooing had just been going on in that part of the coast and Wade reaped the benefit of our measures.

I hope you have good news from Lady Parkes and your little family which must be very much grown up by this time; kindly remember me to Lady Parkes when writing to her.

Goodbye for today, my dear Sir Harry, I shall write to you again as soon as something interesting happens here and I do count upon your promise of not letting me wait too long for an answer.

With very best wishes for your welfare.

Yours very truly.
[Mr. Braus]

J.G. Kennedy (1880. 3. 14) ➔ Salisbury (1880. 5. 2)

井上馨와 회견 보고 (1)

Mr. Kennedy to the Marquis of Salisbury.—(Received May 2)

(No. 52 Confidential)

My Lord,　　　　　　　　　　　　　　　　　　　　Yedo, *March* 14, 1880

I HAVE the honour to inform your Lordship that during a conversation which I held to-day with the Minister for Foreign Affairs, his Excellency, after remarking on the importance of the news recently reported from Peking, that the Chinese Government would refuse to abide by the terms of the Treaty lately negotiated with Russia respecting the Kuldja district, proceeded to denounce as groundless the newspaper reports which hinted at an understanding between Japan and Russia on a combined course of action towards China.

Russia, remarked his Excellency, is extremely desirous of obtaining a footing in Corea, and wished to share in the commercial privileges secured to Japan in the port of Gensan. But Japan, although anxious that all other nations should conclude Treaties with Corea, is herself unable to assist other nations in their attempts to put themselves in direct communication with Corea.

Japan, continued his Excellency, in rendering such assistance would neutralize, and probably annul, the advantages she had with much difficulty obtained in Corea. No symptom had, as yet, been exhibited by the Corean authorities of a decrease in their marked hostility to all foreigners.

This hostility, which had always existed, said his Excellency, had been strengthened by the savage proceedings of some foreigners, who, a few years ago, landed on a small island off the Corean coast, and, in the belief that many of the Corean Kings had been buried in gold and silver coffins in that island, these sailors commenced to excavate in the burial-grounds in the hope of plunder. Such proceedings had naturally outraged the feelings of the Coreans, and had even for some time hampered the progress of the Japanese, but, nevertheless, continued his Excellency, Japan has now obtained a firm footing in Corea, and we have hopes of receiving here a permanent Corean Mission before the end of this year, and we trust that by intercourse with the foreign Representatives in this city, the Corean Envoy may learn to modify the prejudices of his countrymen against foreigners.

I assured Mr. Inouyé that I had learnt with much satisfaction that no understanding existed between Japan and Russia with regard to China, and pointed out the advantage of settling the Loochooan question by direct understanding with China.

His Excellency replied that the advantage of settling the Loochooan question without any foreign intervention had always been evident to Japan, and that he felt sure of an amicable settlement of the dispute before long.

In concluding his remarks, Mr. Inouyé informed me that any suspicions which Great Britain might harbour of Russian endeavours to obtain influence with Japan were reciprocated by Russia, because quite lately M. de Struve, the Russian Minister, had inquired of him, whether it was true that Her Majesty's Government had offered to mediate between China and Japan.

His Excellency also informed me that the United States' Minister had announced the intention of his Government to send a surveying ship to the coasts of Corea, and requested the friendly support of Japan, to which request Mr. Inouyé replied by explaining to Mr. Bingham the difficulty of acceding to his demand.

On the subject of intercourse with Corea, Mr. Iwakura, the Third Minister of State, recently informed me that Corea should be approached through China, and not through Japan.

I have, &c.
(Signed)   J.G. Kennedy

J.G. Kennedy (1880. 3. 25) ➔ Salisbury (1880. 5. 8)

청-러 개전 가능성 및 일본, 조선의 동향 보고

Mr. Kennedy to the Marquis of Salisbury.—(Received May 8)

(No. 55 Confidential)

Yedo, March 25, 1880

My Lord,

    WITH reference to my despatch No. 52, Confidential, of the 14th instant, I have the honour to inform your Lordship that the Minister for Foreign Affairs to-day assured me emphatically, and authorized me to assure your Lordship, that Japan would remain neutral in the event of war between China and Russia.

    His Excellency stated that Japan could have no inducement to go to war with China, and many reasons made it expedient for Japan to remain quiet.

    In the first place, Japan had no wish to possess either Formosa, or Corea, or Saghalien, as had been reported. She was not prepared for war and besides these reasons she had on hand the Treaty revision question, and the agitation for popular representative institutions, which gave no little trouble to the present Government. This latter question alone would suffice to prevent Japan going to war.

    In Europe, remarked his Excellency, Governments are reported to have plunged their country into war in order to divert the attention of their countrymen from domestic grievances, and, by an appeal to patriotism, have joined opposing parties into an united force against the foreign enemy; but the Japanese, said his Excellency, cannot be thus influenced.

    As soon as this country became involved in difficulties, or in war with another country, the agitators for representative government would avail themselves of the opportunity to press their demands.

    Mr. Inouyé, after arguing against the probability of war between China and Russia, again assured me that by no promises could Russia induce Japan to join her. Japan, said his Excellency, by a careful avoidance of any attempt to profit by the difficulties of China, would obtain from the latter a favourable settlement of the Loochoo question, and an assurance of increased friendship for the future.

In concluding his remarks, Mr. Inouyé said that the Japanese Charge d'Affaires in Peking had reported the presentation to Chung How of the white silken cord, which signified the infliction of capital punishment, and that all the foreign Representatives, excepting those of Russia and Japan, had protested against such a severe sentence.

This conduct of the Japanese Representative had been approved, because Japan and China had bound themselves by Treaty not to interfere in the internal affairs of each other.

I have, &c.
(Signed) J. G. KENNEDY

J.G. Kennedy (1880. 5. 25) ➜ Salisbury (1880. 7. 14)

井上馨와 회견 보고 (2)

Mr. Kennedy to the Marquis of Salisbury.-(Received July 14)

(No. 90 Confidential)

Yedo, May 25, 1880

My Lord,

WITH reference to my despatch No. 75m Confidential, of the 1st instant, I have the honour to inclose a French translation of a letter addressed to the leading Japanese paper "Nichi Nichi Shimbun" ("Daily News"), on topics connected with Corea.

In reply to my inquiries, Mr. Inouyê informed me to-day that the information contained in this letter respecting the visit of the United States' ship of war "Ticonderoga," the arrival of a Corean Envoy in Japan, and the mission of a Russian Agent to Corea, was substantially correct.

His Excellency stated that since the return to Japan of the "Ticonderoga," Commodore Schufelt had sought an interview of him in order to express his disappointment at his failure to open communications with the Corean authorities at Fusan, and to declare his intention of renewing his efforts to communicate with the Coreans by proceeding straight to the River Koka, and if possible to the capital, Seoul.

In reply to Mr. Inouyé's declarations that the Japanese Government could render no assistance, and that the Corean authorities had evinced a special aversion to Americans, Commodore Schufelt rejoined, according to his Excellency, that he founded his hopes of success on the strength of a polite exchange of letters which had occurred between himself and the Corean authorities of the city of Seoul some twelve years ago, and that his name alone would awaken pleasant memories in the breasts of the Corean authorities; besides which, continued the Commodore, the orders of the United States' Government enjoined him to make a decided effort towards the conclusion of a Treaty of Commerce with Corea.

With regard to the prospects of success of Commodore Shufeldt, Mr. Inouyé remarked to me that any pleasant memories connected with the Commodore's name would have been effaced by the subsequent bombardment by United States' ships of war of the villages and forts on the River Koka, and that he confidently predicted a complete failure of the Commodore's renewed attempt to enter into friendly communication with Corea. But his Excellency believed that Commodore Schufelt would not have recourse to force on this occasion.

Respecting the presence of a Russian Envoy in Corea, Mr. Inouyé informed me that, according to reports received by his Department, a Russian agent had arrived in a ship of war coming from Vladivostock at the mouth of the river Toman, which forms the frontier-line between Corean and Russian Siberia. After proceeding some distance up the river the Russian Agent had requested the local Corean authorities to receive and transmit a letter addressed to the Government at the capital. Upon the refusal of the local authorities to comply with this request, the Russian Agent had declared his intention of taking the letter himself to Seoul, whereupon the local authorities undertook to transmit the letter, and the Russian Agent departed with and intimation that he would return for the answer at the expiration of a year. The object of the Russian Envoy was, in Mr. Inouyé's belief, to conclude a Treaty of Commerce with Corea.

Form the foregoing observations your Lordship will perceive that Corea forms an object of interest to more than one Great Power. My french colleague, M. de Balloz, who also takes an interest in Corean affairs, has suggested to me the expediency of assisting and encouraging this American expedition, because the result of success on the part of the United States would be to open the Corean ports to all other nations. To this suggestion I have replied that, whilst wishing success to the American operations, I must decline to say or do anything openly in that respect.

I have held this language because it is clear, both from the Report of Mr. Consul Troup, forwarded to your Lordship in my despatch No. 82 of the 5th instant, and from the Returns of trade between japan and Corea inclosed in my immediately preceding despatch, and in my despatch No. 189 of 27th October, 1870, that British trade with Corea, through Japan, is already on a satisfactory footing and that it may be still further encouraged by modifications in respect of drawbacks and bonded warehouses for the attainment of which an opportunity will be afforded in the impending Treaty revision with Japan.

It is meanwhile evident that the japanese Government dread the possibility of Russian success in Corea, and much desire the conclusion of Treaties of Friendship and Commerce by other nations with that country.

I have, &c.
(Signed) J.G. Kennedy

J.G. Kennedy (1880. 6. 29) ➜ G.L.G. Granville (1880. 8. 13)

청-러 개전 가능성 및 조선과 조약 체결 필요 상신

Mr. Kennedy to Earl Granville.-(Received August 13)

(No. 113 Confidential)

Yedo, June 29, 1880

My Lord,

I HAVE the honour to acknowledge the receipt of the Marquis of Salisbury's despatches Nos. 10 and 33 of the 29th January and the 3rd April respectively, transmitting to me copies of despatches from Her Majesty's Ambassador at St. Petersburgh on the subject of the strength of the Russian squadron in the Pacific.

Hitherto it has been impossible for me to obtain any trustworthy information in the above subject, as no Russian vessels of war have come to Japanese waters, exception one or two vessels of the so-called volunteer fleet, which have called for coals at nagasaki, on their way to Saghalien with convicts.

But within the past fortnight the increase of the numbers and strength of the Russian fleet in and on the way to the Chinese seas, and the impending presence of three Russian Admirals with four iron-clads has attracted universal attention.

The return also to Yokohama of the British and French Admirals, and of the Italian ship "Vettor Pisani" has afforded opportunities for obtaining information respecting the intentions of Russia in the Chinese seas.

The Russian Minister here, M. de Struve, has stated in conversation with Admiral Coote and with Admiral Duperré, and also with me, that the prospect of war between Russia and China has become so serious that the Russian Government has decided to send a formidable fleet to the Chinese coast, in order to prove to the Chinese Government the hopelessness of attempting to fight Russia on the sea, and also to place Russia in a position to act with promptitude in the event of a declaration of war.

I have had opportunities of discussing the question of the probabilities of war between Russia and China with most of my colleagues, as well as with the British and foreign naval authorities. As a result of these conversations, I have the honour to report that, in the opinion of the French authorities, Russia is bent on war with China in order to maintain her Eastern prestige, and possibly with a view to the annexation of the Corea.

Another, and perhaps more generally accepted opinion, is that Russia will, on the pretext of enforcing the observance of the Treaty of Kuldja, organize a blockade of the Gulf of Pechili, and of the three Treaty ports within it, and will eventually obtain from China a heavy money indemnity, with the addition of important commercial concessions, by which the interior of China will be opened to Russian trade.

The French authorities are certainly most anxious as to Russian designs, and for two reasons: in the first place, they fear that any hostile act towards China would be the signal for general massacre of Europeans in China, and especially of French missionaries; and, secondly, they believe that Russia would probably annex part or the whole of the Corea, which country France, and also Italy, is desirous to see opened to European trade.

The fate of Corea is supposed to depend on the solution of the difficulty pending between China and Russia. The Japanese Government and the foreign Representatives here believe that, unless Corea be permanently opened to foreign trade within a short time, by the conclusion of Treaties of Commerce with Europe and with America, she is destined to be annexed to the Russian Asiatic possessions. Such annexation would be deplored by the Japanese Government and the French and Italian Representatives especially. The two latter have both urged upon me the advantage of a combined action towards Corea, and have represented that a naval demonstration by the leading maritime nations before the capital of Corea would compel that Government to accede to a demand for opening the country to foreign trade. Both the French and Italian Representatives are under the impression that Corea would afford a new market for the supply of silk, besides which, the French have an additional motive in the fact that many French missionaries reside in Corea and also that they ought to efface the records of their failures to force themselves on Corea by obtaining a permanent right of trade with that country.

On this subject the Minister for Foreign Affairs lately informed me that the Russian Minister, in referring to the recent visits to Corean ports of British,

French, and American vessels of war, declared to his Excellency that the Russian Government had no intention whatever of annexing any part of Corea. In reporting this conversation to me, Mr. Inouyé suggested that circumstances might alter the intentions of the Russian Government, and his Excellency strongly urged the expediency of the conclusion of Treaties of Friendship and Commerce by maritime nations with Corea as the only means of baffling the designs of Russia. His Excellency added that such an object could easily be attained by direct and combined action with the Government at Seoul, instead of isolated attempts at Fusan and Kanghoa, as had hitherto been the case.

Some hopes are entertained by my colleagues and by the Government of Japan of effecting friendly communications with the Corean Government through the Corean Envoy, who is expected to arrive here next month.

The Chinese Minister has repeatedly assured me that his Government has advised the Corean Government to open their country to foreigners.

In conclusion, I have the honour to state that, in all conversations on the subject of Corea, I have confined myself to the general statement that, so far as I am aware, Her Majesty's Government have no present intention of entering into communication with the Government of Corea.

I have, &c.

(Signed)   J.G. Kennedy

J.G. Kennedy (1880. 7. 27) ➜ G.L.G. Granville (1880. 9. 16)

李裕元-李鴻章 왕복 서한 및 조선관련 정보 보고

Mr. Kennedy to Earl Granville.—(Received September 16)

(No. 131 Very Confidential)

Yedo, July 27, 1880

My Lord,

I HAVE the honour to inclose a memorandum, together with copies in translation of three letters, giving much interesting information respecting the past history and present political state of Corea.

These documents have all been furnished to me by Mr. Satow, who informs me that the letters were confidentially communicated to him in Chinese by a native of Corea, and that the information contained in the memorandum was derived from the same person.

Mr. Satow's informant is an enlightened young Corean, who has managed secretly to leave his country with the object of obtaining general information respecting the outside world for benefit of his own countrymen.

During his stay in this city he has been in constant communication with Mr. Satow, to whom, besides the inclosed papers, he has confided much trustworthy information respecting the hopes and prospects of the liberal party in Corea. He is now about to return home, but promises to keep Her Majesty's Legation informed of the progress of events in Corea, and to give timely notice of any changes likely to prove favourable to the admission of foreigners.

Your Lordship will observe from a perusal of the inclosed letters that they clearly prove the existence of friendly relations between Corea and China, whilst the presence of the Japanese is submitted to as an unvoidable evil. The Corean ex-Prime Minister alludes to China as the superior or suzerain Power, and asks the advice of Li Hung Chang as to the designs of foreigners. It is also clear that the Coreans thoroughly dislike all foreign Powers with whom they have come in contact, except perhaps Great Britain. This may be accounted for by the fact so pointedly designated by Li Hung Chang, that British communications with Corea have been confined to the transmission of thanks for kindness shown to British shipwrecked crews by the inhabitants of Corea.

The memorandum, as your Lordship will perceive, gives much novel and interesting information respecting the system of government and the internal organization of Corea. It also states names and details respecting the progressive party which exists in Corea, headed by young men of rank who desire to reform the present oppressive system of government, and to develop the resources of the country by the aid of skilled foreigners.

It will not escape your Lordship's notice that Mr. Satow states, on the authority of his Corean informant, that although the exchange of courtesies between the British and the Corean authorities has undoubtedly had a good effect, yet it is not probable that an Envoy would be received by the present Corean Government unless he were accompanied by a force sufficient to overwhelm resistance.

Mr. Satow has also expressed to me the opinion, in which I quite concur, that any attempt to open communication with Corea by force is to be deprecated on two grounds: first, because it is known that the Coreans have been steadily arming ever since the Japanese forced a Treaty upon them in 1875, and therefore the amount of resistance to be overcome would be far greater than on previous occasions; and secondly, because the experience of the Japanese shows that very little way can be made in Corea by the employment of pressure, and that the chief result of such a policy would be to inspire a feeling of enmity, which might drive Corea into the arms of the very Power from whom all the rest of the world, including China and Japan, is interested saving her.

If the force of the above arguments be admitted, it would appear more politic to await the development of events in Corea which cannot be long delayed.

I have also the honour to inform your Lordship that the above statements have, in the main, been confirmed in conversation both by the Minister and the Vice-Minister for Foreign Affairs. Mr. Wooyeno recently informed me that the people as well as the Government of Corea are more opposed than ever to the admission of foreigners, and that the Corean Government has begun to show distrust of the Chinese Government since the recommendation of the latter through Li Hung Chang to open Corea to foreign nations.

Mr. Wooyeno also admitted to me that the Japanese are obliged to go about armed in their newly-opened Treaty Port of Gensan, and to maintain a body of Japanese police for protection against the hostility of the natives.

His Excellency further mentioned a small circumstance which shows the strength of the spirit of exclusiveness evinced by the Coreans, namely, that the newly appointed Corean Envoy to Japan, before signing the contract for the Japanese steamer which was to convey him to his post, insisted on the insertion of a clause forbidding the presence on the steamer of any European of American whatever, even in the capacity of engineer.

As opposed to these evidences of hostility to all foreigners, I have the honour to report that Captain Hood, of her Majesty's ship "Pegasus," lately informed me that during his recent visit to Port Lazaraff in Broughton Bay, more than fifty natives came on board to inspect the ship, and that the Coreans always, whether afloat or ashore, displayed most friendly feelings towards Captain Hood and his officers and crew.

Captain Hood further informed me that the Japanese Consul at Gensan (also in Broughton Bay) did not seem pleased to see a British ship-of-war in his district, and that he and the other Japanese authorities appeared disconcerted on hearing of the friendly intercourse between Her Majesty's ship "Pegasus" and the Coreans.

In concluding this despatch, I beg to suggest that the information contained in it and especially in the inclosures may be considered as confidential, because in the event of publicity it is probable that the safety of the persons mentioned would be compromised, and Her Majesty's Legation deprived of its present means of information.

I have, &c.
(Signed) J.G. Kennedy

Inclosure 1

Reply of Li Hung Chang to the ex-Prime Minister of Corea.

(Translation)

In the gracious letter, dated the 15th of the 10th moon of the year 1877, which my revered elder brother Küh-Shan, his Excellency the Preceptor, sent by the hands of Prefect Yü, of Yung Ping, he speaks of our brotherhood in terms of exceeding modesty, and his cultured regards for me are most affectionate. I opened the letter, spread out the paper, and read it over repeatedly with pleasure. Then I received sixteen kinds of valuable gifts, more valuable than the finest gems, and beg to return thanks for the presents bestowed on me. Nothing but the want of an opportunity has prevented my replying earlier, so that time has seemed to gallop away, and winter has been succeeded by summer. I trust that your honourable record of services is perpetually increasing, that you are careful of your diet and health, that you govern the black-haired race with success, maintain your boundaries intact, and that you faithfully serve the King in the execution of your lofty policy.

It is now three years or so since Japanese and your honourable country entered into a Treaty of Peace and a commercial port established at Tong-nê, so that the merchants of both nations could mix, and high and low be mutually at peace.

Since the time of hideyoshi that country,* presuming on its cunning arts, has been troubled and unquiet. More recently, Saigô Takamori, fond of fighting in a dirty puddle, took up arms and brought about his own destruction;** but the Sovereign and his Ministers, observing that their country was small, and its difficulties many, seem to have taken warning by the past, and to be more inclined to keep in their proper place.

Last year, when the Junior Expositor Ho, appointed Chinese Envoy to Japan, proceed[ed] thither, I, being concerned about the relations between your honourable country and Japan, begged him to keep his attention fixed on that subject, and to take every opportunity of obtaining information. I have recently received a letter from him, from which it appears that Japan, feeling that the Russians are deceitful, and unceasingly greedy of fresh territory, is seriously thinking of taking precautions, and feels as frightened as a man who sees a savage tiger by the side of the couch on which he is reposing. Although Japan is not altogether innocent of evil sentiments towards your honourable country, she would like to attach you as the second wheel to her cart, and get you to play lips to her teeth (i,e., Japan feels that the destruction of Corea's independence would lead to her own downfall, and that Corea acts as a sort of outward buffer to Japan against Russia), but she feels considerable doubt as to whether your honoured country will, with unreserved loyalty, meet her views.

---

*[원주] i.e., Japan.
**[원주] An allusion to the satsuma rebellion of 1877, headed by this celebrated man.

When I reflect upon the political situation, it appears to me that England and America are to far off to have any other objects than commercial intercourse, and do not seek to extend their territory. Russia, on the other hand, straddles across three continents, and her territory is conterminous with ours on the north and west. She is always occupied in thinking of appropriation and annexing.* Both your honourable country's shores and those of Japan are washed by the Eastern Sea, and the Russian men-of-war are always hovering about on the look out for an opportunity, which they will eventually discover. The State of things is like that when Yü and Kwoh were preparing to defend themselves against Chin, or when the Han and Wei were afraid of Tsin.

I hear that when Japan was desirous of opening a port at Uon-Sam, in the province of Ham-gyang-do, in your honourable country,** The Russians secretly tried to dissuade them, fearing lest, if they should eventually go to war (with Corea), the Japanese commerce there would prove an obstacle to their designs, and that, when the English sought to induce Japan to obtain for them permission to trade, the Russians again persuaded her to do nothing. If this be true, then the Russians wish to isolate your honourable country and deprive it of succour, and, if at any time an opportunity should occur, then they would be quite free, and there would be nothing to hinder their doing as they like. Such are their plans, and it becomes necessary, therefore, to make secret preparations for defence.

In ancient times, after the defeat of the Sovereign of Chu at Hu-ting, he entertained profound enmity toward Wu, but Chu-ko persuaded him to make peace with the Wu in order to subdue the Wei, which is held to have been a sagacious policy. Tê Tsung, of the T'ang dynasty, had long hated the Husi-hoh, but Li Yeh persuaded him to overcome that feeling, and to enter into a Treaty with them, on which the power of the barbarians immediately decayed. Such examples of great men, called by heaven to direct affairs, disregarding trifling matters in order to carry out a wise policy, are frequent in history.

I hear that Russia has lately made peace with Turkey, and affairs in the West being thus settled, she is now turning her attention to her Eastern schemes. Your Excellency is accustomed to devot[ing] yourself to the conduct of your national policy, and your measures are always well considered. Now is the time to take precautions against the coming storm. I look upon Corea as a wall to China, and the two countries are united by mutual obligation and

---

*[원주] Literally, devouring like the silk worm and swallowing like the whale.
**[원주] Called "Gensan" by the Japanese in Broughton Bay in our charts.

trust, so that I feel myself compelled to confide to you my inmost thoughts. Of course, I am quite ignorant of plans of your Government and of the state of its foreign relations. I have the honour to be Viceroy of the Home Provinces, but am ashamed at my own incompetence to fill the post. Fortunately, the weather has been very seasonable throughout the summer, and there are prospects of an abundant harvest both here and in the north generally, so that the people feel like a withered tree restored by cooling breezes.*

I take this opportunity of offering you some trifling objects, to the number of sixteen, in return for your kindness. Our boundaries are far distant from each other, but I always feel great interest in your welfare.

May you have fine weather, and take care of yourself.

With respect, &c.
(Signed) LI HUNG CHANG of Ho-fei.
4th day, 9th moon, 1878

Inclosure 2

Reply of the ex-Prime Minister of Corea to Li Hung-Chang.

(Translation)

When the tribute-bearing Envoy visited China in the 10th moon of this year, he must have briefly inquired after your Excellency's health. I had addressed you by way of Yung-pin Fu, and now have had the honour to receive your instructions dated the 4th day of the 9th moon of the present year, in reply to my letter. I learn from it that your Excellency preserves his health, and I have received the various articles you have deigned to bestow on me, each of which is gloriously bright, and there is not a corner of my heart which does not feel intensely grateful.

How could I have hoped that your calculations with regard to foreign affairs would extend beyond the seas and to my own remote country, or that you would have drawn examples from the remote periods of Han and T'ang to illustrate the present circumstances with regard to Europe and Japan. You put

---

*[원주] An allusion to the recent famine in the north of China.

things so lucidly explanations are at once understood. Being in a position of dependence, these things engrave themselves on my heart, and I shall never forget them.

The English, on the pretext of thanking us for kindness shown to rescued shipwrecked people, came lately to Tong-ne, and asked to see the officials.

The Russians have been continually decoying away the inhabitants of our northern frontier, and we find it impossible to prevent this.

The Japanese are not on bad terms with us, but they are very uncertain-tempered. They send us cannon and books, and they generally speak the truth, but as soon as anything goes a little contrary to their wishes, they easily get up a complication. The other way after we had liberated the European teacher,* in consequence of a despatch from the Tsung-li Yamên, the Japanese wrote to us on the same subject, to which we answered that by the instructions of the "Superior Country"** we had already released him. Then we received a letter from Hanabusa, in which he spoke so rudely about the words "Superior Country" being elevated above the line in our note to him, that we were extremely surprised and disgusted. The whole world is well aware that my little country is subject to the Superior Country. In 1876, when your Excellency administered a rebuff to Mori Arimori,*** the latter learnt that my small country receives the calendar (from China), so that how can they pretend to be ignorant of the connection between us, and use such language as Hanbusa? Then he used such violent language about Tôkuôn**** that it was impossible to get along with him; but we brought him to reason eventually, and remonstrated against his obstinacy. We have written a despatch (to the Chinese Government), and I humbly suppose that your Excellency must have seen it. I could not make out what was their special object in insisting upon Uon-san***** in Tk-uon, but by the letter which your Excellency has been so good as to send to me, I have at last understood. The question is therefore at present under discussion. In fact, but for the details communicated by you, I should have been quite in the dark about Russian, European, and Japanese questions. Whatever people may come to complain to you, no matter whence, or about what, pray deign to favour us by keeping them quiet. This is not the prayer of my humble self alone, but the

---

*[원주] French Missionary Bishop, who had been imprisoned in Corea.
**[원주] China
***[원주] Who had asked Li Hung-Chang if he had an objection to Japan making war on Corea, and received for answer: "Make war if you like, but be assured we shall not stand quietly by and look on."
****[원주] i.e., Broughton Bay.
*****[원주] The Japanese call this port Gen-san.

whole country with one voice implores.

Since the opening of the port Tong-nê,* this is the first year that we have imposed duties on the inhabitants, in consequence of which their Envoy, Hanbusa Yoshikata, came to Tong-nê, and protested that the due time had not yet come, and his threatening voice resounded everywhere. But as this was a thing [in] which strictness could be relaxed, we deferred the term and both parties retired. The letter he wrote on that occasion was very rude, and spoke of indemnities for commercial losses. I do not know what is going to happen next spring.

I take advantage of the departure of our Ambassador to entrust this to Governor Yü for transmission. My sentiments towards your Excellency are too profound for expression, but I tremble myriad-fold at the myriad-fold discourtesies of which I am guilty. Incomplete, but respectfully presented.

10th moon, 27th day, 1878

Inclosure 3

Second reply of Li Hung-Chang to the ex-Prime Minister of Corea.

(Translation)

LAST year, in the beginning of the 9th month, I sent a reply to my revered elder brother, Hüh-shan, his Excellency the Grand Preceptor, in which I briefly exposed the thoughts that had occupied my mind. I hear that it was first safely delivered in the middle of the 10th moon.

From your benevolent letter of the 25th of the 10th moon, forwarded through Prefect Yü, of Yung-ping, I learn that my previous letter had not yet reached you. I have received fifteen articles as gifts from you, precious friends from afar off; and, though I have not yet been able duly to reciprocate, I humbly and respectfully thank you for them. The portrait of my humble self in the Koh-wu Che-chi Pien has been copied so frequently that it has lost all its truth. Your flattering commendations are more than it deserves, and only serve to make me feel more ashamed of it. I have here a small portrait taken from the life, which I

---
*[원주] i.e., Fusan.

beg to offer you, to take the place of a personal meeting.

As the year is just beginning, I hope that your meritorious record is continually increasing, that you may have much happiness, and render diligent aid to your Prince, give ease to the people and protect your boundaries. Last year your honourable country suddenly was thrown into mourning,* and the ceremony of conferring a title took place-an auspicious and inauspicious celebration thus coming close together.

I can imagine that your Excellency, directing public business and sedulously attending to the funeral, must have been overwhelmed with labour.

When the French missionary entered your boundaries, and your honourable country arrested and imprisoned him because he taught a different doctrine, our Tsung-li Yamên, fearing lest the French should make trouble about it, purposely sent in haste to counsel his reease [release], purely with the object of avoiding a complication. The French Envoy was extremely pleased, and there is nothing more to fear. Of course, foreign missionaries declare that their object is to persuade man to be better, but your honourable country reveres the genuine doctrine;** and if any heresy starts up, you strictly and legally seize the persons and enforce order, which is undoubtedly in accordance with right reason and entirely justifiable. But the foreigners make use of the protest that the missionaries have been maltreated, and, therefore, if a case of this kind should occur again, you had better send the person, out of the country, and certainly not to readily visit him with cruel treatment, by which course you will prevent foreign complications.

I lately received a letter from sub-Expositor Ho, our Minister in Japan, telling me that an English merchant-ship, having been driven by continuous gales ashore at Chyon-'iu, in your honourable country's Island of Choi-jyu (Quelpart), the local officials and inhabitants rendered assistance to the crew in danger of drowning and saved the cargo, which was on the point of being engulphed; that the shipwrecked mariners were provided with food and lodgings, for which all payment was refused, and the English Minister, Par Hali (Sir Harry Parkes), sent an officer to return thanks, who also was very courteously treated by your honourable country, and their panegyrics continue even yet. So you see that Occidental nations honour and understand kindness and ties of obligations, and are not altogether incapable of being amenable to

---

*[원주] By the death of the late King's widow, on whom the Emperor of China conferred a posthumous title.
**[원주] i.e., that of Confucius.

reason and reformed by virtue.

He says the Japanese having sent to make surveys and open a port, your honourable country said it was not convenient to do so, because the place was close to the Temple of the founder of your country and the tombs of your kings. If you oppose them with correct language they will give way.

I hear that, in consequence of duties having been levied at Tong-nai (i.e, Fusankai), the Japanese merchants do not care to trade there, and that, owing to the disturbance, Japan was going to send a man-of-war to the spot to discuss the question. Sub-Expositor Ho, anxious that no trouble should arise, went to the ministry of Foreign Affairs and suggested a peaceful solution. I also dispatched a letter, instructing him to arrange the affair, and I imagine that you must have heard of the affair. Have there been any further trouble or not?

The Japanese are by natural disposition vainglorious and fond of novelty although they sometimes say that they profoundly comprehend the great policy, and desire to get your honourable country to play the part of lips to their teeth, and to join them in repelling a powerful foe (Russia) whenever they think their petty interests are involved, they cannot control their anxiety, and make a great outcry.

Your honourable country's policy towards them should be to lean on reason, observe good faith, and take your stand upon the Treaty, but also be sedulous in regulating your internal affairs and watching over your own safety, so as to give no one an opportunity to take advantage of you.

The Japanese of late have taken to imitate the Europeans in everything, including what is quoted as "International Law," so that they cannot, without provocation, seize on the territory of another. If you keep on good terms with them, they cannot transgress the limits of the law or venture to carry out their plans further than commercial intercourse goes.

I am an old block of stone as ever, and ashamed of my uselessness, but by good luck the harvest has turned out well, and the army and people are tranquil, which enables me in a slight degree to requite the Imperial favours. At present foreign affairs occupy much of my attention, and the times are troubled.

Your Excellency has great experience of affairs, and is much beloved by the people; you direct the great policy of your country, and, enjoying your Prince's favour, are permitted to go backwards and forwards to your country seat. Henceforth take care of your health and prolong your life, and continue to give loyal counsels, but pray do not continue in your previous resolution.

Feeling the greatest respect and affection for you I had intended to send some trifling articles in return for your great kindness, but the tribute-bearing Envoy's departure is so close at hand, that I cannot get them ready in time. Permit me to forward them on a future occasion. I beg to inquire again after your welfare. This letter is insufficient to say all I feel.

(Signed) LI HUNG-CHANG of Ho-féi
22nd day of the 1st moon, 1879

Inclosure 4

Memorandum

ACCORDING to the present constitution of Corea, the Government is carried on in the name of the King by a Prime Minister and two colleagues of almost equal rank, next to whom are the Presidents of the six Boards, an institution borrowed from China. But the power is not really wielded by those who are its nominal depositories, and the influence of the King's relations generally overrides the authority of the Ministers.

At the present moment the Prime Minister (Riyong-ui-chyong) is Ri Ch'oiung, uncle of the King, but his authority is weak in comparison with that of Min T'ai-ko, ex-President of the Board of Ceremonies, and uncle of the Queen, who in her turn rules the King.

The reigning King is not the son of his predecessor. When the late King died at the early age of 37, the mother of the last King but one managed to obtain possession of the Royal Seal, and was thus enabled to nominate a successor of her own choice. This was in 1864, and the King being only 11 years old at the time, the power naturally fell into the hands of his real father, Tai-won-Kun, who maintained his authority almost unimpaired during a period of about ten years, in spite of various unpopular act. In the meantime, however, the King grew up to man's estate, and had married the daughter of Min-Sung-ho, a lady one year his own senior, who appears to possess great influence over him.

In 1874 the residence of Min-Sung-ho was destroyed by fire, and he himself perished in the flames. It was supposed that the King's father, fearing his rising influence, caused his rival's dwelling to be set on fire with the object of compassing his death, and from that moment the King, urged by his wife to take the reins into his own hands, forbade his Ministers to consult any more with his father, who, finding himself entirely deserted, retired into private life, and his place was taken by the brother of his rival, uncle of the Queen.

When this change was made, a rumour found its way abroad that the Government had adopted a more liberal policy towards the Christians, and was more favourably inclined toward foreign countries than hitherto owing to the fact of the fallen statesman having held extreme anti-foreign views, but subsequent events have shown that there was little ground for this sanguine belief. There is very little chance, as long as the persons who succeeded to the power in 1874 continue to hold it, of overtures from foreign Powers for the conclusion of Treaties being listened to, and the only hope of the Corea's being brought out of her seclusion lies in that fact that some of the younger men are beginning to take an interest in what goes on beyond their own borders, and to desire to enter into relations with foreign Powers. Perhaps the letter of Li Hung-Chang to the predecessor of the present Prime Minister, in which he urges upon Corea the necessity of cultivating the friendship of Foreign Powers in order to maintain her independence, may have contributed to promote these ideas. But there seems, at any rate, no doubt that there exists a progressive party headed by young men of rank who are desirous of reforming the present oppressive system of government, and of developing the resources of the country with the aid of skilled knowledge from foreign countries. Amongst them the most prominent are the son (aged 23) of the present Prime Minister and the son-in-law of the late King, Pak Yong-hyo (aged 20), and even some high officials belonging to the six Boards, such as Chyo Syong-ha, President of the Board of Civil office (aged 38 years), and Kim Ok-Kyun (aged 29 years), nephew of the elder Queen-Dowager, who occupies a high position in the University.

Hitherto Corea has had intercourse with two Asiatic Powers alone, China and Japan. In spite of the numerous attempts made by the Mongols, Manchus, and Japanese to conquer her, she has always contrived to recover her liberty. In the end of the sixteenth century she was overrun by the armies of the famous Japanese soldier of fortune known to us as Taikosama, but eventually, with the aid of the Chinese, freed herself from the invader. The wrongs inflicted during that unprovoked war have never been forgiven by the Coreans, who only submitted to conclude a Treaty of Commerce with Japan because they felt they were not strong enough to resist.

In the seventeenth century Corea was again conquered by the Manchus, who made a sudden raid upon the capital, and seizing the Queen and her son, forced the King to accede to their demands. Corea has ever since acknowledged the suzerainty of China, although it does not appear to be known what were the conditions upon which she retained her autonomy.

Of Western Powers the Coreans know little, and that little is scarcely of a kind to inspire friendly feeling. They dislike France more than any other nation on account of the troubles caused by French missionary enterprize, and also because they consider themselves to be still at war with her, no further communications having passed between the two countries since the failure of the French expedition in 1866.

They also look upon the United States as their enemy, and it is almost certain that any persistent attempts on the part of American Agents to enter into relations would give rise to renewed hostilities.

Russia is disliked on account of the insidious manner in which she seduces Corean subjects across the border into Manchuria, and also because it is feared that she designs to annex the peninsula whenever a favourable opportunity may offer.

Of Austria, Germany, Italy, and the other Powers who have Treaties with China and Japan, they are absolutely ignorant.

Great Britain alone is the Power toward which they at any rate do not entertain feelings of aversion. She has never made any attempt to force commercial relations upon them, and has always steadily declined to interfere with them in any way. The only occasions on which they have come into contact with Englishmen have been when British vessels have been wrecked on the Corean coast, and British officials have been sent to return thanks for the kind treatment experienced by the shipwrecked crews. That a good effect has been produced by such little courtesies cannot be doubted, but at the same time there is no probability that an Envoy would be received by the present Corean Government unless accompanied by a force sufficient to overwhelm resistance.

(Signed) E. SATOW
July 26, 1880

45

J.G. Kennedy (1880. 11. 21) ➔ G.L.G. Granville (1881. 1. 3)

조선의 개국 가능성 보고

Mr. Kennedy to Earl Granville.—(Received January 3, 1881)

(No. 179 Very Confidential)

Yedo, November 21, 1880

My Lord,

  WITH reference to my despatch No. 131, Very Confidential, of the 27th July last, I have the honour to report that trustworthy information has recently reached me of a great change having taken place in the attitude of the King and Government of Corea towards foreign Powers, and that they are now inclined to receive in a friendly manner both Envoys and communications from Powers desirous of entering into relations with them. This information has been conveyed to me, through Mr. Satow, by the native of Corea mentioned in the above despatch, who has now returned to Japan as the recognized Confidential Agent of his Government.

  This Corean gentleman states that the recent change of attitude of the King and Government of Corea towards foreigners is due to several causes, amongst which he cites the leading ones to be: —The letter addressed by the Chinese Minister here to the Corean Envoy during his recent mission to Japan; the advice given by the Japanese Second Prime Minister and the Minister for Foreign Affairs to the same Corean Envoy, urging on the latter, as a measure of policy in the interests both of Corea and Japan, to open the country to foreigners; and lastly, the alarm felt by the King because of the presence of a formidable Russian fleet in Eastern waters.

  Of these three causes the last mentioned has doubtless been the most efficacious; but it appears that the letter addressed by Mr. Ho to the Corean Envoy has produced its effect, for the Confidential Agent has communicated to me a draft of the reply which has been prepared to Mr. Ho's letter, and of which the chief passages are to the following effect: —

  "The suggestion that Corea should enter into relations with America and other foreign Powers in order to obtain support against Russia is a good one, but from ancient times the practice of Corea has been not to have intercourse with foreign countries, and besides, the distance is so great that they cannot venture to make the first approaches towards entering into alliances for the purpose of obtaining help in their difficulties. But if a vessel came with a letter, they would receive the letter and reply courteously; and if navigators asked help in difficulties they would do all in their power to help. In this way they would discharge the duties of hospitality, and afterwards that country (America) would say that they had been well received, and propose to enter into relations."

The letter winds up by expressing the opinion that the interests of China and Japan, as well as those of Corea, are involved in the success of this plan, and that the time is not one in which dreams of peace and ease should be indulged.

The Agent has shown to Mr. Satow, as his credentials, a passport for safe-conduct furnished to him by the King of Corea, and bearing his Majesty's seal, wherein the bearer is described as travelling on confidential business of the Corean Government, and is specially recommended to all authorities.

He has also communicated to Mr. Satow two letters recently received by him from the capital whilst awaiting in the port of Fusan an opportunity of returning to Japan.

The first letter says that a Council had been held; that the King had very much changed his views; and that Hanabusa's (The Japanese Minister to Corea) demands were likely to be conceded. That if an American Minister came to the capital they would be guided by circumstances as to granting his demands; that it seems probable that the residence of a Japanese Minister at the capital, the free circulation of Japanese throughout the country, and the opening of Ninsen would be conceded, and also, before long, the questions respecting the export of rice.

The second letter is from the son of the Prime Minister, who tells the Agent that the King and Court had very much changed their views, and he hoped that some Japanese of importance would pay them a visit. The writer also begs the Agent to communicate the above to Iwakura (Japanese Second Prime Minister) and Ito (Councilor of State), and persuade them to undergo a little present fatigue for the sake of future ease.

In communicating the above documents to Mr. Satow. the Agent strongly urged the advisability of the dispatch, without delay, of a British Envoy to the capital, accompanied by two or three ships of war, and furnished with full powers to conclude a Treaty of Commerce and Friendship.

In support of his proposal, the Agent alluded to the presence of the Russian fleet, and urged that under pressure of this danger the Corean Government would probably readily enter upon negotiations, whereas a few months hence the fleet might be dispersed or actively employed against Corea, whereby the opportunity might be lost.

The Agent also sketched out a draft Treaty of Commerce and Friendship, framed in a liberal spirit, with a fixed Tariff at 10 percent, upon the chief articles only of import.

The Agent is also in communication with my Chinese and German colleagues, but as yet I have no knowledge of his proceedings in those quarters, and, as his intercourse with Her Majesty's Legation is conducted solely with Mr. Satow. I do not pretend to know of his existence, and abstain from inquiries respecting him.

My Italian colleague has recently again expressed to me his desire to effect the opening of Corean ports, and his hope that Great Britain, Italy, France, Germany and the United States will decide on a combined demonstration against Corea.

My German colleague likewise hopes for instructions from his Government.

There exists a general impression in official quarters, and especially amongst Japanese and Americans, that before long Corea will be opened to foreign commerce.

As regards Great Britain, I apprehend that Corea will not be much importance commercially, but, in view of possible complications between Russia and China, it has acquired a political importance for all nations trading in the far East.

I have, &c.
(Signed) J.G. Kennedy

J.G. Kennedy (1880. 11. 22) ➜ G.L.G. Granville (1881. 1. 3)

何如璋의 조약 체결 권고 보고

Mr. Kennedy to Earl Granville.—(Received January 3, 1881)

(No. 180 Very Confidential)

Yedo, November 22, 1880

My Lord,

IN continuation of my immediately preceding despatch, I have the honour to invite your Lordship's attention to the change of attitude and language assumed by the Government of Corea towards foreign nations, as evidenced by a comparison of the letters embodied in my preceding despatch, with the inclosures in my despatch No. 131, Confidential, of the 27th July last, as well as of the language held to Mr. Satow by the Corean Agent, as reported in the same two despatches.

The changed attitude in a sense favourable to intercourse with foreign nations has been confirmed to me to-day by the Chinese Minister. His Excellency informed me that he himself had written to the Government at Peking, to Li Hung Chang, and to the late Corean Envoy to Japan in the same sense, begging them to urge and advise the King and Government of Corea to make Treaties with foreign Powers as a measure conductive to the interests of both China and Corea, and as a safeguard against possible designs of annexation or occupation by Russia of the latter country.

Mr. Ho promised me immediate communication of the answer he was still expecting to the above letters, but stated his conviction that the present moment was opportune for opening intercourse with Corea.

His Excellency explained to me that the Coreans were like children; that rough measures were of no use against them, but that they were easily influenced and led by kindly and conciliatory treatment, supported by a judicious display of force kept in reverse.

In submitting the above information to your Lordship, I beg leave respectfully to record my opinion that if your Lordship should see fit so to instruct me, I could, with fair prospect of success, proceed within the next few months to Corea and conclude a Treaty with that country. For such purpose I should require the assistance of Mr. Satow and of Mr. Aston, of Her Majesty's Japanese Service, and also of two of Her Majesty's ships of war.

I have, &c.
(Signed) J.G. Kennedy

T.F. Wade (1881. 1. 7) → G.L.G. Granville

러시아의 조선 영토 일부 점령가능성 보고

No. 5

January 7, 1881

Confidential

My Lord,

    I had the honour to address to Your Lordship this day the following telegram—In cypher.

    Confidential. Peace with Russia seems nearly certain, but a Japanese Under Secretary for Foreign affairs has arrived and I fear that China is receding from the engagements she had nearly concluded with Japan. Under Secretary has not visited any legation.

    It is generally thought that Russia will seize something in Corea in Spring.
    I hear confidentially that a telegraph line inland from Peking to Shanghai has been sanctioned by the Imperial Decree; also that a railway from Peking to the Great River is strongly supported.

I have the honor to be, with the highest respect,
My Lord, Your Lordship's most obedient, humble servant,
Wade.

F.O. (1881. 1. 20) ➜ T.F. Wade

조영조약 체결을 위한 청국의 중재 가능성 확인 지령

Draft.
Tel. No. 2

F.O. Jan. 20, 1881

"H. M. Govt. have need intimation that Corea is now favourably disposed to conclude a Treaty with Great Britain.

Ascertain whether Chinese Govt. can confirm existence of such disposition and, in that case, if H.M. Govt. may count on their good offices in carrying matter to a successful termination."

H.S. Parkes (1881. 1. 11)

조영조약 체결 시기에 관한 Memorandum

Memorandum by Sir H.S. Parkes.

[Mr. Kennedy's despatches Nos. 179 and 180, Very Confidential]

IT is very satisfactory to learn from these despatches that the King and Government of Corea are now alive to the importance of abandoning the policy of strict seclusion hitherto maintained by that nation towards all European States, and that they now desire to conclude Treaties with those States, of the same character as the Corean Treaty with Japan. As that Treaty is formed on the lines of the British Treaty with Japan, a similar one would satisfy our requirements.

The presence of the large Russian force in the immediate vicinity of Corea has doubtless convinced the more intelligent members of the Corean Government of the wisdom of the advice given to them both by China and Japan, as to the imminent danger they will incur if they delay any longer the opening of their country to European intercourse.

It is obviously desirable that we should avail ourselves of this favourable disposition without loss of time. We should, I think, find it much easier and more expeditious to act by ourselves that in combination with other Powers. The papers inclosed in Mr. Kennedy's despatch No. 131 of the 27th July, 1880, show that the Coreans are better disposed towards Great Britain than the other European Powers with whom they are acquainted (see Mr. Satow's memorandum), and combination with the latter might, in some respects, prejudice or impede our action. But if our co-operation should be invited by other Powers, it would, of course, be undesirable to withhold it.

It is probable that some of the Powers will not be backward in moving in the matter. Although the endeavours made by the United states and Italy last year to open communications with Corea were not attended with success, those Powers will probably be ready to repeat the effort when they become acquainted with the changed attitude of the Corean Government. It would appear from these despatches that the change of feeling in Corea has been made known to the American and German Ministers in Japan, who would doubtless communicate it to their Governments. If the latter, or any other Power, should desire the co-operation of Great Britain, they would probably communicate their wishes to Her Majesty's Government.

The desirability of acting promptly is suggested by two considerations: (1) that Russia may employ the force she has now on the spot either to occupy territory in Corea, or to coerce Corea into granting her exclusive advantages (see Lord Dufferin's despatch No. 341 of the 13th August, 1880); and (2) that if any settlement arrived at between Russia and China should relieve the Corean Government of the apprehensions they now entertain as to the hostile designs of the Russian force, they may change their views and return to their old policy of seclusion.

The most convenient season of the year for sending a Mission to Corea would be April or May. I am aware that it is the intention of Admiral Willes, who is about to relieve Admiral Coote, in the command of the China and Japan station, to proceed to Shanghae about the end of April, and his presence there at that date would be opportune, either to support the Minister charged with a Mission, or to carry out, as suggested by Sir Julian Pauncefote, any instructions that might be deemed necessary. I need not add that it would afford me pleasure to be charged with a Mission to Corea if Her Majesty's Government should see fit to entrust it to me.

If such a course should be decided on, I think it would be desirable that a preliminary visit should be paid to the Corean capital by an Agent of lower rank than a Minister, and I venture to suggest that Mr. Satow is well fitted, from his knowledge of the subject, to undertake such a duty. If he preceded the Mission by a few weeks he would be able to feel the ground, to ascertain whether a mission would be well received, and in that case, to make preparations for the reception of the Minister. If circumstance should permit, he might commence the discussion of the details of the proposed Treaty with the Corean authorities. And he might meet me at Shanghae to report results or might communicate with me by letter, if he found it more expedient to await my arrival in Corea.

It might, I think, be found possible and advisable to convey earlier notice to Corea of the intended dispatch of the Mission through the medium of the Chinese Government at Peking. It may be presumed that the Chinese Government would approve of the Mission, and would give it their support. If the Corean Government were timely apprized that they might soon expect a British Mission they would be the less inclined to agree to exclusive arrangements' with Russia (if such should be proposed) or to disavow the overtures made by the King's Agent in Japan.

                                      (Signed) HARRY S. PARKES
                                                                        January 11, 1881

50

T.F. Wade (1881. 1. 14) ➜ G.L.G. Granville (1881. 1. 27)

러시아 동향 보고

Sir T. Wade to Earl Granville.—(Received January 27)

(No. 5 Confidential)

Peking, January 14, 1881

(Telegraphic)

WITH reference to my telegram No. 5 of last month, Chargé d'Affaires of Russia has become much more moderate as regards China; also more communicative.

He believes there was a serious crisis at St. Petersburgh between 5th and 15th December, after which the situation improved.

He declares that annexation in the east would be ruinous to Russia, but holds outlet for Russian enterprise" along the shores of the Black Sea" to be indispensable.

French Minister has shown me a despatch of October last, in which French Chargé d'Affaires at St. Petersburgh reports Russian Government much disquieted by sale of German rifles to China.

German Minister says prospect of peace with Russia is illusory.

China has, at any rate, contract for 100,000 German rifles, of which one-fifth have been delivered.

Fear of rupture with Russia is disappearing fast, but rumour of misunderstanding with Japan gains ground. Russia desires this, I suspect, because she has designs on Corea.

German Minister desires it because he believes trouble between China and Japan of advantage to all of us.

G.L.G. Granville (1881. 1. 20) ➜ T.F. Wade

조약 체결에 대한 청국의 입장 확인 지시

Earl Granville to Sir T. Wade.

(No. 7. Extender)

Foreign Office, January 20, 1881

Sir,

INFORMATION to which they are disposed to give credence has recently been submitted to the notice of Her Majesty's Government, to the effect that a disposition has of late manifested itself in the Corea which encourages the hope that a Mission with the object of concluding a Treaty between that country and Great Britain would be favourably received there and its purpose successfully attained.

I have accordingly to request that you will inquire of the Chinese Government whether they are in a position to confirm the assurances above referred to; and will also sound them as to the extent to which their good offices may be relied upon by Her Majesty's Government in the event of a dispatch of such a Mission to Corea towards bringing the negotiations to a fortunate issue.

I am, &.
(Signed) GRANVILLE

52

T.F. Wade (1881. 2. 9) ➡ G.L.G. Granville (1881. 2. 23)

청국의 중개를 통한 교섭 추진 보고

Sir T. Wade to Earl Granville.—(Received February 23)

(No. 10 Very Confidential)

Peking, February 9, 1881

(Telegraphic)

YOUR telegram no. 2 regarding Corea arrived 6th instant.

I had anticipated your Lordship's instructions that day. Chinese Government has been for some time urging that country to open its ports, and is now expecting answer to last letter sent.

Belief is general that Russia will seize some place on that coast, if not more.

It had occurred to me that the attempt of any one Power to establish Treaty relations alone would create jealousy, and most likely precipitate Russian action. I had therefore recommended Chinese Government to persuade those people to request Chinese Government to inform Treaty Powers by Circular that they were ready to open their country and would at once admit Agents to examine country, and frame Report on which Commercial Treaty might be based.

The Yamên approved my proposition very warmly.

The thing should not be talked of, but I am writing confidentially to Admiral to prepare him. If the invitation comes I propose to send Chinese Secretary. More in a few days.

Memorandum by Sir H.S. Parkes.

[Sir T. Wade's Telegram, Very Confidential, of February 9, 1881]

IF I may do so without presumption, I beg to express entire concurrence in the course taken by Sir Thomas Wade.

I may mention that when I found that the Japanese Government had settled their relations with Corea by their two Treaties of 1876, I recommended them to follow the same course as that which Sir Thomas Wade has now suggested to the Chinese Government, namely, to advise the Corean Government to invite the Western Powers, through the Japanese Government, to enter into relations of friendship and commerce. My recommendations failed in effect, either because the relations of the Japanese with the Coreans were not of a sufficiently cordial nature to permit of their offering such advice, or because the Japanese wished to keep to themselves the advantages of an exclusive trade with Corea.

Later on I had frequent opportunities of conversing with the Chinese Minister at Yedo on the same subject, and I pointed out to him that, in view of the advance of Russia on the Pacific, his Government would greatly consult their own interests, and would at the same time gain credit for liberal opinions, by inducing the Corean Government to open their country to foreign trade. The Chinese Minister warmly concurred in this recommendation, and informed me that he had strongly supported it in letters to Li Hung Chang. The friendly communications of the latter to the ex-Prime Minister of Corea (inclosed in Mr. Kennedy's despatch No. 131, Very Confidential, of the 27th July, 1880), show that he was influenced by these considerations.

If Russia, however, according to the general belief referred to by Sir Thomas Wade, should seize one or more place in Corea before friendly relations are established between that country and Western Powers, a new position, affecting British interests in The China and Japan seas scarcely less gravely than those of the Coreans, would then be created.

(Signed)   HARRY S. PARKES

H.S. Parkes (1881. 2. 26)

Wade의 기밀보고서에 관한 Memorandum

Memorandum by Sir H. Parkes.

[Sir T. Wade's Telegram, Very Confidential, of February 9, 1881]

IF I may do so without presumption, I beg to express entire concurrence inthe course taken by Sir Thomas Wade.

I may mention that when I found that the Japanese Government had settled their relations with Corea by their two Treaties of 1876, I recommended them to follow the same course as that which Sir Thomas Wade has now' suggested to the Chinese Government, namely, to advise the Coreim Government to invite the Western Powers, through the Japanese Government, to enter into relations of friendship and commerce. My recommendations failed in effect, either because the relations of the Japanese with the Coreans were not of a sufficiently cordial nature to permit of their offering such advice, or because the Japanese wished to keep to themselves the advantages of an exclusive trade with Corea.

Later on I had frequent opportunities of conversing with the Chinese Minister at Yedo on the same subject, and I pointed out to him that, in view of the advance of Russia on the Pacific, his Government would greatly consult their own interests, and would at the same time gain credit for liberal opinions, by inducing the Corean Government to open their country to foreign trade. The Chinese Minister warmly concurred in this recommendation, and informed me that he had strongly supported it in letters to Li Hung Chang. The friendly communications of the latter to the ex-Prime Minister of Corea (inclosed in Mr. Kennedy's despatch No. 131, Very Confidential, of the 27th July, 1880), show that he was influenced by these considerations.

If Russia, however, according to the general belief referred to by Sir Thomas Wade, should seize one or more places in Corea before friendly relations are established between that country and Western Powers, a new position, affecting British interests in the China and Japan seas scarcely less gravely than those of the Coreans, would then be created.

(Signed)　　HARRY S. PARKES

February 26, 1881

T.F. Wade (1881. 2. 18) ➔ G.L.G. Granville (1881. 4. 16)

Spence의 부산, 원산, 영흥만 조사 보고서

Sir T. Wade to Earl Granville. —(Received April 16)

(No. 5 Confidential)

Peking, February 18, 1881

My Lord,

I SHOULD have reported to-day *in extenso* my proceedings with reference to the Corean question which were summarized in my telegram No. 10 of the 9th instant, but I received yesterday some information which I wish to lay before your Lordship with the rest.

Meanwhile, I inclose copy of a Memorandum of the visit of the "Vettor Pisani" to that country, prepared by Mr. Spence; who, at the request of Signor di Luca, the Minister Resident of Italy, was allowed by Mr. Clement Allen, then Acting Consul at Shanghae, to accompany the Duke of Genoa.

I was under the impression, until within the last few days, that Mr. Spence's interesting paper had been forwarded by Mr. Allen directly to your Lordship.

I have, &c.
(Signed) THOMAS FRANCIS WADE

Inclosure in No. 38

Report by Mr. Spence of his Visit to Corea with His Royal Highness the Duke of Genoa. *

[Map not received.]

---

*[원주] Copies of this Report were sent to St. Petersburgh, Rome, Peking, Yedo, and the Admiralty.

HAVING received an invitation in July to accompany His Royal Highness the Duke of Genoa to Corea, I proceeded, with the sanction of Her Majesty's Consul, to Japan, to join the Prince's ship, the "Vettor Pisani," at Kobe. I joined the vessel on the 26th July, and received a most cordial and hospitable welcome both from the Prince and his suite.

Before our arrival on the shores of Corea, the Prince informed me that he had no special powers from the Italian Government to enter into negotiations on any specific subject with the Corean authorities. His object, he said, in visiting Corea was mainly one of curiosity to see what was possible to be seen of a country and a people so secluded, and to make an attempt to enter into friendly relations with such of the Corean authorities along the coast as he might meet with.

The Prince asked me if I had any ideas as to the best way he could attain these objects, and I told him that, as far as I could judge from recent events and from the experience of the foreign officials who had attempted to approach the Corean authorities through the Japanese Consuls there, his best plan would be to go to ports where there were no Japanese. This opinion, I knew, coincided with M. de Luca's, and before leaving Shanghae I had had an interview with Captain. Fourmier, of the "Lynx," who informed me that his experiences in Corea led him to believe the same. Indeed, Captain Fourmier said that the Japanese authorities were in league with the Coreans to frustrate every attempt on the part of Representatives or I officers of European nations to enter into relations with Corean officials. I also informed the Prince that it was a very natural thing that the Japanese should be anxious to keep a monopoly of such foreign trade as they could coax into existence in Corea, and should, with that view, adopt the extreme measure of assisting the Coreans to remain in the most. complete isolation. This view is, of course, no novel one, and I found that the Prince, who had heard it from other sources, was inclined to believe it. However, he said he was anxious to find out for himself whether it was true or not, and though he did not expect to be able to communicate with the Corean authorities through the Japanese Consuls, he hoped to be able to form some idea whether the influence they possessed would be used for or against Europeans.

I had furnished myself before leaving with the books on Corea written by E. Oppert and the Rev. John Ross. These worthless publications gave us but a meagre idea of the country we were about to visit; but I am happy to say that by the kindness of Mr. Aston, our Consul at Kobé, I was supplied with several much more useful books, notably the "Histoire de l'Eglise dans la Corée,"* by far the best book on the country I have seen, and vol. iv of Siebold's "Japan." He also gave me several Corean books., written in Chinese by Coreans, to show me. how far, if at all, their Chinese differed from the language now current in China, and the maps of Corea published by the Japanese Government. All these proved of the greatest interest and use.

We left Simonoseki on the 28th July, and sailed across the Corean Channel in a single night, passing the Island of Tsushima on our way, and cast anchor next day at the south-east corner of the peninsula in Chosen Harbour, where is situated the most southerly of the two Corean ports open to the Japanese, Fusan.

The harbour of Fusan, or Chosen, is well known. Its surroundings are fully and accurately described on p. 68 of vol. iv of the "China Sea Directory" of 1873. It affords a magnificent anchorage for many more ships than are likely to frequent the port, and it is open all the winter. I have little to add to the description given in the pUblication mentioned. All the sides of the harbour, except the south, are studded with villages, containing a resident population of 10,000 or 12,000, engaged in fishing. At certain times of the year there is an enormous influx to these fishing-towns of people from the interior, to catch and cure the ribbon-fish, which visit the harbour in shoals. The southern shore of the harbour is formed by Deer Island, a densely-wooded pe'§:k some 1,500 feet high. It is a Government reservation, where the Government stud of diminutive ponies is turned out to graze. At the time of our visit there were several hundreds of these "horses" roaming about the lower slopes of Deer Island, and, with the exception of their keepers, it is uninhabited. It abounds with pheasants, hog-deer, wild pig, and even tigers, as I myself can testify.

The country round the harbour is all within the jurisdiction of the Prefect of Tung Tsaifoo, or, as it is called by, the Coreans and Japanese, Toraifoo. The walled city of Torai is situated a few miles inland, and is the seat of the Local Government. It is with this official, dignified by the name of Governor, that Commodore Schufeldt, on behalf of the United States, and Captain Fourmier, on behalf of the French Minister at Peking, tried to enter into official relations. Both these officers availed themselves of the services of the Japanese Consul at Fusan to convey their letters to the Prefect; but, in both cases, the Prefect not only refused to receive or open them, but did so in a rude and offensive-manner.

---

*[원주] Par Ch. Dallet. Paris: Victor Palme, 25, Rue de Grenelle St. Germain.

Immediately on anchoring in the harbour CounJ; Candiani, the Prince's First Aide-de-camp. and myself, went on shore to the Japanese Settlement to visit the Consul, and to present him with the letters with which the Prince was furnished by the Foreign Minister at Tokio. After a short interview we took him off to the ship to call on the Prince. In the course of conversation he warned us not to land anywhere except on Deer Island, lest we should have our heads broken with stones; and, with regard to communicating with the local authority at Torai, he offered to forward a letter, but he gave it as his opinion that the Prefect would decline to receive it.

The Prince, however, in spite of this warning, directed Count Candiani next day to write a despatch to the Prefect, and to send it under flying seal through the Japanese Consul, with a note to him asking him to read and forward it. Both note and despatch were duly translated into Chinese by myself, and sent to the Consul on the 1st August. The following was the substance of the note:-

"Fusan Po, August 1, 1880

"Count Candiani presents his compliments to the Japanese Consul, and begs to hand him herewith a letter to the Prefect of Torai, under flying seal. He begs the Consul to forward it, as an inclosure, in a cover addressed by himself to the Prefect.

"Count Candiani is well aware of the indisposition of the Corean authorities to enter into communication with the officials of foreign nations not in Treaty relations with Corea, but he hopes that, in the present case, the Prefect will not be so ungracious as to refuse to receive a simple letter of thanks.

"Count Candiani would be glad if the Consul would state in his covering letter that the 'Vettor Pisani' has come to Corea simply to express the thanks of the Italian people for the kind treatment by Coreans' of a shipwrecked Italian sailor.

"The Count takes this opportunity of thanking the Consul for his good offices, and the Consul may rest assured that His Royal Highness the Duke of Genoa will bring the services of the Consul to the notice of his Government."

The despatch inclosed in the foregoing note ran as follows. It sufficiently indicates the main purpose of the Prince's visit: —

"To Shen, Prefect of Torai, &c.

"Fusan Po, August 1, 1880

"Sir,

"Two years ago an Italian merchant-ship, named the 'Bianca Portica,' was wrecked on the coast of Quelpart, and the whole of the crew were drowned with the exception of one sailor, Santolo.

"This sailor received the greatest kindness at the hands of the population, and, subsequently, the Corean authorities took charge of him, gave him food and clothes, and kept him until he was able to get back to his country.

"This instance of the humane treatment of Italian sailors having come to the notice of our Government, it has excited a feeling of gratitude, and as the Italian ship 'Vettor Pisani,' under my command, is at present on the Japan Station, I have been commissionpri by the Government to come here to thank the Corean Government and people for their kindness. I am charged, at the same time, to reimburse you for all the expenses which may have been incurred by either officials or people in saving Santolo's life.

"In view of the good relations which ought to subsist between our respective countries, it would be a great pity if the 'Vettor Pisani' had to leave Fusan and return home without accomplishing the present mission of courtesy to the Corean Government. It is in order to accomplish the orders I have received that I have now the honour to address this despatch to you, and I beg you to communicate its contents to your Government.

"I have, &c.

(Signed) "CANDIANI"

While the Prince was waiting for the Prefect's answer, I employed the intervening days in conversing with the Corean merchants in the Japanese Settlement, in visiting the different Japanese shops to find. out the classes and qualities of goods most readily saleable, and in trying to get such information regarding the government and trade of the Settlement as would be either useful or interesting. Conversation with the Coreans was conducted by the slow but not unsatisfactory method of written Chinese characters, and I found the Coreans in the south much more reticent and suspicious than in the north. The

Japanese Consul also furnished me with the statistics I asked for.

The Settlement of Fusan has been inhabited by Japanese ever since the Treaty of 1615 between Japan and Corea with which Fidejoshi concluded his victorious campaigns. It was garrisoned by the Japanese Princes of Tsushima for two centuries with 300 or 400 soldiers, but,-far what purpose, it is hard to say. The garrison was kept under the most severe restrictions by the Corean Government, similar to those imposed by the Japanese themselves on the Dutch at Decima.

From the sea the Settlement has the appearance of an ordinary Japanese town, the houses being of wood and of the usual Japanese type. It is pleasantly situated in a magnificent grove of fir-trees of fabulous age and enormous size. Immediately on the port being opened the Japanese population rose to 700, and it has gone on increasing until there are, to-day, over 2,300 residents.

Every inducement is held out by the Japanese authorities to encourage settlers to come to Corea. The land on which the Settlement is built is leased by the Corean Government to the Japanese for a nominal rent of 50 dollars per annum. On application by any Japanese wishing to settle in Fusan, a lot of land is assigned and made over to him by the Consul, free of all charge and expense whatever; whether of initial price or annual rent. On this lot he is at liberty to build, and he may sell or mortgage his land to any other Japanese subject, provided the consent of the Consul is obtained. The Municipal Government of the Settlement is entirely in the hands of the Consul, but in matters where he desires to have the opinion and support of the public he takes no steps until he has consulted the leading merchants. The police, draining, and lighting are all attended to after the manner of European Settlements in Japan; there is a Chamber of Commerce, a public hospital with duly qualified surgeons, and, I believe, a large Japanese Buddhist temple.

Fusan is, as yet, a free port. There is neither an import nor an export Tariff. The Corean authorities have stationed a small custom-house at the jetty where goods are landed, but its functions are confined to preventing the importation of articles which are, in Corea, a Government monopoly, or articles whose importation has been forbidden by Treaty. A Tariff is at the present time in process of negotiation, and as soon as the amount of duty is agreed upon it will beput in force.

In the year 1879 the imports were of the value of 560,000 yen. They consisted of English cotton goods, Japanese copper, foreign dyes, and Japanese silk goods and notions. I visited nearly all the shops in the Settlement, and carefully examined the cotton goods which were exposed for sale. I was surprised to 'find that they consisted entirely of ordinary English grey and white shirtings of 7 lbs. to 8 lbs. per piece. It is notorious in China that Corea is one of the principal markets for American shirtings, and for the heavy and more expensive cotton cloths imported into Shanghae. In the Settlement of Fusan, however, I could not find a single piece of heavy cotton cloth, either English or American. All the goods were light weight, had come from Shanghae, and bore the names and marks of Birley, Brand, Reiss, Holliday, Thorne, and other well-known importing houses. The present consumption of piece-goods is from 5,000 to 7,000 pieces, a-month, and is increasing.

The exports in 1879 amounted to 670,000 yen. They consisted of rice, furs, gold-dust, dried fish, seaweed, and medicines. There is no restriction at present to the export of grain.

The volume of the trade of the port is increasing, and for the half-year ended the 30th June last it amounted to 760,000 yen. It is very surprising that so small a trade can support 2,300 residents. In other ways, however, than legitimate commerce the Japanese try to make money in Fusan, for I saw more than one large tea-house where Japanese girls were entertaining crowds of Coreans with tea, music, singing, &c.

The currency of the port is Corean cash, which are more valuable and better made than Chinese. It is, however, only suitable for small transactions, and, in order to make the smallest purchases, a Corean visitor to the Settlement has to have two or three servants to carry the few strings of cash he means to spend. The few transactions of any magnitude which take place are done by means of barter-so many pieces of cloth for so many bags of rice. A short time ago the Corean Government suddenly interdicted the export of rice, and the consequence was that the Japanese merchants lost heavily through the inability of their Corean customers to complete their contracts, and the whole trade of the port was, deranged until the prohibition was removed.

The Settlement swarms 'with Coreans during the day, who come in from the towns and villages in the neighbourhood. They are ordered by law to leave every night, but many of them do not do so, and some are engaged by and live permanently with the Japanese as domestic servants. Every Corean merchant intent on buying is accompanied apparently by half-a-dozen friends, who advise him regarding the transaction he is about to make, and by his servants, who carry a load of the international currency. The transactions, as a rule, are trifling in amount, and preceded by an interminable conversation, which, in many cases, leads to nothing.Accusations of cheating are freely bandied about on both sides, and it is only after much strong language and rigorous measurement that a piece of cloth is sold.

There is communication by steamer twice a-month with Japan. The trade besides gives employment to about a dozen Japanese schooners of foreign type, which ply between Fusan, Simonoseki, Nagasaki, and Osaka.

The Japanese Consul is in official communication with the Prefect of Toraifoo, with whom he corresponds on a footing of equality.

The Japanese in Corea live under their own laws, administered by their Consuls. Attached to the Consulate at Fusan is a Court, a gaol, a staff of police, and the usual official machinery for the arrest, trial, and punishment of offenders. In deciding mixed cases, as between Coreans and Japanese, in theory a most wise course is pursued. When a Corean brings a case against a Japanese, the Consul tries the case by Japanese law; and, *pari ratione*, when a Japanese brings a case against a Corean, the Prefect of Torai tries the case by Corean law. It has taken us many years of experience in China to find out that the only practical and logical solution of the difficulty of mixed cases is for the forum and the *lex fori* to be that of the defendant; but Japan 'and Corea have blundered upon it at the very outset of their Treaty intercourse.

In practice, however, any supposed offence by a Corean in the Settlement is summarily dealt with by the first policeman who catches him, or by any Japanese who cares to assume the task of beating the offender. I regret to say that the Japanese treat the Coreans who come to the Settlement merely as visitors out of curiosity very badly. They buffet and kick them as they would beasts, and it seemed marvellous to me how these strong, stalwart men put up with the vile treatment they received from the Japanese pigmies. I have no doubt that it is for this reason that stones are thrown by the Coreans at foreigners When they try to approach any of the villages which fringe the shore of the harbour of Fusan, and that the timidity and submissiveness which we found elsewhere in Corea were said to be wanting here.

I was not sanguine that the Prefect of Torai would reply to Count Candiani's despatch, but I thought that as the Japanese Consul knew that Italy was not a great commercial Power in the East, and one far from aggressive, he might in this case make an exception. I therefore did not tell the Consul that I was an Englishman. Unfortunately, our pilot, who was asked on the evening of the 2nd August to conduct the Consul from the ship to the shore, was indiscreet enough to tell him that the British Consul from Shanghae was on board the "Vettor Pisani," and to indulge in some silly threats as to what would happen if the Prefect did not reply to Count Candiani's letter. This of course made the prospect of any answer hopeless, and after such a misadventure I was not surprised to find that next day Count Candiani received the following letter from the Japanese Consul:-

"The Consul had the honour to receive two days ago from Count Candiani a letter inclosing, under flying seal, a despatch for the Prefect of Toraifoo, and requesting the Consul to send it on to its destination, and to explain to the Prefect that it was merely a letter of thanks to the Corean Government for rescuing and saving a shipwrecked Italian seaman.

"On receipt of Count Candiani's instructions the Consul sent on the despatch at once to the Prefect, and explained its purport carefully to him. To-day the Consul has received the Prefect's reply. It is to the effect that no Corean law empowers him to receive Count Candiani's despatch.

"The Consul has done everything in his power to assist Count Candiani. He is mortified at this untoward result, and his regret is infinite. He has now the h9nour to inclose a copy of the Prefect's reply, which he begs to place before Count Candiani. He begs that Count Candiani will, out of his great bounty, forgive him."

The Prefect's reply to the Consul's letter covering Count Candiani's despatch ran thus: —

"Shên, Prefect of Toraifoo, &c., makes a communication in reply to the Consul. The Prefect has had the honour to receive, and has read, the Consul's letter; and for the Consul's careful consideration of the subject he is exceedingly obliged.

"Whenever men meet with hardships or accidents, to save and succour them is the ordinary instinct of the whole human race. When the Italian ship was lost two years ago on Quelpart, it was by the aid of Heaven that one man was saved; and in helping and relieving him the local officials and people were but acting on ordinary natural instinct.

"The despatch forwarded to the Prefect by a specially-commissioned Italian vessel expresses the most generous sentiments, and the gratitude of the Prefect is inexpressible. But in the Prefect's country correspondence by letter with foreign countries has never been sanctioned by custom or law. He cannot, therefore, in the present instance, receive the despatch which has arrived, and must send it back.

"The Prefect deeply regrets to have to take this step, for how could it be his wish to be ungrateful for sentiments so noble? The Consul must make allowance for what the Prefect has said, and offer to the Italian ship consolation for the trouble they have taken in coming so far, by explaining to them the customary rule, which he cannpt overstep. Will the Consul explain to them, on the Prefect's behalf; his apparent forgetfulness of all they have done, so that his conduct may not appear to them to be unnatural? This the Prefect earnestly begs the Consul to do.

"A respectful reply, addressed on the 28th day of the 6th moon to the Consul for Japan at :Wusan."

A short note to the Consul was subsequently received on the same day from the Prefect, politely declining an invitation which Count Candiani had sent him, through the Chnsul, to visit the "Vettor Pisani."

On the occasion of my first visit to the Japanese Consul I was shown a photograph of the Prefect of Torai, and as it was the first time I had seen a likeness of a Corean official, I observed it closely. While we were waiting for the Prefect's reply, I was in the Japanese Settlement on the 2nd August during the greater part of the day. To my surprise, I met an old Corean gentleman dressed in official clothes, but accompanied by only two followers, who appeared to me singularly like the Prefect of Torai. I got into conversation with some Coreans in a neighbouring shop, and they informed me that it was the Prefect, and that he had been spending the day with the Japanese Consul. This was strange news to get on the day the Japanese Consul was professing to be waiting for the Prefect's answer, at the very time when the Consul was regretting to me that Torai was so far off, and so much time wasted in sending letters to the Prefect. That it was the Prefect himself there was no doubt, because the Japanese themselves confirmed the story which I got from the Coreans. And in the evening, when the Prince and myself were landing to go to a Corean dinner which was given in honour of the Prince by the Consul, we were watched by the Prefect again, and followed by him, with, apparently intense curiosity, up to the gates of the Consulate. The old gentleman's curiosity had got the better of his discretion. Nothing, however, was said to the Japanese Consul which would have led him to believe that we knew that his distant correspondent had been closeted with him all day.

I have alluded to this incident because it shows distinctly that the answers which the Prefect made to the Consul *á propos* of Count Candiani's despatch were written by the Prefect and the Consul together. It affords the strongest presumption also that the policy pursued by the Corean local authority at Fusan *vis-a-vis* the European officials who visit the port from time to time is not only approved by the Japanese Government, but, as Captain Fourmier surmised, in carrying it out the Coreans have the active co-operation and assistance of the Japanese Consul.

Our visit to Fusan, therefore, was to a certain extent satisfactory in that it was made abundantly evident that no communication whatever with Corean officials is possible at the ports open to Japanese. So far the Prince's future course was simplified.

Before leaving Fusan Count Candiani addressed the following letter to the Japanese Chnsul: —

"'*Vettor Pisani,*' *Fusan, Corea, August 6, 1880.*

"Sir

"I have the honour to acknowledge the receipt of your letter yesterday on the subject of my despatch to the Prefect of Toraifoo. I regret that he is precluded by Corean law from accepting it; but although the result is not such as I expected, it is not the less my duty to thank you for your good offices.

"The letter which I had the honour to address the Prefect of Toraifoo was one of ,thanks and of pure courtesy, such as is customary under similar circumstances between friendly nations. Although I am pleased that the Prefect has become acquainted with what I wish to tell him, I do not conceal from you, however, that I was surprised to learn, from the answer which the Prefect sent to you, that he regretted he could not transmit the contents of my despatch to his Government, because the two nations were not in relations, and because he was forbidden to treat with foreigners in writing by the laws of Corea and the orders of his superiors.

"It appears, then, that Corean laws contain, upon this point, a lacuna which they will be obliged, sooner or later, to fill up. Although in this case of the loss by shipwreck of an Italian vessel everything passed off to the complete satisfaction of our Government, it is possible that this may not always be the case. More than one shipwreck has happened on the Coreancoast where the poor sailors received very different kind of treatment, and our Government has no guarantee of' any kind that in future the laws of humanity will be observed in case of shipwreck by the people or minor officials of Corea. If such a thing were again to happen, or some similar case of bad treatment proved, we should be compelled to take some other measures than the peaceful correspondence which we have, in the present instance, attempted with the Prefect of Toraifoo. And, besides, the exclusiveness of Corea is also prejudicial to herself. For so long as it exists it is difficult for us to punish any Italian sailor who may be charged with a delict within Corean territory.

"For a very long time Italy has in no wise been an aggressive nation, and has not tried to enrich herself at the expense of other countries. Her commerce even is very limited, and the Corean Government would have nothing to fear if they were to put themselves is relations with Italy.

"Moreover, the two great countries whose boundaries are conterminous with Corea have not lately been on good terms with each other, and if a feud breaks out between them Corea is perfectly certain to suffer. In such a case it would be of the greatest advantage for Corea to be in relations with foreign countries.

"On these various grounds it is much to be deplored that Italy and Corea have not yet arranged to be on friendly terms with each other.

"I shall, in the course of time, inform the Italian Government of the reply of the Prefect of Toraifoo, for such decision as it may see fit to make.

"I shall, at the same time, make known to the Italian Ministers at Tokio and Peking that the Prefect was unwilling to transmit to his superiors the thanks which formed the object of my despatch to him. In the meantime, I hold the Prefect of Toraifoo responsible for everything which may happen, and I shall find some other channel than him to communicate to the Corean Government at Seoul the contents of the correspondence which has passed.

"As you are in official and amicable relations with the Prefect. I have the honour, to request that you will be so kind as to forward to him a copy of this despatch.

(Signed)   "CANDIANI"

In the course of the day the Japanese Consul replied courteously that he would have much pleasure in forwarding to the Prefect a copy of Count Candiani's letter. There was no means of finding out whether a copy was really sent to the Prefect or not, nor did the Prince stay to inquire. It will be observed that throughout the official correspondence, here as elsewhere, neither the Prince's name nor rank appears, a precaution obviously necessary, and one to which. M. de Luca had drawn my attention before leaving Shanghae.

During the last two days of our stay at Fusan communication with the shore was difficult, owing to a succession of northerly gales, so we were unable to test the readiness of the Corean inhabitants to break the heads of casual foreign visitors with stones. On this account, and as the limit of profitable correspondence with the officials had been reached, the Prince gave orders to weigh anchor on the afternoon of the 6th August, and sail along the eastern coast of Corea.

During our stay at Fusan I found the Coreans perfectly willing to converse with me in a friendly manner, and to give me the information I desired. Every man carries a roll of paper with him and a pen and ink, and is ready to converse when invited to do so. I do not give here the conversations I had with them, because those which I had subsequently in the north were much more interesting, and because at Fusan I only saw the Coreans under the artificial conditions of Japanese Settlement life.

We sailed from Fusan along the eastern coast of Cor~a as far as Yung Hing Bay. The physical configuration of the country in its g~neral outlines resembles Italy. It is traversed from north to, south by, an axial mnge of mountains which runs close to, and is parallel with, the east coast. The Corean rivers which flow into the Pacific are quite small, the main rivers rising to the west of the axial range and flo~in~ westward to the China Sea. The high east-coast line, which varies in height trom 4,000 to 6,000 feet, with peaks rising to 8,000 feet, is visible from a long distance at sea. On approaching the coast the country is seen to have a wild but attractive appearance. The mountains, which, with their outlying spurs, extend close to the shore, rise in tiers, range behind range, and are clothed from top to bottom in dense, impenetrable. jungle and forest. Some of the ranges are narsh and serrated; others, again, are more soft and rounded j but on all there is the same undergrowth of creepers, roses, dwarf oaks, and stunted conifers on the lower slopes, graduating into wild jungle and forest towards the summits. The narrow, deep Valleys are cultivated and thickly populated, but the mountains are given over to wild beasts. Tigers abound everywhere, and traps to catch them may be seen within a hundred yards of the sea. One is not surprised to learn that they are the plague of the country, for the jungle and forests which cover the hills make it a perfect home for them. Corea is a paradise for sportsmen, and I am sure that an energetic hunter of tigers would be welcomed everywhere as a public benefactor. In the Japanese port of Gensan, which we subsequently visited, tigers have even entered the Settlement at night; and excellent skins may be bought fora few dollars.

On the 8th August we anchored in the northern section of Yung Hing Bay, called by the Russians Port Lazareff. This is one of the points which the Russians are supposed to have designs upon, as a basis of operations against China. It is one of the finest harbours in the world, perfectly land-locked, with waters as unruffled as a lake, and with a practically infinite space of good holding-ground in from 8 to 9 fathoms of water. Though fringed with ice round the shores, the harbour is open in winter. We anchored some 5 miles from the northern end of the bay, at which end two rivers run into it. An extraordinary account of the larger of these, from French sources, is given in the "China Sea Directory," vol. iv, which, however true at the time of the survey, is quite incorrect now. The French Admiral who surveyed it says that he found 10 feet of water on the bar, that he sailed 5 miles up the channel through a smiling and cultivated plain, and that, so far as he could judge from the information he procured, and the configuration of the country, the river led to the capital, and was navigable a long distance. The trend of the mountain-ranges is at right angles to the apparent course of the stream, and to reach the capital the river would have to cross a series of high mountains, and to flow south, instead of north-west, as it does. Of this, however, when we first arrived we knew nothing, and when we came to an anchor we knew no more about the country, the officials, and the people than if we had come to the moon.

The shores of this bay are a series of lovely inlets and coves, with the forest and jungle-dad hills dropping, in a sheet of green, on the border of white sand which marks the sea-shore. Here and there were meadows and valleys covered with rice-fields and villages.

The district was a populous one, at least on the low lands. On whatever part of the shore we landed we were soon surrounded by crowds of inquisitive people. Our first duty was to disarm their suspicions of us by conversing with them, and inviting them to visit the ship. The medium of communication was

Chinese characters traced with the finger, or a piece of stick, on the sea-shore. I was surprised and delighted with a discovery which I made as soon as I landed. Every person in this part of Corea can write Chinese with the greatest facility. Peasants, fishermen, and boys, who are in China quite uneducated, could all write and read Chinese. All were most anxious to converse with us. The news of our invitations to visit the ship spread like wild-fire, and, on the day after our arrival, we were surrounded by Corean junks filled with eaget and excited visitors. Notes poured in upon us containing all sorts of requests, so the Prince directed the ship to be thrown open to all and sundry, and we were at once boarded by a swarm of Coreans, who invaded every corner of the ship. On shore men and boys would scuffle for the privilege of talking to me, and the questions put and answered were watched, read, and criticized with deep interest by a crowd of bystanders.

Next day we had many more visitors of a higher class, merchants and scholars from the neighbouring towns, and as soon as confidence was fairly established, I began, by request of the Prince, a series of formal interviews with them on board ship, with a view to getting some information regarding the Local Government.

I found it difficult to get them to talk about official matters, for various reasons. They were much more anxious to get than to give information, and often answered one question by asking another; and I believe they were really afraid to give information about their officials. I give at length here one conversation, to show the difficulty we experienced at first in finding out anything about the district we were in. It must be remembered, too, that these interviews were a great tax on my own patience; the Coreans crowded round me in a hot cabin; their odour and filth were alike unspeakably nasty; the most irrelevant questions were constantly asked me, and I had to submit to my hair and limbs being pulled and pinched to see if they were real. I eliminate from the conversation all misunderstandings, questions about particular characters, and most of the irrelevant qllestions, such as "Why do you throwaway glass bottles?" &c.

Spence. How far is it to the city of Yung Hing?-Corean. Several hundred li (really about fifty).

 S. Are there any officials there? -C. Yes.

 S. What are their names? -C. How should I know? I live here.

 S. In what jurisdiction is this place? -C. In that of the Prefect of Yung

Hing.

S. Are there any smaller officials under him? -C. Yes, everywhere.

S. Who are the nearest of these? -C. I find it hard to remember.

S. If the people hereabout make disturbances, to whom would they be responsible?-

C. We never make disturbances.

S. If you made disturbances-? -C. (interrupting). A complaint would be first made to the district officer, and he would report. it to the Prefect.

S. What is the name of the district officer here? -C. They are changed every

month. I don't know.

S. We went to send a letter about a shipwreck (details given) to the Prefect; can we do so? -C. This is a matter for the Quelpart officials to deal with.

S. Oh, no. We want it to go to the capital through the Prefect here. -C. Well, do as you like.

S. Do you know anybody who would take our letter; we would pay him well? -C. When foreign ships come here, it is the duty of the district officers to report to the Prefect, and then the Prefect sends mim to make inquiries. His men will be here ina few days. I must be going. (Exit)

S. (To another) What is the name of this place? -C. The West Lake of Yung Hing.

S. Are there any officials about here? -C. No.

S. How far is it to Yung Hing? -C. 120 Ii.

S. Li Chi-ch~ng is the Prefect, is he not? -C. Yes.

S. How long will it take to send a letter to him? -C. Three or four days.

S. Shall we send our letter through the district officers, or by a messenger? C. There are no district officers, and you will never be able to get a messenger.

S. We will pay one well. -C. It is perfectly impossible for any sum.

And so forth.

We found the Coreans ready enough to talk about everything except their Government, and they were all unwilling either to take a letter or hire a messenger to go to Yung Hing. Two or three days were spent in fruitless attempts to hire or bribe a man to take a letter to the Prefect, and in making excursions about the shores of the harbour, where we were always well received by the people. We devoted one whole day to the exploration of the embouchure of the river, in the steam-launch and the ship's boats. We found, however, that there were only 3 feet of water on the bar, and, as Corean junks were grounded quite close to us, it is evident we had not lost our way nor mistaken the channel. It was high water, too, and we had full advantage of such small tide (2 feet) as there is. There was a small town on the alluvial delta formed by the river, called the Yung Hing Saltpits, where the sole industry was salt-making; and though we were unarmed we passed through considerable crowds of Coreans without the slightest molestation. At one time the Prince and I were on the top of a small hill with quite 200 Coreans round us, but we were treated with great courtesy by all, only we had to put up with a somewhat distressing curiosity to examine us. In all my conversations with the Coreans during our excursions and walks, the Prince took the liveliest interest, and he invariably over-rated what appeared to him to be my great talent in being able to communicate with the natives by signs traced on the hand or on the sand. Talking to them was to myself very pleasurable, because every person, young and old, could read, and in addressing one I addressed often a hundred. Their intelligence and intense eagerness to talk with me' were everywhere remarkable.

Hempen clothes are universally worn by the labouring classes, and the thread is spun much finer than would be possible with European hemp. I tried to get some specimens of the fibre, but I was unsuccessful. It must be the same, I think, as the "China flax" which grows in the neighbourhood of Newchwang, and, as the importation of that fibre into England has long been desired by our flax-spinners, and is only restricted on account of its high price, attention will probably be drawn to the Corean hemp whenever the country is opened. Unfortunately I did not know the specific Chinese name for the flax of Chihli and Shing King. The better classes wear white cotton clothes, and many of them boast of an overall made of foreign cotton cloth, the gloss and finish of which they much admire. For that they prefer a heavy "honest" cloth, such as American sheeting. Of silk culture there was none in the country which we saw. They spin, however, the cocoons of the wild *ailanthus*, and I procured hanks of their silk (which to my inexperienced eye seemed closely to resemble Shantung silk) and several sheets of eggs, for Count Candiani, who is much interested in sericulture. Of ornamental art work, such as porcelain, bronze, &c., they have none. We saw some worthless pearls, and some silver work for feminine trappings and official insignia. The ceramic art is quite rudimentary, and they attach an excessive value to the commonest Japanese ware.

The meagre information I have given here is hardly noteworthy on its intrinsic merits, but it affords indisputable evidence of the peaceful and satisfactory relations we had established with the people.

The first person who volunteered to help us to communicate with the authorities was a literary man from the capital. I had begun to despair of inducing anybody to convey a letter to the Corean officials, when, one morning, the following note was handed on board:—"My name is An Keui-shun; I come from the capital; I am a poor man, and I should like to see your ship. Please let me come on board." We welcomed him on board, and I had the following conversation with him: —

Spence. How far is it from here to the capital? -Corean. 50 li by water to Gensan then 550 li overland.

S. Are you a merchant? -C. I am 44 years old, an unsuccessful scholar at the examinations, and of a poor family. I want to go home, but I have no money. Where do you come from?

S. We are from Italy in the great West.-C. Have you the doctrines of the sacred Confucius there?

S. We have our own sacred man, Jesus. He is the foundation of truth in our country. We have come here to thank the Corean Government for (details as usual). Do you think we should send our letter to the Yung Hing Prefect or send it direct to Seoul? -C. Send it to the Prefect. He will send it on to his superiors.

S. Unfortunately, we can't find anybody to take our letter. -C. Yesterday the people of this place reported your arrival to the Prefect.

S. We are uncertain whether he will send anyone to see us. -C. They will probably be here in a few days.

S. We cannot wait so long. Can't you think of any plan by which we could send our letter; we will recompense you handsomely? -C. Give your letter to some of the people of this locality.

S. It is not very far; there is no necessity to employ people because they belong to this locality. -C. Nobody can go without money.

S. If anybody will go, we will give them as much as they want. If you yourself will take it, we will assist" you to get home. -C. Ask some of the local people outside.

S. If you take it to the capital for us, we will assist you with money. -C. If

I took your letter to the capital, the king would cut off my head. Send it to the Prefect of Yung Hing, and there will be no trouble.

S. Can you find a man for us to take it? -C. I will bring one to-day or to-morrow. I have a friend outside who would like to come on board the ship to have a look at it. (Friend introduced) Give your letter to this mall, he will take it.

S. Our letter is not yet ready. Bring your friend to-morrow morning to get it. -C. Certainly.

S. Don't forget. -C. We shall be here to-morrow morning. How could a scholar from the capital speak treacherous words?

He departed with a dollar, as earnest of what was to follow; but he did not appear next morning. He came on the evening of the third day, but by that time we had seen the Prefect ourselves, and had no use for him. I am inclined to think he was a spy.

The same afternoon an official junk came alongside, and the following note was handed on board:-

"In obedience to the commands of the local officials to inspect your vessel, we have come to have a look at her. May we come on board?"

We requested the four principal men to come on board, and of these the two highest in rank to come into the ,Prince's cabin. They told us that they had been sent by the Prefect of YUng Hing; that one was a military officer, the other a clerk of police. We informed them of the object of the visit of the "Vettor Pisani" to Corea, and, upon hearing it, they begged us not to be in a hurry, as the Prefect himself would come to visit the ship in a few days. They could assign no probable date to his visit, however, and the Prince attached but little importance to their statement. They also said that if we wished to send any letter, they would be happy to convey it to the Prefect; and 'they promised faithfully to return next day to fetch it.

They did return next day, and as I had not finished the translation of it in Chinese, I requested them to wait until it was ready. When it was sealed they took the letter, looked at it rather suspiciously, and asked for the steam-launch to tow them to the shore. This they could not have, as steam was not up; and then, without a word of excuse, they laid it down, and said they could not take it.

Candiani. The steam-launch is not ready, and you cannot have her. -Officials. Then there is no help for it. When are you going away?

C. To-morrow. to Gensan. In two months we shall return here for the answer to our letter from your Government. (This discomposed them, and they handed back the letter.) - O. We are forbidden by our Government to receive letters from foreign countries. There is no help for it.

C. This is a simple letter of thanks, and has no other object whatever. Please receive it, and to-morrow we shall go away. Why did you promise to take it yesterday? - O. Yesterday we were in a great hurry, and although we promised as we were leaving the ship, we found the law to be such as we have said when we got home.

C. You told us distinctly you would take it, and when you came on board to-day you asked for it. Why have you just now changed your minds? - O. If we take your letter we shall be breaking our laws. We really cannot.

C. Why did you not say so yesterday? Do you refuse now because the launch is not ready? We will get up steam at once. - O. The Prefect will be here himself to-morrow. You can give it to him then.

C. What did you come back to the ship for, if it was not to fetch our letter? - O. It was to have a better look at the ship. We did not return to fetch your letter. The Prefect will be here himself to-morrow; why, therefore, do you want to compel us to break the laws?

C. When you came on board you asked if the letter was ready. Why do you thus recklessly eat your words? - O. The fact is that a small boat has followed us from the Prefect's, and we have just heard by it that he is coming to-morrow.

C. Well, if you do not take our letter, we will take it ,ourselves, with soldiers. - O. You say you are going to send soldiers. IS it to take your letter, or on account of your wrath at what we have said?

C. We are not angry; we only want to send the letter. - O. We made a report to the Prefect of what you told us yesterday, and he has instructed us in reply to, say that he will come to your ship to-day or to-morrow. Why do you want to give us your letter and bring us into mischief?

C. You appear determined not to take it. If, to-morrow, the Prefect does not come, I will certainly send soldiers to Yung Hing. - O. You don't believe us when we tell you that the Prefect is coming. There is no doubt about it. He is certain to come.

C. In a word, what I have to say is this: if he does not come to-morrow, or send somebody, we will send our letter to him by the hands of our sailors. - O.

Very good.

C. We came here with the best intentions ... If anything happens, the responsibility is yours. - O. How can anything happen? If it did, why should we shirk the responsibility of it?

With this these untruthful officials departed with the usual presents of empty bottles. The threat of sending soldiers was, of course, an idle one, as no one even dreamt of carrying it out. However, in the evening I told the people on shore to keep in their houses, as our soldiers were probably going to Yung Hing to-morrow, and I have little doubt that this was reported at once to the Prefect.

Next morning dawned, and no Prefect was visible. As the day wore on the Prince and Count Candiani began to fear that they would have to leave the Corea without having an interview with a Corean official. However, in the afternoon two large junks appeared with the Prefect, the whole of his staff and retinue. He was an old and feeble-looking man, and he came seated in his sedan-chair, which had been lowered into the hold of the junk. He was carried up the gangway by two youths, who held him as he walked along the deck, one under each arm. This gave him the appearance of being dragged, but whether this was a mere affectation of weakness suggested by his ideas of diplomacy, or the actual feebleness of age, I could not say. His staff consisted of three secretaries; a number of confidential advisers, who hedged him round in the cabin to prevent him replying to any question by his own unaided intelligence; one military officer, with half-a-dozen soldiers armed with rusty swords; with a miscellaneous crowd of musicians and hangerson, similar to the tag-rag retinue of Chinese Mandarins.

The staff poured into the Prince's quarters; some sat on the floor, others stood on the chairs, and all gathered round the officials at the table. The Prince himself was present, speaking in the person of Count Candiani; the Prefect sat opposite, with his advisers behind him, and his secretaries at his feet; and I myself sat next him, with my teacher as scribe. The Coreans were regaled with wines of all kinds, fruits, &c., and, as all Coreans do, they ate and drank everything that was offered to them, and as much more as they could steal.

The Prefect was a courteous and amiable old gentleman. He did his best to keep his staff from begging and pilfering, but it was quite impossible to stop them. The Corean officials and men of the better class are not nearly so well bred as either the Japanese or Chinese. When they deigl! to salute at all they do it in a clumsy manner. They cultivate a grave and staid manner, and seem rather ashamed of any other graces than those comprised in a stolid and apathetic demeanour.

The scene in the Prince's room, when the interview was going on, was a singular one. A silent conversation, conducted in pen and ink; the silence only broken by the whispered mutterings of the advisers and secretaries as they objected to this, or suggested that; a hot cabin crowded with high-flavoured Coreans intent on eating and drinking; the secretaries in a little ring on the floor preparing questions and answers, or making copies of those already put-all these were elements in a very striking picture. After a number of unimportant and desultory questions, the following conversation took place:-

Candiani. We are going to fire a salute of three guns in your honour; please tell your people not to be afraid. - *Prefect*. Do not take the trouble to do that.

C. It is a customary ceremony on board our ship. - P. I was not aware of it.

C. May I ask your name, and what office you hold in your country? - P. My name is Li Chi-cheng. I am an official of the Board of Transmission, and Prefect of Yung Hing-foo.

C. This ship is from Italy, in Europe. Some two years ago an Italian merchantvessel was wrecked on the coast of the Island of Quelpart; the whole of her crew were drowned with the exception of one man, whose life was saved, and who was assisted by the people and officials of Quelpart. They gave him clothes to wear and food to eat, so that he was enabled to get back to Italy. For this our Government is deeply grateful, and has therefore commissioned my vessel to come here to thank the Corean officials and people for their kindness. - P. Whenever foreigners are thrown upon our shores by the waves, or are drowned on our coasts, to succour and pity them is a duty prescribed by Corean law. Why is there any special necessity for thanks in this case? Besides, I am not the local authority of Quelpart. Why must you needs come to this place?

C. This ship is a very large one, and there is no safe anchorage for her on the coast of Quelpart; we have on this account come here. - P. In what year and month did you leave Italy, and what countries did you pass on your way here?

C. We left in May last year. We went to Japan, and while we were anchored there we received instructions from our Government to come to Corea on this mission of thanks. - P. May I ask your name, and your rank in the service of your country?

C. Candiani, Capitaine de Fregate. - P. I should like to know the names and rank of the officers under you.

C. There are twelve altogether: Millelire, Lamberti, Bianco, and Acton, Lieutenants, and eight others of lower rank. Having been entrusted with this mission by our Government, I have prepared a despatch conveying the thanks of our country, which I now beg you to receive, to read, and to send on to the Government at Seoul. - P. It is a law of Corea that no local official can address the Court directly, no matter how important the matter may be. The local officials have first to address the Ying Men (Governor of the province) for such decision as he may think fit to come to.

C. Then I beg you to send on this despatch to the Governor, so that it may go up to the capital by the regular official channel. -Po In all matters of importance it is my duty to make a Report to the Governor, and, on this account, Ican take no step of my own responsibility. Whenever foreign ships come here I have to make inquiries, and having ascertained the purportof their visit, I am compelled by law to report to the Governor. Our present conversation I shall have to send On to him.

At this juncture one of the Prefect's three secretaries seized the sheets of conversation which were already filled up, but Captain Candiani would not allow him to take them. He informed them that they were at liberty to make copies, which they at once proceeded to do, and my Chinese boy was told off to watch them that they did not alter any of the characters.

Candiani. - This is a most excellent law, and my intention in writing you this despatch is that you may thoroughly understand what we have come for. I hope you will peruse it, and send it on. - Prefect. It is a law of our country that its high officials are forbidden to receive any communications from foreign countries unless they have received permission from the King to do so; and as regards the local officials, like myself, *á: fortiori* we dare not act unauthorizedly.

C. We have come here because we have been ordered to do so. If you do not receive this despatch, I see no way of accomplishing my mission. It is a despatch addressed by me to yourself, and to no other official. -'-Po But why should you particularly address me in such a matter? That I cannot understand.

C. Because you are the Corean official ,nearest the coast. We are anxious that the Governor should, through you, become aware of the good intention of our visit. - P. Well, all I have to say is this: action can only be taken in a matter of this kind with the consent of the Royal Government. There is no Corean law which authorizes me to receive your despatch. I must wait for instructions from the Governor; no other course is open to me.

C. Well you are at liberty to receive or to decline my despatch at your pleasure. Still I must ask you to read it once, so that you may know exactly, and be enabled to report to the Governor, the purport of my visit. I shall then have acquitted myself of the responsibility of my mission.

The following despatch was then handed to the Prefect:-

"To the Prefect of Yung Hing.
"'Vettor Pisani,' Yung Hing Bay, Corea, August 14, 1880.

"Sir.

"Two years ago the Italian merchant-ship' Bianca Portica' was wrecked on the coast of the Island of Quelpart, and the whole of her crew were lost with the exception of one sailor, F. Santoro. This sailor met with every attention at the hands of the inhabitants, and subsequently the Corean officials gave him clothes and food, and made arrangements for his being sent home to Italy. These facts having come to the knowledge of the Italian Government, they ordered the 'Vettor Pisani' to come here. I am very happy that it is now in my power to convey the thanks due to the Corean officials and Government for their conduct in the unfortunate accident I have alluded to. In fulfilling' this agreeable duty I beg, at the same time, to reimburse all the expenses which may have been incurred in saving the life of the said sailor. In such a matter I am aware that it would be a more direct course to address the officials of Quelpart~ but as there is no good anchorage in that island for a large ship such as this, we have been obliged to come here. I hope, then, that you will have the kindness to convey to the Government of Seoul the thanks which they deserve. I am also well aware that, up to the present time, the Government of Corea have shown a desire to have no relations with foreign countries, and for that reason I cannot address them directly, so I address them through you.

'We have been here several days, and, in consequence of these Corean laws which interdict all communication with foreigners, we have found it impossible to lay in the provisions which the ship is in need of. The country people who dwell along the shore of our anchorage have told us that by the laws of Corea, we were prohibited from going ashore to procure either fresh water or the shell-fish, which, in every part of the world, are recognized as belonging to the ocean. As we have come here on a mission of thanks, we are desirous to observe your laws strictly; but, at the same time, we feel compelled to make some observations regarding these prohibitions which we beg you to transmit to your superior officers.

"Every person who travels by sea is liable to shipwreck, or is often obliged, by the force of circumstances, to seek shelter in the port most convenient to repair the ship, or to lay in provisions for her crew. This is a fact recognized by every nation of the world, and the right to relief which ships and sailors have is considered to be theirs by the laws of humanity,

"It would be a most vexatious thing if an Italian ship were to put in here in distress in order to repair, or to buy provisions, and found that she could obtain nothing. It is probable that in such a case the crew, constrained by necessity, would employ force to procure the things they were in want of, and would pay no attention to your Corean laws; for,so long as no relations exist between Corea and Italy, so long will it be exceedingly difficult for the Corean authorities to obtain justice in cases where Italian subjects may have broken Corean laws; and, indeed, it is possible they might go unpunished, because they can easily leave your coasts in their ships.

"It would be much more convenient, then, if a Convention dealing with this matter were at once established between Representatives of your country and mine, for it is impossible that the existing state of things can long continue.

"Italy has the strongest desire to be always on good terms with Corea, and a Treaty between the two countries could not be but of the greatest use to you, for your prolonged isolation has had the effect of placing you at this moment in a position I of great inferiority in material resources as compared with other nations. At this moment the two great nations whose territories are contiguous to yours are on the point of going to war, and it will be difficult for Corea to escape the consequences which, sooner or later, such a struggle must entail upon her. Such would not be the case if Corea were a Power recognized by the leading nations of Europe, for they would in that case be interested in the protection of the independence of your country.

"I hope, then that you will bring these consideration to the notice of your Government. In less than two months, in all probability, we shall return here, or proceed to Fusan, in order to know what the intentions of your Government are, so that I may inform the Italian Government to enable them to come to some decision in the matter.

I have, &c.
(Signed)   "CANDIANI"

This despatch was read most carefully by the Prefect, and, subsequently, by many of his staff. Some of these, indeed, had spent the time of the interview in reading it surreptitiously. I took good care that they found no difficulty in obtaining stolen peeps at it whilst it was lying on the table. The conversation was then resumed.

Candiani. This despatch is rather a long one; if you would like a copy of it I shall be happy to furnish you with one. What do you say?

The Prefect nodded assent, and the despatch was handed to the three secretaries to be copied.

Prefect. When do you intend to leave the port?

C. Whenever this mission of ours is accomplished we shall leave Corea. If you want a copy of our despatch your people i need not take the trouble to copy it. I will remove the seal from the original, and you can take that.

I had purposely placed the ship's seal on an outside slip of paper, which I now detached with some show of reverence and burnt. Count Candiani then. handed the despatch to the Prefect, which he received most courteously.

C. I beg that you will report the purport of our mission to the Governor of the

province. We will come back in two months to ascertain what his views are. - P. How many men have you under you in this ship?

C. Over 250. You see that our intention in coming here is a good one. China and Russia seem to be. about to go to war, and, if they do, such a war may do great damage to Corea. Corea's abstention from all intercourse with foreign nations is a danger to her. ~P. What do you mean by danger?

C. The Russian seaports are closed with ice during the winter, and it is possible that the exigencies of war may compel Russia to occupy one of your seaports in order to garrison troops, to accumulate provisions, and to be a convenient basis for warlike operations against China. This is the danger I speak of. - P. I will report your despatch and the whole of this conversation to the Governor.

C. Very good. Tell him that Italy has long desired to be at peace with all the world, and she is especially anxious to be the friend of Corea. Call his attention to the portion of my despatch referring to the difficulties existing between your neighbours, which is the most important part of it, and tell him that if Corea would only make a Treaty with Italy, it would be of the greatest advantage to her. - P. I will. The day is getting late, and I must be going.

C. I am exceedingly, obliged to you for having taken the trouble to come so far, with your honourable years too, to visit our ship. - P. I came here to ascertain the purport of your visit. I was compelled to do so by our laws. Why do you thank me?

C. We have packed up a few cakes and some bottles of wine, our Italian wine, for you, as a slight mark of our appreciation of your visit. - P. Although you honour me with this mark of your kindness, I must tell you that I cannot take them, for I am forbidden by Corean laws to take any gifts without permission.

C. Wine and cakes are of no value. There will be no harm in accepting them from us. You can give them away to your people. - P. For my reception on board I am exceedingly obliged. I am now going. You are too good, really.

The Prefect and his advisers were men of considerable intelligence, as the foregoing conversation will show. In answering or asking the more important questions he invariably consulted his advisers, who closely encircled him throughout the interview. Count Candiani had the same advantage in that he could similarly consult the Prince before requesting me to translate anything. This of course made the interview a lengthy one. As against that a conversation so conducted, and by such a medium, has more permanent interest than one merely viva voce, for, as each party carries away copies of it, it at once becomes a written record, with all the importance attaching to it as such. The copies of the conversation which were made by the secretaries sitting on the floor, sheet by sheet, were compared by myself with the original before the Prefect departed. The original sheets I retained for the Prince.

During the interview, and at its close, the numerous staff which crowded the room regaled themselves with wines, sweetmeats, and cigars. Not one of them showed the respect for Corean laws that was professed by the Prefect, or the same reluctance to take a souvenir of the visit in the shape of an empty bottle or a biscuittin. They wrangled for the possession of the most worthless articles, and many of them slipped up their sleeves the tumblers and glasses they had been drinking out of.

The Prefect and his staff at last left the ship. As before, he was dragged along the deck by his two youths, and literally bundled down the gangway into his sedanchair in the junk. The noisy and hilarious staff poured after him, laden with the trumpery trophies of their visit, with which they had been presented or which they had stolen, all in the highest good spirits. Then came the soldiers and attendants, who had spent the time in wandering about the ship. They were similarly laden with gifts of biscuit, &c., by the sailors, who were much amused at their praiseworthy attempts to devour everything given them, even soap. The Prince gave orders for the steam-launch to tow the Prefect's two junks to the point where he wished to land. They departed in the midst of much din, for amongst the tatterdemalion followers was a numerous and noisy band of music, which blew and banged in the lustiest and most imposing manner. The spectacle of the two junks, crowded with picturesque retainers, as they were towed away in a chorus of shouting, laughter, Corean drums and trumpets, and, finally, the booming of our big guns, was one of the most diverting and impressive I have ever seen.

The interview lasted nearly four hours, and was, in some respects, an unpleasant and trying ordeal. The filth of even the official class is extreme, and, as an example of what is almost too disgusting to write about, I saw one of the secretaries performing, for the hair of his colleague, the same good offices that one monkey may be observed doing for another in the Zoological Gardens. I had to answer also side questions, which were stuffed into my pockets and hands, whilst the interview was going on, by the Prefect's too curious followers. However, for such slight trouble and responsibility as the interview entailed on Count Candiani and myself, we were amply rewarded when the Prince kindly told us, after reading the translations I made of the conversation, that one of his main objects in visiting Corea had been most satisfactorily attained.

The Prince had all along taken great pleasure in our intercourse with the Coreans, and watched, with keen interest, every attempt made by myself to communicate with them. The whole of the formal conversations (i.e., in pen and ink) I had with them I translated for his information. To the hundreds of Coreans, rich and poor, who flocked from all parts of the Prefecture to see the foreign ship, he extended a cordial welcome and a generous hospitality, and I have little doubt that the visit of the "Vettor Pisani" to this part of Corea will be pleasantly remembered for many a day by the inhabitants with whom we came in contact.

We paid a final visit to the villages along the shore on the evening of the 15th August, and found that they were well aware of the visit of the Prefect. I was more than ever embarrassed with the number of people who wished to talk with me, and if I stopped anywhere for a minute, the sand all round me was at once covered with characters. We took a cordial farewell of those with whom we had been most intimate.

From first to last we had been on excellent terms with the villagers. They did not sell us any supplies, partly because they had little or nothing to sell, and partly because we had no Corean cash. They said that if they were found by the authorities with a foreign coin in their possession they would be heavily punished, and run some risk of losing their heads. Even Chinese sycee is of little use; it can be easily distinguished from Corean, and the possession of it may entail the most unpleasant consequences.

We had only one unpleasantness with the people. As the incident shows graphically two important traits in the national character, I make no excuse for referring to it. The shores of Yung Hing Bay have many large oyster-beds, and soon after our arrival one or two boats' crews were sent to gather a supply for the ship's use. The sailors took the readiest method of gathering these oysters; they took off their clothes, and enjoyed the luxury of a bathe at the same time as they gathered shell-fish. In the course of our evening walk, we were told by the Headmen of the villages that the capture of oysters was forbidden by the Government, and, on inquiry, I could get no reasonable explanation of this mystery. We sent for more oysters next day, which were procured by our sailors in the same manner, and several Coreans entreated them to desist, but they paid no attention. A posse of men came from some of the neighbouring villages, and beat the Coreans who had failed to make our men desist, and, naturally enough, the people who were beaten felt sore about our conduct. The following note from one of them was sent to me:-

"Your intercourse with us during the past few days has shown us that you know what decency is. How comes it that to-day you have forgotten the rules of propriety? Your sailors have taken off all their clothes, both from the upper. and lower parts of their bodies, and gone into the sea. stark naked to get oysters. Why are you so indecent? The capture of shell-fish on the beach is prohibited by our country's laws. I told your people'this, but they would not hear me; and because they would not hear my people have been. beaten. If your sailors are coming for oysters again, please come and arrange matters."

The letter was anonymous; but to prevent any danger of disturbance I went on shore to try and elucidate the mystery. I was at a loss to understand why the Government had interdicted oyster-fishing, for the shores were strewn with empty shells. On shore I saw no one, so I wrote the character "clam" on the beach in monster strokes, and in ten minutes fifty people were looking at it. Finally, the writer of the oyster-letter appeared.

Spence. Did you write that letter to me? - *Corean*. Yes.

S. What do you mean by saying that the Government does not allow the capture of oysters? - C. (after a long pause). Because it is against the law.

S. But what is the reason for the law? - C. (Another pause) Men and women were made to live together in harmony. Harmony cannot exist without courtesy; and courtesy is impossible if men go about without any clothes on. It is a bad custom.

S. What harm is there? - C. If your men go about naked it is impossible for our women to leave the house, and for the past,two days they have had to keep in doors.

S. Then, if I tell our sailors to keep their trousers on, may they take oysters? - C. Certainly; and you will find the best ones by that fir-tree clump, half-a-mile to the west. So the matter was arranged. The incident shows how ready the Coreans are to use the stereotyped phrases "Forbidden by the King," "Against the law," &c., to answer inconvenient questions. This , indeed, may be seen in all the conversations I have given already. It also shows what a modest people they are. It was hateful to them to see naked men, and distasteful to write about such a thing even. The poorest classes at work in the fields are always decently clad, and the women never show even their faces to strangers. I must Qnce more refer to the extraordinary familiarity of all classes, the poorest, and the youngest of the poor, with the Chinese written characters. Misunderstandings wer,e, of course, not infrequent, but one character was quickly substituted for another, until the sentence became intelligible. Any person of modest attainments in Chinese, who has a facility in reproducing on the shoJCtest notice the characters he knows, can communicate with any Corean pleasantly and intelligently.

We left our anchorage on the 15th August, and steamed to the southern end of the bay, where, about 12 miles distant from our late position, is situated the lately-opened port of Gensan, the second of the three ports open to the

Japanese by Treaty. The third port has not yet been agreed to, as the Japanese wish it to be on the west coast, and in proximity to Seoul. To this the Coreans object. Gensan has only been open four months, and, as yet, there is no trade. The only communication with Japan is one steamer every two months. There are at present 300 settlers, but of these nearly one-third are soldiers or policemen. The houses in the Settlement are being built in the Japanese adaptation of European style which is common in the modern parts of Tokio. The bay ,at this part, is so exposed that the harbour is virtually an open roadstead, and the site of the Settlement does not appear to me to have been wisely selected, either for an anchorage, or as possessed of the best communications with the interior. I understand, however, that the Coreans would not consent to give a site at the Yung Hing end of the bay. A Consul-General is stationed at Gensan, and he is in official correspondence with the Prefect of Te YUan. He has a large staff of student interpreters, who are studying the Corean language. Communication between the new port and the capital is bad: a mere foot-path over high ranges of hills.

At this port, again, I regret to say I have to bear witness to the brutal manner in which the Japanese settlers treat the Coreans. I do not think that the worst class of European rowdies would ever behave so badly to harmless and inoffensive Asiatics as one finds the Japanese in Corea behaving to the Coreans. For example, I saw one Japanese take a pailful of dirty water and throw it into the face of a grave, dignified, and well-dressed Corean, for no other reason than that he was gazing with some interest at the new houses, and probably to make the bystanding Japanese laugh, which they did, heartily. I have little doubt that in a year or two it will be as difficult for foreigners to land in the neighbourhood of Gensan as it is reported to be now in the vicinity of Fusan. I told the Consul-General what I thought of the conduct of his nationals, but he seemed to" think that all Coreans were bad, and that a promiscuous kick could not fail to fall upon a Corean who richly deserved it. He gave the Prince the usual caution about the danger of walking outside the Settlement limits, unless for a short distance with an escort. The Prince himself had some experience of Coreans by this time, and had no fear of the unpleasant consequences of country walks. Accompanied by his Aides-de-camp and myself, he spent three days very pleasantly, shooting, fishing, and roaming about the hills and coasts near Gensan. We were molested by nobody. The demeanour of the inhabitants was the same here as we had found it elsewhere. Fine men physically, much finer than the Chinese or Japanese, they have an upright, bold manner, and the timidity they exhibit at strange sights and sounds is the timidity of ignorance, not of a craven spirit. For the rest, they are exceedingly inquisitive, and filthy in their persons.

We left Corea on the 19th August, and I quitted the "Vettor Pisani" at Tsuruga Bay on the 22nd. I had been twenty-six days on board, and they were days of unvarying kindness from the Prince, his immediate staff, the officers, and everybody on board. It would not be fitting, in an official paper, to repeat even a tithe of the pleasant things that were said to me in grateful recognition of my services before leaving. The Prince, however, told me that he had attained both the ends which he proposed to himself in visiting Corea; and he was good enough to appreciate, in a far too flattering measure, the little I had been able to do for him, by insisting that it was to myself alone that the success and the pleasure of his expedition was due.

The Prince was anxious that I should see something of Japan before returning to China, but as I had heard by telegraph, with extreme pleasure, of my appointment to Chefoo, I took a hurried leave of His Royal Highness, and crossed over to Kobé in fourteen hours, to catch the steamer for Shanghae. I returned on the 1st September.

I attach to this Report a map of Corea, showing the Prince's route, and copies, in Chinese, of the despatches and conversations I have referred to.

         (Signed) WM. DONALD SPENCE;

Shanghae, September 9, 1880.

J.G. Kennedy (1881. 3. 24) ➡ G.L.G. Granville (1881. 5. 9)

러시아 함대의 원산항 점령 가능성 보고

No. 41

   Mr. Kennedy to Earl Granville*—*(Received May 9)*

(No. 30 Confidential)

Yedo, March 24, 1881

My Lord,

  I HAVE the honour to report that the Russian fleet of about seventeen ships of war of all descriptions, which during the past winter months has been dispersed in the three Treaty ports of Yokohama, Kobe, and Nagasaki, has now been summoned by Admiral Lessoksky, the Commander-in-chief, to assemble at Nagasaki.

  Admiral Lessoksky, as your Lordship is aware, had the misfortune on the day before his arrival at Nagasaki from Vladivostok to break his leg during a storm at sea, and consequently has been unable to leave Nagasaki since his arrival in Japan.

  The desire to confer with the commanding officers and to inspect the vessels composing his fleet would sufficiently explain the orders of Admiral Lessoksky for a general rendezvous at Nagasaki; especially at this season when the break up of the ice will enable the ships to revisit the Russian ports on the North Pacific.

  The public press, however, both foreign and native, concur in attributing to Admiral Lessoksky the intention of developing Russian designs in the East by making a descent on the coasts of Corea with the object of annexing Port Lazareff and the intermediate country to the Russian possessions.

  This view is shared by my French and Belgian Colleagues, who have both assured me as a personal conviction that Russia intends to occupy Port Lazareff before the withdrawal from these seas of their existing powerful fleet.

  On the other hand, the Russian Chargé d'Affaires at Peking has, I hear,

---

*[원주] copies sent to Sir T. Wade and Admiralty, May 23.

distinctly informed the French Minister in China that Russia has no designs on Corea, and M. de Struve, the Russian Minister in this country, has given me assurances in the same sense.

In allusion to the above subject, M. de Struve told me that, should such a design still exist, he certainly had no knowledge of it; that in the event of war with China an occupation of Port Lazareff might have been possible and even necessary, but that, as peace seemed now assured, such necessity no longer existed.

I informed M. de Struve that I fully concurred in his view, and further stated to his Excellency that If Russia would open Corea to general commerce all nations would benefit thereby, but that if Russia should forcibly annex to her own territory any part of Corea, such a proceeding would be considered by all Powers as unjustifiable, and such conduct would set a bad example, which might be followed by others.

I do not know what value can be attached to the assurances of the Russian Representatives at Peking and Tokio, but I venture to suggest that the only person fully acquainted with possible Russian designs would be Admiral Lessoksky.

Many persons assert that the present moment is most favourable for Russian designs upon Corea, owing to the presence in these waters of an unusually large Russian fleet, and to the almost total absence of ships of war of other nations; but, on the other hand, it appears hardly possible that Russia, having just concluded a Treaty with China, should perpetrate an act of virtual hostility against that Power.

The Government of Japan, although in a perpetual state of alarm as to Russian designs, do not appear to apprehend any immediate action of Russia against Corea.

On the whole, it would appear that any immediate action by Russia on the Pacific is improbable.

The more likely course would seem to be that the greater part of the fleet should be ordered to the Mediterranean, and a smaller portion to Vladivostock for the summer months.   But I presume that this, as well as other questions of Russian policy, may be affected by the recent untimely death of the Emperor of Russia.

I have, &e.

(Signed)   J.G. KENNEDY

J.G. Kenndy (1881. 6. 8) ➜ G.L.G. Granville (1881. 8. 2)

조사시찰단(朝士視察團) 일본 파견 및 何如璋 문서 보고

Mr. Kennedy to Earl Granville.—(Received August 2)

(No. 61 Very confidential)

Yedo. June 8, 1881

My Lord,

    WITH reference to my despatches marked Very Confidential, No. 179 of the 21st December, and No. 131 of the 27th July last, upon the subject of Corea, I have the honour to inclose copy of a Memorandum prepared by Mr. Satow, giving the latest account of the state of parties in Corea, together with a copy in translation from the Chinese by Mr. Satow of a document addressed to the late Corean Envoy to Japan by the Secretary of the Chinese Legation in Tokio.

    The letter or private Memorandum of the Chinese Secretary, of which the authenticity is undoubted, develops the policy which the writer considers to be most advantageous for adoption by Corea in order to secure her national existence against the aggressive designs commonly attributed to Russia. It counsels Corea to draw closer the existing ties which unite her to China and Japan, and to enter into Treaties of amity with Europe and America. By this means, it is suggested, she would enter the comity of nations, and become entitled to invoke the protection of international law in the case of any attempt upon her independence. The United States are extolled as being especially disposed to treat Asiatic nations in a spirit of fairness, and Corea is advised, by concluding a favourable Treaty with America in the first place, to guard against having to make excessive concessions to England, France, and Germany. The various objections which a Corean statesman might make to the course proposed are combatted in turn with considerable ingenuity.

    I may observe that the tone of the Memorandum throughout indicates that the writer considers Corea to be practically an independent State in her external relations as well as regards her internal affairs, and the tie which binds her to China to be merely one of respect and gratitude for favours received in past times.

The secret Agent of the King alluded to in Mr. Satow's annexed Memorandum is the same of whose proceedings I reported to your Lordship in my two above mentioned despatches. On his return to Seoul, this Agent was appointed adviser to the newly-constituted Department of Foreign Affairs, and exercised much influence over the King. His sudden elevation, however, excited the jealousy of the reactionary party, by whom his life was threatened during a recent agitation, now reported to have subsided. He is now in concealment, awaiting the triumph of liberal ideas, which, so far as an opinion can be formed, will not long be delayed.

The arrival in Japan of the Corean Mission, alluded to in the concluding paragraph of Mr. Satow's Memorandum, confirms the reports already received of the recent growth in that country of an inclination to make acquaintance with the arts and sciences of Europe. Although not ostensibly possessing any public character, there is every reason to suppose that this Mission now in Tokio, consisting of eleven principal officers, representing both the Conservative and Liberal parties, and a following of fifty minor functionaries and servants, is provided with secret credentials from the Government of Corea, which might be produced if necessary.

The members of the Mission, since their arrival about a fortnight ago in Tokio, have been chiefly occupied in visiting the various Government establishments, such as administrative departments, arsenals, factories, and schools. I may add, that individually they manifest a friendly and courteous demeanour whenever they come in contact with Europeans.

In concluding this Report, I beg to state that since the conclusion of peace between Russia and China, and the dispersion of the Russian fleet, the political advantage of opening communications with Corea has greatly diminished, if not disappeared.

Corea, it is believed, has profited much by the importance given to her, and by the interest she has awakened amongst European nations during the past twelve months, and evidence is not wanting that Corea will before long herself offer to enter into friendly relations with foreign Powers, commencing probably with the United States, which country, as your Lordship is aware, made an unsuccessful attempt to communicate with the Corean Government last year, and has recently appointed to Commodore Shufeldt, late Commander of the United States' ship "Ticonderoga," to be Naval Attaché at Peking.

My German colleague recently informed me that he had received a despatch from his Government acknowledging his reports on Corea, but stating that in the opinion of the German Government the time for action towards Corea had not yet arrived.

                                                                I have, &c.
                                        (Signed)   J.G. Kennedy

57

J.G. Kennedy (1881. 9. 28) ➜ Tenterden

조영조약 체결 관련 업무의 잠정 중단 보고

28 Sep.   Tokio
                                                                     Japan

My dear Tenterden,

    I thank you much for your letter of 5. Aug on the proposed Chamberlain jobs. I concur in every word you say my language to Satow was identical with yours to me. I was weak in giving way to Satow's pressures, but at the time I was under special obligation to him. The terms of your reply would I anticipated have exhausted the topic. To Chamberlain himself I have never mention the subject. I take a real interest in this consular service, connected as it always will be with my first reasonable appointment. There are a few inferior articles which terms will dispose of, but on the whole the service is in good working order; the last 4 students promise very well & are socially superior to most of their immediate predecessors. Russia will tell you of a little plan we assert for Dohmen's finale. We propose that Hakodate should be reduced to a Vice Consulate & Dohmen seat there. Dohmen's misfortune in that he is very unpopular & he allows his personal feelings to influence his action. He is perpetually involved in small personal squabbles in as he is generally in the wrong for the settlement of which in his own favour he supplies to me. Such a character is a drawback to the harmonious transaction of busyness at Yokohama whereas at Hadodate it would not signify—a Vice Consulate at Hadodate would answer all purposes. I have just given Mr. acting Consul Lewis a strong hint that before he takes any leave he must send me some proof of his official existence in the hope of a Report—The Russian alone of Foreign nations have a Vice Consul at Hadodate but he has only been there this year for six weeks.

    I have dropped the topic of Korea as a favourable opportunity for opening communication with that Country will hardly present itself for a year or two to come. Meanwhile the American Commodore Schufeldt is working the subject at Peking with Li Hung Chang—Messeigneur Ridal the celebrated informing declared that Korea abounds with mineral wealth, silk & so on—however I shall have all this to Sir Harry of where departure for Japan I shall soon expect to hear by telegraph. Tourists abound 2 of the Cricketing Walker family & Harry & Zouche—2 generals form India & etc.

 I have relieved Inouye's mind somewhat since the receipt of last corres. between Granville & Mr. Mori. I have told Inouye that that style & context of Mori's note is offensive & would indispose his St to oblige Japan. I also urged the foolish of employing 2nd Chief Pointshere & Yankees to write this despatches for them—I myself complain to Inouye of the language of a note addressed to me & since them the notes have been in Japanese & always polite. Out merchants are just mow much irritated by combination of Japanese agst. them—supported it is strongly believed by the govt. I have settled a kerosine oil difficult & have to do either by a silk trouble—our Doyen the U.S. Minister is no good & we all long for Sir Harry to return & to take the lead in representations the negotiations with this Govt.

 The Mikado returns from his northern trip on the 11th & will therefore arrive in time to receive our Prince W. Chanielles has we hear been very ill—I beg to remain sincerely yours.

J. Kennedy

58

V. Drummond (1881. 10. 22) ➡ G.L.G. Granville (1881. 11. 5)

러시아의 조선 점령 가능성 및 미국의 조선 교섭 계획 보고

Mr. Drummond to Earl Granville.—(Received November 5)

(No. 310 Most Confidential)

Washington, October 22, 1881

My Lord,

I HAVE the honour to inform your Lordship that, in a conversation with one of my colleagues here, he mentioned to me most confidentially that both the United Sates and Russia are desirous of obtaining a foothold in Corea. Both countries will make use of China and Japan for their own purposes to obtain an entry into that mysterious country, supposed to contain enormous mineral wealth.

My colleague says that Russia will ultimately endeavour to obtain possession of Corea, and with this intention will use China as the point of the wedge to enter there, and is trying to obtain from China some point of territory on the coast of Chinese Tartary, ostensibly as a coaling-station for her vessels of war, but in reality as an arsenal for future operations.

The United States, on the other hand, will make use of Japan in her dealings with Corea, and take advantage of her relations with that country to induce her to bring her influence to bear on the Coreans for permission to allow the entry and reception of a Untied States' Envoy.

The Americans wish to be the first in the field, but the Russians will use all their diplomacy and power to win the race.

I have, &c.

(Signed) VICTOR DRUMMOND

J.G. Kenndey (1882. 1. 10) ➜ G.L.G. Granville

Shufeldt의 교섭 시도 보고

Most Confidential
No. 5
The Earl Granville K.G.

Yedo, January 10, 1882

My Lord,

I have the honor to acknowledge the receipt of Your Lordship's Despatch marked Most Confidential, No. 78 of the 15th of November last, enclosing copy of a Despatch from Her Majesty's Charge' d' Affaires at Washington stating that he learns that both the United States and Russia are desirous of obtaining a foothold in the Korea.

After careful consideration of the statement contained in Mr. Drummond's above mentioned Despatch, I am disposed to think that they are merely the echoes of impressions as to the designs against Korea of Russia and the United States which existed here during the summer of 1880 and during the winter months of 1880-81.

During the former period, Commodore Shufeldt, of the United States ship "Ticonderoga," made two unsuccessful attempts to make a Treaty with Korea under the patronage of Japan, and during the latter period much anxiety was felt by the Government of Japan lest Admiral Lessofsky with his powerful fleet should take possession of a portion or at least a Port of Korea.

On the above point I had at the time the honor to report fully to Your Lordship in a series of Despatches relating to Korea, and especially as regarded the movements of Russian and American Commanders in my Despatches marked Confidential, Nos. 90, 85, and 135 of May, June, and August 1880, and, as regards the Russian designs, in my Despatch Confidential No. 30 of the 24th of March 1881. Since the latter date I have ceased to report to Your Lordship on Korean affairs, because the Treaty of Kuldja, the dispersion of the Russian fleet, and the return home of Commodore Shufeldt has greatly lessened the interest taken by my Colleagues, by myself, and by the Government of Japan in the politics of Korea.

The only recent event which may be said to point to American designs upon Korea was the return last spring to Peking from Washington of Commodore Shufeldt.

This event was duly reported to Your Lordship in my Despatch Confidential, No. 61 of the 8th of June last, and it is doubtless the Commodore's presence in China which gave rise to the suspicions [_____] impending American designs upon Korea.

In my above mentioned Despatch Confidential, No. 30 of 1881, I reported to Your Lordship the assurances given to me here by the Russian Minister and reiterated at Peking by the Russian Charge' d' Affaires to the effect that Russia had no designs upon Korea. During the past few weeks Mr. Koyander, who, as Your Lordship is aware, was in charge of the Russian Legation at Peking during the Kuldja negotiations and who is now here on his way home, has frequently conversed with me on Eastern politics. He declares that Russia has never wished to annex any portion or Port of Korea, although such an operation might have become a necessity in case of war with China, and in support of his assertion he cites the inaction of Admiral Lessofsky towards Korea during the spring of last year when the Admiral had under his orders the most powerful Russian fleet ever collected in the same waters. To the above argument other reasons for Russian inaction may be added, such as the untimely death of the late Emperor and the domestic and financial difficulties of the Empire.

As regards the presence at Peking of Commodore Shufeldt, Mr. Koyander tells me that the Commodore is very reticent about himself and his plans, and answers all enquiries by stating that he has been sent to Peking by his Government as Naval Attache' to the United States Legation. Mr. Koyander, however, believes that Commodore Shufeldt is trying to get appointed Commander in Chief of the Chinese navy and that he still cherishes the design of opening Korea to American trade to the glory of himself and his country and, it may be added, to the advantage of all other nations.

Information respecting Commodore Shufeldt will doubtless have been furnished [_____] and Korea, in reply to Mr. Drummond's allusion to Korea as "that mysterious country supposed to contain enormous mineral wealth," I would say "omne ignotum pro magnifico." As a result of communications with many Koreans and Japanese residents in Korea, I incline to the belief that Korea is a poor country and that, whatever riches may exist, they have [_____]

In speaking of their country Koreans as a rule are influenced by their personal feelings. Those who wish to see the country opened to foreign intercourse describe Korea as teeming with undeveloped resources whilst the Conservative or anti-foreign party assert that Korea is miserably poor in all respects.

I do not believe, as I have already had the honor to inform Your Lordship in previous despatches, that it would be worth the while of Great Britain to enter into Treaty relations with Korea unless it could be done on the invitation of the Korean Government and with the concurrence of the Suzerain Power of China.

From a commercial point of view Korea offers but poor and vague prospects. The cotton goods imported into the country are mostly of British manufacture, transshipped into Japanese ships at Nagasaki for conveyance to Fusan.

Politically speaking the opening of Korea might obviously under certain circumstances be of advantage to Great Britain and to other European Powers, but in that case, in my humble opinion, combined and not isolated action should be taken towards Korea by the Powers of Europe and America.

I have the honor to be with the highest Respect,

My Lord,

Your Lordship's most obedient, humble servant,

J.P. Kennedy

R.Hall (1882. 4. 17) → G.O. Willes

최혜국대우 균점(均霑)을 위한 교섭 권한 부여

(ADM 125/142/3)

Vice Admiral Willes
Admiralty
17th April 1882

Sir:

I am commanded by my Lords Commissioners of the Admiralty to send you herewith a copy of the letter from the Foreign Office, enclosing a printed copy of a dispatch from H.M. Charge d'affaires at Yedo, relative to the alleged intention of the Americans to negotiate a treaty with the Coreans, in order to open up that district to American trade.

2. As Sir Thomas Wade, in a telegram which is alluded to in the Foreign Office letter, states that the treaty is now about to be negotiated, and is likely to be restrictive as regards opium, missionaries and jurisdiction, and as Sir Harry Parkes reports that the Expedition will be supported by the American Admiral on the Station a telegram in the following sense was sent to you on 14th instant.

"The American Admiral is about to proceed to Corea to support Commodore Shufeldt in negotiating a treaty with the Coreans, watch the proceedings of the Americans and if it is necessary you are authorized to hold negotiations with the authorities of Corea with a view to obtaining the advantages of the most favoured Nation for this country. There is no objection to the Squadron cruising in that neighbourhood and you are to report on the matter."

I am Sir,
Your obedient servant,
(Signed)   Robert Hall

H.S. Parkes (1882. 4. 18) → G.L.G. Granville (1882. 6. 7)

Willes의 조선행을 지시한 외무부 전신 수령

No. 53

Tokio, April 18 1882

My Lord,

I have the honor to acknowledge the receipt this day at 3.30 p.m. of the following telegram from your lordship in cypher:-

"London. april 17. 2.10 p.m.
"your telegram of the eigth instant"
"Admiral Willes has been instructed by telegraph to proceed to the Corea to watch and report, and if necessary negotiate agreement securing the most favored nation treatment for this country."

I have the honor to be with the highest Respect,
My Lord,
Your Lordship's most obedient, humble servant,
Harry S. Parkes

62

H.S. Parkes (1882. 4. 21) ➜ G.L.G. Granville (1882. 5. 29)

조선의 수입관세율 전망 보고

Confidential
No. 57   Tokio, April 21 1882

My Lord,

    Mr. Kennedy in his Despatch No. 8 of the 18th of January of this year reported that the negotiations between the Korean Envoy and this Government respecting the Tariff proposed by the Korean Government had fallen through and that further discussion was deferred until Mr. Hanabusa, the Japanese chargé d'affaires in Korea could return to his post.

    Mr. Hanabusa had been absent from his post for a year and the Japanese Government appeared indifferent as to the time of his return until it became known that Commodore Schufeldt was about to process there. They are now apprehensive that the American negotiator will be willing to concede to the Koreans a similar Tariff to that which the Japanese Government have reject and this is not improbable as that Tariff is almost a counterpart of the one attached to the American Treaty with Japan of 1858.

    I learn from Mr. Hanabusa that the Japanese Government offered to negotiate a Tariff with Korea on the basis of 5 per cent, but that this offer has been declined by the Koreans, who at first refused to accept a lower basis than 20 per cent which was the principal rate of the Tariff of the American Treaty above-mentioned. Mr. Hanabusa thinks that Korean Government have now been advised by the Grand Secretary Li Hung Chang to agree to a 10 per cent basis, but the Japanese Government consider that this rate would be too high for a trade which is still in its infancy while 20 per cent would ruin it entirely.

    As the United States Government cannot expect to participate largely in any trade which may spring up between Korea and the Western World the Japanese Government conclude that they will make little effort to promote the commercial interests of other nations and will not be disposed to allow considerations of that nature to interfere with their opportunity of making the first treaty with Korea. But, as Mr. Hanabusa observed, if they concede a high

Tariff to the Koreans it will be very difficult for Japan or for any Foreign Power to effect an abatement of such a concession, and the argument that high duties are destructive of trade would have little influence on the Korean mind. The example is also likely to have a prejudicial influence on those other Oriental Powers who have hitherto agreed to low Tariffs, and Japan, as Your Lordship is aware, is now demanding a considerable increase in the rates of her Tariff, although she objects to the imposition of similar duties on her trade with Korea.

I have the honor to be with the highest respect,
My Lord,
Your Lordship's most obedient, humble servant,
Harry S. Parkes

63

H.S. Parkes (1882. 5. 12) ➡ G.L.G. Granville (1882. 6. 19)

조미조약 체결 이후 일본의 조선정책 전망 보고

No. 62   Tokio
                                                                May 12, 1882

My Lord,

　　With reference to my dispatch No. 57, Confidential, of the 20th instant, I have the honour to report that Mr. Hanabusa left Tokio for Korea on the 26th ultimo. As he expected that his voyage to the capital Seoul would occupy about ten days, he will probably arrive there only a very short time in advance of Commodore Schufeldt, who left Shanghai for the same destination via Chefoo on the 2nd instant.

　　I enclose translations prepared by Mr. Satow of two articles from two Japanese newspapers in the interest of the government, in which the policy of Japan in Korea is discussed. Finding that the United States have resolved to open that country it is urged that the Japanese Government should not lose time in agreeing with the Koreans to a Tariff of Ten per cent. The Americans will be followed by the French and the English, but it cannot be expected that Korea will enter into relations with foreign nations without serious internal disturbance. These relations will in the end prove of great advantage to Korea because she will thus be saved from Russian aggression, but in consequence of the fanaticism of the antiforeign party the establishment of foreign intercourse will at first be attended with some degree of danger. Japan should endeavour to attract the confidence of Korea (which it is admitted she does not how enjoy), and escorting herself to maintain the independence of Korea should be prepared to act in concert with China in order to protect that country from European dictation.

　　It may be doubted however whether China will be disposed to cooperate with Japan for the above named object, or that her action will be guided by any desire to support the interests of Japan in Korea. I imagine that she seeks, on the contrary, to make her influence in that country paramount to that of Japan, and it is rather with the view of protecting herself against Russia, and possibly also of recovering her position in them undefined way as quasi Suzerain of Korea that she is now interesting herself in the mission of Commodore Shufeldt.

An unfortunate affair has recently occurred at Gensan, the port open to Japanese trade on the Eastern Coast of Korea. A party of Japanese having proceeded, when on an excursion, beyond the Treaty limits of that port were attacked by the Koreans—one of them was killed and two were dangerously wounded. The Japanese press which in opposed to the Government demand that energetic measures should be taken for the redress of this outrage. I add an extract from one of these papers which maintains that it is only by the strong hand that Japan can secure the faithful execution of her treaties with Korea and control the antiforeign spirit which is so strong in that country. Like the Government papers it also observes that Korea can only be saved from Russia by entering into the comity of nations, and that Japan should therefore endeavour to induce her to do so. And in support of the argument that strong measures should be used when necessary, it ass the remark that if Kagoshima and Shimomoseki had not been bombarded by the European Powers at a time when disorder prevailed in Japan, the Japanese would not have made the rapid progress they have since achieved.

I have the honour to be with the highest respect,
My Lord,
Your Lordship's most obedient, humble Servant,
Harry S. Parkes

64

T.F. Wade (1882. 5. 11) ➡ 李鴻章

조선에 제시할 소개 서한 요청

The Grand Secretary Li

Tientsin
11th May, 1882

My Dear Sir,

By letters which arrived yesterday from Japan I am informed of a report that Your Excellency had dispatched an agent to Corea to inform the Government of that country that the American Squadron now on its way to Corea was to be presently followed by a British Squadron for the purpose of negotiating a treaty. From my conversation with Your Excellency a few days ago, I cannot suppose that you have made any intimation of the kind, but the emphasis with which you dwelt upon the timidity of the Coreans induces me to suggest that the simplest method of preventing propagation of rumours so likely to alarm that people would be that, as I have proposed to you, Your Excellency should write a letter to the High Officer in charge of Foreign Affairs in Corea, acquainting him with the plain facts as slated by me in my interview with Your Excellency; namely, that there is in the first place no desire on our part to do anything that may embarrass the negotiations of the Representative of the United States; that the British Admiral proposes to appear off the coast with no more than a single vessel; and that he is prepared to accept a treaty identical in form and conditions with the Treaty which the United States Government is about to conclude.

If it be in Your Excellency's power to forward me a letter to the above effect and to supply me at the same time with a copy of the Chinese text of the draught treaty, I will hand the letter and the draught to Admiral Willes, whose tender is now in the river. The Admiral could then so time his visit to Corea as in no way to interfere with American negotiations. I should wish of course to be furnished with a copy of the Chinese letter that the Admiral is to carry with him.

I will at the same time telegraph to London to explain the nature of the article which declares the relation of the Kingdom of Corea as a dependency to the Empire of China as her suzerain, and will recommend that upon this point also the Government of Her Majesty shall engage to be content with whatever arrangement may be considered satisfactory by the Government of the United States.

　　I assume that Your Excellency would wish communication between me and yourself on this subject to be regarded as confidential.

　　I have, etc,

(Signed) T.F. Wade

65

T.F. Wade (1882. 5. 12) ➜ G.L.G. Granville

李鴻章의 일시 사직 보고

Granville
No. 16

Tientsin
May 12, 1882

My Lord,

    Your Lordship will have learned from my Telegram dispatched some weeks ago, that the United States Government had it in immediate contemplation to conclude a Treaty with the Government of Corea. Having subsequently received from Vice Admiral Willes, Commander in chief of her Majesty's Squadron in these seas, an intimation that he would be glad of some more precise information upon this subject, I came here on the 4th instant to meet him.

    The temporary retirement of the Grand Secretary Li consequent upon the death of his mother, which I have earlier reported, has deprived me to a certain extent of the assistance for which I might otherwise have hoped at His Excellency's hands, as he has been in effect the representative of the Government of China in the negotiations which have led at last to the opening of Corea. I have been enabled nevertheless to communicate with him non-officially, and I have satisfied him that nothing is further from the wishes of Her Majesty's Government than to take any step that may tend either to alarm Corea or to embarrass the negotiations of the Representative of the United States. I have further undertaken, as I am telegraphing to Your Lordship, to recommend acceptance by Her Majesty's Government of whatever terms the United States may have authorized their Representative to accept. I am in hopes, consequently, that if Admiral Willes present himself about the end of next month he will at least find nothing to complain of in the manner of his reception.

    I have promised Admiral Willes to place Mr. Spence at his disposal. Mr. Spence is not only a good Chinese scholar, and a very competent agent, but he has the advantage of having visited Corea, as your Lordship is aware, as Interpreter to the Duke of Genoa.

I cannot but rejoice at the evidence of progress afforded by the decision now taken by the Chinese Government and its dependent to abandon the ancient exclusivist policy. I say this at the same time without venturing to ascribe to my own counsels or those of others, who for years have been recommending the change, an event in chief part due to the pressure of circumstances the gravity of which China has at last acquired sufficient experience to appreciate.

I have the honour to be, with the highest respect,

My Lord,

Your Lordship's most obedient, humble servant,

Thomas Francis Wade

66

T.F. Wade (1882. 5. 12) ➡ G.L.G. Granville

조선 문제 관련 李鴻章 및 總署와 교섭 보고

No. 17 Confidential

Tientsin
May 12, 1882

My Lord,

    In continuation of my Despatch No. 16 of this date I have the honour to lay before Your Lordship some matter that will more particularly explain the position of the Corean question.

    It has not a very ancient history as far as we are concerned. It is eighteen years only since, during my first charge, the Tsungli-Yamen was urged to impress on Corea the importance to her own independence of intercourse with foreign Powers, but the answer of the Yamen, throughout, has been almost invariably that, although dependent on China as her Suzerain, Corea had an autonomic constitution, and that China could go no further than the tender of advice, which the ultra-conservatism of Corea was certain to reject. Various instances of her indisposition to change were adduced by the Chinese Ministers; among the rest, her opposition to the introduction of Buddhism notwithstanding its very general adoption in China.

    The truth, I cannot doubt, has been that although the Chinese Government, thanks to the continued representations of foreign advisors, became more or less awake to the danger to which her exclusivism was exposing Corea, it could not bring itself directly to recommend its dependent to break with its old traditions. Both Suzerain and dependent again were of course confirmed in their adherence to these by the unfortunate expeditions of France and America in 1866 and 1872.

    The petty encroachments of Russians along the Corean frontier, complaints of which from time to time reached us, had not to all appearance committed either Government to any serious effort, if even to remonstrance; but within the last few years the attitude of Japan had begun to excite considerable alarm. The intercourse between the Japanese and Coreans at the few points of contact recently become accessible to Japan was not such as to dispose the latter to an extension of their acquaintance with foreigners; but the Chinese were more directly affected by the absorption by Japan of another of their dependencies, Lewchewan which touched their pride.

As usual however, their first thought was to relieve themselves alike from danger and humiliation by the employment of an intermediary, and they accordingly appealed to General Grant when, on his tour round the world, he visited Peking. I arrived shortly after General Grant's departure from Tientsin in the Spring of 1879, and was also requested to move Her Majesty's Government to intervene by the Grand Secretary Li. As my report to the Marquess of Salisbury will show, I recommended the association of France and Germany in any negotiation of the kind desired, premising however, that the good offices of the latter could not be counted on till the revision of the German Treaty, as I believed needlessly postponed, should be completed. The cooperation of the four Powers secured, I did not think that Russia would care to be left out. The Grand Secretary dropped the negotiation with me abruptly. The Yamen never referred to it. The mediation of General Grant at Yedo produced at the same time no result beyond the recommencement of pourparlers between China and Japan which at this moment appear as far from termination as ever. It will be seen presently why I return here to this Lewchewan question at such length.

Meanwhile, during the earlier part of the quarrel with Russia in 1880, which at one time looked so ugly, the Japanese secured to neglect no opportunity of disturbing the Chinese, and their disquiet was naturally increased to the utmost by the appearance in Japanese waters of the imposing Russian Squadron known as the "patriotic" or "commercial."

Admiral Coote, then commanding in these seas, as was but natural, found little disposition on the part of the Russians to show him or tell him anything that they could conceal: but with the French Commander in Chief, Admiral Charles Duperre, they were or affected to be very much more outspoken. He went over all their ships and they informed him with much detail of their resources and designs.

They said that they had in all fourteen thousand men at Vladivostok; which was certainly an immense exaggeration, though the statement fell short of what was accepted as accurate at Peking.

But the main object for which this fleet had been collected, he gathered, was the annexation of so much of Corea as would give the Russians Port

Lazareff. Admiral Duperre had himself, in 1855, made a survey of this port which he communicated to the Russians. When peace was concluded without concession of it, the Russian Naval Officers did not conceal their disappointment. Monsieur Koyander the Charge D'Affaires, it is true, had loudly protested throughout that annexation of any kind was the thing farthest from the thoughts of the Russian Government.

The impression produced at Peking, however, was that Russia contemplated annexation not only of a slice of Corea, but of the whole peninsula, and when I was on my way through Tientsin to Chefoo, in October 1880, the Grand Secretary Li, begged me to persuade Admiral Coote, whom I was going to meet, to carry me over at once to Corea for the purpose of making a Treaty.

I pointed out that, however high His Excellency's position and credit still in a step of this kind I could do nothing as British Minister without an understanding with Tsungli-Yamen, which arrived at, I must next apply for authority to my own Government. The Grand Secretary was very instant notwithstanding; assuring me, when I reminded him of the danger of irregular movements towards the Coreans, as proved by the reception of the French and Americans, that he could secure me against failure etc. Admiral Coote, with whom I communicated on the subject at Chefoo, as I expected, was entirely of the same mind as myself.

I returned to Tientsin from Chefoo within the week, and visiting the Grand Secretary the night I landed, I found him still full of a Treaty with Corea. On the following day, however, he called upon me, and as I had proposed as soon as I should reach Peking to approach the Yamen on the subject, I began as soon as he was seated, "Well then, as regards Corea, Your Excellency assures me that you can secure our reception as friends."

To my utter surprise, he threw up his hands in manifest terror, and almost shrieked out "Not I! Not I! I would not venture to secure it. Wait a little. The Russians desire the northeast corner where they wish for a port. The Coreans will resist them but will be beaten. When they are beaten then you and other nations will present yourselves and make treaties."

I ascertained presently that on his way to see me he had spent an hour at the Russian Consulate. The news that negotiations between Tseng-How-Yeh and Monsieur de Giers were at last under way, had been very recently received, and the Russian Consul had been evidently instructed to disabuse the Grand

Secretary of the idea that the mere renewal of the discussion assumed to have been ended by the Treaty signed by Ching how, had by any means rendered a rupture with Russia impossible. A beginning had been made but nothing more. A similar intimation, I learned at Peking, had been made by Monsieur Koyander to the Yamen, of which the leading Minister was the late Grand Secretary Shen, the most trickey and cowardly of men.

I may have casually sounded the Yamen regarding Corea in the course of the following two or three months, but I find no record of any conversation on the subject before the 7th of February 1881. When I availed myself of the known currency of certain rumours to speak.

I inclose an extract from the Journal of my interviews with the Ministers of what passed on that day.

The executed item of the convention, my recommendation, namely that, in order to avoid the offence to Russia which the action of any single Power eminently that of England, might occasion, Corea should be prompted to invite all Powers alike to enter into relations with her, was telegraphed the same afternoon to Your Lordship in reply to a Telegram which reached me as I returned to the [_____].

I followed this up next day by a second visit to the Yamen, hoping that I might have turned the receipt of Your Lordship's Telegram to account. But the Ministers who received me were uninfluential men, and some time elapsed before I was enabled to get the ear of the Vice President Wang-Wen-Shao who, since the recent death of the Grand Secretary Shen, had become the Minister of most real importance in the conduct of foreign affairs. He was at the same time member of the Grand Council.

The Vice President Wang discouraged any attempt on my part to open Corea. The time he said was not come etc. But the Chinese Government, as I have since satisfied myself, was entertaining already definite proposals to open Corea to the United States.

I shall here close this dispatch.

I have the honour to be, with the highest respect,

My Lord,

Your Lordship's most obedient, humble servant,

Thomas Francis Wade

Inclosure

Corea
Interview with Ministers of the Tsung-li Yamen, February 7th 1881

Sir T. Wade remarked that, as Their Excellencies were doubtless supplied with translations of matter from the foreign press that bore upon questions affecting China, they had probably informed themselves of the speculations that were rife as to the designs of Russia with regard to Corea.

The Minister Wang replied in the affirmative, and added that the suspicious that seemed to be universally entertained appeared to him to be well grounded.

Sir T. Wade went on to say that without attributing this or that or any motive to Russia, there could be no doubt that the presence of so large a force on the Corean frontier would enable the Russian Government, if they felt so inclined, to discover a pretext for entering Corea, whether for purposes of annexation or otherwise; and, as he had several times already urged upon the Yamen, they would do well in the interests of Corea, and indeed on their own, to press the Corea Government to open the country to foreigners.

Wong ta jen replied that they had been urging this course upon Corea any time the last two years. At first without any success; for the opposition was almost universal. Of late, however, there had been a considerable change in their tone, and since last autumn the majority including the Court, had come round to the opinion that the country should be opened. He might almost say that they had been convinced, and the Yamen were now only waiting for a definite pledge from them that they would accept any overtures that might be made to them by a foreign power.

The Minister Mao added that if they were given time, he felt sure that the Coreans would overcome their prejudices against foreign intercourse.

Delay, Sir T. Wade pointed out, was just what was dangerous. If Russia meant to do anything in Corea, though, he repeated, he did not say positively she did, she certainly would not wait for the Coreans to overcome their prejudices. At the same time, it had occurred to him that matters might be so managed that some delay might be secured. It was perfectly certain that a feeling of jealousy would be caused if any one power were to be beforehand with another power in visiting Corea for the purpose of negotiating a treaty and the Russian Government in particular would resent any attempt to steal a march upon them. In suggesting a means of avoiding the ill feeling that might be caused by any one nationality obtaining precedence over another, Sir T. Wade would assure the Yamen that he was not actuated by any interested motives. Corea was not so wealthy a country, and the establishment of relations with her did not promise such enormous commercial advantages, as would induce any country to struggle to be the first in the field. To avoid, however, the ill feeling which he had explained might be caused by the visit of one representative to the country in advance of others, Sir T. Wade would suggest that the Yamen should obtain from the Corean government an authorization to announce to the Treaty Powers the readiness of the Corean Government to enter into commercial relations with foreign countries; and that the Yamen should then invite the Representatives of the Treaty Powers to send agents to Corea to travel through the country and acquaint themselves with its commercial conditions, with a view to concluding treaties with the Corean Government at a future date. Previous rebuffs had rendered most Representatives wary of subjecting themselves to any further incivilities from the Corean Government, and it was this consideration that had deterred Sir T. Wade on two occasions, namely in 1876 and 1880, from visiting Corea, as he did not wish to cause any complications which his government might feel bound to take notice of. In his opinion a definite promise that they would receive Foreign Representatives if they came to the Corean Capital, should be obtained from the Corean Government; after which the plan he proposed might be adopted.

The Ministers replied that this statement was all that they were at present waiting for. Meanwhile they were greatly obliged to Sir T. Wade for his advice, which they would take careful note of.

Inclosure

Interview with Ministers of the Tsungli Yamen—February 8, 1881

Sir T. Wade called at the Yamen to communicate to the Ministers the substance of a telegram he had found waiting him on his return from the Yamen on the previous day, on the subject of the opening of Corea.

The only Ministers present were Mao Changhoi and Chungli who said that careful note had been taken of the remarks that had been made by Sir T. Wade on the previous day, and they would shortly be submitted to the Prince of Kung. As yet no decision had been taken as to the action that would be adopted; but as spoon as any arrangement had been come to, the Yamen would communicate with Sir T. Wade.

T.F. Wade (1882. 5. 12) ➡ G.L.G. Granville (1882. 7. 22)

Shufeldt의 청국 해군 임용 실패와 조미조약에 대한 청국 태도 보고

Granville (received 7. 22)

No. 18 Confidential

Tientsin
May 12, 1882

My Lord,

I closed the foregoing Despatch with a reference to an understanding between the United States and China on the subject of Corea.

Commodore Shufeldt, as I have before reported, returned to this country in the course of last year ostensibly as Naval Attache to the United States Legation. He had been in China many years ago. When I first knew him in 1867, more particularly, he was engaged in examining the coast of Corea. He was again out here during the visit of General Grant, who was always spoken of as one of his Chief supporters, and it was rumoured that in return for the mediation with Japan promised by General Grant in the matter of Lewchew, a promise was given by the Grand Secretary Li, that Commodore Shufeldt should be created a sort of administrator-in-chief of the Chinese Navy now in process of formation.

It is not improbable that something of the kind was promised. China was not only irritated by the absorption of her dependency by Japan, but I think strongly impressed with a belief that Japan contemplated further acts of aggression. Though not regularly Minister for war, the Grand Secretary Li was the official on whose shoulders the responsibility of securing the empire against war with any power beyond sea was more especially laid, and believing as firmly as anyone in the hostility of Japan, not perhaps unassisted by European allies, he was turning in all directions for help. The American Navy was already supplying him with an officer to form a Torpedo service. He is still here. Two Commandants of the French Navy were engaged in 1879-80 at very liberal salaries; also believing themselves to be Directors General of Chinese Marine. One of these, disgusted at finding that there is really nothing for him to do, has retired. That Commodore Shufeldt was also promised employment is hardly to be doubted, but I am assured by a person who should know, that he never did receive from the Grand Secretary any promise such a position as he returned to China to hold. And this is very possibly true. The Agents through whom communications between the Commodore and the Grand Secretary are stated to have passed not improbably misled the Commodore, and my informant further states that when he, the Commodore, required as the condition of his acceptance of Office the establishment of a sort of Board of Admiralty of which he was to be the direct Agent in Chief, this proposal was negatived by the Grand Secretary.

Be all this as it may, Commodore Shufeldt is a bitterly disappointed man, and his wrath with the Chinese will account for the angry Letter of which I sent Your Lordship a rough copy some weeks ago.

This Letter has now been printed with some modifications which can hardly be taken to improve it. I inclose copy of it taken from a local paper.

Meanwhile the Chinese have been made aware of his feeling towards them, and it is impart to their desire to propitiate him, and his countrymen, that both the Central Government and the Grand Secretary have shown comparative alacrity in furthering his wishes as far as Corea is concerned. There are, it must be admitted, other reasons. They feel that they owe America, that is General Grant, something far friendly intervention in 1879. They imagine and perhaps with justice, that the Americans are likely to grant easier terms to Corea than any other Western Power, and they hope that what one western Power accepts may be accepted by all. Lastly I think they have at length convinced themselves that it is only by opening her ports that Corea will secure her independence.

As regards this, their fear of the intentions of Russia and Japan, which may be described as chronic, has I doubt not been stimulated by the proceedings of the French in Tonquin.

I have, &c.

Thomas Francis Wade

T.F. Wade (1882. 5. 12) ➔ G.L.G. Granville (1882. 7. 22)

조미수호통상조약안 분석 보고

Sir T. Wade to Earl Granville – (Received July 22)

(No. 19 Confidential)

Tientsin
12 May 1882

My Lord,

To come to the Treaty which the United States are about to conclude with Corea, I have the honour to inclose a précis which I have made from the Chinese text of a draught communicated to me, in confidence and for perusal only, by Mr. Holcombe, Charge d'Affaires of the United States.

On my return from Shanghai last December, I found Commodore Shufeldt here at Tientsin, but, although apparently frank about other matters, he was mute regarding Corea. I asked him indeed no question with reference to his mission thither. A Corean official was still here, and in communication with the Grand Secretary Li upon the subject. That high officer none the less assured me that the Coreans continued as deaf as ever to his counsel that they should open their coasts. I shall, however, return to His Excellency later.

Some time after I got back to Peking, Mr. Holcombe began to speak openly to me upon the subject, and having in due time acquainted me that a Treaty was at last under way, I telegraphed that information to Your Lordship. He has since requested me in the event of our following up the American lead, to use my influence in preventing any such intervention as, from its character or its unreasonableness, might embarrass Commodore Shufeldt's proceedings; I do not say negotiations, for these may be said to have been already concluded here, the agents concerned being the Grand Secretary Li, Commodore Shufeldt and Mr. Holcombe himself. I readily gave him the promise he required and he subsequently put in my hands the draught form from which my précis was made, assuring me at the same time that no other of his colleagues had seen it.

Mr. Holcombe asked me if I contemplated myself proceeding to Corea. I told him that some years ago, when submitting the contingency of negotiations to the Foreign Office, I had suggested that the Corean Government should rather be approached from Yedo than Peking; partly, because from the position of the country, geographically, this course appeared the more natural; partly, because I regarded Sir Harry Parkes as more competent than myself to frame a commercial Treaty. Mr. Holcombe rejoined, with some emphasis, that any difficulty that now might exist would be much aggravated if negotiations were supposed to be inspired from the Japanese tide. Both China and Corea, he said, in relation to this question, most suspect Russia and Japan of hostile designs. In the late negotiations with the Grand Secretary Li, in which he, Mr. Holcombe, had played a chief part, he had found obstacles, more than once, removed by a hint that if China would not help America in this matter, America must fall back on Japan who had already tendered her good offices. On these, of course, he did not much rely; the manifest policy of Japan being to keep Corea closed to everyone but herself.

The points specially deserving of notice in the draught treaty are the following.

In Art. 2, America agrees to appoint none but paid consuls. None of the larger powers has in express terms conceded this to China. America, in particular, although for some years past appointing no merchant a Consul, has more than once distinctly declined to surrender her right to make such appointments where she found it convenient.

In the same Article, it is provided that a Consuls' exequatur may be withdrawn on appeal to the United States Minister; but only when he, the Minister sees ground. This is new.

In Art. 4, the Administration of Justice in civil and criminal suits, in mixed cases, is provided for much as in this country; but a clause is added pledging the United States Government to surrender its title to exterritoriality whenever the laws shall be brought into harmony with those of the United States. I think well of this.

The Tariff provided under Art. 5, is a novelty, and appears to me more liberal to the native than to the foreigner. As no inland charges exist in Corea, the stipulation that nothing more shall be levied on imports when the Tariff duty is paid, is of no great value. However, as revision of the Treaty is virtually guaranteed in five years, I should be for giving it a fair trial.

Art. 6 will dissatisfy our people, for it restricts them, as in China from

1842 to 1860 they were restricted, to the seaports, and the carriage whether of imports inland or produce from the interior by American citizens, renders the goods so carried liable to confiscation.

Corean officials are not in repute above those of China or Japan, and against the exactions for which we must be prepared at their hands, I see no remedy so long as the interior is inaccessible to the foreigner. I am, nevertheless, for a five years' trial.

Opium is specially excluded by Art. 7. This was to be looked for. The Coreans have long declared against its introduction. The Grand Secretary declares them equally opposed to the advent of missionaries. But of these no mention is made, and if those interested in mission work are moderately discreet, they will find means, under Art. II, to do all that they could hope to do were their admission formally stipulated for.

There is one Article not in this draught to which I shall request Your Lordship's attention in the following dispatch.

I have, &c.

Thomas Francis Wade

P.S. In the copy of the treaty fro. which my first précis was made the first Article was omitted. Hence the numbers referred to in this dispatch will all have to be advanced one place; 2 read as 3, 4 as 5, etc.

69

T.F. Wade (1882. 5. 12) ➡ G.L.G. Granville (1882. 7. 22)

조미조약안의 조선 속방론 규정에 관한 보고

Granville
No. 20

Tientsin
12 May 1882

My Lord,

    The Article to which I have alluded at the close of my dispatch No. 19 of this date stands thus.

    "Corea is a dependency of China, but autonomic in both domestic and foreign relations. Corea and the United States agree that while the King of Corea engages faithfully to observe as an independent sovereign the different provisions (articles) of this treaty, the Ruler of the United States engages positively to recognize the dependence of Corea upon China, and never to interfere with it."

    When I was here in December last, the Grand Secretary Li, in the course of a conversation upon possible future intercourse with Corea, informed me with some explicitness that in any treaty between Corea and a foreign power, China would look for a clause admitting her suzerainty; and he gave reasons for the tenacity of his government on this point. The prestige of China, he said, was suffering by the extinction of some dependencies, and the withdrawal of others from their historical relation with her. Of the last incident, if I remember rightly, he mentioned Siam as an instance. Of the first, one instance was Anam, or Cochin China, which the French were by degrees annexing; Lewchew, which the Japanese had abruptly sent away, was another. He did not at the time allude to Burma, but, a few days since, when speaking of the most recent action of the French in Tonquin, he did make a slight allusion to the possible absorption of Burma by ourselves. But, to return, with reference to Corea, he made a good deal of the condition I have mentioned, and when Mr. Holcombe took me into his confidence, it was nearly the first point on which he also consulted me.

    I suggested a separate article much in the sense of that above translated, and which is so phrased in Chinese as to avoid a particular stumbling block. If the Chinese Empire were spoken of as the Ta Tsing, the dynastic designation by which the Empire is described in all our Treaties, the words representing Kingdom of Corea would have to take a lower place. To this Corea, as the vassal of China, could not object; but America, treating with Corea as an equal could not, as the equal also of China, accept such a position.

In the text of the Article to be adopted, if any be adopted, China will stand simply as Chung Kuo, the central State, the familiar equivalent of China; a term capable of being used officially, but not necessarily requiring a superior place in the column. Thus, while, in substance, the inferiority of Corea to China is asserted, there is nothing either in form or substance to put in doubt the equality of China and the United States.

The provision being something new in a diplomatic instrument, Mr. Holcombe has telegraphed to Washington for instructions, and as Commodore Shufeldt started from Chefoo for Corea on the 9th instant, it may be presumed that his Government has accepted the Article; or he must, I think, have returned hither to reopen the discussion with the Grand Secretary Li.

In the following dispatch, I shall report my interview with the Grand Secretary.

I have, &c.

Thomas Francis Wade

70

T.F. Wade (1882. 5. 17) ➜ G.L.G. Granville

베트남, 조선 문제에 관한 李鴻章과 회견 보고

Granville

17 May 1882

My Lord,

As I stated in my Despatch No. 16 of this date, I arrived here on the 4th instant. I had been given to understand at the Tsungli Yamen that although obliged to live in his inner apartments, His Excellency Li would receive me as a private friend and on the 6th instant I paid him a visit.

Upon conversation had reference principally to the action of France in Tonquin, which Mr. Stayfair, the acting Consul at Pakhoi, tells me that he has reported to Your Lordship, and to the treaty between Corea and the United States.

As to the first, he seemed disposed to solicit our good offices, but did not press the matter much. I told him, as I had already told him last December, when he suggested, as a check to French influence in Anam, a treaty between Anam and Great Britain, that with the position asserted by France in Anam above twenty years ago, and all this time undisputed, intervention on our part would be scarcely possible. The French, I reminded him, had extorted a treaty in 1874, of the non-fulfillment of which they had frequently complained, and their late expedition, which had evidently much alarmed the Chinese Government, would be justified, I felt sure, by them, as a measure necessary to secure them the exercise of the rights they claimed.

There is another reason given for their action, ominously resembling the plea for occupation of Ili or Kuldja by the Russians in 1864-5, and unhappily of equal validity, viz., that the frontier of Anam is vexed by affiliated brigands, whom the Chinese Government makes no efficient effort to restrain.

The French expedition, however, explained, has troubled the Chinese on two grounds. First, the autonomy of a dependency, Anam, is compromised; next, the suzerain himself, the Emperor of China, is more or less threatened by the establishment alongside him of a very restless neighbour, whose declared object it is to push a foreign trade across the southern frontier of China.

As to the latter consideration, the French, in my belief, will be disappointed. They have no import trade to speak of. They have shown a disposition (see Lord Lyon's correspondence 1874) to fetter the import trade of others. Lastly, had they trade and were they more liberal, the line they have chosen is not, geographically, the best. To reach the country they hope to open, as I pointed out to His Excellency, trade ought properly to ascend the great western river which, after traversing Kuang Li, joins the confluence at Canton. Imports would then pay import and transit duties to China; whereas by the other route, everything carried must of course pay something to France; and this without equivalent conceivable advantage.

As for any other dangers, I did not see how they were to be arrested until China should address herself seriously to organization of a land force. I recalled the advice I had given His Excellency and the Ministers of the Yamen in the spring of 1880. This will be found in my reports of that date. He begged me to call the attention of the Yamen once more to this matter; but he spoke in a half hearted sort of way. With the exception of one or two of the Ministers of the Yamen, he had manifestly not more faith in them than I am bound to admit they are entitled to.

As regards the extinction of the autonomy of Anam, he seemed more excited, repeating what he had earlier said about Lewchew, and adding with a sad smile that Birma, he presumed, would one day be ours. I assured him that, to the best of my belief, Birma was in no danger from us if she abode by her engagements. War with Birma in past years, it might be fairly said, had been forced upon us. We had, at all events, no designs upon the territory of Birma.

We passed on to Cashgaria, of which I shall speak elsewhere, and to Corea. I told His Excellency that Mr. Holcombe had concealed nothing from me about Corea; that I had promised him, so far as in me lay, to guard against any action on our part that might embarrass American negotiations; that I would recommend adoption of the draught treaty approved by Mr. Holcombe; that Admiral Willes, who was now here, had received a telegram from the Government on the subject and was quite prepared to proceed to Corea with nothing but his tender, accompanied by an interpreter of our Consular service whom I had promised to place at his disposal. I urged His Excellency Li to give me the Chinese text of the American draught treaty, and a letter to the Corean Secretary of State. I had learned from Mr. Holcombe that the Corean

Government had already established a Tsungli Yamen. There seems no doubt, either, that Sir Robert Hart, the Inspector General of Customs, has been commissioned to organize a foreign inspectorate in Corea; a measure most favorable, in my opinion, to commerce.

His Excellency promised me the Chinese text of the Treaty, but made some difficulty about a letter. He had been charged, he admitted, by the Emperor with the conduct of intercourse with Corea. This he had told me in December, adding that the arrangement had been made to save the face of the Tsungli Yamen at Peking. The Yamen, I imagine, would have had difficulty in treating with a tributary state, (which should properly be referred to the Board of Ceremonies,) on the same footing as the Powers which are by treaty recognized as the equals of China. That His Excellency Li, therefore, should write to Corea about our coming, did not seem to me much to ask; but he would not promise it. He could hardly promise, he said, a verbal message, for Ma Taotai, the officer sent last year to India, had already started for Chefoo to join Commodore Shufeldt. He would see, however, what could be done, and would be obliged to me to ascertain the views of my Government regarding the Article translated in my Despatch No. 20. I hinted, but without making very much of it, that, failing the support of China, we might have to ask the Japanese to help us.

Meanwhile, Admiral Willes received from Sir Harry Parkes a letter mentioning a report prevalent in Japan that he, the Admiral, was presently appear off the coast of Corea with a large fleet. On hearing this, I immediately wrote to His Excellency Li, pointing out that if the Coreans were not enlightened as to the real nature of our intentions, rumours of this kind would produce the very mischief in Corea that, in our interview, he had so deplored as possible. He had insisted much on their timidity and ignorance.

I inclose copy of my letter, on receipt of which His Excellency sent a subordinate to me to say that a Corean official now here should immediately communicate with his Government, and that he himself would forward me in a few days copy of the draught treaty to be placed in Admiral Willes' hands. He wished to know at the same time if I expected a reply to my letter. I suggested that, as His Excellency had difficulties about writing to Corea direct, he could not do better than reply to one in the Chinese fashion. The Chinese, in a case of this sort, reproduce the whole or the greater part of the letter under acknowledgment in the answer, and then conclude with a statement of what can or cannot be done. Copy of such a reply in the hands of Admiral Willes, I urged, would be nearly as good a paper to lay before any Corean authority who might receive him as the letter I had asked His Excellency Li to write to Corea. He sent back word to say that he would prefer to wait for the arrival of the Vice President Wang, who, as I have reported, was to be sent to him *a latere to* enjoin acquiescence in the Imperial decision about his mourning.

Admiral Willes left this on the 15th for Chefoo, having already learned that Commodore Shufeldt had quitted that port, in the course of the previous week, with a single American war-steamer accompanied by two Chinese gun vessels. Wang tajen arrived here I fancy on the 15th but having made no sign, I sent a message privately this afternoon to His Excellency Li to know how matters stood. I added that if my visits embarrassed him, or if, under the special circumstances of the case, Wang tajen would prefer not to come down to the foreign settlement, I would waive ceremony and call upon him. Properly, as the later comer, Wang tajen should at least have sent me his card.

His Excellency Li has sent me a reply, which, so far as the text of the treaty is concerned, appears to me evasive; but his messenger at the same time informed me that Wang tajen would be happy to receive me; indeed wished very much to see me.

It is not impossible that this wish, if Wang tajen has indeed expressed it, may have reference merely to a farther discussion about opium. Mr. Samuel has at last laid a memorandum of his propositions before the Chinese.

I have, &c.

Thomas Francis Wade

71

T.F. Wade (1882. 5. 22) ➡ C.T.Maude

조미조약초안의 한문본 전달 및 馬建忠 접촉 지시

관련문서 Willes에게 보낸 Maude 파견시 지참 문서 내용(1882. 5. 22)

Maude

Tientsin
22 May 1882

Sir,

  I have to request that you will proceed to Chefoo tomorrow by the steamer "Taku" carrying with you the Chinese text of the draught treaty about to be concluded between the United States and Corea, a translation of this draught, and a letter addressed to Ma Taotai by the Grand Secretary Li, instructing him, as I believe, to assist Admiral Willes in the negotiations which, as you are aware, the Admiral had been instructed to attempt.

  Admiral Willes, I have reason to think, will have left Chefoo, but Commander Bridger, H.M. gun vessel "Sheldrake," has promised to carry you over to Corea, and the Admiral has been apprised by telegraph that you are on your way thither.

  I shall give you a farther letter to Commander Bridger, to request him to wait until Admiral Willes arrives.

  When you reach Corea, you should lose no time in communicating with the Taotai Ma, whom you will find on board one of the two Chinese gunboats that were ordered to accompany Commodore Shufeldt, the American Plenipotentiary.

  I have promised Admiral Willes the services of Mr. Spence as Interpreter, but I cannot doubt that your experience in the Chancellerie will enable you to be useful to the Admiral, should he have treaties, protocols, or similar papers to prepare.

  For such money as you may require you will draw upon the Shanghai Consulate. Mr. Hughes will be instructed to honour your draughts.

  As soon as Admiral Willes can dispense with you, you will make the best of your way back to Peking.

    I am, etc.

Signed,
T.F. Wade

【관련문서】

Admiral willes

Tientsin
22 May 1882

Sir,

    I am happy to be able at last to forward Your Excellency by the hand of Mr. Maude, Second Secretary of Legation, copy of the Chinese draught of the Treaty believed to have been negotiated between Corea and the United States, with an English translation of the text. Mr. Maude carries also a letter addressed by the Grand Secretary Li to Ma Taotai, a very intelligent Chinese, who was sent over at the same time as Commodore Shufeldt's mission. Ma Taotai speaks French well. He has also some acquaintance with English.

    I only received the text of the treaty on the evening of the 19th, and the letter to Ma Taotai only yesterday morning. Hence the delay, which, however, I trust has not seriously inconvenienced Your Excellency.

    Commander Bridger who, on learning from me that I had nothing as yet to send you, had taken his ship down to Taku, was as good as to come up and see me on the 20th, and I have requested him to wait at Chefoo until the arrival of Mr. Maude and, if Your Excellency should have left Chefoo, to carry him over to Corea.

    I have etc,

(Signed) T.F. Wade

P.S. I have this evening written a second letter to Commander Bridger, requesting him to remain in the waters of Corea until you arrive.

T.F. Wade (1882. 5. 22) ➡ D.Spence

Willes 통역 지시

D.Spence
No. 24

Tientsin
22 May 1882

Sir,

You will I trust have received from Mr. Hughes, H.M. Consul at Shanghai, a message transmitted through the senior naval Officer at that port directing you as soon as you could to proceed to Shanghai, leaving the papers of the Ichang Consulate in charge of the Commissioner of Customs.

On your arrival at Shanghai you are to consider yourself at the disposal of Admiral Willes who may possibly require your services in Corea. You have been selected for this service on account of your known ability as an official agent, but also especially because the experience acquired by you during your former visit to Corea cannot fail to be useful.

Admiral Willes will let you know when your services are required. When he has no further occasion for them you will come up to Peking.

I am etc,

Signed,
T. Wade

P.S. It would be well to take a good Chinese clerk with you. He will require high salary, say $50 a month. I will sanction this for two months from the date of his engagement. He will easily return to Shanghai before that term expires.

73

T.F. Wade (1882. 5. 22) ➜ Bridger

Willes에 앞서 조선에 갈 것을 지시

Tientsin
22 May 1882

Sir,

Since I saw you upon the evening of the 20th I have decided to request you, when you have reached Corea, to remain there until the arrival of Admiral Willes. I have telegraphed to the Admiral that you will give Mr. Maude a passage on board the "Sheldrake" and until the Admiral does arrive, I am not sure that Mr. Maude will be able to find a lodging on shore. By letter received from Admiral Willes this morning, I am led to believe that he will meet the squadron at Nagasaki, and will proceed very shortly afterwards to Corea. You will not therefore be delayed long in any case.

Mr. Maude has a letter addressed to a Chinese Mandarin who is on board the "Wei-yuen" Chinese gunboat which should be lying off an island known as Kan-hua, or otherwise as Hu-tao, that is Tiger Island. This is at the mouth of the river called in Chinese Li Ho but by the Coreans …, how by them pronounced I cannot say. In the maps you will find Li Ho written Sa-erl or Sa-eull.

I am &c,

(Signed)   T.F. Wade

T.F. Wade (1882. 5. 23) ➜ G.L.G. Granville

조미 교섭에 관한 李鴻章, 總署 王大臣과 면담 보고

Granville
No. 23

Tientsin
23 May 1882

My Lord,

    The copy of the Treaty for which I was still waiting when I wrote my Despatch No. 22 of the 17th instant, was not forwarded until the evening of the 19th. I called on the Minister Wang on the 18th, after receiving from the Grand Secretary Li, (I find that he is still to be so designated), a promise to send me the Treaty in a day or two. Wang Ta-jen himself did not admit any knowledge of this promise, though he undertook to speak to the Grand Secretary next day. The attitude of both was so little encouraging that I felt bound to inform Admiral Willes of my misgivings. The Admiral had warned me privately that, as his squadron was assembling at Nagasaki, he could wait at Chefoo only a few days.

    My note to him was dispatched on the 19th, but in the afternoon the Grand Secretary sent to say that the Treaty was on its way, and in the evening it arrived. The Minister Wang returned my call upon the 20th and informed me that he had recommended the Grand Secretary to supply me with a letter to Ma Taotai; also that Ma Taotai should be for a time left in Corea. This of course, to watch proceedings in the interest of China and Corea. On the 21st the letter to Ma Taotai was forwarded me. As it was sealed, of course I know nothing of its contents.

    I give these details, for they are illustrative of the difficulty of dealing with officials in this country, even when it might be supposed that their position was eminent enough to secure them against their own fears of accepting responsibility. The Grand Secretary who has gone farther in a forward direction than any man in China, although he knows the fairness of my intentions and positively desires that England should be the first power after America to make a treaty with Corea, for he believes that if England accepts what is accepted by America, all the rest will follow suit, the Grand Secretary Li was nevertheless afraid of being named as the single supporter of a treaty between England and Corea, either by his own countrymen or by foreigners. When he first promised me the Chinese draught, he conjured me not to let M. Von Brandt know that I had got it from him. But the Minister Wang learned from M. Von Brandt that he was already in possession of the text, although he declined to say whence he had obtained it. I think it most likely that he got it from the Grand Secretary Li himself, who cannot possibly love him but is surely in fear of him. As the matter now stands responsibility for anything that has been done will be divided between the two Ministers.

The papers being all now in my hands, I resolved to send Mr. Maude over to Admiral Willes with them by a gun vessel, the "Sheldrake" which was by the Admiral's orders, waiting to take anything I had to send. This I explain in a separate Despatch.

I had much conversation with Wang Tajen regarding opium, as I shall report elsewhere.

I have, &c.

Thomas Francis Wade

T.F. Wade (1882. 5. 23) ➡ G.L.G. Granville

Willes의 芝罘 출항 보고

Granville
No. 24

Tientsin
23 May 1882

My Lord,

In my Despatch No. 16 of the 12th instant, I informed Your Lordship that I had placed Mr. Spence at Admiral Willes' disposal, for the purpose of assisting in the negotiations which the Admiral had been instructed to charge himself with in Corea.

Admiral Willes left Chefoo on the 20th, being unable longer to wait for certain information which I was to have obtained for him; but Her Majesty's gun vessel "Sheldrake" had, by his orders, remained within reach, and the papers I had been anxious to procure being at last complete, I determined to send Mr. Maude forward with them. I inclose copies of my instructions to Mr. Spence and to Mr. Maude, of which I trust Your Lordship will approve.

I add copies of my letters to Lieutenant Bridger commanding the "Sheldrake," and to Admiral Willes.

I have this afternoon received a telegram from Admiral Willes, requesting me to direct the "Sheldrake" to meet him in Imperatrice Gulf. The spot named in my letter to Lieutenant Bridger is that, however, at which the Chinese gun boat, on board of which Ma Taotai is to be found, is lying, and I do not fear any misadventure.

In the treaty signed there will be, of course, many details to be discussed; more especially in matters affecting trade. In a private note to Admiral Willes I have taken on me to suggest the expediency of securing, if possible, an eligible factory site, sufficient for the location of a few houses of business. Mr. Spence's opinion will be valuable on such a subject.

I have, &c.

Thomas Francis Wade

76

T.F. Wade (1882. 5. 27) ➜ G.L.G. Granville

Maude의 조선행 보고

Granville
Confidential 27

Tientsin
May 27 1882

My Lord,

In continuation of my Despatch No. 24 of the 23rd instant, I have the honour to state that Mr. Maude started for Chefoo in a merchant steamer on the morning of the 24th instant. Her Majesty's gunboat "Sheldrake" had left Taku a day on two before. She was to wait there until Mr. Maude's arrival when she would proceed with him to the mouth of the river upon which the capital of Corea stands. It was hoped that Mr. Maude would there find the Chinese gunboat on board of which Ma Taotai had embarked for Corea. The letter to Ma Taotai, I was informed, desired him to remain for some time longer in that country. I have since received a note from Mr. Maude dated the 25th instant, 8 am, informing me that the "Sheldrake" was just getting under way.

It is possible that under these circumstances he may not find Ma Taotai in Corea, for that officer was originally to return here as soon as Commodore Shufeldt had signed his treaty. This, it should be noted, will not be the fault of Mr. Maude, who has not lost a moment since the necessary papers were received here. These, the papers, might easily have been supplied to me a week earlier, and would, in that case, have reached Admiral Willes at Chefoo. He only left that port on the 20th.

I have, &c.

Thomas Francis Wade

T.F. Wade (1882. 5. 27) ➙ G.L.G. Granville

조영조약에 조미조약 원용 건의

Granville
No. 28

Tientsin
May 27 1882

My Lord,

    In a telegram dated the 19th instant, I recommended adoption of the treaty accepted by the United States. The treaty will be found less liberal than the treaties between China and foreign States. I am, nevertheless, an advocate of its acceptance, partly because, with my knowledge of the trouble it has given the Americans to obtain it, I am satisfied that we shall not obtain any terms more advantageous without a resort to action such as there is not a shadow of a pretext to justify; secondly, because provision is made for reasonable modification at the end of five years. It must be remembered how reluctantly the exclusivism of this people has yielded to proposals to which the ultra-conservative majority of the upper class, unless we are misinformed, is still bigotedly opposed; and, unless perhaps in the rates of taxation of imports, which will, I presume, be discussed more in detail when the Tariff is fixed, I can honestly say that I should not have been more exacting than the Americans have shown themselves. I say this without forgetting that the Coreans have been guided mainly, if not entirely, by the Chinese in their negotiations, and that an attempt may one day be made to turn our concessions to the wishes of the Corean Government to account in negotiations between ourselves and the government of China. Thanks to the establishment of missions abroad, the relations of China with foreign Powers have so changed in character in the last few years that I am not afraid of this difficulty. Every day adds to the number of those who perceive that the ancient methods of restrictiveness avail nothing to the safety of advantage or this Empire

    I have, &c.

Thomas Francis Wade

馬建忠(1882. 5. 27/光緒八年四月十一日)

馬建忠・Willes 회담

十一日晨六點鐘 遣人持銜柬至國王與王世子處辭行 國王與王世子亦遣趙秉鎬賫帖來送 無何 金宏集徐相雨諸人先後至館候送 申櫶以老病遣其子來代 九點鐘起程 至漢江渡 時日使花房亦遣隨員持刺追送 十二點鐘至梧里洞 食 三點鐘至富平 易轎而馬 疾馳三十里 四點一刻 抵濟物浦 丁軍門躍馬先至 知英國兵舶二艘 一名味齊朗至自長崎 十二點鐘下椗 一名賽得落 至自津門 一點二刻下椗 尋登舟 而英國駐京參贊懋德偵余歸 先以一書請見 未幾 卽攜傅相函至 叩余行期 答以遲明卽發 則固留 余謂俟讀傅相函後 再定行止 懋德辭去 讀悉書意 旋至味齊朗兵舶答拜懋德 兼晤其議約使臣水師提督韋力士 告以暫緩起程 韋使略詢薛斐爾先後議約情事 與所開口岸 小坐回舟 七點鐘伴接官趙準永登舶送行 留之晩膳 本傅相意作書 致申金二使 俾轉達國王 交準永令星夜賫去

丁汝昌, 馬建忠(1882. 5. 27/光緒八年四月十一日) ➡ 申櫶, 金弘集

영국과 조약 체결 권고

丁·馬兩使抵大·副官書
威堂·道國仁兄大人執事

敬啓者 早間登程後 於五點種抵舟 適英國水師提督韋力士 乘兵艦來此 携有傳相及總理衙門致僕函件 其中 頃駐英國使臣威妥瑪來悟云 其國現派韋提督赴朝鮮議約 如能在美國之後 第二次立議 不再讓他國爭先 則諸事或可俯就 刻下朝鮮已與日美通商 則諸國援例而來 勢難閉關相絶 英國爲歐州大邦 尤非美比 此次欲約事速成 無可稍從遷就 朝鮮若乘此機會 從速與議 或可仍照美約定儗 則微特隨後德法諸國相繼前來 有英美兩國成議在先 不至過爲要挾 卽日人所議稅則等項 亦可屈於兩大國公議 不至終始執拗 此誠朝鮮外交最要機會也 已令金允植由陸路回國報知 不卜能趕及否 玆韋使東來 仍請執事代達朝鮮政府 囑其速與定議 毋失事機等語 用特飛書佈達 希卽轉奏貴國王 於一二日內 妥速計議 以毋負我中堂總署諸王公維持籌畫之至意 僕本儗明晨起碇 刻因英使初來 不得不少作周旋 然至遲於三四日後 卽當鼓輪四渡也 手此飛佈 敬頌均祺

　　　十一日燈下 愚弟 馬建忠 頓首
　　　　丁禹翁 統此請安 幷道謝悃

統理機務衙門(1882. 5. 28/高宗十九年四月十二日)

趙寧夏・金弘集 협상 전권 부여

命經理事趙寧夏等除下直下送于仁川
統理機務衙門啓言卽見京畿監司金輔鉉狀啓謄報則英國船兩隻到月尾島後洋云而際又見淸使抵大副官書7辭則英國使臣自中國摠理衙門帶書信專來商辦云矣凡異船之來泊也遣譯問情自是例也而上國使臣之送書旣若是的據經理事趙寧夏金弘集以全權差下副主事徐相雨仍差從事官經理事趙準永仍差伴接官並使之明日內除下直請下送于仁川地允之

馬建忠(1882. 5. 29/光緒八年四月十三日)

馬建忠·韓文奎·高永周 회담

十三日夜九點鐘威遠舟次與韓文奎高永周筆談

韓高曰　英使現有國書持來耶　有副本否　若有國書持來　則答國書當與美使時
　　　　一例耶　約條旣無異同於美使時云　則照會文字又當有之耶　大副官全
　　　　權諭旨亦如前一例耶
忠曰　　君等此來　是國王之意否
韓高曰　果然奉命而來　謹此相問
忠曰　　所問各節亦出於國王之意否
韓高曰　逐條奉命也
忠曰　　國王有意與英國作速成約否
韓高曰　欲速成約
忠曰　　英使持有全權電報字據　國書尙未遞至　但旣有全權　便可立約　英使旣
　　　　無國書　無需答書　至照會文字　當在議約之先　一如與美國者　所以正外
　　　　交之名　英使已屢言之　而中堂來諭　亦曾及此　惟約係與美約有無異同
　　　　則在貴國王遣員議約之遲速耳　大副官全權諭旨一如前例
韓高曰　約條異同　遣員議約時　可以知之乎
忠曰　　大約可以相同　諸君可卽回王京否
韓高曰　還仁川後　卽欲專撥上達
忠曰　　照會一事　祈卽轉告繕就送至　以便與英使計議
韓高曰　當如敎速達矣　抵大副官書則有曰　約稿視前約一字不錯矣　今承大約
　　　　相同之敎　不無些兜致訝也
忠曰　　前致申金二公函內云　若貴國王作速派員議約　約款或可相同　與今玆
　　　　所云大約相同　並無二致　新派大副官已至仁川否也
韓高曰　想已抵府也　日使聞此消息　似有急來干預之慮　必於明日內與英使相
　　　　接　仍行議定條約　惟置畫鈴一事　更待幾日了勘恐妥
忠曰　　英使來此　携有傳相之函　且再三託僕爲之介紹　可致意大副官　明日來
　　　　舟一見　照會作速寄至　以便商議　日使若來　僕當令其不得攪越
韓高曰　卑職等歸　卽轉達朝廷　當以照會文字全權諭旨斯速送來之意爲最要耶

忠曰　然 再英國兵船來此 不必饋送禮物 彼來有求於貴國 若彼以禮物來饋
　　　則可還答 否則 旣費公帑 亦且貽笑外人 甚無謂也 惟彼等需日用食物
　　　如牛豕雞鴨菜之類 可派人送至該舟 取其價値

韓高曰 禮物之不繁 所敎非不穩當 而已行於美船 則今不可缺之 至於船丁一
　　　犒 係是勞問之意 何可廢之乎 日用食物旣已聞命 固當不有遲滯 但本
　　　地方貧薄 無產畜 就細微之需 必求於京城 故每致汗漫也 望恕諒亦以
　　　此言及於英船恐好也

忠曰　禮物犒賞乃出自貴國王之惠 不送英船 英人必不見怪 大副官明日可
　　　登舟一談否

韓高曰 蕃以至則朝以登舟

高宗(1882. 5. 30/高宗十九年四月十四日) ➡ Queen Victoria

속방조회문(屬邦照會文)

大朝鮮國大君主 爲照會事 窃照朝鮮素爲中國屬邦 而內治外交向來均由大朝鮮國大君主自主 今大朝鮮·大英國彼此立約 俱屬平行相待 大朝鮮國大君主明允 將約內各款必按自主公例認眞照辦 至大朝鮮國爲中國屬邦 其一切分內應行各節 均與大英國毫無干涉 除派員議立條約外 相應先行聲明 爲此備文照會 請煩大英國大君主查照辦理 須至照會者
右照會
大英國大君主
大朝鮮開國四百九十一年卽中國光緖八年四月十四日

83

馬建忠(1882. 5. 30/光緒八年四月十四日)

馬建忠·趙寧夏 회담

十四日文一品兵曹尙書趙寧夏偕金宏集來舟筆談

趙曰 敝邦幸蒙 皇上字小之德 中堂大人原眷 與兩位大人襄助之順成立約 不勝萬幸 國王感荷不已

忠曰 貴國事大 素稱恭順 故凡有裨於貴國 我 中堂無不奏明皇上 設法保護 至僕等來此 只守成命 何力之有焉

趙曰 幸於兩大人在敝邦之時 英舶又至 多費兩大人尊神 實用歉悚 於敝邦事情 尤屬萬幸 國王亦爲感荷 使僕等轉致

忠曰 英舶至此 適逢其會 且携有傳相來函 飭僕等爲之介紹 僕等當少俟約事告蒇 方可西歸 此亦義不容辭耳

趙曰 僕等辭陛時 國王有敎 今此英船之來 適在上國船未擧椗之前 幸甚幸甚 前頭事機亦未可預算 汝等須備懇此由於大人 望須久留敝邦 期賴終始之襄助 意○○有敎 望乞垂諒焉

忠曰 貴國王旣有意挽留 僕等應遵明諭 惟僕等行止非可自專 務祈貴國王將挽留之意 否行北洋大臣轉奏 或自行奏明方可

趙曰 謹當具由馳奏 望須貴艦明晨差遲椗

忠曰 前此兩日內 迭晤英使與其參贊 彼意欲將美約署爲增減 僕堅待不得一字更易 奈彼等尙有三事欲特爲聲明 一則爲所開口岸 因美約未曾提明所開何口 須由執事備一照會 內言所開口岸卽釜山元山仁川三口 但英使謂仁川一口水淺 上下貨物不便 須在京畿道忠淸道海濱另指一口 以換仁川之口 二則貴國三面濱海 島嶼林立 並無精細海圖 須遣兵舶到處測量 並非另行貿易 一如貴國與日本約款內所載 三則英人來此在美國之後 於心怏怏 願於畫押後進見國王 庶足以驕美使 此三事在諸君裁度之耳

趙曰 另指一口 萬難議擧 隨處測量 已有日人之事 進京謁見國王 非僕等所敢擅對

忠曰 另指一口 非於三口外多開一口 彼以仁川一口不便上下貨物故欲另換他

　　　　口耳至進京謁見之說 乃彼之私意 以爲英人苟能進謁國王 在他人之先
　　　　較爲光寵耳
趙曰 仁川與日人爭辨五六年而許之 今若另指一口 則日人之開仁港必無遷動
　　　　此非多開一口耶 謁見一款 我國不見外人 恐致驚疑 英人若以後來欲勝
　　　　於他人 則日後別國若又來欲更勝於人 則將何以應之乎 垂諒焉
忠曰 此二節出自英使托僕代達 故敢轉告 少頃往拜英使 執事當面與之言明
趙曰 惟在大人居間主持 善爲說辭 令彼使開晤 諒我事情 幸勿以此相煩爲幸
忠曰 僕自當盡力爲之
趙曰 感謝感謝
忠曰 執事全權事據可不必携去 晤時第言貴國王遣執事來 矢守美約 一字不
　　　　敢僭易 況貴國臣民以初次通商 未識外交之道 全恃中堂主持 若於中堂
　　　　所議約稿有所增損 甚難以服臣民之心 如是立論 英使想不至始終執拗
　　　　也
趙曰 荷此指敎 萬萬感銘 不知何以仰謝垂眷

午後往拜韋力士趙寧夏筆談
忠曰 英使云遣兵舶測量一節 若由執事自行備文於約外聲明 則事易就緒矣
趙報(Sic.) 政府圖所以方便約事歸正 千萬千萬 照會今明間來到矣 鈐印早爲
　　　　完妥望乞
忠曰 英使現俟彼繙譯官至到時 卽可定日畫押 大約不出四五日
趙曰 若遲延四五日 而日使突至 有碍約事 豈非可慮
忠曰 日使雖來無妨 進京謁見之說 英使務乞執事代達爲幸
趙曰 當轉達 而惟在處分之如何耳
忠曰 英使云除備文聲明兵舶測量之事 彼已明允悉照美約畫押
趙曰 莫非大人紹介主持之力 感銘 感銘

T.F. Wade (1882. 6. 2) ➡ G.L.G. Granville

Dillon 영사 내방과 조불조약에 관한 의견 보고

Lord Granville
Confidential 31

Tientsin
2 June 1882

My Lord,

    I sent off yesterday a series of Despatches which will put Your Lordship in possession of the history of the Corean treaty, so far as the United States are concerned, and of my own action here, in furtherance of the instructions received by Admiral Willes.

    My aid has since been invoked in another quarter. On the 25th or 26th May, Monsieur Dillon, the French Consul here who had been on a visit to Peking, returned with a message from his Minister, Monsieur Bouree, to the effect that, as regarded Corea, the French Government wished him to do whatever I might be doing; not to precede me, but to follow close. He accordingly begged for information. I gave him an outline of what I had been about, and, at the instance of Monsieur Dillon, I endeavoured to procure for him copy of the Chinese text of the Treaty and a letter to Ma Taotai, the Chinese Agent now in Corea; the same papers, in short, as I had been enabled to obtain for Admiral Willes.

    The Grand Secretary Li, to who I applied, through an Agent in his confidence, for these papers, replied after a day's delay, that he had handed over all his archives to his acting successor, the Governor General Chang Shu-sheng. The latter had sent me his card by a subordinate, with an expression of regret that he was as yet too busy to call on me. Accordingly, on the following day, 29th May, I called upon His Excellency.

    When I told him of what had passed between Li Chung-tang and myself the day before, he professed ignorance of the whole question. He had not had time to read half the papers handed over to him. However, after an hour's talk, during which he certainly showed no disposition to do what I asked, he promised either to let me have a letter for Ma Taotai when he came to return my visit next day, or if not then, perhaps in a day or two.

His Excellency, I knew, was coming to the settlement next day, 30th, to take leave of the Grand Secretary Li on board the steamer which was to convey the latter South. He came to me at 4 o'clock, and almost at once, of his own accord, opened the question. He had consulted Li Chung-tang, he said, on the subject of a letter to Ma, and the Chung-tang had pointed out a difficulty in the case of the French, which did not exist in the case of any other power. The only interest of the French was the Romish Missionary interest. The Coreans were hostile to Romish missionaries. Not a year passed without some trouble in connection with them; murders even not being uncommon. Mr. Holcombe, the American Charge d'Affaires, had been pressed to allow the insertion of an Article, prohibiting missionary teaching. To this he had replied that his Government could not in decency accede; so it was eventually agreed that nothing should be said about missionaries one way or the other. In answer to some observations of mine regarding the invidiousness of obliging France to make a different treaty from those of other powers, Chang ta-jen replied that that was not his desire; but that the relation of France to the missionary question being peculiar, he wished to have a clear understanding arrived at beforehand between France and Corea. He could hardly adopt my suggestion that, in that case, the French had best address themselves direct to Corea. Monsieur Bouree had better discuss the matter either with the Tsung-li Yamen at Peking, or if he could make it convenient to come to Tientsin, with Chang ta-jen himself.

All this was urged with sufficient politeness. On my side it was argued that, France being prepared to sign exactly the same treaty as England and the United States, if a treaty were refused her, she could hardly fail to feel offended both with China and Corea. It would be vain to expect France to declare in a treaty that she would not allow missionaries to preach Christianity. No western power, indeed, would make such a declaration. The simplest solution, beyond a doubt, would be to follow the course adopted by Mr. Holcombe in his draught treaty, namely, to leave the question untouched. This would enable France at once to conclude a treaty. I remarked, farther, that France was not the only country whose missionaries were of the Church of Rome. There were at this moment in China, British, German, Dutch, Belgian and Spanish missionaries of the same persuasion. "Yes," said Chang ta-jen with a laugh, "but you do not support your missionaries to the same extent as the French."

I forgot at the time that, as Governor General of the Two Kuang Provinces, Chang ta-jen has had to take part in a very angry discussion regarding a Romish missionary establishment in Kuangsi. If the French version of the Affair be correct, the vicaire apostolique concerned had accepted a compromise proposed by the Chinese Authorities themselves, but from the terms of which they subsequently receded. This alas! Is too possible.

To return as soon as Chang ta-jen was gone, I drew up a memorandum of what had passed between us. This I read to Monsieur Dillon. I may here state that I have known him ever since he arrived in Peking as a student twenty years ago, and that I have the highest opinion of his character. He is an exceedingly devout Catholic, but I have none the less heard him complained of indirectly for his insufficient support of certain missionary reclamations. I am satisfied that Monsieur Dillon would not support any claim that he thought not justified by the treaty. On the other hand, being the devout man that he is, he would be prepared, I feel sure, to go all lengths in advancing whatever he conceived to be the interest of his church.

He was naturally much shocked at learning the grounds of the Governor General's reluctance to put him at once in the way of carrying out his Minister's instructions, and begged me to suppress my memorandum. This, I pointed out to him, would be useless, as Chang ta-jen had spoken in the presence of three persons, two of whom were certain to repeat what they had heard. He left me to say goodbye to Li Chung-tang. I should mention that in reply to a question put to him, a month or two ago, at Shanghai, by a Romish missionary, Commodore Shufeldt is reported to have said that he purposed securing religious tolerance in Corea. Monsieur Dillon had counted upon this.

On the other part, to anticipate a little, he has since been informed, he says, by Chang Tajen, that Mr. Holcombe, when he agreed to leave out of his draught all reference to religious propagandism, did, under pressure from Li Chung-tang, verbally engage, in some sort, to prevent American missionaries from entering the country. I am satisfied that Mr. Holcombe, who himself commenced his career in China as a missionary, could never have given any promise of the kind.

I went later to take leave of Li Chung tang. I found Chang ta-jen seated with him. Monsieur Dillon, whom I met on my way to the ship, told me that he had found means to say a word regarding Corea, and that he thought that the two great men would yield if I supported him.

My intention had been not to speak of business, but Their Excellencies both began at once, and we had a warm, though very good-humoured, discussion for the best part of an hour, at the end of which an interpreter was sent for and was all but instructed to write the letter to Ma Taotai that I required.

I reckoned without my host, and Monsieur Dillon, who had received orders from his Minister to start at once with the papers he did not doubt the Chinese would supply him with, now proposed that he himself should be considered merely as a delegate of his Minister, sent to inform the Coreans of the desire of France to enter into friendly relations with Corea, and of the intention of the French Government shortly to make a treaty. Pending negotiation of this, France was prepared to accept for French citizens precisely the same conditions as the treaties of America and England might impose on their nationals.

I wrote this on the 31st, through a native interpreter, to Chang ta-jen, insisting much on the inutility of attempting to isolate France in the matter, and the danger of such a course. His answer was discouraging. Remarks, conveyed to me through two different channels, were to the effect that Monsieur Dillon wanted something more than I had put forward. On the first instant, however, Chang ta-jen did send me a letter addressed to Ma Taotai, which I was requested to hand to Monsieur Dillon.

Monsieur Dillon now appeared to fear that this letter, which of course was sealed, might contain instructions unfavourable to his mission, and he hesitated as to whether he should proceed. I admitted as a certainty that the letter would review the situation from the standpoint of the Chinese. The interpreter who brought it could tell me no more than that Ma Taotai had been enjoined to lend a helping hand. I thought that, if after pressing so eagerly for the letter, Monsieur Dillon were now to decline to make use of it, the Chinese would simply be confirmed in the suspicion already attributed to them, that the French had some policy in Corea not yet sufficiently declared. Monsieur Dillon's great fear was not only that the anti-missionary question, to him personally most offensive, might be raised; I felt sure, of course, that it would be; but that the form of reference to it might be affronting to his Government. I recommended him to talk the matter well out with Ma Taotai, himself a Roman Catholic, though not, I fancy, one of the strictest, and to impress on him the expediency if formulation of objections on the part of Corea proved unavoidable, of so turning the phrase as to make it diplomatically acceptable. If from Ma Taotai he learned that there was more difficulty ahead than he had expected, the check would not be as serious as if a higher officer of his Government had been concerned: the gunboat that was to carry him was really under orders for Nagasaki, there to meet the French Admiral Meyer. Leaving his letter with Ma Taotai, if the latter could do nothing, he might inform him that he would accompany the gunboat to Nagasaki, and explain the case to Admiral Meyer. Monsieur Dillon had assured me most positively that his Admiral, to whom there appears to have been some idea originally of entrusting negotiations, would not, in any case, take more with him than a single vessel to Corea. Otherwise I should certainly not have given this counsel. But I must add that communication with Admiral Meyer was not to be avoided; the French gunboat, as I have stated, being under orders for Japan. Monsieur Dillon, indeed, left this in doubt whether the Commandant would be persuaded to regard the proposed visit to Corea, en route, as within his instructions.

The "Lutin" had already dropped down to the mouth of the river on the 31st. Monsieur Dillon finally determined to join her, and as soon as he left me, rode down to Taku for the purpose.

Your Lordship may reasonably inquire why I took all this trouble, and why I have reported it with so much minuteness. To answer the last question first, I think it not improbable, I regret to say, that we have not heard the last of this matter, and I think it right that Your Lordship should be aware how far I have made myself responsible for what may happen. I took the trouble, not only in recognition of a general obligation to render good offices, but in the hope of averting a complication that would, I think, be serious.

With a people so exclusive as the Coreans, I have been on the side of extreme moderation in this first beginning of intercourse with them. It is not unlikely that, in accepting so unambitious a treaty as Commodore Shufeldt's, we may be thought to have exceeded in abnegation. Looking to the disastrous results of the French expedition in 1866, and of the American expedition in 1872, when in effect, after a somewhat pretentious demonstration, two great powers were obliged to retire, re infecta, before a fourth-class state's resistance, I can imagine nothing more unfortunate than a renewed attempt to force upon these ignorant semi-savages, by violence, conditions of intercourse to which they are opposed. I am actuated, I need hardly affirm, by no feeling of hostility to the Romish missionary, in Corea or elsewhere. The cause of Romish missions, besides, appears to me to be receiving less political support from France at this moment than at any time since 1860; but there is not field of mission enterprise with a more tragical history, and I should be relieved if I could think any reliance were to be placed on the discretion of the adventurous Missions Etrangeres, the particular body to whom the Chistianisation of Corea belongs. No power can stay them but the Pope, and they are nationally French to a man. Herein, of course, is a special danger; but the attempt to exclude them would, I fear, result in even greater danger; for, as I have tried to make the Chinese here understand there are thousands of Frenchmen who, although indifferent to the cause of missions as a religious cause, would be perfectly ready to take up arms if they are thought their flag insulted. And this I conceived would be the natural impression of a Frenchman, on hearing that while China declined to help France as she had helped America and England, Corea refused to receive France as she had received the other two powers. Without a commencement of relations, France would be free, of course, to take what line she pleased, and unless I am greatly mistaken, nothing would better please some of those who are at this moment very loftily condemning the deplorable proceedings of France at Tonquin, than to see China entangled in a misunderstanding which after the part she has taken as the adviser of her vassal, she might be considered responsible for not preventing. In a word, if Corea were to be struck by France, I should expect trouble, on one side or the other from Russia, Japan, and as she is at present represented, from Germany.

I have chose, therefore, rather to assist France in establishing relations with Corea, than to encourage Corea, by my silence, to persist in a policy of exclusion which could not fail to be irritating to France.

I have, &c.

Thomas Francis Wade

85

T.F. Wade (1882. 6. 3) ➡ G.L.G. Granville (1882. 7. 22)

Hughes 영사의 Shufeldt 면담 보고

Sir T. Wade to Earl Granville.—(Received July 22)

(No. 33)
Confidential

My Lord,　　　　　　　　　　　　　　　　　　　　　　*Tien-tsin, June* 3, 1882

　　I HAVE the honour to forward in original a despatch marked Confidential, which I received last evening from Mr. Hughes, Her Britannic Majesty's Consul at Shanghae. I have of course approved his action.

　　Your Lordship will observe what Commodore Shufeldt said to Mr. Hughes on the subject of Japanese intervention. This more or less confirms what Mr. Holcombe said to me regarding the desire of the Japanese to associate themselves with the negotiations, and the objection of both China and Corea to Japanese mediation.

　　I am sorry to learn that Mr. Spence has not yet reached Shanghae. It was originally understood that we were not to approach Corea until towards the end of June. Mr. Holcombe did not expect Commodore Shufeldt's negotiations to be terminated sooner, he told me, and he begged me, it will be remembered, to prevent as far as in me lay, any proceeding on our side that might interfere with the Commodore. Admiral Willes, to whom I communicated this, was perfectly prepared to spend the month of June up the Gulf of Tartary. But on learning from the Admiral, on the 20th May, that, according to a member of Commodore Shufeldt's family who was staying at Chefoo, the Commodore might be expected almost immediately at Chefoo, I urged him to proceed at once to Corea. This he did as I have reported, upon the 25th May. A telegram had been sent to Mr. Hughes at my suggestion, on the 14th, to hurry down Mr. Spence from Ichang, of which port he is in acting charge. Mr. Spence is not a likely man to lose time in such a case, but communication with Ichang is not so frequent as with the ports lower down the river.

　　　　　　　　　　　　　　　　　　　　　　　　　　　　　　　　I have, &c.

(Signed) THOMAS FRANCIS WADE

P.S.—In my Report of what I tried to effect for my French colleague, I have omitted to state that when discussing the matter with their Excellencies Chang and Li, the latter observed that M. Bourée would be able to do nothing with the Tsung-li Yamên, that the Yamên is not going to class Corea among the foreign Powers with which it has to deal on a footing of equality.

T. F. W.

Inclosure

Consul Hughes to Sir T. Wade.

(Confidential)

Sir, *Shanghae, May* 29, 1882

I HAD an interview with Commodore Shufeldt this morning, and congratulated him upon the conclusion of a Treaty with Corea. The Commodore did not feel himself at liberty to give me any details respecting the provisions of the new Treaty. He mentioned, however, that although he found the Corean Government very anxious to conclude a Treaty, their Representatives discussed the terms which had been partly agreed upon at Tien-tsin, and modified them to some extent. The Treaty was signed, as I understand, at a place between the capital and the port nearest to it. It is a Treaty of Amity and Commerce, and contains provisions similar to those which exist in American Treaties with China. Corea is treated as an independent kingdom, and a United States' Minister is to reside at the capital. The three ports to be opened are, I believe, the same as those at which the Japanese are entitled to trade.

The Commodore thinks that no one will succeed in making a Treaty with Corea, excepting with Chinese or Japanese help. The Japanese Envoy in Corea was dismayed at the action of Commodore Shufeldt in treating without Japanese intervention. He had armed himself with a letter of recommendation to Commodore Shufeldt from the United States' Minister in Japan.

The German Commodore is to leave for the Corean coast on Thursday next.

　　I reported by telegraph, in cypher, to Lord Granville the conclusion of the Treaty, and trust you will approve of my having done so. I sent transcript of the message to you in a telegram, copy of which I have the honour to inclose.

I have, &c.

(Signed)　　P.J. HUGHES

86

馬建忠(1882. 6. 5 이전) ➡ 李鴻章

조영조약안 결정 경위 보고

照錄馬道建忠稟 少荃中堂函 敬稟者 竊忠於本月初四日肅泐寸稟 並日記筆談照會稿各件 交鎭海兵船賚送回津 諒卑上○ 鈞鑑矣 旋於初六日美高兩國使臣 在近岸濟物浦支立帳房 會集畫押 當將朝鮮國王照會與國書條約並交美使 美使卽於初八日起椗歸國 忠亦於是日偕丁提督同赴漢城 初十日見朝鮮國王於便殿 行賓主禮 十一日申刻回舟 則英國使臣韋力士已乘兵舶於是午駛至漢江口 傍我舟下椗 忠登舟後 韋使尋遣其參贊懋德來詢行期 告以明日起椗 遂乃殷殷挽留 囑爲介紹 並出憲臺鈞札 莊誦之餘 祇領壹是 卽夕本書中大意作函飛佈朝鮮申金二使 令其轉達國王妥速計議 嗣復與韋使論及約稿第一條 韋使謂威使在津與中堂言明一切條約 均照美國辦理 至朝鮮爲中國屬邦素奉中國爲主 美國如何辦理 英國亦應照辦 若必列入約內 則未奉本國電復 斷難擅自允行 忠因思條約僅兩國使臣所擬 照會則由朝鮮國王向英國君主自行聲明 似樹義尤覺正大 且此條美國旣不允列入約內 使英國允之 不特於平行有碍 亦且將貽笑墨洲 其意斷難聽從 計不如仍依美國成例 令朝鮮國王於議約前 先備照會聲明 而朝鮮國王亦甚欲約事速成 卽於十三日派兵曹尙書趙寗夏爲大官 經理機務事金宏集爲副官 來與英使會議 今午登舟來謁 遂與同赴英舶 與韋使相見 韋使初膺使命 諸務未諳 狐疑特甚 云美約略擧大網 似涉掛漏 擬從中添註數條 以期周密 忠告以此係初次立約 僅能略擧大網 俟五年後彼此交誼審熟 乃可商酌損益 向來各國立約均係如此 因爲之反復開陳 其參贊懋德亦明決善斷 復從旁代爲剖悉 於是韋使乃無異言 大約一切可照美約定擬 惟須俟英國繙譯官到來 便可擇期畫押 玆因 憲旌卽發 隨後上稟 必須多費時日 或致重勞 鈞注 用特將英高議約情形先行具稟 附以筆談一冊 令揚威快船賚至烟台途次探投 並令就便添備火食 日記則以總促不及備錄 俟隨後續呈 專肅具稟 恭叩崇祺 伏乞 垂鑑 職道馬建忠 謹稟

87

G.O. Willes ➡ 趙寧夏, 金弘集(1882. 6. 5/高宗十九年四月二十日)

조영조약 외 추가 3개조의 성명을 요구하는 조회

관련문서 조선측 회신(1882. 6. 6)

大英國特派全權大臣水師提督統領韋 爲照會事 照得 大朝鮮國·大英國業經立俱通商條約 其有約內未及詳載者三節 合於約外另俱照會聲明

一 英國商民通商口岸 約內雖未言明 自應遵照日本現開元山 釜山 仁川三口辦理
一 按照公法 各國兵舶皆准駛進與國各口 玆 大朝鮮國·大英國自簽約之日 英國兵舶 於朝鮮無論何口均可駛入 凡買取食物淡水 或需修船等事 悉聽其便
一 朝鮮海濱至今未經詳細測量 駕駛極爲危險 應聽英國兵舶 將朝鮮海岸所有島嶼礁石水線 審其位置 測其深淺 用繪海圖 俾航海者得以穩渡

以上三條 均係 大朝鮮國·大英國議明 於約外聲明 爲此 本大臣備文照會 請煩查照施行 須至照會者
右照會
大朝鮮國議約全權大臣 趙·金

【관련문서】

答照會交鈐時
大朝鮮國議約全權 大官趙·副官金照覆事 本月二十日 接准貴大臣照會內開 約內未及詳載 另行聲明三節等因 准此本大官等 查各節 旣係約內 未及詳載之款 自應按照公法辦理 其第二第三節 應由朝鮮政府 轉飭沿海地方官 於貴國兵舶進口 妥爲照料 惟朝鮮民人 向未習與他國往來 誠恐曷涉驚疑 應請貴大臣 嗣後於爲兵舶進口時 務飭兵弁 格外持平 俾得互相體諒 不致意外議生事端 實爲公便 相應先行聲明 爲此備文照覆 請煩貴大臣 查照辦理 須至照會者

右照會 大英國議約全權大臣韋

大朝鮮國開國四百九十一年 卽中國光緖八年四月二十一日

88

G.O. Willes (1882. 6. 9) → Admiralty

조영수호통상조약 체결 보고

Reporting Signature of Treaty between Great Britain and Corea.

(ADM 125/142/5)

"Vigilant" at Nagasaki
9th June, 1882

Sir,

    I have the honour to report, for the information of the Lords Commissioners of the Admiralty, the steps which I have taken to carry out the orders conveyed to me by telegraph on the 15th April, authorizing me to negotiate with the Corean authorities to secure advantages by Treaty.

    2. As I have already reported, I at once visited Tientsin to confer with Her Majesty's Minister at Pekin, and succeeded after much delay, consequent on the Viceroy of Chibli, the Grand Secretary, Li Hung Chang, being retired in mourning, in obtaining from the latter a copy of the American Treaty and a letter of introduction to the Corean Authorities.

    3. I had ascertained that there was no intention on the part of the American Admiral to make any demonstration of force during Commodore Shufeldt's negotiations, and was assured by Sir Thomas Wade, who understands the native character that there would be more prospect of marking terms with the Coreans were I to follow his example. I therefore determined to proceed alone in the "Vigilant" to the Port of Jin Chuen, which lies in the Salee River, within easy reach of the capital of Corea.

    4. I arrived on the 27th May, and found that Commodore Shufeldt had already negotiated a Treaty and sailed in the "Sawtara" for Shanghai.

    There were two Chinese men-of-war, and one Japanese, at the anchorage. One of the Chinese vessels bore the flag of Admiral Ting, and had also on board a Chinese Mandarin named Ma Taotai, who had been sent by Li Hung Chang to assist the American Commodore's negotiations. In fact, I am told on good authority that the American Treaty with the Coreans had been prepared under the auspices of Li Hung Chang, and that a Corean Envoy at Tientsin had so far approved it as to leave nothing but the signature to be obtained in Corea.

The Japanese man-of-war was in attendance on the Japanese Minister Resident at Seoul, who is in vain endeavouring to negotiate a Treaty on better terms than exist at present between the two countries. He may succeed, in which case the benefits will accrue to England.

5. Ma Taotai was absent at the capital, Seoul on the day of my arrival at Jin Chuen, but he returned on the following day and, though he had intended to sail at once for China, he considerately consented to remain at the anchorage and introduce me to the Corean Officials.

6. I informed the Corean Authorities at Seoul of the object of my mission, and His Majesty the King at once graciously sent two Members of His Council, the one being his own brother-in-law, as Plenipotentiaries to meet me.

7. Our first meeting took place on board Her Majesty's Ship "Vigilant" on the 30th May, when the Plenipotentiaries informed me that they had received authority from the King to conclude with me a Treaty similar to that made with Commodore Shufeldt. We discussed its various clauses, and, though I found their Excellencies very conciliatory, they were evidently determined to abide by their instructions to accept no other conditions.

They were willing, however, to admit a protocol naming the open ports, giving immediate permission for Her Majesty's ships to pay friendly visits to any port in Corea, with freedom to survey the coast line forthwith.

8. I learnt at Tientsin that the first article of the American Treaty admitted the suzerainty of China over the Corea, but autonomy in her domestic and foreign relations.

The questions was not, however, raised in our discussion, but after the signing of the Treaty on the 6th instant the Plenipotentiaries presented me with a letter addressed to Her Majesty the Queen by the King of Chosen (Corea) acknowledging the suzerainty of China. His Majesty, I was told, had forwarded a similar letter to the President of the United States, and I saw no harm in receiving the document for transmission to Her Majesty.

I observe that in the Treaty between Corea and Japan, dated 26th February, 1876, Corea is spoken of as an independent State.

9. It is needless for me here to discuss at length the different articles of the Treaty now made. Each carries on its face its own interpretation; but there are one or two points which call for remark.

10. As regards the Treaty Ports, which are Yen San (or Port Lazareff), Fusan and Jin Chuen, I fear that the latter will not be likely to become a port of trade for large vessels, from the shallowness of the water at low tide, the great rise and fall (about 30 feet) and extensive mud banks: but it is of importance as being the nearest approach to the capital, 25 miles by land and 60 miles by a river, which is navigable by boats only, for 12 miles below the capital. I have reason to believe that the southern part of the Corea is more fertile, and I can apprehend no difficulty in getting a suitable Treaty Port opened there, should one be found to exist, after the survey which I have at once put in operation.

11. I hope that I have only anticipated the wishes of Her Majesty's Government in accepting the clause which forbids the importation of opium into Corea. It is not grown in the country, and the use of the drug is a vice which the Coreans have not yet learnt.

12. As Seoul, the capital, is reported to have a very large population, it seemed but reasonable to consent to the prohibition of [the export of] rice and breadstuffs at Jin Chuen; for the country in the neighbourhood, though apparently fertile, seemed only partly cultivated, and a bad impression might be caused if the first intercourse with foreigners should lead to want or scarcity.

13. No importance need to be attached to the clause forbidding the export of "red ginseng." As their lordships are no doubt aware, it is the root of a species of Panax (belonging to the ivy tribe of plants) which is believed by the Coreans and Chinese to possess great medicinal virtues, but which is of no particular use to any other people.

14. The Americans gave the Coreans a high tariff in their Treaty.

After ineffectually combating the point, I was content to accept the same terms, remembering that the tariffs fixed are the maxima, and little doubting that after some friendly intercourse and the establishment of diplomatic relations, a conciliatory minister at Seoul will be able to arrange matters by a satisfactory agreement; the most favoured nation clause will also give us the benefit of any improved succeeding Treaty or Agreement with any other Power.

15. Having arranged all preliminaries with the Envoys, I was invited to land at Jin Chuen to conclude the Treaty. I accordingly, on the 6th June, met the Plenipotentiaries in a tent on a hill-side some distance from the beach. I was accompanied by my staff and by the officers of ships present, H.M. ships "Flying Fish" and "Shelrake" having arrived during negotiations.

The tent was surrounded by a cordon of good-looking, well-built soldiers, unarmed, and every effort seemed to have been made by this simple people to give befitting dignity to the ceremony. The Plenipotentiaries received me with much courtesy, and, after a short discussion, the Treaty was signed by myself on behalf of Her Majesty's Government, and by the two Plenipotentiaries on behalf of the King of Corea.

I then expressed to their Excellencies that I hoped that this Treaty would be the commencement of a long and cordial friendship between the two countries, a desire which they heartily reciprocated on the part of their King.

16. It may here be well to advert briefly to the condition of public feeling in the Corea.

The Government is vested in the King as an absolute despotic monarch. He calls to his assistance a board of Councillors. At the present moment there are two parties in the State, of almost equal strength; the one is progressist, headed by the King, and ready and anxious to admit foreign intercourse; the other, entirely opposed to any such policy.

The King appears determined to open Corea to strangers, in spite of the opposite party. He has now done so by these Treaties with America and England, which will probably be followed by similar conventions with other Powers, all of which will give general moral strength to the Kings' Government, and materially assist friendly intercourse with the people.

17. I fear it may be considered that the Treaty now made is somewhat bald in its provisions, and that better terms would have been more satisfactory. I have felt this, but have at the same time borne in mind that the first desideratum was to gain a footing in the country; and, unable by any means to obtain wider concessions than the United States, except those which are granted by the Protocol, I deemed it wise to accept them, and at the same time obtain the confidence and secure the friendship of a People who, since these seas have been navigated by Europeans, have never hitherto willingly received them into their country.

18. I do not, however, consider that in the immediate future any great commercial advantages will arise—at least, not until the country is opened up, and its resources discovered and developed.

But its being opened to foreigners will have considerable political significance, and I have no doubt that the King (urged by the Chinese) has been originally induced to take his present line of action for this reason—fearing the absorbing power of his northern neighbour.

19. The Coreans, whom I have seen in my various excursions on shore, live in a very primitive fashion. They are a simple, modest folk, industrious only to an extent which will cover the necessities of life.

Their villages are composed of small thatched cabins, each with its own inclosure, and they appear to have the usual Eastern views as to the seclusion of their women. We never succeeded in penetrating into their hamlets, though I believe they prevented us more from the memory of severe punishments which their laws imposed for harbouring strangers, than for any individual dislike to our society. This will wear off by degrees. Before we left the anchorage the vessels were often thronged with native visitors, and they were beginning to treat our officers who landed with great cordiality. They would not receive money.

20. Their mode of living is what might be expected of any primitive people under a patriarchal dynasty of three thousand years' duration, educated through a long history of naught but their own seclusion, cultivating a few needful arts, such as weaving &c., satisfied with their own productions, and content to live at the expense of the least exertion possible.

I doubt whether their own energy will ever put them in the possession of much purchasing power; but if it be true that Corea possesses valuable metals and minerals, the coming generation may profit from resources which only European industry is likely to develop.

21. With this letter I forward the Treaty in Chinese and in English, and retain another original of each until instructions are received as to ratification. The Protocol to Treaty, which I enclosed in my letter to the Plenipotentiaries, was admitted by them, and replied to by letter, of which I retain the original in Chinese, and forward a copy.

I also have the honour to forward the letter from the King of Corea to Her Most Gracious Majesty the Queen, which I undertook to send. A translation is appended.

The title of the King of Corea is King of Chosen, and the country of Corea is called Chosen by the people.

I have forthwith diverted the "Flying Fish" to commence surveying operations of the approach to the Capital, and of the west and south coasts, and I hope this summer to visit Fusan and Yensan, with the Squadron of Evolution.

I have the honour to be, Sir,

Your obedient servant,
(Signed) GEORGE O. WILLES,
Vice-Admiral Commander-in-Chief.

P.S. I have this day forwarded to their Lordships a telegram in cypher (No. 4) informing them of the signing of the Treaty, and giving the heads of the several Articles.

Inclosure*

To their Excellencies the Representatives of His Majesty the King of Chosen.

It being considered desirable that an understanding should be come to on certain points with reference to the Draft Treaty, the undersigned proposes that a Protocol of the nature of the enclosed document should be attached to the Treaty.

(Signed) GEORGE O. WILLES
Vice-Admiral, Commander-in-Chief,
Representative of Her Majesty, the Queen of Great Britain and Ireland.
June 3rd, 1882

Protocol of Supplementary Articles to Treaty between England and Chosen.

I. It is understood that the Ports opened to British trade by the foregoing Treaty (though not designated by name) are the three at present open to Japan, namely, the Portof Yensan (Port Lazareff), the Port of Fuzan, and the Port of Jin Chuen.

II. It being recognized by international law that men-of-war of any nation can freely enter the ports of any other friendly power, it is hereby agreed that from and after the signing of the Treaty between Great Britain and Chosen,

*이 문서에 부속된 조영수호통상조약 원문은 부록의 '조영수호통상조약' 참조.

British ships of war may visit ports within the dominions of the King of Chosen, and shall receive every facility for the purchase of provisions, for procuring water, fuel, and, if necessary, for repairs.

III. The coasts of Chosen, being hitherto imperfectly surveyed, are dangerous to vessels approaching them, and in order to prepare charts showing the position of islands, rocks, and reefs, as well as the depth of water, vessels of the British Government may survey the said coasts.

(Translation)

The Plenipotentiaries for the negotiation of the Treaty of Great Chosen, that is to say, Chief Plenipo. Chao, and Assist. Plenipo. Kim, beg to acknowledge receipt of your Excellency's communication of the 20thof this month, enclosing a supplementary Protocol, in three articles, as to matters not expressly mentioned in the Treaty.

As regards the several items thereof, whatever has not been expressly stipulated must, of course, be arranged in accordance with international law.
As regards the 2nd and 3rdArticles, it will be for the Chosen Government to issue instructions to the local authorities on the seaboard, that in case of men-of-war of your nation entering our ports, they(the authorities) are to attend carefully to their wants. But inasmuch as the people of Chosenare, as yet, unversed in intercourse with people of other nationalities, our Government are apprehensive that our people may easily take alarm. We must, therefore, beg your Excellency to give orders that, for the future, whenever a ship of war enters our ports, the officers and men are to be especially fair in their dealing; in which case we may anticipate that mutual forbearance will prevail, and no unforeseen outbreak occur.
For convenience sake we mention this subject to your Excellency beforehand, in replying to your dispatch, and we trust you will make arrangements in accordance with the purport hereof.
The above reply to his Excellency Wei, Plenipotentiary of Great Britain for negotiation of the Treaty.
21st day of 4th month of Kwang Sii, Chinese Calendar, corresponding to 491st year of the era of Great Chosen

(L.S.)

Inclosure

Translation of a letter from His Majesty the King of Chosen to Her Most Gracious Majesty the Queen of England.

(Translation)

The King of Great Chosen makes a communication.

He begs to say as regards Chosen that it is simply a dependency of China, but that its internal administration and its external intercourse are entirely and in all respects within his discretion and control as an independent king. In now making a Treaty with each other, the States of Great Chosen and Great England shall conduct their intercourse in every respect on the footing of equality. The King of Great Chosen expresses his willingness that all the stipulations of the proposed Treaty shall be arranged in strict accordance with the international usage of independent States. On the other hand, Great Chosen, being a dependency of China, shall fully discharge in all particulars the duties of that relation, but this shall in no wise affect or concern Great England. Moreover, before deputies are appointed to negotiate the Treaty has deemed it incumbent to set forth clearly, as above, his position, and he begs the Queen of Great England that the matter may be arranged on the understanding herein above set forth.

In testimony whereof he makes the foregoing communication.

The Queen of Great England.

Dated the 13th day of the 4th month of the 8th year of the Chinese (year term) Kwang Sii, corresponding to the 491st year of the era of Great Chosen, equivalent to the 30th day of May, 1882.

The above is a true copy of a translation made from a copy of the original letter by her Majesty's Consul at Nagasaki on the 9th June, 1882.

I have ascertained that this letter is written in original in all due form and style.

GEORGE O. WILLES
Vice-Admiral, Commander-in-Chief.

89

H.S. Parkes (1882. 6. 12) ➡ Hallell (1882. 7. 17)

조선주재 외교관 임명에 관한 상신

12 June 1882

My dear Mr. Hallell

    We have just rec'd the news of the treaty that has been made with Corea as it appears 3 ports are to be opened. I am very anxious to get the appointment of Consul or Vice-Consul to one of the ports. I understand the Home Government will select men of some experience in the East to fill the ports. I venture to hope that my long experience in Japan may have some insight and that I may have the good luck to be one of their appointers. I have had a good schooling of it with the Japanese & have followed closely every charge politics as otherwise through which this country has passed as the responsible position in which I have been placed in command of men belonging to the Japanese Naval & Marine Forces has given me an amount of influence that might prove of use to one holding the position of Consul in Corea a country which recent pass through a course of political change and trouble very similar to, though perhaps not so violent, as that through which Japan has passed. My knowledge of the Japanese language, also, is a great help I find toward acquiring the Corean Language, now I feel confident I could creditably fulfill the duties of the port of consul in Corca. Thought the Japanese service is very pleasant, & I can speak very well of the way the government treat me, still, there is no future attached to the career in it, and at the configuration of one's agreement there may or may not be a removal & if it ceases, there is no retiring pension, I am therefore very anxious to get something permanent & possible, and now this chance of Corea has turned up Jane writing to all the friends I know to act them to exert their interest at the Foreign office on my behalf. I now could say how much indebted I have if your could help at all in the matter I do not.

H.S. Parkes (1882. 6. 21) ➡ G.L.G. Granville (1882. 7. 27)

조미조약 한문 초안의 번역문 보고

No. 58

Sir H. Parkes to Earl Graville.—(Received July 27)

(No. 74)

Tôkiô, June 21, 1882

My Lord,

I HAVE the honour to inclose four copies of a translation prepared by Mr. Satow of a Chinese draft of the Treaty lately concluded by Commodore Schufeldt with Corea, as published in several Japanese newspapers.

The Publication of this document in that mode attracted much attention, as it appeared as soon as the conclusion of the Treaty became known here by wire, about a week after it was signed, and before the Japanese Government, as the Foreign Minister assured me, had received any copy. The latter, indeed, were inconvenienced by its publication, as they were assailed on their Corean policy by the editors who have the Treaty publicity.

It is obvious, therefore, that the latter must have obtained a copy at Tien-tsin simultaneously with, if not antecedent to, Commodore Schufeldt's departure from that place to Corea.

I understand from Admiral Willes that the 1st Article, acknowledging the partial dependency of Corea and China, which gives considerable umbrage to the Japanese, has been omitted in the Treaty signed by Commodore Schufeldt, having been transferred, as in the case of the British Treaty, to a letter from the King of Corea.

I have, &e.
(Signed) HARRY S. PARKERS

Inclosure in No. 58

Chinese Draft of the Treaty between the American Admiral and Corea.

(Translation)

Corea and the United States of America being desirous of Strengthening their friendly relations, and of facilitating commercial intercourse between their respective peoples, the Sovereign of Corea and the President of the United States have appointed Plenipotentiaries, who, having communicated to each other their respective full powers and found them to be in good and due form, have agreed upon and concluded the following Articles:—

ARTICLE I

Corea is a dependency of China, but has always been autonomous as regards both internal government and foreign relations. Corea and America having mutually agreed that the king of Corea enters into this Treaty in accordance with international law relating to autonomy, the latter undertakes to carry it out faithfully, while the President of the United States will not interfere with Corea's relationship of dependency on China.

ARTICLE II

There shall be perpetual peace and friendship between the King of Corea and the President of the United States and their respective peoples. Should any other country act unjustly or oppressively the sufferer shall at once inform the other Contracting Party, who shall endeavor to bring about an amicable arrangement of the question, thus showing friendly feeling.

ARTICLE III

The two countries having now entered into a Treaty of Commerce and Friendship may appoint Diplomatic Representatives to reside at the respective capitals, and Consuls-General or other officers to reside at each other's open ports, as they may find expedient. These officers, in their intercourse with the officials of the country where they are appointed to reside, shall be on a footing of perfect equality. The Diplomatic Representatives and the Consuls, and other officers of the two country, shall respectively enjoy all the privileges accorded to the officials of the most favoured nation. The Consuls shall obtain the exequatur of the country to which they are appointed before they can enter on their functions. The consuls appointed must be regular officials, and must not be merchants, or engage in trade. When no Consul is appointed, the Consul of another country may be requested to discharge the duties, but in no case can they be discharged by a merchant. Or the local authorities may discharge them, in accordance with the present Treaty. Should any American Minister in Corea disagree [sic] with the Corean authorities, his exequatur may be withdrawn.*

ARTICLE IV

American Vessels encountering storms off the coast of Corea, or being in want of food, fuel, or water, at a distance from an open port, may anchor wherever convenient, either for shelter or for the purpose of obtaining supplies or repairing, and all the expenses thus incurred will be paid by the master or owners of the ship. The local authorities shall treat them with kindness, render them assistance, and supply their requirements. If American vessels shall attempt to smuggle at an unopen port, their cargoes shall be confiscated. If an American vessel is wrecked on the coast of Corea, the local authorities on hearing of it shall immediately give orders for the crew to be protected and supplied with food, and at the same time measures shall be taken for the protection of the vessel and cargo, and the Consul shall be informed, in order that he may send the crew back to their own country. All expenditure for the recovery of the cargo shall be repaid either by the master or owners, or by the United States.

ARTICLE V

American citizens residing in Corea, and peaceably pursuing their callings, shall be protected in their persons and property by the local Corean authorities, who shall not allow them to be insulted or injured. If any lawless person should attempt to damage the house or property of an American, the local authorities shall immediately inform the Consul, and send officers to

---

*[원주] There is evidently some error or omission in the Chinese text in the pessage. Many misprints are scattered through the document. - Translator's note.

maintain order, search for and arrest the ringleaders, and punish them severely, according to law. If any Corean subject insult an American citizen, it shall devolve upon the Corean authorities to punish him in accordance with Corean law. If any American citizen, whether on shore or afloat, should insult, molest, or injure a Corean subject in his person or property, it shall devolve upon the American Consul, or other officer appointed by America, to arrest and punish the offender according to American law. If a cause of action shall arise between Corean subjects and American citizens in Corea, the authorities of the nationality of the defendant shall decide it according to the laws of their own country, but the authorities of the plaintiff's country may appoint officers to watch the case. The judicial officers shall treat each other with courtesy, and may summon witnesses to give evidence as to the facts of the case, if they deem it desirable. If the judicial officer's judgment is considered unjust, appeal may be made to the Governments of the United States and Corea for decision. If Corea should hereafter establish laws and a judicial system which shall be in harmony with those of the United States, then the right of American officials to exercise jurisdiction in Corea shall be revoked, and United States' citizens in Corea shall thereafter come under the jurisdiction of the local authorities.

ARTICLE VI

Corean merchants and merchant-vessels proceeding to the United states to trade shall pay duties, shipping dues, and all other charges in accordance with the Customs Regulations of the United States, but no higher or other rates of dues and duties shall be levied on them than those which are levied on United States' citizens, or on the subjects or citizens of the most favoured nation. American merchants and merchant vessels proceeding to Corea for the purpose of trading shall pay duties on all goods imported and exported; the right of imposing duties being inherent in Corea's autonomy.

Import and export Tariffs and Customs Regulations for the prevention of smuggling shall be established by the Corean Government, and be communicated in advance to the American officials, that they may notify them to their citizens for their guidance. The Tariff, as at first arranged, shall not exceed on imports 10 per cent, *ad valorem* on the necessaries of life, and 30 per cent, on luxuries, foreign liquors, Manila tobacco, clocks, watches, and such like goods, and on exports of all kinds shall not exceed 5 per cent. Imported goods shall pay no other dues or charges than the regular duties, whether transported into the interior or remaining at a port. American merchant-vessels entering Corean ports shall pay 5 mace per ton, per quarter, according to the Chinese calender.

ARTICLE VII

Corean subjects proceeding to any place in the United States are at liberty to reside there, rent or buy houses, and build godowns, as they may find desirable, may engage in commerce, or follow mechanical trades, and may buy and sell all kinds of produce and manufactures not being prohibited. American merchants proceeding to Corea may reside at the open ports within the limits set apart for the purpose, and may therein rent houses or land, and build houses, as they may find desirable, may engage in commerce or follow mechanical trades, and may buy and sell all kinds of produce and manufactures, not being prohibited. But in the leasing of land the parties shall be subject to no constraint, and rent shall be paid according to the rates established by the Corean authorities. The land thus rented continues to form part of the territory of Corea, and, with the exception of the jurisdiction over American citizens which is herein conceded to the American authorities, shall be entirely under the jurisdiction of the Corean local authorities. American citizens shall not transport foreign goods into the interior for sale, nor shall they go into the interior to purchase native goods, nor transport native goods form one port to another. Contravention hereof will be followed by the confiscation of the goods, and the trader so offending will be punished by his Consul.

ARTICLE VIII

Corea and America hereby agree that Corean subjects shall not be permitted to import opium into the ports of the United States, nor shall United States' citizens import opium into the ports of Corea, or transport it from one port to another. All trading in opium is, moreover, prohibited. The respective Governments will for ever prohibit and prevent their subjects or citizens from hiring the vessels of their own or any other nationality, either for their own account, or on account of the merchants or citizens of any other nationality, for the transport of opium, and any infringement of the prohibition so enacted shall be most severely punished.

ARTICLE IX

If Corea should have any reason to apprehend a scarcity of food within her own borders, the King of Corea may for a while prohibit the export of grain, and after this has been communicated through the local authorities, the United States' officials shall notify it to their citizens at the ports for them to observe. The export of red ginseng has always been prohibited by Corea, and, should American citizens attempt to smuggle it out, it shall all be confiscated, and the offenders shall be severely punished.

ARTICLE X

Cannon, fire-arms, weapons of all kinds, gunpowder and ammunition, and all other material of war, can only be purchased by the Corean authorities, or imported by United States' citizens provided with the express written permission of the Corean authorities. Any such articles secretly imported will be confiscated, and the offenders shall be severally punished.

ARTICLE XI

Officials and merchants of either nation residing at places open to trade may freely employ any class of person in any lawful occupation, but Corcans having violated the laws of their country, or being implicated in any charge, who conceal themselves in the residence, godown, or merchant-vessel of an United States' merchant, shall, on the application of the local authorities to the United States' Consul, be either arrested by the (Corean) police, or by the Consul's deputy for surrender to the Corean police, and no United States' citizens shall harbour or detain such persons.

ARTICLE XII

All possible facilities and assistance shall be given to students of either nationality to study the languages, laws, arts, and industries of the other, in order that friendly feelings and goodwill may be promoted between the two countries.

ARTICLE XIII

This being the first Treaty entered into by Corea, it has been sought to make its provisions as simple as possible, and all the provisions it contains shall be duly carried out for the present. As to what it does not contain, the [Contracting Parties] shall wait for five years, until their respective languages shall be better known to each other, when a revision shall take place.

The Trade Regulations in all their details shall be equitably arranged in accordance with the principles of international law, on a footing of perfect equality.

ARTICLE XIV

In the present Treaty and all subsequent communications Corea shall use the Chinese language, and America either Chinese or English with a Chinese rendering, so as to avoid error or misunderstanding.

ARTICLE XV

All special favours, grants, or privileges, whether relating to navigation, commerce, or intercourse, not contained in this Treaty, nor previously acquired by any other nation, which shall, subsequent to the conclusion of the present Treaty between the two countries, be accorded to any other country or its subjects or citizens, shall be equally accorded to the United States' officials and citizens, and with regard to favoured treatment in the nature of concessions accorded to another country and secured by special stipulations, for which something has been given in return, the United States may enjoy the advantages of the favoured treatment of those special stipulations by agreeing to the same reciprocal conditions.

The foregoing Articles have been agreed to and put in writing by the Plenipotentiaries of Corea and America in Corea, and six copies, identically worded, having been made, three in Chinese and three in English, they have been signed and sealed as evidence thereof, and will be ratified by the two

Governments, and the ratifications having been exchanged in Corea within one year from this date, this Treaty will be notified to the officials and people of the two countries, in order that they may know and observe the same.

  In the Corean year,*   month   day.
  1882 year of the American era,   month,   day.

---

*[원주] which is the eighth year of Kwang-hsü in China

H.S. Parkes (1882. 7. 5) ➜ G.L.G. Granville (1882. 8. 12)

Willes의 통역으로 Aston 파견 보고

Tokio, July 5, 1882

No. 76

My lord,

I have the honor to report the circumstances under which I recently instructed Mr. Aston (Her Majesty's acting consul for Hiogo and Osaka) to proceed to Korea, in order that Admiral Willes might have the benefit of his services as Interpreter in the Korean Language.

As soon as Admiral Willes received at Hong Kong his instructions by telegraph to watch American proceedings in Korea and to secure by negotiation with the Korean authorities, if necessary, the advantages of the most favored nation, he consulted me by private letter to the best means of obtaining a competent interpreter. I at once recommended Mr. Aston on the ground that, besides being familiar with the Chinese character, he possessed an exceptional knowledge of the Korean language, both oral and written. I am not yet aware that the ability to speak this language has yet been attained by any officer of the China Consular service.

Admiral Willes subsequently visited Peking, and he there arranged with Sir Thomas Wade to take with him Mr. Spence of that service as interpreter. Mr. Spence, however, had to make the long journey from Ichang for this purpose, and on the 1st of June I received a note from Admiral Willes, written at the moment of his departure from Nagasaki to Korea, stating that it was doubtful whether Mr. Spence would be able to join him.

I therefore telegraphed to Mr. Aston to proceed at once to Nagasaki by a mail steamer which had already left Yokohama and would call at Hiogo the next day. To wait until I could give Mr. Aston written instructions would have involved the loss of a week, and in adopting this step I was supported by the receipt of Your Lordship's Despatch, No. 35 Confidential of the 17th of April, in which you instructed me to act in concert with Admiral Willes as far as we practicable.

The Admiral had arranged that Her Majesty's Gunvessel "Kestrel" should bring on Mr. Aston from Nagasaki to Korea in case his services were required, and presuming from the doubt expressed by the Admiral as the possibility of his being joined by Mr. Spence that they would be so required, I requested the commander of that vessel to convey Mt. Aston to the Admiral, I also instructed the former to place himself under the order of Admiral Willes and to make the best use of any opportunities that might offer for collecting information in Korea.

On the 9th of June Admiral Willes telegraphed to me from Nagasaki that he had returned there after concluding his Treaty and thanking me for sending Mr. Aston. The latter unfortunately had not joined the Admiral until two hours after he had started on his return. The Admiral added that Mr. Aston remained behind in the surveying vessel "Flying Fish" to collect information to Nagasaki by the end of the month.

I therefore instructed Mr. Aston to come on to Yokohama as soon as he arrived at Nagasaki in order that he might report the result of his observations to Admiral Willes. Mr. Aston accordingly arrived at yokohama yesterday morning, but Admiral Willes had already left on his cruize to the north of Japan and the Russian settlements two days previously.

Mr. Aston has prepared a Report for the Admiral, but in consequence of the departure of the latter he addressed it to me instead, and I am submitting a copy of it to Your Lordship in my succeeding Despatch.

I have the honor to be with the highest respect,
my Lord, Your Lordship's most obedient, humble servant,
Harry S. Parkes

(3) 제1차 조약 이후 청조(清朝)의 대응

高宗(1882. 6. 9/高宗十九年四月二十四日) ➜ 禮部

조영조약의 체결을 알리는 자문(咨文)

朝鮮國王爲咨會事 小邦與美國定約一摺 已差副司直李應浚 附揚威艦專往備達 本年四月十一日 英國水師提督韋力士 乘兵艦來泊仁川港 適馬道丁提督 未及回棹 接到總理衙門暨北洋大臣函內指意 飛書相告 嗣又領選使金允植 專人由陸回國報知 當職卽以經理統理機務衙門事趙寗夏金宏集 充差大副官 前往商酌 迺於本月二十一日 面同英國提督韋力士 講定修好通商條規十四款 按照美約 不容更易 鈐印畫押 用昭憑信 此莫非中朝王公大人暨北洋大臣 克體皇上綏靖之眷 深軫小邦交涉之宜 維持籌畫 靡不用極 並囑馬道丁提督 仍留會辦 裏助協議 務須十分妥善 當職與一國臣民 益加感激 鐫結衷曲 謹將條約冊子照會備文等各槁 悉行鈔錄 庸備轉奏在案 以冀小邦無事不達之忱 茲法國亦要通好 前頭接應 不得不預爲講究 深望部堂諸大人 先賜指導 亦卽請旨更派馬道丁提督 重來商辦 俾小邦終始徼惠 區區幸甚 爲此合行移咨 請照驗轉奏施行 須至咨者
右咨
禮部
光緒八年四月二十二日咨會事
藝文提學 臣 鄭範朝製 進
二十四日 撥送
光緒八年四月 廿六日*

---

*이 문서는 같은날 李鴻章에게도 발송되었음.

93

T.F. Wade(1882. 6. 13/光緒八年四月二十八日) → 總署

조영조약 체결 통보

관련문서 總署의 회신

四月二十八日 英國公使威妥瑪函稱 日昨本大臣接准本國水師提督由日本長崎所發電咨內載 本軍門於四月二十一日 已與朝鮮國定約矣 本大臣准此 合卽備函奉達貴親王暨列位大臣 卽希查照可也 順頌日祉

【관련문서】

五月初二日 致英國公使威妥瑪函稱 昨准函開 接准本國水師提督電咨內載 於四月二十一日已與朝鮮國定約 備函奉達等因 本大臣等備悉一切 相應函復貴大臣查照可也 順頌日祉

張樹聲(1882.8.6/光緒八年六月二十三日)

조영, 조독 조약 체결 전말 상주

直隷總督兼理通商事務大臣張樹聲奏朝鮮與英德議約事竣摺

光緒八年六月二十三日 英國咨文等件見八年六月初十日禮部摺附件

署直隷總督兼辦理通商事務大臣兩廣總督臣張樹聲跪奏爲朝鮮與英德兩國議約事竣恭摺奏陳仰祈聖鑑事 竊朝鮮與美國議定和好通商條約後請留北洋委員二品銜候選道馬建忠及統領北洋水師記名提督丁汝昌商辦他國交涉經臣奏明如英法德三國相繼東往議約仍令馬建忠等襄助以資熟手在案伏查英國所派使臣水師提督韋力士於本年四月十一日乘兵船駛至朝鮮漢口 其時馬建忠尙未起椗西回當爲代達朝鮮該國王卽於十三日派經理統理機務衙門事趙寗夏金宏集爲議約大副官至漢口與英國會議韋力士初以美約略擧大綱尙涉罣漏欲添註數條以期周密 又欲於約內註明索巨文一島爲兵船停泊之地意在專踞險要馬建忠告以初次立約向僅擧其大綱沿海諸島照約皆可停泊船據各國公例反覆開陳韋力士之議 始阻一切照美約定擬惟議另備照會聲明約內未及詳載者三節 一通商口岸請照日本現開三口辦理 二兵船可駛入朝鮮各口 三朝鮮海岸請允測繪圖 馬建忠以核與約款公法均無違礙因告趙寗夏等轉請國王照准卽於四月二十一日會集簽押英約蔵事 德國亦派駐京使臣巴蘭德爲朝鮮議約全權大臣來津晤商巴蘭德就美約增改數款先以擬稿相示臣先以峻詞拒之嗣復連日籌商再三論辦巴蘭德乃欣然從命允照美約一字不易臣仍派馬建忠同往襄助並令丁汝昌酌帶兵輪偕行五月初八日馬建忠等低漢江口巴蘭德已先至朝鮮仍派趙寗夏金宏集爲議約大副官於十一日馳至次日會議十五日會同簽押所有約款及聲明朝鮮爲中國屬邦照會悉照美英兩國原稿其間亦有兩端稍異者一德文通曉者較少此次約稿照中國與巴西定約故事參用法文一冊以便校對 二巴蘭德恐朝德換約需時另備照會請於他國通商時遣德國商民先來貿易馬建忠因與約款無關出令朝鮮使臣卽照覆允行而與文內添未換約前領事官來口僅以賓禮相待未便以公文議事一層於通融之中仍示以確守公法之意 此英德兩國使臣先後在朝鮮定約情形也 竊惟西人好勝性成朝鮮與泰西各國立約通商美人首

導先路英德繼起若一無可以據異之處 其心必有不甘或能橫生枝節今於約款一成不變而於約外無關利害之事略徇其請彼謂立約雖後於別國而另有微與別國不同者則好勝之心旣慰一切邃易就範圍然以英國之領袖商務德國之崛起爭雄而此次赴朝議約匪特妥速成盟不致另滋轇轕抑且鼓舞歡欣感謝朝廷派員襄助之力則亦由創定美約善立始基而該委員等尙能相機操縱之所致也至朝鮮國王咨送朝德約冊係交馬建忠代爲攜呈其與英國所訂約冊先由陸路齎遞玆准禮部將朝鮮國王咨文及朝鮮約冊咨送到臣謹一併抄錄兩次原咨及條約各件恭呈御覽伏乞皇太后皇上聖鑑訓示謹奏

光緖八年六月二十三日 軍機大臣奉旨該衙門知道單五件幷發欽此

(4) 제2차 조약 체결 과정

95

H.S. Parkes (1882. 6. 21) ➡ Tenterden

1차 조영조약에 대한 비판 및 조선 영사관 설치 건의

My dear Lord Tenterden

Tokio, June 21, 1882

  Would you consider me intrusive if I offer a few remarks on the British Treaty with Corea?

  This and the American Treaty are believed here to be Li Hung Chang's work. Besides opening Corea to the Western Powers, which had become essential to the security of China, there is, I fancy, much in these Treaties which is intended to the address of Western Powers in China, as well as to that of Japan. The declaration of dependency on China is a *tu quoque* to Japan for having persuaded Corea to declare herself independent in the Japan Treaty, and for Japan's action in Loochoo. It may also be intended to guard against Corea acting wholly independently of China, as Siam has done. How we are to recognize this *quasi*-dependent condition, and at the same time to treat Corea as an equal, the King being placed on the same footing as the Queen, appears to me rather a puzzling problem. This declared suzerainty will be annoying to Russia and Japan, and will promote the aim of the former to attach the latter to her interests.

  I am very sorry that Admiral Willes had no interpreter with him. He was, therefore, entirely in the hands of the Chinese Ma Taotai. Early in the day I had offered him Aston, who speaks Corean, and also knows the Chinese character; but the Admiral, on conferring with Wade, seems to have formed the idea—which, I think, is rather an extreme one—that any one coming from the side of Japan would be objectionable to the Coreans. As it appears, Aston is well and favourably known to the latter, as many of them have lately visited Japan, and been in constant communication with him at Kobe. Aston would, at least, have secured that the titles of the Queen would have been learned by the Corean Government, the capital would probably have been reached, a reception by the King arranged, and at least some information obtained as to the state of the country and its Government. Eventually I sent Aston on my own responsibility, because, in a note which I received from the Admiral, I saw that there was a possibility that Spence would fail him, as proved to be the case. Aston reached the Admiral just two hours after he had started on his return, but he allowed him to remain in the surveying vessel to collect information, and I have no doubt we shall receive an interesting Report.

If the Treaty is to come into operation in a year from this time a great deal of preparatory work should be done beforehand, or we shall have trouble at the commencement of our relations. A Tariff should be settled that will determine specific rates of duty on as many articles as possible. The *ad valorem* rates mentioned, and the tonnage dues (Article V) are very high, and are those which Li Hung Chang would like to see adopted in China. If we give them to Corea, will it not be difficult to withhold them from China and Japan? I have just been engaged in persuading the Japanese Government to abate their demands for high Tariff; but in view of this Corean Treaty, they may fly back to their original claims. The concessions, *i.e.*, sites for the settlements of foreigners at the port, should be arranged, if possible, before the latter arrive, or we may have the same trouble which we had at first in Japan, and from which we have not yet recovered. By Article VI foreigners are not to carry native produce between the open ports, which is an unfortunate condition. In Japan I am specially instructed to maintain this privilege; but the Japanese will certainly continue to contend for it when they see that it is surrendered in the Corean case. It would please Li Hung Chang largely to deprive us of this right in China for the benefit of his Company of Chinese steamers. Article VI also reserves to the Coreans every power and function not expressly provided for in the Treaty. This, we may believe, will be used to cut down the privileges granted to the lowest possible limits, and in some cases to take away privileges which are necessary to the enjoyment of those expressly granted. The opium Article (VII) appears to me rather embarrassing, as it will be difficult for our Government to apply the "appropriate legislation" spoken of to foreign vessels. I am inclined to doubt whether the Chinese version says anything about "this appropriate legislation;" but of course Admiral Willes does not know what he signed in Chinese.

I venture to suggest that it would not be necessary—in the first instance, at least—to station a Diplomatic Agent at Seoul, and that our Minister at Peking would be our most fitting Agent. Seoul could be visited from Peking sooner than Shanghae. But I would strongly recommend that we should get a staff of three of four men at least on the ground as soon as possible, and these might be contributed both from the China and Japan Service. I am not aware that any of the men of the former Service know Corean. Aston has an extensive knowledge of it, and there is another man here who also knows it—Basil Hall Chamberlain—a very able man of about thirty, who is anxious to get into the public Service. Mr. Kennedy wrote to you about him last year. He knows the Chinese, Corean, and Japanese languages, having been out here nine years, and he is just leaving the Japanese Service. Of course it was hopeless, as I told him long ago, to look for employment in the China or Japan Service; but Corea is a new field, and it would be certainly to our interest to secure him. He might be first engaged as an Interpreter, and placed subsequently with reference to the claims of the Service men who may be sent to Corea. I presume that a Consul and an Assistant would at first be required at each of the three ports, and a Secretary of Consul at the capital, who might also be Consul for the port of Jinchyon (or Jinchuen), close at hand. I certainly think that Aston would be the best man for service at the capital, at least in the commencement; but on this point I may be better able to judge when he returns. If three or four men could be sent to Corea in the autumn, and allowed to reside at the capital, they would learned much of the language and acquired much information by the end of next spring, and might have put in train the Tariff (unless this is to be confided to the Chinese Customs), and other necessary arrangements.

Chamberlain, I may mention, is a nephew of General Sir Neville Chamberlain, of India. His grandfather was Sir Henry Chamberlain of our Diplomatic Service fifty years ago, and, curiously enough, his maternal grandfather was the celebrated writer, Captain Basil Hall, the first Englishman to visit Corea (1816) and to write upon it. I merely mention these particulars to show that the man comes of good stock.

It will be interesting to notice what action is taken by the German and French Ministers in Peking. I should think it probable that they will not be disposed to accept Commodore Schufeld's Treaty without modification. Of course, in our case there was no negotiation whatever; the Coreans handed us Commodore Shufeldt's Treaty, and we took it. The favoured nation clause alone would have been decidedly more advantageous, but I doubt whether the Coreans would have given it the Admiral; they had learned their lesson from Li Hung Chang at Tien-tsin, and were doubtless required to keep to it.

I have been obliged to write very hurriedly, which I beg you to excuse. Pray accept my few remarks for the little they may be worth, and acquit me of any desire to interfere in a question which may not be considered to come within my sphere. The trade in Corea must be very small for some time to come, and if the conditions under which we are to conduct it are to create disadvantages for us in China and Japan, we may not have acquired very valuable privileges. But perhaps there may be some opportunity of modifying or adding to the present Treaty by some supplementary clauses.

Very faithfully, &c.
(Signed)   Harry S. Parkes

96

H.S. Parkes (1882. 7. 5) ➜ G.L.G. Granville (1882. 8. 12)

아산, 인천 등 서해안 개항장 후보지 조사 보고

No. 68

    Sir. H. Parkes to Earl Granville.—(Received August 12)

(No. 77 Confidential)

                                                      Tôkiô, July 5, 1882

My Lord,

    WITH reference to my proceeding despatch No. 76 of this day's date, I have now the honour to place before your Lordship a copy of Mr. Aston's Report on his recent visit to Corea, accompanied by a Memorandum in which he has carefully examined the relative merits of Asan and Inchhyön as a port of trade. Inchyön is the Corean of Jin Chuen, which latter is an approximate Chinese pronunciation of the name.

    The Corean Government are under an engagement with the Japanese Government to open Inchhyön in September next, and Mr. Aston is of opinion that a more thorough examination of the Asan anchorage should be made before Inchhyön is definitely fixed on as the open port for that part of Corea. I am aware, however, that Admiral Willes attaches importance to Inchhyön for the same reason that induced the Japanese Government to select it, namely, its proximity to the capital.

    I beg to invite your Lordship's attention to the friendly communications which passed between Mr. Aston and Mr. Hanabusa, the Japanese Minister of Corea. He made two journeys from the capital in order to visit Mr. Aston at the anchorage of Inchhyön, and also at Asan, and stated that he would offer no objection to the surrender of Inchhyön in case another port, should be preferred by the foreign Powers. It was obviously politie on his part, as Mr. Aston points out, to show the Coreans that he was disposed to make common cause with those Powers, but it was creditable to him to bear so well the disappointment he doubtless felt at finding that Corea had openly acknowledged the suzerainty of China, and that all his endeavours to negotiate a low Tariff had been defeated by the new Treaties. There is good sense in his remarks that as the dependent relationship of Corea to China was an indisputable fact—a fact, however, which the Japanese Government have hitherto disputed—one acknowledgement of it, more or less, did not much matter, although he thought it would have the effect of causing his Government to withdraw their Minister and to appoint a Consul-General instead. Mr. Hanabusa also supplied some useful particulars as to the political conditions of the country, the leading men of the recently formed Administration, and the opposition with which the liberal-minded King has to contend. He also dwelt pointedly on the necessity of any foreign diplomatic officer appointed to reside at the capital being supported by a strong guard.

Mr. Aston draws attention to the difficulty which, owing to the poverty of the land, will be experienced in obtaining house accommodation for foreign officers either at the capital or the ports. He also points to the importance of foreigners in Corea being restrained by strict rules from intruding into the dwellings of the Coreans, in consequence of the great jealousy entertained by the latter for the privacy of their women, and he observes that Commodore Schufeldt mentioned to him, as his reasons for discarding the intervention of Japan, and for preferring the friendly offices of China, that Japan having free trade with Corea, would not make the concessions in favour of a high Tariff with which he wished to propitiate the Coreans. From China, it appears, he could readily obtain the desired concurrence in the imposition of high import duties, especially when accompanied by an acknowledgement of the suzerainty of China over Corea, to which Commodore Schufeldt affects to attach but slight importance.

It is evident, from Mr. Aston's description of the country, that the capacities of Corea for commerce are exceedingly limited, and, as what little foreign trade she now has, though comparatively free from duties, is not increasing, it is not probable that it will be developed by the high Tariff which has been successfully promoted by Commodore Schufeldt and his influential coadjutor, Li Hung Chang.

I feel that I may confidently recommend Mr. Aston's Report and proceedings to your Lordship's approval, and I only regret that he could not possibly arrive in time to be of service to Admiral Willes, who had to trust to the kind and gratuitous offices of a Chinese officer for the means of interpretation.

I have, &e.
(Signed) HARRY S. PARKES

Inclosure 1 in No. 68

Mr. Aston to Sir H. Parkes

Yedo, July 5, 1882

Sir,

I HAVE the honour to submit to you the following notes of information collected by me during my recent visit to Corea in Her Majesty's ships "Kestrel" and "Flying Fish."

I arrived at Roze Island anchorage on the 7th June, and on the same day received a visit from Mr. Kondo, the Secretary of the Japanese Legation in Corea, who said he had come down to express to Admiral Willes the regrets of Mr. Hanabusa, the Japanese Minister, that ill-health had prevented him from coming to call on him sooner. Mr. Kondo was very sorry that Admiral Willes' departure had now made it impossible for him to do so at all. Mr. Kondo could not conceal his annoyance at the manner in which the Treaties had been negotiated, and was full of curiosity as to their provisions, but, as I had had no opportunity of seeing them myself, I was unable to gratify his desire for information. I subsequently found that the Japanese Minister had soon after made himself acquainted with all their principal stipulations.

As I was aware that the anchorage of Inchhyön had only been selected by the Japanese Government owing to their inability to find a better port on the west coast, and that it was open to some obvious objections, I thought I could not employ my time better than by collecting what information I could respecting any alternative port in this neighbourhood. I accordingly dispatched a message to the authorities asking that some Corean official who knew this part of the country might be sent to me, but the stay of Her Majesty's ship "Flying Fish" at this anchorage was so short, and the Corean authorities are so slow to move, that there was no time to carry out this arrangement satisfactorily. The information gathered on this subject will be found in the separate Memorandum inclosed along with this Report. It will be seen that it points to the desirability of a thorough examination of the Asan anchorage before Inchhyön is definitely fixed on as the open port for this part of Corea.

Having written to Mr. Hanabusa, the Japanese Minister to Corea, an old acquaintance of mine in Japan, asking him to communicate to me any remarks he might have to make on the choice of Inchhyön as an open port, he was good enough to come down to Chémulpho, and to visit me on board the "Flying Fish," where he staid over night in preference to sleeping in the very poor quarters available on shore. Mr. Hanabusa showed none of irritation betrayed by Mr. Kondo at the recent negotiations. He remarked that, personally, he had been treated with greater courtesy than on any previous visit, and had received invitations to the houses of some of the leading officials, a civility which none of them had ever effered him before. As to the recognition by Corea of the suzerainty of China, it was an indisputable fact that the dependent relation existed, and one acknowledgement of it more or less did not matter. He thought, however, that one effect of it would be that his own Government would take the firm opportunity of having a Consul-General in Corea instead of a Minister, and he presumed the British Government would not appoint a Minister to a country which had so pointedly brought to their notice its dependent condition. Mr. Hanabusa has evidently determined to resign himself to the situation, and to make the best of it, and I fancy his two visits to the "Flying Fish," one at Chémulpho, and a week later at Asan, were intended not only as a friendly attention to ourselves, but as a little demonstration to the Coreans of his intention to make common cause with European Powers. On both visits he came attended by a suite of seven or eight persons, consisting of Secretary, Attachés, Interpreter guard, and servants.

Mr. Hanabusa informed me that the political state of affairs in Corea remained unaltered. A great blow had been struck at the anti-foreign party for or five months before, from which he believed it would not soon recover. Some had been imprisoned, some executed, and the remainder banished to provinces remote from the capital. The leader of this party was an elder brother of the King, the present Sovereign, though a younger son, having been chosen by the late King as his successor. The king is himself the principal leader of the movement in favour of opening the country, and his efforts are seconded by a number of his own relations (mostly young men) who hold many of the high offices of State. It is expected that the Foreign Department ("Tongumusa") which is now being organized, will be presided over by a brother of the King named Ni Chè-Myön. An uncle of his, Ni Chhoi-ung, is now Prime Minister, or Keni-mu-Puthongri-Taisin. There is another official whose position is somewhat like that of Prime minister. His name is Heung Syun-mong, and his title is Lyŏng-sy-ang. To him Mr. Hanabusa attributes a good deal of the convert opposition to the pro-foreign movement of which a strong under-current is still felt when any important step has to be taken. Cho-nyŏngha, the younger of the two men who signed the English Treaty, is a cousin of the King. The Heir-Apparent, a boy of 9 years of age, has recently been married to a cousin of his own by the mother's side. Ning-yŏng-ik, the Queen's nephew by adoption, is considered one of the most influential members of the party of progress. He is at present in mourning for his mother, and this, according to the Corean custom, will exclude him from public life and the discharge of official duties for some time to come.

Mr. Hanabusa said he had had a good deal of difficulty in persuading the Corean Government to accept Inchhyŏn as the port for the west coast of Corea. They would have preferred one further from the capital. He said fe felt some reluctance to give it up after all the trouble he had had to obtain it, but that, if the other foreign Powers preferred a different port, he would not allow his own personal feelings to stand in the way. He had said so to the official who at present discharges the duties of Foreign Minister, at an interview which was the consequence of my message asking that an official should be sent to supply me with information. Mr. Hanabusa had urged that my request should be complied with, but this trivial matter appears to have been made a Cabinet question, and so many people had to be consulted that it was impossible to make arrangement in time. The only result of it was that Mr. Okam, a young man who has been studying in Japan for the last two years, came down to Asan with informal instructions to find out the ideas of Lieutenant-Commander Hoskyn and myself on the subject. I said to him that the advantages of Inchhyŏn and Asan seemed pretty equally balanced, and that we would report any information which we might be able to collect.

Mr. Hanabusa spoke with some emphasis of the necessity of any Diplomatic Agent stationed at Sŏul being provided with a foreign guard, less for safety, though there is occasionally some danger of being stoned by the populace, than to keep off the Coreans, whose intrusive curiosity is intolerable. Their own countrymen cannot be depended on to do this. Besides, all Coreans of rank are accompanied, when they go out, by a crowd of fifteen or twenty retainers, who are fond of shouting and hustling out of the way any passenger who seems of less consequence than their own masters. The Japanese Legation has a guard of ten mounted police, and Mr. Ma Taotai was escorted by a guard of ten men on his visit to the capital before the conclusion of the Treaties.

Mr. Hanabusa was satisfied with this house accommodation in Sŏul, but one of his Attachés said their Legation was no better than a pig-stye, and, from all I have heard, I am inclined to believe that it will be no easy matter to find any native buildings suitable for the residence of foreign Diplomatic Officers.

At the various places touched at by the "Flying Fish" in the course of her surveying work, I had frequent opportunities of conversing with the local officials and people, but as our conversation was chiefly confined to an exchange of civil speeches, and to my answering some out of the multitude of questions constantly being put to me on all manner of subjects, it does not afford much material for a Report.

The ship was also visited by a good number of people, but, proportionally, far fewer than would have been the case under similar circumstances in Japan. The visitor of highest rank was the chief civil and military official of the district, which contains the Island of Yŏng Jong. He came alongside in a large junk, accompanied by his three sons and a suite of thirty or forty persons of different ranks. He had on a purplish-coloured outer dress, and his girdle had a leathern strap hanging from it, with a knob containing a wooden ticket, on which was inscribed his name and office with the seal of the Government—his commission, in short. As usual in the case of Corean officials of rank, he was attended everywhere by two pages, who supported him under the arms whenever the least exertion was required, and took care that his dress did not get entangled in anything. They carried the tiger-skin which he sat on, which also served to indicate his rank. In a second junk were a bullock, twenty fowls, and 100 eggs, a very acceptable present for the ship's company. In acknowledgment he was given a binocular glass, with which he seemed much pleased. On coming on board he sent me his card, and was conducted to the bridge, where he did his best to make himself agreeable, asking all our names and ages, and producing a stanza of Chinese poetry, which he had composed for the occasion. It ran as follows:-

> "From afar you have crossed the wide sea,
> Already your toils and miseries have been many.
> To your honourable self I wish ten thousand happinesses.

Peace and prosperity be with all your followers."

He received with every mark of respect and interest photographs of Her Majesty the Queen and of His Royal Highness the Prince of Wales which were presented to him by one of the officers. This gentleman staid on board for two or three hours conversing with myself in Corean, and, in my absence, with one of the Chinese stewards on board by means of the Chinse written character. His courteous and friendly behaviour left a very favourable impression on every one on board.

On another occasion I landed on the Island of Ny-önheung with Mr. Jenkins, Paymaster of Her Majesty's ship "Flying Fish." We were soon surrounded by a crowd of people of lower class, one of whom introduced himself as Mr. Min, and said he was a salt manufacturer and had a small farm. He was 23 years of age, and had a fair acquaintance with the Chinese character, which he occasionally resorted to when his Corean was not understood. He wore a clean unbleached hempen upper garment and a large basket hat with scolloped edges. His other clothes were of the usual white cotton materials almost universal in Corea. We walked inland some distance towards a small village, the crowd increasing as we weat, and constant appeals being made to me at every grassy knoll we came to sit down and have a talk. Our clothes, watches, money, etc., were closely scrntinized, and innumerable questions put to us. Here are a few of them—Of what country are you? Japanese? Russian / European? What is your name? Why have you come ashore? What has your ship come here to do? There are the invariable questions everywhere, and are the ones usually written in Chinese on slips of paper handed to foreigners who land on the Corean coast. At the Sir James Hall's group Lieutenant-Commander Hoskyn had received a number of them. These with England, that trading vessels would come next year, and as they did not know these coast, our Government had sent this ship to make a survey of them. Other questions were: What age are you? Why are your skins whiter than ours? Why don't you wear a mang-kön? Have you rice, wheat, cattle, rain, &e., in England? What is the price of a cow there? Have you a King? When she (the Queen) returns to the place from whence she came, who will be her successor? and if her eldest son dies, who will then succeed to the Throne? Have you a Government? What kind is it? Are your hearts like ours? What do you think of our way of life? our scenery? Where did you learn Corean? Are you really a foreigner? When is your ships going away? What makes your steamers move? How is it they sometimes get along without making any smoke? These are but a tithe of the constant stream of questions which were put to us. Mr. Min, the salt-maker, was very anxious to trade. He was pleased to be able to exchange his Corean pen for Mr. Jenkins' lend pencil, and wanted to barter a large pair of horn-rimmed spectacles, quite innocent of any enlarging powers, against my watch. He was most eager, however, to get possession of Mr. Jenkins' many-bladed knife, for which he offered a number of things in exchange, finally writing out in the Corean alphabetical character, "Please say to this gentleman that I wish very much to make the exchange. He is going on board the ship where he can get plenty of knives, but I shall never have another chance. If he does not care for the bargain, let us make an exchange out of friendship, so that we may have something to remember each other by." Mr. Min made as many polite speeches at parting, expressing his regret that we were going, and hoping that we would come back to Corea when the ports are opened—all which we duly reciprocated. Here, as at other places, I found the people decidedly friendly, though they want the polished manners which are found even among the lowest classes in Japan. The officials we met with were in all cases not only friendly, but most courteous. No armed men were seen anywhere. On no occasion, however, did any of our Corean friends invite us into their private houses, and the only interiors I had an opportunity of seeing were those of official residences. This is owing to the seclusion in which they keep their women, who are supposed never to see any man except their own near relations. It is important that this jealousy of strangers entering their houses should be respected. The French draft Treaty of Kanghoa, 1866, contains the following provisions on this subject, no doubt inserted at the suggestions of the French Missionaries to Corea, who were well acquainted with the feelings of the people on this point:-

"(1) L'entrée de toute maison Coréenne, sauf les auberges et les édifices publiques, leur (i.e., to foreigners) est absolument interdite, s'ils ne sont pas invités à entrer par le maître de la maison."

"(4) Si un étranger viole la maison d'un noble, …. le peuple pourra, s'emparer de sa personne, et le conduire aux autorités locales, qui en aviseront le Gouvernement, lequel pourra réclaimer l'expulsion du délinquant du royaume et même une peine plus sévère, s'il y a lieu."

We have no difficulty in getting supplies of cattle, fowls, eggs, and occasionally fish at reasonable prices. Mexican dollars were preferred to japanese silver yen in payment.

Two German men-of-war, a corvette with a commodore's flag at the fore, and national ensign at the main, and a gun-boat arrived at the Roze Island Anchorage on the 21st June. I afterwards learnt that t hey had been expected earlier.

The United States' ship "Monocacy" left Nagasaki about this time with orders to show the flag for 48 hours at Pusan, Wŏusan, and the Sŏul River, and then to proceed to Chefoo.

A French gun-boat left Nagasaki for Corea on the 29th June.

On my arrival at Kobé I saw Commodore Schufeldt, and he was subsequently a fellow passenger with me in the mail-steamer to Yokohama. He mentioned to me in conversation that he believed the reason the French had not made a Treaty with Corea was that they wished first to obtain some satisfaction for the murder of French missionaries.

He also said that the Japanese had not supported him heartily in his attempt to make a Treaty with Corea two years ago. They had got free trade themselves and would not make Corea the concessions in the direction of customs duties, which would have enabled them to support him effectively. Mr. Hanabusa had told me that the difficulty between Schufeldt and himself had been that the former had insisted on addressing a letter to the King, which, as he had no regular credentials, Hanabusa thought he had no right to do. Commodore Schufeldt said he had objected to the clause describing the dependent relation of Corea being inserted in the Treaty. He seemed desirous of attaching as little importance as possible to the letter of the King to the President of the United States which referred to this dependent position. He thought that the United States would appoint a Minister Resident and Consul-General to Corea.

The trade of Corea has been falling off of late. The total imports and exports to and from Japan for the whole country for last year are now estimated by Mr. Hanabusa at 3,000,000 paper yen, or about 2,000,000 dollars, and as the prospects of the grain crops are not very favourable at present, the current year is thought unlikely to show an increase

I have, &e.
(Signed) W.G. ASTON

Inclosure 2 in No. 68

Memorandum of Considerations bearing on the Selection of a Port to be opened on the West coast of Corea.

IT may be premised that a choice in this matter is still open, no final determination having been yet come to on this point between the Japanese Minister at Söul and the Corean Government. It is true that Inchhyön has been provisionally fixed upon by them, but I gathered from Mr. Hanabusa and from the Corean officials with whom I had some conversation on the subject that if any other port were considered preferable by the other Treaty Powers, there would be no objection to the question being reopened. The date fixed upon for opening Inchhyön to Japanese trade is September next, and arrangements are now being made for sending over a ship in advance of that date with materials for the erection of a Japanese Consulate. It is, therefore, important that steps should be taken at once to ascertain whether some other port would not be preferable, more especially as there are some obvious objections to Inchhyön, and there is another port which, on a cursory examination, seems to present at least equal advantages. If a decision cannot be come to at once, I believe that the Japanese Government would readily consent to postpone the opening of Inchhyön for the present, and to act in concert with the other Powers in this matter. It is, I think, desirable for many reasons that they should do so.

Several places on the west coast of Corea which have been suggeseted as suitable for opening to foreign trade may be briefly noticed.

Sonto, Sunto, or Syong-to, one of the places named in the draft Treaty prepared by the French in 1866, is another name for Ke-Syöng, a city in the metropolitan province, a short distance north of the capital. It is a place of some commercial importance, but it is difficult to see why an inland city, close to the capital, should have been selected for opening to foreign commerce.

Kang-hoa, on the Söul River, another place mentioned in the French Treaty, is open to the objection that it is on an island, and I also understand that the channel at this point is no narrow and the tide so strong as to render this place quite unfit to be selected as a port for foreign trade. A Corean book describing Kanghoa gives the population of the town at 5,402, and of the island at 31,285.

Basil Bay. The river which falls into the sea at this point was examined by two officers of the Japanese navy in 1879, and from their Report, a translation of which is annexed to this Memorandum, it will be seen that they found no anchorage here capable of accommodation any except very small vessels. They found a considerable native trade here, and the banks of the river are lined with large villages. Syöpho, the town near the entrance, is reckoned by the Coreans with Wönsan (Gensan), Pusan (Fusan), Masampho (on the south coast near the head of Ashby inlet), and the capital itself, as one of the chief commercial ports of the country.

Ping-yang, Commodore Schufeldt mentioned to me that he thought Ping-Yang, in the province of Hoang hé do, was the best port on the west coast to open to foreign commerce.

There only remain the anchorage of Chémulpho, in the district of Inchhyön and the port at the head of Prince Jerome Gulf to which the Japanese, who surveyed it, gave the name of Asan, a town lying some distance inland, and it may be assumed that the choice will be between these two places.

Inchhyön (ö as in German) called by the Japanese Jinsen, and also written Jinchuen, Inchen (Jenshan is a mistake), is the name both of a Pu (the Chiness Foo) or city, and of the district belonging to it. This district borders on the southern branch of the Söul estuary, and at high tide the sea reaches within a mile or two of the city, but the extensive mud banks which are left dry hear at low water shut out all communications with the sea except from the direction of Chémulpho, the village near which the Treaties were signed.

I visited Inchhyön, and found it to be a straggling village of 185 houses. As the number of inhabitants to each house is small in Corea, this may be taken to represent a population of about 750 souls. I may mention here that I inquired the population of Pupiöng, Nam Yang, Kimpho, and a number of other so-called cities in this neighborhood, and found that none of them were of much greater importance than Inchhyön. Inchhyön has a decayed, desolate appearance. The streets are unpaved and, in the more open parts, overgrown with grass. The houses are built of small stones, with a liberal allowance of mud for plaster, and are thatched. I only saw three houses with tiled roofs. One was the house of Pusa, or chief civil and military officer; the second, of his Lieutenant; and the third was the temple of Confucius. I was told that one or two more existed, but, though I had a tolerably complete view of the city from a rising ground, I could not see any others. There was not the smallest sign of any trade going on. No shops were to be seen, and the fact that neither chairs nor saddle-horses were procurable is a significant indication of the slender resources of the place. As in other Corean towns, what trade there is conducted at periodical fairs or markets. I was informed that, if Inchhyön is selected as the open port in this part of Corea, it is intended by the Government to incorporate with it several of the other Pu in the vicinity, so as to add to its importance, and justify the appointment to it of an official of higher rank.

Chémulpho, the nearest point in the district of Inchhyön to the anchorage where foreign ships must lie, and the only point where it is practicable to load and discharge cargo, is a hamlet of fifteen houses, or rather cabins, built of stone, with mud plaster, and thatched. I visited two of these houses, which, as they had been selected, one as the stopping-place of the Japanese Minister and his suite when travelling to or from Japan, and the other as the official residence of the principal native authority, were, no doubt, not unfavourable specimens of the houses of the Corean peasants. The former of these consisted of three rooms, with a small kitchen. One of these rooms was open to the air on two sides, and in winter would count for nothing. The chief room was about 12 feet by 8 feet, the roof being barely high enough to stand upright in. The flues from the kitchen pass under the floor of this room into a chimney at the other side, and by this means it can be efficiently heated in winter—a matter of great importance in a country where the rivers are frozen a foot thick for two months of the year. This room has a mud floor, covered with matting, and the walls were covered with mud and plaster. It had two small windows, of the same construction as the Japanese paper slides. The other room was smaller, and had no arrangement for heating. It had one window, a foot square, and a small door, some 2 and 1/2 feet by 3 and 1/2 feet. This, I was told, was the women's apartment. The other house I visited was, if anything, worse. I mention these details that it may be seen that there is absolutely no accommodation here fir for even the temporary use of Europeans, and that some steps must be taken in advance of the opening of the port to provide houses in which they can lodge. The same remarks apply still more strongly to Asan. Chémulpo is 5 or 6 English miles distant from Inchhyön. There is a tolerably level road to it, 3 to 6 feet wide, leading through a gently undulating country. A few small clusters of houses are seen here and there, but the land is only cultivated in patches, and the agriculture is much below the Japanese standard. Judging from what I could see of the district in this neighbourhood, it supplies no material for commerce;

and if Inchhyön, or rather Chémulpho, is selected as the open port, it must be regarded simply as a depôt for the trade with the Corean capital. Another road, 4 to 7 feet wide, levelled with a ditch in parts to caryy off water, and made of soft earth, without macadam or gravel, leads from Chémulpho direct to the capital, which is 18 miles distant in a direct line and about 21 miles by the road. This road is used only by foot-passengers and horses, and no traces of wheeled vehicles were visible. The 3 or 4 miles of it which I walked over could easily be made practicable for jinrikishas. The whole way to the capital is through a gently undulating country, without any high mountains to cross or other difficulties of travel, except the Söul River, on the north bank of which Sangé, the commercial port of Söul, is situated. The castle and official quarter lie a mile or two further north, on the other side of a hill. The capital is by far the most important commercial town of Corea. It is said to contain 60,000 houses, which would give a population of about 250,000 persons, and 400 to 500 junks are sometimes seen lying in the river here at one time.

By water, Chémulpho is 55 miles distant from the capital. The Söul River, which forms the channel of communication, is well known from the charts which have been made of it; and I need only say that although the strength and great rise and fall of the tides, and the narrowness of the channel, render it unsuitable for navigation by large vessels above Chémulpho, it is well sheltered, and affords great convenience for communication with the capital by means of lighters or small steamers, in which latter class of vessels the traffic in foreign goods will doubtless be ultimately conducted.

Chémulpho means "creek for the ferrying over of merchandize," and the place, no doubt, received this name from the fact that it is the point through which communication is kept up with the mainland from the opposite Island of Yöng-jong. The statement in one of the charts that the road to the capital from Kanghoa passes through this village is incorrect.

As there is a plan of the anchorage of Wölmi (Roze Island) prepared by Lieutenant-Commander Hoskyn and the officers of Her Majesty's ship "Flying Fish," it is unnecessary for me to enter into a detailed description of it. It is safe, roomy, and accessible, with good holding-ground. There are, however, two objections to it. One is the strength of the tide, which runs about 3 knots at springs and about 2 at neaps. This would, of course, be of little consequence to ships at anchor, and would not much interfere with well-manned ships' boats, but in view of the distance between the anchorage and the landing-place it would be a very serious obstacle to the movements of heavy cargo boats, and might necessitate the aid of small steam-tugs or steam-lighters. The native boat and junk men here never attempt to do anything against an adverse tide, and the question of how the tide will serve is constantly being discussed among them. But the great objection to this anchorage is its distance from the landing-place of Chémulpho, which is about 1 and 3/4 miles. Under ordinary circumstances of wind and tide, this takes a man-of-war's boat twenty to twenty-five minutes, and the Japanese Minister, when he came on board the "Flying Fish" here in a large Corean boat propelled by sculls, said he had been an hour on the way. To obviate this objection it had occurred to Mr. Hanabusa, the Japanese Minister to Corea, to have the foreign settlement on Wölmi (Roze Island), and to connect it by a causeway with the mainland. The same idea had presented itself to Lieutenant-Commander Hoskyn and myself, but, apart from other objections to this scheme, it would involve an expense which all that we know of the prospects of trade here would not justify. The rise and fall of the tide at springs is 30 feet, and the causeway for a considerable part of its length (nearly half-a-mile) would have to be a good deal higher than this.

In the Report on this place made by Commanders Aoki and Yamazaki, of the Japanese navy, who surveyed it in 1879, considerable prominence is given to the creek, called by the natives Ankol (the Olbee Strait of the charts), between Roze Island and the mainland, where small vessels, they say, might be moored bow and stern even at low-water springs. The Japanese survey makes the depth of this creek, opposite Chémulpho, at low-water springs, 2 fathoms, and their plan shows a continuous channel of a somewhat less depth connecting it with the outer anchorage. The survey of the "Flying Fish," however, gives the depth at 1 and 1/2 fathoms only, showing that either the Japanese surveyors did not reduce their soundings to a sufficiently low level, or that this channel is silting up. The latter alternative is by no means improbable in a river which always holds suspended a large quantity of mud, and Mr. Hanabusa mentioned to me that the channel had altered for the worse during the last three years. On the other hand, a channel of this kind could doubtless be improved by judicious treatment, if there were any funds available for such a purpose. I believe that Lieutenant-Commander Hoskyn's opinion is that, however useful such a channel might be for keeping up the communication by cargo boats between the ship and the shore at low tides, it could not be depended on for the accommodation of larger vessels.

There is a sufficiently convenient site for a foreign settlement at the village of Chémulpho. I examined this neighbourhood along with Mr. Hanabusa, and quite agree with him that the site which he has selected, and which is shown in the annexed plan prepared under his directions, is unquestionably the best obtainable at this place.

As at every other part of this coast, there is here a wide foreshore of mud at low water, but at one point the distance between high and low water mark is inconsiderable, and it would not be difficult to construct a pier for the use of cargo boats. The black dotted line on the Japanese plan shows the present high-water mark, and Mr. hanabusa has proposed, as will be seen from his plan, that the foreshore should be reclaimed, so as to give a water frontage to the settlement of a little less than half-a-mile in a straight line between the islet of Nap-szöm and Chémulpho Head, at which last-named place this proposed pier would be situated. This whole frontage would be available as a wharf for landing and loading cargo except at low tides. Something of this kind is highly desirable, but it would, I fear, entail a heavy expenditure, which the Corean Government would doubtless expect to be reimbursed to them by increased ground-rents. I have some doubts of its feasibility. The filling-in of this part, however, would probably have some tendency to create scour, and so deepen the channel in from of the settlement.

Asan.—As Her Majesty's ship "Flying Fish" arrived at this port on the forenoon of one day, and was obliged to leave on the following morning, there was little opportunity for an examination of this place. However, Lieutenant-Commander Hoskyn and I climbed Norui-san, the highest hill (600 feet) of the promontory in the centre of this inlet, from the top of which we had an extensive view of the Prince Jerome Gulf and the surrounding country. Four of five branches of this gulf were seen running far up into the adjoining country, and although we were told that the most navigable of these creeks was available for not more than 30 miles, and for small craft only, they must be of some value as means of communication with the interior. The promontory in question, which occupies a conspicuous place in the Japanese chart of this anchorage, is about 3 miles long by half-a-mile broad. Though it is hilly, there are plenty of level spaces, and there is an excellent site for a settlement, with just enough slope for drainage, in front of the anchorage on the south side of the promontory, and near its western end. It is protected by a hill from the north-west winds, which are much felt in Corea during the winter. There is the usual foreshore of mud, but it slopes down steeply near the low-water level, and much of it is little below high-water mark, so that it could be reclaimed at very small expense. At one end of the suggested site is a projecting reef which could be converted into a pier without much difficulty.

All works of this kind at Asan are rendered easier by the fact that the rise and fall of the tide here is much less than at Chémulpho, being only 22 feet at spring tides instead of 30 feet, as at the latter place. The Japanese plan shows that vessels can anchor here in 5 fathoms, two cables' length from the shore. The cost of preparing this site would be very much less than that of the plan of the Chémulpho settlement, proposed by Mr. Hanabusa, and this, I could gather, is a point of great importance with the Corean Government. Vessels anchored here would probably escape the full force of the tide, which is in any case less in this harbour than at Chémulpho. There is also a basin to the north of the promontory with 3 to 3 and 1/2 fathoms at low water, closed by a bar, on which there are 1 and 1/2 fathoms of water. If the trade here developed much, this would be found a very useful anchorage for native craft. There are several very easy paths from one side of the promontory to another. Commanders Aoki and Yamazaki, of the Japanese navy, who spent three weeks in surveying this harbour, formed a somewhat unfavourable opinion of it, as will be seen by their Report. But the only positive objection to it which they urge is that there are sand-banks in the channel leading to it. No complete survey has yet been made of the Prince Jerome Gulf, but we already know that a deep practicable channel of no great difficulty exists, and it is almost certain that Asan anchorage is perfectly easy of access for vessels of the largest size. The Japanese plan itself goes far to show that this harbour is, in all respects, an excellent one. I was informed by a native fisherman that it is the only place for a long distance approachable by large ships. The country in the neighbourhood of this inlet presents a somewhat more cultivated aspect than the district of Inchhegön, but there are no large towns, and Asan itself, which is a village of 200 houses, is 18 or 20 miles from the anchorage. The Prince Jerome Gulf is the northern limit of Naipho, which has the reputation is Corea of being the most fertile grain-producing district in the country; and as rice is one of the staple exports, there would be an obvious convenience in having an open port situated in this neighbourhood. But, on the whole, it is safer to disregard the local trade, and to consider Asan mainly as a port for the capital, and in a less degree, as a depôt for supplying European goods to the other native ports on the western coast of Corea. Regard should be had to the fact that a foreign trade with Northern Corea already exists through Newchwang and Wöusan (Gensan), and that, although the capital is far the most important commercial town, the commercial centre of gravity, as it, were, of the country is much to the south of this point, so that there is not the same objection to a port situated some distance south of the capital as there would be to one an equal distance to the north of it. All the writers on Corea agree in describing the three southern provinces as the most fertile and prosperous part of Corea, and this opinion is borne out by the following statement of the number of houses, militia, and extent of cultivated land derived from native sources :-

	Houses	Militia	Cultivaled Land	Remarks
Phyöng-an-do, or North-West Privince	218,019	29,465	Kyöl. 103,802	The Kyöl is the limit of assessment for purposes of taxation, and varies according to the quality of the land and other curcumstances.
Ham-Kiöng-do, or North-east Province	93,482	30,209	304,043	
Hoang-hè-do, west coast, north of Metropolitan Province	116,151	13,499	209,244	
Kang-wön-do, east coast, Middle Province	67,012	9,636	203,802	
Kiöng-ki-do, Metropolitan Province	160,615	19,180	103,466	
Chung-Chöng-do, west coast, south of Metropolitan Province	219,768	23,399	315,181	
Chölla-do, South-west Province	286,598	31,949	538,888	
Kyöng-syang-do, South-east Province	388,629	41,775	436,477	
Total	1,550,274	199,112	2,254,910	

The number of houses in the three southern provinces alone is 894,995, or more than half the number for the entire kingdom, and a glance at a map of Corea shows that in extent they comprise about one-third of it. Allowing four inhabitants to every house, this estimate would make the entire population a little over 6,000,000, and though this may be an under-estimate, it is probably far nearer the truth than the estimates of 15,000,000 or 16,000,000 found in some books on Corea. An estimate prepared by the French missionaries in 1850 gives 1,705,920 (adding 60,000 houses for the capital, which is omitted in it) as the total number of houses in the country. This would make the population about 7,000,000. The distribution of it between the northern and southern provinces is the same as in the estimate already given.

The chief objection to Asan is its distance from the capital, which, measured from the anchorage, is 95 miles by water, Inchhyön being only 55. The whole way is sheltered by islands, and it would be only in exceptionally bad weather that small river steamers could not make the passage. Such weather would naturally be principally in the winter months, when the Söul River, for fifty to sixty days, is frozen 1 or 1 and 1/2 feet thick between the capital and the bend above Kang-hoa, and all traffic is interrupted. Possibly a shorter and more sheltered passage may yet be discovered.

By land the anchorage is 40 miles in a direct line from the capital, and by road about 50 miles. Asan itself is said to be 220 Corean li, or 60 miles, from the capital. Mr. Hanabusa, to whose courtesy I am indebted for much of the information contained in this Memorandum, was good enough to furnish me with some notes of his journey from the capital to Kowonpho, a small village on the north side of the Asan harbour. From these notes I have taken the following account of the road between these places:-

From capital to north bank of river, 1 Japanese ri (2½ English miles); road level.

North bank of river to Namthé-regöng, 1 ri; half bed of river, half level road.

(At the capital the river passes through a gorge between two hills, but the river valley widens about this point, leaving a broad, level space covered by water in floods, and at other times a waste of sand and gravel.)

Namthé-regöng to Kwa-chhyön, 1 ri; half hilly, half level, one small pass.

Kwa-chhyön to Syu-wön, 4 ri; level road, 24 to 30 feet wide, compared by Mr. Hanabusa to the Tokaido in Japan.

Syu-wön to Toll-yöng, 4 ri; for 20 chô (1½ miles) a wide road, the remainder a narrow bye-road with numerous low hills and acclivities.

Toll-yöng to Palan-chang, 1 ri; numerous hills.

Palan-chang to Kowonpho, 4 ri; half hilly, with numerous slight ascents and descents, half level but narrow road.

The whole distance Mr. Hanabusa reckoned at 16 ri, or 40 English miles.

He said that although much of the road was hilly, there were no mountain-passes or other serious difficulties. He was two days on the way, leaving the capital at 7 A.M. on one day, and arriving at Kowonpho at 3. P.M. on the following day. He travelled with a suite of six or seven persons, some in chairs and some on horseback.

The road from the capital as far as a little to the south of Syu-wön is one of the three great roads which, leaving the capital, gradually diverge as they go southwards. It passes about 20 miles in a direct line east of the anchorage at Asan. There are two other roads from this port to the capital. The promontory where the suggested site is situated is now used pasturage. There are only half-a-dozen houses on it, and two or three small patches of cultivation. A dozen native junks were anchored near it, and perhaps forty or fifty more were seen in various parts of the inlet.

Mr. Hanabusa's first visit to Asan Harbour with Commanders Aoki and Yamazaki was in very unfavourable weather, which may have prejudiced them against it, and they seem to have given their attention to the anchorage off Kowonpho, hardly noticing that on the southern side of the Asan promontory.

(Signed) W. G. ASTON

Yokohama, July 4, 1882

Inclosure 3 in No. 68

Memorandum by Japanese Naval Officers on Chémulpho as a Port on the West Coast of Corea.

(Translation)

WITH a view to examine the ports on the west coast of Corea, our two ships proceeded in the first place to Basil Bay, and explored the Chinkang River, which forms the boundary between the Provinces of Chöllado and Chung-chong-do. This is rather a fine river. It has numerous large villages and towns on both banks (such as Syöpho, 150 houses; Ungpho, over 300 houses; Kang-kyöng, 700 houses, which are seen along the banks within the space of 20

English miles), and is therefore visited by a considerable number of junks. As will be seen by the "Amaka Kan's" rough survey, the width of the river is about 2 miles, and at first sight it presents a favourable appearance. At its widest part, however, shoals appear at various places at low tide, amongst which there is an unequal depth of from 1 to 3 fathoms, where even a small steamer would get aground, and the place is quite unfit for an anchorage for vessels like ours. There are several places with a depth of 5 to 6 fathoms, where the river winds and forms bays, but they are all of so limited an extent that it would be unsafe to remain here without mooring bow and stern. From the mouth of the river, as far as the Island of Keyado, the water is shallow, with numerous sand-banks and hidden reefs, so that in order to enter the river it is necessary to wait for high tide. Again, the anchorage of Yöndo, though well sheltered against northeast winds, is exposed to a heavy sea when the wind blows from the south-west. This happened just while we were there, to our no small distress. Neither the bay nor river can therefore be thought good as harbours, and so we abandoned the survey of them.

We next proceeded to Asan Bay. There are few large towns or villages here in comparison to the River Chinkang, and not more than one-tenth as many junks are to be seen entering and leaving. There are also sand-banks in the bay, and it is of course not a good harbour, but from Fourmier Island as far as the Kowompho anchorage, it is inclosed on all sides by points and islands, and there is no danger from a heavy sea. There are also places where the shore can be closely approached, so that, if no better alternative offered, this place might be accepted as a tolerable port, and we therefore made a survey of it, to which we beg to refer you.

We next proceeded to Inchhyön Gulf. At this place the Wölmi (Roze Island) anchorage seems exposed on all sides, but it is really inclosed by Yöngjong, Tèpu, Sopu, and other islands, so that even in gales of wind there is nttle danger from any heavy sea. The strength of the tide also does not exceed 3½ knots, which cannot be called excessive, and there is nothing to prevent large vessels anchoring here at all times. There is also, as shown in a separate plan, a second river at low tide between Wölmi and Chémulpho, and near the Wölmi Bluff there is *a depth of water at low spring tides of more than 2 fathoms* (italics in original). By putting down buoys here, *vessels with a draught of 12 feet might, by waiting for the tide, safely lie moored bow and stern and discharge and take on board cargo.* The facilities for communicating with the shore here are such as are not to be found at Chinkang or Asan, and from the natural formation of the place a pier could easily be constructed at no great expense. In addition to these considerations, it is near the capital by land and sea, and communication with it is easy. For these reasons, we consider it the most suitable place for an open port on the coast of the various provinces. We have the honour to present this as an opinion.

                (Signed) AWOKI SUMISADA, *Commander, His Imperial Japanese Majusty's ship "Takao-maru.'*
                YAMAZAKI KAGENORI, *Commander, His Imperial Japanese Majusty's ship "Ho-Sho-kan."*

June 25, 1879.
To his Excellency Hanabusa Yoshimoto,
Minister Resident

T.F. Wade (1882. 7. 6) ➡ G.L.G. Granville (1882. 8. 31)

1차 조영조약 체결 과정에 관한 Maude Report

Sir T. Wade to Earl Granville.—(Received August 31)

(No. 51 Confidential)

My Lord, *Peking, July* 6, 1882

IN continuation of my earlier despatch of this date, I have the honour to inclose, confidentially, copy of Mr. Maude's Report of his visit to Corea.

Mr. Maude himself attaches but little importance to his Report, but I think that it does him credit, and do not doubt that it will be perused with interest by your Lordship.

I have, &c.
(Signed) THOMAS FRANCIS WADE

Inclosure

Mr. Maude to Sir T. Wade.

(Confidential)

Sir, *Peking, June* 24, 1882

IN compliance with your request to be furnished with a Report on my visit to Corea with Admiral Willes, I have the honour to lay before you the following details :—

As I have already reported in my letter of the 28th ultimo, Her Majesty's gun-boat "Sheldrake," on board of which I left Chefoo on the 25th May for Corea, was fortunate in falling in with the Admiral's dispatch-boat "Vigilant" off the westernmost group of islands of the Corean Archipelago. By Admiral Willes' invitation, I at once went on board the "Vigilant," and before noon on the same day, the 27th May, we can't anchor about 27 miles from the capital, in what has now been called the anchorage of Jin-chuen, a part of the southern estuary of the Seoul River, which is called the district of Jin-chuen. Lying close to us were the two Chinese gun-boats, the "Wei-yuan" and the "Yang-wei," and also a Japanese gun-boat, which had brought Mr. Hanabusa, the Japanese Envoy, to Corea a few days before. Our anchor was hardly down when an officer came alongside from the "Wei-yuan" to ask "what we wanted." The Admiral said that he wished to see Ma Taotai, to which the officer replied that Ma Ta-jên had on the previous day gone to the capital on a visit to the King, but that he was expected back that evening. I begged the Chinese officer to say that I would have the honour, that evening, if possible, of delivering to Ma Ta-jên the letter from the Grand Secretary Li with which I was charged. In the meantime, I accompanied Admiral Willes a short distance up the river in his steam-launch. Going first to the western shore, which was about a mile from the ship, we saw that this part of the coast was or had been strongly fortified, according to the ideas of the inhabitants, for within a distance of not more than 1½ miles four or five batteries were to be counted, with five or six embrasures in each. I had not an opportunity of examining any of these works closely, as, in the only one which I approached subsequently, the guns, if there were any, were concealed from view by wooden screens; but the Admiral, on another occasion, saw some oval-bore guns in one of the forts. We did not, however, land the first day, but, after passing near the west shore, kept more to the middle of the mouth of the river, whence we had a good view of the surrounding country. All this portion of the coast appears to be hilly. To the north some higher peaks were visible, but we did not appear to be within sight of any mountain over 3,000 feet high.

The scenery of the mouth of the river is certainly picturesque. The soil seems to be a red loam, the colour of which, mixed with the bright spring foliage of small trees and underwood which grow luxuriantly on the hill-sides, made an effect which we were, perhaps, not inclined to underrate from having just come from the hideous sterility of North China.

On our way back to the "Vigilant," we first noticed evidences of the great rise and fall of the tide on this coast, places which we had steamed over not half-an-hour before having become a mass of brown rocks, and miles of mud-flats having appeared on each side of the river.

On returning to the "Vigilant" I found that Ma Taotai had come off to his ship, and I lost no time in going to pay him a visit. Though evidently very tired by a hot journey from the capital, he begged me to tell Admiral Willes that, as soon as he had read the letter which I had brought him from Tien-tsin, he would come to see the Admiral on board the "Vigilant." In about half-an-hour he arrived, and said that he was charmed to find that his instructions gave him the opportunity of being of service to Admiral Willes, and that we might rely on his best assistance in the negotiations with the Coreans. He said that he had been invited to pay the King a visit, otherwise he should have left immediately the American Treaty was signed, on the 22nd May. He had, however, made all his arrangements to leave the next morning, so that we had arrived exactly at the happy moment. The journey to the capital and back was the most painful he had ever made; it was very hot, and the conveyance was a Corean chair, a machine like a dog-kennel, on poles, in which, as it had no seat, the traveller is obliged to crouch or sit cross-legged; the only other alternative being a wild-looking pony, with an uncomfortable saddle.

On the following day I paid Ma Taotai another visit. He told me he had already written to the Corean Envoys, asking them to fix a day for an interview. That if Admiral Willes was ready to accept the American Treaty as it stood, he apprehended no difficulty in signing the Treaty at once. I replied that I feared it would be necessary to wait for the arrival of Mr. Spence, who was to be charged with comparing the Chinese and English texts. The only version of the Chinese which was in the Admiral's hands was a rough translation made in a hurry at Tien-tsin, and though I understood it was Admiral Willes' intention to adopt the terms of the American Treaty in substance, it would be more satisfactory to us that our text should be carefully drawn up by an experienced sinologue, who would be responsible for the English and Chinese agreeing accurately. Ma Ta-jên replied that he quite understood the desirability of our text being carefully drawn up, but that he would give me a copy of the English text of the America Treaty, which he could guarantee to be an exact translation of the Chinese.

This document only differed from the translation of the Chinese draft Treaty made at Tien-tsin in that the first Article, respecting the dependency of Corea on China, was omitted and that a clause was inserted in Article VIII prohibiting the export of breadstuffs from Jin-chuen.

The first alteration was made owing to Commodore Shufeldt objecting to the question being raised in the Treaty, and an arrangement was made by which the King of Corea wrote a letter to the President of the United States explaining his relations with China, which, however, had nothing to do with his relations with foreign Powers. The insertion of the stipulation respecting the non-exportation of rice from Jin-chuen was a compromise. The Coreans proposed to prohibit the exportation of bread-stuffs from all the open ports, but they were persuaded at last to agree to limit the permanent prohibition to Jin-chuen, the port nearest to the capital, where in case of famine the greatest distress would be felt.

Admiral Willes being anxious to know whether the King of Corea would receive him, I begged Ma Taotai to sound the Corean Envoys. He said he would be happy to do so, but he did not seem to think a visit to the capital would be feasible. He proceeded to say that, though the King of Corea was an autocratic Ruler—the Government being "une espèce de féodalité"—and though the Sovereign himself was convinced of the necessity of entering into relations with the outside world, he stood almost alone of his family in holding this opinion. There was a strong anti-foreign party in Corea, which had not yet given up the struggle to maintain the old system of isolation.

In consequence, the Envoys were unwilling to do anything, or encourage any demands which might be taken advantage of to their detriment by their adversaries of the anti-foreign party. "To give you an instance," said Ma Taotai, "of their timidity, I was invited to pay the Plenipotentiaries a visit at the village in which they are living, about 3 miles inland, and took with me Captain Clayson (an Englishman, Naval Instructor in the Chinese service). No sooner did they notice his presence than they became evidently disturbed, and even when told that he was in Chinese employ were not reassured, but said they feared they had compromised themselves by receiving him."

Whether this picture of the state of Corean feeling was quite accurate, I had, of course, no means of judging, but I took its intention to be to deter the Admiral from making any demands beyond the American Treaty, which would be sure to protract the negotiation.

Ma Taotai's description of the country was that it was very fertile but ill-cultivated. The capital, he said, contained 350,000 inhabitants, a statement which I ventured to doubt, the more so when he estimated the population of Corea at 30,000,000, whereas all other accounts agree in putting it at between 8,000,000 and 10,000,000 at most.

With regard to industries he did not seem to have much information. On arriving in Seoul he had been conducted to the apartments provided for him, and was given to understand that, should he wish to buy anything, it would be sent for, but that he could not go out to get anything. His chief purchases had been books, but he had been unsuccessful in trying to get a copy of a History of Corea, which be knew existed, and he attributed this to the suspicious timidity of the Coreans. What had most surprised Ma Ta-jên was the demeanour of the Corean Court. In a purely Oriental country he had never heard of a throne surrounded with so little of ceremony or restraints. He had been entertained at the Palace as at a family party. The King moved about and talked with every one. His age is a little over 30, and he has one son, an intelligent boy. The Crown is not strictly hereditary, but, as in China and Japan, the Sovereign chooses his successor from the Royal family.

During the two or three days which elapsed between our arrival and the visit of the Corean Envoys, we paid frequent visits to the shore, and Admiral Willes gave it as his opinion that, owing to the great rise and fall of the tide (30 feet), which would oblige ships to anchor at a distance of a mile and a half or more from the shore, it was impossible ever to expect to open a port with any success at Jin-chuen. He was therefore inclined to insert a clause in the Treaty providing for the opening of another port on the west coast, if a suitable harbour could be found. I was asked to speak to Ma Taotai in on the subject. He said he believed it would be useless to ask for such a concession from the Coreans. The Japanese were going, he believed, to open the port of Jin-chuen in the autumn. They were probably negotiating on the subject at Seoul at that moment. The Coreans would not be at all pleased to be asked for another port, as they thought they had given too much in having allowed the Japanese to select Jin-chuen as a port. On my relating to Admiral Willes what Ma Ta-jên had said, he abandoned the idea of making such a demand, and quite coincided with the latter's view that, the Treaty being only for five years, nothing would be lost by not making an effort to obtain an advantage which, as the capabilities of the country were quite unknown, would be more than doubtful.

The Admiral was, however, anxious to arrive at an understanding on three points. He wished to have the ports named; to provide for visits of the fleet to Corean waters; and to have permission granted that the coast might be at once surveyed by a British vessel. I therefore, at Admiral Willes' request, drew up a draft, copy of which I have the honour to inclose, of three Supplementary Articles to the Treaty, which the Admiral proposed to ask the Coreans to sign. I was indebted to Ma Taotai for the form of the IInd and IIIrd Articles. The form of Article II I had taken form Article III of the Treaty of Tien-tsin, 1858, but, at his suggestion, the law of nations was quoted in support of our demand. The last provision, respecting the survey, which was the most important of all, would, Ma Taotai said, be much more easily agreed to by the Coreans if it was put in exactly the same terms as Article VII of the Treaty between Corea and Japan of 1876. At Ma Ta-jên's suggestion. the draft was sent to the Corean Plenipotentiaries, with a covering letter merely saying that the Admiral desired to arrive at an understanding on the points raised in it. The reply of the Corean Envoys, which was only handed in on the day the Treaty was signed, though Ma Taotai had previously informed the Admiral of its sense, I shall refer to further on.

At the interview which took place on board the "Vigilant" four days after our arrival between the Admiral and the Corean Envoys, Ma Taotai acting as interpreter, it was agreed that the terms of the Treaty between Corea and the United States should be accepted for our Treaty, and that immediately on the arrival of Mr. Spence, who was then expected in a day or two, the Admiral should pay the Plenipotentiaries a return visit at the village in which they were living, and arrange to sign the Treaty at an early date.

The two Corean Plenipotentiaries, Tsao-Ling-Hsien and Ching-Hung-Chi, were accompanied by another official, whom I understood to hold the position of an Under-Secretary of State in the Government, and two interpreters. These last, though they were brought to talk Chinese, could not converse with Ma Taotai, and, in fact, soon left the Admiral's cabin and the restraints of business for the congenial occupation of exploring the ship. With the exception of the two Plenipotentiaries, who, in their manners, resembled educated Chinese, none of the Coreans whom we saw seemed to stand on any ceremony with strangers or with one another, the Under-Secretary of State going to sleep during the interview on board, and only being aroused by receiving a kick which the interpreter rose to administer.

The preliminaries as to signing the Treaty being arranged, there was nothing to be done but to await the arrival of Her Majesty's ship "Swift," which was to bring Mr. Spence from Shanghae. During the next few days I went on shore several times, more often on the island to the west of the anchorage called in the French survey "Teung Tchong." The natives always received us with a rough good humour, which found expression in shouts and slaps on the back. They seemed entirely devoid of the natural politeness of the Japanese or the studied ceremoniousness of the Chinese. But, unlike the latter, the Coreans never appeared the least timid, even the smallest children coming out boldly to stare at and touch the foreigner. Their greatest peculiarity seemed to be the jealousy with which the women are secluded. At no time, as far as I know, did any one on board our ships see a woman or girl on shore, and though, when we were walking, we occasionally saw figures precipitately retreating to the houses at the warning signal of a man who always preceded us, we were never close enough to guess to what sex they belonged. Ma Taotai even told me that in his visit to the capital he had not been able to perceive a single woman among the crowds which surrounded him.

The only thing which appears necessary to make the country very productive is more industry in the people. The crops we saw, though only sown in patches, were very promising; they consisted of barley, rye, and rice. The inhabitants, however, seem satisfied to live in their mud cabins in a very primitive way, and their chief occupation, like that of the Irish peasantry, seemed to be smoking. Though rough in manners, the ordinary people whom we met were far better educated than the same class in China, for they could write and read Chinese. My servant, a Pekingese, who was the only interpreter we possessed, and who carried on conversation with them in writing, generally found his stock of knowledge of characters not equal to theirs. In appearance, the Coreans that we saw were generally well built and tall; there is a great diversity of type, however. Sometimes we saw men with finely-cut features, others resembled more the Japanese, and others, again, looked like the Chinese of the North; nearly all were dark, but at least once or twice I saw a man with grey eyes and regular features of the purest Caucasian type.

With regard to the state of native industries in Corea, it would be presumptuous in me to set up an opinion. I may mention however one or two facts, which had me to believe that the idea I have heard universally expressed that there exists nothing worthy in the name of manufactures in the country to be exaggerated. Corean paper, as is well known, is of excellent quality, and even with the present small encouragement given to trade, is much used in China. The Corean hat, the most characteristic part of the national costume, is beautifully made of woven strips of bamboo, covered with light cotton or silk gauze. Though it must be as inconvenient a headdress as could well be imagined, the ingenuity of the workmanship might well be turned to account in other directions. Among the better dressed inhabitants white leather shoes are very commonly worn; these are extremely well made, apparently of fine deerskin; they have leather soles, studded with nails which resemble exactly those put into shooting-boots at home; both leather and nails are of much superior manufacture to anything I have seen in China, and, as far as I know, they are not Japanese exports. The dwelling-houses which we saw were for the most part mere hovels, with mud walls and thatch roofs, but we occasionally came on a house built of rough stones and brick, with a tile roof; there was, however, evidence of the use of stone for monuments. I observed near graves the two stone pillars with carved capitals which often in China are placed at the entrance to tombs, and also some square blocks of what appeared to be marble set up as grave-stones. On one occasion we came upon a small building resembling a Chinese mortuary temple, inside of which was an upright square pillar about 4 feet high, apparently of cast-iron; it was covered with Chinese characters in relief, and my Chinese servant, who professed to read them, pronounced it to be a mortuary tablet; as it stood near the road, with no bank or inclosure round it, I was inclined to suppose it was a complimentary monument.

Never having had an opportunity of entering a dwelling-house, I can say nothing as to the materials to be found there. Any cups or basins which we saw were of the coarsest earthenware; but on one occasion, when we were hospitably entertained by a village official in an open shed in his yamên, the wine-bottle and cups with which we were served were apparently of Japanese porcelain.

Several days elapsed, and nothing having been heard or seen of Her Majesty's ship "Swift," Admiral Willes began to fear that something had occurred to detain Mr. Spence. On the 5th June Ma Taotai and Admiral Ting, who was flying his flag on board the "Wei-yuan," had invited the Admiral, Captain Lindsay, of the "Vigilant," Captain Hoskyn, of Her Majesty's ship "Flying Fish," and Mr. Perry, the Admiral's Secretary, and myself to dine on board the Chinese gun-boat. While we were at dinner the French gun-boat "Lutin" arrived, and dropped anchor. A note almost immediately came on board from M. Dillon, the French Consul at Tien-tsin, who had come in the "Lutin," saying that he should be glad to pay Ma Taotai a visit. It was then that Admiral Willes, fearing that the French negotiations might interfere with ours, and seeing the impossibility of ascertaining whether Mr. Spence was coming or not, told Ma Taotai, in answer to the latter's inquiry whether he thought it necessary to wait for Mr. Spence any longer, that he would be happy to rely on his (Ma's) assurance that the Chinese text was in strict accordance with the English, and that he would sign the Treaty the next day.

Owing to the regrettable absence of Mr. Spence's assistance, it was impossible to alter the language of the American Treaty without risk of departing from the sense of the Chinese, and the phraseology of the English text of Commodore Shufeldt's Treaty was adopted throughout.

The Corean Plenipotentiaries proposed to meet Admiral Willes in a tent near the beach at 4 o'clock on Tuesday the 6th June. At the appointed time the Admiral, accompanied by most of the officers of Her Majesty's ship "Vigilant," and some of those from Her Majesty's ships "Flying Fish" and "Sheldrake," together with myself, went on shore, and were conveyed in chairs to the tent. We were there received by the Plenipotentiaries, who immediately conducted the Admiral to the centre one of five large wooden sentry-boxes, which were placed fronting the entrance. In each box was room for three persons, and we were all invited to walk into them. It did not appear, however, that we were required to stay inside, as, the ceremony of introducing us over, the Corean Plenipotentiaries walked away. We therefore came out and stood or sat in the tent.

Within a short time Ma Taotai and Admiral Ting appeared, accompanied by Captain Clayson, and, after a little delay, the ceremony of signing and sealing the Treaty was gone through. The Corean Plenipotentiaries then handed over to Admiral Willes the letter from the King of Corea to the Queen, and also their reply to the Admiral's note on the subject of the supplementary understanding. Admiral Willes said a few words, expressing a hope that the negotiations just brought to a satisfactory conclusion by the signing of a Treaty between Great Britain and Corea might be the beginning of a long and friendly intercourse between the two countries. Ma Taotai communicated the Admiral's speech to the Corean Plenipotentiaries in writing, who replied in suitable and cordial language; and we then took leave of them and returned as we came. The Admiral, who intended to leave for Nagasaki at daybreak next morning, also said good-bye to Ma Taotai and Admiral Ting.

Admiral Willes, I know, quite appreciates the valuable assistance which he received from Ma Taotai in negotiating with the Coreans. But I must take this opportunity of stating my conviction that if the termination be considered satisfactory, it is mainly to Ma Ta-jên's ready and able intermediation to which the success will be due. To his good offices I attribute the concession which we obtained to be allowed to survey the coasts, really, perhaps, at this moment the most valuable of any obtainable, and one which, as I shall have occasion to show further on, Commodore Shufeldt gave up as unobtainable. In taking leave of Ma Ta-jên, I had good reason to thank him on my own account for his courtesy and kindness to myself.

At Admiral Willes' invitation, I accompanied him to Nagasaki in the "Vigilant," the only other alternative being to have stayed at Jin-chuen on board the "Sheldrake," which was to remain there till the arrival of Her Majesty's ship "Swift," and then take Mr. Spence back to Shanghae, should he arrive in her. Events proved that by going with the Admiral to Nagasaki I took the quickest route to return by.

We left the anchorage at daybreak, and at 8 A.M. sighted a vessel, which was at first supposed to be the "Swift," but which turned out to be Her Majesty's ship "Kestrel," coming from Japan with Mr. Aston, Her Majesty's Consul at Kobé, who had been sent by Sir Harry Parkes to be of assistance to the Admiral if possible. Mr. Aston, who has studied Corean, and is one of the few authorities on the country, was also accompanied by a Corean interpreter, and it was disappointing both to him and to us that he should have arrived too late. He, however, went on in the "Kestrel" as far as Jin-chuen to pay a short visit to the coast.

On the 9th June the "Vigilant" got to Nagasaki, and the next morning, as he was leaving at once to rejoin the fleet, I took leave of Admiral Willes, after thanking him for the kindness and hospitality which I had enjoyed on board the "Vigilant" for a fortnight.

MR.Hall, Her Majesty's Acting Consul at Nagasaki, made a translation of the note from the Corean Plenipotentiaries in reply to Admiral Willes' note inclosing the Protocol, and he called my attention to the fact that no answer was given to the first point respecting the names of the ports. Learning this after the Admiral had left, I wrote to him to remind him that Ma Taotai, in telling us the contents of the note which we afterwards received, had said that it was understood that the ports were those open to the Japanese, though, at the time, it did not occur to me that he meant to say there was no answer in the note to this point. The omission does not appear of any great moment, as the ports of Gensan and Fusan, being open to the Japanese, would naturally come under the head of ports open to foreigners, and the port of Jin-chuen, which has not yet been opened, is expressly denominated an open port in Article VIII in the clause prohibiting the export of rice.

Hearing that Commodore Shufeldt was in Nagasaki, I went to call on him. In conversation about his visit to Corea I asked him why the ports had not been named in the American Treaty. He said he had thought it better to leave it to be inferred that the ports were those open to the Japanese. He had heard that the Coreans were anxious about having allowed the Japanese to fix on Jin-chuen, but the Japanese had no intention of giving it up. I asked about the survey of the coast. He said he had desired to put an Article in the Treaty providing for it. This had, however, been met with opposition and suspicion by the Coreans, and he had relinquished it. I may mention, in confirmation of what Commodore Shufeldt said about Jin-chuen, that the Captain of the Japanese Government mail-steamer, in which I crossed to Shanghae, told me he had been told he would have to go with his ship to Jin-chuen at some time in the summer, as he said, "to show her to the Coreans."

In closing this account of my proceedings, I must apologize for venturing to offer crude observations on a place and population which will soon be visited by able critics.

I have, &c.

(Signed)   C.T. Maude

H.S. Parkes (1882. 7. 24) ➡ G.L.G. Granville (1882. 8. 25)

1차 조영조약에 따른 일본의 조약개정 요구 보고

No. 3

Sir. H. Parkes to Earl Granville.—(Received August 25)

(No. 92)

Tôkiô, July 24, 1882

My Lord,

I WISH to report briefly, as time will not permit me to do more by this opportunity, that the Japanese Foreign Minister has proposed to the Conference that the new Treaties, when revised, shall continue in force—the commercial clauses for only eight years, and the other clauses for only twelve years from the date of ratification; and that after the lapse of the said periods of eight and twelve years, any one of the new Treaties may be terminated in whole or in part by either of the Contracting Parties on twelve months' notice.

This proposal was made at a meeting held on the 19th instant, and although it has not yet been finally formulated, I have been assured by the Japanese Minister for Foreign Affairs that his Government will make it a *sine quá non* of any revision. He has also observed to me that, if the Governments of the Treaty Powers should not accept it, his Government would regard the refusal as denoting a want of confidence on their part in the progress and good intentions of Japan, and in that case they would prefer to maintain the present order of things under the existing Treaties until the justice of their claim, which would not be lost sight of, should be recognized by the Treaty Powers.

On hearing this proposal made at the Conference, I at once observed that it so seriously affected all the work in which we had been engaged during the last six months, that I could have wished that it had been brought forward at the earliest instead of at the final stage of those proceedings. When the Conference commenced its sittings the Minister for Foreign Affairs had himself proposed that the Austro-Hungarian Treaty should be taken as the basis of the preliminary negotiations. That Treaty, like all the others, was permanent, and not terminable in its character, it was open to revision but not to abrogation, and—the knowledge that the Treaties could be so revised from time to time, and amended as experience should prove desirable, but without being annulled—had given a stability to foreign relations with Japan which had proved of great value to all concerned, and could not be lightly relinquished. The present proposal of the Japanese Government was in effect a proposal to abrogate the Treaties, and, if it should prove unacceptable to the Treaty Powers, and be adhered to by Japan, then all the proceedings of the Conference would prove useless. I added that all that I could do would be to submit it to Her Majesty's Government, if the Japanese Government so desired, but that I should find it difficult to recommend to the former any basis for the revision of the Treaty between Great Britain and japan that contained a condition for the abrogation of that Treaty.

The French Minister marked his disapproval of the proposal as strongly as I did, but it was warmly supported by the American Minister. The German Minister observed that he believed his government wished the permanent character of the existing Treaties to be maintained, but that much would depend upon the exact wording of the proposal, which he would submit to his Government with the President's explanations. Most of the other Representatives, who seem at a loss to speak on the subject, expressed concurrence in the rather indefinite views of the German Minister. The Russian Chargé d'Affaires stated that he was in favour of the termination of the commercial clasuses of the Treaties, though this does not accord with the action of his Government in their recent Treaty with China.

I have reason to think that the Minister for Foreign Affairs would not be disappointed of this proposal were to have the effect of postponing the revision of the Treaties. He is charged, I believe, by his colleagues in the Government, with having made overtures of too liberal a nature, and he has only reconciled them to his offer to open the whole country to foreigners by assuring them that he would satisfy national pride by recovering in return entire jurisdiction over the latter. He now sees that it is doubtful whether the Governments of the Treaty Powers will accept the above offer on such terms, and he probably wishes to retreat from a position which he feels he may not be able to successfully maintain.

He has another reason, however, for that desire in the great dissatisfaction which has been occasioned to his Government by the recent Corean Treaties, the conditions of which they regard as far more favourable to Corea than those of the existiing Treaties are to Japan. They consider that whatever Corea has gained should be conceded to Japan; or, rather, that the latter, as being a more advanced nation, and having long held relations with Western Powers, is entitled to conditions superior to those which have been granted to Corea at the very outset of her foreign intercourse.

The Minister for Foreign Affaris has exprressed this feeling in unmistakable language to the German Minister, and it clearly appears in the following passage in the "Japan Mail" of the 22nd instant, which is reported to be the foreign organ of the Government, and has evidently been made acquainted with the discussions of the Japanese Government, observes: "So long as Japan's twelve years of progress—rapid enough to excite the admiration of the world—avails her so little that our very first Treaty with Corea accords to that semi-barbarous and bigoted coutry rights which to this day we refuse to Japan, so long as her adoption of our own Codes and ger appointment of our own experts to be her Judges fail to obtain any relaxation of a system which no free people could tamely endure, and which, moreover, has been extended beyond the utmost limits contemplated in the Treaties: so long, we say, as all this obtains, not mush prescience is needed to foresee the sentiments that are likely to influence Japan's behaviour toward us. There can no longer be any mistake about her policy. She will grant us no new commercial privileges until we, on our side, practically demonstrate our faith in the reality of her progress."

I notice a considerable resemblance between this language and that used to me by the Foreign Minister on the day when he made the above-mentioned proposal to terminate the Treaties. He then mentioned that his Government and people attached the utmost importance to that condition (possibly for this region, among others, that Corea has not obtained it), and that. If it was refused to Japan, and the existing Treaties could consequently not be revised, such an unfortunate result might create a reactionary feeling in the public opinion of this country, which the Government would be obliged to respect by closely adhering to the conditions of those Treaties, and by strictly maintaining all the restrictions on the trade and liberties of foreigners, which may be imposed under their provisions.

I have, &c,
(Signed) Harry S. Parkes

T.F. Wade (1882. 8. 3) ➜ G.L.G. Granville (1882. 9. 26)

조선의 개항과 수출입 현황에 관한 Spence Report

Sir T. Wade to Earl Granville.—(Received September 26)

(No. 67)

My Lord, *Peking, August* 3, 1882

I HAVE the honour to lay before your Lordship a Report by Mr. Spence of his visits to Corea, which, I cannot doubt, will be perused with interest.

Mr. Spence, as your Lordship is aware, did not arrive in Corea early enough to act as Admiral Willes' interpreter, the duty which he was detached to perform, but this was not Mr. Spence's fault, nor, I may add, was it mine. Admiral Willes, on arriving at Tien-tsin, had mentioned his desire to take Mr. Spence with him to Corea, his experience, acquired when he visited the country with the Duke of Genoa, making him of necessity a valuable assistant.

On the 14th May, having received a promise that the papers required by Admiral Willes should be forthcoming, I requested him to telegraph to Mr. Hughes, Her Majesty's Consul at Shanghae, to desire Mr. Spence to come down with all speed from I-chang, of which port he was in acting charge. At this time it was assumed that Admiral Willes' negotiations would not commence before the end of June. The Chargé d' Affairs of the United States had stated to me that Commodore Shufeldt's business would hardly be concluded sooner, and as he had expressed some anxiety about the non-appearance of other negotiators until he had himself left the field, Admiral Willes, on learning this from me, proposed to spend the intervening time up the Gulf of Tartary. Meanwhile, on the 19th May, we heard from the best authority that Commodore Shufeldt was expected at Chefoo in a week, and I then took the liberty of recommending him to proceed immediately to Corea. Sir Harry Parkes had already one or two gentlemen at hand should the Admiral require them. One of them, Mr. Aston, did eventually proceed to Corea. That he was not there earlier is possibly to be ascribed to my advice. I had been assured that a belief on the part of the Coreans that Admiral Willes was drawing counsel or assistance from the side of Japan would retard rather than accelerate his proceedings. I now believe that, so far as British officers of the Consular service in Japan are concerned, this was a mistake, and if, as I suspect, it was owing to what I told him, that Admiral Willes did not also engage the services of Sir Harry Parkes' men, I must express my regret. But to return to Mr. Spence; the letter forwarded by Mr. Hughes was detained four days at Hankow, on its way to I-chang, reaching that port only on the 29th May; Mr. Spence was unable to leave I-chang before the 2nd June. Steam communication between I-chang and Hankow is regular but not frequent. He arrived at Shanghae on the 8th, and embarking on board the man-of-war which was waiting for him on the 9th, arrived in Corea on the 11th to find the Treaty signed and the Admiral departed.

The particular duty which would have fallen to the lot of Mr. Spence was the verification of the Chinese text. For this Admiral Willes was obliged to refer to Ma Taotai.

Mr. Spence is a very competent scholar in Chinese, written and spoken. It will be seen, I think, from his Report of what importance is a conversance with the former, the written language, in Corea.

It will be seen from the same Report that we must not be over ready to credit the pessimists who are preaching that Corean trade is worth little. On the other hand, it is, I think, undoubtedly true that, whatever foreign trade is done there will pass through the hands of the Chinese factor rather than of the Western trader, but this, I take leave to say, is not, in my opinion, against the interests of the Western producer. The western trader has heavy expenses to pay and a fortune to make. The Chinese factor's expenses are comparatively slight, and his notion of fortune making not extravagant. Consular surveillance is necessary, but rather to fight the battle of the trade than of the trader.

I have, &c.

(Signed)　　THOMAS FRANCIS WADE

Inclosure

Notes on the newly-opened Ports of Corea, and Trade prospects thereat.

Gensan

GENSAN, the most northerly of the two ports on the east coast of Corea, is situated in Broughton Bay, in latitude 39°. It is only a Corean village, built on a strip of level ground lying between the great axial range of mountains which runs parallel with and close to the whole eastern coast and the sea. The port is easily made, and is, though more of a roadstead than a harbour, a good anchorage in all winds except those between north and east. The well-known harbour of Port Lazareff is only a few miles off, and as some confusion exists between the two places, I attach a rough map of the Corean coast near Gensan, showing their relative position. Port Lazareff, it will be seen, lies directly to the north of the new port. It was minutely described by me in the report of my visit to Corea with His Royal Highness the Duke of Genoa, printed by the Foreign Office the 10th May, 1881, and I need not refer to it here except as a safe haven in a north-easterly gale for the shipping which may frequent the open port of Gensan. The anchorage has a gently sloping, sandy bottom, shallowing from 15 fathoms about 1½ miles from shore to 7 fathoms when half-a-mile. Wooden landing piers were put up by the Japanese in 1880, but it is not likely that the trade of the port will ever be sufficiently large to necessitate any other means of landing cargo than that which exists at present—viz, in open harbour into cargo boats. The maximum rise and fall of the tide during the three weeks I spent near Gensan was 2½ feet. The shores of the harbour and of Port Lazareff are fringed with ice during winter, but both places remain open and accessible throughout the year. Navigation is much impeded by the fogs during spring and autumn.

Gensan is at the southern extremity of the north-eastern province of Hsien Ching. Its connections with the towns of this province, which lie to the west of the axial range, are fairly good, but with the capital, about one hundred miles off as the crow flies, communication is difficult. In the trade with Seoul, the capital of Corea, and the populous valley of the Hankiang, Gensan will be unable to compete with the port to be opened on the west coast of the country, owing to the height of the mountain passes and the badness of the roads. From the great range which throws up near Gensan several peaks of from 7,000 to 8,000 feet high, spurs run down to the sea shore, inclosing along the whole east coast a series of narrow valleys of limited extent, but of enchanting beauty, which are well tilled and populous. In the bottom lands, where irrigation is easy, rice is cultivated; but on light soils, or where the supply of water is short, millet, hemp, and sweet potatoes are grown. No terracing has been done anywhere, not even on the lowest slopes of the hills. All are covered with a dense jungle of brushwood, ferns, conifers, rose trees, stunted pines, and dwarf oaks. Trees get more frequent as the hills get higher, and the lofty ranges, from a distance, appear to be an unbroken mass of forest. The narrow valleys, however, teem with people, and it is the wants of their hardy population of farmers and fishermen, and of the towns in the province of Hsien Ching that Gensan will supply, rather than those of cis-montane Corea.

Two small streams flow into the sea near Gensan. A river of considerable size flows into Port Lazareff by two or three embouchures, erroneously described in the "China Pilot," Vol. iv., as navigable. It is navigable for light draught Corean boats, but by none of its mouths in 1880 could we find an entrance for a steam launch drawing only 3 feet. This river forms a considerable delta, in which is situated extensive Government salt works. It is covered with drysalters' huts and ponds, through which the river meanders in a dozen different channels. We followed the river a short way inland, sufficiently far to prove that Admiral Roze's remarks regarding its course and importance are quite misleading.

Until the opening of Gensan by the Japanese in 1879 it was an unimportant collection of huts. In that year the Japanese chose, or were alloted, a site for a Settlement to the west of the Corean town, picturesquely situated near a wooded headland in the position I have marked in the map. When I visited it in 1880 the Settlement was marked out, a Consulate-General erected, and a dozen substantial two-storied European houses, besides a number of Japanese houses, built. Communication with Japan was maintained by a steamer once every two months, and trade had hardly begun. The year 1881 may be considered to be the first year of the port, the trade done amounting to 770,000 yen of imports, and 728,000 yen of exports; in all, a trade of about 225,000ℓ. The imports were all European or American goods, in the main, cottons of heavy weight. The exports were hides, gold-dust, hemp, and silk. The cotton piece-goods go to Corea by way of Shanghae, being sold by English to Chinese merchants there, and by the latter to Japanese merchants in Nagasaki and Kobé. Eighteen vessels entered and cleared at Gensan during the year.

The Japanese have a Consul-General here, with a staff of student interpreters, learning Corean for colloquial purposes and Chinese for official correspondence. The nearest local authority to Gensan of sufficient rank to be in relations with the Consul on a footing of equality is the Fu-shih, or Prefect of Tê Yüan-fu, a city of the first rank some 10 miles to the south-west. All business regarding international matters, as between Japan and Corea at this port, is entrusted, on the Corean side, to the Tê Yüan Prefect. There is another city of equal rank some 20 miles to the north-west, Yung Hing-fu, the Prefect of which visited the Duke of Genoa's ship in 1880. These places I have dignified by the name of cities, as they are designated "fu" by the Coreans, but they are in no way to be compared in point of buildings, defences, population, or trade to Chinese cities of that rank. "Fu" denotes in Corea, as in China, the first territorial division of a province, or the capital city of such division, or the rank of the officer having jurisdiction. The provincial Superior of the Prefect is the Ying-mên, or Governor, but I am unable to say whether the Japanese authorities are in direct relations with him or not.

The Settlement area at Gensan was given by the Corean Government to the Japanese on the most liberal terms, and in the event of the acquisition of a British Settlement site being contemplated by Her Majesty's Government, it will in all probability be secured with little or no expenditure of money. If the promontory marked in the map is not all included in the Japanese Settlement, and I feel sure it is not, is would be a most desirable site for the houses of British subjects resorting to Gensan, provided fresh water in plentiful supply exists. One more convenenient could not be found, and one ore healthy or more beautiful it would be difficult to conceive. In this connection I may add that the Corean huts in the neighbourhood and in the native town are not only not fit habitations for Europeans, but cannot by any transformation short of rebuilding, be made so. There may be in the fu cities of Corea temples and stone houses sufficiently well constructed to serve as residences for a time, but in Gensan there was none. When under the new treaty a British Consul is first sent to Gensan he will either have to apply for accommodation to the Japanese Consul General, or remain on board ship until a place can be run up for him. There are plenty of Japanese carpenters and masons in the port, and there will be no difficulty in getting temporary quarters erected.

I shall consider later on in this paper the prospects of British trade at this port, but I may state here one field of usefulness and pleasure which the opening of Gensan will secure to some of my countrymen. The jungle-clad mountain range I have described as the backbone of Corea is given up to the undisputed possession of the tiger, and near Gensan the hills, great and small, are abandoned to him and other wild beasts. Tiger pits are to be seen on farms contiguous to the jungle, and in winter, which at Gensan is bitter, the tigers come down to the valleys by the sea in search of food. They have at times invaded the Japanese Settlement even, and the Consul General informed me that one broke into the guard-house of the Settlement in the winter of 1879, and devoured a policeman. The natives, being defenceless, hold them in horror, and the Englishman with his rifle will be hailed in this part of Corea as a deliverer.

Fusan

Fusan, is latitude 35°, is situated exactly at the south-east corner of the peninsula where the great Corean range loses itself amongst barren hills and sand dunes. The harbour is one of the finest in Eastern seas. The black-looking hills of the mainland bound it to the east, west, and north; on the south it is protected by Deer Island; and it is a magnificent anchorage, easy of access, and safe in all weathers. The shores of the harbour are fringed with villages containing an aggregate population of from 10,000 to 12,000, mostly engaged in fishing, for I believe the neighbourhood of Fusan is as barren as it looks. Deer Island, on the contrary, is uninhabited, and, with the exception of a space which has been cleared as a Government reservation for horses, is densely wooded to its summit, 1,500 feet high, and well stocked with game. Ships can lie at anchor within a short distance of any of its shores. Tides are very small, only 2 or 3 feet rise an fall, and the harbour, of course, is free from ice. The whole of this part of the coast, including Fusan Harbour, has been carefully surveyed by Her Majesty's ships, and is accurately described in Vol. iv of the "China Pilot." Fusan is only a few hours steaming from Simonoseki in Japan, and is about the same distance from Shanghae as Nagasaki.

One hundred and twenty miles south of Gensan the Corean range divides into two branches, one continuing to run along the east coast, and the other trending south-west to the south-west corner of the peninsula. These two branch-ranges inclose the watershed of a considerable river, the Wu, with its tributary, the Ching, which flows into the Channel of Corea a little to the west of the port of Fusan.

This watershed forms the Province of Ch'ing Shang, which is over 7,000 square miles in extent, and comprises a great extent of rice lands. This section of the country produces far more grain than it can consume, and since the opening of Fusan to Japanese trade it has exported a considerable amount, and taken payment for the exports in British cotton goods. This and the neighbouring Province of Chuan Lo, of which I know nothing, is the country which will supply, and be supplied from, Fusan.

Owing to its proximity to Japan, Fusan has long had relations with that country, although till 1876 they were not those of commerce. It was the last stronghold of the Japanese in Corea after Fidejoshi's campaigns, and it has been inhabited by a garrison of Japanese from the Island of Tsushima ever since 1615. The little town where the Princes of Tsushima kept their garrison under the old Treaty of 1615 is now transformed into the Japanese trading Settlement under the Treaty of 1876. It is situated as I have marked in the foregoing rough map. Its area has been extended to meet the large influx of Japanese which the hope of gain has drawn hither, but the modern settlement is built under the shadow of the rees planted by their military predecessors 200 years ago.

Shortly after Fusan was open to trade 700 Japanese found their way there, and when I visited the port in 1880 there were over 2,000 residents in the Settlements. Trade in 1879 was of the value of 560,000 yen of imports, and 670,000 yen exports. The imports were mainly English cotton goods and foreign dyes; the exports, rice, stock-fish, and medicines. Owing to the great increase in the export of rice lately, trade is reported as having increased to a total volume of over 2,000,000 yen a year, of which 700,000 yen represents rice exports. Trade is much impeded, both here and at Gensan, by the cumbrous nature of Corean money,copper cash, there being no such system of banking as we have in China, enabling the defects of a bad currency to be entirely obviated by means of notes and bills of exchange. Transactions are conducted at present between Japanese and Coreans at Fusan are frequently in barter.

The Japanese have a Consul and a large Consular staff at Fusan. He is in relations with the territorial Prefect* living at Tung-ts'ai Fu, a city some 8 miles off. It is with this official we shall be in relations in event of the British Treaty being ratified. There is a second prefectural city some 16 miles off, at the mouth of the river which drains the whole province.

In striking contrast to the barren hills round the harbour the Japanese Settlement nestles in the midst of a grove of magnificent fir-trees of phenomenal size. It strikes me as occupying the best site also for trade purposes. However, between it and the Corean town of Fusan, which lies 2½ miles to the north-east at the head of a little bught, there are plenty of sites along the high road to

---

*[원주] ____ in the Prefect is whose jurisdiction Fusan ___.

Tung-ts'ai. Should Her Majesty's Government desire to acquire a Settlement here for the use of British subjects resorting to Fusan, it will be obtained, in all probaility, on a simple understanding to pay a nominal rent, annually, without any initial purchase. Such, at least, I was told by the Japanese Consul at Fusan was the arrangement made with the Japanese Government when their Settlement was enlarged, and this affords a presumption that a similar courtesy will be extended to other Treaty Powers.

Jên Ch'uan

Jên Ch'uan is the port opened on the west coast, near the mouth of the Hankiang River, and within a few miles of the capital. When I crossed over to Corea in June, by order of Her Majesty's Minister, to join Admiral Willes, I was only a few hours at the anchorage of Ile Boisée, and had no opportunity of seeing this port. The extraordinary rise and fall of the tide, some 30 feet, and the velocity of the tide currents, appear to me to be great obstacles to the success of this port as a trading mart. This is all the more to be regretted, inasmuch as its proximity to the capital and to the valley of the principal Corean river points to it as the port where trade in British products is likely to be largest, and where the products of the country which can be profitably purchased will be most easily discovered. However, this is a matter on which I speak with insufficient knowledge. Her Majesty's ship "Flying Fish" has been surveying off the mouth of the Hankiang, and Commander Hoskyn, or Mr. Aston, the Consul at Kobé, who is on board, should be able to give Her Majesty's Government accurate information regarding the convenience and safety of Jên Ch'uan, or any other port near the capital. Until such information is received the selection of the port on the west coast should, in my opinion, be left an open question for a time. I hear, however, that the Japanese are to commence trading at Jên Ch'uan in autumn. In that case, a change of port, even if proved to be desirable, will be impossible. The small part of the Jên Ch'uan Prefecture which came under my eyes was not much cultivated; but it would be as unfair to argue the poverty of the country from that, as to judge of China from the mud flats of Taku.

Trade Prospects

The three ports are well selected. Corea is divided naturally into three sections by its mountain system. These I may term Southern Corea, cis-montane Corea, and trans-montane Corea. The first of these is served by Fusan, the second by Jên Ch'uan or some other port near the capital on the west coast, and the last by Gensan. No part of the country, except the strip along the Tumen River, on the Russian frontier, is 100 miles from a Treaty port.

British shipping will be at once engaged in the Corean trade as soon as the Treaty is ratified, and permission given to British subjects to proceed to Corea. A British line of steamers has recently been running between Vladivostock, in Russian Tartary, and Shanghae, with considerable success. The agents of it, Messrs, Jardine, Matheson and Co., of Shanghae, intend to make the two Corean ports, Fusan and Gensan, ports of call for the steamers of this line, on both outward and inward voyages. It is their intention also to station agents at these ports. The port on the western coast being only a few hours out of the regular course of steamers plying between Shanghae and Tien-tsin, it will probably, shortly after its opening be in constant communication with these important cities.

Imports

The main import will be British cotton goods. There is an impression that Coreans wear nothing except white cotton cloths, which is not correct. All classes, of all occupations, are fully clothed in all weathers in white garments, but most of the poorer people wear a singularly fine species of hempen cloth, which may easily be mistaken for coarse cotton. I found, however, that it was an object of ambition to all people clothed in hemp to have an outer cloak or gown of foreign cotton cloth, the superior fineness and finish of which they have a high admiration of. For this, which one sees worn by every person of means, they insist on having the best cotton cloth, American sheetings being the favourite stuff in the north, and the heaviest makes of English goods in the south. Indeed, it is an axiom in Shanghae that "There is no market in Corea for rubbish," and that "A Corean is a gentleman who pays a high price for a good article." A large quantity of cottons are imported into Corea at present overland from Newch-wang, through the palisade frontier known as the Corean Gate. Some are taken from Tien-tsin, and 200,000 or 300,000 pieces find their way into the country through Japanese ports and hands. In all cases the goods come first from Shanghae; and I have it on the authority of Shanghae importers that the total amount which is now sent from that port in these various channels is much larger than it is the custom to assert. I am of opinion that the opening of Corea to British trade will be followed by a large increase in the consumption of our cotton goods in that country, particularly at the port on the west coast, which will be the inlet to the capital and the Han-kiang Valley, a new and extensive market. The 10 per cent. Tariff provided for in the British Treaty will not be a bar to the trade, for this reason:—The goods sent into Corea by way of the northern ports of China pay, at present, a 5 per cent. Tariff duty at Shanghae, besides three or four profits to brokers and middlemen; whereas, sent direct from Shanghae to Jên Ch'uan or Gensan, a drawback on re-export for the Chinese duty would be given, and the middlemen's profits saved. Individual transactions in imported cottons at the new Corean ports will, in most cases, be small, owing partly to the clumsy currency and the want of bills—a subject to which I have already alluded—and partly to the timidity of the natives, who, as far as I was able to judge in the Fusan shops, spend much time and many words over the purchase of one piece of cloth. On these grounds, I think it probable that the distributors of our goods will be eventually all Chinese or Japanese, and not English. None the less will the trade be a British one, and an advantage to us, in the interests of our manufacturing classes, to secure, especially at a time when, in more civilized parts of the world, market, after market is shut against us. There will be a great demand, too, at Corean ports for inexpensive European knick-nacks of all kinds—metal ware, glass ware, and the like, for the country has hitherto been in such complete isolation that grown-up men have the curiosity and desires of children regarding all handy and glittering articles.

Exports

With regard to exports, we are as yet quite in the dark, except in so far as the Japanese trade with Corea has thrown light on the subject. That the southern provinces produce rice in abundance, the non-prohibition of its export in the Treaty proves. Various medicines, notably "ginseng," are at present brought to China; but whether they are of a nature to enrich the European pharmacopoeia we do not as yet know. Hides and skins seem to be obtainable; the fine quality of the hemp I have already noticed; and the gold dust exported to Japan indicates some store in the country of the precious metals. To the north there are, along the Yaloo and Tumên Rivers, great forests of pines, poles cut from which come to Tien-tsin in junks from the Chinese district coterminous with the Corean frontier.

There is a disposition to depreciate the resources of Corea as a producing country, founded on quite insufficient testimony. The country, in any case, has resources to support millions of strong, sturdy men, and in the South it produces, in ordinary years, more grain than can be consumed.

The foregoing notes on trade are sufficiently meagre. Of this, however, we may be assured: whatever imports trade springs up will, in origin, be mainly British. Provided equal privileges are granted to all, trade, both import and export, will, in carriage and distribution, be mainly British. But if commercial privileges, such as the rights of coast trading, be granted to the Chinese, and the feudal relation in which Corea stands toChina be put forth as a special consideration barring a claim by England, under the favoured-nation clause of the Treaty, to equal privileges, Corean trade, in carriage and distribution, will be mainly in Chinese hands. The right of Corea to make such arrangements will, I feel sure, in the course of time be asserted, and, in my humble opinion, it will have to be strenuously resisted.

The Coreans are physically the finest people in Eastern Asia; they are, as a rule, tall, strong men, with a most independent bearing and look; they are much less refined than either the Chinese or Japanese; they are boorish in behaviour even on occasions of ceremony, and seem to know no medium between sulking and rude familiarity; they are very dirty drunken when they get the chance, and dishonest. In 1880 I found them, away from the Japanese Settlements, well-disposed, willing to talk, and even friendly; but in the neighbourhood of Fusan and Gensan I found them the very reverse. The bad usage they have had to put up with from the Japanese settlers has, I regret to say, infuriated the Coreans not only against them, but against all foreigners. The outrages one reads of as constantly occurring by Coreans on Japanese are simply occasional retaliations by the former for the constant tyranny of the latter. To this legacy of hate we shall succeed at Fusan and Gensan when British subjects proceed there; but I have little doubt that, with ordinary circumspection by our people, and watchful supervision by our Consuls, hate will be turned to toleration, and Coreans learn to distinguish between an Englishman and a Japanese. For a time, however, it will be impossible for Englishmen to walk much about alone in the vicinity of the Japanese Settlements.

The right of travelling in the interior is not expressly granted in our Treaty, and it is open to contention whether a prohibition to carry goods into the interior connotes a permission to travel in the interior without goods. If the Corean Government intends, as is more than probable, that our subjects shall have no other or higher privileges than those they have granted to Japanese subjects, we shall have no right to travel, and the question of Settlements will therefore have to be faced at the very outset of our Treaty intercourse. Without permission to travel, and in the midst of a Corean population on thoroughly bad terms with the Japanese, it would be impossible for a handful of British subjects to live at a Corean port except on ground reserved for their especial use. Mindful of this, I have in my notice of the ports above drawn special attention to Settlement sites.

The Coreans, it is known, have a language of their own, and a method of writing it by means of an alphabet. This latter seems to be displaced by the written Chinese character, which I found in universal use. Education is more wide-spread than in China, and I rarely have met with a Corean, however young or however poor, who was not able to read and write sufficient Chinese to carry on an ordinary conversation. Chinese is written by the Coreans exactly in China, only they read it in Corean, so that any person who has a ready knowledge of the commoner characters and combinations of the Chinese written language finds himself quite at home in Corea, and might, armed with pen and ink, travel through the country unharmed from one end of it to the other. All official correspondence in Corea is in Chinese, examinations for official appointments being conducted in that language. Of Japanese, written or spoken, neither officials nor people know anything, and the Japanese Consuls in Corea have to make a special study of Chinese to fit them for their duties. In the service to which I have the honour to belong Her Majesty's Government has there a body of servants from whom may be drawn, without any further linguistic preparation than that which their training in China has already given them, a Consular staff for Corea capable of communicating freely with both officials and people the moment they set foot in the country.

I have given Corean names throughout these notes their sounds in Chinese.

(Signed)　　WM. DONALD SPENCE

前田獻吉(1882. 9. 3) ➡ 吉田淸成

영국 군함의 조선 해안 측량 보고

第七拾七號

去ル七月廿七日午後四時英國軍艦マクバイ號入港艦長海軍大尉カアベルトン氏ニシテ通辨トシテ中村思孝ト申者乘組居同廿八日艦長本館ヘ尋訪熊川近海測量ノ爲渡來ノ義ニ有之就テハ地方長官對面致度候處初メテノ事ニ付都合取計呉候樣依賴相成候ニ付承諾東萊ヘ通報置候處同日東萊府使問勞トシテ該艦ヘ立越シ艦長ヨリ致通辨乘込方各地方ヘ諭達等懇望有之府使承知ノ上歸府同廿九日東萊府ヘ廻禮トシテ立越候處厚ク待遇有之同卅日午前九時三十分昌原馬山港ヘ向ケ拔錨八月十六日同艦廻來ニ付本官尋訪同廿四日投錨一咋一日午後十一時又々入港卽チ通辨ヲ以テ致尋問候處當國巨濟島或ハ統營等ノ沿海測量相濟候ニ付一時當港ヘ拔錨本日午後四時長崎港ヘ向ケ拔錨致候段申聞候竊ニ聞所ニ據レハ右測量ノ趣意タルヤ全ク統營ヲ以テ開港ノ目的ノ由尤モ統營ハ慶尙道水軍ノ統部ニシテ當港ヲ距ル貳拾里[日本里數]程人家三千戶船舶出人ノ便宜慶尙道ノ要港ト申事ニ御座候

右具狀仕候也敬具

　　　明治十五年九月三日

　　　　　　　　　　　　　　在釜山浦
　　　　　　　　　　　　　　總領事　前田獻吉

外務大輔　吉田淸成殿

101

H.S. Parkes (1882. 9. 12) ➜ G.L.G. Granville (1882. 10. 21)

조선의 국제적 지위에 관한 井上馨와 회견 보고

Sir H.S. Parkes to Earl Granville.—(Received October 21)

(No. 128 Secret)

My Lord,   *Tôkiô, September* 12, 1882

  AT my interview of yesterday with the Foreign Minister, which I have reported in my immediately-preceding despatch, his Excellency observed that he desired to mention, in the strictest confidence and secrecy, his views on a point connected with the Corean question which his Government regarded as one of great moment. This was, whether Corea should exist in future as an independent State, or be recognized as a dependency of China.

  In considering this point he was prepared, he said, to admit at once that it would be difficult for Corea to preserve her integrity, unless she received either the material or the moral support of some more powerful State. If material support were needed it would be natural that that should be extended to her by a neighbouring Power. The countries adjoining Corea are China, Russia, and Japan. Japan was exceedingly desirous that Corea should occupy a position of independence, but Japan would not undertake the charge of her protection. China, on the other hand, seemed disposed to claim the position of Corea's Suzerain, which would or should involve the responsibilities of protection; but was China able to defend Corea in case of need against the other Power which he had named? He was satisfied that she was not, and he was equally assured that Russia desired that Corea should be regarded as a dependency of China, because in the event of a conflict occurring between those two Powers, Russia would then be at liberty to fasten on Corea.

  In saying this he was scarcely dealing with a hypothetical case. Russia was not satisfied with the Ili settlement, and her long line of contiguous frontier to China offered constant occasion of misunderstanding. She was continually adding to her military strength on the Corean border; she had 8,000 troops at Vladivostock, and had found two other strong posts, one at Khabaroffka, at the junction of the Usuri with the Amur, and another at a point in the same neighbourhood which he could not distinctly name. In case, therefore, of a dispute occurring between her and China, she was prepared at a moment's notice to take possession of the Corean ports of Gensan and Fusan, which were points of the greatest strategic importance, and China was wholly incompetent to prevent the capture or recover the loss of these places.

Russia, he knew, viewed with strong disfavour all attempts to bring Corea into relations with Western Powers. As an instance of this he might mention that when Commodore Shufeldt applied to Japan to assist him in his mission to Corea in 1881, the Russian Representative at Tôkiô strongly urged him to withhold all aid, using as an argument that by the opening of Corea to other nations Japan would be deprived of the monopoly of the trade. He (the Foreign Minister) had then replied that he could not actively assist the American Commodore because the Corean Government would resent any endeavour on the part of Japan to introduce Western nations to Corea, but, on the other hand, he could do nothing to thwart the efforts that any of those nations might see fit to take in order to establish relations with that country.

The recent action of China in Corea raised the question of the *status* of the latter, which would now have to be seriously considered by all those Powers who had relations with that country. He had therefore telegraphed on the 7th instant to the Japanese Ministers at London and Berlin, and to Mr. Ito, the Cabinet Minister, now travelling in Europe, informing them of the settlement recently effected by Mr. Hanabusa at Söul, but pointing out that the true position of Corea must now be determined. He had instructed them, therefore, to seek the opinion of the British and German Governments, and to express the hope of the Japanese Government that those Powers would ratify their Treaties with Corea as with an independent State, as he believed those Treaties contained no conditions which were in the least opposed to such independence. He had heard of letters of a compromising character having been written by the King of Corea; but it would be unsafe, he thought, to allow such letter, which were probably dictated under exceptional influences, to supersede or detract from the conditions of the Treaties themselves.

The importance of Corea, his Excellency added, should not be weighed by her commercial capacity, which appeared at present, it is true, to be very limited. But the country was known to possess gold and silver (500,000 dollars' worth of the former having been bartered to Japan last year at Gensan alone), and, also, it was believed, deposits of iron and coal. Her material resources might, therefore, admit of development, but there was no doubt of the great political importance of her position, and viewing the question of her *status* from that point, he felt confident that the loss of her independence would prove positively disastrous, not only to Corea herself, but also to other nations who had large interests in the extreme East.

He did not expect, nor did he desire, that any of the Western nations who had concluded Treaties with Corea should directly undertake the protection of that State, but he hoped that in her case, as in that of the minor States of Europe, the moral support of greater Powers would prove sufficient to guard her against exterior aggression. He also hoped that free communications with the West would quickly stimulate a desire on the part of the Coreans for internal reforms, which would lead to the establishment of a stable Government, and, by quelling factional strife among the ruling classes, would afford the people opportunities of industrial effort, and of thereby ameliorating their present poverty-stricken condition.

His Excellency having asked my opinion on the subject, I replied that, while I appreciated the singleness of view which characterized his arguments, I could only report the latter to my Government for their consideration. He then begged me to do so both by wire and despatch, and I therefore forwarded to your Lordship my telegram of yesterday's date.

I have, &c.
(Signed)   HARRY S. PARKES

N.R. O'Conor (1882. 9. 22) ➜ 趙寧夏, 金弘集

조영조약 비준 요청에 대한 회신

大英署理欽差駐劄中華便宜行事大臣頭等參贊格 爲照覆事 光緒八年八月初八日 接准由總理衙門遞到貴大臣照會一件內開 本國六月初九日之事 係屬內難 玆幸壹是敉平 本署大臣准此捧讀之餘 勿任欣慰 又稱 前經簽押條約 自應按照公法 悉遵原議辦理 如貴國批准 派員前來 即請馳往仁川互換 以便兩國人民一體遵守 共享利益各等語 本署大臣自應譯錄原文 即日杏會本國 轉爲入奏 以俟批准遵辦可也 爲此照覆 須至照會者
右照會
大朝鮮國欽差全權大副官趙金
一千八百八十二年九月二十二日 光緒八年八月十一日

H.S. Parkes (1882. 9. 25) ➜ G.L.G. Granville

Aston의 조선 개항장 조사 보고

The London Gazette
Published by Authority
FRIDAY, DECEMBER 22, 1882

Foreign Office, December 21, 1882

DESPATCH from Her Majesty's Minister in Japan forwarding a Report on Corea.
Sir H. Parkes to Earl Granville. Tokyo, September 25, 1882.

My Lord,

I HAVE the honour to forward a copy of a Report which I received this morning from Mr. Aston, containing the information he has collected at the places on the east coast of Corea visited by the squadron under the command of Admiral Willes, namely, Wönsan (Gensan), Pusan (Fusan), and Port Hamilton.

In order that I may not delay the transmission to your Lordship of this interesting Report by the mail of to-day, I venture to forward it without remark. Wönsan and Pusan, as your Lordship is aware, are two of the ports which are believed to be opened to foreign trade under the new Treaties with Corea; and the importance of soon selecting building sites for the use of British subjects at those ports is clearly shown in this Report. The existing limited trade which is carried on there by Japan is fully described by Mr. Aston, and also the predominant share in that trade which is already enjoyed by British merchandize. The Commercial Returns which he mentions as Inclosures are in Japanese, and shall follow as soon as they are translated. But I am able to add a copy of the Municipal Regulations of the Japanese Settlement at Pusan, which, like that of Wönsan, is administered, as Mr. Aston observes, under the exclusive control of the Japanese Consul, and without any interference on the part of the Corean Government.

It is very satisfactory to notice the friendly manner in which the squadron was everywhere received by the Coreans.

I have, &c.,
HARRY S. PARKES

Inclosure 1
Mr. Aston to Sir H. Parkes

"*Iron Duke*," at Port Hamilton,
September 13, 1882

(Extract)

I HAVE the. honour to submit to you the following notes of information collected during a visit to the Corean ports of Wönsan (Gensan), Pusan (Fusan), and Port Hamilton, in ships of Her Majesty's squadron, under the command of Admiral Willes.

I arrived at Wonsan in Her Majesty's ship "Swift" on the 22nd August. The only other ship then in the harbour was the Japanese gunboat "Banjokan," or "Iwakikan," which had been sent here a fortnight previously for the protection of the Japanese Settlement, and had also brought up the new Consul, Mr. Soyeda, formerly stationed at Pusan.

Admiral Willes arrived at Wönsan on the 24th, and the Japanese Consul and the Pusa called on him the same day. The Pusa is the chief local magistrate. He resides at Tökwön, a town of about 300 houses, situate two or three miles inland. The Pusa and his suite wore the greyish hempen garments which in this country denote mourning. He informed Admiral Willes that the whole nation had gone into mourning for a year for the Queen, who had died in consequence of the shock to her feelings caused by the proceedings of the rioters at Söul. The whole population at the other places visited was in mourning, and the acts of the rioters were spoken of with disapproval.

Admiral Willes returned the Pusa's visit on the 26th, and was entertained by him at a dinner in the Corean style. Both these interviews, were of the most friendly character.

During the stay of the squadron at Wönsan the ships were visited by many hundreds of Coreans, the dress and appearance of many of whom showed that they did not belong to the lowest class. A large number were merchants, and a few "Nyangpan," or Samurai. Leave was freely given to the offices and men of the squadron but it was thought prudent not to allow them to, visit the native town of Wönsan.

The ships were tolerably plentifully supplied during their stay with cattle (10 to 12 dollars, ahead), fowls (1 dollar per dozen), and eggs. Fish and vegetables were also procurable in small quantities.

At the time of our arrival no news had been received from Sŏul later than that of the attack on the Japanese Legation, but the Panchalkwan subsequently informed me than 3,000 Chinese had landed at In-chhön, that an American ship wad also there, and that the Japanese Minister was at the capital. No important changes were made in the local staff of officials at Tökwön or Wönsan in consequence of the events at Sŏul.

A German ship-of-war visited Wönsan on the 25th July, and the Commander exchanged visits with the Pusa.

The United States' ship "Monocacy," which visited this port in June last, left again without anchoring or communicating with the shore.

The harbour of Wönsan is on the whole a good one. It is easy of access, sheltered, and has good holding ground, with a convenient depth of water. The principal objection to it is that it is too large, being about 10 miles in length from north to south, and about the same from east to west, so that in stormy weather a sufficient sea gets up within the harbour to interfere with the movements of boats. An otherwise excellent site for a Settlement at the southern end of the harbour was rejected by the Japanese in consequence of the sea which sets in here during the prevailing northerly gales of the winter months. In easterly gales a considerable swell finds its way between the islands at the entrance of the bay, and sometimes interrupts the communication with the ships lying at anchor opposite to the Japanese Settlement on its western shore. The Mitsu Bishi steam ship "Tsurnga Maru," of 486 tons, anchored here at a distance of about three-quarters of a mile from the shore in 4 or 5 fathoms. A more sheltered anchorage exists in the northern arm of this inlet, but all accounts agree that the commerce of this locality, is centred at Wönsan at its southern extremity.

A good deal of ice forms in this harbour in severe winters. Last year there was none, but during a hard frost in the previous winter the bay was frozen as far out as the Island of Changdökdo, and the native junks had to anchor at a considerable distance from the town of Wönsan.

The town of Wönsan is considered by the Coreans one of the great commercial centres of their country. It extends for more than a mile along the southern shore of the bay, and consists of about 2,000 houses, with a population of perhaps 10,000 inhabitants. One main street of some 10 or 12 feet in width winds through it from end to end, and into this open numerous narrow and crooked alleys. The Coreans disliked our entering these lanes, no doubt because in passing along them one is apt to surprise their women, whose delicacy is shocked by the near approach of a foreigner. Near each end of the town there is an open space where a market, chiefly for agricultural produce, is held on the 5th, 10th, 15th, 20th, 25th, and 30th days of the Chinese month.

The houses strongly resemble those seen at In-chhön on the western coast. They consists of a kitchen with an earthen floor, and two or three other rooms, seldom more than 8 or 9 feet square, with ceilings about 6 or 7 feet in height. The kitchen has one or two large clay fire-places, the smoke from which passes into flues underneath the rest of the houses, warming it comfortably, and finding a vent at the other side in a chimney of stone cemented with clay and surmounted by a hollow log, or by several earthen pots lashed together by straw ropes. Many of these chimneys project into the street, giving it a very odd appearance. The doors do not slide like the Japanese doors, but are on hinges, and are not more than 4 or 5 feet in height. The windows are wooden lattices covered with paper, and no glass is to be seen. All the houses are of one story only, with thatched roofs, the eves being only 6 or 7 feet from the ground. The framework is of wood, the interstices being filled with woven reeds plastered with clay. The floors are matted and carpets of thick oil-paper are sometimes seen. There is no furniture. I saw no godowns, but was told there were three which were used for the storage of grain. There are not many shops, and those that are have a very poor appearance, the whole stock-in-trade amounting in value to a very few dollars. In only two or three were there any European goods exposed for sale. Read making at Wönsan consists in filling up the hollows with soft earth, and there seem to be no arrangements whatever for cleaning the streets. There are numerous pig-styles in front of the houses in the main street, and the passenger is constantly in danger of stumbling over their occupants, black, bristly animals, with pendent bellies dripping with mud. Almost the only pleasant thing to look at is the luxuriant growth of melon and pumpkin with grey fruit and white orange blossoms showing amid a mass of green leaves which cover many of the houses.

The clothing and personal appearance of the inhabitants contrast favourably with the aspect of the towns. Nearly everyone is decently dressed, and a really well-dressed Corean, in his broad hat and white robes, has an eminently respectable, well-to-do appearance.

The soil in the valleys near Wönsan seems fertile, but much of the country is mountainous, and the proportion of cultivated land is not large. The principal crops are rice, millet of three different kinds, a sort of French bean, and jute. The agricultural is of a rude description.

The Japanese Settlement of Wönsan is on the western side of the bay, opposite to the Island of Changdŏkdo, and about a mile from the western end of the native town of Wönsan. The site is low and marshy, and disease is very prevalent especially in the spring and early summer. Few of the Japanese residents have escaped attacks of remittent fever, and kakke, another disease of malarious origin, is common.

A hill of 300 or 400 feet in height rises immediately behind the Settlement, and would afford more healthy sites for residences.

The Settlement contains about forty houses, including the Consulate, a Buddhist Mission-house; and twelve or thirteen merchants' offices, the rest being shops or restaurants. There are numerous vacant lots, less than half the available space having been built on. A small stream, which for a short distance from its mouth has a sufficient depth of water for cargo-boats, flows through the Settlement. The Consul informed me that 15 yen per annum* was paid by him for each house in the Settlement to the Corean authorities in lieu of ground-rent; and a Japanese resident told me that from this year 3 yen per annum were to be paid to the Consul for each lot of 300 tsubos, no ground-rent whatever having been paid hitherto. The Settlement is infested by Corean thieves, who rob the godowns of the Japanese by picking the locks or removing the foundation stones, and the markets at Wönsan are also said to swarm with them: "Tigers abound in the neighbouring mountains, and last year two Coreans were carried off by these animals from the immediate neighbourhood of the Settlement.

The Japanese Consul corresponds on equal terms with the Pusa of Tökwŏn, the latter, however, ealling first on the Consul; but all ordinary business is transacted with the Panchalkwan, who has an office in the native

---

*[원주] Probably a mistake 15 yen for the whole Settlement – W. G. A.

town of Wönsan. The Kamsa, or Governor of the Province of Hamkyongdo, resides at Ham-Leung, some 50 or 60 miles north of Wönsan. He has no relations with foreigners.

The following table shows the imports and exports to and from Wönsan since it was opened to Japanese trade in 1880. The amounts are given in paper yen of which 150 to 170 may be reckoned as equal to 100 Mexican dollars:—

IMPORTS

	Paper yen
July to December, 1880 … …	269,173
January to June, 1881 … …	380,972
July to December, 1881 … …	389,472
January to June, 1882 … …	358,184

EXPORTS

	Paper yen
July to December, 1880 … …	135,880
January to June, 1881 … …	301,082
July to December, 1881 … …	426,355
January to June, 1882 … …	419,816

This shows that the trade for the year ended June, 1882, amounted to 747,656 yen for imports and 846,171 yen for exports, the total of both being 1,593,827 yen, or about 1,000,000 Mexican dollars. Detailed statistics of the trade and shipping of Wönsan for the half-year ended on the 30th June last are inclosed herewith. The second half of the year is expected to show larger totals, as the Myöngthai fishery brings large numbers of junks here in the early winter, and the rice and pulse, which form the principal exports, come to market at that time. For some time past, however, there has been little demand for these last named articles in Japan, owing to favourable seasons there, and trade, both here and at Pusan, has suffered in consequence. To the same cause is due the large outflow of bullion from Wönsan during the half-year. It amounted in value to 288,135, paper yen, or about seven-tenths of the entire exports. The only other exports of any importance were pulse (27,232 yen) and ox hides (65,912 yen).

I was told by a Corean at Wönsan that the export of red ginseng, which appears among the exports in these tables, is prohibited by the Corean Government, and the draft of the American Treaty with Corea, which was lately published, contains a similar prohibition. I believe the truth is, that the Corean Government has granted a monopoly of the export of this article, which is in great demand in China, to a company of merchants in Sunto or Kaisyŏng.

The imports to Wŏnsan consist chiefly of shirtings, muslins, and other piece-goods, which are almost without exception of English manufacture. During the half-year in question these articles were imported to the value of 285,233 yen, or about four-fifths of the total imports; and if 37,681 yen in Corean copper cash, which were brought from Pusan, be deducted, the proportion becomes still larger. As the national costume consists of flowing garments of a white or grayish cotton material, it is highly probable that the import of shirtings and similar goods will be large in proportion to the numbers and means of the population. A preference is given to the better qualities, but I was told that no American shirtings reached this port.

The only other important import is European dye-stuffs, of which 19,549 yens' worth was imported. Japanese imports only reached the value of 6,773 yen, but to this should be added the greater part of the articles imported for the use of the Japanese residents, which amounted for the half-year, to 5,623 yen.

The most important fact to be noted in regard to the foreign trade of Wŏnsan is, that seven or eight-tenths of the goods imported are for the consumption of the cities of Sŏul and Phyŏngyang, which can be far more conveniently supplied from In-chhŏn, when that port is opened to trade, and that the gold and silver, which are so prominent articles of the export trade, are produced in Phyŏngando, the province on the west coast bordering on China. Shirtings can be seat from Wŏnsan to Sŏul on pack-horses in six days, each horse carrying a load of twenty-five to fifty pieces, according to his size and strength. It should be added, however, that Mr. Mayeda, the Japanese Consul-General for Corea, who spent two years at Wŏnsan, has a high opinion of its capabilities for commerce, and does not believe that the opening of In-chhŏn will greatly check its prosperity.

The Japanese at Wŏnsan complain loudly of the difficulty of doing business with the Corean traders. They say that it is impossible to give them credits, that the petty officials and interpreters levy an exorbitant black-mail on even the most trivial transactions. In the agricultural districts, it is said that the peasants are often prevented by the same class of Coreans from sending their rice and pulse to the Wŏnsan market for sale to the Japanese, and that in consequence the crops are sometimes allowed to rot in the fields.

Japanese money is not current outside the Settlement, and even in Wŏnsan all purchases have to be made by means of the inconvenient Corean copper coin.

The trade of Wŏnsan is carried on chiefly by the Mitsu Bishi steamship "Tsuruga Maru," which visits the port monthly. An occasional schooner or junk is also sometimes seen here. The "Tsuruga Maru" goes on to Vladivostok, where there is a colony of 200 or 300 Japanese engaged in commerce, and there appears to be some probability of commercial relations springing up between the two places. A Corean whom I met at Vladivostok told me he had come there from Wŏnsan with cattle and ponies for sale, and that others of his countrymen were engaged in the same business. There are now in Russian Tartary about 10,000 Coreans from the north-east province. Many of these have settled down as farmers, wood-cutters, and graziers, and there is a fluctuating population of about 2,000 Coreans in Vladivostok itself, where they are employed as labourers, earning about a rouble a day. The Corean authorities no longer molest or put to death those who return to their country after having settled in or visited the Russian territory.

I arrived at Pusan on the afternoon of the 3rd September. Two Japanese men-of-war were lying there, one of which had arrived from Inchhŏn on the previous night, bringing news of the results of Mr. Hanabusa's negotiations at Sŏul.

The news of the attack on the Japanese Legation had caused much excitement at Pusan. Trade had been suspended for some time before our arrival, and was still far from having resumed its usual course.

Leave was freely given at this port to the officers and men of the squadron. Large numbers of Coreans came off to see the ships, and the usual official visits passed off in a cordial and satisfactory manner.

The native town of Pusan is a collection of low thatched cabins, with a population of about 2,000 inhabitants. No signs of trade are to be seen, there being hardly anything deserving the name of shop. A wooden tray containing a little fruit or tobacco set on a clay platform in front of the window is the most common representative of commerce. The Castle of Pusan is surrounded by a wall 15 or 20 feet high, and has rather a fine granite gateway.

Tongnai (or Tŏrai) is a walled city of 300 or 400 houses, about 8 or 9 miles from the Japanese Settlement. The only signs of trade I saw were a few articles of food set out in one or two mean-looking shops, and some wares of no great value laid out on mats in the open space in front of the Pusa's residence. More business is probably transacted at the markets, which are held here every fifth day.

I visited the Pusa, who received me in the most friendly way. We conversed for about two hours on a variety of subjects, and I was surprised to find him well-informed on such matters as the proposed canal through the Isthmus of Panamâ, the recent events in Egypt, and the importance to England of the Suez Canal.

The agriculture in this part of Corea is much superior to that of the country about In-chhŏn or Wŏnsan, and approaches closely to the Japanese standard. The soil and climate are more favourable to the cultivation of rice, which is the staple article of food in these countries. The climate is a little like that of Nagasaki, with a somewhat lower temperature, both in winter and in summer. 90° to 92° were spoken of as the maximum summer heat at the Japanese Settlement, and there is a little frost in winter, but not enough for skating.

The Japanese Settlement of Pusan is on the mainland, opposite to the Island of Chŏlyŏngdo, from which it is separated by a strait of about 400 yards in width and 2 or 3 fathoms in depth. This part of the harbour is well-sheltered from any sea from without, but it is rather exposed to the strong winds which, in winter, blow from the north-east side of the harbour, a distance of about 3 miles, and raise a sea which would be troublesome to small vessels lying alongside the wharf, were it not that it is protected by a small mole. Inside of this mole there is a depth of water of about 2 fathoms, and while the squadron was at Pusan six schooners of 80 or 90 tons, a large Japanese junk, and five or six Corean junks were lying here. Three or four times as many vessels of this description could be sheltered here, if necessary.

The Japanese town has a clean, well-kept appearance. The streets are moderately wide, and paving and scavenging are not neglected. There are several police-stations, occupied by policemen in uniforms of a European pattern. The whole Settlement is under the exclusive control of the Consul, in whose name all police and other regulations are issued. The Consul is assisted by an elective Municipal Council, which, however, can take no important step without his sanction. The title-deeds for the lots of land in the Settlement are also issued in the Consul's name, and the Japanese residents pay him ground-rent at the rate of 6/10, 1, or 1 and 6/10 sen per annum for each tsubo, so that a good-sized lot, of say, 300 tsubos, costs the occupier, on an average, about 2 Mexican dollars per annum. A head-rent of 60 yen per annum is paid by the Consul to the Corean authorities for the whole Settlement. Several desirable lots are for sale at present, and houses could be readily rented or purchased; but if other foreigners are to become permanent residents in the Japanese Settlement, it is evident that its municipal arrangements would have to be considerably modified. The present Japanese population here is about 2,000, and some time ago was nearly 3,000. The site is only moderately healthy, and fever is rather common.

Two sites have been suggested for the foreign Settlement at Pusan. One is on the northern side of Deer Island, about three-fourths of a mile from the Japanese Settlement. There is here a convenient level space of ground, fronting a well-sheltered part of the harbour. The objections to it are the fact of its being on an island, and the strong tide (3 knots) which runs in front of it.

The best site, on the whole, seems to be a spot on the mainland just to the south of the Corean village of Kokwen, and about two-thirds of a mile to the north of the Japanese Settlement. There is a level space here of sufficient extent unoccupied by houses, and lying opposite to that part of the harbour which is least affected by the strong tides. The soil is gravelly. There is anchorage here in from 4 to 5 fathoms at one-third to half-a-mile from the shore, and in 6 fathoms at a distance of three-fourths of a mile. I was told by old residents that a heavy sea seldom finds its way in here; and this statement was borne out by the appearance of the beach and of the pine trees along it, which all bend towards the sea. There are facilities for the construction of a pier or camber for the protection of cargo boats. This site is on the main road from the Japanese Settlement to Pusan, Tongnai, and the interior, and by having the Settlement at this point more than half-a-mile of a rocky precipitous path would be avoided. Far the greater part of the import trade finds its way into the interior by land along this road. A Settlement on this site would be more exposed than one on Deer Island in case of any riot or attack by the Corean population.

The following table shows the value of the imports and exports to and from Pusan for the four years 1878-81:—

1878—					Paper yen
Imports	…	…	…		205,281
Exports	…	…	…		244,545
Total	…	…	…		449,826
1879—					
Imports	…	…	…		677,062
Exports	…	…	…		566,955
Total	…	…	…		1,244,017
1880—					
Imports	…	…	…		1,237,792
Exports	…	…	…		730,763
Total	…	…	…		1,968,555
1881—					
Imports	…	…	…		640,233
Exports	…	…	…		572,951
Total	…	…	…		1,218,184

Among the imports for 1881 there were European goods to the value of 470,971 yen, of which 250,000 yen represented shirtings alone. American shirtings to the value of 6,000 yen were imported during the year. Goods imported from Wŏnsan amounted to 39,138 yen. This sum included ox hides to the value of 13,371 yen, which were brought to Pusan in Japanese ships—a practice which is not prohibited by the Japanese Treaty as it is in that negotiated for America by Commodore Schufedt. Japanese schooners sometimes visit the unopened port of Masanpho, but I was told by the Consul that this was only when driven by stress of weather, and not for purposes of trade.

The falling off in the trade of Pusan in 1881 is due to the opening of Wŏnsan in May of the previous year. The trade of the two ports may now be considered nearly equal, the gross imports and exports for each amounting to about 1,000,000 dollars.

The enclosed table gives details of the import and export trade of Pusan for the six months ended on the 30th June last. It contains no return of shipping, but I learnt that the trade is carried on by the Mitsu Bishi steam-ship "Tsuruga Maru," which visits this port monthly, and by schooners which come here from Nagasaki and Osaka.

The trade of Pusan is, on the whole, similar to that of Wŏnsan, but for the six months in question cereals take the place, to a large extent, of the billion exported from the latter port.

The squadron remained for some days at the group of islands known as Port Hamilton. There are five or six villages here, with a total population of about 2,000 people. Every available spot of ground is under cultivation, the principal crop being millet. There are no cattle on any of the islands, and supplies of other kinds are not plentiful.

Throughout this cruize the relations with the Corean officials and people have been of a very amicable nature, and nothing occurred to mar the favourable impression which the visits to these places must have left behind.

At all the places visited I conversed with large numbers of Coreans, and found them invariably friendly, though sometimes inclined to be unpleasantly familiar. Their desire for information knew no bounds.

I should not omit to report to you the friendly assistance which I received from Mr. Mayeda, the Japanese Consul-General at Pusan, and Mr. Sayeda, the Japanese Consul at Wŏnsan. To their courtesy I am indebted, amongst other things, for nearly all the information on the foreign trade of Corea which is contained in this Report.

Inclosure 2
Municipal Regulation of the Japanese Settlement of Pusan* in Corea.

Notification No. 16

IT is hereby notified that the Temporary Municipal Regulations of the 28th January, 1881, are now amended as in the annexed paper, and will now be called "Municipal Regulations."

KONDO MASASUKE, Consul

November 9, 1881

MUNICIPAL REGULATIONS

I.—General Regulations
1. Residents are divided into two classes, those who have leased land and

---

*[원주] Corean pronunciation of the place known in Japan as Fusan.

erected houses in which they reside, and who are called "permanent residents;" and those who lodge in the houses of others, who are called "temporary residents."

2. On the permanent residents devolves the entire charge of the municipal affairs of the Settlement. But persons who, although renting houses from others, have established their own name (i.e., householders), are all to be considered as permanent residents.

3. One mayor is to be elected for the Settlement, who shall have an office where all municipal business shall be transacted.

4. The Settlement shall be divided into wards of twenty houses each, for which wardsmen will be appointed to transact the business of the ward, according to Regulation 13, taking it in monthly turns, one after another.

5. Each ward shall elect a representative, who will represent it in the Municipal Council, and take a share in all the deliberations of that body in accordance with Regulation 14 and the succeeding Regulations.

II. The Mayor

6. The election of the mayor shall rest with all the permanent residents.

7. The elected person need not be a permanent resident. It is sufficient if he has lived in the Settlement for more than one year. The following classes of persons, however, are excluded: Persons under 25 years of age. Persons sentenced to penal servitude or to imprisonment for treason for one year or upwards. (The last clause not to apply after seven years from the expiration of the term of sentence.) Bankrupts.

8. The mayor shall hold office for two years, at the expiration of which term a new election shall be held.

Note.—The salary of the mayor shall be fixed by the Municipal Council.

9. The duties of the mayor are as follows:—

To circulate all notifications, examine and forward all petitions, inquiries, and reports.

To keep the registration books.

To conduct the election and discharge from office of members of the Municipal Council, and to arrange for the monthly wardsmen.

To provide for the repairs and maintenance of roads, bridges, drains, wells, aqueducts, and public buildings and privies.

To attend to all municipal payments and receipts, and to take charge of the municipal chest.

To superintend public schools.

To superintend the management of public shrines ("Shinto") and cemeteries, and measures for the prevention of contagious diseases.

The superintendence of fire brigades.

To attest sales and mortgages of buildings in the Settlement.

To attest conveyances of leases of land in the Settlement.

To keep a register of the seals of residents.

To attest petitions by attorneys for others.

To manage bankrupt estates.

To manage the property of persons who have run away or died without leaving heirs.

To report all extraordinary events whenever urgent action is necessary.

To take charge of persons who have fallen down in the street, or who have died a violent death.

In the above cases, wherever expenditure is necessary, the sanction of the Municipal Council must be obtained before it is incurred.

10. In order to assist the mayor in the discharge of his duties, he may appoint a clerk and other employés subject to the approval of the Council, whose wages, however, are to be fixed by the Council.

11. The mayor shall have power to call extraordinary meetings of the Council in addition to the ordinary ones.

12. No alteration of, or additions to, these Regulations can be carried into effect without the sanction of the Council and the approval of the Consul.

III. The Wardsmen

13. The duties of the wardsmen are as follows:—

To circulate in their wards notifications communicated to them by the mayor.

To collect the balloting papers of residents in the ward.

To report to the mayor any extraordinary occurrence in the ward.

From time to time to consult with the mayor generally on all matters relating to the ward.

IV. The Municipal Council

14. The Municipal Council shall deliberate on all matters concerning the

public interests of the Settlement, and the receipts and expenditure of the same.

15. The rules of the Council are to be drawn up as may be found convenient, subject to the approval of the Consul.

16. All resolutions of the Council shall be carried into effect at once by the mayor whenever routine matters are concerned, but in other cases the Consul's approval must be obtained.

17. If, in the opinion of the mayor, any deliberation of the Council is contrary to law, he shall adjourn the meeting and refer the matter to the Consul.

18. If the Consul shall be of opinion that any deliberation of the Council is contrary to law he may cause the meeting to be adjourned, or he may dissolve the Council and cause a new election to be held.

V. Municipal Expenditure

19. The funds for the municipal expenditure are to be provided by a tax on buildings and persons within the Settlement, and by a tax of so much per tsubo on land leased. (Kitahama-machi, outside of the Settlement, also falls within the last clause.)

20. The expenses to be defrayed out of this fund are as follows:—

Police, maintenance and construction of roads, bridges, sewers, wells, aqueducts, and all public buildings, public shrines, and cemeteries; subsidy to public schools, prevention of contagious diseases, prevention and extinction of fires, salary of mayor and his staff, expenses of mayor's offices. The taxes and expenditure detailed in the last two clauses are all subject to the sanction of the Council and the approval of the Consul.

Police Regulations of the Japanese Settlement of Pusan in Corea.

It is hereby notified that the annexed police regulations came into force on the 11th instant.

They do not apply to offences comprised under the section of the Criminal Law from section 425 onwards.

All previous police regulations are hereby cancelled.

KONDO MASASUKI, Consul

February 3, 1882

The penalty for the offences specified below is imprisonment from one to ten days, or a fine of from 5 sen to 1 yen 50 sen.

1. Offences against land regulations.

2. All offences against industrial regulations for the residents in the Settlement with the exception of offences against the brothel and singing-girl regulations.

3. Offences against the regulations requiring persons to report their arrival in and departure from Corea; also to report themselves periodically while residing there.

4. Offences against the regulations for the construction of houses.

5. Offences against the scavenging regulations.

6. Anchoring vessels so as to obstruct the fair way, fastening nets to buoys unauthorizedly.

7. Indecent or other drunken conduct.

8. Men wearing women's clothes.

9. Importuning people for contributions to religious festivals.

10. Music, singing, or other noisy behavior after twelve o'clock P.M., interfering with other persons' sleep.

11. Committing nuisances in the streets, except in the places provided.

12. Keeping public baths for both sexes indiscriminately.

13. Throwing open the doors of bathhouses, or exposing the person indecently.

14. Going to fires on horseback, not having any business there.

15. Throwing rubbish or tiles into gutters or drains within the limits of the port.

16. Using for drying fish any places except the sardine drying place, or interfering with fish-drying places.

17. Scavengers carrying tubs without lids.

18. Challenging to wrestling, or forcing on people wares for sale.

19. Newsmen reading aloud newspapers in the streets.

20. Discharging fire-arms near houses.

21. In general, interfering with people's liberty, or clamour of a nature to cause alarm.

H.S. Parkes (1882. 10. 16) ➡ G.L.G. Granville (1882. 11. 20)

수신사 朴泳孝 일행 임무 보고

No. 144

Tokio,
October 16, 1882

My lord,

In continuation of my despatch No. 138 of the 7th instant, I have now to report that the Koran Mission arrived here on the evening of the 13th instant.

The foreign Minister informed me today that the powers of the Envoys are at present confined to the exchange of the Ratifications of the recent convention between Japan and Korea and to the delivery of the letter of apology from the King of Korea to the Mikado in fulfillment of the Sixth Article of that convention. The Envoys will be received in audience by the Mikado on the 19th instant.

The foreign Minister also mentioned that in contrast to the two previous Korean missions to this Court, which had been instructed by the Korean Government to hold no intercourse with foreigners when in Japan the Envoys in this case have been authorized to cultivate friendly communications with the Foreign Representative at Tokio.

I have the honor to be with the highest respect
My Lord
Your lordship most obedient humble servant
Parkes

H.S. Parkes (1882. 10. 24) ➜ G.L.G. Granville (1882. 11. 28)

金玉均과 면담 보고

Sir H.S. Parkes to Earl Granville.—(Received November 28)

(No. 154 Confidential)

My Lord,　　　　　　　　　　　　　　　　Tôkiô, October 24, 1882

WITH reference to my preceding despatch, in which I have reported a conversation with the Corean Envoys, I think I should also inform your Lordship of some remarks made to me by Kim Ok Kiun, who visited me before I saw the Envoys. Kim Ok Kiun is mentioned in Mr. Aston's Confidential Memorandum (inclosed in my despatch No. 140) as unquestionably much the ablest and shrewdest member of the Mission, in which, however, he holds no official position.

He said that his people were anxious to know what foreign Powers thought of the recent action of China in Corea. Was it in accordance with international law? He thought not. International law ought to support a weak Power when oppressed by a strong one. Corea was unfortunately weak; her low civilization was a disgrace, and the recent disturbances would, he feared, have shaken the confidence of Western Powers. She had no army, and was therefore obliged to submit to China and Japan. Troops from both those countries had recently been imposed upon her, but they came with different objects. China had sent a force to restore order and seize the ex-Regent, and had therefore interfered in the internal affairs of Corea, which she had no right to do. Japan had not so interfered, but had confined herself to the settlement of her own questions. He wanted to know what I thought of all this.

That, I replied, was rather a hard question to ask a foreigner, seeing that the interested parties contradicted themselves and each other in their statements as to the position of Corea. Thus, when difficulties occurred between two Western States and Corea some years ago, China had then declared that she had nothing to do with the affairs of that country, but her present action denoted an active degree of interference. Corea, on the other hand, had declared herself independent in her Treaty with Japan, but had recently stated, in letters addressed by the King to the Sovereigns of several Western States, that she was dependent on China and yet retained the sole control of her internal and external affairs. International law was clear enough in regard to the relations of independent States, but those of dependent States were governed by the circumstances of each case, and the degree of dependence varied in almost every instance. The right of China to interfere in Corea must therefore depend upon the conditions of her suzerainty. If her interference were limited to the restoration of order, she would have done Corea some service.

Kim Ok Kiun replied that whether it would be so limited or not remained to be seen, and the way in which the ex-Regent had been captured and treated by China was offensive to Corea. The letters of the King to which I had alluded proved that China has no right to interfere either in the internal or external affairs of Corea, as those letters were written by the dictation of China. He wished to know whether a dependent country could make such Treaties as Corea had made with the United States, Great Britain, and Germany. He thought not. Those treaties were also the work of China. They, as well as the letters of the King, were drafted by her, and she cannot go back upon them. "You must know," he added, "that Chinese officers managed everything connected with the British Treaty, and were present when it was signed. All these proceedings constitute an agreement on the part of China with Corea, and amount to a recognition of the independence of Corea. He wished to know what Western Powers thought of the question, and if the three which he had named felt any doubt as to the position of Corea. He hoped that they would hear and weight the statements of both sides.

The letters of the King were calculated, I observed, to occasion doubt, as they declared that Corea was both dependent and independent.

"Can the letter to the Queen be withdrawn?" he inquired.

"That," I said, "would scarcely serve your purpose if you rely upon it as a recognition by China of your independence."

"Then you need not answer it," he observed.

"In that ease," I rejoined, "the declaration of dependence would remain, and the letter could be used by Corea or China whenever it suited the purpose of one or the other to do so,"

"Corea would accept the letter if you sent it back," was his next remark.

"That could scarcely be done," I said, "except by the request of the King, as to return the letter of a Sovereign, unasked, would be an affront." Did he think that the King would make such a request?

To this he replied evasively that he thought the Envoy would speak to me on the subject, but it was not referred to by the latter at the interview which I have reported in my preceding despatch.

Kim Ok Kiun closed his remarks by saying that he hoped the British Treaty would be ratified as soon as possible.

I observed that I had no knowledge of the views of my Government on the subject of the Treaty, but that I should not be surprised if some delay were caused, either by doubts as to the position of Corea, or by the recent disturbances in that country, or in consequence of it being found necessary to consider some of the provisions of the Treaty.

I have, &c.

(Signed)　　HARRY S. PARKES

H.S. Parkes (1882. 11. 25) ➡ G.L.G. Granville (1883. 1. 8)

수신사 朴泳孝 일행의 내방 및 조선 정세 보고

Sir H.S. Parkes to Earl Granville.(Received January 8, 1883)

(No. 166)

Tôkiô, November 25, 1882

My Lord,

DURING a visit which the Corean Envoy paid me two days ago he again asked me whether the British Treaty had been ratified, and expressed his desire to see the people of the two countries entering into direct relationship with each other. He also observed that, as Great Britain was a powerful State, and possessed of wide Asiatic experience, Corea, who was weak and uninformed, would count upon her for support. He also hoped that the British Representative in Corea would be well versed in Asiatic affairs.

He also told me that he had heard of the unsettled feeling in Corea, to which I have referred in my despatches Nos. 158 and 162, but that it was never serious, and had been allayed.

MR.Hall, Her Majesty's Acting Consul at Nagasaki, who has paid a short visit to Söul, informs me privately that the Chinese are very popular in Corea, and that strict discipline is now maintained among the troops. He observes that the severe regulations, which I forwarded in my despatch No. 162, were posted up everywhere along the road from the coast to the capital, and that they were rigidly enforced, five men having been executed for infringing them. He could see no signs of the existence of any Corean troops.

The Japanese Vice-Minister for Foreign Affairs told me yesterday that he had heard, though not authentically, that the Chinese Government had increased their loan to Corea to 800,000 dollars, and that the Corean foreign Customs of the future had been hypothecated to them as security.

I have, &c.

(Signed) HARRY S. PARKES

T. G. Grosvenor(1882. 11. 25) ➜ G.L.G. Granville (1883. 1. 16)

Möllendorff의 외교고문 초빙 보고

Mr. Grosvenor to Earl Granville.—(Received January 16, 1883)

(No. 140 Most Confidential)

Peking, November 25, 1882

My Lord,

RUMOURS have from some little time past been current that M. von Möllendorff, a German, had entered into an arrangement with the Corean Envoys, lately in China to serve the Corean Government as foreign adviser. These rumours have now received confirmation.

M. von Möllendorff's career in China has, up to the present, been short but chequered. He came out in 1871 as an employé of the Foreign Customs Service, left that Service in 1874, and was subsequently employed as Interpreter to the German Consulate at Tien-tsin. He left the German service in the course of last year, and has, up to the present, served as one of the many foreign employés in the suite of his Excellency Li Hung-chang.

Mr. Brenan, Acting Consul at Tien-tsin, had some few days ago an opportunity of reading rapidly the agreement in Chinese that has been drawn up between M. von Möllendorff and the Corean Government. Mr. Brenan informs me that the gist of the agreement is as follows:-

M. von Möllendorff agrees to go to Corea to assist the Government in its foreign relations. His former experience in the Chinese Customs will enable him to assist the Coreans in establishing a foreign Customs system. If the Corean Government, or any Chinese Deputy sent to assist the Corean Government, gives him orders with regard to Customs matters, or directs him to proceed to any port, he must obey. He will at first find it necessary to employ foreign subordinates, but they must only be employed from year to year, so that they may gradually make way for Coreans, as these learn that work. At first the Customs revenue will be insufficient to pay expenses, so a certain sum will be allowed from some other source to carry on the service. M. von

Möllendorff must not, however, incur any expense without the sanction of the Corean Government. When the Customs revenue, after a year or two, becomes considerable, a certain sum out of this will be set aside for the purpose of these expenses. M. von Möllendorff is to receive [300 taels (**circa80**)] a-month. He will, besides, be allowed quarters. His agreement is terminable all three months' notice on either side.

Some surprise has been felt and expressed in Peking that the organization of the Corean Foreign Customs was not intrusted to Sir Robert Hart, who has rendered such valuable services to the Chinese Government in this direction, as it is well known that his Excellency Li Hung-chang is the motive power in all matters concerning the relations of Corea to foreign powers. His Excellency's action in this matter, as will be seen further on, appears to have been in opposition to Sir R. Hart's.

A few days after Mr. Brenan had sent me the precis of the arrangement concluded between M. von Möllendorff and the Corean Government, he had a conversation with M. von Möllendorff on the subject of the latter's appointment, in Corea. M. von Möllendorff, stated that Sir Robert Hart began, as soon as he had the opportunity, to offer his assistance in organizing the Corean Customs Service, and suggested to the Tsung-li Yanem that the Corean Customs should be incorporated with the Chinese. The Yamen demurred to this arrangement because it would place Corea in the position of a Chinese province. Sir Robert Hart then, according to M. von Möllendorff, proposed some scheme whereby Corea should have a separate establishment under Sir Robert Hart's supervision. His Excellency Li Hung-chang had, in the meanwhile, made other suggestions to the Corean Envoys, one of which was that M. von Möllendorff should become their adviser on foreign affairs, with a special view to assist them in establishing a Foreign Customs Service. His Excellency Li is stated by M. von Möllendorff to have placed Sir Robert Hart's and his own proposal very fairly before the Corean Envoys; to have requested them to return home and explain matters to the King, and to come back to Tien-tsin with their minds made up as to which plan was most acceptable, and also to bring with them full powers to conclude an arrangement on the subject. The Coreans went, returned, and stated their preference for his Excellency Li's scheme, which has consequently been adopted. M. von Mollendorff went on to say that, previous to the decision of the Corean Envoys, Sir Robert Hart had his plans ready, and had selected two members of the China Foreign Customs staff to commence operations in Corea, and had, moreover, offered the Inspector-Generalship of Corean Customs to Mr. Cartwright, an Englishman who has just resigned the post of Commissioner of Chinese Customs. Mr. Cartwright, however, declined the proffered appointment. One of the gentlemen whom Sir Robert Hart meant to send to Corea has just been appointed to serve in the Inspectorate here. His name is Carral.

I cannot help feeling that the Coreans have made a great mistake in accepting His Excellency Li's nominee as a foreign adviser with the mission of organizing their Customs Service. Whilst crediting M. von Möllendorff, who is almost an entire stranger to me, with the best intentions, both with regard to foreigners in general and Coreans in particular, I cannot but think that his somewhat spasmodic changes of career since he has been in China, and his relations to His Excellency Li, do not offer the guarantee requisite for so delicate an operation as the establishment of a Foreign Customs Service in a new country. I think that Coreans and foreigners alike would have been much safer in the hands of so experienced and able an organizer as Sir Robert Hart, and I am sure that no Customs official in China would have performed the duties for which he was intended by Sir Robert Hart more efficiently than Mr. Cartwright.

Your Lordship will observe in the terms of the agreement given in the earlier portion of this despatch that foreigners are only to be employed temporarily in the Corean Customs Service. In order to enable the Coreans to learn English, of which they must necessarily know something in order to become Customs officials, M. von Möllendorff is taking over to Corea with him six of the Chinese youths who have completed their course of study in America.

M. von Möllendorff spoke to Mr. Brenan of his decided intention of pushing the Coreans to develop the resources of their country in the way of mines, manufactures and other industrial enterprises, and stated, moreover, that the Coreans were, in his opinion, ready to go in for anything that promised future wealth. As M. von Möllendorff has lately seen a great deal of the Corean Envoy, his opinion on this point is worth consideration.

The impression which M. von Möllendorff left upon Mr. Brenan was that he counted upon English support a good deal for the success of his new enterprise, and that he hoped to induce English capitalists to invest money in Corea.

M. von Möllendorff went on to say that he could not hope for much support from his former chief, M. von Brandt, from whom he parted, on leaving the German service, on terms the reverse of friendly; and he did not expect Sir Robert Hart would view his proceedings very favourably. In both these forecasts I should say that his view is correct.

I have, &c.
(Signed)　T.G. GROSVENOR

T.G. Grosvenor (1882. 12. 4) ➡ G.L.G. Granville (1883. 1. 22)

조청상민수륙무역장정 영역문 보고

Mr. Grosvenor to Earl Granville.—(Received January 22, 1883)

(No. 147)

Peking, December 4, 1882

My Lord,

I HAVE the honour to forward to your Lordship herewith a translation of the Regulations lately drawn up at Tien-tsin between the Corean Envoys and two Chinese officials acting under the orders of his Excellency Li Hung-chang, in his quality of Imperial Commissioner for Trade at the Northern Ports. These Regulations define the conditions under which the subjects of either Power may resort to each other's country for purposes of trade.

I have the honour to forward the translation at once to your Lordship without further remark than that his Excellency Li Hung-chang would appear, according to these Regulations, to intend asserting a position for China in Corea more favourable than that accorded to the other foreign Powers who have already signed Treaties, and expressly to guard himself against the application of the most favoured-nation clause which Corea grants to China. That such a pretension as this, which is arrogantly put forward in the preamble of the Regulations, will be admitted by the other Powers who have signed Treaties with Corea, seems to me to be very doubtful.

The translation of these Regulations only reached me yesterday, and I have consequently not the time necessary before the departure of this day's mail to subject them to a careful comparison with the Treaty signed by Admiral Willes.

I am indebted to Mr. Brenan, Acting Consul at Tien-tsin, for the translation of this important document. .

I have, &c.

(Signed)　　T. G. GROSVENOR

Inclosure in No. 7

Regulations for Trade between Chinese and Coreans, camed on by Sea.

(Translation)

COREA has long been considered a feudatory country, and all matters of ceremonial are by law prescribed. No change is called for in this respect, but as foreign 'Powers are now to engage in maritime trade with Corea, it becomes necessary to rescind the prohibition against intercourse by sea, so that natives of both countries may similarly engage in commerce, and share its advantages. The Rules regarding trade over the frontier also require modification. The Regulations now framed respecting trade both by land and by sea are due to China's wish to treat a tributary State with special favour, and are not such as other countries may claim the benefit of.

These Regulations are as follows:-

No. 1. The imperial Commissioner for the North will appoint Commercial Agents to reside at the open ports of Corea for the purpose of looking after Chinese merchants. These Agents, in their relations with Corean officials, will be on terms of equality, and they shall be treated with courtesy. Should any question of importance arise, these Agents shall not take upon themselves to settle it with the Corean officials, but shall refer to the Imperial Commissioner for the North, who will address the King of Corea on the subject, so that be may instruct his Executive Council how to deal with the matter.

The King of Corea will likewise appoint a high official to reside at Tien-tsin, as well as Commercial Agents to reside at the open ports of China. These Agents will be on a footing of equality with the Chinese Taotais, Prefects, and Magistrates at the several ports.

Should any difficult question arise, they shall be at liberty to refer it to the Corean high official at Tien-tsin, who will request the Imperial Commissioner for the North, or for the South, as the case may be" to settle the matter. The Commercial Agents of the two countries may not levy contributions, but shall defray their own expenses. Should any such official act in an improper rn.anner he will be recalled immediately the Imperial Commissioner for the North represents the case to the King of Corea, or *vice versd*.

No. 2. Disputes arising between Chinese subjects at Corean ports shall be referred to the Chinese Commercial Agent for settlement. In all civil and criminal cases, if the plaintiff is a Corean subject and the defendant a Chinese subject, the case shall be dealt with by the Chinese official; if the plaintiff is a Chinese subject and the defendant is a Corean subject, the Corean official shall produce the accused and, together with the Chinese official, try the case according to law. Corean subjects at Chinese open ports shall, in all civil and criminal cases, no matter what is the nationality of the plaintiff or defendant, be tried by the Chinese authorities, who will send a report of the case to the Corean Agent. Should the Corean subject be dissatisfied with the decision, the Corean Agent may request the high authorities to rehear the case.

Should Corean subjects, in their own country, have occasion to lay a plaint against a Chinese subject at the office of the Chinese Agent; or, in China, to make complaint at the office of a Chinese official, the Court underlings shall not extort fees of any kind. Offenders in this respect shall be severely punished by the official under whom they are serving. Subjects of one country who, having committed an offence against their own laws, either in their own country~ or at the open ports of the other country, take refuge in the other country, shall be delivered up by the local authorities to the nearest Commercial Agent for conveyance to their own country, on representation being made by the Commercial Agent of the country interested. While being so conveyed, however, the prisoner shall only be subjected to restraint, and shall not be exposed to any cruel treatment.

No. 3. The ships. of either country may frequent the open ports of the other for purposes of, trade, under the Regulations already agreed upon affecting the loading and unloading of merchandize and the payment of maritime duties.

Vessels which may be stranded on the shoI:es of either country may remain there to buy provisions or effect repairs, but any outlay shall be at the expense of the master of the vessel. Should any vessel break up, the local officials will give assistance, and send the passengers and crew to the Commercial Agent at the nearest port for conveyance to their home, and thus avoid the expense hitherto incurred in sending back distressed subjects to their own country. Except in case of vessels wrecked or seeking repairs, any ship of either country proceeding to a non-open port for purposes of trade shall, with her cargo, be confiscated. Fishing craft, however, of either nation, from the coast of Corea, or the shores of Shantung or Féngtien, may come and go at pleasure in pursuit of their avocation, and may purchase provisions or water ashore. They may not carryon a clandestine trade, and boats so offending will, with their cargo, be confiscated. Persons guilty of offences at such places shall be apprehended by the local authorities and sent to their national Agent at the nearest port, to be punished in accordance with Article No. 2. After the expiration of two years, Rules shall be framed regulating the fish duties to be paid by the fishing-boats of either nation. [Owing to the fish having been frightened by steamers over to the opposite coast, Shantung fishermen go by thousands to the islands on the Coast of Corea.]

No. 4. Subjects of either Power resorting to each other's country for purposes of trade, being well-conducted persons, shall be at liberty to rent land and premises, or build houses; and also to trade in local produce, and any merchandize, not contraband. Imports and exports shall pay duty and vessels shall pay tonnage dues as specified in the Maritime Customs Regulations. Merchandize may also be carried from one port to another on payment of a half import duty at the time of reimportation, in addition to the export duty already paid at the time of exportation. Corean subjects are by law allowed to trade at Peking, and Chinese subjects to open establishments at Yanghua and Chinghan in Corea. But this apart, they are not allowed to convey merchandize into the interior.

Subjects of either country may proceed into the interior to purchase native produce, provided they first obtain a pass in the joint name of their Commercial Agent and the local official, specifying the place where the produce is to be purchased. The horses, carts, or boats shall be hired by the purchaser, who will also pay all *li-kin* and duties leviable *en route*.

Persons intending to travel in the interior may do so upon obtaining a passport in the joint name of their Commercial Agent and the local official. Should such persons while travelling be guilty of any offence, they shall be sent by the local officials to the nearest port, to be there dealt with as provided in Article No. 2. While being so sent they shall merely be kept under restraint, and shall not be exposed to any ill-usage.

No. 5. The trading stations hitherto existing on the frontier, such as Yi-chou, Huining, and Ch'ing-yuan, have been under the control of officials, a system which gave rise to many difficulties. It is now proposed that at Cha-men and Yi-chou, on the opposite bank of the Ya-lu River; and at Hun-ch'un and Hui-ning, on the opposite bank of the T'u-nien River, the people shall be at liberty to trade as they please. At the marts thus opened Customs stations shall be established for the detection. of bad characters and for the receipt of duties. All merchandize, imported or exported, with the exception of red' ginseng shall pay an *ad valorem* duty of 5 per cent. The system of fees for the maintenance of the stations hitherto in force shall be abolished. Civil and criminal cases shall continue to be dealt with by the officials of either country as the law directs.

Special and detailed Regulations cannot be put in force until the Imperial Commissioner for the North and the King of Corea each send officers to the spot to draw up these conjointly; after which they shall be submitted to the throne for approval.

No. 6. Munitions and implements of war and opium, both foreign and native, may not be imported for sale by the subjects of either country, at any port or at any place on the frontier. A breach of this Regulation will lay the offender open to the infliction of the severest penalty.

Corean merchants are allowed to bring red ginseng into China on payment of an *ad valorem* duty of 15 per cent. If Chinese subjects are detected in conveying ginseng out of Corea. without the express permission of the Corean Administration, the goods shall he confiscated.

No. 7. Postal communication between the two countries has been hitherto carried on overland by way of Cha-men at great expense. Now that communication by sea is allowed, it is expedient to profit by this more convenient way. Corea, however, having no merchant or war steamers at present; the King of Corea may apply to the-Imperial Commissioner for the North to detail a merchant steamer to come and go once a-month, the Corean Administration paying a certain sum as subsidy. But Corean officials will no longer have to supply the wants of Chinese men-of-war which may cruize on the coast of Corea or anchor in her ports for her protection. All expenses for provisions and stores shall be defrayed by the ships. The Commanders of such ships and their subordinates shall have intercourse with Corean officials on terms of equality. The officers of the ship shall exercise strict control on sailors going ashore, and prevent them from causing any disturbance.

No. 8. These provisional and brief Regulations are to be strictly conformed to by both officials and people of either country. Should it hereafter become necessary to make any alterations, the Imperial Commissioner for the

North will consult with the King of Corea, as the occasion requires, and submit any change for the approval of the Throne. The above Regulations have been framed by the Corean Envoy Chao Ning Hsia, the Corean Assistant Envoy Chin Hung Chi, and the Coreanofficial Yu Yûn-chung, in consultation with Chou Fu, Customs Taotai at Tien-tsin, and Ma Chien-chung, an expectant Taotai, all acting under the instructions of Li, Acting Imperial Commissioner for the North, &c.

T.G. Grosvenor (1882. 12. 14) ➡ G.L.G. Granville (1883. 2. 14)

조러 육로교섭 보고

No. 24

Mr. Grosvenor to Earl Granville—(Received February 14)

(No. 155 Most Confidential)

Peking, December 14, 1882

My Lord,

I LEARN on good authority that M. de Bützow, Russian Minister here, endeavoured shortly before his departure to negotiate with the Tsung-li Yamên a set of Regulations between Russia and Corea for overland trade between the two countries.

M. de Bützow was met by the assurance that it was impossible to persuade the Corean Government to enter into arrangements regarding overland trade with any country, China herself included.

The appearance of the Regulations lately framed for trade by sea and overland between China and Corea (see my despatch No. 147 of the 4th December) consequently caused no little surprise, I am informed, at the Russian Legation here; and I have good reason to believe that these Regulations formed the subject of a rather angry disenssion between M. Waeber, at present in charge of the Russian Legation, and the Ministers of the Tsung-li Yamên.

I have, &e.

(Signed)　　T. G. GROSVENOR

H.S. Parkes (1882. 12. 21) ➜ G.L.G. Granville (1883. 1. 29)

조청상민수륙무역장정 체결에 따른 1차 조영조약 개정 건의

Sir H.S. Parkes to Earl Granville.—(*Received January 29, 1883*)

(No. 172 Confidential)

Tôkiô, December 21, 1882

My Lord,

  IN the course of a visit which I paid to the Foreign Minster on the 18th instant, his Excellency spoke with evident displeasure of a new Treaty, as he called ti, which had been concluded between China and Corea. It denoted, he observed, that China intended to assume great powers of control over Corea, and to secure exclusive commercial privileges in that country. He believed this action to be chiefly directed against Japan, although it also materially affected the interests of those nations who were about to enter into Treaty relations with Corea. China evidently intended to keep her troops in that country; she continued to send there munitions of war; she had appointed a Chinese officer as Adviser to the Corean Government, and had attached to him foreigners in the China service to organize the Customs and to prospect the mines. He understood that she held the future customs revenue of Corea and certain of her mines as security for the loan of 500,000 taels which she had made to Corea. He believed that she even intended to remove the King of Corea to China because Japan had taken a similar course in regard to the King of Loochoo, and that she would not rest until she had made Corea a Chinese province. All this was done under the pretext of guarding against Japanese aggression in Corea, although Japan, by the moderation of her recent proceedings when her Legation was attacked, had given substantial proof that she entertained no designs of that nature. It was really retaliation for the past action of Japan in Formosa and Loochoo, but it would also have the effect of depriving other nations of the advantages they might expect to obtain from their new relations with Corea. He was anxious to know what course would be taken by the Powers who had made

Treaties with Corea, and he desired that the action of the Japanese Government should be influenced by and should conform, if circumstances so permitted, with their proceedings.

I asked his Excellency to allow me to see the so-called Treaty between China and Corea, and eventually furnished me with a copy. I inclose a translation, which has been somewhat hastily prepared. It is not termed a Treaty, but Regulations for the Trade by Sea and Land between China and Corea, and the following is a summary of its conditions.

The preamble declares that Corea is a feudatory of China, and that, as intercourse on the seaboard of Corea has now been admitted with foreign nations, it becomes necessary to remove the prohibitions on maritime trade which have hitherto existed between China and that country. But it also clearly indicates that the relations between China and Corea rest on a different basis to those of Corea with foreign countries; the latter being governed by international compact and the former by the conditions of dependency in which Corean stands to China. Foreign nations, therefore, cannot claim identical treatment with China.

The 1st Article provides for the reciprocal appointment at the ports open to trade in China and Corea of officers or Commissioners who will have the management of commercial affairs. A higher functionary will be appointed by the King of Corea to reside at Ten-tsin and be in communication with the Minister superintendent of Northern Trade, but the latter is to be placed in direct relation with the King of Corea, and they, the Minister Superintendent and the King, will determine together the recall of any of the above-mentioned officers when misconduct may render this necessary.

The 2nd Article gives to the Chinese Commissioners of Trade in Corea large judicial powers. They are to have complete jurisdiction over Chinese subjects and joint jurisdiction with the Corean authorities in cases in which Corean subjects are defendants. The Corean Commissioners of Trade in China on the other hand, are to have no powers of jurisdiction over their own people. It also provides for the mutual extradition of offenders.

The 3rd Article stipulates for trade at the open ports, subject to the payment of such customs dues as have been determined between the two countries. These dues are not particularized, but the 5th Article, which treats on the trade by land, states that "the customs dues on imports and exports shall not exceed 5 percent. *ad-valorem* except upon red ginseng," which by the 6th

Article is to pay 15 percent. It does not appear clear whether it is intended that this or a different Tariff is to govern the maritime trade. Proceedings in shipwreck and fishing rights are also provided for.

The 4th Article stipulates for residence, the carriage of goods coastwise on payment of half duty, and also for access to the interior under passport either for purposes of travel or the purchase of native produce.

The 5th Article frees the land trade from the old restrictions and exactions, and provides that the necessary Regulations for this trade shall be made by the Minister Superintendent of Northern Trade and the King of Corea, subject to the approval of the Emperor of China.

The 6th Article prohibits all trade in foreign or Chinese opium, and the smuggling of ginseng.

The 7th Article provides that the King of Corea shall pay a subsidy to the Chinese Merchants' Steam Navigation Company for a monthly steamer to run between China and Corea, and also that "the vessels of the Chinese navy shall furthermore visit the coast of Corean and call at the different ports to afford protection," it being probably intended that such protection shall extend to Corea as well as to the Chinese subjects and their interests in that country.

The 8th Article provides for the revision of these Regulations when necessary by the Minister Superintendent of Northern Trade and the King of Corea, subject to ratification by the Emperor of China.

It is not surprising that these arrangements should occasion the japanese Government great annoyance, and the Foreign Minister is correct in his view of the effect which they are likely to have on the commercial interests of those nations who have recently concluded Treaties with Corea. If Chinese subjects in that country are to possess exclusively the advantages contained in these Regulations, it would be vain for foreign merchants to endeavour to compete with them, and the expense of providing commercial establishments in that country had better be avoided.

Although I cannot suppose it probable that the Chinese Government entertain the idea, as stated by the Foreign Minister, of removing the King of Corea, these Regulations show very clearly that they only regard him as the equal, in point of rank, of a Chinese Viceroy, and in entire subordination to the sovereign of China. It would be strangely inconsistent for the King to occupy such a very inferior position towards the latter, and at the same time one of perfect equality with Her Majesty and other sovereigns of Europe, although it would doubtless be flattering to Chinese pride to see the King accepted as an equal by those Sovereigns.

The extent to which China is disposed to clam authority over Corea is also indicated by the stipulation that in mixed cases occurring in Corea between Chinese and Coreans, Chinese officers are to exercise jurisdiction over Corean subjects even on Corean soil.

The feeling of the Foreign Minister is already being reechoed in the native Japanese press. I inclose a translation of a long article which appeared in print last evening, and is evidently inspired.* It is intended as an appeal to the people to sanction the increase of the Japanese armaments, for which additional taxation is required. The identity of a portion of the following passage with the language used to me by the Foreign Minister is noteworthy, and the apprehensions expressed by the writer as to the consequences of the action of China in Corea, when viewed in regard to her relations with Russia, though possibly exaggerated, are not altogether groundless:-

"If China sees any chance she will annex Corea, and add it as a new province to her other eighteen. The father of the Corean King is already her prisoner. How much more, then, would she not unhesitatingly carry off the King? Corea is to be thus appropriated and converted into a province. The result at this critical moment will be that China's complications with Russia on the North-West will extend as far as Corea, and that Russia will endeavour to recoup herself in the East for her losses in the North. Wonsan (Port Lazareff) will then be immediately occupied by a Russian fleet. In such a crisis other European Powers will doubtless interfere to frustrate the plans of Russia. All this will, of course, result in great misfortune to Corea, and China, in the absorption of the peninsula kingdom, will have brought calamity to herself."

I regretted to hear from the Foreign Minister that the new Japanese Minister to China, Admiral Enomoto, had met with only a cool reception at Peking, and that the Grand Secretary Li Hung Chang, in conversation with the United States' Minister at that capital, had used very unfriendly language towards Japan.

Although it may be considered that I am out of place in alluding in this despatch to such a very different subject as the revision of our Treaty with Japan, I nevertheless venture to offer the brief remark that if Admiral Willes' Treaty with Corea should be ratified as it stands, it would then be hopeless

---

*[원주] "Japan Daily Mail." December 20, 1882.

to expect that the Japanese Government would make any of the concessions which I named in my Report on the Tôkiô conference as desirable to obtain in return for a higher Tariff. Those were: a more liberal passport system, access to the interior for the purpose of trade, and the employment by Japanese subjects of foreign shipping in the coasting trade. Admiral Willes' Treaty secures none of these advantages in Corea, and even debars British subjects from carrying native produce between the open ports, while it at the same time grants to Corea a far higher Tariff than that proposed by Japan. It is not likely, in the event of that Treaty being ratified, that Japan, knowing well that it was the work of the Grand Secretary Li hung Chang, and seeing Corea obtain by it a higher Tariff than she claims, on the strength of her progress and long friendly relations, will make concessions to us which we have not even sought to gain in Corea, and which China, while she has secured them for her own people, has required Corea to withhold from all other Powers.

I have, &c.

(Signed)   HARRY S. PARKES

H.S. Parkes (1882. 12. 29) ➔ G.L.G. Granville (1883. 2. 5)

朴泳孝와 1차 조영조약 개정 협상 보고

Sir H. Parkes to Earl Granville.—(Received February 5, 1883)

(No. 176 Confidential)

Tôkiô, December 29, 1882

My Lord,

THE principal Corean Envoy to Japan, Pak Yöng-hyo, visited me on the 23rd instant to take leave, as he was about to return to his country. He excused the absence of the Second Envoy on the ground of indisposition.

He at once directed the conversation to the subject of our Treaty with Corea, and inquired if I had heard anything as to its ratification. Having answered in the negative, he observed that he regretted the delay as he feared that if it were to continue, his country, owing to the high-handed course which China was adopting towards her, would sink without hope of succour. He was anxious to know what I thought on the subject.

I replied that I was not surprised at the delay, because I thought, as I had told him in our previous conversations on this subject (reported in my despatches Nos. 153 and 154 of the 24th October), that the unfortunate events which had occurred in Corea since the Treaty was made would oblige my Government to proceed with caution, even if they approved all the conditions of the Treaty, which I also thought was doubtful. And now, again, I had heard of the recent arrangements made between China and Corea at Tien-tsin, which I thought would place additional difficulty in the way of ratification. By these arrangements China would be able to trade with Corea on far more favourable terms than the Western Powers who had made Treaties with Corea. Japan was also placed by her Treaty in a much more advantageous position than those Powers. It would be useless, it appeared to me, for British or any other foreign merchants to endeavour to compete against the favoured treatment which Corea had accorded to those two nations.

The Envoy observed that the Tien-tsin arrangements to which I had alluded had been forced upon Corea by China, and this was the high-handed action to which he had referred. An Agreement had been concluded, but it had not yet been ratified by the King.

I replied that I did not doubt that he spoke his true feelings, but his language did not appear to be reconcilable with the action of the Corean Envoys who represented his country in China. The Agreement in question was the outcome, I believed, of much negotiation at Tien-tsin; the Envoys, I understood, had gone backwards and forwards between China and Corea while it was being conducted, and it might fairly be presumed, therefore, that the arrangements which had thus been concluded with China had been willingly made with the full knowledge and consent of the Corean Government and King. But, however this might be, that Agreement, I thought, must have the effect which I had named.

The Envoy said that he wished to talk with me very frankly, but begged me to accept all he had to say in strict confidence, and as emanating from himself alone. That, I rejoined, was exactly the character of my own remarks. He then made the following observations:—

"I grant that, judging from appearances, you may naturally conclude that the recent agreement between China and Corea has been made with the consent of the latter, but this is not the fact. It has been forced upon us by China, who has taken advantage of Corea's weakness to dictate it. Japan made her Treaty with Corea direct, and, therefore, it is a satisfactory one. But when Corea had to negotiate with Western Powers, China intervened and drafted the Treaty, which she told us we should make with those Powers. In our ignorance of the subject, we thought that China must know what was the most proper course, and would advise us for the best. The unfavourable conditions of those Treaties were therefore adopted at her suggestion. We now perceive that, taking advantage of our inexperience, she has acted entirely with a view to her own interest and to the disadvantage of Corea, and that she now wishes to subordinate Corea completely to herself. We hoped that by entering into Treaty relations with Western Powers we should be guarded against such a result, and we still trust that the latter will afford us their support. Corea's position is this. She has no army, as she did not need one for the government of her own people. She is, therefore, in the grasp of China, whom she cannot resist, and who can, therefore, compel Corea to do whatever she wishes. You are doubtless aware that in the draft of the Western Treaties a clause was inserted declaring Corea to be a dependency of China, but entirely independent both in her external and internal affairs. This clause was removed from the Treaties as signed, but it was transferred to the letters which the King addressed to the Sovereigns with whom he concluded those Treaties. This declaration of the independent position of the King was made with the full knowledge and approval of China, Now, however, she is interfering in every way in Corea, both in internal and external matters, and is depriving the King of his rights and his Government of their liberty of action. I have no words to express my indignation at the flagrant injustice of her proceedings."

I inquired whether the above views were simply his own, or whether they were shared by the King and his Government. It was important also to know what were the feelings of the Corean people on the subject, as it was open to a nation to surrender its independence if it desired to do so. The Tien-tsin Agreement certainly seemed to greatly lower the position of the King of Corea, and might render it difficult for other Sovereigns to regard him as an equal.

The Envoy replied that when tie left Corea to come to Japan the King had expressed to him his strong repugnance to the aggressive spirit which was then being shown by China, and had desired him to lose no opportunity of making his feelings known. But the Agreement recently forced upon Corea at Tien-tsin, which places the King in a position of utter subjection to China, was a serious aggravation of anything that had before occurred. As to the feeling of the nation and the Government, he regretted to say that the people of Corea, in their present low condition, could not be taken into account; while, owing to so many of the public offices being held by hereditary tenure, a large proportion of the governing class were either spiritless or under the influence of old Chinese ideas; but the King and his party were strongly imbued with a desire to maintain the national independence. They perceived that if China continued in her present oppressive course, and if foreign Powers did not make Treaties with Corea, and there by recognize her national status, she would sink and never rise again.

I asked the Envoy whether his Government would be willing to give Western Powers the same privileges as they had given to China under the Tien-tsin Agreement. He replied that he was not authorized to say so, but he thought that they would willingly extend to those Powers any of the conditions of that Agreement that were not disadvantageous to Corea, provided that those Powers made proposals for amending their Treaties, or making new ones direct to

Corea, and not through China.

Having asked him to name the conditions of the Tien-tsin Agreement which he regarded as disadvantageous to Corea, the Envoy observed that the conditions which they chiefly objected to were all those passages which subordinated the King to the Government of China, and practically deprived him of his sovereign rank; but that in addition to these they disapproved of the stipulation which opened the interior of Corea to China for purposes of travel and trade, as they considered that in the present state of the former country the safety of foreigners in the interior could not be guaranteed.

I observed that the said Agreement provided that the import and export duties to be paid by Chinese were 5 per cent, *ad valorem*. Would his Government be willing to admit foreign goods on the same terms?

The Envoy replied that he thought the Tariff of 10 to 30 per cent, on foreign imports, which was named in the Treaties with Western Powers, was too high, and would crush a nascent trade, but it had been specially recommended by China, 5 per cent., on the other hand, he thought was too low.

That rate, I observed, is the basis of the Tariffs concluded by China, and also by Japan, with all Western Powers.

In that case, he replied, Corea might also agree to it, though he still thought that it was too low.

It would be a very proper rate, I remarked, on some classes of goods, though I admitted that the more valuable commodities might bear a higher rate.

As to his observation that any proposals to amend their Treaties or to conclude new ones should be made by Western Powers direct to Corea, it appeared to me, I remarked, that a foreign Government would probably wish to receive some assurance that overtures of that nature would be favourably entertained by Corea before they made them.

He replied, that although he was leaving Japan, Kim ok Riun would remain here, and would serve, if necessary, as a channel of communication. And although I had told him that I was in no way concerned officially in Corean affairs, he begged me to do what I could to make known to the British Government the difficulties of his country, and also that Corea earnestly looked for the support of the Western Powers with whom she had made Treaties.

On returning his visit on the 26th instant I met both the Envoys, who remarked that they hoped I would report favourably about their country to my Government, and that the latter would approve of the British Treaty coming into force. I told them that as this was the last time I should have the pleasure of seeing them I would unreservedly state to them, but as my personal opinion only, that the present Treaty was of no value to my country. The remark led to a conversation between themselves, at the conclusion of which the Senior Envoy remarked that they agreed with me, and that if the British Government had any objections to offer to the present Treaty his Government would be glad to know them.

I then inquired whether a report, which had reached me, was true, that the Corean Government would object to foreigners in Corea observing their religion to the extent of erecting places of worship within the concessions that would be set apart for the residence on the latter.

The Senior Envoy replied that he feared the erection of churches would excite the people and occasion disorder. To this I observed that it was incumbent on any Government that made a Treaty to maintain order among its own people. Foreign churches were allowed by Treaty in China and Japan, and foreigners who respected their faith would rather not go to Corea than be deprived, if they went there, of liberty of religion. The Envoy observed that he could perceive that to prohibit the building of churches would offend the feelings of foreigners, but their erection, on the other hand, would offend the feeling of the Corean people, and if the Government endeavoured to repress that feeling, it might only make matters worse. He believed that this was a question which would eventually settle itself. If foreigners would refrain from building churches during the first two or three years of their stay in Corea, the hostile feeling towards foreign religion which was at present prevalent among the Corean people would abate, and the latter would become accustomed to the idea that the free observance of their worship should be permitted to foreigners.

I referred to this subject because my French colleague had told me that he had discussed the missionary question with the Envoy. He had stated to the latter that though liberty to proselytize might not be claimed for missionaries, still a foreigner being a missionary and a subject of one of the Powers who had lately concluded Treaties with Corea, would have the same rights as to residence in Corea as any other subject of the same Power, and that he saw no reason why a clause should not be inserted in a Treaty giving foreigners the right of building churches in their own concessions. The Envoy had replied that he thought this was impossible in the present state of popular feeling in his country. M. Tricon, I should add, entertains the opinion that the Corean

Government is powerless to control its own people, and that the advent of foreigners there will not be unattended with trouble. He told the Envoy that the French Government had suspended their wish to negotiate a Treaty with Corea on hearing of the murders at Söul, because they considered that the country was not in a condition to enter into relations with foreign Powers, and to incur the responsibilities which those relations involved.

I should observe to your Lordship that in the course of the preceding conversations in which I have closely reported the language of the Envoy, I refrained from passing any criticisms on the action of China. The Envoy, Pak Yŏng-hyo, is a young man of much intelligence and self-possession, and he spoke forcibly but without excitement. His remarks I thought of sufficient importance to justify the telegram which I sent to your Lordship on the 24th instant. He evidently feels strongly against China, and this feeling it may be presumed will not have been diminished by his communications with the Japanese Foreign Minister, and I believe I may add with the United States' Minister at Tokio, as the latter in conversation with myself has unreservedly condemned the assumption by China of control over Corea, and has observed to me that his Government consider that the independence of Corea should be maintained.

Corea being a weak and an uncivilized State, may be expected to be insincere; her people are violent and ill-mannered, and greed and rapacity appear to be prominent characteristics of her officials. Though the various parties in her divided and incapable Government will pay court from time to time either to China or to Japan, as may best promote their own particular aims, or thwart those of their opponents, they all probably entertain for both those countries about an equal degree of aversion. Though glad to derive such a degree of support from China as will effectually protect them against Japan, they are equally ready to resent the patronage of the former when it involves subjection, and as a counterpoise to her domination, which has recently been imposed upon them in a way and to an extent which they did not anticipate, they now look for aid to the intervention of Western States. It would be vain, however, for the latter to suppose that the Coreans have conceived any real regard for foreigners, or are prepared to suddenly lay aside their old traditional hostility. A wide field, however, is presented for intrigue and dissimulation, and Corea may find that Japan and Russia will both be inclined to encourage them in resistance to China.

I have evidence that the discussions which led to the Agreement of Tien-tsin were not conducted between the Chinese and Corean Representatives in a way that was acceptable to the latter, and Pak Yŏng-hyo was not incorrect in stating to me in the above conversation that that Agreement was dictated by China, and unwillingly concurred in by the Corean Agents. When the latter urged that other nations would probably claim the same privileges as were thus accorded to China, the Grand Secretary Li Hung Chang stated to them, in terms which must have wounded their susceptibilities, that they should remember that China was not the equal of Corea, but her superior, and that she did not make Treaties with Corea, but "Regulations," which were communicated by order of the Emperor. The nations who treated with Corea were therefore in a wholly different position to China, and could not claim the same privileges, and he tauntingly added that if Corea really desired to silence any demands for equal treatment with China, she should inform the nations which made such demands that the Regulations in question were granted by China as a favour to one of her dependencies.

It will be evident, I think, that our ability to promote harmony between these Oriental nations, and to stimulate the impoverished Coreans to enter on industrial and commercial pursuits, must depend on the position we shall occupy in our earliest relations with Corea. It would be better, I submit, to hold entirely aloof from that country than to enter it on conditions inferior to those which we possess in China and Japan, It may be foreseen that the first foreign settlers in Corea will need foreign protection, and other Western nations will probably not be more eager than ourselves to incur, without the prospect of any adequate return, the cost of that obligation.

I have, &c.
(Signed) HARRY S. PARKES

112

H.S. Parkes (1882.12.31) ➜ G.L.G. Granville

朴泳孝의 전권 소지여부에 관한 회신

No. 180

Tokio, December 31, 1882

My Lord,

I have the honor to acknowledge the receipt this day at 12 noon of the following telegram from your Lordship in cypher:

"Parkes Tokio
"N.B December 30 3.50 p.m. your Telegram of 24th instant,
if Korean Envoys can get authority from their Government to negotiate on basis suggested Her Majesty's Government will be happy to entertain their proposals Granville"

I have the honor to be with the highest Respect
My Lord,
Your lordship's most obedient Humble servant
Harry Parkes

J.P. Mollison (1883. 1. 9) ➜ G.L.G. Granville (1883. 2. 20)

1차 조영조약에 대한 橫濱 상공회의소 의견 상신

Mr. Mollison to Earl Granville.—(Received February 20)

Yokohama General chamber of Commerce, Yokohama,
January 9, 1883

My Lord,

I HAVE the honour to acknowledge receipt of your Lordship's letter, dated 10th October lst, intimating that you would be glad to receive and give due consideration to any observations the Yokohama General Chamber of Commerce might wish to make on the proposed Treaty with Corea; and I have also to acknowledge receipt of copy of said Treaty under cover from his Excellency Sir Harry S. Parkes.

The Committee of the Chamber have carefully considered the proposed Treaty, and now venture to submit to your Lordship the following comments upon its provisions;-

Tariff.—The Tariff, or rather the absence of a Tariff, is the first conspicuous feature, for the simple statement that a duty not exceeding 10 per cent. shall be charged on articles of daily use, and not exceeding 30 per cent. on luxuries, amounts to nothing, in the absence of provision for allowing British officials a voice in the question of whether a particular article shall be charged as a necessary or a luxury, and especially as it is reserved to the Corean authorities to fix all duties without reference to British officials. This of itself is a bad precedent; but when taken in conjunction with the excessive rates of duty proposed to be levied becomes doubly so, bearing in mind the revision of the Treaties with Japan now pending, and also possible future negotiations with China having the same end in view.

Further, it is not clear from the Treaty whether the percentage of duty is to be estimated on the first cost at the place of production, or on the lay-down cost of the goods in Corea, as per invoice, including freight and insurance charges.

It may be noted here that, in their intercourse by Treaty with Corea, the

Japanese pay no import duties whatever, and also, in the same connection, that in the matter of tonnage dues those proposed to be levied on British vessels are out of all proportion to what are paid by Japanese vessels.

Leasing Land.—Here again advantages are granted to Japanese by Treaty which are denied to British subjects, the most noticeable being that the former are only required to pay the same ground-rent as is charged to Coreans themselves, whereas the latter, it is stipulated, shall pay whatever rent the Corean authorities may see fit to impose. Moreover, the British Treaty would appear to contemplate the foreign settlements being subject to Corean municipal law, an arrangement which, judging from the accounts which have been received as to the state of Corean towns, roads, &c., it is feared would be found extremely unsatisfactory.

Coast Trade.—The stipulation closing the trade between the open ports in Corea, in native produce, to British shipping is a feature in the proposed Treaty open to several objections, besides again affording a precedent that Japan and China would not be slow to avail themselves of. Such trade, denied to British ships, would not fall into the hands of Coreans, who have practically no mercantile marine, but of the japanese and Chinese, who are not affected by any similar prohibition. One of the Chinese Shipping Companies is believed to have already secured exceptional privileges in this respect. In connection with the coast trade, it may not be out of place to notice here that in cases of smuggling it is stipulated in the British Treaty that both vessel and cargo shall be seized and confiscated, whereas the Japanese Treaty states that cargo only shall be so dealt with.

Export of Grain.—The entire prohibition of the export of grain from Jin'chuen, the port nearest to the capital of Corea, seems unnecessary in view of the preceding clause, by which the Government of Corea reserves to itself the right of temporarily suspending the trade at any or all of the ports whenever it may appear desirable to do so. It should be remembered that Corea has no manufactures, and for a long time to come must pay for imported goods, as she in now doing, by agricultural produce, and any restrictions on the export of grain will therefore have a directly injurious effect on the import trade. In the event of the exercise of this right of prohibition being contemplated, ample notice should be given beforehand to prevent the injury to trade which a sudden measure of this kind would undoubtedly cause. It may be pointed out that, according to the terms of the Japanese Treaty, the export of grain is free from all the open ports, without exception, and that no right of prohibition is reserved.

Trade Regulations.—These it is stipulated shall be framed in conformity with international law, but there is no provision that British officials shall have the voice in their preparation which the comparative importance of British interests (shown by the fact that almost the whole of the imports at present are of British origin) demands. It is also stated that these Regulations shall be drawn up after an interval of five years, whereas it is patent that they should be ready when the country is opened. The Japanese Treaty of 1876 with Corea provided for the drawing up of Trade Regulations "by Special Commissioners appointed by the two Countries" prior to the opening of the ports, and at a later period provision was made for revision whenever necessary "by Commissioners appointed by each country."

Treaty Ports.—The Treaty does not mention what ports are to be thrown open to British trade, but it is presumed they will be the same as the Japanese have fixed upon, viz, Wönsan, Fusan, and Jin'chuen. As the last-named is in some respects objectionable, it is desirable, before finally deciding on it, to ascertain whether some more eligible port cannot be found near the capital.

Opium.—The stipulation prohibiting Coreans from importing opium into England seems unnecessary, and could not be enforced (should the occasion arise) without special legislation.

Article XIV.—From a commercial point of view, this is the most objectionable clause in the whole Treaty, as by it British merchants are excluded from advantages previously acquired by other nations in Corea, and Great Britain is therefore placed in the position, not of the most favoured nation, but after both Japan and China.

The Japanese, as has already been stated, pay no import duties, and only insignificant shipping fees, and it is not likely that they will consent to allow the Coreans to charge the high rates of duties, &c., of the British Tariff. Under these circumstances, it is plain that it will be totally impossible for British merchants to compete with them, except by resorting to the somewhat ignominious plan of conducting their business in the names of Japanese.

The commercial position of the Chinese in Corea is not quite so clear, as we have no precise knowledge of the privileges they possessed in that country prior to the negotiation of the proposed British Treaty. Whatever these privileges may be, however, that Treaty debars British subjects from any participation in them. And According to intelligence just received from China, it appears that arrangements have recently been concluded, which gives to China a Tariff of 5 per cent. on imports and exports, and to her merchants the right to go into the interior of Corea to purchase native produce, and to trade in native produce between the open ports, both of which are expressly prohibited to British merchants under the proposed Treaty. It is understood, moreover, that it is maintained by China that foreigners are to be excluded from participation in the above-named privileges.

All that is claimed by British merchants in Corea is a fair field and no favour. But so long as the Treaty places them at such a manifest disadvantage in respect to the Japanese, and no doubt also to the Chinese, it may be confidently predicted that British trade with Corea will be carried on, as at present, by these intermediaries, and that few British merchants will establish themselves in the country.

Jurisdiction.—It hardly falls within the province of a commercial body to offer an opinion the Jurisdiction Clauses of the Treaty, but the Committee may be pardoned for saying that it appears strange, while reserving British jurisdiction in all case in which a Corean is plaintiff and a British subject defendant, to leave to Corean law and Corean Tribunals cases in which both parties are British subjects, and cases between British subjects and foreigners.

The arrangements as to criminal jurisdiction are open to similar objection. This result, we presume, could never have been intended, but it is essential that on an important point of this kind no doubt should be left possible. There is none in the case of Chinese or Japanese subjects in Corea; they are amenable in their persons and property solely to the jurisdiction of their own authorities, and they are expressly exempted from the control of Corean law.

In view of the considerations above named, the Committee regret that they can only report to your Lordship on the proposed Treaty in an unfavourable sense. They have to object to its containing no Tariff, Customs, Trade, or Municipal Regulations, nor any provision for negotiating these before the opening of the ports to trade; to the excessive duties which, under its provisions, could be imposed on British trade by the Corean Government at will; to the liberty given to the latter to determine, as they may see fit, the land-rents to be paid by British subjects; to the power which they will possess to confiscate ships and cargoes, and subject British subjects, in many important respects, to Corean laws and Corean Tribunals, which are known to be in a barbarous condition; and they object to and burdened by disadvantages which would render it impossible for them to compete with the latter, and would, in short, deprive them of all inducement to establish themselves in business in that country. Believing, as they do, that little or no commerce could be conducted by British merchants under this Treaty, they respectfully recommend that it should not be ratified by Her Majesty's Government.

I have, &c.

(Signed)   JAMES P. MOLLISON, Chairman

114

H.S. Parkes (1883. 1. 12) ➜ G.L.G. Granville (1883. 2. 20)

조일 관세율 협정에 관한 朴泳孝·井上馨의 회담 보고

Sir H.S. Parkes to Earl Granville.—(Received February 20)

(No. 3 Confidential)

Tôkiô, January 12, 1883

My Lord,

  I REPORTED, in my despatch No. 177 of the 30th ultimo, that the Corean Envoys had returned to Corea, and that they were accompanied by Mr. Takezoye, the new Minister Resident appointed by the Japanese Government to the Court of Söul.

  I have since learned from the Foreign Minister that the Corean Envoys had desired the Japanese Government to empower Mr. Takezoye to negotiate a Commercial Treaty at Söul. The Foreign Minister, however, had objected to this course, on the ground that any negotiations conducted at the Corean capital would be controlled by the Agent of the Chinese Government—the brother of Ma Taotai—who is now stationed there, and who directs or interferes with all the foreign affairs of the Corean government. He had told the Envoys, however, that Japan was quite willing to negotiate such a Treaty with Corea, the principal object of which would be the arrangement of a Tariff, provided the Corean Government would send a Minister Plenipotentiary to Tôkiô for that purpose; but he clearly intimated to them that Japan could not agree to a higher Customs Tariff than that which Corea had lately accorded to China, and which was settled on a basis of 5 per cent.

  He also pointed out to the Envoys that Corea could not expect Western Powers, any more than Japan, to accept a Tariff of 10 to 30 per cent. on their imports when those of China were to be admitted at 5 per cent., as it would be impossible for other foreigners to compete with Chinese under such conditions. He therefore advised them, if they wished to secure Treaties with those Powers, to negotiate afresh with the latter also. He suggested that if a satisfactory Commercial Treaty and Tariff were concluded by the Corean Government with

Japan at Tôkiô, the Western Powers might be disposed to negotiate direct with Corea on the same terms.

I observed to his Excellency that I thought he had given the Envoys sound advice, and I concurred with him that the Japanese mercantile communities now settled in Corea would be ousted from that country if their trade was burdened with higher duties than those paid by the Chinese.

His Excellency also remarked that he thought the Grand Secretary Li Hung-chang was going too far in his interference with Corea. He had the impression that he was encouraged in this course by the Representative of a Power at Peking, as that Power was actively engaged in supplying ships and munitions of war to China. I could perceive that his Excellency referred to Germany, but he can scarcely, with justice, complain of that country selling ships of war to China, as I know from himself that the Japanese Government are now in treaty for the purchase of two gun-vessels at Kiel. He observed to me that he could procure these two vessels for 102,000*l.* without their arrangement, and that Japan required them at once, as only four of her ships of war are at present in a serviceable condition.

I have, &c.
(Signed)   HARRY S. PARKES

115

H.S. Parkes (1883. 1. 12) ➡ G.L.G. Granville (1883. 2. 20)

조약 개정에 관한 金玉均과 회담 보고

Sir H.S. Parkes to Earl Granville.—(Received February 20)

(No. 4 Confidential)

Tôkiô, January 12, 1883

My Lord,

YOUR Lordship's telegram of the 30th ultimo was delivered to me on the following day. I could not then communicate with the Corean Envoys, as they had left Tôkiô on the 28th to return to Corea, but, on the 1st instant, I received an opportune visit from Kim Ok-kiun, the influential agent named in Mr. Aston's Memorandum of the 3rd October (forwarded in my despatch No. 140), and whom the Senior Envoy, Pak Yöng-hyo, had told me would serve, in his absence, as a channel of communication.

I found, as I expected, that he was acquainted with my conversations with the Envoys which I reported in my despatch No. 176. As he holds no official position, I did not think it desirable to inform him of your Lordship's telegram; but I told him that, looking to the change in the position of affairs which had been created by the arrangements recently concluded between China and Corea, I thought there was now little doubt that the conditions of the Treaty signed in May could not be regarded as satisfactory by Her Majesty's Government. If Corea, therefore, really desired to enter into Treaty relations with Great Britain, she should lose no time in signifying her willingness to negotiate a new Treaty on a basis similar, in regard to commercial matters, to that of the agreement she had recently made with China.

Kim Ok-kiun replied that he shared the opinion of the Envoys that it was of great importance in the interest of his country that she should promptly be brought into Treaty relations with Great Britain, and he could perceive that, in order to attain this object, a new Treaty became desirable, but he felt it impossible to say whether his Government would be disposed to invite fresh negotiations for that purpose. He knew that the Tien-tsin Agreement was disapproved by the King.

I observed to him that the Envoy Pak Yöng-hyo had stated to me that, though he was not authorized to say so, he thought his Government would be willing to extend to those Powers who had signed Treaties with Corea any of the conditions of the above-mentioned Agreement which were not disadvantageous to the latter. It would be vain, I thought, for Corea to suppose that the Western Powers would accept inferior terms to those which Corea had granted to China and Japan, as it was obvious that their people could conduct no trade in Corea unless they were placed, in regard to commercial advantages, on an equal footing with the subjects of those two nations. If his Government, therefore, wished to expedite the conclusion of a Treaty, they should intimate their readiness to extend to Western Powers the concessions they had lately made to China. I added that the question possessed much greater importance for Corea than it did for England.

Kim Ok-kiun inquired whether a Treaty with Great Britain would secure the independence of Corea.

I replied that various conditions were essential to the independence of a State, and one of these was the possession of the Treaty-making Power.

The King of Corea had written to her Majesty that he had complete control of all his internal and external affairs, and if this were so, he possessed the Treaty-making power; whether Western Powers would regard Corea as an independent or a subject State, must depend greatly upon her own action.

The conversation concluded by Kim Ok-kiun observing that he would communicate it to Corea by the first opportunity. He was convinced of the importance of all that I had said, but he could not forecast the opinions of his Government on the subject.

As your Lordship mentioned in your telegram of the 30th ultimo that Her Majesty's Government would be glad to entertain proposals from Corea if the Envoys could get authority to negotiate, I was particular in suggesting to Kim Ok-kiun that his Government should offer to amend the Treaty of May. The Envoy, Pak Yöng-ho, however, had told me, as I reported in my telegram of the 24th and despatch of the 29th ultimo, that he thought his Government might be disposed to give to us the same terms as to China, provided that we applied to Corea direct and not through China. I am afraid that the fear of offending the latter Power may deter the Corean Government from making such proposals themselves, although they might be willing to entertain them if made by a

Western Power, as they could then represent to China that they had not acted voluntarily, but on the demand of a foreign Government.

I have, &c.
(Signed)   HARRY S. PARKES

E.G. Low (1883. 1. 17) ➜ G.L.G. Granville (1883. 2. 28)

1차 조영조약에 대한 上海 상공회의소 의견 상신

Mr. Low to Earl Granville.—(Received February 28)

Shanghae General Chamber of Commerce,
Shanghae, January 17, 1883

My Lord,

I HAVE the honour to convey to your Lordship the thanks of the Committee of this Chamber for the copy of the British Treaty with the Corea which you have been good enough to forward, as well as for the expression of your willingness to listen to their views upon the question.

Acting upon your kind permission, I now have the honour to lay before you the Chamber's observations carry weight, and are worthy of consideration.

It must first be noticed that the Treaty is said to have been drawn up in the Tsung-li Yamên, and negotiated through the Chinese Government, and this alone is a sufficient reason for examining carefully how far the making of Concessions to the Coreans may bear upon existing Treaties with the neighbouring countries, in the event of their revision at a future time, when the waiving of certain privileges contained in the latter may be claimed on the ground that they are omitted from the former, and this knowledge of the real origin of the Corean Treaty makes it almost certain that it has been framed with this object, while it further appears that the Concessions made are so hampered with restrictions as to be in many instances useless for the purposes of trade, which it is understood it is the main object of the Treaty to develop.

Taking the Articles *seriatim* then:

Article I. Under the guise of friendly feeling, as the object of making the Treaty is to be very plainly seen that the real object was to hinder the carrying out of the threatened annexation of the Corea by Russia, a step to be dreaded alike by both Chinese and Coreans.

Article [II] provides for the appointment of Consuls at the open ports, which, however, are not specified; and as merchant Consuls are prohibited, the maintenance of these officials will be rather a serious burden in a country where the resources of the trade are not for some time likely to be very great, more especially under the restrictions contained in subsequent Articles.

Article III may be passed without comment, as a necessary provision in the event of accident.

Article IV deals with the punishment of criminal offences and the settlement of differences between foreigners and natives, but it contains no provision that the judgements of the native Courts will be enforced in the event of a foreigner suing a Corean, and experience of such matters in China gives little hope that the foreign interest will have due protection without some special proviso for the purpose.

The concluding paragraph with regard to the cessation of exterritoriality so soon as the laws of Corea are assimilated to those of Great Britain is hardly likely to come into effect, and as other nationalities whose laws differ from ours may claim the same privilege, there might be some difficulty in compiling such a Code as would meet all the exigencies of the case. It is true that the British Government is to be the Arbiter in such a case, but the clause is likely to be claimed for insertion into neighbouring countries' Treaties, and may lead to complications which at the least will be vexatious and troublesome.

The same general remark applies to the 4th paragraph of Article V, which states that "articles of daily use" are to pay duty at not exceeding 10 per cent. *ad valorem*, while the duty on "luxuries,"—foreign wines, foreign tobacco, clocks, and watches, is not to exceed 30 per cent. *ad valorem*; but although there is a proviso that no further duties are to be charged on such goods on passing into the interior, it will be very difficult to provide with certainty for the free passage of such goods, and still more difficult to get proof in the event of the imposition of further inland taxation, which will probably only be discovered when such goods are found to be unremunerative and declined by the natives by reason of the extra imposts.

The term "articles of daily use" is extremely vague, and includes, no doubt, "stores" imported for foreign consumption, which are duty free under the Chinese Treaties. Foreign tobacco is also specifically mentioned as distinct from Chinese, so that Chinese tobacco will escape, while the article imported for foreign use will bear a heavy tax.

The tax, moreover, is put at too high a figure, at all events until the capabilities of the country for trade are ascertained with more certainty than at present, unless, which is not improbable, the object is to hold out as little inducement to foreign residence and trade as possible, and at the same time secure all the advantages of an alliance with a powerful nation.

The rate of tonnage dues is in excess of that charged in China, and there is, moreover, no provision for the application of the moneys arising therefrom in lighting and guarding the coast, so that foreign vessels will have to pay the tax and take the chances of any dangers which may exist, without any efforts on the part of the native authorities to prevent them.

Article VI is again very one-sided, as, while allowing Coreans free access to Great Britain and her possessions, British subjects are to be confined to the Treaty ports without leave to go into the interior for any purpose, or to send or purchase goods there. Such a stipulation nullifies the value of the whole Treaty, and reduces the prospects of any advantage of trade to such a point as to make it very unlikely that any one would avail of it. Moreover, the Japanese in their Treaty have a radius of 30 miles from ports which are open to them, while the Chinese are free of the country for mining purposes and the purchase of any goods they may require, and although Article XIV specially introduces the favoured nation clause, which would apparently render that part of Article VI a dead letter, the clause has doubtless not been introduced for nothing.

It will be further observed that Article VI allows British subjects to pursue (at the ports) their various "callings and avocations," and they are permitted to traffic there in "all merchandize," but not a word is said about the various "industries," the introduction of which will probably be the most remunerative trade that will be done for some years to come. It is the ambiguous wording of the similar clause in the Tien-tsin Treaty which gave the Chinese the opportunity to attempt to stop several such industries in Shanghae at a recent date, and it would certainly be advisable that the legality of such institutions should be placed beyond question.

Article VII prohibits all dealing in opium, the only result of which will be to encourage the smuggling of the drug, while it will be a most convenient precedent for the Chinese to obtain the removal of the opium clauses from their Treaty.

The remaining clauses may be passed without remark, further than those made with regard to Article XIV, which would seem to render Article VI unnecessary, as the restrictions therein provided have been relaxed in the Treaties with both Chinese and Japanese.

Taken as a whole, the Treaty appears to have drawn up with two distinct objects, neither of which is in any way to the advantage of the Western Power. Corea, while securing for herself the alliance with a nation powerful enough to keep her dreaded enemy in check, gives little more than the empty privilege of residence in certain fixed spots, of which few will care to avail, since the facilities to trade are so hampered with restrictions as to leave but little hope of any profitable result. The coasting trade is given to the Chinese, while both Chinese and Japanese are more or less free of the interior. The imposts are heavier than in either China or Japan, and there is not the slightest warranty that even these will not be exceeded, and the so-called "privilege of trade" be practically nullified. But although it is not perhaps intended that Great Britain should be a gainer in any way by a Treaty which circumstances have forced on Corea to enable her avoid a threatened danger, it is pretty evident that China, under the pretence of assisting Corea, has been looking well after herself, and that the restrictions and Tariffs suggested by them to the Coreans as the basis of their Treaty with Great Britain are to serve as the foundation of a claim for similar stipulations in their own Treaties with foreign Powers when the time comes for their revision.

I have, &c.

(Signed) E.G. LOW, Vice-Chairman

F.B. Johnson (1883. 1. 20) ➜ G.L.G. Granville

1차 조영조약에 대한 香港 상공회의소 의견 상신

Mr. Johnson to Earl Granville

(Private and Confidential)

Hong Kong General Chamber of Commerce,
Hong Kong, January 20, 1883

My Lord,

I HAVE the honour to acknowledge the receipt of Sir Julian Pauncefote's despatch of the l0th October, 1882, replying to the communication I made on behalf of this Chamber to your Lordship on the subject of the Treaty recently negotiated between Great Britain and the Kingdom of Corea.

I have now to convey to your Lordship the thanks of the Chamber for the courteous and confidential invitation extended to the Committee to express its views upon the Treaty, a copy of which was inclosed with Sir Julian Pauncefote's letter, and to set forth, with as much brevity as the subject permits, the opinions of the Committee upon the operation of the clauses which relate to trade and commerce.

The Committee has no doubt that Her Majesty's Government, when entering into political relations with Corea, has regarded that kingdom as a State which is completely independent in respect of its domestic administration and its international responsibilities, though subject to a certain undefined suzerainty exercised by China, similar to that acknowledged by Annam and Burmah and hitherto satisfied by the rendition of an annual tribute. That such has also been the view held, until recently, by China herself, is clear from the evidence furnished by the express declarations of the Tsung-li Yamen of Peking in 1866 and 1871 on the occasion of French and American difficulties with Corea, when the Chinese Government disclaimed all responsibility for Corean affairs, and by her acquiescence in the recognition of the complete independence of Corea which was declared in the Japanese Treaty with that country concluded in 1876.

Since, however, the attack upon the Japanese Legation at Seoul last year, the Chinese Government appears to have changed its attitude, and to have asserted its claims to exercise control not only over the administration of the internal affairs of Corea, but also over its foreign relations. The Edict published some months ago in the "Peking Gazette," notifying the punishment of the Dai-in-Kuri, refers to the King of Corea as being subject to Chinese law and authority, and in a document recently made public, styled "Regulations for the Conduct of Trade by Sea and Land between Chinese and Corean subjects," the Grand Secretary Li Hung-chang, late Viceroy of Pechili, is designated in terms of official equality with the King of Corea, as if the Ruler of that country were occupying a position delegated to him by the Emperor, analogous in point of rank and authority to that of a Governor-General of a Chinese province.

The Committee may hereafter deem it necessary to consider, in a separate communication to your Lordship, the terms of these Regulations and the special privileges which they appear to confer upon Chinese traders, and refer to them now, when discussing the bearing of the British Treaty, in order to bring prominently before Her Majesty's Government the desirability of ascertaining the precise character of the relationship claimed by the Government of China *quoad* that of Corea, before Her Majesty is advised to ratify the Treaty negotiated by Admiral Willes.

As the Kingdom of Corea has never been claimed to be an integral part of the Chinese dominions. it is either a mediatized State under the protection of China, in which case the authority of its King to conclude Treaties with foreign nations may hereafter be questioned, or it is an independent country, with whose autonomy the Regulations referred to are inconsistent. It would be unfortunate if the recent interference of the Chinese Executive in the internal affairs of Corea should be hereafter adduced to throw doubt upon the international validity of any of the provisions of the foreign Treaties, on the faith of which commercial intercourse with Corea will have been entered upon and is to be conducted. The Committee, however, accepting the independence of Corea as a recognized international fact, ventures in the first place to offer to your Lordship some observations upon the Treaty as a whole, and, in the second, to consider seriatim the several clauses of that document which may seem to call for special comment.

The Committee assumes that Her Majesty's Government has had some cogent reason, arising out of the political situation, for pushing forward to a rapid conclusion the negotiations with the Core an authorities, but admitting that there were good grounds of policy for entering into immediate relations with the country, the Committee respectfully submits that that object would have been as successfully, and much more conveniently, attained if preliminary negotiations had been confined to drawing up a short Treaty, expressive of national amity, and providing generally for political and commercial intercourse, leaving a Tariff of duties, and the special conditions under which foreign trade is to be carried on, to a supplementary and carefully considered Convention. The frequent disputes which have arisen about the interpretation to be placed upon certain clauses of the Treaty of Tien-tsin show the importance of drafting with peculiar care agreements, affecting national interests, which have to be drawn up in a language so full of obscurities even to the most experienced Sinologue as that of China, so as to avoid all misunderstanding when the stipulations and covenants to be observed on either side come to be made effective. The Committee cannot fail to perceive that the diplomatic instrument signed by Admiral Willes at Jin Chuen in June last has been very loosely compiled in point of form, and that many of its most important provisions have been expressed in most indefinite language, and further, that imperfections, similar to those now generally recognized as existing in the Treaties with China and Japan, have been repeated and intensified in this new Treaty. Moreover, after a careful consideration of the whole scope of the document, the Committee is apprehensive that the limitations which some of its stipulations impose upon foreign intercourse and trade will not only be injurious to the operation of the Treaty itself, but will seriously prejudice the position hitherto consistently maintained by the Representatives of Western nations at the Courts of Peking and Yedo in combating proposals to place similar restrictions upon trade with China and Japan.

There can be no doubt that, notwithstanding the vast material benefits which have resulted to the people of China during the last twenty years from the great increase in all branches (excepting in opium) of the foreign and coasting trade of the Empire, and which have been the direct consequence of the extended foreign intercourse opened up by the Treaty of Tien-tsin, the ruling classes of China are actuated at the present time by a desire to restrict, as far as possible, the application of foreign capital and enterprise to the further development of the resources of the country. The Committee may adduce the strenuous attempts which have recently been made to prevent the organization of various industries under foreign auspices at Shanghae in evidence of the present unsatisfactory attitude of the Chinese authorities, and earnestly desires to draw your Lordship's attention to the great accession of strength which the reactionary party in China would derive from the stipulations of a Treaty voluntarily entered into by the Western Powers with a dependency of the Empire, if the opponents of progress should be able to point to conditions of exclusion in that Treaty disadvantageous to the foreigner, which have been yielded to the tributary State, but are denied to the country of the Suzerain.

In conclusion of these general remarks, your Lordship need hardly be reminded of the difficulty which would be placed in the way of a successful conduct of the existing negotiations for a revision of the Treaty with Japan, if the arguments of Her Majesty's Minister at Yedo in favour of the adoption of a liberal foreign policy by the Japanese Cabinet should be met by unfavourable precedents, cited from the recent Agreement with Corea.

Proceeding now to consider some of the special stipulations of the Treaty -

Article II relates to the character of official relationship and communication between the two countries, with which it is scarcely the province of this Chamber to deal; but so great has been the inconvenience sustained in former years by the merchants in China under the provisions of the Treaty of Nanking, which seriously hindered free communication between foreign Consular officials and the provincial authorities, that the Committee feels it necessary to advert to the paragraph in the first clause of this Article which stipulates that "Officials shall have relations with the corresponding local authorities of equal rank upon a basis of mutual equality." This stipulation is a very vague one according to the English text, and what it may imply in the Chinese text the Committee is unable to say. It may be read in an exclusive sense, and be taken to mean that officials of the one country may only communicate with officials of the same rank in the other. The war with China, commenced in 1856, would probably have been averted if Consul Parkes could have insisted upon personal communication with Governor-General Yeh, and the Committee suggests the expediency of providing that the commissioned officers of both countries, whether civil, naval, or military, shall be entitled to hold official intercommunication on terms of social equality, while observing the ordinary rules of precedence relating to official rank.

Article III, in the clause which provides that a British vessel shall, with her cargo, be seized and confiscated if found engaged in clandestine trade, is remarkable for repeating a grave shortcoming in the Tien-tsin Treaty which has been the occasion of a lasting controversy. Under this Article a vessel, alleged to be engaged in trading to a port not opened by the Treaty, may be confiscated by the Corean authorities of their own motion, and with or without trial, subject to no investigation by or appeal to British officials.

The Committee desires to enter the strongest protest against the confirmation of this clause, on two grounds:-

1. That the absence of any recognized practice or system of jurisprudence in Corea renders it impossible to repose confidence in the decisions of Corean officials who would be judges in their own cause without appeal; and

2. Because the power of confiscation is granted without the safeguard of any provision as to the nature of the proceedings which shall be taken to prove that the vessel shall have been really quiltyof the offence with which it may be charged.

The Treaty between Japan and Corea provides that in the event of a Japanese vessel being found engaged in smuggling goods "into any non-open port in Corea, it shall be seized by the Corean local authorities, and delivered over to the Agent of the Japanese Government residing at the nearest port. Such goods to be confiscated by him, and to be handed over to the Corean authorities."

In the clause relating to the wreckage of British vessels on the coast of Corea, the local authorities should be made responsible, not only for taking the necessary measures for rendering assistance to the crew, and salving the vessel and cargo, but also for inflicting condign punishment upon all plunderers or wreckers.

Article V mainly relates to fiscal obligations, and the Committee cannot conceal its surprise and regret that after the e:-perience which has been gained of the unsatisfactory working of the Tien-tsin Treaty, owing to the looseness of certain of its stipulations which provide for and limit the Tariff of duties, Her Majesty's Representative should have given his assent to clauses which cannot fail in operation to revive, in the case of Corea, difficulties and controversies similar to those which have arisen and still exist in carrying on trade with China.

It is no doubt necessary to concede to Corea, in principle, the right to levy duties and protect its own revenue laws; but before the Tariff which the Treaty prescribes is assented to, the Corean Government, as having had no previous experience in such matters, may reasonably be required to furnish to the British officials a Code of Customs Regulations, and of proceedings for adjudication in the case of a breach of fiscal rules. The want of such a Code, and the absence of any provision in the Tien-tsin Treaty for a system of trial or adjudication, led to the grossest miscarriage of justice during the earlier years of the establishment of the Foreign Customs Inspectorate in China, and the Committee hopes that Her Majesty's Government will take adequate precautions for the protection of the property of British subjects against unjust Customs seizures when Corea becomes opened to foreign trade.

The Committee is of opinion that the Tariff of customs duties upon imports and exports generally should not exceed those levied in China under the Treaty of Tien-tsin, and considers that the scale of *ad valorem* duties upon imports therein, viz.,5 per cent upon entry and 2% per cent. commutation of inland dues, should be adopted also in Corea, and would not be excessive, provided that measures should be taken to give satisfactory and complete effect to the stipulation in the concluding lines of paragraph 4 of this Article: "that no other dues, duties, fees, taxes, or charges of any sort shall be levied upon such imports either in the interior of Chosen or at the ports." Here, however, appears to be repeated another defect in the Treaty of Tien-tsin, which provides no guarantees for redress in the event of a breach or evasion on the part of local officials of a similar stipulation in that document. The Committee suggests that the clause should run, "and that any other dues, duties, fees, taxes, or charges of any sort, which may be levied upon imports either in the interior of Chosen or at the ports, shall be recoverable from the Chosen Customs at the port of entry of such imports."

The distinction between articles of daily use, which are to be subject to an *ad valorem* duty of 10 per cent., and articles of luxury, which are to pay more, is much too vague, and cannot fail to be productive of endless disputes. The Committee would propose that schedules of the several articles be drawn up and agreed upon with British officials before the Treaty is confirmed, and has, moreover, to point out that no provision is made for any drawback of duty in the case of goods which have paid import duty beingre-exported.

As regards tonnage dues, no stipulation appears that these levies shall be applied to their usual and legitimate purposes, viz., the lighting of the coast, and the improvement to rivers and harbours. No definition is given as to the character of the ton, whether of register or burthen, or of the money in which payment is to be made as to its being Corean or Chinese currency. In Chinese money the tax would be far too heavy.

A serious, and in the opinion of the Committee, a fatal objection remains to be urged against this Article as a whole, because it places British subjects on a more unfavourable footing than Japanese, who, by their Treaty of 1876 are, as the Committee understands, relieved from the payment of any import duties. As the "favoured nation clause" in Article XIV is not made retrospective in its effect, and as the Chinese under their "Regulations" claim a right in the case of the" subject State" of Corea to favoured treatment, different in its character from that which other nations on the ordinary footing would obtain, it is certain that, if duties are to be levied upon British trade on the scale authorized in Article V, British vessels and subjects will be virtually excluded from commerce with Corea. Article VI-The second clause of this Article refers to ports in Corea open to foreign commerce, and to the "concessions" within the limits of which British subjects may alone reside. The list of such open ports is not given in the Treaty, and no provision is made for the marking out or setting aside such "concessions." Under the Treaty of Tien-tsin, the British Government became the lessee from the Government of China, at equitable prices, of an allotment of land at each port newly opened by the Treaty, for the purposes of occupation by British subjects, but the provisions of the Core an Treaty leave it to be a matter of conjecture us to the meaning which is to be attached to the term "concession."

The second clause proceeds to stipulate that buildings or land may be leased and residences or warehouses may be constructed within the "concessions," that no coercion or intimidation (presumably by British subjects) in the acquisition of land or buildings shall be permitted, and the land-rent shall be paid as fixed by the authorities of Corea; These stipulations imply that the acquisition of land is to be a matter of private arrangement between intending purchasers and the native owners, and while the language of the clause permits an unmerited and offensive imputation to be thrown on the character of British merchants, no safeguard is taken that exorbitant or prohibitory prices will not be demanded for land, and that the rents to be fixed by the authorities will not be excessive.

The third clause provides that all rights of jurisdiction over persons and property within the concessions remain vested in the authorities of Corea, except in so far as such rights have been expressly relinquished by the Treaty. As the only rights relinquished are those reserved by Article IV, and relate solely to civil and criminal cases between natives of Corea and British subjects, it follows that cases in which British subjects are concerned against each other, or those in which they are engaged with foreigners of other nationalities, will have to be adjudicated by the Corean authorities. The Committee cannot suppose that Her Majesty's Government will sanction such an arrangement.

It is further to be remarked that it appears doubtful whether, by the terms of this Treaty, the native Government, as in the cases of the Treaties between China and Japan and Great Britain, has wa:ved the ordinary right of the Sovereign of the soil to tax the persons and property of British subjects within the areas of the concessions, and that no provision is made in it for the municipal government of those concessions. The difficulties which have from time to time arisen in the conduct of the municipal affairs of the foreign Settlements in China and Japan show the necessity of making arrangements, such as experience has shown to be adequate, to meet the serious questions and controversies which otherwise cannot fail to arise under similar circumstances in Corea. The Committee has now before it "a Code of Municipal Regulations of the Japanese Settlement of Fusan, in Corea," dated the 9th November, 1881, under which "the entire charge of municipal affairs devolves on the permanent residents in the Settlement," and does not doubt that Her Majesty's Government will not permit British subjects to be placed in a more unfavourable position in the country than those of Japan.

The fourth clause prohibits British subjects from transporting foreign imports to the interior, or from proceeding thither to purchase native produce, and from transporting native produce from one open port to another open port.

As to the prohibition against British subjects visiting the interior, it will be seen that this stipulation involves a retrograde step, placing British subjects at a great disadvantage, when it is compared with the freedom of travel granted to foreigners in China and Japan, and with similar facilities given to Chinese and Japanese traders in Corea. Under the Chinese "Regulations," Chinese merchants may open commercial establishments in Yang Wha Chiu and in the capital, and by applying to the Commissioner of Trade they may obtain passports to go into the interior for the purpose of trade or pleasure.

The prohibition against the transportation by British traders the clause does not mention British ships, though the stipulation may be supposed to includethem-of native produce between the open ports, the Committee regards as one of the most objectionable provisions in the Treaty. This prohibition cannot be defended on the ground that it affords a necessary protection to

Corean shipping, because the Japanese enjoy the right of trading between the ports opened to them under their Treaty of 1876, and the Chinese under their "Regulations" will assuredly claim a similar privilege. The carrying trade, under such a disability as this attaching to British and foreign shipping generally, would be virtually handed over to the Japanese and Chinese flags, notwithstanding that the larger proportion of imports to Corea would be goods of British origin, and the Committee needs hardly remark upon the onerous charge for freight which the existence of a local carrying monopoly would impose on the manufactures of the United Kingdom and the trade generally of Corea, or as to the unfavourable effect which the abandonment of the coast trade with Corea would not fail to exercise upon the course of future negotiations for the revision of the existing Treaties with China and Japan.

The importance of the issues which are at stake in the maintenance of the provision that foreigners may share in the intermediate trade between the open ports is not to be measured by the effect which the abrogation of that provision would have upon the interests of foreign shipping alone, extensive as those interests are.

If foreign vessels should be excluded from the coast trade, foreigners would be practically shut out from all business, excepting at the ports which would have direct trade with foreign countries. Coasting freights under Chinese and Japanese flags alone, and the establishment of native guilds and monopolies which would follow the absence of competition in general business by other foreigners, would cause the control of the distributing traffic to pass into a few hands, and trade of all kinds, under the weight of exorbitant profits, would languish and decay. The evil effect of these monopolies may be understood when the stagnation of industry which prevails at the ports in China not open to foreign trade is compared with the activity and enterprise which are displayed by native merchants at the open ports, where they are exposed to competition with foreigners; and the Committee does not doubt that the maintenance of the progressive character of the external commerce and internal industry of China and Japan is very greatly dependent upon the possession by foreigners of the privilege of competing with natives for a share in the coasting traffic of these countries.

Article VII.-The extraordinary and apparently useless stipulation in this Article that subjects of Corea shall not be permitted to import opium into any British port would necessitate a legislative enactment on the part of the Imperial

Parliament, and the Committee is unable to understand how the prohibition, declared in the second clause,against the engagement of foreign vessels other than British, is to be enforced, or offenders against it are to be punished, by any legislation which it is possible to devise on the part of the British Government.

Article VIII.-In the second clause, instead of the words "shall be confiscated; the Committee, for the reason already given in the case of vessels charged with offences, suggests the insertion of "may be seized, and shall be liable to confiscation, on satisfactory proof of intention to evade the prohibition being furnished to the British authorities."

Article IX.-To the first clause there should be added: "Fire-arms and ammunition for sporting purposes or for purposes of self-defence. may be imported under special permits describing the quantity, value, and object of introduction."

Article X.-In the second clause, after the words "local authorities, "the words "on being satisfied as to the justice of the charge made" should be inserted.

Article XII, while admitting that the Treaty is "incomplete in its provisions," nevertheless stipulates that it shall remain in force for five years. The Treaty with Japan provides that the "Regulations under which Japanese trade is to be conducted" may be "revised whenever it may be found necessary by Commissions appointed by each country,"and a similar stipulation is to be found in the Chinese "Regulations." The Committee is of opinion that the term of five years, as arranged by the British Treaty, would not be too long, provided that the covenants and engagements entered into on either side should be drawn up with carefulness and completeness by experienced negotiators.

Article XIII does not provide as to whether the English or Chinese text of the Treaty is to be accepted in the event of a dispute as to the proper meaning of its provislons. The Committee suggests an addition to this clause of "the English version is to be considered the accepted text in case of dispute."

Article XIV.-The Committee regards the qualification of the ordinary "favoured nation clause," admitted by this Article in its last lines, with great distrust. Under that qualification the provisions of all Treaties with Corea will be liable to be set aside, or rendered nugatory, by the grant to one foreign nation of favourable conditions, in which it may be specially interested, in exchange for nominal concessions in which it has no interest at all, but which may be of vital importance to the trade of other countries having Treaties with Corea. This qualification, if yielded to Corea, will probably be demanded by China and Japan, and be made use of in forcing the policy of the British Government in relation to the Treaties with these Powers to an extent which may not at present be foreseen.

The objection to this Article, as not being retrospective in its operation, has been already alluded to, and the Committee feels confident that Her Majesty's Government will not permit British subjects trading with Corea, or residing in the country, to be placed under disabilities from which natives of China and Japan are exempted.

No stipulation is to be found in the Treaty as to the currency in which commercial operations are to be carried on, or in which duties are to be paid, and no provision is made for drawing up a detailed Tariff of duties. No mention is made of any regulations as to the standard weights and measures to be used in trade between foreigners and natives.

The Committee desires to refer to the great importance of the issues which are at stake as its apology to your Lordship for the length at which the provisions of the Treaty have been examined in this communication, and does not seek to disguise its expectation that sufficient cause has been shown why Her Majesty's Government should be asked to refuse ratification of that document in its present shape.

The Committee trusts that your Lordship will use the authority and influence of Great Britain to secure beyond question the recognition of the national independence of the Corean Kingdom, which is obviously threatened by the recent highhanded declarations and proceedings of the Chinese officials, and will depute an experienced Diplomatic Representative to reopen communications with the Corean Government. It should not be difficult, in the light of the experience gained in China and Japan, to draw up an amended Treaty, under the wise and well-considered provisions of which not only would the people of Corea be admitted to the benefits of free commercial intercourse with the rest of the world, and their rights and interests be fully protected, but the trade of the United Kingdom with that country would be promoted and be placed on an equality of privilege with that enjoyed by other nations.

I have, &c.

(Signed)   F. BULKELEY JOHNSON, Chairman.

J. Saumarez (1883. 1. 24)

조청상민수륙무역장정과 1차 조영조약 비교

Memorandum comparing the Regulation for Trade between Chinese and Coreans with the Provisions of the British Treaty with Corea.

*Foreign office,
January 24, 1883*

The points in which the provisions of the Chinese and Corean Trade Regulations differ from those of the recent Treaties are such as are affected by the suzerainty which has hitherto been exercised by China over Corea, the superiority of China in power and civilization, the geographical position of the two countries as neighbours, and the fact that both Regulations and Treaties were framed under the supervision of Li Hung-chang, who, while he might be expected to further therein his country's commercial interests in his capacity of Imperial Commissioner for the North, might be trusted to secure his own personal interests as one of the principal shareholders of the Chinese Merchants Steamship Company.

Chinese and Corean Regulations	British and Corean Treaty
Appointment of Commercial Agents.—With reference to the "suzeraineté," the title accorded to the officials of each country who will reside at the open ports of the other is *Commercial Agent* instead of Consul. The Chinese Agents are appointed by the Imperial Commissioner for the North, to whom they will refer important cases, the Corean Agents being appointed by the King. The latter Agents will refer important	

cases to a high Corean official, who will reside at Tien-tsin (the seat of government of Li Hung-chang).

No mention is made of the residence of a Chinese official at the Corean capital.

"Commercial Agents may not levy contributions, *but shall defray their own expenses.*"

An incidental allusion to the "suzraineté" is made in one of the later provisions, by which Corean officials will no longer have to supply the wants of Chinese men-of-war which may cruize on the coast, or anchor in her ports for her protection.

Jurisdiction.—With regard to jurisdiction, China exercises jurisdiction in her own ports over Coreans, but reserves it in Corean ports over her own subjects. Coreans at Chinese open ports shall in all cases be tried by the Chinese authorities, who will send a report of the case to the Corean Agent. Should the Corean be dissatisfied with the decision the Corean Agent may request the High Authorities to rehear the case, whereas in Corean ports Chinese defendants will be tried by the Chinese official, and in cases where the Coreans are defendants and the Chinese plaintiffs the Corean official shall produce the accused, and, together with the Chinese official, try the case *according to law.*

This term would seem to imply that the Commercial Agents are to be permitted to trade, although by the terms of the British Treaty it is laid down that "no merchants shall be permitted to exercise the duties of the Consular office," &c.

British defendants in Corean ports will be tried by their Consul, and Corean defendants by the Corean authorities, an official of the plaintiff's nationality being permitted to attend the trial and to examine and crossexamine witnesses. If he is dissatisfied with the proceedings, he shall be permitted to protest against them in detail.

(In the Chinese version of the United States' Treaty the wording is "appeal may be made to the

Extradition is to be carried out of persons who have committed offences against the laws of their respective countries (China and Corea), and take refuge in the other country.

The prohibitions as to ships of either country entering non-open ports for purposes of trade is maintained as in the Treaties, exception being made in the case of fishing-boats.

"Fishing craft of either nation from the coast of Corea or the shores of Shantung and Fengtien may come and go at pleasure in pursuit of that avocation, and may purchase provisions and water ashore."

"They may not carry on a clandestine trade, and boats so offending will, with their cargo, be confiscated.

"After the expiration of two years, Rules shall be formed regulating the fish duties to be paid by the fishing-boats of either nation."

With regard to port dues and tonnage dues, reference is made to Regulations which do not accompany the present document, viz., "The ships of either country may frequent the open ports of the other for purposes of trade *under the Regulations already agreed upon* affecting the loading Governments of the United States and Corea for decision.")—See Sir H.S. Parkes' notes on British Treaty, Article IV.

Coreans guilty of the violation of the laws of the kingdom, or against whom any action has been brought, to be delivered up to the Corean authorities if they conceal themselves in the residences or warehouses of British subjects or on board British merchant-ships.

While by Article V of the Treaty British merchants and merchant-vessels visiting Corea for the purpose of traffic shall pay duties upon all merchandize imported and exported.

The right of fixing their Tariff is also here asserted, and notice is given that both the Tariff and the Customs Regulations will be fixed by the Corean authorities, and communicated to the proper officials of the British Government, &c.

and unloading of merchandize, and the payment of maritime dues." And again, "Imports and exports shall pay duty, and maritime vessels shall pay *tonnage dues*, as specified in the Maritime Customs Regulations."

All merchandize imported or exported shall pay an *ad valorem* duty of 5 per cent.

Tonnage dues are to be paid by English ships entering Corean ports at the rate of 5 mace a-ton.

The Article goes on to say that it is agreed as a general measure that the Tariff upon such imports as are of daily use shall not exceed an *ad valorem* duty of 10 per cent., and for luxuries of 30 per cent., and that native produce exported shall pay a duty not exceeding 5 per cent.

It is further agreed that the duty upon foreign imports shall be paid once for all at the port of entry, and that no other dues, duties, fees, taxes, or charges of any sort shall be levied upon such imports either in the interior or at the ports.

Ginseng.—Corean merchants are to be allowed to bring red ginseng into China on payment of *ad valorem* duty of 15 per cent.

But in the case of British subjects, if they clandestinely purchase it for export, it shall be confiscated and the offenders punished, "Corea having of old prohibited the exportation of red ginseng."

Terms of Residence.—Chinese and Coreans resorting to each other's countries for trade—being well-

But in the case of British subjects, by Article VI these advantages of residence are restricted to the limits of

conducted persons—are to be at liberty to rent land and premises and build houses, and also to trade in local produce and any merchandize not contraband.

Trade between the Ports and in the interior.—Merchandize may be carried from one port to another on payment of a half import duty at the time of reimportation, in addition to the export duty already paid at the time of exportation.

Corean subjects are by law allowed to trade at Peking, and Chinese subjects to open establishments at Yanghua and Chinghan in Corea, But, this apart, they *are not allowed to convey merchandize into the interior.*

New Frontier Trading Stations are proposed "where the people shall be allowed to trade as they please. At the marts thus opened customs stations shall be established for the detection of bad characters, and for the receipt of duties."

It is added that "special and detailed regulations cannot be put in force until the Imperial Commissioner for the North and the King of Corea each send officers to the spot to draw up these conjointly, after which they shall be submitted to *the Throne* for approval."

the concessions, and their traffic to the limits of the port.

The land rent also is to be fixed by the Corean authorities, a point which is not mentioned in the case of the Chinese.

Subjects of either country may proceed into the interior to purchase native produce (or to travel), provided they first obtain a pass in the joint names of their Commercial Agent or the local official, specifying the place where the produce is to be purchased. The horses, carts, and boats to be hired by the purchaser, who will also *pay all li-kin* and duties leviable *en route.*

Whereas, by Article VI, British subjects are not permitted to transport native produce from one open port to the other. Violations of this rule will subject such merchandize to confiscation, and the merchant offending will be handed over to the Consular authorities to be dealt with; and by Article III, "if a British vessel carries on a clandestine trade at a port not open to foreign commerce, such vessel, with her cargo, shall be seized and confiscated."

But British subjects are not permitted either to transport foreign imports to the interior or to proceed thither to purchase native produce (are

Munitions of War (Article VI) *and Opium.*—Their importation *for sale* is prohibited to the subjects of either country.

Postal Communication (Article VII).—The King of Corea may apply to the imperial Commissioner for the North to detail a merchant steamer to come and go once a-month (no details as to ports supplied), the Corean Administration paying a certain sum as subsidy.

A report that this was his intention is mentioned by Sir H.S. Parkes in his notes on the British Treaty (Article VI).

they allowed by the text of the Treaty to go into the interior at all?) (See Sir T. Wade, No. 63 of the 28th July) The German Minister, Herr von Brandt, does not read the Treaty as authorizing circulation in the interior, even for pleasure.

Article VII. *Opium.*—In the English Treaty the words *for sale* are omitted, and British subjects are not permitted to import opium into the open ports, to transport it from one open port to another, or to traffic in it in Corea.

Arms, &c., may be imported only by British subjects under a written permit.

It is by means of this arrangement respecting the postal service, which is to be undertaken by Chinese merchant-steamers, that Li Hung-chang has obtained for his Steam-ship Company above alluded to the monopoly of the passenger and goods traffic both to and from the Chinese and Corean ports and between the Corean open ports.

No time is stated during which the Regulations will remain in force, but alterations will be made "as the occasion requires," the Commissioner for the North consulting with the King of Corea, and submitting any change for the approval of the Throne.

J. SAUMAREZ

P. Currie (1883. 1. 29)

조영조약의 개정을 위해 독일과 공조 필요 상신

Regulation for trade between China & Corea

These Regulation are in fact a treaty between China & Corea, in which China achieves the position of suzerain & the right of making special & exclusive arrangements with her dependency.

Li-hung-chang having first suggested a draft Treaty which has been signed by the United States, England & Germany, in which we have treated with the Sovereign of Corea on equal terms, now concluded a treaty in which the King of Corea appears merely as a vassal of China—as Sir H Parkes points out, the position is one which we cannot accept.

Either the king of Corea is an independent Sovereign with whom other sovereigns can make treaties, in which case the M.F.N. clause of our treaty gives us an equality with China:

Or, he is a vassal of China, in which case we may maintain that our treaty with China applies to this dominion.

A Mem is annexed which has been prepared in the China Dept, confirming the 'Regulations' with our treaty.

It will be seen that in expand to jurisdiction and customs Duties the Chinese have obtained much more favorable terms than we have.

I would suggest that we should in the first place communicate with the German Gov. & prepare to act together in the matter; and that the course we should then take, either jointly with them or alone, should be to instruct Sir H Parkes, (if he thinks it can be done without danger), to send Mr. Aston at once to Corea to inform the Corean Gov. that we claim the same treatment as China under the M.F.N. clause of our treaty, but that we should be prepared to negotiate a new Treaty in place of the unsatisfactory are concluded by Admiral Willes in which we should not insist on these clauses of the China Regulations which may not be suitable for the relations between England and Corea:

And that his Governor should be instructed to inform the Chinese Gov. that we claim the application of the M.F.N. clause in our treaty to their regulations.

P.C.

Jan 29/83

Pauncefote (1883. 2. 2)

조청상민수륙무역장정에 대한 미국의 견해 확인

I concur – We might also ask SCHUFELDT to ascertain the views the U.S. Govt on the new trade regulations between China and Corea.

It is clear that Li-Hung-Chang has been pulling the strings of all the negotiations between Corea & other powers.

PF 2/2/83

121

K.B. Murray (1883. 2. 16) ➜ G.L.G. Granville (1883. 2. 17)

1차 조영조약에 대한 London 상공회의소 의견 상신

Mr. K. Murray to Earl Granville.—(Received February 17)

The London Chamber of Commerce, 84 and 85, King William Street,
London, February 16, 1883

My Lord,

I Am in due receipt of your Lordship's letter of the 6th December last, transmitting to the London Chamber the correspondence which has passed between Her Majesty's Government, Admiral Willes, and Her Majesty's Ministers in China and Japan, relative to the conclusion of a Treaty between this country and Corea. I have consulted both the Executive Committee and the Council of this Chamber as to the advisability of ratifying this Treaty, and am instructed, in reply, to convey the following answer to your Lordship.

This Chamber is particularly desirous that every opportunity to open up and develop new markets for British manufactures be turned to the best account. Such being the general policy of this Chamber, it cannot but express its satisfaction at the promptitude with which Sır T. Wade and Admiral Willes followed the action of the American Government in seeking to negotiate a Treaty with the King of Corea. The London Chamber would be prepared, when necessary, in the instance of new countries, to support, as a means of encouraging commercial relations with Eastern nations, the acceptance of conditions less favourable to this country, during the first years of a new Treaty, than the stipulations of our Treaties with China.

It also appears most desirable that the British Government should obtain, through these Treaties, the right of appointing Consuls, of establishing merchants, and of owning land in Corea, both as a means of intercepting Japanese influence in that country, and of anticipating the commercial efforts of the American Government, but particularly with a view of securing every means of access to China, and developing our influence with and upon that country with the purpose of ulterior trade extension.

The principal objection to present ratification of Admiral Willes' Treaty appears to lie in the high rate of the proposed Tariff, influenced, as this seems to have been, by Chinese intervention, and the future possibility of the Chinese Government claiming from Her Majesty's Government the right to exact similarly high duties. Since the drafts of the new American and British Treaties differ from the old Corean-Japanese Convention by the insertion of a Tariff and the pretended dependence of Corea on China, would it not be possible to take advantage of this real or pretended dependence to add, on the force of it, a clause to the proposed Treaty, providing that, on the expiration of the admittedly provisional measure, the rates of duty to be charged by Corea should not then exceed those now in force under our Treaty with China? With such a proviso this Chamber would recommend the ratification of the Treaty, for fear of encouraging at some future date Chinese pretensions to be placed on a similar footing.

I have purposely omitted to allude to the minor objections to Admiral Willes' Treaty, such as the stipulations for paid Consuls and the possible withdrawal of their exequatur, the restrictions as to trading in the sea-ports and not in the interior, the exclusion of hides from the list of imports, &c., due relief having been given to these objectionable items in the correspondence submitted by your Lordship. If fresh negotiations, however, arise, the Chamber is confident that these items will be carefully dealt with by Her Majesty's Representatives.

This Chamber has noted with satisfaction the interesting and thoughtful reports of Mr. W. Donald Spence and Mr. W.G. Aston, and will be obliged by such further communication as circumstances will permit of information as to the economical condition of the Kingdom of Chosen, and of the progress of negotiations for a Treaty with that country.

I am, &c.

(Signed) K.B. Murray, Secretary

122

H.S. Parkes (1883. 2. 16) ➜ G.L.G. Granville

Aston의 조선행 보고

No. 22

Tokio
February 16, 1883

My Lord,

I had the honor to despatch to your Lordship this day at 5.30 P.M. the following telegram in cypher:

Granville
　　　Foreign Office
　　　　　London

"Your Despatch No. 116 – Recommend despatch of Aston in a man-of-war now in Japan to Korea for the purpose.

"If unsuccessful would still obtain valuable information as to state of affairs Parkes."

I have the honor to be, with the highest respect,
Ny Lord,
Your Lordship's most obedient, humble servant,
Harry S. Parkes

H.S. Parkes (1883. 2. 17) ➜ G.L.G. Granville (1883. 3. 28)

김옥균 및 井上馨와 회담 보고

Sir H.S. Parkes to Earl Granville.—(Received March 28)

(No. 26 Confidential)

Tôkiô, February 17, 1883

My Lord,

WITH reference to my despatch No. 4 of the 12th ultimo, reporting my conversation with the Corean Confidential Agent, Kim Ok Kiun, consequent on your Lordship's telegram of the 30th December, I have now to add that on the 13th instant he informed me that he had heard nothing from Corea in reply to his report of that conversation. He observed spontaneously that he was unable to say whether his government would go on following blindly the dictation of China, or whether they would be bold enough to take a course of their own in regard to their foreign relations. He had heard that the United States had ratified their Treaty, and this act, he thought, would serve to test Corea's position and bring to an issue the question of her dependency on China.

He wished that that test could be made more forcible by the ratification of the British Treaty.

I replied that I thought my Government might think it necessary to understand the position of Corea before ratifying a Treaty with her, and that the disadvantageous conditions of the Treaty negotiated by Admiral Willes were a further impediment in the way of its ratification. I had, therefore, pointed out to him, in our conversation of the 1st ultimo, that if Corea wanted a Treaty with Great Britain, she should lose no time in offering to negotiate one that would be acceptable.

He then inquired whether Her Majesty's Government would be disposed to ask Li Hung Chang whether Corea should make with Great Britain a Treaty including similar arrangements to those recently concluded between Corea and China, to which I replied that my Government would not lose sight of their own dignity in any course they might see fit to take.

In a conversation which I had yesterday with the Japanese foreign Minister, His Excellency stated that he had received no reply from the Corean Government to his proposal (which I reported in my despatch No. 3 of the 12th ultimo), that a Corean Plenipotentiary should be sent to Tôkiô to negotiate a new Commercial Treaty with Japan. This was the only overture, his Excellency added, which his Government could make, and Corea could show, by accepting or declining it, how far she was now acting under the domination of China. Japan had hitherto treated with Corea as an independent State, and if any change had taken place in the relations of Corea to China, the Governments of those two countries should inform Japan of it, and this they had not done. Japan's relations with Corea continued, therefore, to be based on the Treaties of 1876, and if China had assumed the control of Corea she must also fulfill the obligations of those Treaties. Japan could not allow her people in Corea to be placed in a worse position than Chinese subjects.

His Excellency also observed that Japan was said to be arming against China, but that there was no foundation for such a report. A certain increase of naval and military force had been authorized, but not more than was necessary for efficient defensive strength. He strongly deprecated collision with China, for which indeed there was no cause, and he invariably endeavoured to suppress such an idea whenever it found expression either among Japanese officials or the people. Military men were inclined at all times towards military enterprise, but he had shown how effectually he had discouraged this feeling when it naturally evinced itself at the outset of the recent Corean difficulty. He had heard with regret that the French Minister, when conversing lately at his, the Foreign Minister's house, with three members of the Cabinet, General Oyama, the Minister of War, Admiral Kawamura, the Minister of Marine, and General Saigo, the Minister of Agriculture and Commerce, had asked them why they did not send 20,000 men to China, as with such a force they could easily take Peking, and if Japan were to undertake an operation of this nature she would be supported by French action in Tongking.

He believed that this was only said in jest, but he thought it was a bad jest, as it might excite the minds of those who heard it.

I observed that he might feel assured that such a postprandial remark could not have been seriously intended, and that the Ministers who heard it could of course not regard it in any other light. I was very glad to hear his Excellency express himself so decidedly against hostility to China, as he was aware that my opinion had always been that Japan should do all in her power to cultivate friendly relations with that Power, as she could only contend with her on very unequal terms, and that nothing but manifest wrong or insult would ever justify Japan in perilling her own interests by engaging in any military undertaking except such as might be required for self-defence.

I have, &c.
(Signed)　HARRY S. PARKES

124

H.S. Parkes (1883. 2. 20)

Aston의 조선행 승인

My Lord,

I have the honor to acknowledge the receipt this day at 11 a.m. of the following telegram in cypher from Your Lordship

"To Sir H. Parkes
Tokio
Send Aston as you propose to Korea Granville."

I have the honor to be, with the highest respect,
My Lord,
Your Lordship's most obedient humble servant,
Harry S. Parkes

G.L.G. Granville (1883. 2. 28) ➔ Ampthill

조청상민수륙무역장정 이후 조선의 국제적 지위에 관한 보고

Earl Granville to Lord Ampthill.

(No. 102 Confidential)

Foreign Office, February 28, 1883

My Lord,

  I HAVE to acknowledge the receipt of your Excellency's despatch No. 61 of the 16th instant, from which it appears probable that Germany intends to ratify the Treaty that was signed last autumn between that Power and Corea.

  Her Majesty's Government have recently received from Peking and Tôkiô information in regard to Regulations which have been drawn up at Tien-tsin between the Envoys of the King of Corea and two Chinese officials acting under the orders of His Excellency Li Hung-chang in his capacity of Imperial Commissioner for Trade at the Northern Ports.

  I inclose herewith, for your Excellency's information, copies of the Reports which have been received from Mr. Grosvenor and Sir H.S. Parkes on the subject of these Regulations,* together with a duplicate copy of the Regulations themselves.

  There is but little doubt that the drafts of the Treaties which were signed last year with Corea by the negotiators on behalf of Great Britain, Germany, and the United States were prepared generally under the suggestions of Li Hung-chang.

  In the Treaty between this country and Corea, which was signed on the 6th June last, the Sovereign of Corea is treated on equal terms with Her Majesty the Queen, but according to the Regulations recently drawn up at Tien-tsin, China assumes the position of Suzerain towards Corea, and the right of making special and exclusive arrangements with her dependency.

  The position is not, therefore, clear on what footing the relations of Corea

---
*[원주] Nos. 7 and 16.

with foreign Powers are to be based.

Either the King of that country is an independent Sovereign with whom Treaties can be concluded by other Sovereigns, in which case the most-favoured-nation clause of the Treaty signed by Admiral Willes would give to this country all the advantages accorded to China;

Or, he is a vassal of China, in which case the provisions of any Treaty existing between Her Majesty the Queen and the Emperor of China would also extend to the vassal State of Corea.

It will be seen that, in regard to jurisdiction and customs duties, much more favourable terms have been obtained for China by these Regulations than are secured to Great Britain by the Treaty of the 6th June, 1882.

You will have observed from the Confidential Memorandum which accompanies my despatch No. 98 of the 27th instant that on different occasions China has declined all responsibility for events occurring within the territory of the King of Corea, and that it was only last year that the Chinese Government, contrary to the policy which she has pursued during recent years, has interfered with the internal affairs of that country by sending a military and naval expedition to restore order there.

Her Majesty's Government are disposed to think that it would be desirable to treat with Corea as an independent Power, so as to avoid any closer union between the two countries than has hitherto existed, in order to prevent the possible contingency of its absorption by China.

I have now to request that Your Excellency will communicate to the German Government a copy of the Trade Regulations concluded at Tien-tsin between China and Corea. You will at the same time state that Her Majesty's Government would be glad to act in this matter with that of Germany; and that they are very desirous to ascertain the views of the Imperial Government as to the basis on which the relations of Corea with foreign Powers should be conducted.

As the period of twelve months within which the ratifications of the Treaty of the 6th June last should be exchanged will shortly expire, Her Majesty's Government hope that they may be favoured with the opinion of the Imperial Government on this matter at their earliest convenience.

I am, &c.

(Signed)　　GRANVILLE

H.S. Parkes (1883. 3. 9) ➡ G.L.G. Granville (1883. 4. 14)

Aston의 조선행 및 지시 내용 보고

Sir H.S. Parkes to Earl Granville.—(Received April 14)

(No. 35)

Tôkiô, March 9, 1883

My Lord,

  VICE-ADMIRAL WILLES having been so good as to place the services of Her Majesty's ship "Moorhen" at my disposal to convey Mr. Aston to Corea, I have arranged that he shall leave Nagasaki about the 14th instant.

  I inclose copies of the instructions I have furnished to Mr. Aston, and also of three letters which I have addressed to the Prime Minister and Foreign Minister of Corea, and to the late Corean Envoy to Japan, in order that the Corean Government may be clearly informed of the objects of Mr. Aston's mission.

  As the American mail, by which I am writing, is on the point of departure, I am unable by this opportunity to furnish the observations which I wish to submit to your Lordship on those instructions and letters; but as the instructions themselves are very detailed I trust that, in the meantime, they will carry with them sufficient explanation.

  I can only now add that I attach considerable importance to Mr. Aston being accompanied by Kim Ok-kiun, the Confidential Agent of the King of Corea; that the latter cordially concurred in my view that Mr. Aston should be sent as soon as possible, and that his co-operation would probably not have been secured unless Mr. Aston had gone at once, as he (Kim Ok-kiun) was on the point of leaving Tôkiô when I informed him that I intended to send Mr. Aston to Korea.

  I had these circumstances in view when I telegraphed to Vice-Admiral Willes (as I have reported in my despatch No. 33 of this date) that I had additional important reasons for desiring that Mr. Aston should be promptly dispatched.

I have, &c.
(Signed)   HARRY S. PARKES

Inclosure 1

Sir H.S. Parkes to Consul Aston.

(Confidential and Separate)

Tôkiô, March 6, 1883

Sir,

I HAVE to instruct you to proceed to Corea on service which appears to me to call for the following explanation:

In a despatch, dated the 15th December last, Earl Granville instructed me that, having had under consideration your Memorandum of the 12th October, in which you point out the difficulties which will be met with in securing suitable house accommodation for the Diplomatic or Consular officers who may eventually be appointed to reside in Corea, his Lordship deemed it desirable that I should make further inquiry as to the places most suitable for the establishment of Consular residences in that country, and obtain the refusal of eligible sites at the ports where they are likely to be required.

Knowing that I should be unable to prosecute such an inquiry in Japan, I obtained, by telegraph, the sanction of his Lordship to dispatch you to Corea for this purpose. I am sensible that his Lordship, in approving this step, may have been influenced in some measure by my representation that, even if you should not be successful in securing the refusal of such sites, you would still be able to obtain valuable information as to the existing state of affairs in Corea. The latter forms, therefore, another object of your mission, and, in view of its general and important character, I think it more convenient to consider it first, and to put you in possession of some particulars which will enable you to understand the character of the information which it is desirable you should endeavour to gain.

In the despatch in which Earl Granville instructed me to make inquiry as to Consular sites his Lordship also informed me that Her Majesty's Government are not yet prepared, without further information on various points raised in the Treaty between Great Britain and Corea, which was signed by Vice-Admiral Willes in May last, and with regard to which investigation is being made, to ratify that Treaty as it stands. It is not impossible, I think, that this view may be confirmed by the information his Lordship will have received, subsequent to the date of that despatch, relative to the arrangements concluded towards the close of last year between China and Corea, which confer on the former country commercial privileges of greater value than those secured to British subjects under Vice-Admiral Willes' Treaty.

I had occasion to discuss these arrangements with Pak Yonghyo, the senior of the two Corean Envoys who were lately accredited to Japan, and he assured me that though he was not authorized to pledge his Government to such a step, he believed that the latter would be willing to make a new Treaty with Great Britain, conceding the same Tariff as that granted to China, provided Her Majesty's Government made proposals to the Corean Government direct, and not through China. Having telegraphed this information to Earl Granville, his Lordship replied that if the Corean Envoys could get authority from their Government to negotiate on the above-mentioned basis, Her Majesty's Government would be happy to entertain their proposals.

The envoys had unfortunately left Tôkiô on their return to Corea when I received his instruction, but I advised Kim Ok-kiun, the Confidential Agent of the King of Corea, who, together with the Envoys, had repeatedly assured me that His Majesty was most anxious to see Treaty relations speedily established between his kingdom and Great Britain, that if the Corean Government wished to promote that object they should lose no time in intimating their willingness to negotiate with Her Majesty's Government a new Treaty based in regard to commercial matters on similar conditions to those which Corea has granted to China and Japan.

Kim Ok-kiun assured me that he would convey this intimation to the senior Envoy, but when speaking with me on the subject on the 20th ultimo, he observed to me that though his government were sensible of the importance of such a step, they had yet taken no decision on the subject.

At the interview which I held with him on the 2nd instant, and at which you were the medium of communication, he stated that he was confident that commercial conditions were altogether secondary in the estimation of the King to the friendly relations and recognition of political position which Corea would secure by Treaties with foreign Powers, and that His Majesty attached special value to the friendship of Great Britain. But that, as the United States had ratified that Treaty with Corea, it would now be difficult for the latter to offer to alter the Treaty with Great Britain. He admitted that the high duties of those Treaties were unparalleled in the East, and would prevent the growth of trade; but he believed his Government, after some experience of the working of the Treaties, would themselves perceive that the duties were too high, and would spontaneously offer to reduce them. He therefore hoped that Great Britain would follow the example of the United States, that is, ratify the Treaty first and trust to its being subsequently amended.

I replied that I doubted whether such a course would be acceptable to Her Majesty's Government, as it was manifestly undesirable to ratify a Treaty that was known to be defective, and the injurious consequences of our doing so in this instance might not be limited to our interests in Corea alone, but might also affect those in China and Japan, which were of much greater importance than the former. If Corea really wished for friendly relations with Great Britain, which were obviously of more importance to the former than to the latter, she should offer Great Britain sufficient inducements to enter into those relations.

She could now understand the deficiencies of the Treaty made last spring, and could perceive that a friendship based on such conditions was not likely to be valued by Great Britain or to prove advantageous to Corea. The former, with due regard to her own dignity, could not occupy in Corea an inferior position to China or Japan, and if Corea desired a Treaty with Great Britain, she should signify her willingness to extend to the latter the treatment of the most favoured nation.

Both the friendship and the political status of Corea would necessarily be judged by her action. If she were willing to treat on the above basis she would attest by doing so the reality of her friendship, and also her independence in regard to her relations with foreign States. It seemed to me very important that my Government should obtain definite information as to her disposition and her power in these respects, and as he had informed me that his Government had taken no decision on the communication already made to them through the Envoys, I thought it would be desirable to send an officer to the capital in order to ascertain what their views and position in regard to independent negotiations really were. You are aware that Kim Ok-kiun cordially concurred in this suggestion, and on my saying that I should depute you to proceed on this service he at once volunteered to accompany you.

I reached this point, as you will have noticed, without having had occasion to inform him that I had been instructed by Earl Granville to send you to Corea for the particular purpose of selecting Consular sites, although I subsequently apprized him that this would be one of the objects of your visit.

This recital appears necessary, in order that you may perceive the character of the overtures which it is desirable that the Corean Government should make to that of Her Majesty, and the tone which you should use in discussing the subject with them. Although I see no objection to your acquainting them that the views of Her Majesty's Government in regard to the ratification of the Treaty are likely to be influenced by similar considerations to those which I expressed to Kim Ok-kiun, I do not think that you should press the Corean Government to negotiate a fresh Treaty, but should rather appear to leave it to them to elect the course which their own interests may prompt them to adopt. It is impossible at present to judge either of their own inclinations in this respect, or as to how far they are able to act independently of China in regard to their relations with foreign Powers. But your communications with them will oblige them to make some declaration of their views, and whether these should be favourable to the negotiation of a fresh Treaty or not, the information cannot fail to be valuable to Her Majesty's Government. It would be desirable that you should communicate to me by telegraph any definite information that you may obtain on this subject, and if you can do so more expeditiously by way of Shanghae you should send your message (in Cypher N), under cover, to Her Majesty's Consul at that port.

The question of the selection of sites for the residences of Diplomatic or Consular officers will afford you, I think, a practical opportunity of eliciting from the Corean Government some disclosure of their policy and opinions, and it therefore possesses a value apart from its own merits. In treating with them on this subject, you will be entirely guided by the instructions contained in Earl Granville's despatch to me, of which I inclose a copy.* I think, however, that the field of this inquiry may advantageously be extended to sites for settlements, of which it would also be desirable to secure the refusal, if such can be obtained. At several of the ports in China the site of the settlement appropriated to British subjects has been leased by the Chinese Government to that of Her Majesty, who have sublet it to British occupants, and as similar arrangements have been

---

*[원주] Earl Granville, No 116, Confidential, November 15, 1882.

made by Japan in Corea, the Corean Government may see the reasonableness of extending those arrangements to ourselves.

Chemulpho (or Jinchuen) will, I presume, have to be selected as one of the three ports to be opened to foreign trade, and I conclude that the remaining two must be Pusan and Wönsan. In view of the distance of the latter port I trust it will not be necessary for you to visit it, on the present occasion at least, but trust that your knowledge of the locality will enable you to indicate, when at Söul, the site which you think suitable at that port. It may be necessary, however, that you should visit Pusan to effect a selection, and I have accordingly to authorize you to request the Commander of Her Majesty's ship in which you will proceed to Corea to take you there on returning from the capital. You will also endeavour to bespeak a site at Yang-hwa-chin (or the town close to Söul, which will be opened under the Japanese Convention of last August), and it is particularly desirable that you should endeavour to secure at the capital accommodation for the residence of any diplomatic officer that may eventually be sent to Corea. As to the terms upon which such sites may be obtainable, I can, of course, say nothing, and you will be careful, in accordance with Earl Granville's directions, not to commit Her Majesty's Government to any expenditure, present or prospective, in this account; but in discussing the subject with the Corean authorities, you will naturally be guided by the terms under which the Japanese Government hold their settlements at Pusan and Wönsan, and the arrangements which you may find they have already concluded at Chemulpho, which was formally opened to Japanese trade on the 1st January last.

I need not point out to you the desirability of obtaining as much information as possible relative to the constitution and organization of the Corean Government, and their ability to control their people, the state of political parties, the conditions under which Chinese and Japanese are residing and trading in Corea, and the disposition of the people toward foreigners.

Another important subject of observation is the position assumed by China in that country, and the manner in which this is regarded by the Corean Government, the strength of the Chinese force now stationed there, and the objects and probable duration of this military occupation. The relations of the Japanese Minister of Söul with the Corean government, and the circumstances attending the maintenance there of a considerable guard, are also deserving of notice.

You will also naturally obtain all the particulars you can collect relative to the recent action of the Corean Government (taken mainly, it is believed, under the advice of Chinese Agents) as to the framing of the Customs Tariff, the organization of a Customs Service, or as to any other arrangements which they may be making for the management of foreign commerce. It is manifestly undesirable that your communications with the Corean Government should be conducted through the intervention of Makien-chang[sic] or M. Möllendorf (whose precise position in Corea you will endeavour to ascertain), but I must leave it to you to judge how far you should endeavour to check interference on their part in your affairs, or to avail yourself of their assistance if one or the other should be willing to render you any.

As it is necessary that the object of your visit should be authentically stated to the Corean Government and that you should be introduced to them in some official form, I have thought it advisable to address the two letters which I inclosed to the Prime Minister and to the Member of the Government who hold, I believe, an analogous position to that of Minister for Foreign Affairs. The first you will perceive is general in its tenour, while I specify in the latter that I send you to Corea under instructions from Her Majesty's Government to endeavour to make arrangements respecting building sites, the selection of which, owing to the utter absence of any houses in Corea suited to the requirements of foreigners, should obviously precede the arrival either of Diplomatic or Consular officers and merchants. I also add a semi-official letter to the late Senior Envoy in Japan, which may serve to remind him of the prospect he held out to me, that his Government was disposed to grant to Great Britain similar commercial advantages to those which they have conceded to China, although I have avoided committing him to the direct statements which he made to me on this point.

Having applied to Vice-Admiral Willes for one of Her Majesty's ships to convey you to Corea, and represented to him the importance of your being able to proceed there immediately, his Excellency has been so good as to order the "Moorhen" on this service, and I understand that she will be at Nagasaki and ready to embark you by the 14th instant. By proceeding from Kobe in the Peninsular and Oriental steam-ship "Khiva," you will reach Nagasaki about that date, and Kim Ok-kiun and his coadjutor, Sö Kwang-pöm, will leave Yokohama in the same vessel on the 10th instant, in order to join you at Kobe. I trust these Corean functionaries, who have given proof of their friendly earnestness by their offer to accompany you in Her Majesty's ship "Moorhen," will be able to render you material assistance when in Corea.

On arrival at Chemulpho you will have to determine your own course of proceeding. Judging from the statements of Kim Ok-kiun, I do not anticipate that any obstacles will be placed in the way of your going to the capital, which would obviously be the best point of observation and the most convenient place for the transaction of business, and I trust you will find that the Corean Government will be disposed to provide you when there with the necessary accommodation. I should, however, enjoin you to avoid as far as possible personal risk, not only on your own account, which to yourself would not be a paramount consideration, but also in view of the political complications to which any untoward occurrence would give rise. If the result should prove that the visit of a public officer in your position to Corea is attended with insecurity, Her Majesty's Government might naturally infer that the time is inopportune for authorizing private subjects of Her Majesty to resort to that country.

I must also leave it to you to determine the length of your stay. An officer who is tied to time in dealing with Orientals is deprived of one of the first elements of success, and as the Corean Government may perceive that your visit will have the effect of causing them to show their hand, they may not be over-prompt in responding to your lead. You will have, however, to consider the requirements of Her Majesty's ship which takes you to Corea, and which will remain to support you when there, and also the importance of acquiring as speedily as you can, for the guidance of Her Majesty's Government in regard to their approaching relations with Corea, the information you are sent to obtain.

As Her Majesty's ship "Moorhen" cannot convey you nearer to the capital than Chemulpho, and in view of the isolated situation in which you would be placed at Söul, I think it expedient that you should be accompanied by another Consular officer as your assistant, and I have accordingly instructed Her Majesty's Acting Consul at Nagasaki to give you the services of Mr. Bonar, who will join you on your arrival at Nagasaki.

Although in confiding to you this delicate mission I have endeavoured to aid you with the fullest instructions in my power, it is due to you to add that I leave it to your discretion, on which I feel I can place implicit reliance, to be guided as you may judge best by the information you may obtain on the spot, and by circumstances which I am unable to foresee.

I have, &c.

(Signed) HARRY S. PARKES

Inclosure 2

Sir H.S. Parkes to Hong Sun-mok, Prime Minister of His Majesty the King of Great Chôsen.

Tôkiô, March 9, 1883

Your Excellency,

THIS letter will be delivered to your Excellency by Mr. Aston, one of Her Majesty's Consuls in Japan, whom I have been authorized by my Government to send to Corea in order to obtain certain information from your Government, which may have an important bearing upon the future relations of our respective Government, and also to make certain preliminary arrangements as to building sites which he will explain to the Foreign Minister of Corea.

Mr. Aston is an officer of rank and long experience in Her Majesty's service, is acquainted with your language, and, having twice visited Corea, is well known to several of your high authorities. As the object of his mission is to advance friendly relations between Great Britain and Corea, I confidentially trust that he will receive from your Excellency and the Government over which you so ably preside such friendly treatment and careful protection as you would wish your own officers to receive in my country, and which would certainly be extended to them by Her Majesty's Government.

In making this important communication to your Excellency, I beg to offer you the assurances of my most distinguished consideration.

(Signed) HARRY S. PARKES, *Her Britannic Majesty's Envoy Extraordinary and Minister Plenipotentiary to Japan.*

【漢譯文】

日本東京英吉利公使館 三月九日千八百八十三年

奉此照會 要日本在留領事官阿須頓代達閣下 僕今奉我大英國政府命 代送阿須頓氏 一爲兩國交際上重大事件要貴國政府知悉 一爲審察建築房屋地界等事 伊當委細辦理于貴外務衙門 閣下諒之 阿須頓氏久仕我政府 官階高顯 又略解貴國語言 今再到貴國 貴國官紳亦有知之者 概伊君之此行 特爲兩國將來交際速趨敦密 閣下以寵幸邦國 克善隣交之道 特別款待 如禮保護焉 他日貴國官弁到敝國時 可徵今日貴國待我之誼 此呈照會于閣下 以盡恭敬之儀

大英國特命全權駐劄日本東京公使 巴
大朝鮮國議政府領議政 洪 閣下

Inclosure 3

Sir H.S. Parkes to Cho Yong-ha, Minister for Foreign Affairs of His Majesty the King of Great Chôsen.

Tôkiô, March 9, 1883

Your Excellency,

I HAVE the honour to inform your Excellency that I have been instructed by my Government to make inquiry as to the means of obtaining building sites in Corea for the residences of the Diplomatic or Consular officers whom it will be necessary to appoint when Treaty relations between our two nations shall be established.

As the houses of your country are not adapted to the requirements of foreigners, the erection of Consulates will be indispensable, and foreign merchants resorting to Corea will also be obliged to construct their own residences. It is obvious, therefore, that the selection of suitable sites for these purposes should precede the arrival both of public functionaries and private individuals, and my Government, in authorizing me to send Mr. Aston, one of Her Majesty's Consuls, to Corea, to make inquiry as to building sites, is giving a proof of their willingness to advance the establishment of Treaty relations.

I have, therefore, the honour to request your Excellency to afford Mr. Aston full facilities for selecting, in conjunction with officers deputed on the part of your Government, suitable sites for the above-mentioned purposes, both at the capital and at the ports to be opened to foreign trade, and my Government, on receiving Mr. Aston's Report, and becoming acquainted with the conditions on which such sites can be obtained, will then be able to arrive at a decision on the subject.

I have also the honour to invite your Excellency's attention to another important subject. Your Government, having studied the conditions which govern international intercourse, will now be aware that equality of treatment is the only satisfactory footing on which relations between different States can be conducted. They will, therefore, I trust, perceive that the commercial and other arrangements which they have recently concluded with China must materially influence the consideration of the Treaty between Great Britain and Corea, and I have consequently been instructed by Her Majesty's Government to apprize your Excellency that, if the Government of Corea is willing to enter into further negotiations with them on the basis of those arrangements, they would be happy to entertain proposals of that nature. Mr. Aston is accordingly authorized to receive any communication which you may wish to make to Her Majesty's Government on this subject.

I gladly profit by this opportunity to offer to your Excellency the assurance of my highest consideration.

(Signed) HARRY S. PARKES, Her Britannic Majesty's Envoy Extraordinary and Minister Plenipotentiary to Japan.

【漢譯文】

癸未三月初九日 日本東京英吉利公使書譯漢文 三月九日千八百八十三年
貴國與敝國 行將修睦交通 凡係交際官員及領事官駐留地面 先察形便 爲交際之先務 所以我大英國政府命僕審問于貴政府 閣下其諒之 貴國家產之制 不便於外國人所處 至於商民居留地界內 亦各因其便而建築爲可 今命派阿須頓領事航往貴國 足徵我政府樂與貴國修好之誼也 望閣下簡拔委員 京城及各港口通商界內便利之地使之指定 則我政府當以阿須頓氏所覆爲允准也 又有一重大事件奉告者 閣下諒察 今天下交通之道 惟以公允相待 平均無異 爲不

易之公法 想貴政府今焉燭知 然則貴國向來與淸國所訂通商約款及其外各節 視與敝國所立擬案大有關係者 貴政府亦應體察 貴國若以平均無異之權理以 對我國 則我政府樂而顧聞 貴政府所有議論 阿須頓氏均能代達我政府 今奉 照會 備悉禮儀

　　　　　　　　　　大英國特命全權駐劄日本東京公使 巴

大朝鮮外務衙門 趙寧夏 閣下

Inclosure 4

Sir H.S. Parkes to Pak Yŏng-hyo.

(Semi-official)

Tôkiô, March 9, 1883

Your Excellency and my Friend,

　　RECOLLECTING with pleasure the friendly communications which passed between us when Your Excellency, as the Envoy of your Government, formed one of the body of foreign Representatives at Tôkiô, I am glad to have this opportunity of writing to you by the hand of Mr. Aston, who is so well known to you.

　　I send Mr. Aston to Corea under instructions from my Government to make inquiry on a particular subject which I have explained to the Minister for Foreign Affairs, and also to acquire information as to the views of your Government in regard to Treaty relations. You will remember that when you were in Tôkiô I pointed out to you the material differences which are observable in the Treaties which your Government made last spring and those which you have concluded with Japan and China. I trust your Government will now perceive that friendly relations between State may best be secured by treating all nations on equal terms, and if they have adopted this view, we may then hope that your country will soon be able to participate in that profitable commercial intercourse with western Powers which has been productive of so much benefit to the people of China and Japan.

　　I was glad to be able to accommodate Mr. Kim Ok-kiun and Mr. Sö

Kwang-pöm with a passage in the ship of war which conveys Mr. Aston to Corea, and I am satisfied that no effort will be wanting on their part and on yours to promote arrangements which will conduce to durable friendship between our respective countries.

I take this opportunity to send you the photograph of myself which I promised you, but which had not been taken in time to present it you before your departure from Tôkiô, and I beg to offer with it the assurances of my most friendly regard and esteem.

(Signed)   HARRY S. PARKES

127

洪淳穆(1883/高宗二十年) ➡ H.S. Parkes

Parkes 조회에 대한 회신

大朝鮮國議政府領議政洪 謹覆書大英國特命全權駐劄日本東京大臣巴閣下 由阿須頓氏 接奉手教幷漢文譯本 藉知來意 乃辱獎譽過當 愧悚愧悚 所有一切事件 悉經我統理交涉衙門與阿氏酌設 可應代達 公使久駐東洋 蔚有令聞 深切馳欽 所願兩國永敦友誼 幷受其福 敬此泐佈 順頌台安

淳穆 頓首

H.S. Parkes (1883. 3. 10) ➜ W.G. Aston

조선 관세율에 관한 井上馨와 회견내용 통보

Sir H.S. Parkes to Mr. Aston.

(Confidential)
Sir,

Tôkiô, March 10, 1883

I THINK you should be informed that I yesterday acquainted the Foreign Minister that you were going to Corea, and I explained to him the object of your mission, but without mentioning the detail of Consular sites. He told me that he had heard the same that morning from Kim Ok Kiun, who had observed that he had gathered from his conversations with me that it was very doubtful whether the British Treaty would be ratified, and inquired what the Foreign Minister thought should be done. Mr. Inouyé replied that, if the Corean Government wished to have a Treaty with Great Britain, they should intimate to you their readiness to lower their proposed Tariff and to give to England equal commercial privileges to those they had granted to China. That he recommended a Tariff on a 5 per cent. basis in the first instance, as a higher one would prevent the growth of trade, but that five or ten years hence, when trade had been fairly established, it might then be possible to raise the Tariff. He added that Kim Ok Kiun had said that he was returning home, and had taken leave of him. He (Mr. Inouyé) entirely concurred in your being sent to Corea in order to ascertain what the Corean Government were willing to do. He thought that it was a very opportune step, and the sooner it was taken the better.

I thereon informed Mr. Inouyé that Mr. Kim Ok Kiun had asked me to give him a passage to Corea in Her Majesty's ship which conveys you there, and that I had willingly assented.

His Excellency has sent me this morning, by the hand of his Private Secretary, the inclosed despatch, which he wished you to deliver to Mr. Takezoye, the Japanese Minister at Sôul. The Secretary informed me that Mr. Takezoye is therein instructed that you are being sent to Corea to learn the views of the Corean Government on the subject of the Treaty. That as the action of Her Majesty's Government may be greatly influenced by the disposition of that of Corea, Mr. Takezoye is to advise the latter to offer to reduce the Tariff to a 5 per cent. basis, and to signify their readiness to make such other reasonable modifications in the Treaty as will render future relations acceptable to the British Government. Mr. Takezoye is also instructed to render you any assistance that may be in his power.

    I need not point out to you the desirability of reciprocating in your communications with Mr. Takezoye the confidence of the Foreign Minister, if you find that the former is acting in the spirit of the above instructions.

I have, &c.
(Signed)   HARRY S. PARKES

R.G.W. Herbert (1883. 3. 19) ➡ P. Currie(1883. 3. 20)

1차 조영조약에 대한 香港 상공회의소 의견 상신

Mr. Herbert to Mr. Currie.—(Received March 20)

Downing Street, March 19, 1883

Sir,

I AM directed by the Secretary of State for the Colonies to transmit to you, for the information of Earl Granville, with reference to the letter from this Department of the 19th October last, a copy of a despatch from the Administrator of Hong Kong Chamber of Commerce on the Treaty with Corea.

I am, &c.
(Signed) ROBERT G.W. HERBERT.

Inclosure 1

Administrator Marsh to The Earl of Derby.

(Confidential)

Government House, Hong Kong, January 30, 1883

My Lord,

THE Chairman of the Chamber of Commerce of Hong Kong has requested me to transmit, through your Lordship, the inclosed letter addressed to Her Majesty's Principal Secretary of State for Foreign Affairs, containing the observations of the Chamber on the Commercial Clauses of the Treaty with Corea, which Lord Granville promised to take into consideration on receipt thereof.

I have, &c.

(Signed)   W.H. MARSH

Inclosure 2

Mr. Johnson to Earl Granville.

(Private and Confidential)

Hong Kong General Chamber of Commerce,
Hong Kong, January 20, 1883

My Lord,

I HAVE the honour to acknowledge the receipt of Sir Julian Pauncefote's despatch of the 10th October, 1882, replying to the communication I made on behalf of this Chamber to Your Lordship on the subject of the Treaty recently negotiated between Great Britain and the Kingdom of Corea.

I have now to convey to your Lordship the thanks of the Chamber for the courteous and confidential invitation extended to the Committee to express its views upon the Treaty, a copy of which was inclosed with Sir Julian Pauncefote's letter, and to set forth, with as much brevity as the subject permits, the opinions of the Committee upon the operation of the clauses which relate to trade and commerce.

The Committee has no doubt that Her Majesty's Government, when entering into political relations with Corea, has regarded that kingdom as a State which is completely independent in respect of its domestic administration and its international responsibilities, though subject to a certain undefined suzerainty exercised by China, similar to that acknowledged by Annam and Burmah and hitherto satisfied by the rendition of an annual tribute. That such has also been the view held, until recently, by China herself, is clear from the evidence furnished by the express declarations of the Tsung-li Yamên of Peking in 1866 and 1871 on the occasion of French and American difficulties with Corea, when the Chinese Government disclaimed all responsibility for Corean affairs, and by her acquiescence in the recognition of the complete independence of Corea which was declared in the Japanese Treaty with that country concluded in 1876.

Since, however, the attack upon the Japanese Legation at Seoul last year, the Chinese Government appears to have changed its attitude, and to have asserted its claims to exercise control not only over the administration of the internal affairs of Corea, but also over its foreign relations. The Edict published some months ago in the "Peking Gazette," notifying the punishment of the Dai-in-Kun, refers to the King of the Corea as being subject to Chinese law and authority, and in a document recently made public, styled "Regulations for the Conduct of Trade by Sea and Land between Chinese and Corean subjects," the Grand Secretary Li Hung-chang, late Viceroy of Pechili, is designated in terms of official equality with the King of Corea, as if the Ruler of that country were occupying a position delegated to him by the Emperor, analogous in point of rank and authority to that of Governor-General of a Chinese province.

That Committee may hereafter deem it necessary to consider, in a separate communication to your Lordship, the terms of these Regulations and the special privileges which they appear to confer upon Chinese traders, and refer to them now, when discussing the bearing of the British Treaty, in order to bring prominently before Her Majesty's Government the desirability of ascertaining the precise character of the relationship claimed by the Government of China *quoad* that of Corea, before Her Majesty is advised to ratify the Treaty negotiated by Admiral Willes.

As the King of Corea has never been claimed to be an integral part of the Chinese dominions, it is either a mediatized State under the protection of China, in which case the authority of its King to conclude Treaties with foreign nations may hereafter be questioned, or it is an independent country, with whose autonomy the Regulations referred to are inconsistent. It would be unfortunate if the recent interference of the Chinese Executive in the internal affairs of Corea should be hereafter adduced to throw doubt upon the international validity of any of the provisions of the foreign Treaties, on the faith of which commercial intercourse with Corea will have been entered upon and is to be conducted.

The Committee, however, accepting the independence of Corea as a recognized international fact, ventures in the first place to offer to your Lordship some observations upon the Treaty as a whole, and, in the second, to consider *seriatim* the several clauses of the document which may seem to call for special comment.

The Committee assumes that Her Majesty's Government has had some cogent reason, arising out of the political situation, for pushing forward to a rapid conclusion the negotiations with the Corean authorities, but admitting that there were good grounds of policy for entering into immediate relations with the country, the Committee respectfully submits that that object would have been as successfully, and much more conveniently, attained if preliminary negotiations had been confined to drawing up a short Treaty, expressive of national amity, and providing generally for political and commercial intercourse, leaving a Tariff of duties, and the special conditions under which foreign trade is to be carried on, to a supplementary and carefully considered Convention.

The frequent disputes which have arisen about the interpretation to be placed upon certain clauses of the Treaty of Tien-tsin show the importance of drafting with peculiar care agreements, affecting national interests, which have to be drawn up in a language so full of obscurities even to the most experienced Sinologue as that of China, so as to avoid all misunderstanding when the stipulations and covenants to be observed on either side come to be made effective. The Committee cannot fail to perceive that the diplomatic instrument signed by Admiral Willes at Jin Chuen in June last has been very loosely compiled in point of form, and that many of its most important provisions have been expressed in most indefinite language, and further, that imperfections, similar to those now generally recognized as existing in the Treaties with China and Japan, have been repeated and intensified in this new Treaty. Moreover, after a careful consideration of the whole scope of the document, the Committee is apprehensive that the limitations which some of its stipulations impose upon foreign intercourse and trade will not only be injurious to the operation of the Treaty itself, but will seriously prejudice the position hitherto consistently maintained by the Representatives of Western nations at the Courts of Peking and Yedo in combating proposals to place similar restrictions upon trade with China and Japan.

There can be no doubt that, notwithstanding the vast material benefits which have resulted to the people of China during the last twenty years from the great increase in all branches (excepting in opium) of the foreign and coasting trade of the Empire, and which have been the direct consequence of the extended foreign intercourse opened up by the Treaty of Tien-tsin, the ruling classes of China are actuated at the present time by a desire to restrict, as far as possible, the application of foreign capital and enterprise to the further development of the resources of the country. The Committee may adduce the strenuous attempts which have recently been made to prevent the organization of various industries under foreign auspices at Shanghae in evidence of the present unsatisfactory attitude of the Chinese authorities, and earnestly desires to draw your Lordship's attention to the great accession of strength which the reactionary party in China would derive from the stipulations of a Treaty voluntarily entered into by the Western Powers with a dependency of the Empire, if the opponents of progress should be able to point to conditions of exclusion in that Treaty disadvantageous to the foreigner, which have been yielded to the tributary State, but are denied to the country of the Suzerain.

In conclusion of these general remarks, your Lordship need hardly be reminded of the difficulty which would be placed in the way of a successful conduct of the existing negotiations for a revision of the Treaty with Japan, if the arguments of Her Majesty's Minister at Yedo in favour of the adoption of a liberal foreign policy by the Japanese Cabinet should be met by unfavourable precedents, cited from the recent Agreement with Corea.

Proceeding now to consider some of the special stipulations of the Treaty-

Article II relates to the character of official relationship and communication between the two countries, with which it is scarcely the province of this Chamber to deal; but so great has been the inconvenience sustained in former years by the merchants in China under the provisions of the Treaty of Nanking, which seriously hindered free communication between foreign Consular officials and the provincial authorities, that the Committee feels it necessary to advert to the paragraph in the first clause of this article which stipulates that "Officials shall have relations with the corresponding local authorities of equal rank upon a basis of mutual equality." This stipulation is a very vague one according to the English text, and what it may imply in the Chinese text the Committee is unable to say. It may be read in an exclusive sense, and be taken to mean that official of the one country may only communicate with officials of the same rank in the other. The war with China, commenced in 1856, would probably have been averted if Consul Parkes could have insisted upon personal communication with Governor-General Yeh, and the Committee suggests the expediency of providing that the commissioned officers of both countries, whether civil, naval, or military, shall be entitled to hold official intercommunication on terms of social equality, while observing the ordinary rules of precedence relating to official rank.

Article III, in the clause which provides that a British vessel shall, with her cargo, be seized and confiscated if found engaged in clandestine trade, is remarkable for repeating a grave shortcoming in the Tien-tsin Treaty which has been the occasion of a lasting controversy. Under this Article a vessel, alleged to be engaged in trading to a port not opened by the Treaty, may be confiscated by the Corean authorities of their own motion, and with or without trial, subject to no investigation by or appeal to British officials.

The Committee desires to enter the strongest protest against the confirmation of this clause, on two grounds:-

1. That the absence of any recognized practice or system of jurisprudence in Corea renders it impossible to repose confidence in the decisions of Corean officials who would be judges in their own cause without appeal; and

2. Because the power of confiscation is granted without the safeguard of any provision as to the nature of the proceeding which shall be taken to prove that the vessel shall have been really guilty of the offence with which it may be charged.

The Treaty between Japan and Corea provides that in the event of a Japanese vessel being found engaged in smuggling goods "into any non-open port in Corea, it shall be seized by the Corean local authorities, and delivered over to the Agent of the Japanese Government residing at the nearest port. Such goods to be confiscated by him, and to be handed over to the Corean authorities."

In the clause relating to the wreckage of British vessels on the coast of Corea, the local authorities should be made responsible, not only for taking the necessary measures for rendering assistance to the crew, and salving the vessel and cargo, but also for inflicting condign punishment upon all plunderers or wreckers.

Article V mainly relates to fiscal obligations, and the Committee cannot conceal its surprise and regret that after the experience which has been gained of the unsatisfactory working of the Tien-tsin Treaty, owing to the looseness of certain of its stipulations which provide for and limit the Tariff of duties, Her Majesty's Representative should have given his assent to clauses which cannot fail in operation to revive, in the case of Corea, difficulties and controversies similar to those which have arisen and still exist in carrying on trade with China.

It is no doubt necessary to concede to Corea, in principle, the right to levy duties and protect its own revenue laws; but before the Tariff which the Treaty prescribes is assented to, the Corean Government, as having had no previous experience in such matters, may reasonably be required to furnish to the British officials a Code of Customs Regulations, and of proceedings for adjudication in the case of a breach of fiscal rules. The want of such a Code, and the absence of any provision in the Tien-tsin Treaty for a system of trial of adjudication, led to the grossest miscarriage of justice during the earlier years of the establishment of the Foreign Customs Inspectorate in China, and the Committee hopes that Her Majesty's Government will take adequate precautions for the protection of the property of British subjects against unjust Customs seizures when Corea becomes opened to foreign trade.

The Committee is of opinion that the Tariff of customs duties upon imports and exports generally should not exceed those levied in China under the Treaty of Tien-tsin, and considers that the scale of *ad valorem* duties upon imports therein, viz., 5 per cent upon entry and 2 per cent. commutation of inland dues, should be adopted also in Corea, and would not be excessive, provided that measures should be taken to give satisfactory and complete effect to the stipulation in the concluding lines of paragraph 4 of this Article: "that no other dues, duties, fees, taxes, or charge of any sort shall be levied upon such imports either in the interior of Chosen or at the ports." Here, however, appears to be repeated another defect in the Treaty of Tien-tsin, which provides no guarantees for redress in the event of a breach or evasion on the part of local officials of a similar stipulation in the document. The Committee suggests that the clause should run, "and that any other dues, duties, fees, taxes, or charges of any sort, which may be levied upon imports either in the interior of Chosen or at the ports, shall be recoverable from the Chosen Customs at the port of entry of such imports."

The distinction between articles of daily use, which are to be subject to an *ad valorem* duty of 10 per cent. and articles of luxury, which are to pay more, is much too vague, and cannot fail to be productive of endless disputes. The Committee would propose that schedules of the several articles be drawn up and agreed upon with British officials before the Treaty is confirmed, and has, moreover, to point out that no provision is made for any drawback of duty in the case of goods which have paid import duty being re-exported.

As regards tonnage dues, no stipulation appears that these levies shall be applied to their usual and legitimate purposes, viz., the lighting of the coast, and the improvement to rivers and harbours. No definition is given as to the character of the ton, whether of register or burthen, or of the money in which payment is to be made as to its being Corean or Chinese currency. In Chinese money the tax would be far too heavy.

A serious, and in the opinion of the Committee, a fatal objection remains to be urged against this Article as a whole, because it places British subjects on a more unfavourable footing than Japanese, who, by their Treaty of 1876 are, as the Committee understands, relieved from the payment of any import duties. As the "favoured nation clause" in Article XIV is not made retrospective in its effect and as the Chinese under their "Regulations" claim a right in the case of the "subject State" of Corea to favoured treatment, different in its character from that which other nations on the ordinary footing would obtain, it is certain that, if duties are to be levied upon British trade on the scale authorized in Article V, British vessels and subjects will be virtually excluded from commerce with Corea.

Article VI.—The second clause of this Article refers to ports in Corea open to foreign commerce, and to the "concessions" within the limits of which British subjects may alone reside. The list of such open ports is not given in the Treaty, and no provision is made for the marking out or setting aside such "concessions." Under the Treaty of Tien-tsin, the British Government became the lessee from the Government of China, at equitable prices, of an allotment of land at each port newly opened by the Treaty, for the purpose of occupation by British subjects, but the provisions of the Corean Treaty leave it to be a matter of conjecture as to the meaning which is to be attached to the term "concession."

The second clause proceeds to stipulate that buildings or land may be leased and residences or warehouses may be constructed within the "concessions," that no coercion or intimidation (presumably by British subjects) in the acquisition of land or buildings shall be permitted, and the land-rent shall be paid as fixed by the authorities of Corea. These stipulations imply that the acquisition of land is to be a matter of private arrangement between intending purchasers and the native owners, and while the language of the clause permits an unmerited and offensive imputation to be thrown on the character of British merchants, no safeguard is taken that exorbitant or prohibitory prices will not be demanded for land, and that the rents to be fixed by the authorities will not be excessive.

The third clause provides that all rights of jurisdiction over persons and property within the concessions remain vested in the authorities of Corea, except in so far as such rights have been expressly relinquished by the Treaty. As the only rights relinquished are those reserved by Article IV, and relate solely to civil and criminal cases between natives of Corea and British subjects, it follows that cases in which British subjects are concerned against each other, or those in which they are engaged with foreigners of other nationalities, will have to be adjudicated by the Corean authorities. The Committee cannot suppose that Her Majesty's Government will sanction such an arrangement.

It is further to be remarked that it appears doubtful whether, by the terms of this Treaty, the native Government, as in the case of the Treaties between China and Japan and Great Britain, has waived the ordinary right of the sovereign of the soil to tax the persons and property of British subjects within the areas of the concessions, and that no provision is made in it for the municipal government of those concessions. The difficulties which have from time to time arisen in the conduct of the municipal affairs of the foreign Settlements in China and Japan show the necessity of making arrangements, such as experience has shown to be adequate, to meet the serious questions and controversies which otherwise cannot fail to arise under similar circumstances in Corea. The Committee has now before it "a Code of Municipal Regulations of the Japanese Settlement of Fusan, in Corea," dated the 9th November, 1881, under which "the entire charge of municipal affairs devolves on the permanent residents in the Settlement," and does not doubt that Her Majesty's Government will not permit British subjects to be placed in a more unfavourable position in the country than those of Japan.

The fourth clause prohibits British subjects from transporting foreign import to the interior, or from proceeding thither to purchase native produce, and from transporting native produce from one open port to another open port.

As to the prohibition against British subjects visiting the interior, it will be seen that this stipulation involves a retrograde step, placing British subjects at a great disadvantage, when it is compared with the freedom of travel granted to foreigners in China and Japan, and with similar facilities given to Chinese and Japanese traders in Corea. Under the Chinese "Regulations," Chinese merchants may open commercial establishments in Yang Wha Chiu and in the capital, and by applying to the Commissioner of Trade they may obtain passports to go into the interior for the purpose of trade or pleasure.

The prohibition against the transportation by British traders the clause does not mention British ships, though the stipulation may be supposed to include them—of native produce between the open ports, the Committee regards as one of the most objectionable provisions in the Treaty. This prohibition cannot be defended on the ground that it affords a necessary protection to Corean shipping, because the Japanese enjoy the right of trading between the ports opened to them under their Treaty of 1876, and the Chinese under their "Regulations" will assuredly claim a similar privilege. The carrying trade, under such a disability as this attaching to British and foreign shipping generally, would be virtually handed over to the Japanese and Chinese flags, notwithstanding that the larger proportion of imports to Corea would be goods of British origin, and the Committee needs hardly remark upon the onerous charge for freight which the existence of a local carrying monopoly would impose on the manufactures of the United Kingdom and the trade generally of Corea, or as to the unfavourable effect which the abandonment of the coast trade with Corea would not fail to exercise upon the course of future negotiations for the revision of the existing Treaties with China and Japan.

The importance of the issues which are at stake in the maintenance of the provision that foreigners may share in the intermediate trade between the open ports is not to be measured by the effect which the abrogation of that provision would have upon the interests of foreign shipping alone, extensive as those interests are.

If foreign vessels should be excluded from the coast trade, foreigners would be practically shut out from all business, excepting at the ports which would have direct trade with foreign countries. Coasting freights under Chinese and Japanese flags alone, and the establishment of native guilds and monopolies which would follow the absence of competition in general business by other foreigners, would cause the control of the distributing traffic to pass into a few hands, and trade of all kinds, under the weight of exorbitant profits, would languish and decay. The evil effect of these monopolies may be understood when the stagnation of industry which prevails at the ports in China not open to foreign trade is compared with the activity and enterprise which are displayed by native merchants at the open ports, where they are exposed to competition with foreigners; and the Committee does not doubt that the maintenance of the progressive character of the external commerce and internal industry of China and Japan is very greatly dependent upon the possession by foreigners of the privilege of competing with natives for a share in the coasting traffic of these countries.

Article VII.—The extraordinary and apparently useless stipulation in this

Article that subjects of Corea shall not be permitted to import opium into any British port would necessitate a legislative enactment on the part of the Imperial Parliament, and the Committee is unable to understand how the prohibition, declared in the second clause, against the engagement of foreign vessels other than British, is to be enforced, or offenders against it are to be punished, by any legislation which it is possible to devise on the part of the British Government.

Article VIII.—In the second clause, instead of the words "shall be confiscated," the Committee for the reason already given in the case of vessels charged with offences, suggests the insertion of "may be seized, and shall be liable to confiscation, on satisfactory proof of intention to evade the prohibition being furnished to the British authorities."

Article IX.—To the first clause there should be added: "Fire-arms and ammunition for sporting purposes or for purposes of self-defence may be imported under special permits describing the quantity, value, and object of introduction."

Article X.—In the second clause, after the words "local authorities," the words "on being satisfied as to the justice of the charge made" should be inserted.

Article XII, while admitting that the Treaty is "incomplete in its provisions," nevertheless stipulates that it shall remain in force for five years. The Treaty with Japan provides that the "Regulations under which Japanese trade is to be conducted" may be "revised whenever it may be found necessary by Commissions appointed by each country," and a similar stipulation is to be found in the Chinese "Regulations." The Committee is of opinion that the term of five years, as arranged by the British Treaty, would not be too long, provided that the covenants and engagements entered into on either side should be drawn up with carefulness and completeness by experienced negotiators.

Article XIII does not provide as to whether the English or Chinese text of the Treaty is to be accepted in the event of a dispute as to the proper meaning of its provisions. The Committee suggests an addition to this clause of "the English version is to be considered the accepted text in case of dispute."

Article XIV.—The Committee regards the qualification of the ordinary "favoured nation clause," admitted by this Article in its last lines, with great distrust. Under that qualification the provisions of all Treaties with Corea will be liable to be set aside, or rendered nugatory, by the grant to one foreign nation of favourable conditions, in which it may be specially interested, in exchange for nominal concessions in which it has no interest at all, but which may be of vital importance to the trade of other countries having Treaties with Corea. This qualification, if yielded to Corea, will probably be demanded by China and Japan, and be made use of in forcing the policy of the British Government in relation to the Treaties with these Powers to an extent which may not at present be foreseen.

The objection to this Article, as not being retrospective in its operation, has been already alluded to, and the Committee feels confident that Her Majesty's government will not permit British subjects trading with Corea, or residing in the country, to be placed under disabilities from which natives of China and Japan are exempted.

No stipulation is to be found in the Treaty as to the currency in which commercial operations are to be carried on, or in which duties are to be paid, and no provision is made for drawing up a detailed Tariff of duties. No mention is made of any regulations as to the standard weights and measures to be used in trade between foreigners and natives.

The Committee desires to refer to the great importance of the issues which are at stake as its apology to your Lordship for the length at which the provisions of the Treaty have been examined in this communication, and does not seek to disguise its expectation that sufficient cause has been shown why Her Majesty's Government should be asked to refuse ratification of that document in its present shape.

The Committee trusts that your Lordship will use the authority and influence of Great Britain to secure beyond question the recognition of the national independence of the Corean Kingdom, which is obviously threatened by the recent high-handed declarations and proceedings of the Chinese officials, and will depute an experienced Diplomatic Representative to reopen communications with the Corean Government. It should not be difficult, in the Light of the experience gained in China and Japan, to draw up an amended Treaty, under the wise and well-considered provisions of which not only would the people of Corea be admitted to the benefits of free commercial intercourse with the rest of the world, and their rights and interests be fully protected, but the trade of the United Kingdom with that country would be promoted and be placed on an equality of privilege with that enjoyed by other nations.

I have, &c.

(Signed)　　F. BULKELEY JOHNSON, Chairman

H.S. Parkes (1883. 3. 24) ➜ G.L.G. Granville (1883. 5. 8)

Willes의 지시에 따른 *Moorhen*과 *Darling*의 임무 교대 보고

Sir H.S. Parkes to Earl Granville.— (Received May 8)

(No. 39)
My Lord,

Tôkiô, March 24, 1883

IN continuation of my despatch No. 33 of the 9th instant, reporting that Vice-Admiral Willes had kindly met my request in respect to the prompt conveyance of Mr. Aston in Her Majesty's ship "Moorhen" to Corea, I now beg to add a copy of a letter in which I acknowledge the Vice-Admiral's despatch of the 28th February, and explained to him the grounds which rendered it advisable that Mr. Aston should proceed there without delay.

The Commander of Her Majesty's ship "Daring" has now informed me that he has been instructed by Vice-Admiral Willes to proceed to Jinchuen (or Chemulpho) to relieve Her Majesty's ship "Moorhen" of the duty in which she is now engaged, and this arrangement will afford me the opportunity I had desired of maintaining communication with Mr. Aston.

The "Moorhen" having been detained by bad weather at Nagasaki did not leave that port until the 17th instant, and Mr. Aston and his party of Corean functionaries probably arrived at Chemulpho on the 20th instant. The "Daring," leaving here to-morrow, may be expected to arrive there on the 5th proximo.

I have, &c.
(Signed) HARRY S. PARKES

Inclosure

Sir H.S. Parkes to Vice-Admiral Willes.

Sir,

Tôkiô, March 10, 1883

ON the 4th instant I had the honour to address your Excellency the following telegram:—

"'Daring' cannot be repaired and reach Nagasaki before the 28th (instant), or possibly later. Aston can be there by the 14th. There are now important additional reasons for dispatching him promptly; (I) strongly recommend that 'Moorhen' should proceed with him. If you approve, (she) might subsequently be replaced by 'Daring.'"

On the evening of the 5th I received from your Excellency the following reply:—

"In consequence of urgency 'Moorhen' at your disposal. 'Daring' was supposed to be ready for the 14th."

I now beg to return my best thanks to your Excellency for having so kindly met my wishes in this respect.

In explanation of my desire that the departure of Mr. Aston should not be delayed until the "Daring" was ready to proceed with him, I should observe that, as the authorities and workmen of the Yokosuka Dockyard cannot be relied on for dispatch, the date of the completion of the repairs was attended with some uncertainty; that on receipt of your Excellency's telegram of the 23rd ultimo, informing me that the "Daring" would convey Mr. Aston to Corea "when he was ready," I had at once relieved him of the charge of his Consulate, and he had consequently left Kobé; and that I had also arranged for his being accompanied by two high Corean functionaries who were then on the point of leaving Tôkiô, and who will now join him at Nagasaki, and proceed with him in the "Moorhen." I had also to consider that the value of the information which Mr. Aston will obtain in Corea, on other points that those connected with the selection of Consular sites, will be in proportion to the promptness with which it is gained.

I have now the honour to acknowledge the receipt of your Excellency's despatch of the 28th instant. I have fully explained to Commander Eliott the nature of the assistance I wish Mr. Aston to receive, and he has been so good as to show me his orders of the 7th instant to the Commander of Her Majesty's ship "Moorhen," which are entirely in accordance with my wishes.

The distance of the Jinchuen or Chemulpho anchorage from the capital, to which Mr. Aston will endeavour to proceed, and the indecision and delay of the Corean authorities which he will probably have to encounter, render it impossible for me to estimate the length of time he may be detained in Corea, but I am satisfied that he will not protract his stay there longer than is absolutely necessary.

I can clearly understand from your Excellency's despatch that Mr. Aston cannot be conveyed nearer to the capital than Jinchuen in Her Majesty's ship, but your Excellency will, I trust, permit me to mention that that anchorage appears to be free from ice throughout the winter. It was formally opened to Japanese trade on the 1st January last, and Japanese ships of war and merchantmen, and I understand Chinese vessels also, have been going there since that date.

I am further reminded that the Japanese Expedition, consisting of eight or ten vessels, which was sent to Corea in 1876, proceeded to Jinchuen in the month of January of that year, and the Treaty which occupied a month in negotiation was signed on the 26th February.

I have, &c.

(Signed)　　HARRY S. PARKES

131

H.S. Parkes (1883. 4. 7) ⇒ G.L.G. Granville (1883. 5. 23)

조선 광산 탐측 결과 보고

Sir H.S. Parkes to Earl Granville.—(Received May 23)

(No. 48)

Tôkiô, April 7, 1883

My Lord,

I HAVE the honour to inclose two Reports on Corean mines, one by the enterprising Chinese Tong-king-sing, and the other by the Corean officer who accompanied him in a tour he lately made in Corea for the purpose of mine prospection.

The tour having been undertaken in the depths of winter, was conducted under disadvantageous circumstances. Numerous veins of various ores appear to have been observed and superficially examined, but it is important to notice that the explorers failed to discover any deposits of coal. The views of Mr. Tong-king-sing as to the wisdom of encouraging industrial enterprise by means of mines and railways are interesting as coming from a Chinese, and though, to judge from these Reports, the working of Corean minerals does not give promise of high remuneration, his disposition to secure a monopoly of that interest to his own country may not be discouraged by his powerful patron, Li Hung-chang.

I have, &c.

(Signed) HARRY S. PARKES

Inclosure 1

Report of the Corean Officer who escorted Mr. Tong-king-sing and party on an Expedition with the object of investigating Mines.

(Translation)

ON the 24th day of the 11th month of the year of the "Horse" (January 3, 1883) I received instructions, and at 4 o'clock in the afternoon of the same day, having changed my dress, I left secretly by the eastern side gate, taking with me five officials. I travelled 10 miles, and then, as the evening was far advanced, I stopped at an inn for the night. The foreigners (*lit.* the party of those other fellows) had arrived beforehand. We were supplied with refreshment by the local official, the Governor of Yang-shin. The official attendants guarded the apartments of "those other fellows," and, remaining on duty in the vicinity during the night, kept watch against anything unusual which might happen. During the day some went ahead and some followed in the rear so as to prevent any disturbance along the road.

On the 25th I went 17 miles, and took my midday meal at Song-thang-chang. Starting again, I went 6 miles, and stopped for the night at An-chön. The local officials of the Pho-chhön Ken supplied us with refreshment.

Starting early on the 26th I went about 2 miles. The road was skirted on each side by a big river, and boulders polished by contact with the water were strewed in every direction. The Englishman got out of his chair and walked quietly along with his head bent down. He appeared to be looking for something on the bank of the river, and picked up several small pebbles. These he struck with an iron hammer, listened to the sound, and then threw them away. He selected one kind of pebble, and he and Tong-king-sing exchanged specimens of this and examined them alternately. They laughed and talked, and I inferred from their excitement that the stones indicated the probable existence of gold in that place. They then got into their chairs and proceeded some 5 miles, reaching a place called Mansé-kyo-chöm, in the Yöng-phyöng district. About half-a-mile to the east of Mansé-kyo-chöm there is a green peak. It is very precipitous, and a mass of rock; it is called Keum-chin-san. A vein of stone also appears at the foot of the mountain. In some places the colour of the stone is red, in others green; this is said to be copper ore in its primitive condition. In the 4th or 5th month of this year Tha-hoing-kwan went there with several hundred soldiers and made extensive workings in the mine. He extracted and smelted the ore, but no copper was produced. After spending much money, with no result, he relinquished the undertaking. The mining engineer went to the spot and, striking a light, entered the mine; he broke off and brought out pieces of stone which sparkled. These he examined carefully with a glass, and said, "This one contains silver, copper, iron, and sulphur, and the quality is very good. It is truly a national treasure. It is a pity that the people of the country do not know how to make use of it, and that they only succeed in wasting their resources."

Proceeding on for 6 miles we stopped at a place in the Yŏng-phyŏng district. In the engineer's baggage there were, amongst other things, an iron furnance and a kettle. In the night he lighted a fire in the furnace and put into it about a *sho* weight of stone taken from Kim-chin-san. In a short time the ore was melted, and silver was produced; the weight of silver thus extracted was one or two *sen*. Both of them were very pleased.

At daylight on the 27th I met Tong-king-sing and Mr. Burnett, and expressed to them the sentiments of my Sovereign. I said, "His illustrious Majesty appreciates the exertions made by both of you great men in coming here from so great a distance at this inclement season of the year. I have been instructed to make inquiries after your health, and have therefore come to act as your escort, and to guard against the occurrence of any disturbances on the road." Both were very pleased, and made profuse acknowledgments and thanks. Staring early, we proceeded 3 miles from Yŏng-phyŏng in an easterly direction, and reached a place called Pha-su-tong. Lime is produced here. The mining engineer examined the quality. From Pha-su-tong we proceeded 3 miles in a south-easterly direction; high rocks flanked the road like a wall on each side. The path was rocky and winding, and there was an abundance of ice and snow. The party (of foreigners) went on foot. In a precipitous gully there was a solitary village called San-nai-chi. There was a shop for the sale of iron at foot of the hills. It is said that in the summer of this year a north-countryman came to this place, and was the first to discover trace of iron. He worked the mine and obtained iron from it. The mine is at the top of the mountain in a very precipitous place. The engineer entered the mine and examined the opening; he took measurements, and stated that the vein of iron was very narrow. He added that the production would not be very great, but it was of some value. We then descended the mountain, and, turning to the west, followed a winding road for some 16 miles, stopping for the night at the town of Phung-chhŏn. The officials of the Chhŏl-wŏn Fu provided for our wants.

On the 28th day we went a distance of 16 miles, and stopped at Kim-hwa-ken.

On the 29th, starting early, we proceeded to the eastward along a small road for about 7 miles, and reached Sampha-ri. In a willow-tree valley (or Yang-kok) there is an iron mine. The people in the neighbourhood have opened shops and smelted the iron ore for many years past. The depth of the mine (existing workings) is about 80 or 90 feet. The engineer entered the opening of the mine and examined the ore; he pronounced it to be of good quality. From this valley of willows (or Yang-kok) we proceeded about a mile, and reached a place called Ri-sil-tong. In the summer of this year Tha-hoing-kwang brought soldiers with him to this place, and opened up more than forty mines. The depth of the openings thus made varied from between 30 and 40 feet to between 50 and 60 feet. The veins of copper became thicker as the work progressed, and more prominent, but the resources for working the mines were small, and the undertaking was stopped. The soldiers, however, stayed on the spot, waiting for the time when operations would be recommenced. The engineer took some of the copper ore, pounded it into small pieces in a mortar, and then put into a glass bottle. The bottle was 4 or 5 inches long and about as thick as a man's thumb. He put a preparation into the bottle and then warmed it over a fire; he added a little more of the preparation and heated it again over the fire. The ore gradually melted into a liquid substance of a green colour. He then put into the bottle some other preparation, what it was I do not know, but the colour of the contents of the bottle became much deeper; he then said, "Good, good." We next proceeded 12 miles in a northerly direction from Ri-sil-tong, and stopped at Kim-söng. The Kenrei* of this Prefecture came out to meet us, and saw the two foreigners. In his interview with them he entered into very precise details, and was very polite.

  We left Kim-söng early in the morning, and went 10 miles in a westerly direction by a small road. We took our midday meal at Sim-hyöp; there is a village called Hyn-an. We proceeded 7 miles to the north of Hyn-an. The road was very narrow and precipitous; we stopped the night at a shop for the sale of lead; the place is called So-kok. The General residing in the mountain Paik-hak-san, called Kim-hakkeum, opened shops here and sold lead. The soldiers brought lead ore from Tang-hyöng to this place, where it was smelted.

  The people of the district, hearing that the appearance and dress of foreigners were different from that of Coreans, flocked to see them in crowds. In all the villages we passed through the streets were blocked with people, who stared at the foreigners, but the latter were not alarmed at the demonstration.

---

*[원주] Han-chhang-yang

Some of us, concealing our identity, mingled with the crowd of sightseers, in order to learn their feelings and to hear what they said. We found that, though the suspicions of the people were excited, there was no reason to apprehend any improper behaviour. An old man addressed the crowd, explaining to them the necessities of the times. He said, "The various Western countries in Europe have powerful armies, and they are clever in arts. They travel thousands of miles round the globe, both for pleasure and for commercial profit, like tigers on the crouch and wolves on the prowl. China, again, is an immense country, with great warlike resources, and it is impossible to resist her. We must, therefore, remove the interdict by sea altogether, and, concluding Treaties, enter into commercial relations with other countries. We must endeavour to understand the changes in the dispensation of Heaven, and in the affairs of men. How can such a small country as Corea preserve an independent attitude, and alone and unaided defend her frontiers against foreign encroachments? We must alter our national policy. Our Sovereign is wise and knows all the affairs of the country. He has established friendly relations with Japan, and has permitted the promotion of similar relations with the Western Powers. He understands how to inaugurate modern reforms based on the wisdom of the past; how to lay aside what is useless amongst Corean customs in exchange for advantageous methods borrowed from foreign countries. By the adoption of Western systems of drill the army will be made strong; by the development of the mines the country will become rich; by respecting international law foreign countries will be prevented from attacking Corea just as they please, and the nation will thus enjoy lasting peace. An official and a commercial mining expert have accordingly been allowed to travel through the country. This is a custom common to all countries, and need not therefore cause either alarm or suspicion. Be tranquil, and exhort each other to behave properly." The misconceptions of many were corrected by this address.

On the 1st December Tong-king-sing remained in the lead-shop, and the rest of the party went on towards Tang-hyŏng. The mountains were high, their tops reaching into the heavens. The road was very steep and slippery with ice, so that it was difficult to secure a foothold, and there were many falls. We proceeded 3 miles, and having traversed the mountain ridge descended, arriving at the place called Tang-hyŏng. The lead mine has two openings, one goes down straight to a depth of several hundred feet, and from this numerous side-workings branch off. The other descends straight for about 800 feet, and from this also numerous side-workings branch off, following the direction of the veins of ore. Some of these, it is said, extend to a distance of 1½ to 2 miles. The engineer and all of us took off our hats and clothes and entered the mine with lights. We descended only some 500 feet, when the air began to be exhausted and noxious vapours rose from the soil; we all felt unwell and began to perspire and choke for want of air. The engineer was afraid, and as we found it impossible to penetrate further into the mine we came out. We caused the soldiers to fetch a great many pieces of ore out of the mine, and then returned to the lead-shop. The engineer asked the General who sold the lead, how much lead was extracted from the mine every day. The General replied that the workings were deep, and it was therefore difficult to extract the ore; the amount of lead obtained in one day was about 30 or 40 *kin*.* The engineer laughed and said, "It would not be that under my system. I should place several thousand *kin* of gunpowder in the furthest depths of the workings, and explode the powder by means of a slow-match. The mountain would be rent asunder, the rocks split in fragments, and the daily yield after this operation would be several thousand *kin* of lead." He appeared to be telling the truth, but his hearers would not, for all that, believe him. There is also a copper mine in this place, So-kok, which was opened in the summer of this year. It lies, however, in a very deep glen, and we were unable therefore to visit it, for the evening began to set in, and we returned to Hyn-an, where we passed the night. That evening we melted the lead ore and tested the quality of the silver.

 On the 2nd we left Hyn-an and went eastward for 5 miles. We arrived at Chhang-dô and saw a sulphur deposit. The country skirting the river for some 3 miles was rich in sulphur. We struck southwards, and followed a steep mountain-road for about 9 miles. After crossing a lofty ridge we descended to a place called Chong-rô, where there is a copper mine with two openings. Each of these is deep, extending over 100 feet. We examined some of the ore we took from the mine, and found it to be of a bright green colour. We then went 1½ miles in a westerly direction, and stopped the night at Chök-mokri, on the borders of Kim-söng. That evening we tested the copper of Chong-rô, and the engineer pronounced the quality good.

 On the 3rd we went 18 miles in a south-westerly direction from Chök-mok-ri, and had our midday meal at the town of Lu-un. We proceeded 5 miles, and stopped the night at Chu-pha-chöm, on the borders of Kim-söng.

---

*[원주] 40 to 53 lbs.

On the 5th we left Rang-chhön and went 7 miles, reaching a place called Wön-chhön. Lime is produced here. We then went on another 7 miles, and crossing the Mu-chin-kang River, took our midday meal at the town of In-ram. Officials of the Chhun-chhön Prefecture visited us and provided for our wants. We then proceeded some 13 miles, and crossing the So-yang-kang River, stayed for the night at the village of Chhun-chhön.

On the 6th we went 10 miles, and took our midday meal at the town of Wön-chhang. Officials of the Chhun-chhön Prefecture met us and provided for our wants. They treated the foreigners with much courtesy. We proceeded 13 miles, and stopped the night in the Hong-chhön Ken. The chief magistrate (or Governor), Sü-ha-sun, of this Ken, visited the two foreigners.

On the 7th we started from the village of Hong-chhön and went eastward 19 miles, reaching a place called Phyöng-chhön. On the top of the mountains there is a vein of lead. Workings were begun here, it is said, this spring, but were abandoned. The engineer examined the ore, and said, "Bad iron is mixed with the lead; the ore is worthless." We went on 1 mile, and stayed the night at Chhön-kam-ri.

On the 8th we left Chhön-kam-ri, and went back some 16 miles to the village of Hong-chhön, where we had our midday meal. From there we went 10 miles, and stayed the night at Yang-tök-wön.

Sixteen miles to the east of Hong-chhön, at Chhön-kam-ri, and 3 miles to the west, at O-ri-tong, we were informed that much iron is produced. The two foreigners, hearing this, said it was not extraordinary. "But," they added, "at Chhim-to, Yöng-phyöng, Kim-hwa, and Kim-söng there are copper and iron mines which will bear working for the next thirty years, so that it is useless to explore fresh places."

One and a-half miles from Yang-tök-wön there is a place called Ha-kwa-u, and 3 miles from the same place there is a place called Sang-kwa-u. At both these places gold is produced. During the summer of this year we were told that the mines were opened and gold extracted. The mining implements, we heard, had been left on the spot. The foreigners, however, did not care to visit these places, so the country people were made to bring specimens of the ore from those mines. These were packed away in the baggage for examination after our return to the capital.

Western people consider copper, iron, lead, and coal as very profitable things; gold and silver they regard as inferior to these, and they do not, therefore, concern themselves much about them. When they are in the vicinity of copper and iron mines they look at the colour of the stone in the geological formation and examine the nature of it; and they are so clever at drawing their conclusions as to the value of the minerals in these places that they can tell what the ores are before they are extracted from the mines. It is impossible to say how many mines there were in the districts we passed through, but we saw no actual traces of valuable places having been discovered. Copper and iron exist, but as there is no coal they are useless. We regretted our failure to find coal during this journey.

On the 9th we went 13 miles, and took our midday meal at Kwang-thang. The Governor of the Chi-phyöng-ken, Sin-yang-wön, came to meet us, and had an interview with the two foreigners. We proceeded 17 miles, and stayed the night in the district of Yang-hyöng. The district Governor, Ri-wi, came to see us.

On the 10th we went 17 miles, and took our midday meal at the town of Po-an, on the borders of the Province of Kwang. We proceeded 10 miles, and stopped for the night at the town of Phyöng-phai.

On the 11th we proceeded 13 miles, and arrived at the capital.

Inclosure 2

Record by Mr. Tong-t'ing-ch'u (Tong-king-sing) of a trip in the Mountains.

(Translation)

I HAVE prepared the following abbreviated account of towns and mines which I have visited, and I send it for your perusal.

On the 14th November I went to the Prefecture of Kang-hwa, and on the 21st returned to the capital. While in Kang-hwa I visited the various mountains to the south and west of the Castle. On the mountain Mah-tal-san, to the south of the Castle, I observed gold-speckled stone. The country-people said it was gold ore, but in reality it was worthless. There is a mine of loadstone on the mountain Ko-ryo-san. The stone is very good. The iron could be made into steel by forging. Unfortunately the snow lay so thick on the mountain that I was unable to ascertain the depth of the mine-opening. There were two graves at the mouth of opening into the mine. If this mine be worked at some future time these graves will have to be removed to some other spot selected for the purpose.

On the 24th I went north, and on the 26th visited the copper mine in the mountain of Kim-chu-san, at the village of Yŏng-phyŏng-eup. The ore is very good. There is a small river 2 miles from the mine, so that it is easy to obtain water.

On the 27th I was at Chang-ka-ku, a place to the east of Kim-chu-san, and inspected some iron ore, of which the colour was that of the palmetto. The quality of the ore is very good. The vein of the ore in this mine is about 6 feet wide, and extends in a crooked direction about half-way up along the side of the mountain. By opening a boring at the foot of the mountain the ore could be easily extracted.

On the 29th I was at a place about 1 mile from Kim-hwa-eup, where I saw some iron mines. The colour of the stone was blue (or green), and the quality very good. Again, at Ri-sil-tong, in this village I saw two copper mines, but the same vein is being probably worked in each mine. These mines appear to be richer than that of Kim-chu-san, and the quality of the ore is even better.

On the 30th I went to Hyn-am, in Kim-sŏng. It snowed very hard that day. The hills were some 200 feet high, and it was impossible to climb up them.

On the 1st December I ascended the hills and saw some lead ore. The opening into the mine was some thousand feet deep. On inspecting some of the ore I found that it was not very rich in lead. Fortunately, however, in every 100 *riyô* weight of ore there is silver to the value of 2 *sen* (or 2 per *mil*). I will make a further assay of it.

Three miles south of Kim-sŏng there is a place called Ma-hoi-tong, where [_____] is placed.

On the 2nd I went to Chhang-do, to the east of Kim-sŏng, and saw a mine of sulphur. On looking at some specimens I found they were iron sulphur. This might be used for [_____] I was also at Eul-kai-tong and in Chong-ro, and saw there a copper mine. This may be said to be equal to the mine of Kim-hwa.

On the 3rd December I reached Rang-chhŏn from Chang-do. In the hills I passed through I was on all sides [_____] (a kind of stone), from which tiles can be made.

On the 5th I was at a place 3 miles from Rang-chhŏn, where I saw [_____] (a kind of white marble), which could be used for making the tops of tables.

On the 7th I visited a mine 17 miles east of Hong-chhön, called by the country-people a silver mine. On inspecting the ore I found it to be [＿＿＿] (a kind of hard lead). The quality of the ore was not good.

On the 8th I visited Chhöng-kam-ri, a place 150 miles to the east of this village. The iron (in a mine there) in quality was like that of mine at Yong-phyöng-eup.

On the 11th I returned to the capital. My trip had lasted one month. I had travelled through more than ten *fu* and *ken*, and found those districts very mountainous. All the mountains were covered with a kind of stone, in which gold, silver, copper, iron, and lead are found, and which is never found in the same place as coal. The district of Hong-chhöng certainly appears not to be one in which there is coal. A minute examination of the map (of Corea) shows that the country in the three circuits, Hwang-hai-do, Chöl-la-do, and Kyöng-sang-do, is flat almost throughout, and therefore it is not probable that there are any places which produce coal. It may be well to make another investigation next year.

Corea is mostly mountainous, and there is little flat country. The agriculturists consequently find cultivation difficult. The population increases every day, however, and there is no other industry for them to follow. It is well, therefore, to take precautions in time, and to remove the interdict (on trade) by sea, and thus extend the means of earning a livelihood, open up the mines, and thus provide for the wants of the country. This, being the means by which the country can be made rich and powerful, is a most urgent matter. I have travelled twenty days, and have seen more than ten mines. Copper and iron are mostly the produce of these mines, and there was clear evidence of the good quality of the ore. The four iron mines I saw at Kang-hwa, Yöng-phyöng, Kim-hwa, Höng-chhön, and the three copper mines at Kim-chu, Ri-sil-tong, and Eul-kai-tong, could, I think, be worked certainly for a hundred years. There are several other mines in the vicinity which the country-people either knew about but would not show me, or did not even know of. If these good mines are left to the working of the country-people, who follow with reverence ancient methods, and never change their system of work, no profit will be seen. The local system of obtaining ore from a mine is to do first what is easiest, and leave to the last what is difficult. They dig away at the mine, and the hole gets gradually deeper, but there is no ventilation, and no means of furnishing a light; there are many springs which discharge water (into the workings), and no appliances for getting rid of this water. If the mine is under these circumstances abandoned, the capital put into it is lost; while, on the other hand, it can only be worked at risk of life. No profit can thus be made out of these mines under the local method of working them. If, however, machinery is employed, and in other respects the mines are worked according to modern methods, the difficulties of light and water will be avoided, the miners can work as they please, the workings will be developed, the number of men employed will increase, and more and more ore will be extracted from the mine. Under this system the hardest is put first and the easiest last. If modern methods are followed, much capital will be required for the erection of foreign machinery, and, in employing foreign artizans, care must be taken to select good men. Japanese furnaces for forging iron are used (by the country-people), but they are useless. They engage as workmen coal miners who work the coal mines at Ho-puk, but no practical results are visible. They ought to take warning by these failures. Therefore, although there is plenty of ore in the mines in the various Prefectures, there is no coal to be obtained in the vicinity of the mines which can be used for the purpose of smelting the ore; and, moreover, as the ore is found in lofty and steep mountain ranges, it is not easy to transport it.

The working of the mines of Corea is not only attended with more difficulties than the working of mines in foreign countries, but it is even more difficult than it is in China. Railways are the only means of overcoming these difficulties. The construction of railways and the opening of mines are two things which necessarily go together; railways are constructed in consequence of the opening of mines, and the ore, when extracted, is transported by means of the railways. When there is no coal in a country which produces the five metals (*i.e.*, gold, silver, copper, iron, and lead), either the ore must be transported to where the coal is, or the latter must be taken to the latter mines. One of the two things must be done.

In working the various five metal mines, the first thing to be done is to look for places where there is coal; the second is to construct connecting lines of railways. Both are essential. To carry out these three objects, many millions of *riyô* (taels) will be required. If these undertakings were all carried out with enthusiasm, not only would all the mines in the various circuits be opened up, but railways would be gradually extended throughout the country, as far as Wŏnsan in the north and Pusan in the south, and it would thus be the most effectual means of securing the wealth and strength of the country.

It is now six years since I, Tong-t'ing-ch'u, have been charged by the Office with the duty of exploring mines in China, and now for the first time practical results have shown themselves. I have at present been actually selected for this work by a majority of merchants, and have investigated various coal, iron, copper, and lead mines in An-hwai. Already 31,000 *riyô* (taels) have been collected as capital, and it has been decided that I shall go to England in the ensuing spring, and, having obtained machinery, return to Peking, taking with me foreign artizans as employés, and make the necessary arrangements. If it be considered that Corean mines and railways are urgent matters, and should be proceeded with at once, I beg that a decision may be arrived at in respect to the two methods of work hereinafter mentioned.

With regard to the rules of the merchants' Association, and the regulations affecting mines and railroads, I await the decision of the Head Office before doing anything. In drawing up the rules and regulations, reference will be made to the regulations of great Western countries on this subject, and I shall give them careful consideration.

1. Merchants have unrestricted control of all mines throughout the world, and no limit of time is assigned to this control. Matters affecting mines in Corea should be placed under the control of Corean merchants, subject to the payment or not of certain taxes to the Government. If the Corean Government assumes control over the mines, they should be responsible for loss or profit. If I, Tong-t'ing-ch'u, am instructed to buy machinery and to engage Chinese and foreign skilled workmen, I will give my assistance as requested.

2. Corea was formerly a part of China, and cannot be regarded in the same light as other foreign countries. Should the mines in the various circuits be placed under the control of the merchants, and should there be at the time no one to assume the management of the undertaking as Head Director, I, Tong-t'ing-ch'u, will apply for this post, and (having obtained it) I will allow both Corean officials and Corean private individuals to become shareholders; and, should there be still a deficiency in the number of shareholders, I will make arrangements for the admission of Chinese as shareholders on the same terms as to profit as the Coreans. With regard to the lands (the locality in which a mine is situated) to be obtained, the value will be estimated, and it will either be paid to the proprietors or they can receive the value of the lands in shares, according as they may wish.

Ampthill (1883. 4. 10) ➜ G.L.G. Granville (1883. 4. 12)

조독조약 비준 연기를 알리는 Bismarck의 통지 보고

Lord Ampthill to Earl Granville.—(Received April 12)

(No. 126)

Berlin, April 10, 1883

My Lord,

WITH reference to my despatch No. 110 of the 29th ultimo and to previous correspondence respecting the Anglo-Corean Treaty, signed by Admiral Willes on the 6th June last, I have the honour to inclose translation of a note which I have received from his Highness Prince Bismarck, explaining the views of the Imperial Government on the recent negotiations with that kingdom.

The Chancellor states that, in the opinion of the Imperial Government, the recent Treaties concluded with Corea are less favourable than those existing with the neighbouring countries of China and Japan, and considers it probable that the United States' Government will formally ignore the question of suzerainty between China and Corea, on the ground that the United States only conclude Treaties with independent States, and will therefore, by virtue of their most-favoured-nation clause, claim the concessions made to China by Corea.

The German Government would, under these circumstances, prefer to postpone the ratification of the German Corean Treaty until it is seen whether, in virtue of their most-favoured-nation clause, the Americans will obtain the benefits of the concessions granted to the Chinese; and, should difficulties arise on this point, the Imperial Government would then enter into negotiations for adequate supplementary Articles.

Or they would be willing to follow the example of Her Majesty's Government in laying the Treaty before Parliament, should such a course be ultimately decided on, provided it be understood that the exchange of the ratifications could only be carried out if the Government succeeded beforehand in removing the doubts as to the interpretation of the existing Treaties either by the conclusion of adequate supplementary Articles, or by a Declaration binding the Corean Government so to interpret the most-favoured-nation clause as to include the concessions made to the Chinese.

I would venture to call your Lordship's attention to the concluding paragraphs of his Highness' note, with regard to the proposed mission of an English official to Corea to reopen negotiations with that country, which would appear to have been referred to by our Lordship in conversation with Count Münster.

Prince Bismarck expresses an earnest desire to be informed whether Her Majesty's Government still hold to their intention, and if so, in what manner they propose to carry it out.

I have, &c.
(Signed) AMPTHILL

Inclosure 1

Prince Bismarck to Lord Amphill.

Foreign Office, Berlin, April 7, 1883

(Translation)

THE Undersigned, Chancellor of the Empire, has the honour to give the following answer to the communications of the 4th, 16th, and 23rd ultimo, from his Excellency Lord Ampthill, &c., &c., respecting the Treaties with Corea.

The Imperial Government recognizes the justice of the essential doubts expressed by the several Chambers of Commerce in Eastern Asia as regards the tenour of the Treaties concluded with Corea in the summer of last year. These Treaties are, as regards matters of commerce, navigation, settlement and Consular relations, less favourable than the existing Treaties with China and Japan, and in their concessions to Corea exceed the limit which has been set down as acceptable in the negotiations for the revision of the Treaties with China and Japan.

It must be especially remarked that the impediment, which the exclusion from the coasting trade and the high customs rates will cause to the development of European trade with Corea, will become still greater if the concessions obtained by China in its agreements with Corea of October last should be refused to other Treaty Powers. So long as there is a doubt upon this point, the Imperial Government would only unwillingly decide to lay the German-Corean Treaty of the 30th June last before the Bundersrath and the Reichstag for their assent.

As the Treaty between the United States of America and Corea has been already ratified, and the documents of ratification must be exchanged by the 22nd May next, the Imperial Minister at Washington was, in consequence of his Excellency Lord Ampthill's note of the 4th ultimo, instructed to ascertain whether America would, by virtue of the most-favoured-nation clause, claim the concessions made to China by Corea. Herr von Eisendecher was informed that the American Envoy named to Corea had been instructed to report fully, at once, upon the trade privileges conceded to the Chinese, and that the United States would probably claim equal rights.

It may be assumed from former reports that the United States will formally ignore the question of suzerainty between China and Corea, as America only concludes Treaties with independent States.

Under these circumstances, the Imperial Government considers it advisable, in the first place, to postpone, still further the ratification of the German-Corean Treaty, and to take into consideration the prolongation of the period, which will expire on the 30th June next, within which the ratifications must be exchanged. Should America meet with difficulties in the attempt to obtain the benefits of the most-favoured-nation clause from the China-Corean Agreements, it would be all the more necessary to try to remove the essential doubts as to the advisability of ratifying the Treaty of the 30th June last by entering into negotiations for adequate supplementary Articles.

In the second place the Imperial Government would follow the example of the Government of Great Britain, if the latter should decide to lay the Anglo-Corean Treaty before Parliament in its present form, in spite of the essential doubts as to the advisability of its ratification, which they have recognized; the Imperial Government would, however, in this case consider it advisable that it should be distinctly understood that the exchange of ratifications would only be carried out if the Government could succeed beforehand in removing the essential doubts as to the Treaties, either by the conclusion of adequate supplementary Articles, or by a binding Declaration by the Corean Government, that the most-favoured-nation clause extended to the concessions made to the Chinese.

The undersigned has learnt, from the Reports of the Imperial Ambassador in London of his conversations with Lord Granville and his representatives, that the Government of Great Britain had a short time ago taken into consideration the advisability of sending an English official in Eastern Asia to Corea to reopen negotiations.

It would be of great value, as regards the decision of the German Government, to learn whether the British Government still have this intention, and, if so, in what manner they mean to carry it out.

The Undersigned would be especially grateful if His Excellency the Ambassador would inform him of the decisions of his Government on the above-mentioned points.

Meanwhile, he avails, &c.

(Signed)   v. BISMARCK

閔泳穆(1883. 4. 12/高宗二十年三月六日) ➜ H.S. Parkes

공관부지 선정 및 공법 준수요청에 대한 회신

癸未三月初六日

大朝鮮督辦交涉通商事務閔 謹覆書大英國特命全權駐劄日本東京大臣巴閣下 阿君來 奉手書及譯本謹悉 來敎有以公允相待 平均無異 爲不易之公法 敢不奉以周旋 無有失墜 所有京城及各港口通商界內 應擇形便 爲將來批約後 貴國官商居住之地 謹當遵照已訂約章 並遵均平相待之道 無使厚此薄彼 有違尊敎 讀來函 又有與淸國所訂通商約款云云 由阿君晤語 得以少窺緖論 除已面答阿君外 敢此肅覆 恭請崇安

泳穆 頓首

H.S. Parkes (1883. 4. 20) ➜ G.L.G. Granville (1883. 6. 4)

Darling 함장 Eliott의 해임 경위 보고

Sir H.S. Parkes to Earl Granville.—(Received June 4)

(No. 58)

Tôkiô, April 20, 1883

My Lord,

IN my despatch No. 49 of the 13th instant I reported to your Lordship that Vice-Admiral Willes had ordered Commander Eliott to proceed with the "Daring," the ship under his command, to Corea to relieve the "Moorhen," which had conveyed Mr. Aston there, that I had thanked the Vice-Admiral for having afforded me this opportunity of communicating with Mr. Aston, and that I had requested Commander Eliott to receive my despatches for Mr. Aston at Nagasaki, at which port I understood he would have to call in order to fill up with coal.

For convenience of reference, I beg again to inclose copies of the two letters I inclosed in my previous despatch, one to the Vice-Admiral thanking him for this means of communication with Mr. Aston, the other to Commander Eliott, requesting him to receive my despatches for that officer.

I now greatly regret to have to inform your Lordship that I have received a reply from Vice-Admiral Willes, of which I inclose a copy, stating that by requesting Commander Eliott to visit Nagasaki I had caused him to disobey his (the Admiral's) stringent orders against touching at that port, and that Commander Eliott could have received my letters equally well at Simonoseki, as that port is in the direct route to Jinchuen (Chemulpho). The Admiral adds that Commander Eliott will be removed from the position of Senior Officer in Japan immediately he returns from Corea.

Your Lordship, I feel assured, will readily understand that it has occasioned me much pain to learn that I have been the cause of this severe censure being passed upon that officer, and from a feeling of justice to Commander Eliott, who appears to have been thus punished for complying with a service request of mine of a very simple nature, and also from a sense of the wrong done to myself as Her Majesty's Minister in being thus publicly discredited in making that request, I have felt compelled to address Vice-Admiral Willes the accompanying despatch, in which I have protested against this sentence, and have informed him that I shall appeal against it to your Lordship.

My action, which Vice-Admiral Willes has thus condemned, consists solely in my having requested Commander Eliott to receive at Nagasaki the despatches which I wished to be conveyed to Mr. Aston. In accordance with the Admiral's orders, the "Daring" left Yokohama very suddenly, and I could not have prepared those despatches, for which I required to obtain some information, before she took her departure. This circumstance, however, occasioned me no inconvenience, as I knew that letters forwarded by the Japanese mail-steamer four days after the "Daring" departure would be delivered at Nagasaki, owing to the slower speed of the latter vessel, as soon as she would arrive there. I did not actually request Commander Eliott to visit Nagasaki, because I understood from him that he would be obliged to call at the port for coal, and I had therefore only to beg him (as your Lordship will perceive from my letter) not to leave Nagasaki before the arrival there of my letter for Mr. Aston, which would be sent by the mail-steamer.

But the Vice-Admiral states in his letter to me that, by requesting Commander Eliott to visit Nagasaki, I caused him to disobey his (the Admiral's) stringent orders against his touching at that port. Now, the orders which were shown me by Commander Eliott are those which I inclose, and your Lordship will perceive that they do not contain a word against his touching at Nagasaki. Commander Eliott being absent, I cannot now ascertain whether he had received any further directions than these; but, being thereby instructed to inform me of the nature of his order, he would, I presume, have communicated to me any instructions forbidding him to visit Nagasaki when engaged on this service if he had been in possession of such orders.

Had I been made acquainted with their existence, I should, of course, have respected them, and should in that case have requested Commander Eliott to receive my despatches at Kobê, which would have involved a delay of twenty-four hours (he having left that port on the morning of the 29th March, and the mail-steamer having arrived there on the morning of the 30th). But I named Nagasaki because I understood that the "Daring" must call there for coal. For the same reason I had sent Mr. Aston to Nagasaki to meet the 'Moorhen' and the Admiral in his communications with myself had distinctly approved of the latter vessel going there. Why the "Moorhen" should have been authorized by the Admiral to call at Nagasaki, and the "Daring" "stringently ordered" not to call there, is entirely unknown to me, though, seeing that both these vessels have been sent to Corea to enable me to carry out the instructions I have received from your Lordship, I think that it would not only have been considerate, but right, that the Commander-in-chief should have apprised me of any orders he saw fit to issue for the regulation of the movements of those vessels.

It is not for me to judge of the requirements of Her Majesty's ships in regard to supplies of fuel, and I do not for a moment pretend to do so, but it would surprise me to learn that it was not deemed necessary or judicious for a gun-vessel to fill up with coal at the last available point of departure from Japan after being more than a week at sea (the time occupied by the "Daring" in getting as far on her voyage as Simonoseki, which is about 130 miles distant from Nagasaki), and being bound to a country where coal is wholly unobtainable, and where, in taking up the duties of the "Moorhen," she would have to convey Mr. Aston to one or more ports in that country, which are situated at a considerable distance apart.

I have pointed out in my despatch to the Vice-Admiral that his Excellency is mistaken in stating that Commander Eliott could have received my letters equally well at Simonoseki. I have no right to ask the master of a Japanese mail-steamer to drop letter for me at a Japanese town which is not opened to foreign trade; if he had been willing to take them, he could only have intrusted them to some irresponsible Japanese on passing Simonoseki, and the liability of mistake or misdelivery is in that case obvious. To have placed them in the charge of Japanese officials would have required a correspondence on my part with the Japanese Government, which was also unadvisable. Such a course, indeed, would never have occurred to me, and if I had known that the "Daring" was forbidden to call at Nagasaki I should, as I have already observed, have sent my letter to Kobé.

I greatly regret to have to trouble your Lordship with details of such minor moment, and in particular to have to report that so small a question should have occasioned a misunderstanding between the Commander-in-chief and myself; but the painful position in which I am placed by an act of mine being assigned as the cause of the Senior Naval Officer in this country having been removed from his post will not permit me to accept His Excellency's judgment, as it imposes upon that officer the blame which, if any is due, should fall upon myself. I trust, therefore, that your Lordship will allow the case to be submitted to the consideration of the Lords Commissioners of the Admiralty, and to their decision and that of your Lordship I shall, of course, readily submit. I do not wish to dwell upon the feeling, though it is disadvantageous in the interests of the public service, which I cannot but perceive the Vice-Admiral's action in this matter denotes. As I have observed to the latter in my letter, he has unfavourably construed my proceedings in the only two instances in which, in the execution of a public duty, I have had occasion to seek his co-operation. In the first of these, the visit of Her Majesty's ship "Flying Fish" to Corea in July last, your Lordship was so good as to approve my proceedings by your despatch No. 89 of the 10th October, and I shall also hope to be sustained by your Lordship in the present case. The regret which this misunderstanding causes me is materially increased by the reflection that during the course of my eighteen years' service at this post, during which period I have had the pleasure of being associated with seven Commanders-in-chief prior to the appointment to this command of Vice-Admiral Willes, I have never had a difference with any of those officers, either on public or private grounds, and it is painful to me to find that at this stage of my service I should be exposed to this unpleasant experience.

I have, &c.

(Signed)   HARRY S. PARKES

Inclosure 1

Sir H.S. Parkes to Vice-Admiral Willes.

Tôkiô, March 24, 1883

Sir,

COMMANDER ELIOTT has informed me of the nature of your

orders, dated the 12th instant, in which you direct him to proceed to Jincheun (Chemulpho) to relieve Her Majesty's ship "Moorhen."

I feel that I should thank your Excellency for furnishing me with such a good opportunity of communicating with Mr. Aston, and I inclose a copy of a letter in which I have ventured to request Commander Eliott's assistance in that object.

I have, &c.
(Signed)　HARRY S. PARKES

Inclosure 2

Sir H.S. Parkes to Commander Eliott.

Tôkiô, March 24, 1883

Sir,

I HAVE to thank you for having informed me that you have been instructed by His Excellency the Commander-in-chief to proceed in Her Majesty's ship "Daring," after her defects have been made good, to Jinchuen (Chemulpho), to take up the duty now being performed by Her Majesty's ship "Moorhen," which will then return to Kobé. You have also apprised me that you will be ready to sail to-morrow.

I feel indebted to the Commander-in-chief for an arrangement which enables me to maintain communications with Mr. Aston, and in furtherance of this object I beg to make the following requests:-

1. That you should call at Kobé on your way through the Inland Sea for any letters for Mr. Aston that Her Majesty's Acting Consul at that port may desire to send.

2. That you should not leave Nagasaki before the arrival there of any letters for Mr. Aston, which I shall send under cover to Her Majesty's Acting Consul at that port by the Mitsu Bishi mail-steamer leaving Yokohama on the 28th instant, and which steamer will probably arrive at Nagasaki simultaneously with yourself.

3. That you will allow Mr. Aston sufficient time to communicate with me by Her Majesty's ship "Moorhen" before you send that vessel away from Chemulpho.

As Mr. Aston may be at the capital when you arrive at that anchorage, and as he will not be expecting your arrival, communication with him may not be easy, and may possibly involve delay, if he is allowed to take full advantage of such a good opportunity of reporting proceedings.

I have, &c.
(Signed)　HARRY S. PARKES

Inclosure 3

Vice-Admiral Willes to Sir H.S. Parkes.

"*Audacious,*" *at Hong kong, April 5*, 1883

Sir,

I HAVE the Honour to acknowledged the receipt of your letter, dated the 24th ultimo, inclosing a copy of your letter to Commander Eliott, of Her Majesty's ship "Daring."

I am glad that you found it convenient to send your despatches by that vessel; but your Excellency will, I feel sure, regret that, by requesting Commander Eliott to visit Nagasaki, you caused him to disobey my stringent orders against his touching at that port, and Commander Eliott could have received your letters equally well at Simonoseki, that port being in the direct route to Jinchuen.

Commander Eliott will be removed from the position of Senior Officer in Japan immediately he returns from Corea.

I have, &c.
(Signed)　GEORGE O. WILLES

Inclosure 4

Sir H.S. Parkes to Vice-Admiral Willes.

Tôkiô, April 18, 1883

Sir,

I HAD the honour to receive yesterday your despatch of the 5th instant, in which you state that, by requesting Commander Eliott to visit Nagasaki, I had caused him to disobey your stringent orders against touching at the port, that he could have received my letters equally well at Simonoseki, and that he will be removed from the position of Senior Naval Officer in Japan directly he returns from Corea.

Apart from the painful position in which I am placed by your having thus severely censured an officer under your command for having aided me in the execution of a public duty, I cannot but perceive that that censure is directed against myself as well as against Commander Eliott, and believing it to be wholly unmerited, I feel that I should not allow it to pass without protest and appeal to a higher judgment than that of your Excellency.

I am therefore obliged to note in detail my proceedings in this matter, although I am sensible that these only derive importance from the unfortunate result to which they have led, and I shall proceed to show in this letter:-

That I had no knowledge of Your Excellency's stringent orders against the "Daring" touching at Nagasaki which I now learn have been disobeyed;

That it was because I understood that the "Daring" was obliged to touch at Nagasaki to fill up with coal that I requested Commander Eliott to receive at that port my letters for Mr. Aston;

That the first vessel sent on this service (the "Moorhen") had touched at Nagasaki for coal in the same way, and that Your Excellency had approved of her doing so; and

That Your Excellency is wholly misinformed in stating that Commander Eliott could have received my letters equally well at Simonoseki.

Your Excellency will remember that when I suggested, for your consideration, in my despatch of the 21st February, that, in view of the difficulty of estimating the duration of Mr. Aston's stay in Corea, it might be desirable to send a second vessel in order to secure means of communication, your Excellency replied, in your despatch of the 28th February, that it did not appear to you necessary to dispatch a second vessel on that service.

I was agreeably surprised, therefore, when Commander Eliott called on me on the 23rd March, and showed me your Excellency's orders of the 12th of that month, directing him to proceed to Jinchuen to take up the duty being there performed by the "Moorhen," and to communicate to me the nature of your orders.

On reading these orders, which did not contain a word against the "Daring" touching at Nagasaki, I asked Commander Eliott when he would proceed, and what course he would take. He replied that he would be ready for sea early on the 25th, that he would go through the Inland Sea, and that, expecting to meet with strong westerly winds, it would be necessary to call at Nagasaki for coal. I then made to him, verbally, the requests which I repeated in my letter of the following day (referred to in your despatch under acknowledgement), namely, that on passing Kobe. He should call for letters for Mr. Aston from the officer acting for Mr. Aston as Her Majesty's Consul at that port, and that he should not leave Nagasaki before the arrival there of my despatches for Mr. Aston, which might be expected to reach the latter port as soon as the "Daring," by the Japanese mail-steamer leaving Yokohama on the 28th March.

In my telegrams to Your Excellency of the 28th February and 4th March I requested that the vessel which was being sent with Mr. Aston to Corea (the "Moorhen") should call at Nagasaki to embark that officer and the Corean functionaries who accompanied him, and who overtook her at Nagasaki in the same way that my letters overtook the "Daring." Your Excellency approved of the "Moorhen" calling at Nagasaki, and I had no reason to suppose that the course approved by you in the case of that vessel would be disapproved in the case of the "Daring."

I regret that Your Excellency did not apprise me of your "stringent orders" against the "Daring" touching at Nagasaki, as, if I had been acquainted with them, I should not have sent my despatches for Mr. Aston to that port, but should have requested Commander Eliott to wait for them at Kobe. This would have involved a delay at the latter port of about thirty-six hours; but I presume that your Excellency in sending a second vessel to Corea intended to afford me an opportunity of communicating with Mr. Aston, and the short and unexpected notice (twenty-four hours) given me of the departure of the "Daring" from

Yokohama did not permit of my preparing in that interval the despatches which I wished Commander Eliott to convey.

Owing to bad weather which the "Daring" encountered in the Inland Sea after leaving Kobé, she did not arrive at Nagasaki until three days after the Japanese mail which carried there my despatches for Mr. Aston, and I am informed by Her Majesty's Consul at that port that in less than twenty-four hours, or as soon as he could possibly take on board the coal which he required, Commander Eliott left again for Corea.

It is not for me to judge whether it was necessary or not that one of Her Majesty's ships going to a country where coal is wholly unobtainable, and being charged with the duty of conveying a public officer to several points in that country, should fill up with coal at the last point of departure after having been some time at sea, and having therefore reduced her supply of fuel; but I must distinctly repeat that, in sending my despatches for Mr. Aston to Nagasaki, I acted on the understanding that it was considered requisite that the "Daring" should coal at the port, and that I was wholly unaware that your Excellency had ordered that vessel not to touch there.

Your Excellency, I beg to point out, is mistaken in supposing that Commander Eliott could have received those despatches equally well at Simonoseki. That port is not open to foreign intercourse, and I do not see how the safe delivery of my despatches to Commander Eliott could have been secured unless the "Daring" had chanced to be waiting at anchor off that town when the mail-steamer passed through the Straits, and unless I had succeeded in making some special arrangement for their delivery through the intervention of the Japanese authorities, which would, at least, have involved prior official correspondence. It would certainly have been preferable, therefore, to send my despatches to Kobe if the "Daring" was not to call at Nagasaki. As a fact, the mail-steamer passed through the Straits of Simonoseki several days before the "Daring" arrived there.

I am unwillingly compelled to enter into these particulars because, in sending to Earl Granville, as it is my duty to do, a copy of Your Excellency's despatch of the 5th instant, I consider that I should accompany it with the vindication of my proceeding which I submit this letter contains.

The regret which Your Excellency justly thinks I should feel on learning that by an act of mine your orders have been disobeyed goes further than Your Excellency implies. Having been kept in ignorance of those orders by Your

Excellency, I cannot be responsible for their infringement; but I do deeply regret that for such a simple act as requesting Commander Eliott to receive my despatches for Mr. Aston at Nagasaki when he called at that port for coal, Your Excellency should have seen fit to discredit me as Her Majesty's Principal Secretary of State for Foreign Affairs, and to visit Commander Eliott with so sever a penalty because he complied with that simple request.

My regret is further increased by the reflection that on the only two occasions on which I have had to seek Your Excellency's co-operation in carrying out the public service in this country, namely, that of the visit of Her Majesty's ship "Flying Fish" to Corea in July last, and the present instance, you have unfavourably construed my action, and have obliged me in both these cases to trouble Her Majesty's Principal Secretary of State with an explanation of my proceedings. I am not at liberty to speak in defence of a naval officer who has fallen under your censure; but Your Excellency must be sensible of the pain I feel on learning that that censure was occasioned by an act of mine, and if it is only on account of that act that Commander Eliott has been thus blamed, and if any blame has been justly incurred in this case, I shall trust that the Home authorities will allow it to fall wholly upon myself, and not in any degree on that officer.

I have, &c.

(Signed)   HARRY S. PARKES

Inclosure 5

"Audacious," at Hong kong, March 12, 1883

(Memo)

WITH reference to telegram relating to the visit of a vessel of war to the Corea to convey Mr. Aston on a mission to that country, I acquaint you that I desire to be informed of the orders which you have given to the "Moorhen" in consequence of my telegram to you to place her at the disposal of Her Majesty's Minister.

So soon as the "Daring" is ready for sea, after her defects have been made good at Yokoska, you will proceed to Jinchuen in the "Daring" and take up the duty which is there being performed by the "Moorhen," dispatching the latter vessel to Kobe, if you do not require her services in Corean waters.

You will communicate with Her Majesty's Minister, and inform him of the nature of your orders.

You will telegraph to me the date (when fixed) of your intended departure from Japan.

You will bear in mind that fresh provisions are not easily obtained in the Corea, the supply being doubtful.

(Signed) GEORGE O. WILLES, *Vice-admiral,*
Commander-in-chief

To Commander Eliott,
Her Majesty's ship "Daring"
(At present Senior Naval officer in Japan)

135

H.S. Parkes (1883. 4. 21) ➜ G.L.G. Granville (1883. 6. 4)

조선의 조약 개정 의도와 정세에 관한 Aston 전보 보고

Sir H.S. Parkes to Earl Granville.—(Received June 4)

(No. 60 Confidential)

Tôkiô, April 21, 1883

My Lord,

    I MENTIONED in my despatch No. 35 of the 9th ultimo that I wished to submit to your Lordship some observations on the instructions I gave to Mr. Aston on sending him to Corea, and which I inclosed in that despatch. I have been backward in doing so because it subsequently appeared to me that I need only trouble your Lordship with remarks on two points connected with those instructions, namely, the wording of my letter to the Corean Minister for Foreign Affairs, and my reasons for promptly dispatching Mr. Aston. In order, therefore, to make that despatch more complete, I now beg to add the following comments.

    It occurred to me that, if the Corean Government were to be induced to entertain the idea of modifying the British Treaty, and to communicate to Mr. Aston their disposition to do so, it was at least necessary that that idea should be suggested to their consideration, and that they should be informed that Mr. Aston was authorized to receive any communication on the subject which they might desire to make to Her Majesty's Government. Such a suggestion had indeed been offered, or I had been told that it had been offered (as I reported in my despatch No. 4, Confidential, of the 12th January), by Kim Ok Kiun to the late Corean Envoys to Japan, but I could not rely on the latter having effectually placed it before their Government, and the request that they would do so had elicited no response.

    I therefore ventured to consider that I might make to the Foreign Minister of Corea a similar communication to that which I had been authorized by your Lordship to make to the Corean Envoys, and I accordingly observed in my letter to his Excellency that I had been instructed by Her Majesty's Government to apprise him that if the Corean Government were willing to enter into further negotiations on the basis of the arrangements which they had recently concluded with China, Her Majesty's Government would be happy to entertain proposals of that nature. It remains for me to hope that Your Lordship will approve of my having made this use of your instructions, and of my having addressed the Prime Minster and the Foreign Minister of Corea in order to satisfy them of the official character of Mr. Aston's mission, and to induce them to treat him with proper consideration.

But lest those functionaries, either intuitively or at the suggestion of the foreign Agents at their capital, should have been disposed to question my right to address them, I attached considerable importance to the presence with Mr. Aston of Kim Ok Kiun, the confidential Agent of the King, which I could only have secured by dispatching Mr. Aston without delay, as the former was then on the point of leaving Japan for China, and he would not have accompanied Mr. Aston unless he could have proceeded with him at once. Kim Ok Kiun professes to be exceedingly anxious to see Treaty relations established between his country and European Powers as a means of checking the predominant influence and, as he considers it, the arbitrary action of China in Corea, and he is therefore interested in desiring the presence at the capital of European Agents, in order that the leaven of new opinion may be introduced into Chinese thought and views which at present prevail in the Corean mind. He may not unnaturally desire that the European Treaties shall be as one-sided in the Corean interest as his present perceptions lead him to think advisable, but I do not question the sincerity of his wish that Corean nationality shall not be absorbed in that of China.

In a conversation with me, he himself observed that if the British Government did not approve of the Commercial Clauses of their Treaty, which, in the face of the ratification of the identical American Treaty, his Government would find it difficult at once to alter, a preliminary Treaty of Friendship of two or three Articles, which would not comprise any commercial stipulations, might first be concluded between Corean and Great Britain, and which, by means of the insertion of the favoured-nation clause, would still enable the latter to claim full participation in the conditions of the American Treaty, if Her Majesty's Government should choose to do so. I accordingly desired Mr. Aston to endeavour to learn whether this idea is favourably entertained by the Corean Government. If so, it might possibly furnish for the moment a convenient alternative course to ratification or rejection, as Kim Ok Kiun stated to me that China has advised the Corean Government, when they have secured the ratification of the American Treaty, to allow the other Treaties to lapse, unless they are also ratified without modification.

As to the date of Mr. Aston's proceeding to Corea, I had to remember that if the information which he might obtain there on the various points named in my instructions to him was to be of service to Her Majesty's Government, if it was desirable that the latter should receive timely intimation of a disposition, if it exists, on the part of the Corean Government to modify the British Treaty, seeing that a decision must soon be taken as to whether that Treaty should be ratified or not, it was obvious that that information should be acquired as soon as possible. If also he was to secure a choice of Consular building sites, it was equally essential that he should be the first on the ground. Dispatching him at the earliest moment that I could obtain the services of one of Her Majesty's ships, that is, in the middle of March, I could not look for his return before the middle or end of April, and I expected that by that time the ratification of the American Treaty would be followed by the arrival of the American Minister to Corea. I had also reason to believe that M. Möllendorff, the protégé of the Chinese Grand Secretary Li Hung Chang, was about to leave Corea for a short interval to report progress to his patron and to promote the advancement of his interested action, and I thought that it would be no disadvantage to Mr. Aston to visit the capital during his absence. The Japanese Foreign Minister (as I reported in my despatch No. 50 of the 15th instant) also concurred with me in the opportuneness of Mr. Aston's mission, and assured me that he would be assisted by the Japanese Minister at Sŏul in endeavouring to induce the Corean Government to adopt reasonable commercial views.

The correctness of these expectations have been sustained by the event. Mr. Aston, on his arrival in Corea, found M. Möllendorf absent, and he did not return there until the 9th instant. The American Minister to Corea arrived here on the 19th instant, and Mr. Aston will return to Tôkiô, as I learn from his telegrams, which I have reported in my despatch No. 59 of this date, about the 25th instant.

In view of these considerations, I trust your Lordship will approve of my having pressed Vice-Admiral Willes, as I reported in my despatches Nos. 33 and 34 of the 9th ultimo, to allow one of Her Majesty's ships to convey Mr. Aston to Corea without delay.

I have, &c.

(Signed)   HARRY S. PARKES

H.S. Parkes (1883. 4. 21) ➜ G.L.G. Granville (1883. 6. 4)

Aston의 조선행 및 지시내용에 관한 추가 보고

Sir H.S. Parkes to Earl Granville.—(Received June 4)

(No. 60 Confidential)

Tôkiô, April 21, 1883

My Lord,

I MENTIONED in my despatch No. 35 of the 9th ultimo that I wished to submit to your Lordship some observations on the instructions I gave to Mr. Aston on sending him to Corea, and which I inclosed in that despatch. I have been backward in doing so because it subsequently appeared to me that I need only trouble your Lordship with remarks on two points connected with those instructions, namely, the wording of my letter to the Corean Minister for Foreign Affairs, and my reasons for promptly dispatching Mr. Aston. In order, therefore, to make that despatch more complete, I now beg to add the following comments.

It occurred to me that, if the Corean Government were to be induced to entertain the idea of modifying the British Treaty, and to communicate to Mr. Aston their disposition to do so, it was at least necessary that that idea should be suggested to their consideration, and that they should be informed that Mr. Aston was authorized to receive any communication on the subject which they might desire to make to Her Majesty's Government. Such a suggestion had indeed been offered, or I had been told that it had been offered (as I reported in my despatch No. 4, Confidential, of the 12th January), by Kim Ok Kiun to the late Corean Envoys to Japan, but I could not rely on the latter having effectually placed it before their Government, and the request that they would do so had elicited no response.

I therefore ventured to consider that I might make to the Foreign Minister of Corea a similar communication to that which I had been authorized by Your Lordship to make to the Corean Envoys, and I accordingly observed in my letter to his Excellency that I had been instructed by Her Majesty's Government to apprise him that if the Corean Government were willing to enter into further negotiations on the basis of the arrangements which they had recently concluded with China, Her Majesty's Government would be happy to entertain proposals of that nature. It remains for me to hope that Your Lordship will approve of my having made this use of your instructions, and of my having addressed the Prime Minster and the Foreign Minister of Corea in order to satisfy them of the official character of Mr. Aston's mission, and to induce them to treat him with proper consideration.

But lest those functionaries, either intuitively or at the suggestion of the foreign Agents at their capital, should have been disposed to question my right to address them, I attached considerable importance to the presence with Mr. Aston of Kim Ok Kiun, the confidential Agent of the King, which I could only have secured by dispatching Mr. Aston without delay, as the former was then on the point of leaving Japan for China, and he would not have accompanied Mr. Aston unless he could have proceeded with him at once. Kim Ok Kiun professes to be exceedingly anxious to see Treaty relations established between his country and European Powers as a means of checking the predominant influence and, as he considers it, the arbitrary action of China in Corea, and he is therefore interested in desiring the presence at the capital of European Agents, in order that the leaven of new opinion may be introduced into Chinese thought and views which at present prevail in the Corean mind. He may not unnaturally desire that the European Treaties shall be as one-sided in the Corean interest as his present perceptions lead him to think advisable, but I do not question the sincerity of his wish that Corean nationality shall not be absorbed in that of China.

In a conversation with me, he himself observed that if the British Government did not approve of the Commercial Clauses of their Treaty, which, in the face of the ratification of the identical American Treaty, his Government would find it difficult at once to alter, a preliminary Treaty of Friendship of two or three Articles, which would not comprise any commercial stipulations, might first be concluded between Corean and Great Britain, and which, by means of the insertion of the favoured-nation clause, would still enable the latter to claim full participation in the conditions of the American Treaty, if Her Majesty's Government should choose to do so. I accordingly desired Mr. Aston to endeavour to learn whether this idea is favourably entertained by the Corean Government. If so, it might possibly furnish for the moment a convenient alternative course to ratification or rejection, as Kim Ok-Kiun stated to me that China has advised the Corean Government, when they have secured the ratification of the American Treaty, to allow the other Treaties to lapse, unless they are also ratified without modification.

As to the date of Mr. Aston's proceeding to Corea, I had to remember that if the information which he might obtain there on the various points named in my instructions to him was to be of service to Her Majesty's Government, if it was desirable that the latter should receive timely intimation of a disposition, if it exists, on the part of the Corean Government to modify the British Treaty, seeing that a decision must soon be taken as to whether that Treaty should be ratified or not, it was obvious that that information should be acquired as soon as possible. If also he was to secure a choice of Consular building sites, it was equally essential that he should be the first on the ground. Dispatching him at the earliest moment that I could obtain the services of one of Her Majesty's ships, that is, in the middle of March, I could not look for his return before the middle or end of April, and I expected that by that time the ratification of the American Treaty would be followed by the arrival of the American Minister to Corea. I had also reason to believe that M. Möllendof, the protégé of the Chinese Grand Secretary Li Hung Chang, was about to leave Corea for a short interval to report progress to his patron and to promote the advancement of his interested action, and I thought that it would be no disadvantage to Mr. Aston to visit the capital during his absence. The Japanese Foreign Minister (as I reported in my despatch No. 50 of the 15th instant) also concurred with me in the opportuneness of Mr. Aston's mission, and assured me that he would be assisted by the Japanese Minister at Söul in endeavouring to induce the Corean Government to adopt reasonable commercial views.

The correctness of these expectations have been sustained by the event. Mr. Aston, on his arrival in Corea, found M. Möllendorf absent, and he did not return there until 9th instant. The American Minister to Corea arrived here on the 19th instant, and Mr. Aston will return to Tôkiô, as I learn from his telegrams, which I have reported in my despatch No. 59 of this date, about the 25th instant.

In view of these considerations, I trust your Lordship will approve of my having pressed Vice-Admiral Willes, as I reported in my despatches Nos. 33 and 34 of the 9th ultimo, to allow one of Her Majesty's ships to convey Mr. Aston to Corea without delay.

I have, &c.
(Signed)   HARRY S. PARKES

137

G.L.G. Granville (1883. 4. 22) → H.S. Parkes

독일과 영국의 조약 비준 연기 통보

Earl Granville to Sir H.S. Parkes.

(No. 42. Ext. 3)

Foreign Office, April 22, 1883

Sir,

YOU will receive with my despatch No. 41, Confidential, of the 20th instant a copy of a despatch from Her Majesty's Ambassador at Berlin, inclosing a note addressed to his Excellency by price Bismark, in which his highness communicated the views of the Imperial Government as to the stops which should be taken by Germany and by this country in regard to the Treaties negotiated last summer with Corea.

In my reply to Lord Ampthill, of which a copy has also been forwarded to you, his Excellency was instructed to ascertain whether the German Government would be prepared to adopt the same course as was proposed by Her Majesty's Government, and whether they would wish that Mr. Consul Aston, who is now on the spot, should make any communication on their part to the Government of Corea.

Having since ascertained that the German Government entirely concur in the proposals made to them by Her Majesty's Government in regard to Corea, I have telegraphed this day to inform you that it has been agreed between the two Governments that the ratifications of their respective Treaties with Corea shall be postponed for six months, on the ground that further consideration is required in respect of certain portions of them.

I have at the same time requested that you will place yourself in communication with your German colleague, who will receive instructions from his Government on the subject.

You will direct Mr. Aston to notify to the Corean Government the desire of both Government to postpone the ratification of the Treaties, and, if desirable, to sign declarations of such postponement.

He should also sound that Government as to whether they would be ready to place Great Britain and Germany on the same footing as China, or whether they would reopen negotiations in order to assimilate the new Treaties to those which are now in force and by which the relations of these countries are regulated with China and Japan.

I am, &c.
(Signed)   GRANVILLE

H.S. Parkes (1883. 4. 28) ➡ 閔泳穆

Aston의 재파견을 알리는 조회

관련문서 閔泳穆의 회신(1883. 5. 16)

大英國駐劄日本欽差巴 爲照會事 據本國阿須領事前自貴國回來 稟本大臣稱 在貴國時 凡往來辦事官員接待極優 及政府所備房屋亦皆如意 該領事實深欣慰等情前來 本大臣聞之 深爲感佩 並將阿領事之言 即行轉咨本國政府 本大臣耑此鳴謝 現因阿領事前赴貴國 仍望相待如前 益敦和睦 相應照會 爲此照會貴大臣 請煩查照可也 須至照會者
右照會
大朝鮮國統理通商事務衙門督辦 閔
西曆一千八百八十三年四月二十八日　照會 三月二十二日

【관련문서】

大朝鮮國督辦交涉通商事務閔 爲照覆事 接准貴大臣照會內開 據本國阿領事前自貴國回來稟稱 在貴國時 凡往來辦事接待極優 所備房屋亦皆如意等情 本大臣聞之 深爲感佩 耑此鳴謝 現因阿領事前赴貴國 仍望相待如前 益敦和睦等因 准此 竊照本國從前不嫺交際 向日貴領事戻止 接待供頓諸多菲薄 常懷歉仄 乃荷貴大臣謬加稱謝 尤增愧汗 貴領事此次再來相對敍舊 喜不可量 從玆兩國益敦和睦 永遠勿替 實有所厚望焉 爲此照覆 請煩貴大臣查照可也 須至照覆者
右照覆
大英國駐劄日本欽差世爵 巴
大朝鮮開國四百九十二年四月初九日

H.S. Parkes (1883. 4. 28) ➜ 閔泳穆

1차 조영조약의 비준서 교환 연기를 통보하는 조회

관련문서 閔泳穆의 회신(1883. 5. 15)

大英國駐劄日本欽差世爵巴 爲照會事 照得 本大臣准本國政府札開 上年西曆六月初六日 在仁川口與大朝鮮國所立之條約 本以一年期滿換約 玆請改期 多緩數月等因前來 本大臣奉此 特派本國駐日本領事官阿前赴貴國 將前由達知貴國政府 蓋本國政府之所以改期者 因約內尚有數語待於商酌 總期先難後易 彼此均臻妥善爲要 故當立約之初 尤宜愼重 玆派阿領事前來 與貴國官員兩面畫押換約之期 即以西曆本年十二月三十一日爲止 相應照會 爲此照會貴大臣 請煩查照施行 須至照會者
右照會
大朝鮮國統理交涉通商事務衙門督辦 閔
西曆一千八百八十三年四月二十八日 照會

【관련문서】

大朝鮮國督辦交涉通商事務閔 爲照覆事 接准貴大臣照會內開 本大臣准本國政府札開 上年西曆六月初六日 在仁川口與大朝鮮國所立條約 本以一年期滿換約 玆請改期 多換[sic]數月等因前來 本大臣奉派駐日本領事館阿前赴貴國 將前由達知貴國政府 與貴國官員兩面畫押換約之期 即以西曆本年十二月三十一日爲止等因 准此 本大臣奉派本衙門參議李與阿領事將上年在仁川口所立條約內載日期今緩訂 互換條約限期之約章 於本年四月初九日西曆五月十五日 在漢陽京城畫押蓋印 以爲憑信 相應備文照覆 請煩貴大臣查照施行 須至照覆者
右照覆
大英國駐劄日本欽差世爵 巴
大朝鮮開國四百九十二年四月初九日 照覆 約章另具

140

H.S. Parkes (1883. 4. 28) ➜ G.L.G. Granville (1883. 6. 19)

조선에서의 협상에 관한 Aston의 despatch 발송

Sir H.S. Parkes to Earl Granville.—(Received June 19)

(No. 64 Confidential)

Tôkiô, April 28, 1883

My Lord,

WITH reference to my previous despatch No. 63 of this date, I beg to inclose copies of the despatches which Mr. Aston forwarded from Söul by Her Majesty's ship "Moorhen."

These consist of a general account of his proceedings, and a Confidential despatch in which Mr. Aston reports the result of two interviews which he held on the 2nd and 9th instant with the Corean Foreign Ministers, and in the course of which the provisions of the Anglo-Corean Treaty signed on the 6th June last were discussed at some length.

As the English mail leaves to-day, I am obliged to reserve for the next opportunity the observations I shall have to submit to your Lordship on these subjects.

I have, &c.
(Signed)   HARRY S. PARKES

Inclosure 1

Mr. Aston to Sir H.S. Parkes.

Söul, April 10, 1883

Sir,

I HAVE the honour to report that, in accordance with the instructions contained in your despatch of the 6th March, I proceeded on the 12th of the same month to Nagasaki in the Peninsular and Oriental steamer "Khiva," along with the two Corean officials, Mr. Kim Ok Kiun and Mr. So Kwang-poin[sic]. We arrived at Nagasaki on the 14th, but the "Moorhen" was prevented from sailing till the morning of the 17th by a strong westerly gale, against which it would have been impossible for her to make headway. We arrived at Roze Island anchorage on the morning of the 22nd. Messrs. Kim and So proceeded to the capital the next day, promising to make arrangements at once for Mr. Bonar and myself to follow as soon as possible; but it was not till the 28th that we were able to start for Söul.

In the meantime, I learnt that Mr. Hong Yöng Sik, Vice-Minister for Foreign Affairs, was with Mr. Ma Kie Tchang, at the village of Hwa-do-chin, near Chemulpho, having come down from the capital in order to examine the proposed sites for a Settlement here. I took the opportunity of calling on the Vice-Minister, and as Mr. Ma was with him, the visit was taken as paid to both, and was returned the same evening. I said nothing about business matters further than hinting to the Vice-Minister that we should expect to be consulted in respect to the selection and laying-out of a Settlement. I learnt here that General Wu had left for China a day or two before; that Cho Nyöng-ha had ceased to be Minister for Foreign Affairs; and that Kim Ok Kiun had been appointed to an Under-Secretaryship in the same Department.

Mr. Ma said that everything was quiet, but that there was still danger of trouble from the anti-foreign party, so that it was necessary to keep the Chinese force at its original strength, viz., about 3,000 men. I was afterwards told by Mr. Takezoye that 2,000 men was nearer the mark, and that General Wu, before leaving for China, had expressed to him his intention of recommending to his Government the withdrawal of half the number. Mr. Ma admitted that there was no danger to himself personally, and said that he was in the habit of going about in Söul alone and unarmed. I observed, however, that whenever Mr. Ma went out at night he was accompanied by a guard of five or six armed Chinese soldiers. The Japanese guard remains at its former strength of about 200 men, and there is no present intention of making any change.

Suitable arrangements were made by the Corean authorities for our journey to the capital, a palanquin carried by four men, with four others to relieve them, having been provided for myself, and ponies for the rest of the party. A Corean luncheon was prepared for us at a halfway village, by order of the Governor of the Province of Kyŏng-ki-do. Two clerks of the Foreign Office had come down from Sŏul expressly to superintend these arrangements.

The house of a Corean nobleman had been prepared for our reception, and although small according to European ideas, it was sufficiently comfortable, and compared favourably with many other houses which we had opportunities of inspecting. Several petty officers were deputed to attend to our wants, and it was the duty of one of these to report to the King every morning how we had passed the night.

Mr. Kim Ok Kiun called on me the same evening. He assured me that the minds of the people had become much more settled, and that no danger whatever was to be apprehended. He said he had found his Government favourably disposed in regard to Treaty matters.

On the 30th I went to the Foreign office and delivered your letter to the present Foreign Minister, His Excellency Min Yŏng Mok. Mr. Ma came in afterwards, and the English version of your letter was handed to him for perusal. I next delivered my letters to the Primes Minister and to his Excellency Pak Yong-hyo. The latter told me that Mr. Kim Ok Kiun was now the real Director of the Foreign Office, though nominally holding a subordinate office. He suggested my calling also on Kim Pyŏng Kuk, the second Minister of State, and on Cho Nyŏng-ha and Min Thai-ho. The first-named Minister received me in a very cordial manner, but the other two were prevented by illness from receiving my visit.

I shall report in separate despatches the result of my interview with the Corean foreign Ministers on the 2nd and 9th instant, and of my endeavours to secure houses and building sites.

My reception has on the whole been as friendly as could reasonably have been expected. The Corean authorities spared no pains to make us comfortable, and have refused to let me refund to them the travelling and other expenses of my visit. I could see, however, that, although personally friendly to me, and sincerely anxious to establish friendly relations with us, they still entertain considerable suspicion of our objects, which it will take time altogether to remove. Amongst other attentions shown to me, a review of 300 of the King's body-guards was given in the Royal park, and before our departure we were entertained by the Foreign Minister and his Excellency Pak Yŏng-hyo at dinners, where a number of the leading officials were invited to meet us. On the other hand, I was told that Mr. Kim Ok Kiun had incurred much censure for bringing me over, and he was obliged to avoid coming to see me as often as he would have wished. There is no real cordial feeling towards foreigners outside a very small circle.

I trust to be able to leave Soul to-morrow, and to embark for Pusan in the "Daring" on the following day.

I have, &c.
(Signed)   W.G. Aston

Inclosure 2

Mr. Aston to Sir H.S. Parkes.

(Confidential)

Söul, April 11, 1881

Sir,

I HAVE the honour to report that, having applied to the Corean Foreign Office on the 1st instant to depute an official to point out to me such available buildings as might be deemed suitable for the accommodation of a British Diplomatic Representative in the city, and to furnish me with information respecting the nature and cost of such building materials as might be procurable, I was invited by his Excellency Min Yŏng Mok, the Corean Minister for Foreign Affairs, to meet him at the Foreign Office on the following day.

On arriving there I found assembled all the senior officials of the Foreign Department, with the exception of Mr. Ma Kie Tchang, the Chinese gentleman belonging to it. In addition to the Senior Minister there were present the Vice-Minister, Hong Yŏng-sik, Kim Hong-jip, one of the signers of the Jinchuen Treaty, Kim Ok Kiun, and Cho Pyŏng-phil.

After some conversation upon the subject of houses and sites for building, the Senior Minister handed me a copy of the Chinese text of Admiral Willes' Treaty, which, as I had never had an opportunity of inspecting it, I had requested permission to see, asking me as he did so whether I thought it would be ratified. I replied that I had no information as to the intentions of Her

Majesty's Government in this respect, and was in no way authorized to speak for them, but that it appeared to me that there were some features in it which I was afraid would make it difficult to ratify it as it stands. He then invited me to point these out to him, which, as a convenient means of eliciting the opinions of the Corean Government, I had no hesitation in doing. I accordingly referred to the omission of Her Majesty's title as Empress of India, and of any provision for the continuance of the present Treaty under the successors of the present Sovereigns of Great Britain and Ireland and Corea. Article II was passed over without remark.

In Article III there is a slight difference in meaning between the Chinese and English text, the clause which is in English, "If a British ship carries on a clandestine trade," being in Chinese, "If such ship" (*i.e.*, a ship which has put into a non-opened port in distress) "carries on a clandestine trade." I showed the Minister that by a strict wording of this clause no punishment was provided in the case of a vessel which, without the excuse of bad weather or want of provisions, went to an unopened port in Corea and carried on a clandestine trade there. The Minster replied that he saw no difficulty here, as if vessels in distress were to be punished for clandestine trading there was still stronger reason for punishing one which did so without any such excuse. I said that in principle the Minister was perfectly right, but that these provisions of the Treaty would have to be applied by judicial officers who could be guided only by what they found before them, and would not be allowed to inflict punishments, however just in principle, which were not distinctly laid down in the Treaty. The provision in this Article for sending shipwrecked crews to their own country, I added, could not be conveniently carried out. This was seldom done in these countries, the usual practice being to send them to the nearest port where they could obtain employment.

Article IV I passed over on this occasion with the remark that the wording of it required to be amended, but at a subsequent interview with the same officials on the 9th instant I asked whether there was any objection to extend the operation of this clause so as to include offences by British subjects against other British subjects and foreigners, together with all judicial matters in which Corea was not concerned. To this the Minister replied that of course there could be no objection to this.

Up to this point the Corean Ministers unanimously expressed their concurrence in my remark, but in regard to Article V, the Tariff Clause, they informed me that they intended to leave it as it now stands, subject, however, to the qualification that no heavier duties would be levied on British commerce than on that of other nations.

I pointed out that a 10 per cent. duty would have a very injurious effect on a trade which was now quite insignificant though no duties whatever were charged, and that if we allowed to Corea a Tariff based on this principle, it might embarrass us in any future Tariff negotiations with China and Japan in which we might be engaged. In reply, the Ministers reminded me that the scale of duties laid down in this Article was a maximum scale only, and made profuse promises to deal liberally with Tariff matters when the Treaties were once concluded. They said a high rate of duty was of no consequence to them in comparison with fostering trade and placing their relations with foreign countries on a friendly footing. It should be remembered, they continued, that England was not the only country interested in this matter, and as America had already signified her intention to ratify the Treaty, it was difficult for them to propose a reduction to one country only. We might rely, however, on receiving favoured-nation treatment in this respect. I asked would the favoured-nation treatment apply to the Convention recently concluded with China. Mr. Kim Ok Kiun said it would, and Mr. Kim Hong-jip remarked that this Convention was not in force (or his word might mean, "would not be enforced"). I was then told that the 5 per cent. rate of duty named in this Convention was applicable to land duties only, and not to importations by sea. I noticed, however, a disposition on their part to get rid of this as well as certain other stipulations of the Chinese Convention. They felt no doubt that it would be used as an argument in favour of a 5 per cent. Tariff at the ports, and were perhaps also influenced by the consideration which the Japanese Minister told me he had brought to their notice, viz., that when Russia made a Treaty she would of course also claim a land frontier rate of 5 per cent. If Japan were granted a 5 per cent. rate, England, they said, would naturally be entitled to a similar privilege, but it must be remembered that it was not correct to say that the Japanese had the right of free trade. The principle of payment of duty had all along been admitted, and it was only the rate which had not been decided. I was led to suspect, by the sanguine tone of their remarks on this point, that they have been led to understand that Japan will not oppose a 10 per cent. Tariff if the other Powers consent to its adoption. The details of the Tariff the Corean Minsters intimated their intention of settling by themselves, and I am inclined to believe that they purpose to take the same course in regard to Customs, Land, and other Regulations.

It was explained to me that the mace according to which tonnage dues are to be reckoned is not the Corean mace of copper money, but the mace by weight of silver, and therefore identical with the Chines mace. This I said was a very high rate, and much heavier than the corresponding charges in China and Japan.

In regard to Article VI, the Corean Minsters informed me that they were averse to allowing foreigners to visit the interior for purposes of trade, and that they hoped to be able to cancel this stipulation in the Convention lately concluded with China. It had been introduced, they said, in return for a similar privilege granted to Corea subjects in China, to which I replied that the same privilege was allowed to Coreans visiting England. I added that so long as we were treated on an equality with other nations in this respect we should not complain, but any concession in this direction to China would certainly lead to similar claims being made by ourselves.

The stipulation in this Article reserving for Corean shipping the interport trade in native produce would, the Minister said, be also subject to the favoured-nation clause, but it was their desire to retain this trade in their own hands for the present, and they were confident that Japan, whose Treaty as it now stands contains no prohibition of interport carriage of native goods, would not object to make this concession to them. From some remarks dropped at various times by Mr. Kim Ok Kiun, I believed that there is a scheme on foot for establishing a native Corean Steam Navigation Company, holding a similar position to that which the Mitsu Bishi Company holds in Japan, and that they wish to retain this prohibition with a view to its protection.

The clause prohibiting Corean subjects from importing opium into England had not been introduced into the Treaty at the desire of the Corean Government, and they have no objection to its being expunged. They also observed that they would not object to insert in the Tariff a provision allowing the importation of opium for medicinal use.

In answer to a question whether it would not be sufficient to prohibit the export of grain from Inchhön (Jinchuen) in seasons of scarcity only, as at the other ports, it was explained to me that this clause was introduced more in order to reassure the minds of the Corean people than from any belief that it was really required. The grain of the Metropolitan province was never sufficient for the wants of the inhabitants, and any surplus for exportation would be found at Pusan or Wŏnsan, and not here. The same opinion was expressed to me by Mr. Sugimura, the Japanese Vice-Consul at Chemulpho, who, for this reason, augured unfavourably of the prospects of foreign trade at this port. He thought the trade here would never equal that of Pusan, but in this opinion I cannot agree with him.

In regard to the concluding Article of the Treaty (the favoured-nation clause), the Corean Ministers made a statement which very materially alters its character. They informed me that the non-retrospective character of this clause in the English version is owing simply to a mistranslation. The Chinese version, they said, was not intended to have, and has not, this force, and it was always wholly foreign to the intentions of the Corean Government to refuse to one nation privileges which they had already allowed to another. I said I had no doubt this statement would be received with satisfaction by Her Majesty's Government, and that it would go far to remove the difficulties in the way of establishing friendly relations between the two countries. I must say, however, that the Chinese text seems capable of both interpretations, and that the circumstances under which the Treaty was drawn up suggest reasons for thinking that the meaning originally intended was that of the English text.

There was then some conversion respecting the necessity in any future Treaty of selecting one version as the authoritative one in case of a divergence of meaning of the two texts. The Senior Minister expressed a preference for Chinese, and Mr. Kim Ok Kiun suggested that a Corean version should be prepared and adopted as the standard. This suggestion is a very sensible one, as the Corean would be understood by a far larger proportion of the people. It is usual to issue notifications to the people in both Chinese and Corean, and if the Treaty is to be notified in the latter language, it would be well to have an officially-authorized version of it. Mr. Asayama, the Corean Interpreter to the Japanese Legation, says that the Corean language is capable of greater precision than the Chinese, and is preferred by the natives in intricate matters where precision is necessary. Mr. Kim Ok Kiun's preference for a Corean version was no doubt prompted by his wish to avoid anything which might suggest the dependent relation of Corea to China. As you are aware, he is the leading man of the anti-Chinese party.

The Corean Ministers then requested me to represent to Her Majesty's Government, through you, that it was their earnest desire to establish Treaty relations between the two countries as soon as possible, and they trusted that, in view of the explanation they had given regarding the favoured-nation clause, no difficulty would be found in doing so.

I said I believed this proposition might lead to a satisfactory result, but that I ought not to conceal from them my apprehension that their attitude in respect to the Tariff would cause difficulty and delay, and might altogether defeat this desirable object. I then said that I had omitted to mention a number of other objections to the Treaty as it now stands, but as none of them were likely to lead to any difference of opinion, I had not thought it worth while to occupy the time of the Ministers by dwelling on them. I subsequently suggested to Mr. Kim Ok Kiun, in a private conversation, that if his Government wished to have Treaty relations established as quickly as possible, some time might be saved if they declared their willingness to conclude a preliminary Treaty consisting of the first and last Articles of the present Treaty, with a provision to the effect that it should come into operation as soon as Her Majesty's Government signified to the Corean Government their intention to ratify it. I made this suggestion knowing that it was nearly in accordance with the instructions of Her Majesty's Government to Admiral Willes, and because it seemed to afford the only chance of allowing Corea to be opened to British subjects at the same time as to those of other Treaty Powers. If adopted, it would also enable us to avoid pledging ourselves to a direct approval of a high rate of Tariff, in case the Corean Government persisted in their refusal to make concessions in this respect. I took no further steps in the matter, but was informed by his Excellency Pak Yong-hyo and Mr. Kim Ok Kiun that this suggestion was favourably regarded by the Corean Government.

I was told that Ma Kie Tchang was not consulted in reference to these communications of the Corean Government, but that they were not concealed from him. I was unable to discover any trace of interference on his part, and believe that the language held to me by the Ministers is the genuine expression of the views of the Corean Government, and was not dictated to them by China. I have no doubt of the sincerity of their wish to enter into Treaty relations with Great Britain. In addition to mere obvious motives, they are aware that, until a Treaty has been concluded, English capitalists will not lend them the money which they so urgently require, and the anti-Chinese party hope that British influence will in some measure act as a counterpoise to that of China, which is exercised in a way very irritating to them. I should not be surprised if the other Treaty Powers were appealed to, under the Ist Article of the Treaty, to use their good offices with China in order to obtain the withdrawal of the Chinese force now stationed here.

I have, &c.
(Signed)　W.G. Aston

141

H.S. Parkes (1883. 4. 28) ➜ G.L.G. Granville (1883. 6. 19)

조선 정세에 관한 Aston의 Memorandum 발송

Sir H.S. Parkes to Earl Granville.—(Received June 19)

(No. 65 Confidential)

Tôkiô, April 28, 1883

My Lord,

WITH reference to my despatch No. 59 of the 21st instant, reporting the purport of two telegrams which I had received from Mr. Aston—one dated Söul, the 11th instant, and the other, Simonoseki, the 20th instant—and observing that I expected Mr. Aston would shortly arrive in Tôkiô, I have now the honour to add that Mr. Aston reported himself to me on the morning of the 26th instant. He had been conveyed in Her Majesty's Ship "Daring" to Simonoseki, and had come on by the more expeditious opportunity of the Japanese mail-steamer which he happened to meet at that place.

Mr. Aston has handed to me a Confidential Memorandum embodying the political information he obtained at Söul on various subjects, and a despatch written after he had left Corea, in which he reports an interview with M. von Möllendorff, the Foreign Adviser of the Corean Government, and his latest communications with Kim Ok Kiun, whose views are not wholly in accord with those of the former gentleman.

I shall beg to submit some observations on these papers in a succeeding despatch.

I have, &c.

(Signed) HARRY S. PARKES

Inclosure 1

Memorandum

(Confidential)

AS to the constitution and organization of the Corean Government, I can add but little to what is already known. The impression I derived from this visit is that the whole machinery of the Government is in an extremely disorganized condition. The court-yards of the various public offices are overgrown with weeds, the buildings in a dilapidated state, and presenting a deserted appearance. The foreign Office is the only place where there is any appearance of activity, and the arrangements here were still very imperfect, as was shown by the repairs and alterations still going on, and the fact that the interviews held there seemed practically open to the public. I was told by the Japanese Minister that the other offices were rarely visited by the officials. Coreans who have once held office retain the title for the rest of their lives. These titles are much coveted, and pressure is always being brought on the occupant of an office to vacate it, so as to allow another person to acquire the title. The consequence is that all the high officials are changed every few months, and no one of any experience in business is to be found in any high position, the work of the office being carried on by third-rate officials. Another evil, Mr. Takezoye informed me, was the want of control of the Treasury over the expenditure; every Department grasping as much as it could get without any regard for the requirements of the other Departments. The revenue is small, but the nominal amount is far from representing the cost of government to the people. In addition to a regular system of so-called presents to officials, from which it is impossible to escape, there are the bribes to land-tax officers to assess the dues payable in kind at a low figure, and, worst of all, the system of forced labour, which works as badly here as it has been found to do in other countries. Several instances of the dislike of the peasants to this burden came under my notice during my stay here.

The police arrangements of the town of Söul are extremely imperfect. There is a police force of seventy-two men, I was told, in charge of the city at night, but robbery is very frequent. The streets are not lighted, and sanitary arrangements are almost non-existent. I was assured on all sides that the temper of the people as regards foreigners had undergone a considerable change owing to recent events, and that the city was now quite safe. That it is so at the present moment I have no reason to doubt; but in the presence of any popular movement I fear the Government would be powerless. The only force at their disposal (leaving the Chinese out of the question) is the King's body-guard of 1,000 men, partially armed with rifles, and not long enough under discipline to be relied on. Mr. Kim Ok Kiun is very positive that no popular movement fraught with danger to foreigners is any longer possible; but I confess I was not convinced by the reasons which he gave for this opinion. It is no doubt true, as he says, that the Coreans are a quiet, peaceable race, but in view of what was last year effected by designing agitators, it is impossible to feel assured that something of the same kind may not happen again.

I learnt little of the state of parties in Corea at present, but I conclude, from the recent appointment of Mr. Kim Ok Kiun to a Secretaryship in the Foreign Office, that the party which he represents has lost none of its influence.

China, according to Mr. Takazoye, has not of late shown any disposition to interfere in Corean matters, except by advice privately given. I was told that Ma Kie Tchang was not the nominee of Li Hung Chang, but had merely his permission to accept the office which he holds in the Corean Government. It is probably by his advice that the King's guards, a fine-looking lot of fellow, wear a semi-Chinese uniform and practise with Lefaucheux muzzle-loading rifles manufactured at Nankin, a semi-Chinese drill in which English words of command sound strangely incongruous. Mr. Ma told me that another step taken by his advice was the adoption of the French system of weights and measures, but I could not see any signs of this having passed into general use. I had noticed some boxes suspended in the front of the houses in several parts of the city, and supposed at first that they were to serve the purpose of letter-boxes, but I afterwards found that they had been hung up at Mr. Ma's suggestion, in accordance with Chinese custom, so that any stray pieces of printed paper which might be dropped in the streets might be placed in these receptacles and preserved from pollution until they could be burnt. Mr. Kim Ok Kiun told me that none of the money of the Chinese loan had been received. He spoke in his usual way about China, saying that the conduct of the Chinese troops created great indignation, and might lead to fighting. They engaged in trade, and insisted on purchasing merchandize at prices fixed by themselves, a statement which I found confirmation of from other sources. I was also told that their demeanour to the Coreans was frequently most offensive, and the Japanese had often had to complain of their men being hustled and insulted in the streets by superior numbers of Chinese. Mr. Asayama, who told me this, added that strict justice was done whenever complaints of this kind were made. I have myself, on two occasions, narrowly escaped being ridden over by Chinese mounted men riding at a gallop through the Corean streets. Mr. Kim Ok Kiun has no patience with Mr. Ma. He says he has no principle, that he consorts with Corean women of the lowest class, that he is feathering his nest at the expense of the Coreans, that the King would be only too glad to get rid of him, as he knows nothing of the business he was expected to do, and his advice is worthless, and that he will be sent off as soon as the Treaties are made.

My relations with Mr. Ma have been most amicable, but we conversed very little on business matters, and then confined ourselves to the question of the site of the Settlement at Chemulpho.

One of the young Chinese lately returned from America has been here for five months for the purpose of establishing a school of English for the Coreans. A building has been set apart, sixty pupils have set down their names, but the classes have not yet begun. He says that M. Möllendorff is organizing a Customs Staff, to consist of six tide-waiters, one clerk, one harbour-master, and one collector, at each of the three ports. The arrangements for the letting of land to foreigners at the ports are in a very backward state. It is hardly too much to say that nothing has been done. M. Möllendorff is spoken highly of by both Coreans and Japanese. I was told that, although he speaks and reads Chinese to some extent, he cannot carry on a conversation in the Chinese character, so that communication with him is difficult. Messrs. Kim Hong-jip and Hong Yŏng-sik speak a very little Chinese.

The relations of the Japanese Minister with the Corean Government were, so far as I could judge, friendly. Allowance must be made for the circumstance that I had no opportunities of hearing the view of the anti-Japanese party. The Minister complained to me that their ignorance of foreign matters was great, and that it was no easy task to contend with the inveterate suspicions which they had of the designs of foreign Powers. He has urged them to adopt a 5 per cent. Tariff, but he avoided giving me any assurance that Japan would resist the imposition of a higher rate.

(Signed)　W.G. Aston.
Soül, *April* 11, 1883

Inclosure 2

Mr. Aston to Sir H.S. Parkes.

(Confidential)

Hiôgo, April 23, 1883

Sir,

 IN continuation of my despatch dated from Sŏul on the 10th instant, I have the honour to report that on the following day I received a visit from M. P. G. von Möllendorff, Inspector-General of Corean Customs, and Adviser to the Corean Foreign Department. He had returned from Shanghae on the previous day. M. von Möllendorff wore a Corean head-dress, but the remainder of his costume appeared to me to be more Chinese than Corean. He said he had adopted the Corean costume for the sake of convenience. He also wore Corean dress when he appeared at Court, the reason given by him being that it is almost impossible for any one in European dress to be received there with the formalities due to his rank. The Corean Court-dress is very costly, and M. von Möllendorff informed me that the purchase of a costume being beyond his means, the King had presented him with one.

 M. von Möllendorff had come over in one of the China Merchants' steam-ships, and he brought with him a sum of 200,000 taels lent to Corea by that Company at an interest of 8 per cent. per annum.

 He informed me that he had complete control of this money, which it was his intention to devote to three objects, viz., to introduce silk culture into Corea, to establish a fishery at Port Lazareff on improved principles, and to organize a plan for the extension and conservation of the Corean woods and forests.

 He had brought over several thousand young mulberry trees, a supply of implements used in the silk industry, and two Chinese to act instructors to the Coreans. He spoke of planting many acres of ground with mulberry trees, and was sanguine of large profits. Merchants at Shanghae had assured him that with the land he proposed to plant he might expect an annual production of 25,000 bales of silk. I may mention that raw silk, as at present prepared in Corea, is unsaleable in the London market.

M. von Möllendorff was strongly opposed to allowing the money to be spent on preparing foreign Settlements, building custom-houses, jetties, &c. He seemed to think they might be allowed to shift for themselves. Two Europeans arrived with him from Shanghae. I heard that one of these men was to organize a Woods and Forests Service.

M. von Möllendorff informed me that the Viceroy, Li Hung Chang, had promised to allow the Corean Government any concessions in commercial matters which they might require in order to place their relations with foreign Powers on a satisfactory footing, reserving, however, all political rights. He said that Mr. Russell Young, the American Minister to Peking, had expressed his "determination to insist" on the maintenance of the high rate of Tariff of the present Treaties, though by what means he proposed to do so was not explained. Japan, M. von Möllendorff added, would be compelled to grant Corea the Tariff she wishes for. The Treaty with that country provided for reciprocity of treatment, and if Japan would not agree to a Tariff, he (M. von Möllendorff) would establish a colony of Corean merchants at Nagasaki, where they would be entitled to import goods free of duty. I pointed out that, as Japan had a 5 per cent. Tariff, this employment of the principle of reciprocity would only enable the Coreans to compel a similar rate. M. von Möllendorff insisted, however, that he had the means of forcing Japan to accept the Corean terms, whatever they might be. He scouted the idea of the Corean Tariff being appealed to as a precedent in future Tariff Regulations between China or Japan and European countries.

He has arranged with Messrs. Jardine, Matheson, and Co. to establish themselves at Inchhön at once, and without waiting for the ratification of the Treaty. He does not believe that the China Merchants' Steamers can carry on the Corean trade. They do not succeed in China, he said, where they have many privileges.

M. von Möllendorff's friends in the Corean Government are Kim Hong-jip, Hong Yöng-sik, and Min Yong-ik. Kim Ok Kiun he spoke of as a clever but dangerous man.

Mr. Kim Ok kiun called on me late on the same evening. He had come direct from the Palace, which had on that day been a scene of more than usual excitement.

He said his policy had had a great success, and had been adopted by the

King. He referred especially to the use to be made of the loan of 200,000 taels, which he informed me it had been resolved to spend on harbours, custom-houses, &c., the object being to provide some security for a foreign loan, which is an essential part of his policy. It is intended, Mr. Kim Ok Kiun says, that this loan shall be of 2,000,000 dollars, and that it shall form the basis of a paper currency, which is much needed in Corea. This, however, I believe to be a secondary object only, the principal one being to provide funds for the reorganization of the army. Mr. Kim Ok Kiun, as you are aware, is the most prominent member of the anti-Chinese party. His policy is to maintain the national independence of Corea, reducing the suzerainty of China to as much of a shadow as possible, and getting rid of all interference by Chinese troops and Chinese officials in the internal administration or foreign relations of Corea.

In order that this policy should be successful, Corea wants a small but well-organized army, clothed, drilled, and armed in European fashion, so as to be able to guarantee internal tranquillity; and for this purpose a foreign loan is necessary, as the Corean finances are at present in a very disorganized state.

Mr. Kim Ok Kiun is of opinion, and my observation leads me to agree with him, that Corea, in her future efforts after progress, will follow in the footsteps of Japan, and adopt Europe as her model, abandoning the guidance of China, under which her condition for several hundred years past has been stationary, or rather, retrograde.

Mr. Kim Ok Kiun drafted the letter written to you in reply to your letter to the Corean Minister for Foreign Affairs. A counter-draft, prepared by Mr. Ma Kie Tchang, was rejected. Mr. Kim's father has been appointed to an office in the Judicial Department.

I learned afterwards that on the same day his Excellency Pak Yŏng-hio[sic], lately Envoy to Japan, had been driven from his office as Governor of the city of Söul by the Chinese party, with Min-thai-ho at their head, the reasons being that he had insisted on the removal of the straw-built booths by which the main thoroughfares of the city were until lately encumbered, and that his action in a dispute between the iron and cotton guilds had been thought injudicious. These straw booths were being re-erected on the day before I left Söul.

I left Söul for Chemulpho on the 12th. Her Majesty's ship "Daring" was detained there during the 13th by bad weather. Three Japanese vessels arrived on the afternoon of that day with merchants who intend to settle at this port. The cargoes consisted of coal for the Japanese men-of-war stationed here, curios, copper, and Corean rice from Pusan, the latter being, of course, an instance of interport trade in Corean produce.

I left Chemulpho on the morning of the 14th, and reached Pusan on the 17th. The Pusa of Tongnai came to call on me, and in course of conversation reminded me of my remarks last year about the stone pillars denouncing friends to foreigners, which, he said, he had the pleasure of informing me had been removed shortly after my last visit. I arrived at Simonoseki on the 20th, and came on here in the Mitsu Bishi mail-steamer, as I had some apprehensions that the "Daring" might fail to connect with her at Kobé. I propose to leave by the same vessel for Yokohama to-morrow afternoon.

Mr. Bonar I left behind at Simoneseki, where I learnt that he would be able to proceed to Nagasaki by the Koiin Maru of the 22nd instant. I take this opportunity of thanking you most cordially for allowing me the advantage of his assistance and companionship.

My hearty thanks are also due to Lieutenant-Commander Corfe, of Her Majesty's ship "Moorhen," and to Commander Eliott, of Her Majesty's ship "Daring," for the facilities they on all occasions willingly afforded me. In the case of the "Moorhen" particularly, the service of conveying the two Corean officials, Mr. Bonar, and myself, from Nagasaki to Inchhön, a voyage of five days, involved no little personal discomfort to Lientenant-Commander Corfe and his officers.

I have, &c.
(Signed)   W.G. Aston

142

H.S. Parkes (1883. 4. 28) ➜ G.L.G. Granville (1883. 6. 19)

Aston의 영국공관, 영사관 부지 선정 보고

Sir H.S. Parkes to Earl Granville.—(Received June 19)

(No. 66)

Tôkiô, April 28, 1883

My Lord,

I HAVE the honour to forward a copy of a despatch, with two inclosures, handed to me by Mr. Aston on the 26th instant, in which he reports the steps he had taken, during his recent visit to Corea, to secure the refusal of building sites for use of the Diplomatic or Consular officers who may be appointed by Her Majesty's Government to that country.

The comments which I shall have to submit to your Lordship in support of Mr. Aston's proceedings will form the subject of a subsequent despatch.

I have, &c.
(Signed)   HARRY S. PARKES

Inclosure 1

Mr. Aston to Sir H.S. Parkes.

Hiôgo, April 24, 1883

Sir,

IN compliance with the instructions contained in your despatch of the 6th March last, to endeavour to obtain from the Corean Government the refusal of suitable sites for Consular residences in that country, I have the honour to report as follows.

On the 2nd and 9th April I had interviews with the Corean Foreign Ministers, at which this subject was discussed.

With regard to the accommodation which might be required for a British Diplomatic Representative in the city of Söul, they said that they proposed to leave the matter altogether to the owners of land or houses and myself, and I was accordingly placed in communication with a house agent, along with whom I visited four residences of Corean noblemen which were for sale. All were in every respect inferior to the house provided for me during my stay in Söul, and, as this was also in the market, I obtained a promise from Mr. Kim Ok Kiun that it would not be disposed of to any one else until Her Majesty's Government had an opportunity of deciding whether or not to purchase it.

This house is within the walls of the city, between the south and west gates, and about a mile from the Palace, the Foreign Office, and the Japanese Legation. There are a large number of detached buildings on the site, none of any great size, and the rooms are low and small. All the buildings have most of the rooms heated by flues underneath the floors in the manner usual in Northern China. Mr. Bonar has prepared a description and plan of the principal building and of the whole premises, to which I have the honour to refer you for further details. (A) and (B) might be joined by a covered gallery so as to form the principal residence; (C) would do for a chancery; (D) might be made to serve as quarters for an Assistant; and there are smaller buildings which might be converted into stabling, &c. The main building is in tolerably good repair, but a good deal of alteration will be required to suit it for occupation by Europeans, and it can only be regarded as a temporary shelter until permanent buildings are erected. There are no houses in Söul suitable for permanent quarters. In making the necessary alterations, stoves, window-glass, wall-paper, locks, hinges, and other fittings would be among the articles required. None of these are procurable in Corea.

As a site for building, this is on the whole an eligible position. It contains 1,700 to 1,800 tsubos (about 7,000 square yards), and occupies a rising ground sloping off in steep banks on three sides, and commanding a fine view of the whole city. On the fourth side, where the entrance is, it slopes gradually to the streets below. The lots immediately adjoining are occupied by Coreans of rank.

The chief objection to this site is that it is approached for some distance through narrow and very filthy alleys, but the same objection applies to nearly every site in Söul that I have seen. There is a somewhat better approach on another side; and as the ground here belongs to the Corean Government, by whom it is used as a timberyard, it would no doubt be easy to arrange with them for a right of way through it. There is no well on the premises. It is indispensable to sink one, as the wells in the neighbourhood from which water is at present procured are close to fetid gutters, and the water, though clear and pleasant to drink, cannot be wholesome. The depth of a well would be 50 or 60 feet,

The price of this site, with the buildings on it, is 7,500 "nyang" of Corean money, equal at the present rate of exchange to a little over 1,400 Mexican dollars. House property has become very cheap in Söul since the disturbances of last year. No rent would be payable subsequently, and there is at present no land or house tax in Söul. The Foreign Minister, however, informed me that houses or land purchased by the British Government in Söul would be liable to pay similar taxes to those which might afterwards be levied on native property, I hardly think that a better permanent site than this can be obtained; but before closing with the offer, further inquiry would be desirable, if opportunity offered.

I was informed on the day previous to my departure that the house of his Excellency Pak Yöng-hio would be for sale. It is in excellent repair, and could be occupied at once. The situation, however, is low and confined, and could not be recommended as a building site. It is close to the public offices and to the residences of the principal high officials.

Some information as to the nature and cost of the building materials procurable at Söul will be found in the Memorandum which I have the honour to annex herewith.

At Yanghwa-chin the only building which is at all suitable for occupation by Europeans is the King's cottage referred to in my Memorandum of the 12th October, 1882. I can now confirm from personal observation the information given there with respect to this building. The formal reply of the Corean Foreign Minister to my request for a refusal of this place was that it would be given to the first Power which asked for it after their Treaty was ratified; but I received private assurances that no difficulty in respect to it need be apprehended. The house is small, and the doors and windows are not in very good repair, but the situation is charming, as it commands a fine prospect in both directions of the river, which is here about 300 yards wide, and 2 to 3 fathoms in depth. It is 4 miles from the capital by an indifferent road, which like all the [____] I have seen in this country, is not passable for wheeled vehicles.

It was discovered that the site originally p.ched(*Sic.*) upon by the Japanese for a Settlement at Yanghwa-chin is flooded every spring to the depth of several feet, and M. von Möllendorff has selected a spot about a mile up the river. The latter site seems well chosen, at least in so far as can be judged with the present imperfect survey of the river. M. von Möllendorff thinks that the chief trade will be here rather than at Chemulpho; but except it turns out that vessels of greater draught than it is at present supposed (9 to 10 feet), can reach this point, this would seem rather doubtful.

I suggested to Mr. Kim Ok Kiun that his Government would do well to reserve this cottage for the accommodation of any British official who might be sent to Corea to make ulterior arrangements respecting the Treaty. The distance from the capital, I said, was of little consequence in comparison with the increased facilities for water transport. The capital, for many reasons is not a pleasant place of residence, and in times of popular excitement there the advantage, on the score of safety, of a residence on the river would be considerable. It is quite near enough to any probable site for a foreign Settlement here to serve for a Consulate, at least temporarily, and it is close to one of the roads from Chemulpho to the capital. Yanghwa-diin is to be opened to Japanese trade in September next.

The site of the foreign Settlement at Inchhön (Jinchuen) is not yet finally determined. I found that M. von Möllendorff and Mr. Ma Kie Tchang were in favour of a site on the north end of Wölmi (Roze Island), and I could see that their opinion had considerable weight with the Corean Government. The Japanese, on the other hand, prefer a site on the mainland at the village of Chemulpho. The Wölmi site has the advantage of being much nearer to an anchorage for large vessels, and a jetty could be easily constructed here for cargo-boats. But it is separated from the mainland by a strait nearly half-a-mile in width, so that a double transport would be necessary for all merchandize transported by land to Söul. The great rise and fall of the tide (34 feet at springs) would make a bridge or causeway here a very costly undertaking.

M. von Möllendorff is of opinion that most of the trade will be carried on by means of the river, but against this it is to be observed that the distance to the capital by this route is 55 miles, as compared with 24 by land; that one part of the river is only passable at certain times of the tide, and that the upper reaches are closed to traffic by the ice for three months every year. Wölmi is a rugged and precipitous island, and does not afford sufficient level ground for the site of a foreign Settlement, chemulpho has the disadvantage of lying 1¾ miles from the place where large vessels would have to anchor, and this, in a river where the tides run so strongly, is a very serious objection. Small vessels could, however, lie in the strait between it and Wölmi, there being at the lowest spring tides 9 feet of water here, and much more at other times. By dredging, this channel could probably be improved. A jetty for cargo-boats could be constructed here as easily as on Wölmi. The Chemulpho site is very suitable for a Settlement, the ground sloping up not too rapidly from high-water mark, and it is capable of being indefinitely extended if necessary. That it is on the mainland is, of course, the chief consideration in its favour. The road to the capital is tolerably level, and could be easily made practicable for wheeled vehicles. The River Hangang would be the chief difficulty, as there is no bridge at present, nor is one likely to be constructed for some years.

Temporary buildings have been erected at Chemulpho for the Japanese Vice-Consulate, and as quarters for a number of Japanese soldiers who are stationed here, but when I first arrived there were no Japanese merchants and no sign of commerce, the only representative of trade being a Corean who sat in front of his cabin with a scanty stock of straw shoes, eggs, and dried persimmons displayed on a mat before him. The site for the permanent Japanese Consulate had been levelled, and the materials for building it were deposited close by, but no work was going on.

I do not think the Japanese will readily consent to abandon the Chemulpho site, more especially as it is in the district of Inchön, as provided in their Treaty, whereas the proposed Wölmi site is in a different district, a fact of which I suspect M. von Möllendorff to be ignorant.

Mr. Ma Kie Tchang gave me to understand that an objection to this site which had great weight with the Corean Government and their advisers was that, if now definitively fixed on, an opportunity would be afforded to the Japanese of establishing themselves here in advance of other Powers, and so getting possession of all the best sites. It is the intention of the Corean Government not to have distinct Settlements for each nationality, but common Settlements, somewhat after the model of those in Japan.

Having come to the conclusion that the Chemulpho site, though open to one serious objection, is not only, upon the whole, the best procurable, but is the only possible palce which answers to the description of Inchhön as laid down in the Treaty, I requested the Foreign Minister to depute a Corean official to select along with me a provisional site for a British Consulate at this place. The Foreign Minister reminded me that this Settlement had not been finally determined on, but said he had no objection to my selecting a Consular site there, subject to conditions as to rent, &c., to be subsequently arranged on the basis of such similar charges as might be fixed upon for the rest of the Settlement. He declined to authorize the selection of a site outside the limits of the Settlement.

On arriving at Chemulpho I selected a vacant space of over 1,200 tsubo, or about. 5,000 square yards, in area, the four sides measuring from 60 to 90 yards each. It is in the centre of the proposed Settlement, and faces the sea. The front of this lot forms a steep bank, rising at one end to about 16 feet above the high-water mark, and at the other to about 7 or 8 feet. It slopes gently upwards towards the hill behind, no part of it having an inclination too steep for building purposes. It will probably be separated from the adjonining Japanese Consular lot by a road. The Corean official who accompanied me remarked that it might be necessary to take earth from this site for the purpose of filling in the sea in front of the Settlement. I replied that this was a matter which could be afterwards arranged by the authorities of the two countries, At my request, this official had pegs, inscribed (*Sic.*) with the Chinese characters for "British Consulate," driven in at each corner of the site, and I subsequently arranged with the Japanese Vice-Consul to have these replaced by substantial posts, 5 or 6 inches square and 5 or 6 feet in height.

It was fortunate that this matter was not longer delayed as on the following day three vessels arrived with a number of Japanese merchants, who had come to establish themselves here, and a large Japanese steamer passed Simonoseki on the 20th instant with her decks crowded with passengers for Inchhön. The Japanese Government, in the exercised of a Treaty right, formally notified that this port was open to Japanese trade from the 1st January last, and some provision for letting land to Japanese subjects must be made at once. Had this site not been reserved, it would, in all probability, have been occupied by them. I pointed it out to the Japanese Vice-Consul in person, so the there can now be no excuse for interference with it by his countrymen.

At Söul I found that the question of the site of a foreign Settlement at Pusan was still undecided. Some of the officials had an idea, which I did my best to discourage, that the Japanese Settlement would do for other foreigners as well. M. von Möllendorff had seen my Report of last year, in which this subject was touched upon, and had translated it into Chinese for the information of the Corean Government. He thought favourably of the site suggested by me, and said that he hoped to examine it personally in the course of a few weeks. Assuming that this spot would be selected, I proceeded to Pusan, provided with a letter from the Corean Minister of Foreign Affairs to the chief local functionary there. With this official I visited the place, and having chosen site for a Consulate, and obtained from him a promise that it would not be interfered with or disposed of to any one else without consulting us, I had a number of stout posts driven in to mark the boundaries. This site comprises the top and slopes of a hill about 100 feet in height. The summit has sufficient flat ground for a Consul's residence, not much above the level of the main road between the Japanese Settlement and Pusan which skirts the site. On the side next the sea there are precipitous cliffs, but on that facing Pusan, where the foreign Settlement would be situated, the slope is not very steep, and there is an eligible position for Consular offices at a point a little above the sea-level. The site is an extensive one, but much of it is too steep for building purposes. It commands, however, a view of the whole harbour, and the elevated situation would be found a great advantage in a climate so hot as that of Pusan, There are one or two graves on it, in removing which it would be necessary to avoid offending the feelings of the natives.

As I observed in my previous Report, all building materials used here are imported from Japan. The timber comes chiefly from the Island of Tsushima, 40 miles away.

I endeavoured to obtain the refusal of houses in the Japanese Settlement which might serve as temporary quarters pending the erection of a permanent Consulate, but I found that the inducements I was able to hold out were not sufficient to tempt the owners to run the risk of refusing eligible offers which might be made to them. I saw two houses which I was told might be had. One had four rooms of 6 mats, or 12 feet square, in the first storey, and three rooms of the same size on the ground floor, besides kitchen, bath-room, servants' room, and a small but substantial godown. The house stands in a side street, and has no garden. The other house is about the same size, new, and in good repair, and in the main street. There is access to it from the sea, and boat davits have been provided. It has also a godown. These are fair specimens of the houses procurable here. They could be had, if engaged now, for about 30 dollars each per month, but when Pusan is opened to foreign commerce they may command much higher rates, as the first settlers will have to rent Japanese houses for a time.

At Söul I requested that the hill immediately above the Japanese Consulate at Wönsan might be reserved as a site for the British Consulate, and I addressed a letter to the Japanese Consul informing him of this fact, and requesting him to make it known to any person who might wish to erect buildings in this locality. It is improbable, however, that there will be any necessity for a permanent Consular establishment at this place, at least for some time to come, I did not visit this port.

I have, &c.
(Signed) W.G. ASTON

H.S. Parkes (1883. 4. 28) ➜ G.L.G. Granville (1883. 6. 19)

조영, 조독조약 비준서 교환 연기 통보를 위한 Aston의 재파견 보고

Sir H.S. Parkes to Earl Granville.—(Received June 19)

(No. 67 Confidential)

Tôkiô, April 28. 1883

My Lord,

I HAVE the honour to report that on receipt of your Lordship's telegram of the 22nd instant, which I acknowledged in my despatch No. 62. of the 23rd instant, I communicated with my German colleague, Count Dönhof, and arranged with him that Mr. Aston should proceed again to Corea to inform the Corean Government that Her Majesty's Government and the Imperial German Government desired to extend for six months the term within which the ratifications of the British and German Treaties with Corea should be exchanged. We also agreed that it would be desirable that declarations of such postponement of ratification should be duly executed.

The arrival here of General Foote, the American Minister to Corea, and his intended departure on the 2nd proximo for that country, rendered essential the immediate dispatch of Mr. Aston on this service. He will accordingly proceed in the Peninsular and Oriental mail steamer leaving Yokohama to-night as far as Simonoseki, where I have arranged by telegraphic communication with Vice-Admiral Willes and the Senior Naval Officer in Japan that he shall be met by the latter in Her Majesty's ship "Daring," in order that he may be conveyed direct from that point to the Chemulpho anchorage (Jinchuen).

I beg to inclose a copy of the note which I have addressed on this subject to the Corean Minister for Foreign Affairs, and of the Declaration which I have instructed Mr. Aston to sign on the part of Her Majesty's Government, together with a translation of a similar note addressed by Count Dönhof to the said Corean Minister, giving cover to a Declaration of the same tenour. I also add a translation of a letter from Count Dönhof to myself, requesting me to authorize Mr. Aston to undertake this service on behalf of the Imperial German Government.

I have furnished Mr. Aston with the inclosed instructions, and have requested Commander Eliott in the accompanying letter to convey him as expeditiously as possible to Jinchuen, and back again to Japan as soon as he is ready to return.

Owing to the immediate departure of the mail I am obliged to be thus brief in reporting these proceedings. I may add that I have named the 31st December in the Declaration between Her Majesty's Government and that of Corea, because an extension of exactly six months in the case of the Anglo-Corean Treaty would have prolonged the term for exchanging the ratifications to the 6th December, and in the case of the German-Corean Treaty to the 30th December, and I thought that unity of action between the British and German Governments would be becomingly attested by naming the same date within which the ratifications of their respective Treaties may be exchanged.

I have, &c.
(Signed) HARRY S. PARKES

Inclosure 1

Sir H.S. Parkes to Min Yöng Mok.

Your Excellency,   Tôkiô, April 28, 1883

I HAVE the honour to inform you that I have been instructed by Her Majesty's government to direct Mr. Aston, one of Her Majesty's Consuls in Japan, to inform your Government of their wish to extend for several months the time fixed for the exchange of the ratifications of the Treaty signed at Jinchuen on the 6th June last by the respective Representatives of our two countries.

My Government are of opinion that certain provisions of this Treaty require further consideration, and your Excellency will, I trust, perceive that their motive in proposing this postponement is an earnest desire to place the Treaty relations of our two countries from their commencement on a satisfactory footing, so as to prevent difficulties in the future.

Mr. Aston is therefore authorized to sign with a Representative of your Government a document declaring that our respective Governments agree to extend the term for exchanging the ratifications of the said Treaty till the 31st December of the present year.

I take, &c.

(Signed)   HARRY S. PARKES

Inclosure 2

Declaration for extending the period stipulated for exchanging the Ratifications of the Treaty between Great Britain and Ireland and Chosen, signed at Jinchuen, June 6, 1882.

WHEREAS the Treaty of Friendship and Commerce concluded at Jinchuen on the 6th June, 1882, between Vice-Admiral Willes, on the part of Great Britain and Ireland, and Isas Ling Hsia and Ching Hung Kie, members of the Royal Council, on the part of Chosen, contains a stipulation that the ratifications of this Treaty shall be exchanged at Jinchuen within one year from the date of its signature, and whereas the Government of Great Britain is of opinion that portions of this Treaty require further consideration, the Undersigned being duly authorized by their respective Governments, have agreed to declare as follows:—

That the period fixed within which the ratifications should be exchanged shall be extended to the 31st December, 1883.

In faith of which they have signed the present Declaration made in duplicate and in the English and Chinese languages, and have affixed thereto their seals.

Done at Söul on the(*Sic.*)

Inclosure 3

M. Dönhof to Min Yŏng Mok.

(Translations)
Your Excellency, Tôkiô, April 28, 1883

ANIMATED by the wish to take into further consideration the German-Corean Treaty, signed at Jinchuen on the 30th June last year, the Imperial German Government desires to prolong the term for exchanging the ratifications of the said Treaty for several months.

I have therefore the honour to inform Your Excellency that I have received instructions to introduce to your Excellency Mr. Aston, one of Her Britannic Majesty's Consuls in Japan, who is hereby authorized by the Imperial German Government to sign, with a Plenipotentiary appointed by your Excellency's Government, a document by which the term for exchanging the ratifications of the German-Corean Treaty is extended to the 31st December of the present year.

I avail, &c.
(Signed) G. DÖNHOF, German Minister

Inclosure 4

M. Dönhof to Sir H.S. Parkes.

(Translations)
Your Excellency, Tôkiô, April 28, 1883

THE Imperial German Government have decided, in concert with your Excellency's Government, to postpone the ratification of the Treaties with Corea.

In obedience to instructions received from my Government, I have the honour to request Your Excellency to be so good as to allow me to introduce Her Britannic Majesty's Consul, Mr. Aston, in the name of my Government to the Government of Corea, and to empower him to sign a document postponing the exchange of the ratifications of the German-Corean Treaty.

I have the honour to inclose the letter of introduction for Mr. Aston, addressed to the Corean minister for Foreign Affairs, and the document for signature, and at the same time beg your Excellency to accept, &c.

(Signed)　　G. DÖNHOF, German Minister

Inclosure 5

Sir H.S. Parkes to Mr. Aston.

(Confidential)

Tokio, April 28, 1883

Sir,

YOU will learn from the inclosed copy of a telegram from Earl Granville, which I received on the night of the 23rd instant, that Her Majesty's Government have agreed with the German Government to extend the period fixed for the ratification of their Treaties with Corea for six months, and that I am instructed, after communicating with Count Dönhof, the German Minister to Japan, to direct you to give notice of this resolution to the Corean Government on behalf both of Her Majesty's Government and that of Germany.

I have accordingly to direct you to proceed to Corea to carry out this instruction. You are aware of the reasons which render it essential that you should sail by the Peninsular and Oriental mail-steamer which leaves Yokohama this evening, and that I have arranged with Commander Eliott, of Her Majesty's ship "Daring," to meet you at Simonoseki. On joining that vessel I trust you will find that Commander Eliott will be able to proceed with you direct from thence to the Chemulpho anchorage. In that case, I hope you will reach that point about the 5th May, and thus anticipate by several days the arrival there of General Foote, the American Minister to Corea. It is obviously desirable that you should do your best to effect within that interval the negotiation with which you are charged.

I am glad to think that, as I have had the advantage of personal communication with yourself, detailed instructions in this case are not indispensable. I inclose under flying seal a note, in which I have informed the Corean Minister for Foreign Affairs of the object of your mission, and that you are authorized to sign a Declaration by which the British and Corean Governments will agree to the time for the exchange of the ratifications of the Anglo-Corean Treaty being extended until the 31st December next. Duplicate copies of this Declaration in English are inclosed.

I have also to hand to you, on the part of the German Minister, a similar note which he has addressed to the Corean Foreign Minister, and duplicate copies in German and French of a Declaration of the same tenour.

It will remain for you to draw up in concert, and with the aid of the Corean authorities, the Chinese versions of these two Declarations, and when they have been duly signed, you will leave one copy of each version with them, and bring away with you one copy of each version for the British and German Governments.

I trust you will find that the Corean Government will readily perceive the necessity which exists for the execution of these Declarations. It may occur to themselves, without your having occasion to remind them, that the grave events which occurred in Corea last year, and the arrangements recently concluded between Corea and China, render it incumbent on the British and German Governments to act with deliberation, and to obtain fuller information respecting the state of affairs in Corea than they yet possess. It is also to be hoped that the Corean Government will see that this proposal to delay the exchange of the ratifications of the British and German Treaties with their country admits solely of a friendly interpretation, and indicates the desire of the British and German Governments to establish amicable relations with Corea.

Unless you should see reason to delay your departure from Corea, it is desirable that you should return to Tôkiô to report your proceedings to myself and the German Minister as soon as these Declarations shall have been signed, and the Corean Minister for Foreign Affairs shall have furnished you with his replies to my note and that of the German Minister.

I inclose, under flying seal, the despatch in which I have requested the Commander of Her Majesty's ship "Daring" to convey you from Simonoseki to the Chemulpho anchorage as expeditiously as his general instructions will permit, and back again to such port in Japan as he may deem most expedient after having been made acquainted by you with the requirements of the important service on which you are engaged.

I am, &c.
(Signed)   HARRY S. PARKES

Inclosure 6

Sir H.S. Parkes to Commander Elott.

Tôkiô, April 28, 1883

Sir,

WE have already been in telegraphic communication with each other relative to the service on which your are now engaged, namely, the conveyance of Mr. Aston to Corea, in execution of important telegraphic orders which I received from Her Majesty's Principal Secretary of State for Foreign Affairs on the 23rd instant.

The Commander-in-chief, upon my application for a vessel, has been so good as to inform me that your will proceed on this service, and I heard yesterday, from Her Majesty's Acting Consul at Kôbé, that you would leave to-morrow to receive Mr. Aston at Simonoseki, but that there was a possibility of your having to coal at Nagasaki. I therefore at once intimated to you by wire that, in view of his Excellency's instructions (as to vessels not touching at Nagasaki), and also having regard to delay which would be occasioned by your calling on this occasion at that port for coal, I considered it particularly desirable that you should not do so if it could possibly be avoided.

Mr. Aston proceeds to-night in the Peninsular and Oriental steamer "Sumatra," to Simonoseki, and on joining you there will deliver to you this despatch. I earnestly trust that you will be able to convey him to the Chemulpo anchorage (Jinchuen) direct from Simonoseki; and as the service on which he is engaged is of and urgent nature, I have to request you to use all the expedition that your general instructions will permit.

As the speedy return of Mr. Aston is of similar importance, I trust that you will not be detained more than a few days at Jinchuen, and as soon as Mr. Aston shall inform you that he is ready to leave, I have to request you to bring him back to such port in Japan, whether Simonoseki, Kôbé, or Nagasaki, as may best meet, in your judgement, the requirements, of Her Majesty's ship under your command, combined with the best consideration, which I am well assured you will readily give to the exigency of the important public service with which Mr. Aston is charged.

 I gladly profit by this opportunity to cordially thank you for the assistance you have already rendered to Mr. Aston on the occasion of his recent visit to Corea.

I have, &c.

(Signed)   HARRY S. PARKES

H.S. Parkes (1883. 4. 28) ➜ G.L.G. Granville (1883. 6. 19)

Foote의 일본 도착 보고

Sir H.S. Parkes to Earl Granville.—(Received June 19)

(No. 69)

Tôkiô, April 28, 1883

My Lord,

I HAVE the honour to report that General Foote, Envoy Extraordinary and Minister Plenipotentiary from the United States to Corea, arrived at Yokohama on the 19th instant, and that he proceeds on the 2nd proximo to Nagasaki, where a ship of war of the United States is waiting to convey him to Corea.

General Foote is being actively assisted with Interpreters and similar services by the Government of Japan, who welcome his appointment as a recognition on the part of the United States of the independent position of Corea in regard to China which is declared in the Treaty of 1876 between Japan and Corea.

I inclose a translation of an article on the subject of this appointment which has appeared to-day in the semi-official Japanese journal, the "Nichi Nichi Shim bun." It asserts that China has been completely baffled in her pretensions to treat Corea as a subject State by the action of the United States' Government in entering into Treaty relations with that country, and that this action having been followed by Great Britain and Germany, the independence of Corea can no longer be questioned. It also alleges that the letter which the King of Corea was induced by China to address to the President of the United States, stating that Corea is a dependency of China, has been treated by the President as a private communication having no effect, and to which no answer will be returned.

I have, &c.

(Signed)   HARRY S. PARKES

H.S. Parkes (1883. 4. 29) ➜ G.L.G. Granville (1883. 4. 29)

상업 특권 양여에 대한 미국의 반대 보고

Sir H.S. Parkes to Earl Granville.— (Received April 29, 7 · 20 P.M.)

(Telegraphic)

Tôkiô, April 29, 1883, 4 P.M.

YOUR telegram of 22nd.

Communicated with German Minister, and conjointly dispatched Aston to Corea yesterday (he returned here on the 26th); has already sounded Corean Government. American Treaty being ratified, they will resist commercial concession and insist on complete control of Tariff; they hope Chinese and Japanese will accept conditions of American Treaty, in order to promote their own claims on European Powers.

H.S. Parkes (1883. 5. 14) ➔ G.L.G. Granville (1883. 6. 18)

Foote와 회견 및 Foote의 조선행 보고

Sir H.S. Parkes to Earl Granville.—(Received June 18)

(No. 75 Confidential)

Tôkiô, May 14, 1883

My Lord

WITH reference to my despatch No. 69 of the 28th April, reporting the arrival here of General Foote, the United States' Minister to Corea, I have the honour to report the tenour of some observations which he made to me in a conversation I had with him on the 29th ultimo.

He remarked that Corea was considered by his Government to be an independent State, and that his appointment was, of course, a demonstration of that view. They believed that the Chinese Government would approve of this recognition, as the latter had recommended the American Treaty to the Corean Government, and had aided in negotiating it. He could see that some of its details required improvement, which he would endeavour to effect, but he thought the basis of the Tariff named in the Treaty might stand as it was, as the Coreans needed money, and import duties were simply an indirect tax on the Corean People. He considered that the United States could claim any privileges that had recently been gained by China in Corea.

In reply to an inquiry of mine, he observed that no Consuls had yet been appointed by his Government to Corea, and probably would not be until they received his reports, as little or no trade was expected. He would secure sites, however, for Consular residences, and do what he could to promote the satisfactory formation of the future foreign Settlements, which he thought the foreign residents should be allowed to manage themselves.

On my asking what notice had been taken by the United States' Government of the letter of the King of Corea to the President of the United States, I understood General Foote to reply that it was regarded by his Government as a private communication, which did not in any degree affect the Treaty. It had been, or would be only formally acknowledged. He was not precise on this point, and the Vice-Minister for Foreign Affairs mentioned to me, on the 30th ultimo, that Mr. Stevens, the Foreign Secretary of the Japanese Legation at Washington (who was for many years Secretary of the United States' Legation at Tôkiô), had advised the Foreign Office here that no answer had been returned to the King's letter. It may occur to your Lordship that, in my despatch No. 154 of the 24th October last, I reported that Kim Ok Kiun in a conversation with me had suggested that the letter of the King to the Queen need not be answered, or that it might be returned, and it is not improbable that he made similar suggestions to the Minister of the United States at Tôkiô.

General Foote expressed a hope that the British and German Governments would shortly see their way to ratify their Treaties with Corea, to which I observed that I could say nothing as to their views or future action, but that I could not see what compensation would be derived in Corea by my Government in return for the expenses which they would incur in establishing Diplomatic and Consular officers in that country, as it appeared to me that the high duties of the Treaties would prevent the growth both of trade to the foreigners and of revenue to the Corean Government. It was probable also that the outlay would not be confined to civil expenses, for the tide of change which appeared to be setting in Corea could scarcely be attended without some degree of political disturbance. We had already witnessed one serious [convulsion] there since the Treaties were signed, and the occupation of the capital by a Chinese garrison, the presence there of a large guard for the protection of the Japanese Minister, and the known weakness of the Corean Government were indications that order had not yet been securely established there. It appeared to me, therefore, that the early stages of foreign relations with Corea would not be unattended with risk.

General Foote left Yokohama on the 2nd instant, reached Nagasaki on the night of the 6th, and left again early on the 8th in the United States' ship of war "Monocacy," for Corea, where he probably arrived on the 10th or 11th.

The Japanese Foreign Minister had previously apprised the Corean Government of General Foote's arrival in Japan, and had instructed the Japanese Minister at Söul to arrange for his reception. His Excellency has also attached to General Foote Mr. Saito, one of his private secretaries, who has a very good knowledge of English, acquired in the United States.

I have, &c.
(Signed) HARRY S. PARKES

統署(1883. 5. 15/高宗二十年四月九日)

비준서 교환 연기 요청 수락

統理交涉通商事務衙門以英國德國條約互換改期約章畫押蓋印啓
　該衙門啓言去壬午年在仁川口所立英國德國條約本以一年期滿互換爲訂而
　英國領事官阿須頓因英國德國政府意改期緩訂於本年十二月初三日內互換
　故委派本衙門參議李祖淵與該領事官阿須頓訂立約章畫押蓋印矣

閔泳穆(1883. 5. 15/高宗二十年四月九日) ➔ H.S. Parkes

Aston과 협의한 3개조 조약안의 시행여부를 문의하는 조회

大朝鮮國統理交涉通商事務衙門督辦閔 爲照會事 照得 前次貴國阿領事至本國訂立約章之時 已面商先議條約三款 係從阿領事之意 在阿領事以爲貴國政府必所樂行是以本大臣玆將三款另行開錄呈覽 卽請貴大臣將此三款情形轉咨貴國政府可否能行 仰希示覆 以便商辦 相應照會 爲此照會貴大臣 請煩查照可也 須至照會者
右照會
大英國駐劄日本欽差大臣世爵 巴
月 日 照會

朝英訂立條款
大朝鮮國大君主與大英國大君主兼印度后帝 均欲惠顧彼此人民 敦崇和好 是以大朝鮮國特派 大英國大君主兼印度后帝特派 各將所奉全權字樣互相較閱 俱屬妥善 訂立條款開列於左

　　第一款
大朝鮮國大君主 大英國大君主兼印度后帝 幷兩國人民 皆永遠和平友愛 若他國有何不公輕藐之事 一經照知 必須相助 從中善爲調理 以示友誼關切

　　第二款
凡英國人民 在朝鮮遇有財産刑犯等案被控者 應歸英國官員按英國律例核辦 若朝鮮人民或亦有被英國人民控告者 應歸朝鮮官員辦理 原告所屬之國 可以派員聽審 審官當以禮相待 如欲傳訊·查訊·分訊 訂期相見 亦聽其便 如以審公所斷爲不公 亦許其詳細駁辨 大朝鮮國與大英國彼此明定 如朝鮮國日後改定律例及審案辦法 在英國視與本國律例辦法相符 卽將英國官員在朝鮮審案之權收回 以後朝鮮境內英國人民卽歸地方官管轄

第三款

自此條約畫押之日起 凡朝鮮政府有與別國已前曾經允許 及後日再行允許之利益 英國政府及其人民 可一體均霑 其別國條約內 有英國亦要遵行者 則英國亦將該條約一體照辦 至陸路通商 除毗連之隣國外 概不准行 英國人民不得於陸路貿易

G.O. Willes (1883. 5. 30) ➜ Secretary to the Admiralty(1883. 7. 26)

조약 개정에 관한 李鴻章과 회견 내용 보고

Vice-Admiral Willes to the Secretary to the Admiralty.—(Received at the Foreign Office, July 26)

"Audacious," in the Yangtse Kiang River,

(Extract)

May 30, 1883

THE "Daring" returned to Nagasaki on the 21st May, having brought Mr. Aston back from the Corea. She would leave for Kobé on the 22nd, and thence for Shanghae on the 26th. As reported in my letter of this date, Mr. Aston's mission has been unsuccessful. Their Lordships will remember that in a former despatch I presumed to offer an opinion, after my Treaty negotiations, that "Japan was certainly not the point from which our relations with the Corea should be directed," and the observations of Li Hung-chang on the subject seem to confirm the view I then took.

Vice-Admiral Willes to the Secretary to the Admiralty.

Sir,

"Audacious," in the Yangtse, May 30, 1883

I THINK it may be of interest to the Lords Commissioners of the Admiralty to be informed of an interview which I have had with the Grand Secretary Li Hung-chang.

This powerful Chinese statesman arrived at Shanghae on the 28th instant, and I took the earliest opportunity of calling on him. Mr. Hughes, Her Majesty's Consul, was good enough to accompany me.

2. In the course of conversation Li asked me whether Majesty's

Government intended to ratify the Corean Treaty.

I replied that I had no information as regards the intentions of Her Majesty's Government, but that I was under the impression that the merchants of Germany and England were dissatisfied with the commercial clauses of the Treaty, especially those relating to Tariff and coast trade, and it was rumoured that the ratification of the Treaty would be deferred.

3. Li informed me that Mr. Aston had been sent to the Corea, and had endeavoured to induce the Corean Government to modify the two clauses referred to, but he had received despatches from Corea yesterday to the effect that his mission had been unsuccessful. This was the first intelligence I had received of the object of Mr. Aston's recent visit to the Corean capital. Li gave me to understand that his authority was necessary before the Corean Government could take upon itself to alter a Treaty which had been made under Li's auspices and with his assistance; and that he (Li) was of opinion that the Treaty, being a Commercial one, should be ratified as it stands, and that any modifications might be hereafter agreed upon and arranged by Protocol when Diplomatic Representatives had taken residence in the county. He said that at the present time there were many high officials (Coreans) visiting the various open ports in China and Japan in order to report to their Government on the manner in which commerce was regulated under present Treaties with those countries, and he thought that it would be inopportune at the present moment to place obstacles in the way of the ratification of the Corean Treaty, especially as the United States had already ratified the original Treaty.

I offered no opinion, but listened to Li's observations.

4. He then turned to the subject of Annam, and said that, in the same sense as Corea, Annam was a dependency of China, and the only European nations which had made a Commercial Treaty with that dependency were France and Spain. Why not England and other Powers? he asked. Would England make a Treaty with Annam now? She would have China's co-operation, and he could promise favourable terms. He pledged his word that he would then guarantee the acceptance in the Corea of English proposals with reference to the Corean Treaty. He asked me to express these remarks of his to Her Majesty's Government, and the interview, which was of a very cordial nature, ended.

I naturally refrain from the discussion of any of these matters.

5. Li is said to be the guiding power of China's counsels in foreign politics, and I thought, therefore, that it would be proper that I should report his

conversation.

6. He expressed deep regret that his old friend Sir Thomas Wade was not to return to China.

I have, &c.

(Signed)　　GEORGE O. WILLES

150

P.J. Hughes (1883. 5. 30) ➔ T.G. Grosvenor (1883. 7. 23)

李鴻章・Willes 회담 보고

Consul Hughes to Mr. Grosvenor—(Received at the Foreign Office, July 23)

(Confidential)
(Extract)

Shanghae, May 30, 1883

IN my despatch No. 53 of yesterday I reported the arrival at this port on the 28th instant of his Excellency Li Hung-chang. I mentioned that Vice-Admiral Willes called yesterday upon his Excellency, and that I was present on the occasion. After a long conversation on various subjects, Li inquired respecting the probability of the Corean Treaty being ratified. The Admiral informed him that there would be some delay, as both German and English merchants objected to the high rate of duties, and especially desired that the coast trade should be thrown open. The Admiral asked if Li would give his assistance in removing these obstacles. Li replied that it would be time enough to discuss these points after the ratification of the Treaty, but could not be induced to give the assurance that his influence would be exerted in the desired direction. He mentioned that by a letter lately received from Corea he learned that Mr. Aston had discussed these very questions with the Coreans, but without success, and added that the fact of the Americans having ratified their Treaty made any change in ours now more difficult.

In reply to another question, Li said that on political grounds he thought that the earlier our Treaty was ratified the better.

On the Admiral expressing a hope that the difficulty with France might soon be settled, Li assented with evident sincerity. He went on to say that Annam and Corea were on a like footing, both being tributary dependencies of China. He could not therefore understand why a nation with such vast commercial interests as England should not make a Treaty with Annam as well as with Corea. Why should England and other countries make Treaties with Corea, and leave France the monopoly of Annam, England especially, with India and the Straits Settlements so near? Why should the Admiral not proceed to Annam and make a Treaty now? If he did, Li would promise him his aid in obtaining most favourable terms. He would do more; he would engage to exert his influence in obtaining the desired changes in the Treaty with Corea. The Admiral informed his Excellency that it is our wish to maintain peaceful relations with all countries, but he would acquaint Her Majesty's Government with the offers now made. Li hoped he would do so, and remarked that the Chinese Minister in London had already mentioned the subject to Her Majesty's Secretary of State for Foreign Affairs.

151

H.S. Parkes (1883. 5. 30) ➜ G.L.G. Granville (1883. 7. 7)

비준서 교환 연기 협정 보고 (1)

Sir H.S. Parkes to Earl Granville.—(Received July 7)

(No. 87)
My Lord,

Tôkiô, May 30, 1883

IN my despatch No. 58 of the 20th ultimo, I inclosed copies of letters which had passed between Vice-Admiral Willes and myself relative to the censure which he had passed on Commander Eliott, then Senior Naval Officer in Japan, for having called at Nagasaki to coal, and to receive my despatches from Mr. Aston when he proceeded to Corea under orders from the Vice-Admiral at the end of March last.

I have now received from Vice-Admiral Willes the inclosed reply to my letter of the 18th April disclaiming any unwillingness on his part to co-operate with me in the execution of the public service. His Excellency adds that his disapproval of Commander Eliott's conduct related to discipline alone, and that he had abstained from conveying his disapproval to that officer until he could do so personally on his joining the flag.

Under these circumstances, I remain at a loss to understand why the Commander-in-chief should have communicated that disapproval to me, and in terms which showed that in his opinion that I had needlessly caused Commander Eliott to disobey certain "stringent orders" furnished him by his Excellency. I also remain uninformed as to what those orders were, as they certainly were not included in those shown me by Commander Eliott, a copy of which I inclosed in my despatch No. 58. I am left to surmise that they refer to one of the "Station orders," by which, as I have since casually heard, the Commanders of Her Majesty's ships are required not to touch at Nagasaki except for urgent reasons, in consequence, it is believed, of the prevalence of illicit prostitution at that port. If this be the cause of such an order, my despatch No. 73 of the 11th instant will show that it might be assigned with an equal degree of reason for depriving all the other ports in Japan of the visits of Her

Majesty's ships. But I also observe that notwithstanding this order, and since the date of Vice-Admiral Willes' letter to me of the 5th April, Her Majesty's ships continue to call at Nagasaki in the performance of their own service. Both the "Moorhen" and "Daring" did so on their return from Corea, although as the first was bringing me despatches, and the second Mr. Aston himself, I should have greatly preferred that they should not have been obliged to incur the delay occasioned by such a deviation from a more direct course.

The "Sheldrake," which left Yokohama on the 23rd ultimo to proceed to Hong Kong, also visited Nagasaki on her way down. I understood that each of these three vessels found it necessary to call there for a supply of coal, and it was this same reason, and not any particular requisition of mine, which obliged Commander Eliott to go there on his way to Corea. It was for contributing to that particular visit (out of the four that I have named) by requesting Commander Eliott to receive, when at Nagasaki, my despatches for Mr. Aston that the Commander-in-chief informed me in very decided terms that I had needlessly caused Commander Eliott to disobey his stringent orders against touching at that port.

Whether the language of the Vice-Admiral's letter to me of the 5th April justified my reply of the 18th of that month will now be determined by your Lordship and the Lords Commissioners of the Admiralty, but I have not hesitated to assure the Vice-Admiral, in acknowledging in the inclosed letter his rejoinder of the 11th instant, that I gladly accept his Excellency's assurance that I have misinterpreted the meaning of his previous communications, and that I earnestly reciprocate his desire for cordial co-operation in all matters relating to the discharge of the Queen's Service.

I have, &c.

(Signed)　　HARRY S. PARKES

Inclosure 1

Vice-Admiral Willes to Sir H.S. Parkes.

"Audacious," at Woosung, May 11, 1883

Sir,

I HAVE the honour to acquaint your Excellency that I have forwarded your despatch of the 18th April, 1883, to the Lords Commissioners of the Admiralty, with such remarks as it calls for.

I cannot too strongly express my regret that you should have been disposed to interpret a question, which was exclusively one of discipline between myself and Commander Eliott, into a want on my part of a willingness to co-operate with your Excellency for the public service.

It was Commander Eliott's duty to have informed you that he had received my express orders not to visit Nagasaki, and then if you still wished him to go to that port it was his duty to communicate with me by telegraph, knowing that I was within reach. For this neglect I have felt bound to remove him from the possibility of making similar mistakes, and in good faith I informed you of the result of his proceedings.

Far from discrediting you in the eyes of a junior officer (as you suggest I have done), I have up to the present moment purposely abstained from conveying to Commander Eliott my disapproval, which I had intended to communicate to him personally on his joining my flag.

The whole question is a simple one of naval discipline, and separate from any possible argument between your Excellency and myself. I need not assure you that I shall not allow the offence of Commander Eliott, whose cause you have so warmly espoused, to interfere with the cordial co-operation which it has always been and always will be my duty to afford your Excellency in the Queen's Service, whenever it may be my good fortune to have the opportunity given to me.

I have, &c.

(Signed)　　GEORGE O. WILLES

Inclosure 2

Sir H.S. Parkes to Vice-Admiral Willes.

Tôkiô, May 23, 1883

Sir,

I HAVE the honour to acknowledge the receipt of your Excellency's despatch of the 11th instant, and feel that I should not omit to express the satisfaction I derive from the assurance it conveys, that I have misinterpreted the meaning of your Excellency's previous letter of the 5th April, by thinking that it indicated an unwillingness on your part to afford me your valuable co-operation.

Whether the wording of Your Excellency's letter of the 5th April justified the terms of my reply of the 18th of that month, will now be determined by our respective superiors to whom that correspondence has been submitted, but I consider that I should not hesitate to assure your Excellency that your desire to cordially co-operate with me in all matters connected with the fulfilment of Her Majesty's Service is earnestly reciprocated by myself.

I have, &c.

(Signed)　　HARRY S. PARKES

152

H.S. Parkes (1883. 5. 30) ➜ G.L.G. Granville (1883. 7. 7)

비준서 교환 연기협정 보고 (2)

Sir H.S. Parkes to earl Granville.-(Received July 7)

(No. 3 Treaty)

Tôkiô, May 30, 1883

My Lord,

I HAVE the honour to forward to your Lordship a copy of the Declaration extending the period stipulated for exchanging the ratifications of Admiral Willes' Treaty with Corea, which was signed at Söul on the 15th May last by Mr. Aston on the part of Her Majesty's Government, and by I Cho-yön on the part of that of Corea.

The original Declaration was signed in duplicate, and one copy having been retained by the Corean Government, I have thought it advisable for the present to retain the other in this Legation rather than risk its transmission to your Lord-ship by post.

I have, &c.
(signed)   HARRY S. PARKES

Inclosure

Declaration for extending the period for exchanging the Ratifications of the Treaty between Great Britain and Ireland and Chosen, signed at Jinchuen, June 6, 1882.

WHEREAS the Treaty of Friendship and Commerce, concluded at Jinchuen on the 6th June, 1882, between Vice-Admiral Willes on the part of great Britain and Ireland, and Isas Ling Hsia and Ching Hung Ku, members of the Royal Council, on the part of Chosen, contains a stipulation that the ratifications of this Treaty shall be exchanged at Jinchuen within one year from the date of its signature; and whereas the Government of Great Britain is of opinion that portions of this Treaty require further consideration, the Undersigned being duly authorized by their respective Governments, have agreed to declare as follows:—

That the period fixed within which the ratifications should be exchanged shall be extended to the 31st December, 1883. In faith of which they have signed the present Declaration made in duplicate, and in the English and Chinese languages, and have affixed thereto their seals.

(L.S) (Signed)　W.G. Aston, *Her Britannic Majesty's Consul for Nagasaki, in Japan.*
(L.S) (Signed)　I CHO-YON, *Secretary of the Foreign Board of Corea.*

Done at Söul on the 15th May, 1883, corresponding to the 9th day of the fourth month of the Kwei-wi year of the Corean reckoning.

153

H.S. Parkes (1883. 5. 31) ➡ G.L.G. Granville (1883. 7. 7)

비준서 교환 연기협정 보고 (3)

Sir H.S. Parkes to Earl Granville.—(Received July 7)

(No. 90)
My Lord,

Tôkiô, May 31, 1883

HAVING expressed in my despatch No. 78 of the 14th instant, the apprehension that owing to the long passage made by Her Majesty's ship "Daring" to Corea, the United States' Minister might arrive there before the conclusion of the business with which Mr. Aston was charged, it affords me satisfaction to point out that, owing to the promptitude of Mr. Aston's action, the Declarations extending the time for the exchange of the ratifications of the Treaty between Great Britain and Corea were signed two days before General Foote arrived at Söul.

I have since heard from the Acting Foreign Minister that the Japanese Minister to Corea has informed him by telegraph from Nagasaki that the ratifications of the American Treaty with Corea were exchanged at Söul on the 19th instant.

I have, &c.
(Signed)   HARRY S. PARKES

H.S. Parkes (1883. 5. 31) ➜ G.L.G. Granville (1883. 7. 7)

비준서 교환 연기협정 보고 (4)

Sir H.S. Parkes to Earl Granville.-(Received July 7)

(No. 89)

Tôkiô, May 31, 1883

My Lord,

    WITH reference to my despatch No. 67 of the 28th ultimo, reporting that in pursuance of your Lordship's telegraphic instructions, and acting in concert with my German colleague, I had sent Mr. Aston to Corea to arrange with the Corean Government that the time named for the exchange of the British and German Treaties should be extended until the 31st December next, I have now to add that Mr. Aston returned to Tôkiô on the evening of the 27th instant, and handed to me the inclosed general Report of his proceedings. This shows that he reached Söul on the 10th instant, and succeeded in signing on the 15th Declarations on the part of the British, German, and Corean Governments, agreeing to the above-mentioned extension of time for the exchange of the ratifications of the said Treaties. Mr. Aston left Söul again on the 16th, one day in advance of the arrival at the capital of the United States' Minister, General Foote.

    The Declaration between the British and Corean Governments was signed in duplicate, one copy of which was retained by the latter, and the other copy has been delivered to me by Mr. Aston. Pending your Lordship's instructions I have thought it desirable to keep the original, but I inclose in my despatch No. 3, Treaty, of this date, a copy which your Lordship will perceive is identical in its wording with the draft which I forwarded in my despatch No. 67.

    I also inclose a translation of the reply of the President of the Corean Board of Foreign Affairs to my note of the 28th April, accrediting Mr. Aston to His Excellency for the purpose of executing this Declaration. His Excellency states, in his reply, that he had empowered I cho-yön, one of the Secretaries of the Foreign Board, to sign the Declaration on the part of the Corean

Government.

I add a copy of a note in which I communicated to Count Doenhoff a copy of Mr. Aston's Report, and it remains for me to express my high appreciation of Mr. Aston's proceedings, and the hope that they will receive your Lordship's approval.

I have, &c.
(Sigend)　　HARRY S. PARKES

Inclosure 1

Mr. Aston to Sir H.S. Parkes.

Kobé, May 25, 1883

Sir,

I HAVE the honour to report that, in compliance with your instructions, I left Yokohama on the 28th ultimo for Shimonoseki, where I arrived on the 2nd instant. There I went on board Her Majesty's ship "Daring," which sailed at daybreak on the following day, and reached Chemulpho anchorage on the afternoon of the 8th, having been detained two days at Port Hamilton by a contrary breeze.

I proceeded to Söul on the 10th, and on the following day received a visit from Messrs. Kim Hong-jip, Hong Yöng-sik, and Min Yöng-ik, Vice-Presidents, and Messrs. Kim Ok-Kiun and I Cho-yön, Secretaries of the Foreign Board. These gentlemen had evidently met at my lodging by previous arrangement in order to find out on what business I had come, and I explained to them that as the Governments of Great Britain and Germany found that some portions of the Treaty required further consideration, they wished to extend the limit fixed for the exchange of the ratifications for a further period of six months, or to the end of the current European year. I had accordingly been sent to Corea to make an arrangement to this effect.

Mr. Min Yöng-ik asked me why more time was required, and why could the Treaties not be ratified at once. I replied that the instructions under which I had come to Corea were telegraphic, and did not give a detailed statement of the reasons for taking this step, but that Mr. Min Yŏng-ik must be well aware that there were features in the Treaties which made it difficult to ratify them as they now stand. I might add that the state of affairs in Corea when the Treaties were concluded was very different from what it afterwards became. There were then no Chinese troops in Sŏul, and the King's father was not resident in China. These important circumstances made it necessary for the Governments of Great Britain and Germany to consider very carefully their future relations with Corea. I was sure, however, that the Corean Government would see that in taking the present step the two Governments were actuated by friendly motives, one of which was no doubt a desire to avoid the discourtesy to Corea which would have been involved in allowing the period fixed for the exchange of the ratifications to expire without any notice being taken of it. I added that I was provided with letters from the British and German Ministers at Tōkiō and also with the necessary document for signature, but as I had not supplied myself with translations into Chinese, preferring to have them prepared with Corean help, I would ask them to allow me the services of one of their Chinese scholars for this purpose.

Mr. Kim Hong-jip here remarked that he did not see the necessity for signing any special Declaration. He thought an answer from the President of the Foreign Board to the letters of the two Ministers would be sufficient, but when it was pointed out that, the object in view being to alter a Treaty stipulation, the document recording this modification ought to follow the form of the Treaties as nearly as possible, Mr. Kim Ok Kiun said that this was the right course, and the other gentlemen present made no further objection.

The next day I received a message from the Foreign Office asking me to arrange with M. von Möllendorf for the translation of the despatches and Declarations, and this having been done, I went to the Foreign Office on the 14th, and handed them to his Excellency Min Yŏng-mok, the President of the Foreign Board, stating in a few words the object of my mission. The president made no difficulty whatever, and 2 o'clock on the following day was fixed for the signature of the Declarations. The signatures were accordingly affixed at the time appointed, in the presence of the President and a number of the other members of the Board, Mr. I Cho-yŏn, one of the Secretaries, signing on behalf of the Corean Government.

On the 16th I returned to Chemulpho, where I found the "Monocacy," which had arrived a few days before with the American Minister to Corea and his suite, and I had an opportunity of calling on General Foote before his departure for Söul on the following morning. The "Daring" sailed on the morning of the 17th. I should have preferred proceeding to Kobé direct by way of Shimonoseki, but want of coal made it necessary to touch at Nagasaki. I arrived at Kobé to-day.

I have, &c.
(Signed)   W.G. Aston

Inclosure 2

The President of the Board of Foreign Affairs of Corea to Sir H.S. Parkes.

(Translation)

MIN, President of the Board of Foreign Affairs of Great Corea, has the honour to communicate this reply.

Your Excellency states in your letter that you have received instructions from your Government that they desire to extend for several months the period of one year fixed for exchanging the ratifications of the Treaty concluded at Inchhön on the 6th June of last year, according to foreign reckoning, between (your country) and Great Corea, and that accordingly Mr. Aston, Her Britannic Majesty's Consul in Japan, who has previously visited this county, has been empowered by your Excellency to return to Corea, and having communicated this intelligence to my Government, to sign with an official of my country, a Declaration extending the period for exchanging the ratifications of this Treaty; the term of such extension to be till the 31st December of the present year, according to foreign reckoning.

Accordingly, I, Secretary of the Board of Foreign Affairs, having been duly empowered by me, has, this 9th day of the 4th month of this year, being the 15th day of the 5th month, according to foreign reckoning, executed with Mr. Consul Aston, at the capital, Han-yang, an Agreement extending the period for the exchange of ratifications stated in the Treaty concluded last year at Inchhön, in proof of which they have together affixed their signatures and seals.

I have the honour to give you this reply, and beg you will take the proper steps in the matter.

The above is the answer addressed to Sir Harry Parkes, Her Britannic Majesty's Envoy in Japan, on the 9th day of the 4th month of the 492nd year of the establishment as a kingdom of Great Corea.

(L.S)

May 15, 1883

Inclosure 3

Sir H.S. Parkes to Count Doenhoff.

Tôkiô, *May* 28, 1883

M. le Ministre et cher Collègue,

WITH reference to the letter which your Excellency addressed me on the 28th ultimo, I have now the satisfaction of informing you that Mr. Aston returned to Tôkiô last evening, and handed to me this morning a Report of his proceedings, which resulted in the signature, on the 15th instant, of the Declarations extending the term for the exchange of the ratifications of the British and German Treaties with Corea until the 31st December next.

I hasten to communicate to you a copy of this Report, and Mr. Aston will wait upon your Excellency this morning to supply your Excellency with any further information you may require as to his negotiations, and to hand to you the declarations which he executed on the part of the German Government.

Accept, &c.

(Signed)　　HARRY S. PARKES

155

H.S. Parkes (1883. 5. 31) ➡ G.L.G. Granville (1883. 7. 7)

조선의 정세에 관한 Aston의 Memorandum 발송

Sir H.S. Parkes to Earl Granville.—(Received July 7)

(No. 91 Confidential)

Tôkiô, *May* 31, 1883

My Lord,

I HAVE the honour to inclose a copy of a very interesting Memorandum by Mr. Aston, in which he has noted the political information he collected during his last visit to Corea.

I shall have occasion to refer to some of the points reported by Mr. Aston in this Memorandum at a later date.

I have, &c.

(Signed)   HARRY S. PARKES

Memorandum of Information collected during Mr. Aston's visit to Sŏul, May 1883.

(Confidential)

I FOUND that no material alteration had taken place in the state of affairs since my last visit.

When the "Daring" touched at Port Hamilton I was on two occasions eagerly questioned by several intelligent-looking village Elders about the Tai-wŏn-kun. They knew of his removal to China, and evidently looked forward eagerly to his return. They said he was a great and good man, and that everybody knew it. Port Hamilton is in the Province of Chŏllado, which contains a large number of the Tai-wŏn-kun's adherents. I found that there was to some extent among the lower classes in the capital a similar feeling.

Having asked what the people said of my coming over again, I was told that the common saying was that they would much prefer to have seen the Tai-wŏn-kun back from China. I observed to Mr. Kim Ok Kiun and Min Yong-ik when at Sŏul that this state of things did not promise well for the future tranquillity of the country, but both were eager in their assurances that there was no danger to be apprehended. It was only the ignorant lower classes, they said, who talked in this way. This topic is not an agreeable one to them. To admit that there is any danger of internal disturbance is to admit the necessity of a continuance of the Chinese occupation, which it is the chief object of their party to put an end to as soon as possible.

M. von Möllendorff is by no means a through going partizan of China, but he is strongly opposed to the withdrawal of the Chinese troops. He says that the soldiers who last year attacked the Japanese Legation and plundered the houses of twenty or thirty Corean high officials were still in the capital, and it was reasonable to suppose that, having once tasted blood, they would attempt something similar on the first favourable opportunity. Such a chance would be afforded them by the withdrawal of the Chinese force. A Corean army would be ineffective, and he also objected to it on the score of expense. Some of the Chinese Generals thought the troops might be withdrawn, but he had opposed this measure.

The antagonism between M. von Möllendorff and Mr. Kim Ok Kiun has become much more pronounced of late. M. von Möllendorff accuses him of wasteful expenditure on his visits to Japan, of furnishing dishonest accounts, of being a dangerous schemer who had unfortunately got the ear of the King, and for his own ends encouraged in him foolish ideas of national independence. If he did not take care, M. von Möllendorff said, Mr. Kim Ok Kiun would be sent after the Tai-wŏn-kun to China, a threat which I know has been made use of by the pro-Chinese party to intimidate Mr. Kim Ok Kiun, who is much hated by them. M. von Möllendorff thinks Mr. Kim Ok Kiun very ignorant, and by no means clever. He ridiculed a scheme he had started for establishing a whale fishery by native boats and nets, not knowing that this mode of catching whales is successfully practised on the coast of Japan, where Mr. Kim Ok Kiun no doubt got the idea. He thinks he will soon be driven out of the Foreign Office.

Mr. Kim Ok Kiun is much more guarded in his language regarding M. von Möllendorff, and praises his abilities and talents. It was a pity, he said, he did not speak Corean, so that it was difficult to communicate with him. Some of the members of the Foreign Board speak a little Chinese, and one, Mr. I Cho-yŏn, speaks it well; but Mr. Kim Ok Kiun, though well acquainted with the written language, cannot speak Chinese. The only way in which his jealousy of M. von Möllendorff showed itself was in a warning to me not to try to transact business through the latter. He did not know Corea, he said. I replied that, as M. von Möllendorff was an official of the Corean Government, we should certainly transact business with him if we found it convenient. If the Corean Government did not like that, they had the remedy in their own hands. I reminded him that neither I nor any other British official could be expected to take any share in their disputes among themselves.

Mr. Kim Ok Kiun is about to start in the Japanese gun-boat "Moshunkan" on a visit to Quelpart and several other islands in the south and east coasts, with a view of seeing whether anything can be done to develop their industries. This scheme is in imitation of the Japanese Kaitakushi, or Colonization Department, and it is probable that, in taking this step, they are influenced by similar political motives, viz., the fear of the annexation by foreign Powers of some of the outlying islands. It is in the last degree improbable that it will prove an economical success. M. von Möllendorff is not friendly to this expedition.

I learned from M. von Möllendorff that Corea and Russia are in and attitude of mutual expectation in regard to the negotiation of a Treaty. Each is waiting for the other to make the first advances. M. von Möllendorff had seen the instructions to the Russian Minister at Peking on this subject, which were to conclude a Treaty similar to those made with other European Powers, with the addition of a clause providing for a frontier trade on the conditions stipulated in the regulations for the frontier trade between Corea and China. There was, however, M. von Möllendorff said, another question with Russia which Corea wished to take advantage of any Treaty negotiations to settle. Russia now possesses a strip of territory (formerly belonging to China) lying along the sea-coast north of the Jumen River, and bounded on the west by a line drawn from a point on that river 30 miles from its mouth, and one north to meet the River Usuri. The southern portion of this strip has been peopled by immigrants from Corea, who have also settled in the Chinese territory for some distance to the west of it, occupying a belt of ground extending 100 miles from the sea, and forming a homogeneous Corean population of about 13,000 souls, all of whom are practically under Russian control. Corea is very anxious to get back her subjects, and Russia offers no obstacle to their returning to their country; but the previous treatment of these Coreans by their own Government has not been of a nature to encourage them to do so, and the Corean Government now wishes to obtain from Russia the promise of active co-operation to this end. From a remark of M. von Möllendorff, I gathered that the Corean Government are thinking of endeavouring to induce foreign Powers to guarantee their national independence, which is exposed to danger, M. von Möllendorff said, on three sides. I understood him to refer to China, Japan, and Russia.

Nothing has been done recently in regard to a Treaty with France. Corea, M. von Möllendorff says, will make no concession in the direction of admitting missionaries, but they have no objection to the erection of places of worship in the Settlements, and he thinks would even make grants of land for the purpose of building churches.

The English school, to which I referred in a previous Memorandum, was opened during my stay in Söul. About seventy pupils attended on the first days. Their ages were from 13 to 28, and they belonged to the upper and middle of the three classes into which the Corea population is divided. These are the nobility, the *literati*, and the industrial and mercantile classes. One of the teachers, a young Chinese who had been educated in America, declared to me that these distinctions would not be recognized in the school, but that all should be treated on a footing of perfect equality. He is probably unconscious of all the results which the inculcation of such principles may lead to.

I visited the school, which is in the Foreign Office itself. The room is well lighted, sufficiently large, and is supplied with suitable furniture. I found about sixty pupils all engaged in learning the alphabet from one of Messrs. Chambers and Co.'s educational series. Several members of the Corean Government came in while I was there, and a strong interest was evidently taken in it. Mr. Kim Man-sik, recently Second Minister of the Special Mission to Japan, is Director. Fourteen young men have lately proceeded to Japan also to study English. This is an idea of Mr. Kim Ok Kiun's, and is objected to by M. von Möllendorff as needlessly expensive.

M. von Möllendorff told me that the Foreign Office is rapidly taking to itself all the functions of the other Departments of the Government. He made this remark apropos of the currency, which is properly the business of the Home and Finance Department. This Department lately issued a series of coins of 1, 2, and 3 mace (a mace is the tenth of the Chinese tael or ounce). They are of pure silver, and are current merely at the value of the silver they contain, thus leaving, M. von Möllendorff says, nothing to pay for the expense of coinage and no profit to the Government. They are very badly made, and are by no means uniform in size or weight. Fortunately no great number has been coined. A scheme for a paper currency, which is fostered by Mr. Kim Ok Kiun, is very strongly opposed by M. von Möllendorff, who seemed ignorant of the projected loan, by the help of which it is intended to place the notes in circulation.

The Coreans have no proper system of banking. There are Government stores of grain from which advances are made on easy terms, repayable at the harvest, but the plan is surrounded with many abuses, and M. von Möllendorff says he will endeavour to get it abolished, notwithstanding that the King looks on it with favour. It is no longer necessary, he says, now that Corea can draw supplies from foreign countries in years of scarcity.

He also informed me that he had arranged with Messrs. Jardine, Matheson, and Co. to establish a line of steamers between China and the open ports in Corea under conditions to be afterwards settled for sharing the profits between that firm and the Coreans by a partnership or otherwise, and for disposing of the steamers at a later period to the Corean Government, should the latter desire to purchase them. The chief partner of the firm at Shanghae was expected in Corea a few days after my departure. Messrs. Jardine, Matheson, and Co. would also be allowed to trade on condition to paying the tariff duties, but this formed no part of the agreement with them. M. von Möllendorff said that the private sanction of the British Government had been obtained to this arrangement. Similar overtures had previously been made to Messrs. Russell and Co., and American firm at Shanghae, but they had refused to entertain them.

I found that M. von Möllendorff had got possession of a copy of the Memorial of the Hong Kong Chamber of Commerce respecting Admiral Willes' Treaty, no doubt through some member of Messrs. Jardine Matheson and Co.'s firm.

M. von Möllendorff's silk culture scheme has proved a failure, as the provincial authorities had refused to assist in carrying it out. The two Chinese engaged to teach the Coreans had been sent back to their country. One reason why it fell through was the dislike of the Coreans to allow foreigners to reside in the interior. Chinese are regarded by the Coreans as foreigners just as much as Europeans or Japanese, and, indeed, one of the commonest appellations for them is "Ora[n]kai," or barbarian, a term which is not applied to ourselves.

Mr. Ma Kien-tchang is about to return to China, and no successor to him will be appointed. M. von Möllendorff informed me that Mr. Ma had been originally appointed simply as a spy on himself, and that he had really no other duty except to make private reports to Li Hung Chang about him. During M. Möllendorff's absence in China he had managed to get a seat on the Foreign Board, but this he had since been obliged to vacate.

Pak Yŏng-hyo, lately Envoy to Japan, whose dismissal, by the influence of the Chinese party, I reported in a previous Memorandum, was recalled to office after a short interval, and he now holds a still higher official position than before.

Sunday has been made a holiday at the Corean Foreign Office.

I was told that a house had been prepared for the American Minister to Corea, somewhat similar to that which I occupied, and certainly not any better. A vice-Minister of the Foreign Office, Mr. Hong Yong-sik, went on board the "Monocacy," at Chemulpho, to welcome him. The Corean flag was saluted with twenty-one guns. Horses from the King's stables, and chairs, were sent down for General Foote and his party, which was to consist of seventeen persons, nine of whom were officers of the "Monocacy." I was told by Coreans that General Foote had said that he was instructed not to avail himself of the assistance of Chinese or Japanese in making his arrangements.

M. von Möllendorff informed me that as soon as the ratifications of the American Treaty were exchanged the Corean Government would proceed to negotiate with General Foote a further Agreement, having for its object to remedy and supplement the defects of the commercial clauses of the present Treaty. He regretted that I was obliged to leave so soon, as the Corean Foreign Office would have been glad to consult me respecting these matters. He also mentioned that the jurisdiction Article required material alteration.

(Signed)　　W.G. Aston

156

H.S. Parkes (1883. 5. 31) ➜ G.L.G. Granville (1883. 7. 7)

조일무역규칙 초안 및 3개조 조약에 관한 Aston의 Memorandum 발송

Sir H.S. Parkes to Earl Granville.—(Received July 7)

(No. 92 Confidential)

Tôkiô, May 31, 1883

My Lord,

I HAVE the honour to inclose a copy of a despatch in which Mr. Aston has reported to me the endeavours he made to ascertain the feelings of the Corean Government in respect to fresh Treaty negotiations. Mr. Aston incloses in this despatch a translation of a draft of General Trade Regulations which the Corean Government have proposed to the Japanese Government, and probably intend to propose to the other Treaty Powers, and also a Memorandum of a project of a three-clause Treaty which the Corean Government appear inclined to entertain.

I shall submit my views on the important subject of this Report in a succeeding despatch.

I have, &c.
(Signed)　　HARRY S. PARKES

Inclosure 1

Mr. Aston to Sir H.S. Parkes.

Sir,

Tôkiô, May 29, 1883

I HAVE the honour to report that I took advantage of my recent visit to

Sŏul to endeavour further to ascertain the views of the Corean Government as to the basis on which they would be willing to reopen Treaty negotiations. I found the President of the Foreign Board, however, in a much more reticent frame of mind than on the occasion of my previous visit. It had plainly been suggested to him, probably by Mr. Kim Ok Kiun, that he ought not to commit himself further to any one but a duly accredited Envoy, and to my inquiries his invariable reply was that he would reserve his answer until the arrival of a Plenipotentiary, and this he hoped he should not have long to wait for. He allowed M. von Möllendorff to supply me with a copy of an English translation of the Trade Regulations lately communicated to the Japanese Government, but with the reservation that it was only a draft for consideration, and was not binding on them. I inclose this document, which I was told had originally been drafted in English by M. von Möllendorff, some alterations are mainly based on the Chinese and Japanese Regulations of Trade. Their most important provision is the permission to foreigners to carry on an interport trade in Corean produce for a period of five years. The Article of the Treaties prohibiting this trade was characterized by M. von Möllendorff as a shallow device of Ma for securing to China a monopoly of this trade. He had, he said, prevailed on the Corean Government to adopt a more liberal course.

Duty at the rate of 5 per cent. *ad valorem* is payable on native goods carried from one port of Corea to another, half of this amount being recoverable afterwards.

These Regulations contain no provision for the importation of medicinal opium.

The tonnage dues remain fixed at the same high rate named in the Treaties.

There is a provision for granting a drawback on re-exports of non-Corean goods within twenty-four months of their importation. In this respect, these Regulations are more liberal than the Japanese Trade Regulations.

Section 5 (miscellaneous).—Article 4 states that "in order to protect native produce the Tariff may from time to time be changed, four months' notice of such change being given by the Custom-house." I believe the meaning of this clause is that such luxuries as are for the present omitted from the list given in the Tariff of articles on which 30 per cent. duties are payable may at four months' notice be again made subject to the higher rate, so as to prevent their competing with similar articles of native production. The principal article affected by this provision is Chinese silk goods, of which a considerable quantity is imported into Corea. The guild of dealers in this article consists of 100 members, and all Coreans of rank wear silks of this description.

Grain is not mentioned among the goods whose export is prohibited.

The Tariff supplies an obvious omission in the Treaties, by providing for the importation of foreign gold and silver coins, ship's stores and personal effects free of duty. It is also more liberal than the Treaties in promising a lower rate than 10 per cent. for medicines, and in omitting from the list of articles subject to a duty of 30 per cent. a number of articles which might fairly be considered luxuries.

As the Coreans have at present no gold or silver currency duties are to be payable in Haikwan (*i.e.*, Chinese Customs) taels of 36 grammes of silver. M. von Möllendorff informed me that by private arrangement orders on Shanghae banks in this medium would be accepted in payment of duties.

M. von Möllendorff spoke with decidedly greater moderation than before about Japan's share in the approaching negotiations, and admitted that much depended on the view she might take. He was confident, however, that Japan would adopt any Tariff which might be consented to by the other Powers.

Finding that the President of the Foreign Board declined to add anything to his former statements regarding the Treaty, I endeavoured to ascertain through M. von Möllendorff and Mr. Kim Ok Kiun, who represent two opposing parties in the Board, whether or not the Corean Government would accept a Treaty consisting of three Articles, viz., peace and friendship, jurisdiction, and a favoured-nation clause. M. von Möllendorff told me that at a meeting of the Board, at which this question was discussed, all the members appeared favourable to such a Treaty, the only objection having been made by Mr. Kim Ok Kiun, who suggested that the Jurisdiction clause should be reciprocal, and that Corean subjects in England should be subject to Corean law. M. von Möllendorff had argued that this was utterly inadmissible, and I do not think Mr. Kim Ok Kiun could have been in earnest in holding this language.

Mr. Kim Ok Kiun informed me himself, at a visit which he paid me on the morning of my departure from Söul, that his Government would accept a three-clause Treaty of the kind described, leaving other matters for subsequent consideration, but that the President was precluded from saying so to me, as I was not a Plenipotentiary. In order to give a somewhat more definite character to this suggestion, I prepared, along with M. von Möllendorff, the

Memorandum, of which I inclose a copy, showing in more detail the character of the three Articles suggested. M. von Möllendorff promised to lay it before the Government, and inform me later on of their views respecting it.

In M. von Möllendorff's opinion, the Chinese version of the Treaty does not contain anything corresponding to the phrase "in the opinion of the British Government," which appears in the English version. He also remarked that the Corean Government would not alter the rate of duty of 5 per cent. payable at the Chinese frontier. They were about to avail themselves very largely of the promise made by the Viceroy Li Hung Chang to M. von Möllendorff personally to alter the existing Regulations to the disadvantage of China, by withdrawing the privilege of visiting the interior for purpose of trade, residence in the capital, and the monopoly of the interport trade, and they felt they could not well go further in this direction. There was also the precedent of the China and Russia frontier arrangement, which showed that the favoured-nation clause did not entitle other foreign Powers to claim similar privileges at the ports to those granted in respect to a frontier trade. M. von Möllendorff admitted that the frontier trade was not likely to be important. Of late years it has been gradually declining, and the opening of Inchön would probably give it its death-blow. English shirtings, for example, could then be laid down at Söul for little more than half the price they now command, and a difference of 5 per cent. in the duty would never compensate for the heavy expense of land transport by way of the Chinese frontier.

I have, &c.

(Signed) W.G. Aston

Inclosure 2

Rough Translation of Draft of General Trade Regulations of Corea.

Article I—*On Entrance and Clearance of Vessels*

THE captain or agent of any merchant-vessel, within two days (forty-eight hours), Sunday excepted, after anchoring in one of the open ports, shall deposit the ship's papers at the Consulate of his vessels' nationality; the Consul informing the Customs authorities of this fact.

The ship's papers should clearly show the length of the ship, the tonnage and name of the ship, the names of her crew, the year when the ship was built, which papers should bear the seal of the Customs and local authorities.

He shall then make an entry of his ship at the Custom-house, by giving a written paper, stating the name of the ship, her tonnage, the names of the captain and the agent, the name of the port from which she comes—which paper shall be signed by the captain or agent of the ship—and by depositing a written manifest of his cargo, setting forth the marks and numbers of the packages, and their contents, as they are described in his bills of lading.

Should there be no Consulate of the ship's nationality at the port, the captain shall deposit the ship's papers at the Custom-house.

2. Should there be any wrong statement, or any omission in the ship's papers, the captain shall pay a fine of 300 Haikwan taels.

3. If any error is discovered in the manifest the captain may correct it at the Custom-house within twenty-four hours; after that time the captain will be fined 20 Haikwan taels each day.

4. All goods not entered on the manifest shall pay on landing double duty.

5. Any captain who shall neglect to enter his vessel at the Custom-house within two days shall pay a penalty of 50 Haikwan taels for each day, but not exceeding the sum of 500 taels.

6. Should any goods be discharged from a ship without a permit to break bulk, the captain of such ship shall pay a penalty of 200 Haikwan taels, and the goods shall be confiscated.

7. Any merchant-ship wishing to clear shall pay all dues and duties and shall then receive from the Custom-house a port clearance, on receipt of which the Consul of the vessel's nationality will deliver to the captain the deposited ship's papers. But if the Custom-house has reason to refuse the port clearance it shall immediately inform the captain or agent of the ship of such reasons, and give the same notice to the Consul.

Article II—*On application at the Custom-house for Import and Export Goods*

1. The owner of any goods who desires to land them, shall make an application at the Custom-house, clearly setting forth therein the name of the

owner and of the ship in which those goods were imported, with the marks, numbers, and packages and value, which application shall be signed by the owner. The original invoice for each merchandize shall be presented on the demand of Custom-house; if this be refused, the Custom-house may not grant the permit to land.

2. All goods so entered may be examined by the Custom-house officers, and for this purpose the merchant shall bring them to the Customs jetty for examination. On opening the packages the Custom-house officers should not injure the goods, nor should they give any unnecessary annoyance. After examination they shall restore the goods to their original condition in the packages (so far as may be practicable) and such examination shall be made without any unreasonable delay to the injury of the merchant.

3. If any goods have been damaged on the voyage of importation, the owner may notify such damage to the Custom-house, and he may have the damaged goods appraised by two or three competent persons, who shall state the actual value of the damaged goods. The Custom-house officers having approved of this, the owner shall then hand in another application signed by him, stating this valuation and the duty will be charged according to it.

4. After the duties have been paid, a permit to land the goods will be issued by the Custom-house.

5. All goods intended for exportation shall be entered at the Custom-house before they are placed on ship-board.

6. The applications for export shall not be different from those for import.

7. All goods which are put on board a ship for exportation before they have been entered at the Custom-house, or which have been secretly placed on board, or which contain prohibited articles, shall be liable to confiscation.

8. A person making a false or incomplete application with the intent of defrauding the revenue of Corea shall be liable to a fine of 100 Haikwan taels.

Article III—*On Protecting the Revenue*

1. The Custom-house shall have the right to place Custom-house officers on board of any merchant-ship in their ports. Those officers shall close and watch the hatches of the ship, they shall be not an object of annoyance, and shall be treated by the crew of the vessel with civility.

2. Goods shall be unladen from any ship or placed on board during

daytime, holidays excepted, except by special permission of the Custom-house. If this is not granted the Customs authorities may secure the cargo by fixing seals on the hatches. Whoever breaks open such seal shall pay a fine of 50 Haikwan taels for each offence.

3. Goods that shall be discharged without having been duly entered at the Custom-house shall be liable to confiscation.

4. Packages of duty-free goods concealing therein dutiable goods shall be liable to confiscation.

5. Packages of goods concealing therein articles of a higher value shall be liable to confiscation.

6. For trading at a non-opened port, ship and goods shall be liable of confiscation.

7. The import of all kinds of opium is prohibited. Should any one try to import it, the opium shall be confiscated and the captain of the vessel shall pay a fine of 10 Haikwan taels for each catty. If the opium has not been found on board the ship, the person carrying it will be fined 10 Haikwan taels per catty.

Article IV—*On Tonnage Dues*

1. All vessels of more than 150 tons' register shall pay tonnage dues at the rate of 5 mace per ton; of between 100 tons and 150 tons, 2 mace per ton; of less than 100 tons, 1 mace. Tonnage dues are payable once every quarter.

2. Vessels remaining less than two days in port pay no tonnage dues if the hatches are not opened.

3. Vessels requiring only victuals, or being driven into port by stress of weather, need not enter at the Customs. Should they, however, commence to trade, then they must act according to 1st Article.

4. Vessels wanting to repair, and therefore to discharge their cargo, must enter at the Customs. No duties are charged if, after repairs, the goods are taken on board again. For each part sold, they come under these Regulations.

5. For transhipments a permit has to be obtained; no duties are charged. If goods are transhipped without such permit, a fine of 100 taels is levied.

6. For re-exports of non-Corean goods a drawback is granted within twenty-four months of importation, which may be exchanged for silver or be used in the payment of other duties.

7. Vessels of war are exempted from all obligations of the above

Regulations.

Article V—*Miscellaneous*

1. Coast trade is allowed to all vessels of all nationalities for the term of five years.

2. Native goods, if carried from on Corean port to another, which have paid export duty, half the export duty is refunded on arrival at the port of destination.

3. Native manufactures will be treated in conformity to these rules—that is to say, no privileges will be given to them.

4. In order to protect the native produce, the Tariff may from time be changed. A four-months' notice of any such change will be given by the Custom-house.

5. To prevent smuggling and defrauding the revenue, the Customs may, from time to time, frame rules, to which all merchants should submit.

6. Each vessel arriving in port shall wait to have her anchorage assigned to her by the Customs.

Article VI—*Tariff*

1. Duty-free goods: Foreign gold, silver, and silver coins, ships' stores, personal effects.

2. All goods exported pay an *ad valorem* duty of 5 per cent. The export of red ginseng is prohibited.

3. All goods imported pay an *ad valorem* duty of 10 per cent.
Medicines will pay less.

4. The following goods pay, when imported, an *ad valorem* duty of 30 per cent.:—

    Tobacco, all kinds.
    Birds' nests.
    Wine and liquors.
    Perfumes and scents.
    Artificial flowers.
    Real and imitation jewellery, and gold and silver ware.

All kinds of coral and jade ware.
Clocks, watches, musical instruments, and musical boxes.
All kinds of furniture.
Grass cloth.
Embroideries.
Carpets.

5. The importation of the following articles is prohibited :—Gunpowder, saltpetre, sulphur, shot, cannon, rifles, muskets, pistols, and all other munitions and implements of war; opium.

Length measure is the metre.

One tael is equal to 36 grammes.

Inclosure 3 in No. 121

Memorandum of Three-Clause Treaty.

HER Majesty the Queen of the United Kingdom of Great Britain and Ireland and Empress of India, on the one part, and the King of Chosen (or Corea), on the other part, being sincerely desirous of establishing permanent relations of amity and friendship between their respective countries, have resolved to enter into a Treaty of Friendship and Commerce, and to this end have appointed as their Plenipotentiaries, that is to say.

Her Majesty the Queen of Great Britain and Ireland and Empress of India,
His Majesty the King of Chosen (or Corea),

Who, after having communicated to each other their respective full powers, and found them to be in due and proper form, have agreed upon the following Articles:—

ARTICLE I

There shall be perpetual peace and friendship between the High Contracting Powers and their respective subjects. If other Powers deal unjustly or oppressively with either Government, the other will exert its good offices, on being informed of the case, to bring about an amicable arrangement, thus showing friendly feelings.

[The substance of this provision to be retained; the wording of it is admittedly defective.]

ARTICLE II

This Article is to contain the substance of section 2, paragraphs 2 and 3, of the Chefoo Convention, followed by the last paragraph of Article IV of Admiral Willes' Treaty.

[The provisions of the Chefoo Convention referred to are as follows:—
"The British Treaty of 1858, Article XVI, lays down that Chinese subjects who may have been guilty of any criminal act towards British subjects shall be arrested and punished by Chinese authorities according to the laws of China.
"British subjects who may commit any crime in China shall be tried and punished by the Consul, or any other public functionary authorized thereto, according to the laws of Great Britain."
"It is further understood that so long as the laws of the two countries differ from each other there can be but one principle to guide judicial proceedings in mixed cases in China, namely, that the case is tried by the official of the defendant's nationality, the official of the plaintiff's nationality merely attending to watch the proceedings in the interests of justice. If the officer so attending be dissatisfied with the proceedings, it will be in his power to protest against them in detail. The law administered will be the law of the nationality of the officer trying the case. This is the meaning of the words "hui ting," indicating combined action in judicial proceedings, in Article XVI of the Treaty of Tien-tsin, and this is the course to be respectively followed by the officers of either nationality."
The last paragraph of Article IV of Admiral Willes' Treaty is as follows:—
"It is, however, mutually agreed and understood between the High Contracting Powers that whenever the King of Chosen shall have so far modified and reformed the Statutes and judicial procedure

of his kingdom, that, in the judgment of the British Government, they conform to the laws and course of justice in England, the right of ex-territorial jurisdiction over British subjects in Chosen shall b abandoned, and thereafter British subjects, when within the limits of the Kingdom of Chosen, shall be subject to the jurisdiction of the native authorities."]

ARTICLE III

This Article to follow the wording of Article XX of the Austro-Hungarian Treaty with Japan.

Article XX of the Austro-Hungarian Treaty with Japan is as follows:—

"It is hereby expressly stipulated that the Austro-Hungarian Government and the citizens of the Austro-Hungarian Monarchy shall, from the day on which their Treaty comes into operation, participate in all privileges, immunities, and advantages which have been granted, or may hereafter be granted, by His Majesty the Emperor of Japan to the Government or subjects of any other nation."

H.S. Parkes (1883. 6. 10) ➜ G.L.G. Granville (1883. 7. 16)

1차 조영조약 개정에 관한 의견

Sir H.S. Parkes to Earl Granville.-(Received July 16)

(No. 98 Confidential)

Tokio, June 10, 1883

My Lord,

  I PROPOSE in this despatch to offer some general observations on the prospect of modifying by future negotiation the Treaty concluded by Admiral Willes with Corea. They are naturally based on the insight gained into the views of the Corean Government by Mr. Aston in the course of his two recent visits to Soul, as reported in his letters to me of the 11th April and 29th May, which I forwarded to your Lordship in my despatches Nos. 64 and 91 of the 28th April and 31st ultimo.

  I will mention at the commencement, as the point which appears to me to be chiefly worthy of your Lordship's attention, that on the first of these visits, and in the course of the discussion on the Treaty reported by Mr. Aston in his despatch of the 11th April, he elicited from the Corean Ministry of Foreign Affairs the important admission that the Corean Government consider that the favoured nation clause, being the XIVth Article of Admiral Willes' Treaty possesses a retrospective character. They declared that the non-retrospective meaning conveyed by the English version of this clause was wholly attributable to mistranslation, that the Chinese version was not intended to have and had not that meaning, and that it was wholly foreign to the intentions of the Corean Government to refuse to one nation privileges which they had already allowed to another.

  It is to be hoped that Government will steadily adhere in future to this formal declaration of the construction which they put upon the Chinese text. It would ill become us to contest an interpretation which is so satisfactory to ourselves, which is declared by the Corean Government to express their meaning, and which may possibly be technically correct. Whether this declaration denotes a change in their original views, or whether, in other words, they ever intended that the said clause should have a non-retrospective application, is at least open to question. I recollect that Admiral Willes observed to me on arriving here from Corea in June last, that he had endeavoured to obtain the insertion in the English text of a sentence which would have clearly given the clause a retrospective character, but that it was omitted at the instance of Ma Taotai, who assured the Admiral that the Corean Government would refuse to admit it. But I believe we have no proof that this assertion was made by Ma Taotai on the authority of the Corean Government, or even with their knowledge, while it cannot be doubted that that officer in arranging the business of the British Treaty, which was marked by an entire absence of negotiation, acted rather as the agent of the Viceroy, Li Hung-chang, than of the Corean Government. It was unfortunate that circumstances should have obliged Admiral Willes to place himself entirely in his hands.

Mr. Aston mentions in his Report of the 11th April that he had never seen the Chinese text of Admiral Willes' Treaty until a copy of it was handed to him by the Corean Foreign Minister (or President of the Foreign Board). This copy is also the first one which I have seen of that text, for although Admiral Willes had kindly and voluntarily communicated to me a copy of the English version of his Treaty, he declined to allow me to inspect the Chinese counterpart.

The objection to the non-retrospective character of the English text, which would at once strike any one acquainted with the subject, and which doubtless occurred to Admiral Willes, is that it would exclude us from the benefits of the Japanese Treaties with Corea of the 26th February and the 24th August, 1876, and from those of any compacts existing between Corea and China which would admit of being applied to ourselves. The conditions of the political and commercial relations between those two countries were lately defined, as your Lordship is aware, by the Agreement or Convention called "Trade Regulations," which was made at Tientsin at the close of last year, and which, apart from its peculiar political stipulations, secures much larger commercial privileges for Chinese subjects in Corea than those obtained by Japan under the above-mentioned Treaties.

The members of the Foreign Board unhesitatingly assured Mr. Aston that their Government would apply the favoured-nations treatment to the said Convention or Regulations as well as to their Treaties with Japan, but they were careful to add that the Convention itself was not in force (or, as the Corean Envoy to Japan observed to me, see my despatch No. 176 of the 29th December last, it had not been ratified by the King), while, in regard to the Japanese Treaties, they expected to prevail on the Government of Japan to agree to some material modifications and to accept a similar Tariff to that named in the European Treaties. The Japanese, I may mention, are trading in Corea without any Tariff at all. They, however, do not deny the right of the Corean Government to levy customs duties on their trade, and some progress had been made in the negotiation of a Tariff, which, would probably have been arranged on a 5 percent. basis, when the offer of a 10 to 30 percent. rate by the American, British, and German negotiators suddenly raised the expectations of the Corean Government, and effectually checked the consideration of the more reasonable proposals of the Japanese Government, which were far better adapted to promote the development of a limited and nascent trade.

The Corean Government, actuated by the party in that Government which is opposed to Chinese domination, and whose views on the Chinese Convention may be gathered from the unfavourable observations of the Corean Envoy to Japan, which I reported in my despatch No. 176 of the 29th December, have, I believe, represented to the Chinese Government, since that Convention was concluded, that it would be difficult for them to withhold from foreign Powers the special privileges granted by that Convention to China, and have therefore urged that those privileges should be withdrawn. The Viceroy, Li Hung-chang, appears to be disposed to meet this demand, as M. von Möllendorff stated to Mr. Aston (see his letter of the 23rd April inclosed in my despatch No. 65 of the 28th April) that the Viceroy had promised to allow the Corean Government any concessions in commercial matters which they might require in order to place their relations with foreign Powers on a satisfactory footing. That the Chinese Government were therefore prepared to relinquish their right of trade in the interior and at the capital, and their promised monopoly of the interport or coasting trade, and would also agree to a similar Tariff on their maritime trade as that of the European Treaties with Corea, reserving, however, a 5 per cent. rate on their frontier trade in which foreigners could not participate.

Although it appears to me that most of M. Möllendorff's sanguine assertions should be accepted with considerable reserve, there may be some truth in this particular statement, because the Viceroy may now perceive that, in obtaining for Chinese subjects under that Convention special advantages of so extensive a nature as would practically secure to them a monopoly of the

Corean commerce, and thus render useless to foreign Powers the Treaties they have concluded at his instigation, he has overreached himself and imperilled the first object he probably had in view in promoting those Treaties, namely, to found upon them claims for similar restrictions and the same high rate of duties in the Treaties between China and European Powers. The surrender of the special advantages of the Corean Trade Regulations would be a small price to pay for the support which such claims would derive -in the way of argument at least -from the acceptance by China of the same terms as those Powers in regard to maritime trade with Corea, especially when it is remembered that prior to the negotiation of the said Regulations China possessed no maritime trade with Corea, and it therefore matters little to her whether that prospective trade is fettered at the outset with restrictions or high duties so long as she exclusively retains a frontier commerce with a Tariff of 5 per cent. and a monopoly of the trade in ginseng.

The willingness of the Corean Government to extend to us the same treatment in respect of maritime trade as they observe towards China would therefore prove of little or no value if the latter should make to Corea the concessions indicated by M. von Möllendorff. It is of more importance to us that the Japanese Government should not agree, in the same way, to the abandonment of their Treaty privileges, and accept, as the Corean Government hope they may be disposed to do, similar disadvantageous conditions to those of the American, British, and German Treaties. The position of the Japanese Government is one of some embarrassment. On the one hand, they are fully aware that the high duties of those Treaties would greatly reduce the Japanese trade with Corea, which, although hitherto exempt from the payment of any imposts, and fostered by advances to dealers from a Japanese bank supported by Government funds, is even now in a stationary condition, and limited to an annual value of little more than 500,000*l*. On the other hand, they are bidding against China for the alliance of Corea, and therefore would not wish to be placed in a less friendly attitude towards that country than that which is assumed by China. The influence of local American agents will not be wanting to prompt the Japanese Government to give to Corea similar terms to those which the United States have accepted, and they may suggest to that Government that the latter may found upon the relinquishment of their present privileges claims for similar concessions from European Powers. The Japanese Government, however, must be aware that the policy of the United States entails no sacrifice on their part, while its adoptions by Japan would seriously prejudice her existing commercial interests in Corea. The postponement of the exchange of the ratifications of the British and German Treaties may therefore have the effect of inducing them to pursue a temporizing course, and to adapt their action to the policy of those Governments, instead of to that of the United States.

I regard that postponement as the most desirable step that could have been adopted in our interest. The United States, I venture to think, will gain but little by their ratification of a defective Treaty; and if the experience which will be acquired in the course of the present year should show, as I believe it will, that the conditions of that Treaty are not calculated to promote trade, and that it therefore fails to satisfy the strong desire of the Corean Government for a Customs revenue, they will be more inclined than they now are to offer us acceptable terms. The Corean Government are anxious, not only to obtain a Customs revenue, but to borrow money from abroad. They will look in vain for such aid from the capitalists of the United States, and they know that, in the absence of Treaties, they cannot hope to obtain it from England or European Powers. The progressive party, as pointed out by Mr. Aston, have a further object in desiring relations with those Powers, namely, a hope that their influence may serve as a counterpoise to that of China, and be exerted, among other ways, in obtaining the withdrawal of the Chinese force which now occupies the capital. They may be disappointed in both these ulterior objects, seeing how limited is the security, according to our present knowledge, that they can offer for loans, and how doubtful is the capacity of the Corean Government, on the admission of M. von Möllendorff, their most earnest advocate, to maintain order among their own people with their own means, and to guard against mutinous outrages on the part of their ill-organized soldiery, such as those which occurred in July last, and which were directed against their King and Queen and the Ministers of the Corean Government.

Your Lordship instructed me, in your telegram of the 23rd April, to direct Mr. Aston to sound the Corean Government as to whether they would be willing to put England and Germany on the same footing as China, or to reopen negotiations with a view of assimilating the Treaties to those in force between us and China and Japan. This instruction, your Lordship will perceive, was in some measure anticipated by Mr. Aston's communications with the Corean Government, which he has reported in his letter of the 11th April, and which elicited from the Corean Government the assurance that they would extend to us the same treatment as they accorded to China and Japan. I did not omit to instruct Mr. Aston, on the occasion of his second visit, to endeavour to ascertain whether they would be willing to assimilate their Treaty with us to those of China and Japan; but his Report of the 29th ultimo, inclosed in my despatch No. 91. of the 31st ultimo, shows that the President of the Foreign Board was unwilling to commit his Government to any further admissions, and that he shielded himself under the reserve that he could only treat on such subjects with a duly accredited Plenipotentiary.

He authorized M. von Möllendorff, however, to communicate to Mr. Aston a draft of a paper prepared by the former, and called "General Trade Regulations of Corea," which shows that the Corean Government are disposed to accept the China and Japan Treaties as their guide as far as they may deem it convenient to do so, seeing that many of the terms of that draft are taken from those Treaties. I feel it unnecessary to enter into a critical examination of this document, seeing that the President stated that it was only a draft for consideration, which was not binding on his Government, and had been simply communicated as a proposal to that of Japan, but I venture to offer a few brief remarks on some of its leading features.

The first thought which occurs to me is that it shows that the draftsman -M. von Möllendorff-does not possess a practical or intimate knowledge of his subject. The arrangement is defective, and he appears to have been chiefly careful to multiply penalties, some of which are manifestly unreasonable, and heavier than those imposed in China and Japan. The most favourable point in it is the offer to open the coast trade of Corea to vessels of all nationalities for a period of five years, which is too short a term to give value to the concession; but it is interesting to observe that the complete interdiction of this trade which is contained in the American Treaty, and is repeated in our own and the German Treaty, was characterized by M. von Möllendorff as "a shallow device of Ma Taotai for securing to China a monopoly of this trade" (see Mr. Aston's Report of the 29th May). It appears to improve the Tariff basis of those Treaties by declaring that "all imported goods shall pay an *ad valoren* duty of 10 per cent., with the exception of medicines, which will pay less, and by limiting the 30 per cent. rate to only a few articles; but this apparent improvement is entirely nullified by the further condition that, "in order to protect native produce, the Tariff may from time to time be changed on four months' notice being given by the Custom-house." Drawback of duty is allowed on foreign goods when re-exported, but in the case of any Tariff above a 5 per cent. basis this would simply be an indispensable condition. The tonnage dues are retained at the exorbitant rate of the three foreign Treaties, which could only be borne by vessels carrying full and valuable freights, such as are not likely to be obtained by those engaging in the Corean trade.

I do not think it probable that the Japanese Government will be willing to agree to these Regulations, as they are open to all the objections which, as I reported in my despatch No. 76 of the 14th ultimo, are taken by the Foreign Minister of Japan to the conditions of the American, British, and German Treaties. The XIth Article of the Japanese Treaty with Corea of the 26th February, 1876, the XIth Article of the Supplementary Treaty of the 24th August of the same year, and the XIth Article of the Regulations attached to the latter Treaty, contain the important and most salutary condition that all the Regulations under which Japanese trade is to be conducted with Corea, or any provisions which it may be necessary to add to the Articles of the first-named Treaty in order to develop its meaning and facilitate its observance, are to be settled by Commissioners appointed by each country. This condition, unfortunately, has not been secured to ourselves by Admiral Willes' Treaty, and it is one which the Corean Government doubtless desire the Japanese Government to abandon, but I scarcely believe that the latter will be persuaded to take such a suicidal step, although they have endeavoured to gain a similar degree of liberty and of Customs autonomy in their own proposals to foreign Powers respecting the revision of their Treaties. In consequence of the Foreign Minister having been absent from Tōkio I have been unable to ascertain his views on the subject, but the Vice-Minister who is temporarily acting in his stead has observed to me that the proposed Trade Regulations of the Corean Government appear to him to be wholly unacceptable.

I reported in my despatch No. 60 of the 21st April that I had instructed Mr. Aston to endeavour to ascertain whether the Corean Government would be willing to agree to a short Treaty of two or three Articles which would give us the advantage of the most-favoured-nation treatment without binding us to the objectionable commercial clauses of our Treaty, and he has reported, in his letters to me of the 11th April and 29th May, that the suggestion was favorably regarded by the Corean Government, but that the President of the Foreign Board was precluded from saying so to him because he was not accredited to the

Corean Government as a Plenipetentiary. To give some degree of definiteness to this proposal Mr. Aston drafted with M. Möllendorff a Memorandum on this subject, which the latter undertook to lay before the Corean Government and of which I inclosed a copy in my despatch No. 93 of the 31st ultimo. Guided by the additional light obtained by Mr. Aston's Reports, and by the determination of Her Majesty's Government to postpone the exchange of the ratifications of our Treaty until the end of the year, I am now less disposed to advocate the adoption of this course. I think it would be preferable that Her Majesty's Government should propose to the Corean Government to negotiate with them a new Treaty in place of that concluded by Admiral Willes, and I trust that I shall not be considered presumptuous in offering to submit to your Lordship's consideration a draft Treaty, which I shall hope to forward by the succeeding American mail. It appears to me that it would be highly unadvisable that we should agree to terms with Corea which we have not already granted or are prepared to grant to China and Japan, and my recommendations will therefore be conceived in that sense.

 I have still to offer to your Lordship some observations on the political information respecting Corea and its Government which has been gained by Mr. Aston, and on his proceedings in the matter of the consular sites, but I feel that I should not longer delay to express the high opinion I entertain of the valuable services he has rendered during his two recent visits to that country. His own Reports speak so forcibly for themselves that I feel it unnecessary to dwell upon the ability, knowledge, and judgement which they so clearly indicate, but I consider it to be due to him to state that, independently of the charge confided to him by your Lordship to secure the postponement of the exchange of the ratifications of the British and German Treaties, the information he gained on his first visit has amply justified his nation on that occasion, even if that information had been limited to the declaration he obtained from the Corean Government that they consider themselves pledged by favoured nation clause of our Treaty to extend to us all the privileges which they had already allowed to any other nation.

I have, &c.

(Signed) Harry S. PARKES

H.S. Parkes (1883. 6. 11) ➜ G.L.G. Granville (1883. 7. 16)

Parkes 서신에 대한 洪舜穆과 閔泳穆의 회신 보고

Sir H.S. Parkes to Earl Granville,-(Received July 16)

(No. 99)

Tokio, June 11, 1883

My Lord,

IN my despatch No. 60 of the 21st April I requested your Lordship's approval of the letters which I addressed to the Prime Minister and the Foreign Minister of Corea, on sending Mr. Aston there in the beginning of March, and I now beg to inclose translations of the replies to those letters which Mr. Aston brought with him on his return at the close of April.

The answer of the Foreign Minister is chiefly interesting as it conveys an acquiescence in my suggestion that the Corean Government, in their international relations should be guided by the principle of equality of treatment, which had a direct bearing on the arrangements recently concluded between Corea and China, and Mr. Aston's Reports will have informed your Lordship that the Corean Government have distinctly admitted that they consider Great Britain to be entitled to the same privileges as Corea may concede to China.

I have pleasure in adding that the translations of these letters, which are written in Chinese, as well as those of the two letters from the President of the Foreign Board, which were inclosed in my despatches Nos, 89 and 94 of the 31st ultimo, have been made by Mr. Gubbins, the Acting Japanese Secretary of this Legation.

I have, &c.

(signed)   HARRY S. PARKES

Inclosure 1

Hong. Prime Minister of Great Corea, to Sir H.S. Parkes.

6th day of the 3rd Month of the year of the Gont

(Translation)

　　I BEG to acknowledge the receipt, though Mr. Aston, of your Excellency's letter in original and Chinese translation, and to state that I have taken note of its contents. I beg to thank you for the cordial acknowledgements you express, which are indeed more than the occasion requires, and which I am quite unworthy to receive. The various points in your letter have all been discussed with Mr. Aston, through the Board of Foreign Affairs, and it will be the duty of that gentleman to report (the result of these discussions) to your Excellency. You, Sir Envoy, have resided long in the East, and you enjoy a high reputation for having industriously performed the duties of your position as Envoy.

　　I trust that the friendly relations between our two countries will continue for ever on the present cordial footing, and that both will enjoy prosperity.

　　I beg to communicate this answer.

With Respectful salutations,
(Signed) (L.S.)　SUN MOK

———

Inclosure 2

Min, President of the Board of Foreign Affairs of Great Corea, to Sir H.S. Parkes.

6th day of the 3rd month of the year of the Glat

(Translation)

　　I BEG to acknowledge the receipt, through Mr. Aston, of your Excellency's letter in original and Chinese translation, and I have respectfully noted its contents.

In this letter your Excellency states that it is a principle of international law that all people should be treated on an equal footing, and with perfect impartiality. It would be impossible, therefore, for me to do otherwise than assist (in the furtherance of the objects mentioned in your note). I have borne carefully in mind (all the points in your letter).

The proper steps have been taken in compliance with your request for the selection at the capital and the various ports, within the limits assigned for the conduct of trade, of suitable sites, which will be established, as places of residence for British officials and merchants after the ratification of the Treaty.

Agreements have already been concluded, in the execution of which the principle of equal treatment has been adhered to; and no favoured treatment having been extended to one (country) more than to another, our action in this respect is in accord with the views expressed by your Excellency.

Your Excellency further alludes in your letter to the Regulations which have been established for the conduct of trade between this country and China. I have been able, in conversation with Mr. Aston, to obtain some insight into your Excellency's views on this matter. I have the honour to give you this reply in addition to the verbal answer I have given to Mr. Aston. I trust you are in the enjoyment of good health.

With respectful salutations,
(Signed) (L.S.) MIN-YOUNG-MOK

G.L.G. Granville (1883. 6. 11) ➡ H.S. Parkes

조약 개정 교섭시 해군 파견에 관한 훈령

Earl Granville to Sir H.S. Parkes.

(No. 55 Confidential. Ext. 5)

Sir, Foreign Office, June 11, 1883

WITH reference to the concluding paragraphs of your despatch No. 34, Confidential, of the 9th March, I have to state to you that the Commander-in-chief on the China Station has inquired through the Lords Commissioners of the Admiralty whether naval officers may be permitted to visit Seoul, and I have requested what Vice-Admiral Willes may be informed that there appears to be no objection to a few officers visiting that place, but that anything in the nature of a demonstration should, under present circumstances, be avoided, and that before giving officers leave to go there it would be desirable that he should consult you in the matter, as it is under your superintendence that the negotiations are being carried on with the Corean Government. The substance of the foregoing was communicated to you by telegraph to-day.

I am, &c.

(Signed) GRANVILLE

H.S. Parkes (1883. 6. 11) ➜ G.L.G. Granville (1883. 7. 25)

2차 조영조약, 무역규칙안, 관세율안 보고

Sir H.S. Parkes to Earl Granville.-(Received July 25)

(No. 108 Confidential)

Tokio, June 22, 1883

My Lord,

IN my despatch No. 98 of the 10th instant I proposed to forward to your Lordship a draft of a Treaty showing the terms which I consider we should endeavour to obtain from Corea in place of these secured by Admiral Willes, and in fulfilment of this proposal I now beg to inclose drafts of a Treaty, Regulations of Trade, and a Tariff, which compose together an instrument.

I venture to adopt this form of submitting my suggestions to your Lordship because it enables me to state them with greater clearness and precision than I could do if I gave them in a general shape. In framing them I have been impressed by the desirability of adhering as closely as possible to the terms of Admiral Willes' Treaty, and if what I conceive to be its deficiencies would admit of being remedied by Additional Articles on a supplementary Treaty, I should greatly have preferred to recommend that course. But the alterations I have to recommend in respect to jurisdiction, the conditions of residence of British subjects in Corea, the Tariff, Custom Rules, and other commercial rights and privileges are so material that it would be impossible to place these in a Supplementary Treaty without practically cancelling the first one, or creating occasion for a conflict of meaning between the two which it is most desirable to avoid. I have, however, endeavoured to observe simplicity and brevity, even at the cost, of some comission, and have thus confined my draft to the same number of Articles as those of Admiral Willes' Treaty, but I have not been able to retain the same order in the subjects.

I now proceed to offer a few explanatory remarks upon the Articles of my draft.

In the preamble I have adopted a somewhat different wording to that of

Admiral Willes, and have added "Empress of India" to Her Majesty's titles.

Article I is made more comprehensive than that of Admiral Willes's Treaty, and is, I think, worded in terms which would be easier of execution.

Article II, which relates to Diplomatic and Consular Representatives, contains some additional stipulations to those of Admiral Willes' Treaty. It provides that a Diplomatic Representative or a Consul-General may reside permanently or temporarily at the capital of either country, and that the Diplomatic or Consular functionaries shall enjoy the same facilities for communication with authorities of the country where they reside and the same privileges and immunities as are enjoyed by Diplomatic or Consular functionaries in other countries. The stipulation in Admiral Willes' Treaty that the latter should correspond with local authorities of equal rank might lead to inconveniences which have been noticed by the Hong Kong Chamber of Commerce in their Memorial to your Lordship of the 20th January last. It also secures to those functionaries the right of free travel in the interior (which has been obtained by the Japanese Government under their Convention of the 30th August, 1882), and provides for the validity of Acting Consular appointments.

Article III deals with the next most important subject, that of jurisdictions, which is mainly treated of in Article IV of Admiral Willes' Treaty, but in a manner which confines within narrow limits the jurisdiction which it is eminently desirable Her Majesty's officers should be able to exercise over British subjects in Corea. By Articles III, V, VI, and IX of the same Treaty jurisdiction in all matters relating to Customs Regulations and confiscations, and also to the persons and property of British subjects within the foreign settlements, is confided to the inexperienced Corean authorities. Article III of my draft would remove these undesirable conditions, which have not yet been conceded to China and Japan. It would place every British subject when a defendant in any civil or criminal case, or when charged with a breach of the Treaty, or of any Regulations made under its provisions, completely under the jurisdiction of his own authorities, and it also provides for a satisfactory procedure, similar to that which is now in force in Japan, in the case of goods that may be seized by the Corean authorities. It likewise inferentially vests entire jurisdiction in the British authorities in non-contentious cases such as probate or intestacy.

Article IV relates to the conditions of residence at the ports to be opened to British trade, which I presume will be the three named in the Protocol to

Admiral Willes' Treaty, but to which I have given the Corean pronunciation of Chemulpho (Jinchuen), Pusan (Fusan), and Wonsan (Gensan). I have also inserted Yang-hwa-chin, which is to be opened to Japanese trade next year under the Convention of the 30th August, 1882, and the capital, Hanyang (or Soul), to which Chinese traders have acquired access by the Regulations of Trade recently negotiated at Tien-tsin. I should add, however, that I at present entertain material doubts as to the desirability of stipulating that our merchants should reside in the capital, as it would be far more difficult to protect them there than at Yang-hwa-chin, which is distant only 4 miles from that city, and therefore near enough for purposes of trade. There exists some question at to whether Yang hwa-chin or another place in its immediate vicinity would be the most desirable place of trade on the Hangang River, and I have therefore provided for this possible change of locality.

In clause 2 of this Article I have provided for the purchase of land by British subjects, and if the Corean Government should object to this stipulation, they might be willing to agree to "perpetual leases," which are in force in China and Japan. I have provided that land should be obtained either by official intervention or by private arrangement between the parties concerned, as may be found most desirable, and that on land thus acquired British subjects may build, not only residences and warehouses, which are alone named in Admiral Willes' Treaty, but also factories-in view of a recent difficulty which has occurred in China-and schools, hospitals, and places of worship, which would meet all the reasonable requirements of missionaries.

Clause 4 of the same Article, which is taken literally from the British Treaty with China (Tien-tsin, 1858), would give British subjects the same right of travel and trade in the interior of Corea as they enjoy in China, and the latter Power has also secured this right for her subjects in Corea by the recent Regulations of Trade. But I insert this Article rather with a view to facilitate, by withdrawing it, the attainment of the other new conditions contained in this draft, and also the ultimate acquirement of the stipulation itself. The Corean Government would certainly oppose its insertion at this date, and, as far as I can at present judge, I doubt whether it would be prudent, in the existing state of Corea, to allow British subjects to penetrate the interior for purposes of trade. Mr. Aston was informed that the Corean Government were pressing the Chinese Government to relinquish this privilege, and had already received a promise from the Viceroy, Li Hung-chang, that it would be surrendered. But, in return for the abandonment at this date of such a proposal on our part, the Corean Government might be induced to engage that, at some future time- possibly in the course of five or ten years —they would allow British subjects to trade in the interior, when the condition of the country and the feelings of the people towards foreigners admitted of the privilege being safely exercised.

Clause 6 would be particularly valuable, not only as giving the British authorities in Corea a voice in the Regulations under which the future Settlements will be governed, but also at conferring power on those authorities to enforce the observance of such Regulations by British subjects.

Article V will secure to British subjects the fullest liberty of trade at each of the ports open to foreign commerce, without interference on the part of Corean officials or any other persons, such as licensed or self-constituted monopolists, on payment of the duties named in the Tariff annexed to the draft, which are very much lower than the rates named in Article V of Admiral Willes' Treaty, but to which (as is stipulated in that Treaty) no other taxes, excise, or transit duty may be added. It provides for drawbacks of such duties being granted on re-exported goods, and for the payment of half-duty only on Corean goods carried between Corean open ports. It proposes such moderate tonnage dues as the probable scant and common quality of the freights of Corean trade will bear (instead of the prohibitory rates of Admiral Willes' Treaty), and it meets the wishes of the Corean Government in regard to the prohibitions they desire to place upon the importation of opium and munitions of war, and on the exportation of red ginseng and grain, without singling out the first-named article for special denunciatory interdiction. The Regulations of Trade attached to this draft provide for the confiscation of prohibited goods (section 3, clause 4), and I know of no more effective means for preventing, in any country the importation of such goods. Few would fail to sympathize with any honest effort of the Corean Government to protect their people against the evils of the misuse of opium, and I submit that this clear but undiscriminating form of prohibition will effectually enable them to do so. The parties who may endeavour to evade it are far more likely to be Chinese than British subjects or any other foreigners.

By the 8th clause of this Article power is given to the British authorities to make, in conjunction with the Corean Government, such Trade, Customs, and Harbour Regulations as may be required to secure the observance of the provisions of the Treaty, I hesitate to say, as in the Japan Treaties, "the Trade Regulations annexed to this Treaty," as it is particularly desirable that full liberty and warrant should be secured to the British authorities, acting in conjunction with the Corean Government, to make and modify such Regulations from time to time as may be found necessary.

Article VI deals with smuggling at non-opened Corean ports, which appears to me to be a subject of sufficient importance to be treated apart from an Article relating to regular trade. It is referred to in the second clause of Article III of Admiral Willes. Treaty relating to shipwreck, but that clause, taken in connection with Article VI of the same Treaty, would give the power to the Corean Government of confiscating any vessel, together with her whole cargo, which may be concerned, in however limited a degree, in clandestine trade. The attempt of a single individual on board such a vessel to trade clandestinely with the shore might thus entail the sequestration of the ship and all her freight. I have therefore, in my draft, confined the consequences of such an illegal act to the Person committing or attempting to commit it, and to the particular goods concerned in the offence or the attempt, and I have provided, in additions, the penalty of imprisonment not exeeding twelve months, with or without a fine not exceeding 1,000 dollars, or a fine not exeeding that amount without imprisonment, combined with the obviously necessary condition that all such cases shall be tried and adjudicated by the proper British judicial authority.

In Article VII, which relates to shipwreck, I have amplified Admiral Willes' Article III, and included in it the details of the arrangement, which I made, under the instructions of The Earl of Derby, with Japan, and reported in my despatch No. 90 of the 19th June, 1877. Although these details form a long Article, it will serve to enable the Corean Government to clearly understand the respective obligations in regard to shipwreck expenses which should be borne by the British Government and by themselves, and will secure a complete understanding on this subject, which, considering the dangerous and unknown nature of the Corean coasts, can scarcely be too soon secured.

Articles VIII and IX contain the stipulations which appear in the Protocol attached to Admiral Willes' Treaty relative to ship of war and surveying vessels, with the additional provision that such vessels shall be free to visit all Corean ports, and shall not be liable to the payment of duties or port charges of any kind.

In Article X I have provided for the right to store at the open ports of Corea naval supplies, which, of course, would include coal.

Article XI will secure the employment of Coreans by British subjects in any lawful capacity, while it repeats the provision as to students which forms Article XI of Admiral Willes' Treaty.

Article XII is the favoured-nation clause. The wording of my draft differs materially from that of the corresponding Article (XII) in Admiral Willes' Treaty in respect of the omission of the conditional portion of that Article, and in rendering it retrospective and also reciprocal, which the Corean Government will probably tenaciously claim. The negotiator of a new British Treaty with Corea would feel the need of receiving special instructions on this subject from your Lordship.

Article XIII provides that of the three languages—English, Chinese, and Corean in which it is proposed that this Treaty should be written, the English version shall be considered the original text.

Article XIV provides for the revision of this Treaty and Tariff by mutual consent in ten years. But, if circumstances should not admit of a complete or fully satisfactory Tariff being arranged at once, it might be desirable to stipulate that the Tariff should be revised at an earlier date.

Article XV provides for the exchange of ratifications as soon as possible, or within such time as may be named; also for the due publication of the Treaty by both Governments, and for its coming into operation on the day on which the exchange of ratifications shall take place.

Owing to want of time, I refrain on this occasion from referring in detail to the Trade Regulations attached to my draft, but I trust your Lordship will find that they carry with them their own explanation, and compare favourably with those drafted by M. von Möllendorff, which I criticized in my despatch No. 98 of the 10th instant.

For the same reason, I am obliged to pass without remark the Tariff which I also annex to my draft, and in which I am only able to give *ad valorem* rates, as I cannot tell under what denomination-whether of coin or bullion-the Corean Government may desire to specify their customs duties. The only existing indigenous coin, namely, the copper cash, would be manifestly unsuited to the purpose, and they will have to elect, therefore, between taking silver by weight, as is done in China, or accepting as their standard a well-known foreign coin, such as the Mexican dollar, which I am at present disposed to think would be a very desirable alternative.

I may, however, mention that this is practically a 7½ per cent. Tariff, as the first item in section 3, namely, "textile fabrics of all kinds, excepting fabrics wholly of silk," would include all British cotton and woollen manufactures, and would probably embrace seven-or possibly as much as eight-tenths of the future foreign Corean trade. Section 2 would secure the importation of all raw materials and metals, the trade in which may gradually admit of considerable development, at the lower rate of 5 per cent., while the articles classed under the higher rates of 10 and 20 per cent. would only be imported to a trifling amount, on account of the inability of the Coreans to purchase extensively such valuable commodities.

It remains for me to add that I do not presume to regard as complete the draft Treaty which I now venture to submit to your Lordship's consideration. I have drafted it since I wrote my despatch No. 98 of the 10th instant, with the effective aid of Mr. Aston, but under pressure of time, and obviously without full knowledge of the views which may be taken by the Corean Government on the various conditions which are not contained in the Treaty of Admiral Willes. It meets, however, all the objections to that Treaty which have been taken, as far as I am informed, by the various Chambers of Commerce who have addressed your Lordship on the subject, and I have the satisfaction of knowing that the provisions relating to jurisdiction are approved by Mr. Hannen, the judge of Her Majesty's Court for Japan. To make those provisions enforceable on British subjects in Corea it will be sufficient, I suppose, to extend to that country the operation of the existing China and Japan Orders in Council.

The signing of the present British Treaty with Corea appears to me to render it incumbent on Her Majesty's Government -if they decline to ratify that Treaty, as I trust they will, in view of the prejudice it is likely to occasion to our large interests in China and Japan -to open fresh negotiations with that of Corea before the extended time named for the exchange of the ratifications shall expire; and the only object I have had in view in framing the drafts which I now beg to inclose is to offer in a convenient and available form the suggestions as to such negotiations which your Lordship may expect to receive from an Agent who possesses some local knowledge and experience of the subject.

I have, &c.
(Signed)   HARRY S. PARKES

Inclosure 1

Draft of proposed Treaty with Corea.

References.   *Draft of Treaty.*

Preamble to Admiral Willes' Treaty.

Proclamation of the 28th April, 1876, with Foreign Office Circular of the 26th May, 1876, instructing Her Majesty's Diplomatic Representatives to notify same to foreign Governments. Also Treaty with Portugal relating to Indian Possessions and draft Convention with Siam of the 11th August, 1880.

Her Majesty the Queen of the United Kingdom of Great Britain and Ireland, Empress of India, and His Majesty the King of Corea, being sincerely desirous of establishing permanent relations of friendship and commerce between their respective dominions, have resolved to conclude a Treaty for that purpose, and have therefore named as their resolved Plenipotentiaries, that is to say:

Her Majesty the Queen of the United Kingdom of Great Britain and Ireland, Empress of India,

His Majesty the King of Corea,

who, after having communicated to each other their respective full powers, found in good and due form, have agreed upon and concluded the following Articles:-

Admiral Willes' Treaty. Article I.

Treaty of Paris of the 30th March, 1856. British Treaty with Japan of the 26th August, 1858. Article I.

British Treaty with China, Nanking, of the 29th August, 1842.

ARTICLE I

1. There shall be perpetual peace and friendship between Her Majesty the Queen of the United Kingdom of Great Britain and Ireland, Empress of India, her heirs and successors, and His Majesty the King of Corea, his heirs and successors, and between their respective dominions and subjects who shall enjoy full security and protection for their persons and property within in the dominions of the other.

> Admiral Willes' Treaty. Article I.
> United States' Treaty with Japan of the 29th July, 1858. Article II.

2. In the case of differences arising between one of the High Contracting Parties and a third Power, the other High Contracting Party, if requested to do so, shall exert its good offices to bring about an amicable arrangement.

> Admiral Willes' Treaty. Article II.
> Chefoo Agreement of 1876. Section 2, clause 1.

ARTICLE II

1. The High Contracting Parties may each appoint a Diplomatic Representative or Consul-General to reside permanently or temporarily at the capital of the other, and may appoint Consuls or Vice-Consuls to reside at any or all of the ports of the other which are open to foreign commerce.
They shall freely enjoy the same facilities for communication personally or in writing with the authorities of the country where they reside, and all other privileges and immunities as are enjoyed by Diplomatic or Consular functionaries in other countries.

> Japanese Supplementary Convention with Corea of the 30th August, 1882. Article II.

2. The Diplomatic Representative, Consul-General, Consuls, and Vice-Consuls of either Power, with their families and the members of their official establishments, shall have the right to travel freely in any part of the dominions

of the other, and the Corea, and shall provide such escort for their protection as may be necessary.

Admiral Willes' Treaty. Article II.

3. Consuls General, Consuls, or Vice-Consuls shall exercise their functions on receipt of an exequatur from the sovereign of the country where they reside, or, in the case of temporary appointments, with the sanction of the Corean Government. They shall be *bondfide* officials, and shall not engage in trade.

Admiral Willes' Treaty. Article IV.
Chefoo Agreement of 1876. Section 2, clauses 2 and 3.
Austro-Hungarian Treaty with Japan, 1869. Article V.

ARTICLE III

1. Jurisdiction over the persons and property of British subjects in Corea shall be vested exclusively in the duly authorized British judicial authorities.
2. If a Corean subject has a complaint against a British subject in Corea, the case shall be heard and decided by the British judicial authorities.
3. If a British subject in Corea has a complaint against a Corean subject, the case shall be heard and decided by the Corean authorities.
4. A British subject who commits any offence in Corea shall be tried and punished by the British judicial authorities according to the laws of Great Britain.
5. A Corean subject who commits in Corea any offence against British subjects shall be tried and punished by the Corean authorities according th the laws of Corea.

Austro-Hungarian Treaty with Japan. Article VII.

6. Any complaint against a British subject involving a penalty or confiscation by reason of any breach of this Treaty or of any Regulations made by virtue of its provisions, shall be brought before the British judicial authorities for decision, and any penalty imposed and all property confiscated

in such cases shall belong to the Corean Government.

7. Goods which are seized by the Corean authorities shall be put under the seals of the Corean and the British Consular authorities, and shall be detained by the former until the British judicial authorities have given their decision. If this decision is in favour of the owner of the goods they shall be immediately placed at the Consul's disposal. In the case of perishable goods, the owner shall be allowed to receive them at once on depositing their value with the Corean authorities pending the decision of the British judicial authorities.

Admiral Willes' Treaty. Article IV.

8. In all cases, whether civil or criminal, tried either in Corean or British Courts in Corea, a properly authorized official of the nationality of the plaintiff or prosecutor shall be allowed to attend the hearing, and shall be treated with the courtesy due to his position. He or the plaintiff or the prosecutor shall be allowed to call and cross-examine witnesses, and to protest against the proceedings in case he is dissatisfied with them.

Admiral Willes' Treaty. Article X.

9. If a Corean subject who is charged with an offence against the laws of his country takes refuge on premises owned by a British subject, or on board a British merchant-vessel, the British Consular authorities, on receiving an application from the Corean authorities, shall take steps to have such person arrested and handed over to them for trial.

Admiral Willes' Treaty. Article IV.

10. As soon as, in the judgment of the British Government, the Corean laws and judicial procedure have become so far modified as to obviate the objections which now exist to British subjects being made amenable to Corean jurisdiction, the right of extra-territorial jurisdiction, granted by this Treaty, shall be relinquished, and thereafter British subjects in Corea shall be subject to the jurisdiction of the Corean authorities.

Admiral Willes' Protocol. June 3, 1882. Clause 1.

Chinese Regulations for Trade with Corea. Article IV.
Japanese Supplementary Convention with Corea the 30th August, 1882. Clause1.

ARTICLE IV

1. The ports and towns of Chemulpho, Pusan, and Wŏnsan, with the city of Han-yang and the town of Yang hwa chin, or such other place on the Hangang river as may be deemed desirable, shall from the day on which Treaty comes into operation be opened to British commerce.

Admiral Willes' Treaty. Article VI.
All Treaties between foreign Powers and China and Japan.
Japanese Supplementary Treaty with Corea, 1876. Article III.

2. At the above-named places British subjects shall have the right to lease or purchase land or houses, to erect dwellings, warehouses, factories, schools, hospitals, and places of worship, and to permanently reside. Land so acquired by British subjects shall be liable to the payment of the same land tax to the Corean Government as is levied on other ground in the vicinity. The rent or price payable to the owners of the land shall be determined by mutual arrangement between the British Consular and Corean local authorities, when this is judged desirable, or they may leave it to the parties concerned to arrange the terms for themselves without any official interference.

British Treaty with Japan, 1858. Article III.
Japanese Supplementary Convention with Corea of 1882. Clause 1.

3. The limits within when British subjects will be allowed to reside at the above-named places shall be determined by the British Consular authorities, in conjunction with the Corean local authorities.
British subjects shall be free to go where they please, without passports, within a distance of 100 Corean li from of these places.

British Treaty with China, Tien-tsin, 1858. Article IX.
Chinese Regulations for Trade with Corea. Article IV.

4. British subjects are, however, authorized to travel for pleasure or for purposes of trade to all parts of the interior, under passports which will be issued by their Consuls, and countersigned or sealed by the Corean local authorities. These passports, if demanded, must be produced for examination in the districts passed through. If the passport be not irregular the bearer will be allowed to proceed, and no opposition shall be offered to his procuring such means of transport as he may require. If he be without a passport, or if commit any offence against the law, he shall be handed over to the nearest Consul for punishment, but he must not be subjected to any ill-usage in excess of necessary restraint. The provisions of this clause do not apply to seamen, for the due restraint of whom Regulations will be drawn up by the British authorities.

Supplementary Treaty between Japan and Corea of the 24th August, 1876. Article VI.
Practice at all open ports in Japan except Nagasaki.

5. The Corean authorities will set apart, free of cost, at each of the places open to trade, a suitable piece of ground as a foreign cemetery, upon which no rent, land tax, or other charges shall be payable, and the management of which shall be left to the foreign Consuls.

General practice in China and Japan.

6. The British Diplomatic Representative, in conjunction with the Corean Government , will make such Land, Municipal, and Police Regulations as may become necessary for the peace, order, and good government of British subjects in Corea.

Admiral Willes' Treaty, Article V.
British Treaty with Japan, Article XIV.
French Treaty with China, Tien-tsin, 1858. Article VII.

ARTICLE V

1. At each of the places open to foreign trade British subjects shall be at

full liberty to import from any foreign port or any Corean open port to sell to or buy from any Corean subjects or others, and to export to any foreign or Corean open port all kinds of merchandize not prohibited by this Treaty on paying the duties of the Tariff annexed hereto.

They may freely transact their business with Corean subjects or others without the interference of Corean officials or other persons, and they may freely engage in any industrial occupation.

Draft Regulations of Trade proposed by Corea to Japan, forwarded in Sir H.S. Parkes' despatch No. 91 of the 31st May, 1883. Article IV, clause 6.
All Treaties with China.

2. The owners of all goods imported from any foreign port upon which the duty of the Tariff shall have been paid shall be entitled, on re-exporting the same to any foreign or any Corean open port at any time within twenty-four months of the date of importation, to receive a drawback certificate for the amount of such import duty. These drawback certificates shall either be paid by the Corean Customs on demand, or they shall be received in payment of duty at any Corean open port.

Draft Trade Regulations proposed by Corea to Japan. Article V, clause 2.

3. Half the duty paid on Corean goods when carried from one Corean open port to another shall be refunded on arrival at the port of destination.

British Treaty with Japan of 1858. Article XVI.
Admiral Willes' Treaty. Article V.

4. All goods imported into Corea by British subjects, and on which the duty of the Tariff annexed to this Treaty shall have been paid, will not be subject to any additional tax, excise, or transit duty whatsoever, either at the open ports or in the interior of the kingdom.

Admiral Willes' Treaty. Article VII, VIII, and IX.

5. The importation of opium, arms, and all munitions of war, and the

exportation of red ginseng is prohibited, except under the express authority of the Corean Government.

Admiral Willes' Treaty. Article VIII.

6. Whenever the Government of Corea shall have reason to apprehend a scarcity of food within the kingdom, His Majesty the King of Corea may, by Decree, temporarily prohibit the exportation of grain to foreign countries from any or all of the Corean open ports, and such prohibition shall become binding on British subjects in Corea on the expiration of one month from the date on which it shall have been officially communicated by the Corean authorities to the British Consul at the port or ports concerned, but shall not remain longer in force than is absolutely necessary.

Admiral Willes' Treaty. Article V, last paragraph.
Draft Regulations of Trade proposed by Corea to Japan, Article IV, clause 1.
Japanese Regulations of Trade in Corea of the 24th August, 1876.
Rules of Trade, signed at Shanghae, 8th November, 1858, by Lord Elgin.
Rule X, 2nd paragraph.

7. All British ships of more than 200 tons register shall pay tonnage dues at the rate of 20 cents (Mexican) per ton; and of 200 tons register, or under, at the rate of 10 cents (Mexican) per ton. One such payment will entitle a vessel to visit any or all of the open ports in Corea during a period of three months without further charge. All tonnage dues shall be appropriated for the purposes of erecting lighthouses and beacons, and placing buoys on the Corean coasts, more especially approaches to the open ports, in deepening or otherwise improving the anchorages for foreign vessels and in providing facilities for the landing and shipment of cargo.

Admiral Willes' Treaty. Paragraph 2.
British Treaty with Japan of 1858. Article III, paragraph 5.
Japanese Treaty with Corea of the 26th February, 1876.
Japanese Supplementary Treaty with Corea of the 24th August, 1876.

8. The Diplomatic Representative of Her Britannic Majesty's Government

in Corea, in conjunction with the Corean Government, shall make such Trade, Customs, and Harbour Regulations as may be required to carry into effect and secure the observance of the provisions of this Treaty. The said Regulations may be modified from time to time by the British Diplomatic Representative in conjunction with the Corean Government.

Admiral Willes' Treaty. Article III, paragraph 2.
Regulations of British Trade in Japan.
Article II, paragraph 5.
Regulations of Japanese Trade in Corea.
Article IX.

ARTICLE VI

Any British subject who smuggles, or attempts to smuggle, goods into any port or place not opened to foreign trade, shall be liable to imprisonment for a term not exceeding twelve months, with or without a fine not exceeding 1,000 dollars, or to a fine not exceeding that amount without imprisonment; and all such goods, together with the boats employed in transporting the same, shall be liable to confiscation. The Corean local authorities may seize such goods and boats, and may arrest any person concerned in such smuggling, or attempt to smuggle, and shall immediately forward the persons so arrested to the nearest British Consul, for trial by the proper British judicial authorities, and if necessary, shall detain such goods or boats until the case shall have been finally adjudicated.

Admiral Willes' Treaty. Article III.
Austro-Hungarian Treaty with Japan. Article XVIII.

ARTICLE VII

1. If a British ship be wrecked or stranded on the coast of Corea, the local authorities shall immediately take steps to protect the wreck and all persons on board from plunder and ill-treatment, and to render such other assistance as may be required. They shall at once inform the nearest British Consul of the occurrence, and shall furnish the shipwrecked persons, if necessary, with means

of conveyance to the nearest British Consular station. The Consul shall have the right to proceed to the scene of the wreck.

Vide shipwreck Conventions between Great Britain and other Powers.

2. All expenses incurred by the Government of Corea for the rescue, clothing, maintenance, and travelling of shipwrecked British subjects, for the recovery of the bodies of the drowned, for the medical treatment of the sick and injured, and for the burial of the dead, shall be repaid to the Corean Government by the Government of Her Britannic Majesty.

3. But the British Government shall not be responsible for the repayment of the expenses incurred in the recovery of preservation of a wrecked vessel or the property on board. All such expenses shall be a charge upon the property saved, and shall be paid by the parties interested therein upon receiving delivery of the same.

4. No charge shall be made by the Government of Corea for the expenses of the Government officers, police or local functionaries, who shall proceed to the wreck, for the travelling expenses of officers escorting the shipwrecked men, nor for the expenses of official correspondence. Such expenses shall be born by the Corean Government.

Admiral Willes' Treaty. Article III.

5. Whenever British ships are compelled, by stress of weather or by want of fuel or provisions, to enter an unopened port in Corea, they shall be allowed to execute necessary repairs, and to obtain wood, coal, and other supplies. All such expenses shall be defrayed by the master of the vessel.

Admiral Willes' Protocol. Article II.
Peruvian Treaty with China of the 26th June, 1874. Article X.

ARTICLE VIII

The ships of war of each country respectively shall be at liberty to visit all the ports of the other, They shall enjoy every facility for procuring supplies of all kinds, or for making necessary repairs, and shall not be liable to the payment of duties or port charges of any kind.

Admiral Willes' Protocol. Article III.
Japanese Treaty with Corea of the 26th February, 1876. Article VII.

ARTICLE IX

The coasts of Corea, being hitherto imperfectly surveyed, are dangerous to vessels approaching them, and in order to prepare charts showing the position of islands, rocks, and reefs, as well as the depth of water, vessels of the British Government may survey the said coasts.

British Treaty with Japan of 1858. Article XI.

ARTICLE X

Supplies of all kinds, for the use of the British navy, may be landed at the open ports of Corea, and stored in the custody of a British officer without the payment of any duty. But if any such supplies are sold, the purchaser shall pay the proper duty to the Corean authorities.

Vice Admiral Willes' Treaty. Article X, paragraph 1.
Supplementary Treaty between Japan and Corea of the 24th August, 1876. Article V.
Austro-Hungarian Treaty with Japan. Article XV.

ARTICLE XI

1. British subjects in Corea shall be allowed to employ Corean subjects as interpreters, teachers, or servants, or in any other lawful capacity, without interference from the Corean authorities, and no restrictions shall be placed upon the employment of British subjects by Corean subjects in any capacity.

Admiral Willes' Treaty. Article XI.

2. Subjects of either nationality who may proceed to the country of the other to study its language, literature, laws, arts, or industries shall be afforded every reasonable facility for doing so.

Admiral Willes' Treaty. Article XIV.
All Treaties with China and Japan.

ARTICLE XII

1. It is hereby stipulated that the Government, public officers, and subjects of Her Britannic Majesty shall, from the day on which this Treaty comes into operation, participate in all privileges, immunities, and advantages which shall then have been granted or may thereafter be granted by His Majesty the King of Corea to the Government, public officers, or subjects of any other Power.

2. In like manner the Government, public officers, and subjects of the King of Corea shall participate in all the privileges, immunities, and advantages which shall then or which may thereafter be granted within Her Majesty's dominions to the Government, public officers, or subjects of any other Power.

Peruvian Treaty with China of 1874. Article XVII.
Austro-Hungarian Treaty with Japan of 1869. Article XXIII.
Danish Treaty with China of 1863. Article I.
British Treaty with China of 1858. Article I.

ARTICLE XIII

This Treaty is drawn up in the English, Chinese, and Corean languages, all of which versions have the same meaning, but in order to prevent dispute as to interpretation it is hereby agreed that, as English is the European language best known in Eastern Asia, the English text shall be considered as the original.

Admiral Willes' Treaty. Article XII.
British Treaty with Japan of 1858. Article XXII.

ARTICLE XIV

Ten years from the date on which this Treaty shall come into operation, either of the High Contracting Parties may, on giving one year's previous notice to the other, demand a revision of the Treaty or of the Tariff annexed thereto, with a view to the insertion therein by mutual consent of such modifications as experience shall prove to be desirable.

ARTICLE XV

The present Treaty shall be ratified by Her Majesty the Queen of the United Kingdom of Great Britain and Ireland, Empress of India, and by His Majesty the King of Corea, under their hands and seals. The ratifications shall be exchanged at Hanyang within months, or as soon as possible, and the Treaty, which shall be published by both Governments, shall come into operation on the day on which the exchange takes place.

In witness whereof the respective Plenipotentiaries have signed the present Treaty, and have thereto affixed their seals.

Done in triplicate at (Hanyang), this day of, in the year 188, corresponding to the day of the month of the year of the Corean era.

Inclosure 2

Draft Regulations of Trade.

I.-*Entrance and Clearance of Vessels*

WITHIN forty-eight hours (Sundays excepted) after the arrival of a British ship in a Corean port, the master or agent shall deliver to the Corean Custom-house authorities the receipt of the British Consul showing that he has deposited all the ship's papers at the British Consulate; and he shall then make an entry of his ship by handing in a written paper stating the name of the ship, of the port from which she comes, of her master, the names of her passengers, if any, her tonnage, and the number of her crew, which paper shall be certified by the master to be a true statement, and shall be signed by him. He shall at the same time deposit a written manifest of his cargo, setting forth the marks and numbers of the packages and their contents as they are described in the bills of landing, with the names of the persons to whom they are consigned, and shall sign his name to the same. When a vessel has been duly entered the Customs authorities will issue a permit to open hatches, which shall be exhibited to the Customs officer on board.

2. If any error is discovered in the manifest it may be corrected within twenty-four hours (Sundays excepted) of its being handed in without the payment of any fee, but for any alteration or post entry to the manifest made after that time a fee of 5 dollars shall be paid.

3. Any master who shall neglect to enter his vessel at the Corean Custom-house within the time fixed by this Regulation shall pay a penalty of 50 dollars for every day that he shall so neglect to enter his ship.

4. Any vessel which remains in port for less than two days (exclusive of Sundays), and does not open her hatches, also any vessel requiring only supplies or driven into port by stress of weather, shall not be required to enter or to pay tonnage dues so long as such vessel does not engage in trade.

5. The master of any vessel wishing to clear shall give twenty-four hours' notice to the Customs authorities, who shall then return to the master the Consul's receipt for the ship's papers. The Consul shall not return the ship's papers to the master of the vessel until the latter produces a clearance in due form the Customs authorities.

6. Should any ship leave the port without clearing outwards in the manner above prescribed, the master shall be liable to a penalty not exceeding dollars.

7. British mail-steamers may enter and clear on the same day, and they shall not be required to hand in a manifest except for such goods and passengers as are to be landed at that port.

II.-Landing and Shipping Cargo and Payment of Duties

1. The importer of any goods who desires to land them shall make and sign-an application to that effect at the custom-house, stating his own name, the name of the ship in which the goods have been imported, the marks, numbers, and contents of the packages and their values. The Custom-house authorities

may demand the production of the original invoice of each consignment of merchandize, and if it is not produced, or its absence is not satisfactorily accounted for, the permit to land the goods may be refused.

2. After the duties have been paid, the Custom-house authorities shall issue a permit to land the goods.

3. All goods so entered may be examined by the Custom-house officers, and for this purpose the importer shall bring them to the Customs jetty for examination. On opening the package the Custom-house officers shall not injure the goods, nor shall they give any unnecessary annoyance. After examination they shall restore the goods to their original condition in the packages (so far as may be practicable), and such examinations shall be made without unreasonable delay.

4. Should the Customs authorities consider the value of any goods paying an *ad valorem* duty as declared by the importer or exporter insufficient, they shall call upon the importer or exporter to pay duty on the value determined by an appraisement to be made by the Customs appraiser; but should the importer or exporter be dissatisfied with that appraisement, he shall, within twenty-four hours, state his reasons for such dissatisfaction to the Superintendent of Customs, and shall appoint an appraiser of his own to make a re-appraisement. The Superintendent of Customs will then, at his option, either assess the duty on the value determined by this re-appraisement or will purchase the goods from the importer or exporter at the price thus determined, with the addition of 5 per cent. In the latter case the purchase-money shall be paid to the importer or exporter within ten days from the date on which he has declared the value determined by his own appraiser.

5. Upon all goods damaged on the voyage of importation, a fair reduction of duty shall be allowed proportionate to their deterioration. If any disputes arise as to the amount of such reduction, they shall be settled in the manner pointed out in the preceding clause.

6. All goods intended to be exported shall be entered at the Corean custom-house before they are shipped. The entry shall be in writing, and shall state the name of the ship by which the goods are to be exported, the marks and numbers of the packages, and the quantity, description, and value of the contents. The exporter shall certify, in writing, that the entry is a true account of all the goods contained therein, and shall sign his name thereto.

7. No goods shall be landed or shipped at other places than those fixed by

the Corean Custom authorities, or between the hours of sunset and sunrise, or on holidays, without the special permission of the Custom-house authorities.

8. No entry shall be required in the case of the baggage of passengers, which may be landed or shipped at any time after examination by the Customs officers.

III.-*Protection of the Revenue*

1. The Corean Government shall have the right to place Custom-house officers on board any British merchant-vessel in their ports. All such Customs officers shall be treated with civility, and such reasonable accommodation shall be allotted to them as the ship affords.

2. The hatches, and all other places of entrance into that part of the ship where the cargo is stowed, may be secured by Corean officers between the hours of sunset and sunrise, and on holidays, by fixing seals, locks, or other fastenings; and if any person shall without due permission open any entrance that has been so secured, or shall break any seal, lock, or other fastening that has been affixed by the Corean Custom-house officers, not only the person so offending, but the master of the ship, shall be liable to a penalty not exceeding 100 dollars.

3. All goods shipped on board or discharged from a British ship, or attempted to be so shipped or discharged without having been duly entered at the custom-house in the manner above provided, shall be liable to confiscation at the discretion of the Court, or the Court may impose a fine not exceeding 500 dollars, with or without imprisonment for a term not exceeding three months, upon any British subject concerned in the said offence.

4. Packages which contain goods of a different description to those described in the import or export permit-application, and packages containing prohibited goods, shall be liable to confiscation.

5. Any person making a false or incomplete permit-application with the intent of defrauding the revenue of Corea shall be liable to a fine not exceeding dollars.

6. Any violation of any provision of these Regulations to which no penalty is specially attached herein may be punished by a fine not exceeding dollars.

IV.-*Miscellaneous*

1. Every British vessel arriving in a Corean port shall take up the berth indicated to her by the duly authorized Harbour-master.
2. Ballast must not be thrown overboard in the harbours or anchorages.
3. Vessels needing repairs may land their cargo for that purpose without the payment of duty. All goods so landed shall remain in charge of the Corean authorities, and all just charges for storage, labour, and supervision shall be paid thereon. But if any portion of such cargo be sold, the duties of the Tariff shall be paid on the portion so disposed of.
4. When cargo is to be transhipped from one vessel to another, an application for a transhipping-permit must be made to the Custom, and upon such permit being exhibited to the Customs officers on board the said vessels, the transhipment may be effected in accordance with such permit. No duty is payable on goods so transhipped.

V.-*Ships of War*

Ships of war shall not be subject to any of the above Regulations.

Inclosure 3

Draft Tariff

I.-Duty Free Goods

Animals, living, of all kinds.
Bullion, gold and silver, and copper, coined or un-coined.
Coal, coke, patent fuel, charcoal, and firewood.
Fresh fish, meat, and vegetables.
Grain, seeds, and pulse of all kinds.
Flour and meal of all kinds.
Bean-cake, oil-cake, and manure of all kinds.

Fish, dried or salted, all kinds.
Salted meats of all kinds.
Salt.
Biscuits and table stores of all kinds, excepting bear, wines, and spirits.
Printed books, maps, and charts.
Gunny bags and gunny cloth.
Packing matting.
Tea lead.
Plants, trees, and shrubs.
Travellers' baggage.
Samples of merchandize in such quantity as shall be approved by the Customs authorities.

II.-Articles subject to Duty at the rate 5 per cent

Raw materials of all kinds, as wool, cotton, silk, or other substances.
Timber and building materials of all kinds.
Hard woods and dye woods, and raw dye stuffs of all kinds.
Tallow, tar, pitch, rosin, glue.
Hides, horns, hoofs.
Skins and leather of all kinds.
Metals of all kinds, manufactured or unmanufactured, excepting manufactured articles otherwise provided for.
Machinery.
Implements or tools for the use of farmers or mechanics.
House utensils, excepting articles otherwise named.
Anchors and chain cables.
Balances and scales.
Cordage and canvas.
Paints and colours of all kinds, and materials used in mixing paints.
Wax and vegetable oils of all kinds.
Earthenwere and porcelain.
Sugar of all kinds.
Matches.
Rattans.
Tea and coffee.

Pepper and spices of all kinds.
Yarn, twine, or thread, all kinds, excepting silk.
Soap, common qualities.
All unenumerated unmanufactured articles.

III.-Articles subject to Duty at the rate of 7½ per cent

Textile fabrics of all kinds, excepting fabrics wholly of silk.
All clothing or wearing apparel not made wholly of silk.
Boots and shoes.
Blankets and rags.
Carpets of all kinds.
Drugs, dyes, medicines, and chemicals of all kinds.
Furniture.
Stationery.
Umbrellas.
Trunks or portmanteaux.
Scientific instruments or apparatus.
Saddlery and harness.
Kerosene and other mineral oils.
Window glass, ordinary and uncoloured.
Cutlery, as table knives, pocket knives, rasors, scissors, steels.
All other unenumerated manufactured articles in metal.
All other unenumerated articles only partly manufactured.

IV.-Articles subject to Duty at the rate of 10 per cent

Textile fabrics, all kinds, wholly of silk.
Silk thread.
All clothing or wearing apparel wholly of silk.
Wines and beer.
Tobacco, all kinds, and pipes.
Clocks, and parts thereof.
Watches, and parts thereof, of common metal, or silver, or silver gilt.
Plated ware of all kinds.
Musical instruments of all kinds.

Pictures, prints, photographs, or engravings, all kinds, framed or unframed.
Glass, coloured or stained.
Glass, plate, silvered or unsilvered, and framed or unframed.
Glass, all manufactures of, not otherwise provided for.
Soap, perfumed, or other superior varieties.
Arms, firearms, fowling-pieces, or ammunition imported under special permit for sporting purposes or self-defence.
All other unenumerated articles completely manufactured.

V.-Articles subject to Duty at the rate of 20 per cent

Amber, coral, tortoiseshell, ivory, jade.
Scented woods.
Perfumes and scents.
Artificial flowers.
Jewellery and precious stones, real or imitation.
Plate, gold and silver.
Watches, or parts thereof, wholly or in part of gold.
Embroideries, in gold, silver, or silk.
Birds' nests.
Spirits and liqueurs of all kinds.
Furs of all kinds.

VI.-Prohibited Goods

The importation of the following articles is prohibited, except under special permit from the Corean Government;-

Arms, munitions and implements of war, as ordnance or cannon and shot and shell, firearms of all kinds, cartridges, sidearms, spears, or pikes, gunpowder, guncotton, and all other explosive substances, salt-petre, and sulphur.

(The Corean authorities will grant special permits for the importation of arms, firearms, and ammunition for sporting purposes, or for purposes of defence, on satisfactory proof being afforded them of the bond fide character of the application)

Opium, except medicinal opium.

The Exportation of red ginseng is prohibited, except under special permit from the Corean Government.

The temporary exportation of Corean rice (or grain of all kinds) may, in time of scarcity, be prohibited by Royal Decree.

VII.-Export Tariff

All articles of Corean production, when exported to foreign countries, will pay a duty of 5 per cent; when exported to Corean ports the same duty is leviable, but half will be refunded at the port of destination.

The above Tariff of import and export duties shall be converted, as far as may be deemed desirable, into specific rates by agreement between Her Britannic Majesty's Diplomatic Representative and the Corean Government as soon as possible.

The standard coin in which all duties will be paid will be the Mexican dollar. Other coins or silver or gold bullion will be received at the option of the Corean Government at such rates as they may from time to time notify.

In the above Tariff the measure of length is the English yard or foot; the measure of weight, the Chinese picul or catty, the latter being equal to 1½ pounds avoirdupois.

H.S. Parkes (1883. 7. 16) ➡ G.L.G. Granville (1883. 8. 25)

金玉均과 면담 보고

Sir H.S. Parkes to Earl Granville.-(Received August 25)

(No. 114 Confidential)

Tôkiô, July 16. 1883

My Lord,

I HAVE the honour to report that Mr. Kim Ok Kiun, whose name has been frequently mentioned in my despatches to your Lordship relative to Corea, and in Mr. Aston's Reports, has again visited Japan, and called on me on the 3rd instant.

In the conversation which ensued he commenced by referring to a point on which he had on previous occasions laid great stress, namely, the anxiety of the Corean Government to establish Treaty relations with Great Britain as soon as possible. He referred to the fact that the 31st December was the limit assigned to the extension of the period for the ratification of the Treaty concluded by Admiral Willes, and stated that his Government looked forward with interest to the appointment, before the expiration of that period, of a Minister Plenipotentiary empowered by Her Majesty's Government to conclude with that of Corea the formalities of ratification, or any further negotiation that might be found necessary.

In answer to his inquiry as to the intentions of Her Majesty's Government, I observed that, in the absence of definite instructions on this point, I could only tell him that I knew that they were indisposed to ratify Admiral Willes' Treaty as it stands, as it contained several objectionable clauses; and the high Tariff on that Treaty would prevent the development of trade between the two countries. I felt confident, however, that in regard to any steps they might see fit to take, my Government would be guided by the consideration of what was expedient in the interests both of Corea and Great Britain, and though they would naturally decline to accept a commercial Treaty containing conditions which would be prejudicial to those interests, they would be willing to negotiate with

Corea similar Treaties to those they had concluded with China and Japan, and which, as Mr. Kim himself must be aware from his own observation, had been productive of very great benefit to both those nations. If Corea earnestly desired Treaty relations with Great Britain, she should be willing to offer the latter sufficient inducements to enter into such relations. Such a Treaty as that which was concluded last year did not contain sufficient inducements: it would entail considerable cost on Her Majesty's Government, without any corresponding advantage.

Mr. Kim earnestly assured me that the Corean Government were quite alive to the fact that, when Admiral Willes' Treaty was negotiated last year, they were inexperienced in Treaty matters, and, as they could now perceive that some modifications of that Treaty might be desirable, they were ready to enter into negotiations having this object. His Government, he said, were not disposed to attach great importance to the Tariff provisions of the Treaty, but were very sensible of the necessity, in Corea's interests, of the establishment of friendly relations with Great Britain at as early a date as possible. He proceeded to state that, in his opinion, the policy adopted by China towards Corea was entirely actuated by motives of self-interest, and that although she had ostentatiously affected regard for the welfare of Corea, she had practically done nothing to facilitate the development of the wishes of the Corean Government in regard to intercourse with foreign countries. In fact, thus far, China, instead of furthering the interests of Corea, had exerted her influence to retard Corean progress. A Treaty of Friendship with Great Britain, and the commercial relations between the two countries which would follow on that Treaty, would do more than anything else to strengthen Corea's hands in resisting the pressure brought to bear upon her by China, and in enabling her to maintain her independence, which, in the absence of Treaties with foreign Powers, could not, he believed, be long preserved.

Mr. Kim was then so good as to add that the experience of Eastern affairs which he conceived I had obtained after many years' residence in China and Japan, and the interest I had taken in Corean matters, caused his Government to indulge in the hope that I might be selected to conduct the negotiations to which he had referred. He expressed his confidence that, in the event of my being instructed to proceed to Corea in the capacity he had indicated, I should find the Corean Government quite disposed to meet the wishes of Her Majesty's Government, and to consider favourably any fresh proposals which were not injurious to the interests of Corea. He added, that his Government might deem it advisable to invite the American Minister to Corea to participate in these negotiations.

In reply, I reminded Mr. Kim that I should shortly leave this country for Peking, and that while appreciating the friendly wish he had been good enough to express, he must understand that the appointment of a Plenipotentiary to proceed to Corea was a matter which Her Majesty's Government alone could decide. With regard to his assurance of a cordial and conciliatory attitude on the part of the Corean Government, I felt obliged to point out to him that Mr. Aston's visit to Corea had furnished the Foreign Minister in that country with a fitting opportunity of communicating on the spot to a confidential Agent of my Government the views of that of Corea. That opportunity had not been taken full advantage of, and I could have wished, in the interests of Corea herself, that the Corean Ministers should have shown the same frankness in speaking to Mr. Aston as Mr. Kim had now observed towards myself.

Mr. Kim explained that, had Mr. Aston visited Corea in the character of a Plenipotentiary, this reticence would have been avoided, but he added that the Corean Government had made no attempt to conceal from Mr. Aston their views in general on the subjects which were discussed during that gentleman's stay in Corea.

He went on to remark that the relations between China and Corea would assuredly lead, at no distant date, to a pronounced disagreement of opinion between the Governments of the two countries. Whenever this rupture occurred, Corea would of course be precluded by her weakness from opposing any armed resistance to China's demands, but he trusted that by the peaceful co-operation of foreign Treaty Powers she might be enabled to establish her rights as an independent state.

He then inquired whether it was the case that England intended to negotiate modifications of the Treaty with Corea through China. To this I replied that I did not think this probable, as it was understood that Corea possessed herself the Treaty-making power; and in answer to a further inquiry of Mr. Kim as to the views entertained generally by foreign Powers on the question of Corean independence, I stated that these views must depend very much on the attitude and action adopted by Corea herself.

In reporting this conversation to your Lordship, I think I should add my opinion that it would not be prudent to accept the assurances of Mr. Kim Ok

Kiun as a complete reflection of those of the Corean Government. He may honestly express his own convictions as to the desirability of Treaty relations, but judging from the reserve he observed before Mr. Aston when in Corea, it is doubtful how far those convictions, and the intelligence he has gained, are yet shared by the ruling class in that country. I gather, however, from his remarks, that the Corean Government are determined to await fresh proposals from Her Majesty's Government, and that they will only consider these when delivered by a Plenipotentiary who would be fully empowered to negotiate a definite arangement.

I have, &c.
(Signed)　　HARRY S. PARKES

G.L.G. Granville (1883. 8. 23) ➜ Baron von Plessen

Parkes에게 조약개정 전권 부여 후 조선 파견 예정 통보

Earl Granville to Baron von Plessen.

M. le Chargé d'Affaires,

Foreign Office, August 23, 1883

I HAVE the honour to acknowledge the receipt of Count Bismarck's letter of the 24th ultimo, with its inclosures, in which he was so good as to convey to me the desire of the Imperial Government to be made acquainted with the intentions of Her Majesty's Government in regard to the amendments to be introduced in the Treaty negotiated by Admiral Willes between this country and Corea.

Her Majesty's Government are very sensible of the readiness shown by that of the Emperor to arrive at a common understanding as to the further steps to be taken in order to obtain an uniform alteration of the British and German Treaties with that country.

Since the receipt of Count Bismarck's letter above referred to a despatch has arrived from Her Majesty's Minister in Japan, forwarding, for the consideration of Her Majesty's Government, a draft of a new Treaty, accompanied by drafts of regulations for trade and of a Tariff to be attached to the Treaty.

In transmitting herewith, for your information, and that of your Government, copies of these documents, I have the honour to request that you will state to them that Her Majesty's Government are inclined to send Sir H.S. Parkes to Corea, with authority to conclude a Treaty based on the lines of his draft Treaty, which, as you will observe, includes nearly all the points contained in the Memorandum forwarded with Count Bismarck's letter of the 26th July.

Sir H.S. Parkes' great experience and acquaintance with the relations of the Western Powers with the eastern countries of Asia entitle him to the entire confidence of Her Majesty's Government in regard to the negotiations with which he may be intrusted in Corea, and it is not proposed, therefore, that he should be strictly bound as to the wording of the Treaty.

Indeed, should he not find it practicable to conclude a complete and satisfactory Treaty, Her Majesty's Government are of opinion that his action for the present should be limited to obtaining from the Corean Government a declaration of most-favoured-nation treatment, and watching events with a view to concluding a more comprehensive Treaty when a favourable occasion presents itself.

But before proceeding further in the matter, they would be glad to learn whether the German Government concur in the course proposed, and whether they also would be prepared to send an Agent to Corea, with powers to negotiate a similar Treaty.

As it will be necessary, in order to enable Sir H.S. Parkes, who has been appointed Her Majesty's Minister in China, to reach Peking before the navigation of the river is closed above Tien-tsin, that his instructions and full powers should be sent from London early in September, I shall feel greatly obliged if you will move your Government to favour me with their views at their earliest convenience.

I am, &c.
(Signed)   GRANVILLE

Queen Victoria(1883. 8. 24) ➜ 高宗

Parkes 전권위임장

英使全權詔勅
奉天承運大英國全境大君主大護法兼膺五印度大后帝御名詔曰 朕惟玆與大朝鮮國大君主議商政務 應行特派賢員 以代朕躬 玆簡我忠勤明敏愛臣頭等邁吉利寶星兼二等拔德寶星欽差駐箚中華便宜行事全權大臣巴夏禮作爲代朕 錫以確實全權 勅其與大朝鮮國大君主所簡同權之全權大臣會擬約款一切事宜 庶將以上議政之端妥爲蕆事 代朕於所擬條款冊內畫押 其續定各節 亦如與朕親允無異 玆特親宣勅旨 凡有我臣巴夏禮所已定諾各事 朕必全行允准 嗣後如有絲毫違犯不遵者 亦必勉爲勅禁 今將我大英國璽用於此書之上 幷御筆書押爲據 布告天下 咸使聞知
英曆一千八百八十三年今上卽位之四十七年八月二十四日

164

G.O. Willes (1883. 8. 31) ➙ Secretary to the Admiralty

조선 개항장 현황 보고

Vice-Admiral Willes to the Secretary to the Admiralty.

(Extract)

"Audacious," at Poisette Bay, August 31, 1883

AT Chosan (Fusan) and Gensan (Port Lazareff) the Coreans came on board the ships in large crowds, and behaved with marked courtesy and hospitality to the officers and men on leave. I found it no longer necessary to impose any restrictions on the recreations of the officers on shore, and they freely penetrated the country in search of game. At each place there were European gentlemen regulating the Customs, but they informed me that trade is diminishing rather than increasing, and the only hope the Coreans have of attracting foreign intercourse is by discovering that their country possesses mineral wealth—a discovery not yet made. The objections made by the Chamber of Commerce to the ratification of the Jinchuen Treaty on the score of Tariff and dues now possess only a ludicrous significance.

P. Currie(1883. 8. 31) ➜ L. Mallet

아편 수입금지 조항에 대한 Granville경의 견해 문의

Mr. Currie to Sir L. Mallet.

Foreign Office, August 31, 1883

Sir,

I AM directed by Earl Granville to state to you, for the information of the Earl of Kimberley, that a Treaty was signed on the 6th June last year by Vice-admiral Willes on behalf of Her Majesty's Government with that of Corea.

Similar Treaties were negotiated, about the same time, with Corea by Germany and the United States of America. The only Treaty that has since been ratified is the American Treaty; while the ratifications of the British and German Treaties have been, by agreement between all the parties concerned, postponed to the 31st December next, in order to give time for a further examination of sundry points enumerated in them, with a view to the introduction of such amendments as may be considered desirable.

By the VIIth Article of the British Treaty, a copy of which is inclosed, the importation of opium by the subjects of either Power into the ports of the other is strictly prohibited. A similar provision exists in the German and also in the American Treaty, the ratifications of which latter Treaty were exchanged at Söul on the 19th May last.

Sir H.S. Parkes, Her Majesty's Minister in Japan, has now sent home, for the consideration of Her Majesty's Government, an amended draft of a Treaty. In this draft the clause affecting opium is thus worded: "The importation of opium, arms, and all munitions of war, and the exportation of red ginseng, is prohibited, except under the express authority of the Corean Government." Sir H.S. Parkes further suggests that an exception in favour of medicinal opium should be mentioned in this clause of the proposed Treaty, as well as in the Tariff to be annexed to the Treaty, where a definition should be given as to what is intended by the term "medicinal opium."

At the same time Sir H.S. Parkes has pointed out that the prohibition to import opium into Corea is almost in itself a recognition of the independence of that country (the sovereignty over which has hitherto been claimed by China as the Suzerain Power), inasmuch as China would claim any concession granted to a dependency.

On this point I am to observe that the King of Corea claims for his country that, while it is simply a dependency of China, its internal administration and its external intercourse are entirely and in all respects within his discretion and control as an independent King.

I am now to request that, in laying this letter before the Earl of Kimberley, you will move him to inform Lord Granville whether he sees any objection, so far as Indian interests are concerned, to the prohibition regarding the importation of opium into Corea, and the definition of "medicinal opium" proposed by Sir H.S. Parkes.

Her Majesty's Government are in communication with that of Germany as to the proposed amendments in the Treaties already signed with Corea by the Representatives of the two countries; and as it is of consequence that a decision on the subject should be taken, in order to enable the negotiators to proceed to the spot not later than the beginning of October, I am to state that Lord Granville would be glad to learn the views of the Secretary of State for India with the least possible delay.

Copies of the Treaty signed by Admiral Willes and of the draft Treaty suggested by Sir H.S. Parkes are inclosed for Lord Kimberley's information.

I am, &c.
(Signed)   P. CURRIE

J.Walsham(1883. 9. 1) ➜ G.L.G. Granville (1883. 9. 3)

Zappe의 조선 파견 통보

Sir J. Walsham to Earl Granville.-(Received September 3)

(No. 255 Confidential)

Berlin, September 1, 1883

My Lord,

ON the receipt of your Lordship's No. 307 of the 23th ultimo, I did not fail to communicate at once to the Acting Minister for Foreign Affairs a Memorandum containing the views of Her Majesty's Government as to the steps now to be taken with regard to the negotiations for amending the Treaties concluded last year on behalf of Great Britain and Germany with Corea, and I furnished his Excellency, confidentially, with a copy of Sir H.S. Parkes' draft Treaty, expressing at the same time the hope that, as the matter was pressing, the German Government would be so good as to let Her Majesty's Government know, as early as they conveniently could do so, whether they agreed with the views expressed in the Memorandum.

On delivering the Memorandum personally to Dr. Busch, and giving him a brief statement of its contents, his Excellency said that the German Government would not in any case send to Corea a Special Representative of the same category as Sir H.S. Parkes, but would probably appoint an official conversant with the subject to act with Sir H.S. Parkes, and he promised to take into immediate consideration the provisions of the draft Treaty. Today Dr. Busch informed me that Herr Zappe, German Consul-General in Japan, had been appointed to act with Sir H.S. Parkes; that he had already started, and that, although owing to the question of urgency, and from a desire to meet the wishes of Her Majesty's Government, there had not been time to submit the provisions of the Treaty to a detailed examination, the German Government agreed in principle with the basis laid down for a renewal of the negotiations.

I have, &c.

(Signed)　　JOHN WALSHAM.M

167

G.L.G. Granville (1883. 9. 3) ➡ H.S. Parkes

조선에 부임하는 Zappe 독일 공사와의 협조 지시

Earl Granville to Sir H.S. Parkes.

(No. 4. Ext)

Foreign Office, September 3, 1883

Sir,

WITH reference to your despatch No. 108, Confidential, of the 22nd June, and to my telegram No. 8 of the 23rd ultimo, I have to state to you that the German Government have expressed to me, through their Chargé d'Affaires in this country, a copy of whose letter is inclosed herewith, their intention of negotiating a new Treaty with Corea, simultaneously and jointly with Her Majesty's Government, and have nominated Herr Zappé, the German Consul-General at Yokohama, who will act as their Plenipotentiary for the purpose. A copy of a despatch from Her Majesty's Charge d'Affaires at Berlin upon the subject is likewise inclosed.

Her Majesty's Government will be glad if you will make arrangements so as to proceed to Corea next month.

You will be furnished with further instructions by telegraph, and your full powers will be dispatched by the mail of the 7th instant.

I have to-day communicated to you the substance of the foregoing by telegraph.

I am, &c.
(Signed)　GRANVILLE

L. Mallet (1883. 9. 25) ➜ P. Currie (1883. 9. 25)

아편 수입금지 조항에 대한 Kimberley경의 견해 전달

Sir L. Mallet to Mr. Currie.-(Received September 25)

India Office, September 25, 1883

Sir,

WITH reference to Mr. Currie's letter of the 31st ultimo relative to a Treaty with the Government of Corea, I am directed by the Secretary of State for India to inform you that his Lordship, having communicated by telegraph with the Government of India, has now received a reply to the effect that while they see no harm in recognizing the prohibition by Corea of the importation of opium, it is feared that if Her Majesty's Government undertake to prohibit its importation, the position of the Government of India in regard to the general opium question will be weakened.

With this opinion I am to state the Earl of Kimberley concurs. Article VII of the Treaty negotiated by Vice-Admiral Willes appears to his Lordship to be inadmissible. Her Majesty's Government could not undertake to punish a British subject for conveying opium or any other exportable article from a port in British dominions, and any interference with this trade on their part would prove extremely embarrassing in negotiations with China on the opium question, especially in view of the relations of Corea with China.

The clause proposed by Sir H.S. Parkes is not open to this objection, and Lord Kimberley does not consider that the making of opium contraband in Corea need in itself be opposed from the point of view of Indian interests; but Lord Granville will doubtless consider whether the insertion in the Treaty of such a clause as is proposed will give China any opening to claim a similar concession.

I am to suggest that it may be better to omit all mention of opium in the body of the Treaty, and simply to enter it as contraband in the Tariff Schedule.

As regards the question of medical opium, the definition of the term proposed by Sir H.S. Parkes does not appear to be given in the letter under acknowledgment, or in the papers which accompanied it. Lord Kimberley, however, does not see any objection to Sir H.S. Parkes' proposal that an exception should be made in favour of medicinal opium, if this can be done without giving rise to practical difficulties in administration.

I have, &c.

(Signed)　　LOUIS MALLET

G.L.G. Granville (1883. 10. 3) ➜ H.S. Parkes

아편 수입금지 조항 및 수정 조약안에 관한 훈령

Earl Granville to Sir H.S. Parkes.

(No. 36. Ext. 23)
Sir,

Foreign Officer, October 3, 1883

I HAVE to state to you that I have been in communication with the Secretary of State for India in Council, with a view to ascertain whether there exists, from an Indian point of view, any objection to the prohibition of the importation of opium into Corea, and to the exception in favour of "medicinal opium," as proposed by you in the revised draft Treaty which you sent home with your despatch No. 108 of the 22nd June last.

For your information, I inclose copies of the correspondence that has taken place on this point.*

You will perceive that, while the Indian Government consider that the provisions of Article VII of the Treaty signed by Admiral Willes are not admissable, they are disposed to think that it would be desirable that all mention of opium should be omitted in the body of the proposed Treaty, and that it should be simply entered as contraband in the Tariff schedule.

Lord Kimberley is further of opinion that an exception should be made in favour of medicinal opium, if this can be done without giving rise to practical difficulties in administration.

I request, therefore, that in drawing up the draft of a new Treaty for submission to the Corean Government, you will be guided in the matter of opium by the views expressed in the letter from the India Office of the 25th ultimo.

The German Government are of opinion, and this view is shared by that of Her Majesty, that both in their political and commercial relations no greater concessions should be made to the Kingdom of Corea than are to be found in the Treaties concluded by the European Powers with China and Japan; and

---

*[원주] Nos.151 and 165.

they have proposed, as will be seen on referring to Baron Plessen's note of the 5th ultimo, a copy of which accompanied my despatch No. 13 of the 7th, that a clause should be added to Article III of the draft Treaty inclosed with your despatch No. 108 of the 22nd June, withdrawing disputes between subjects of two different Treaty powers from the jurisdiction of the native Tribunals.

The German Plenipotentiary will further be instructed to claim a series of concessions included in the draft of a Treaty submitted to the Austro-Hungarian Government on behalf of that of Corea, the text of which was communicated to me by Baron Plessen in his note of the 5th ultimo.

The most important of these are:—

1. The acceptance by the Corean Government of the Strand Regulation which has been in force in China since the 26th May, 1876 (see last paragraph of Article III of the draft Treaty with Austro-Hungary).

2. The issue of drawback certificates, and the application of tonnage dues to lighting the sea-coast and facilitating navigation, as specified in Article V of the same Treaty.

3. The permission to foreign merchants to accompany and to sell their goods in the interior of the country, and the opening of the coasting trade stipulated for in Article VI of the Austro-Hungarian Treaty.

I have now to state to you that Her Majesty's Government are prepared to adopt the above amendments to the draft Treaty sent home by you should you see no objection thereto.

But should you find that any alterations of detail may be necessary or considered by you to be advisable, full discretion is left with you in this respect.

If, however, you are unable to secure a Treaty framed on the lines laid down in your draft with the modification sanctioned in this despatch, you should endeavour to conclude a most-favoured-nation Convention.

In conclusion, you should act throughout the negotiations in concert with the German Plenipotentiary, the probable date of whose arrival at Chefoo will be communicated to you hereafter by telegraph.

The substance of the foregoing instructions was telegraphed to you this evening.

I have, &c.
(Signed)   GRANVILLE

H.S. Parkes(1883. 10. 8) ➡ 閔泳穆

조약 개정 협상을 위한 사전준비 및 전권 임명을 청하는 조회

관련문서 閔泳穆의 회신(1883. 10. 25)

Sir H.S. Parkes to the President of the Foreign Board of the Government of Corea.

Peking, October 8, 1883

Sir,

I HAVE the honour to inform your Excellency that, as my Government deem it desirable to negotiate a new Treaty with Corea, I have been instructed to proceed there as Plenipotentiary, and to cat in concert with M. Zappe, the Plenipotentiary appointed by the Government of Germany for the same purpose.

Count Tattenbach, the German Representative at Peking, together with myself, have also been instructed to notify the intentions of our respective Governments to that of Corea, and Mr. Aston is accordingly deputed to deliver to your Excellency this letter, and one of similar tenour which Count Tattenbach has addressed to your Excellency.

I expect to arrive in Corea in company with M. Zappe about the 25th instant, and Mr. Aston will precede us by about ten days. During that interval I beg your Excellency to afford Mr. Aston all requisite facilities for completing the necessary arrangements for our reception and accommodation at the capital, and also to obtain the appointment of Plenipotentiaries on the part of your Government, so that M. Zappe and myself may be able to enter on the business of our mission immediately on our arrival.

I am obliged to urge on your Excellency's consideration the necessity of these negotiations being conducted with all possible dispatch, as in consequence of the lateness of the season it will be impossible for me to reamin long in Corea.

I do not doubt that your Excellency will see in this offer to negotiate a new Treaty a fresh proof of the desire of my Government to establish the most friendly relations with Corea, and I beg to add the expression of my own satisfaction in being charged with a mission of this character, in the execution of which I feel I may confidently rely upon your Excellency's cordial co-operation.

I take, &c.
(Signed)　　HARRY S. PARKES

【漢譯文】

癸未九月 日

大英欽差駐劄中華便宜行事大臣巴 爲照會事 照得 現因我國擬定 應與貴國 重議和約 玆特欽簡本大臣 錫以全權 派赴貴國 會同大德國欽差全權大臣擦 將一切條款事宜再爲妥議 囑卽先行知照等因 查德國駐華大臣譚 亦已奉命 將兩國重議合約之意 先行奉達在案 爲此 相應特派本國領事官阿 賫此照會 及譚大臣同因之文 先期十日 上下親投貴國 一倂呈覽 本大臣與擦大臣 訂於 本月二十五日約可同抵貴境 當此旬日之間 務望協同阿領事官 將在京城一應 接待居住應辦事宜妥爲料理 並請預行簡派全權大臣相待 以便本大臣曁擦大 臣到日卽可作速會商 原因天時較晩 勢不得不乞亟 未能久延故也 竊思我國 再擬重訂和款 仍期益敦睦誼之旨 貴大臣自能洞悉 而本大臣欣承此差 所有 和衷商辦之處 必能仰藉鼎力 妥爲襄助也 順候蕃祉延釐 爲此照會 須至照會 者
右
大朝鮮國總理各國事務大臣
一千八百八十三年十月初八日 癸未年九月初八日

【관련문서】

大朝鮮督辦交涉通商事務閔 爲照覆事 接准貴大臣來文內開云云等因前來 准 此 查貴國阿領事已於本月十八日到本衙門晤談 一應接待居住應辦事宜妥爲

料理 本大臣奉諭着全權 以便與貴大臣會商 頃聞貴大臣啣命遠涉 已到本國地方 曷任欣喜 玆派本衙門協辦金晩植·主事徐相雨 前往仁川口岸迎接 即同貴大臣到京 惟祈遄臨 順頌勛祺 爲此照覆 須至照覆者
右
大英欽差駐劄中華便宜行事大臣 巴
癸未九月二十五日 照會

H.S. Parkes (1883. 10. 18) ➜ G.L.G. Granville (1883. 12. 7)

조약 개정 협상을 위한 조선행 보고

Sir H.S. Parkes to Earl Granville.-(Received December 7)

(No. 28)

Peking, October 18, 1883

My Lord,

I HAVE the honour to report that, in pursuance of your Lordship's telegraphic instructions, I leave Peking for Corea to-day, having arranged, as I have reported by telegraph on the 12th instant, to arrive there simultaneously with M. Zappe on the 25th.

Mr. Aston will have preceded us, and I inclose a copy of the instructions which I have furnished to him, and a copy of the letter which I have addressed to the President of the Foreign Board of Corea, explaining the intentions of Her Majesty's Government.

I add a copy of a note I have received from Count Tattenbach, the German Chargé d'Affaires at Peking, showing that he has addressed a similar communication to the Corean Government.

I also beg to submit a copy of a despatch in which I have communicated with Captain Fullerton, the Senior Naval officer at Chefoo, on the subject of my own conveyance to Corea, and that of Mr. Aston.

I have, &c.
(Signed)   HARRY S. PARKES

Inclosure 1

Sir H.S. Parkes to Mr. Aston.

Sir,

Peking, October 8, 1883

I HAVE the satisfaction of being informed by Earl Granville that his Lordship has instructed Mr. Trench to place you at my disposal for service in Corea, and being apprised by Mr. Trench that you would be prepared to join me, and by Vice-Admiral Willes that Her Majesty's ship "Sapphire" was to leave Yokohama about the 5th instant, and would take you to Chefoo, I send these instructions to meet you at that port.

You are aware that the object of my mission to Corea is to negotiate a new Treaty with that country, and that the German Government have appointed M. Zappe Plenipotentiary for the same purpose. I expect to reach Chefoo about the 22nd instant, and I believe that M. Zappe will arrive there at the same date.

It being necessary that the intentions of the British and German Governments should be notified to the Corean Government before we arrive in Corea, and that timely preparations should be made for our reception, I have to instruct you to proceed to Chemulpho as soon as the Senior Naval Officer at Chefoo, to whom I have written, shall enable you to do so on the vessel which Vice-Admiral Willes has informed me will be detailed for this service.

I inclose a letter which I have addressed to the President of the Foreign Board of Corea, announcing the object of my mission, and requesting that the necessary preparations may be made for the reception of m. Zappe and myself at the capital. I also beg that Plenipotentiaries may at once be appointed on the part of the Corean Government, so that we may be able to enter on the intended negotiations immediately on our arrival. I add for your own use a copy of this letter and of the Chinese translation.

Count Tattenbach, the German Chargé d'Affaires at Peking, has addressed a similar letter to the President of the Foreign Board, which I inclose in original, together with a copy and translation.

You will take steps for the delivery of these two letters to the President as soon as possible, and you will use your best endeavours to obtain his compliance with the course I have requested. You will perceive that I have pointed out to the President that owing to the lateness of the season it is imperative that the negotiations should be conducted with all possible dispatch, and you will press this necessity on his Excellency's serious attention.

I believe you are in possession of a copy of the draft Treaty which it is proposed to conclude with Corea. It is probable that the negotiations may be accelerated by your communicating and explaining its conditions to the Foreign Board before my arrival, and I therefore authorize you to take any step you may think advisable for advancing the consideration of our proposals by the Corean Government. But you will inform them that the draft is not complete, and that it is subject to modification on some few points by M. Zappe and myself. For your own guidance on this subject, I inclose you a copy of a telegram which I received on the 6th instant from Earl Granville, from which you will perceive that section 5 of Article V, which relates to prohibited goods, should be struck out from the draft.

You will also ask the Corean authorities to provide you at once with such assistance as you may require and they can afford for the translation of the Treaty into Corean. The Acting Chinese Secretary who will accompany me will undertake its translation into Chinese.

I should be glad to be met by you on my arrival at Chemulpho, and you will inform the Corean Government that in order to avoid delay I particularly desire to proceed to the capital immediately on reaching that anchorage.

I am, &c.

(Signed)　　HARRY S. PARKES

Inclosure 2*

Inclosure 3

Count Tattenbach to Sir H.S. Parkes.
Pékin, le 8 October, 1883

M. le Ministre,

J'AI l'honneur de retourner a votre Excellence la note addressee par elle au President du Ministere des Affairs Etrangeres de la Coréa.

---

*본서 170번 문서

J'ajoute la note que j'ai adresse de mon côte a ce fonctionuaire et qui est identique a celle de votre Excellence sauf quelques changements purement formels.

Pour que Mr. Aston ne soit pas ignorant du contenu, j'ajoute pour son usage une copie du texte Allemand de ma note ainsi quo du texte Chinois.

Pour l'usage de votre Excellence je me permettrai d'envoyer demain ces mêmes copies.

Il ne me reste que de remercier notre Excellence de l'extrême amabilité avec laquelle vous avez bien voulu consentir a faire expédier ma note par Mr. Aston.

Agrées, &c.

(Signe)　　GRAF VON TATTENBACH

Inclosure 4

Sir H.S. Parkes to Captain Fulierton.

Peking, October 9, 1883

Sir,

I HAVE been informed by the Commander-in-chief that you would leave Yokohama in the ship under your command about the 5th instant, and would await me at Chefoo. Also that your would take Mr. Aston to that port, and forward him from thence to Corea in advance of myself in one of Her Majesty's ships.

I am now forwarding my instructions to Mr. Aston, and I should feel obliged if you would enable him to proceed to Chemulpho as soon as he receives them.

I shall endeavour to be at Chefoo on the 22nd instant, but as the steamers between Tien-tsin and that port do not run on fixed days, there is necessarily a little uncertainty as to the time of my arrival there.

I may mention that I am informed that the German corvette "Leipzig," which will convey M. Zappe, the German Plenipotentiary, to Corea, is expected to reach Chefoo on the dte above named, and I believe that M. Zappe will also arrive there at the same time.

I shall be accompanied by Mr. Maude, the Second Secretary of this Legation, Mr. Hillier, the Chinese Secretary, a Chinese writer, and four or five Chinese servants.

I have, &c.
(Signed)　　HARRY S. PARKES

Balfour of Burleigh (1883. 10. 18) ➜ G.L.G. Granville (1883. 10. 22)

天津 조약에 준하는 전교, 내지여행권 명문화 요구

Lord Balfour of Burleigh to Earl Granville.— (Received October 22)

National Bible Society of Scotland,

My Lord,

224, *West George Street, Glasgow, October* 18, 1883

ON behalf of the Board of Directors of the National Bible Society of Scotland, I venture to ask your Lordship's good officers in connection with any Treaty arrangements that may be made between Her Majesty's Government and the Government of Corea.

As your Lordship is aware, provision is made under Article VIII and IX in Lord Elgin's Treaty with China, signed at Tien-tsin in 1858, for the protection of persons, native or foreign, who may teach or profess the Christian religion, and for liberty to British subjects to travel, with passports, to all parts of the interior; while under the favoured-nation clause missionaries and Bible Society agents have been able to reside in any part of China to which their duty has called them.

In the interests of their mission, and of possible native converts in Corea, the Directors of this Society are anxious that similar arrangements should, if practicable, be made with the consent of the Government of Corea; and they respectfully solicit your Lordship's powerful sympathy and aid in this behalf.

I may assure your Lordship that any agents we may send to Corea will take care, as those in China have always done, to conduct themselves prudently, and with due regard to local regulations and circumstances.

I have, &c.

(Signed)   BALFOUR OF BURLEICH, President

李鴻章(1883. 10. 21/光緖九年九月二十一日)

李鴻章・Parkes 회담

巴云 本大臣今晚擬卽起程 匆匆不及備文 求中堂轉致粵督 答云 巴大人現擬何往 巴云 前往朝鮮 問 有何公幹 巴云 因和約之事 問 貴國與朝鮮和約去年業經議定 此次前赴朝鮮是否互換 巴云 並非互換 擬另行議改 答云 朝鮮前議和約甚妥 美國業經批准互換 現在所定各口通商章程貨物稅則 亦極允協 美國日本均已照辦 巴云 前議條約英國國家不以爲然 故宜更改 朝鮮本係極窮之國 無甚商務 如欲改易 卽另立約 如不欲改 卽將前約毁棄 因與英商毫無利益也 從前立約時 中國何不勸其仿照天津和約稅則 答云 天津訂約時情形不同 自難援以爲例 朝鮮通商稅則 係照外國通例 斟酌至當 如玩器烟酒等類卽加重稅 日用必需之物則微輕稅 極爲公允 恐巴大人尙未見過 本署却有兩冊可以借閱 巴云 感謝感謝 天津和約雖爲用兵後所定 却甚公允 此約通行後 至今二十餘年 中國百姓受益甚多 我此次來華 看各口商務茂盛 沿海窮民均有生計 可爲確証 夫民樂則國富 國富則兵强 於國計大有關係 不可謂非和約之益也 朝鮮能與各外國通商 日久必受其益 故宜輕稅 以招徠商人 不宜重稅以遏絕商務 答云 我勸朝鮮與歐洲各國立約 本係此意惟日本土地褊小 而志願極大 畏强欺弱 與朝鮮立約通商七八年 出入貨物 均不完稅 復玆中國商令美國與之訂約 今年又定通商稅則 日本不得不照行 然心常懷怨 我朝開國 先平朝鮮 其臣服中國 尤非安南琉球可比 乃東洋屢屢在彼煽惑 欲唆令其不爲中國屬藩 不知朝鮮勢有不能 理有不可也 巴大人在東洋年久 想必習聞此論 此次前往朝鮮 如竟翻前案 適入日本穀中 不免爲倭人所用 巴云 我前在中國廿年 未曾變成華人 後往東洋十八年 亦未變爲倭人 中堂可無庸過慮 惟承中堂明白告以此語 可見心口如一 感佩之至 數年前 東洋全國皆欲與朝鮮打仗 經我極力勸息 此卽本大臣不黨倭人之明証 答云 日本如來攻朝鮮 中國必出兵相助 當時我已以將此語明告日本 如日本不認朝鮮爲中華屬國 或欲呑倂 本大臣不能不與計較 巴檢問朝鮮稅則章程云 大致尙屬妥當 俟帶回細閱 本大臣因奉國家電信 前往朝鮮議約 是以不得不往 去年秋間 本國水師提督韋力士定約末款云 限期一年互換 今已屆期或應互換 或應更議 自應議妥爲是 約須一月竣事 俟回津再細談

The society for the Suppression of the Opium Trade (1883. 10. 31) ➜ G.L.G. Granville (1883. 11. 8)

아편 수입금지 명문화를 촉구하는 청원

The Society for the Suppression of the Opium Trade to Earl Granville.—
(Received November 8)

My Lord,

Queen Anne's Mansions, St. James' Park, October 31, 1883

WE heard last year with the liveliest satisfaction of the signing of a Treaty between Great Britain and Corea, by which, following the precedent set by the previously signed Teaty between the United States and Corea, the opium trade was absolutely prohibited. The United States' Treaty has been ratified, but we observe in the newspapers a statement that Sir Harry Parkes is proceeding to Corea to procure some modifications of the Treaty negotiated by Admiral Willes, or to set it aside, and contract a new Treaty.

Although no expressions of dissatisfaction with the Article which prohibits opium have come to our knowledge from any quarter, and we are far from imputing any such dissatisfaction to Her Majesty's Government, yet we conceive that the grave importance of the subject will justify us in addressing to your Lordship an expression of our earnest hope that the Treaty which will eventually be ratified will contain a clause prohibiting the opium trade, as expressly and entirely as the American Treaty prohibits it.

The terrible evils which have resulted from the opium trade with China, and the embarrassments which it is still inflicting upon our relations with that country, have, we confidently anticipate, induced your Lordship to resolve that from the outset British commercial intercourse with the Kingdom of Corea shall not be infected by so malign an element. In adopting this policy your Lordship will be strengthened, not only by the precedent of the recent Treaty between the United States and Corea, but succeeded by so remarkable a development of trade with that country.

Hoping that your Lordship will be able to favour us with an assurance that we may set our minds at rest in respect to the subject of this letter, we have, &c.

(Signed)　　　SHAFTESBURY, *President of the Society*
　　　　　　　JOSEPH W. PEASE, ⎫ Vice Prsedident
　　　　　　　SAMUEL MORLEY, ⎭
　　　　　　　C.W. TREMENHEERE, *Lieutenant-General*,
　　　　　　　　　　　　　Chairman of Committee
　　　　　　　　　　　　STORRS TURNER, Secretary

H.S. Parkes (1883. 11. 1) ➜ G.L.G. Granville (1884. 1. 2)

조선 입국 보고

Sir H.S. Parkes to Earl Granville.-(Received January 2, 1884)

(No. 36)

Söul, November 1, 1883

My Lord,

I Have the honour to report that on the evening of the 24th ultimo I embarked at Chefoo on board Her Majesty's ship "Sapphire," with Mr. Maude and Mr. Hillier. Captain Fullerton proceeded to sea at 4 a.m. on the 25th and anchored at Chemulpho (or Jin-chuen) at 2 p.m. on the 26th.

I thus arrived a day behind the time I had appointed with Herr Zappe, the German Plenipotentiary, for our rendezvous at Chemulpho, the delay being caused by stormy weather, which detained me at the Chefoo anchorage for thirty-six hours, and rendered it impossible to tranship, during the continuance of the gale, either men or begged to Her Majesty's ship "Sapphire."

I found that Herr Zappe had arrived at Chemulpho in the German frigate "Leipzig" on the evening of the 24th. Instead of proceeding to Söul, as he could have done on the morning of the 26th, he very considerately awaited my arrival.

Mr. Aston boarded the "Sapphire" immediately she anchored. He reported to me that he had arrived at Chemulpho in Her Majesty's ship "Kestrel" on the evening of the 15th October, that he had proceeded the next day to Söul, and had made arrangements with the Corean Government for the reception there of Herr Zappe and myself. He had secured for both the Missions suitable accommodation, which had been placed in habitable condition; he had explained the character of the proposed negotiations to the Ministers of the Foreign Board, and he had been informed that his Excellency the President would be appointed Plenipotentiary to treat with Herr Zappe and myself.

I was at once visited by Herr Zappe, and we arranged to land early the next morning, and to proceed together to Söul.

Shortly afterwards Kim-man-sik (or Chin-wan-chih, according to

Chinese pronunciation), one of the Vice-Presidents of the Foreign Board, and well known to me as the Second Minister of the Corean Mission to Japan of last year, called on board Her Majesty's ship "Sapphire" to deliver a welcome on the part of the Corean Government, and to inform me that he was commissioned to assist me in making the journey to the capital. I begged him to aid Mr. Aston in procuring the necessary number of conveyances and baggage-animals for myself and suite, which comprised, besides my two secretaries, a Chinese writer, two men of my English escort, and eleven Chinese servants.

The arrangements which were eventually made for this purpose were certainly of a very imperfect nature, but I soon perceived that the deficiencies were not attributable to want of will on the part of the Corean Government, but to their limited means for the reception of foreign visitors, and the apparent absence of organization. Landing with difficulty at Chemulpho, on the rude construction called a jetty, two hours were occupied in endeavouring to form a baggage-train, and to provide the various individuals with mounts or portable conveyances. The distance we had to traverse was 25 miles, which is considered in this country a full day's journey. When we had progressed about 5 miles rain unfortunately commenced, and it continued to fall steadily throughout the day. The Corean officers appeared quite unable to cope with the confusion occasioned by this inconvenience, and it soon became evident that every person in the party would have to trust to his own exertions. My officers and myself were mounted upon the small ponies of the country, and we managed to push on through the miry paths and to reach our quarters at Söul in indifferent condition at half-past 5 p.m. Herr Zappe, who had exchanged his pony for the slower conveyance of a chair, was not so fortunate, and having arrived at the city as late as 11 p.m. found difficulty in gaining admission, as the gates were closed. Servants and others continued to straggle in until noon the next day, and the baggage was much longer on its way. I mention these details, in order to show how imperfectly this country is provided with means of transport.

The President of the Foreign Board was so good as to call on me at 8 o'clock on the evening of my arrival. His Excellency and other Corean Ministers had intended to receive Herr Zappe and myself as we entered the city, but the bad weather had disturbed all their arrangement.

On the following day, the 28th, I received visits from several Corean Ministers, and on the 29th I returned these visits when I called officially on the President of the Foreign Board at the Yamên. Herr Zappe paid his official visit immediately after mine. We also called on the United States' and Japanese Ministers. There being no Chinese Representative at Söul of diplomatic rank, I sent Mr. Aston and Mr. Hillier to see Mr. Chin, the Chinese Agent now here, who is charged with the superintendence of Chinese trade, in order to express my desire to be in friendly communication, and to receive a visit from him at his convenience.

In conclusion, I should add that I have every reason to be satisfied with my reception by the Corean Government, which has, I consider, been most courteous and cordial, and I believe that this impression is shared by my colleague, the German Minister.

I have, &c.
(Signed)   HARRY S. PARKES

H.S. Parkes (1883. 11. 3) ➜ G.L.G. Granville (1884. 1. 2)

조선 입국 직전 李鴻章과 회견 보고

Sir H.S. Parkes to Earl Granville.—(Received January 2, 1884)

(No. 37 Confidential)

Söul, November 3, 1883

My Lord,

    IN your telegram No. 21 of the 21st September, your Lordship instructed me that it was not necessary to make any special communications to the Chinese Government on the subject of my mission to Corea. I therefore gave the Yamên no intimation on the subject until three days before my departure, when I had to call there on other business. I then thought it necessary to state to the Ministers, at the close of the interview, that I had to leave Peking for about a month, and that during my absence Mr. Grosvenor would be in charge of the Legation. They asked me where I was going, and on my replying "to Corea," they made no further observation.

    On passing afterwards through Tien-tsin I called on the Viceroy, Li Hung-chang, on the 21st ultimo. I could not have avoided doing so, as he had received me with much friendly demonstration on my way to Peking, and had then particularly desired to see me soon again.

    I also wished to speak with his Excellency on the subject of the recent disturbances at Canton. I told him, as I had already stated to the Yamên, that I considered I had reason to complain of the conduct of the Viceroy of the Two-kuang for having failed to keep the turbulent class of that city under proper control, in order, as it appeared to me, that he might be able to plead popular animosity to foreigners as an excuse for not extending to the latter that ample protection which the Chinese Government were bound to afford. He had even instigated excitement by proclaiming to the people that he had demanded that the man Logan should be tried again; and as that would certainly not be allowed, the Viceroy would be responsible for any fresh outbreak that might be caused by our non-compliance with the untenable demand which he had so imprudently made public.

I spoke at length and with earnestness on this subject, as well as on the communications relating to it which had passed between the Yamên and myself, because I felt it to be important, particularly in view of my absence in Corea, to impress the Grand Secretary, as I had already endeavoured to impress the Ministers of the Yamên, with the view that the Viceroy at Canton must be made sensible of his responsibilities and of the peril of the course he had chosen to follow.

I was glad to find that the Grand Secretary evinced more practical perception than the Ministers of the Yamên. The latter, he observed, had sent him all the correspondence, and he admitted that the objections which the Viceroy at Canton had taken to the legal procedure at Logan's trial, and to the sentence passed by the Chief Justice, were based on mistaken information. He assured me very positively that I need not apprehend any repetition of disturbance, and he appeared chiefly anxious that the claims which I told him his Government would have to meet should not be over stated. On this point, I observed to his Excellency that I had already instructed Her Majesty's Consul at Canton to do his best to see that the claims presented by British subjects should be limited to losses of a substantive character.

His Excellency then remarked that he had been informed by the Yamên that I was proceeding to Corea. "That country," he added, "is a dependency of China, and all business connected with it is in my charge. Why do you not come to me before proceeding there, and what are you going to do there?"

I replied that I was instructed by my Government to negotiate a new Treaty with Corea.

"But why," his Excellency proceeded, "without first coming to me; I made the Treaties of last year with Corea, and without me you would have done nothing. Why are you not frank with me on this subject?"

I replied that I was quite disposed to be frank with His Excellency, and in response to his appeal to my candour would at once express my regret that his Excellency had not made more satisfactory Treaties, as in that case I might have been saved the trouble of an uninviting expedition.

"What is there to object to in those Treaties?" he then inquired.

I answered that it would take up too much of His Excellency's time if I were to engage in a discussion on the merits of those Treaties. I would simply therefore refer to the Tariff alone, which, if it were accepted, would make all foreign trade impossible, and would render the Treaties worthless.

His Excellency then observed that I had been long in Japan, and he feared that I wished to play the Japanese game and prevent the Coreans obtaining a proper revenue from their trade. The Japanese had deceived the Coreans; they had been trading with the latter for eight years, and had not yet paid them a farthing of duty.

I replied that I was not generally charged with playing a Japanese game, and certainly not by the Japanese themselves. On the contrary, I agreed with his Excellency that the Coreans had been unfairly treated by the Japanese in regard to duties, and all that I wanted to secure on that point was a fair Tariff, which would enable the Coreans to carry on a trade with my country which would be advantageous to themselves as well as to us.

His Excellency then observed: "I believe you want more than that; you want to expunge the opium clause from your Treaty."

I remarked that my Government did not object to the import of opium being prohibited by the Coreans, and I myself should be glad to know that the latter would never use the drug in the form of an indulgence, though as a medicine it was simply invaluable. The opium which the Coreans would have to be guarded against would not be Indian, which they could not afford to buy, but the cheaper opium, which was now so extensively grown throughout China, and which I feared would be imported into Corea by Chinese. China was now the largest opium producing country in the world, and his Excellency was doubtless aware that it was grown in Manchuria, on the very frontier of Corea.

His Excellency at once changed the subject, and told me that the Corean Government had recently made a much lower Tariff, and also a set of improved trade Regulations, and he hoped I should be satisfied with them. But what he particularly desired was, I should discuss fully Corean business with himself.

I begged his Excellency to give me a copy of these Regulations and Tariff, and he at once complied with my request. Having taken a cursory glance at their contents, I observed to his Excellency that they appeared to me to contain some substantial improvements on his Treaties of last year, which would doubtless facilitate the work with which I was charged. Our position was simply this. In a couple of months from the present date we were bound either to accept Admiral Willes' Treaty of last year, or to reject it and try to make a new one. My Government having intrusted me with the negotiation required for the latter purpose the brief period I had named was practically reduced to a single month, as I must return before the navigation of the Peiho became closed by ice. I was therefore so pressed for time that a single day was of importance to me, and as passages had been engaged for me and my suite in a vessel that might leave Tien-tsin that afternoon, I regretted that this circumstance would deprive me of the benefit I should derive from his Excellency's intimate acquaintance with Corean affairs, if I could stay to discuss these with him. My mission, however, instead of being conceived, as his Excellency seemed to suppose, in the interest of the Japanese, was in fact opposed to that interest, as eight-tenths of the import trade now being conducted by Japan with Corea consisted of British goods, which we should prefer to supply to the Coreans ourselves. A fair Tariff would enable us to engage directly in that trade, while the Treaties made by his Excellency would effectually exclude us from it, and would enable the Japanese to retain it in their own hands. It was his Excellency, therefore, rather than myself, who might be charged with having hitherto played the Japanese game, and the same charge might be laid against his Government with greater force in regard to other matters than the Corean question.

His Excellency the Viceroy, Li Hung-chang, having asked me what I meant by the latter remark, I proceeded to observe that I had noticed with concern, as I recently passed through Shanghae, that his Government had opposed serious obstructions to the efforts made at the port by foreigners of several nationalities to improve the silk industry of the country. Several filatures had been established at great cost, in which many hundreds of Chinese workwomen were profitably employed in increasing, by superior reeling, the value and quality of Chinese silk, which would enable it to compete with that of Japan. The Governors of Chehkiang and Kiangsu, I had been told, were now placing such a high internal tax on cocoons as would cut off the supply of raw material from those filatures, and would probably cause them to be closed. In that case the Japanese silk industry would greatly gain, as filatures had been actively encouraged by the Government of that country during the last ten years with very satisfactory results. The export of silk from Japan had been steadily increasing, while that of China had shown a proportionate decline, and it was evident that if this state of things continued for a few more years the position of the two countries in respect to the important industry of silk would be reversed, and Japan would excel China in both the quantity and quality of her silk. In this matter China appeared to me to be playing the Japanese game in a degree which was actually suicidal. I intended to take up the question with the Yamên on my return from Corea, but from my brief experience of the unimpressionable character of that Board, I was by no means sanguine as to the result of my representations.

The Grand Secretary seemed surprised at some of my observations, and particularly desired me to give him a Memorandum on the subject. The silk question, he said, concerned the Viceroys of other provinces, who were by no means always inclined to listen to his advice. He stood almost alone as a progressist, and was obnoxious in consequence to many of his countrymen.

On terminating the interview, I observed that I believed the Chinese Government had an Agent in Corea, and that I should be glad if his Excellency would apprize him that, as my mission was calculated to promote the wishes of the Chinese Government in regard to that country, it would be desirable that he should place himself in friendly communication with me. I understood his Excellency to say that he would furnish me with letters to the Agent. Mr. Ma Kien-chang, who is now attached to his Excellency's staff, and was present at the interview, and who took, as your Lordship is aware, an active part in the management of Admiral Willes' Treaty, called on me later in the day and delivered to me an official letter addressed to his brother, Mr. Kien-chang, who succeeded him as Chinese Agent in Corea. He told me that he was not certain whether his brother was then in Corea or Chefoo. On arriving at the latter place I ascertained that he was at Chefoo, and I therefore sent him the letter. When I had left the Chefoo anchorage I was overtaken by a Chinese gun-boat sent out by Mr. Ma Kien-chang, to request that I would take him to Corea in Her Majesty's ship "Sapphire;" but I felt that I could neither impose on Captain Fullerton such a serious inconvenience, nor accede to the delay which it would have occasioned. I am at a loss to understand the object of Mr. Ma in making this request, as I find that he has been superseded here by another Agent, and that he had ceased, before he left Corea, to attract either influence or respect.

I may add that the new Agent, named Ch'ên Shu-tang, who was at one time Chinese Consul at San Francisco, has thus far held aloof from me on the plea of sickness.

I have, &c.
(signed)   HARRY S. PARKES

H.S. Parkes (1883. 11. 7) ➜ G.L.G. Granville (1884. 1. 2)

조선 입국 후 교섭경과 보고

Sir H.S. Parkes to Earl Granville.-(Received January 2, 1884)

(No. 38)

Söul, November 7, 1883

My Lord,

As an opportunity offers of communicating to-morrow with Chefoo by Her Majesty's ship "Kestrel," I propose to report briefly in this despatch the progress made by my German colleague and myself in our negotiations with the Corean Government.

I should first observe that on landing at Chemulpho on the morning of the 27th ultimo the Vice-President, Kim-man-sik, delivered to me a despatch from the President of the Foreign Board, acknowledging the note which I addressed his Excellency from Peking on the 8th ultimo, in order to make known to the Corean Government, in accordance with your Lordship's instructions, that Herr Zappe and myself had been commissioned by our respective Governments to negotiate new Treaties with Corea.

As your Lordship is aware, I requested in the same note that arrangements might be made at once for our reception at Söul, and that Plenipotentiaries should be appointed to treat with us immediately on our arrival. This note was delivered to the President by Mr. Aston on the 18th ultimo, and his Excellency states in his courteous and friendly reply, of which I inclose a translation, that arrangements which were considered satisfactory by Mr. Aston had been made for my accommodation at the capital, that the Vice-President, Kim-man-sik, had been appointed to escort me there, and that his Excellency himself had received full powers from His Majesty the King of Corea to treat with me on the business of my mission. Herr Zappe also received a similar communication from his Excellency.

The President, as I observed in my despatch of the 1st instant, called on me on the evening of my arrival at Söul, and I was thus enabled to thank his Excellency for the kind and adequate arrangements made for my personal convenience, and in particular for the prompt and gratifying consideration shown me by his Sovereign in appointing a Minister of his high rank as His Majesty's Plenipotentiary for the purposes of the negotiation with which I was charged.

Immediately after Herr Zappe and myself had paid the necessary official visits to the Corean Ministers we met to consider our course of action, and we agreed that it would be desirable to deliver our proposals to the Corean Plenipotentiary in the form of a draft Treaty with Regulations of Trade attached, and a Memorandum stating the principles on which we proposed to proceed with the compilation of a Tariff. Taking as a basis the drafts which I submitted to your Lordship in my despatch from Tôkiô No. 108 of the 22nd June last, and amending them in conformity with the instructions of our respective Governments, and so as to include certain valuable commercial concessions which have recently been made by Corea to Japan, together with other additions suggested by our own experience, on the numerous subjects that require to be dealt with in a first Treaty with an Oriental State, we drew up a set of fresh drafts in English, German, and Chinese. The preparation of these documents closely engaged our attention for four days, and early on the morning of the 3rd instant our Secretaries handed them in to the Yamên, and proceeded, as previously arranged, to read them through, clause by clause, with the Corean functionaries appointed for the purpose. The reading occupied a whole day, and the President and the other Ministers then agreed to meet Herr Zappe and myself at the Yamên on the 5th instant to discuss our proposals in detail.

This discussion, which lasted for several hours, was continued yesterday at the same length, and I have the satisfaction of adding that it resulted in a general agreement between the Corean Plenipotentiaries and ourselves on all the points of the Treaty which we had proposed, various objections to our project being withdrawn on the Corean side, and some modifications, which are in no sense disadvantageous, being volunteered on our part, in order to meet the wishes of the Corean Government. But we experienced considerable difficulty in treating on the trade Regulations and Tariff, owing to the differences which exist between our proposals on these subjects and the Regulations and Tariff of the Convention recently concluded between Corea and Japan, and which actually came into operation upon the 3rd instant. We had to take serious objection to the latter on many points, both of form and substance, and although fully disposed to give the utmost consideration in our power to the embarrassment which would be occasioned to the Corean Government by having to modify arrangements which they have so recently concluded with another Power, we felt obliged to adhere to the Regulations and scheme of Tariff which we had proposed. The Corean Plenipotentiary stated that he must take the pleasure of the King on this important subject, and that it would also have to be considered by the Council of State.

To enable his Excellency to take the necessary steps for these purposes, the Conference was adjourned until 9 A.M. to-morrow morning. I am not without hope that I may be able to add before I close this despatch, that the opinions of the Council and the decision of His Majesty may be favourable to our views, as I should deeply regret that a negotiation which has been conducted with very commendable earnestness on the part of the Corean Ministers, and in a most friendly spirit on both sides, should not lead to a result which would be attended with mutual satisfaction.

November 8, noon,

The Conference was continued this morning, and I am happy to state that after careful and prolonged discussion the Corean Plenipotentiary agreed to accept the trade Regulations and [Project] of Tariff proposed by Herr Zappe and myself as a basis of negotiation on these subjects. I am therefore able to confirm the hope I expressed yesterday, that we shall be able to effect a satisfactory settlement of all the points under consideration, and in the end conclude a satisfactory Treaty. As my courier must leave immediately, I am unable to add further particulars.

I have, &c.

(Signed)　　HARRY S. PARKES

Inclosure

The President of the Corean Foreign Office to Sir H.S. Parkes.

(Translation)   *October 25*, 1883

    MIN, Plenipotentiary and Minister Superintendent of Foreign Affairs, makes a communication in reply.

    The Minister is in receipt of his Excellency's note (note from Sir H.S. Parkes of the 8th October, 1883, to the President of the Foreign Office, quoted in full).

    The Minister has to observe that Mr. Aston, Consul of Sir H.S. Parkes honourable nation, came to the Minister's Yamên upon the 18th instant, and personally discussed the arrangements that should be made for the reception and residence of the British Minister, and satisfactorily settled everything.

    The Minister has been honoured with the bestowal of full powers by his Sovereign, in order that he may treat with the British Minister. He has just heard with much pleasure of the British Minister's arrival in this distant country with commands from his Sovereign, and he has accordingly dispatched Chin Wan-chih, one of the Vice-Presidents of his Yamên, and a Secretary, Hsü Hsiang-yü, to the port of Jên-Ch'uan, to meet the British Minister and to accompany him to the capital. His one hope is that the British Minister will speedily arrive, and he avails himself of this opportunity to present his wishes for his well-being.

United Presbyterian Church of Scotland (1883. 11. 13) ➡ G.L.G. Granville (1883. 11. 14)

선교사들의 전교, 내지여행권 명문화 청원

관련문서 T.V. Lister의 회신(1883. 11. 20)

Memorial of the Foreign Mission Board of the United Presbyterian Church in Scotland.—(Received November 14)

Unto the Right Honourable Earl Granville, K.G., Her Majesty's Secretary of State for Foreign Affairs.

The Memorial of the Foreign Mission Board of the United Presbyterian Church in Scotland,

Respectfully sheweth:

THAT the Board of Foreign Missions of the United Presbyterian Church have at present in their service a staff of upwards of seventy fully qualified missionaries, besides a large number of native agents, labouring in several mission fields, whom they support at an expenditure of 37,000l. per annum.

That of these missionaries, three ordained missionaries, one medical missionary, and a lady missionary are located in Manchuria, who make occasional journeys to the Corean border, while some of the native agents are labouring in Corea itself.

That the Board are desirous that their missionaries entering Corea should have the same protection and privileges which were secured to all missionaries in China by Articles VIII and IX of the Treaty signed at Tien-tsin in 1858 and ratified at Peking in 1860.

The Board, in these circumstances, beg most respectfully that in any Treaty arrangements between Her Majesty's Government and the Government of Corea your Lordship's good offices may be used in favour of securing protection to all persons in Corea, native or foreign, who may teach or profess the Christian religion, and of securing liberty to British subjects to travel with passports to any part of the interior.

In name, and by authority of the Foreign Mission Board of the United Presbyterian Church.

(Signed)　　WM. NAIRN, Chairman

JAS. BUCHANAN, *Foreign Mission Secretary.*
United Presbyterian Church Foreign Mission Office,
Edinburgh, November 13, 1883

【관련문서】

Mr. Lister to the Rev. W. Nairn.

Sir,

Foreign Office, November 20, 1883

I AM directed by Earl Granville to acknowledge the receipt of the Memorial of the Foreign Mission Board of the United Presbyterian Church in Scotland, expressing the hope that in any Treaty arrangements between Her Majesty's Government and that of Corea security may be afforded to all* persons who may profess or teach the Christian religion, and liberty be granted to British subjects to travel with passports in the interior of the country.

In reply, I am to state to you that the proposals which will be made to the Corean Government include the concession to British subjects of the right to build schools, hospitals, and places of worship, to travel with passports in the interior, and to enjoy under a most-favoured-nation clause all the privileges and advantages that may be granted by Corea to the subjects of other Powers.

If the above proposals are accepted by the Corean Government, Lord Granville hopes that the objects which the Foreign Mission Board of the United Presbyterian Church in Scotland have in view will be sufficiently secured.

I am, &c.

(Signed)   T.V. LISTER

---

*[원주] N.B.— The Board wish that British protection may be afforded in Corea to all whether *natives* or *foreigners*, who may profess the Christian religion.

高宗(高宗二十年十月)

閔泳穆 전권위임장

督辦全權字據
大朝鮮國大君主勅曰 玆與大英國大君主締訂交好 應行特派大臣 以代寡躬 玆簡我忠亮周慎信臣督辦交涉通商事務一品崇祿大夫議政府左參贊奎章閣提學世子左副賓客全權大臣閔泳穆 錫以確實全權 勅其與大英國大君主所簡同權之全權大臣會議約款一切事宜 庶將以上締好之旨妥善蕆事 於所擬條款冊內互相畫押 玆特親宣勅旨 凡有我臣閔泳穆所已定諾各事 予必全行允准 爲此 盖用大朝鮮國寶 幷御筆畫押爲據
大朝鮮開國四百九十二年十月 日

尹致昊(1883. 11. 7/高宗二十年十月八日)

Parkes와 협상에 관한 Foote의 자문

관련문서 Foote 자문에 대한 국왕, 왕비, 尹致昊의 대화(1883. 11. 7)

是午　李祖淵來訪美使而言曰　余躰我大君主聖意　恃公使之公平　今日之來　一以訪貴躰　一以問些小事件　爲英約請公使　勿惜示敎

美使曰　余恃公以友誼　倍於他人　又以公　貴國大君主所信任也　故凡有所示　余當傾懷以對

李狐曰　閣下得聞英使議約事乎

美使曰　余得聞之而不得知有議案也

李狐　自袖內持出一副稿本而言曰　英使言內　日本章則罰金千圓　太輕云云矣

美使曰　誠是我意亦如此

李狐曰　英使言內　船鈔金及罰金　將以弗銀云云矣

美使曰　誠好　本來我意如此　使日使納稅以銀　又勸穆氏抽稅以銀　不一二次　而穆氏不聽　今英使之言　誠好　合我意

李狐曰　英使言內　彼之來此之時　自其廷府命　定以値百抽七五云云　閣下以爲何如

美使曰　英使氣勝　每事所請　必過於其所欲矣　貴衙門須着力相爭　然後至雖許抽七五　無傷國利之條　可以許之　假似洋人葬地　自國人寺宇等事　可以許之

李狐曰　貴敎誠然　本衙門亦有此意

美使又曰　英使好以威相爭　若逆已見　激怒跳奮　然而貴衙門　須靜肅而接之　勿示弱處　論之以事情　議之以公法　彼若言將往支那定約　貴衙門當曰　我國已與合衆國日本定約　今與貴國論約　已是三次　君若願往支那定之　君請試之云云　則彼必更請和論矣　然后　較之事理　務協其願　爲好好　此是余之忠告　若巴夏里　知余之勸此等事于貴衙門　巴夏理必疑余　不與我議矣　然則余何能紹介左右乎　惟公諒之　勿使他人得知他人指穆氏

李狐曰　敢不如命　余雖愚　能不泄此等忠告也　且余之來此　無人知者　惟閣下諒之　若遇英使　善爲勸勉之地　切仰切仰

美使曰　當如敎矣　李狐退去

【관련문서】

是夜 入侍奏 美使今日言內 英使若請無理之條 外衙門當嚴辭拒絶之言 上曰 諾 因命余往探今日英德使來訪美使與否及其何等議論 余歸館探知 英使不曾來訪 因詣闕奏此事 上敎于閔督辦曰 明日談判 必須整嚴 期勿落抽八權利 敎甚震嚴 當此時坤殿天顔 似帶不平之色 督辦氣色 亦似未安 余莫知其故 而間間中殿下敎內 有美使但恃自己之富强等句 余自不覺怪訝 美使未甞有自恃之言 未甞有無理之行 而是敎何意乎 熊熊思之 頭尾莫捉 少焉李祖淵 閔督辦出後 兩殿合坐 命余坐 中殿曰 英使到此後 對我廷府 似甚和厚 日前彼自草條約 以請外衙門之可否 外務督辦 擇不合我意者十五件 請改正 英使初似難之 終許改正 以從我國所欲 其外日本章則中罰金二千圓 英使改以若有犯禁船隻 將其貨入官 又取罰金 假令船貨値千圓入官 又收罰金如其價 是倍罰 且船鈔 日本二十五文銅錢 英使改以廿五仙銀錢 及罰金 英使改日本納銅錢之條 定爲銀錢 且其外雖多七五之條 而亦多改日本抽八條 定以抽十 此等所爲 宗於我國 有利無害 設使有所小損 當今我國事情 不可不曲從彼所願 以定約爲重 而況彼於我如此和厚 且彼之言內 我旣順從貴國所請幾條 貴國亦不可不使我得伸我願云云 其所謂願者 不過幾件抽七五事也 且彼言內 若全不從彼意 則彼將辭退云云 假令以理言之 彼聽我願 我不可不從彼幾條之願 以事言之 英德使若不定約而退去 是使淸國人拍掌大喜 必尤驕陵(Sic.) 其利害如彼 而若如美使之言 徒爭七五之輕 則英使豈不以爲朝鮮人無知妄貪乎 余聞此敎 不覺汗出沾背 而此事本末 固係分明 故乃奏曰 何以今日李祖淵 來訪美使 而言不及於英使之如此和厚 徒言英使之以七五爲主云云乎 若使美使得知英使之如許公平和厚 美使旣(Sic.)不欣賀乎 臣與美使 但知英使之爭小利也 故美使勸外務督辦 若英使强爭小利 不顧人之利害 督辦可剛辯以折其氣 然後復和議 則英使必不作氣 此所以美使未知英使如許公平故也 若使知之 豈有此言乎 坤殿奏上曰 何以李祖淵 不言其詳于美使乎 上曰 余問於李祖淵 李祖淵言內 何可以如此仔細事情 泄於外國人乎云云 其言亦有理可歎 可歎 余奏曰 不然 李某旣承聖命 以英使意向 請美使公議 則當言英使所議本末無遺 然後美使可言好否

而李某今日訪美使 不曾言及英使長處 但言英使短處 故美使只憤其短處 而公議如彼 若使英使聞知 豈不怒美使之妄議乎 坤殿曰 李某必是恐汝之不能通辨 故不曾詳言也 諸位惑於李狐耶 李狐 善於迷人耶 可歎可歎 余奏曰 蔽一言 美使則一端公議 而若使英使聞知 大有關係於事 穆氏若聞此事 必告於英使矣 伏惟聖裁 無至起言 伏望伏望 兩殿曰 可知汝意 俄已命督辨及李祖淵 勿泄其言。汝須釋慮 於此一端事 李狐 反覆心事 可知 曉退

尹致昊(1883. 11. 8/高宗二十年十月九日)

관세협상 결과

관련문서 Foote의 논평

是夜入侍 得聞今日英使議章則於外衙門 果然罰金及船鈔 俱以銀錢爲定 而增船鈔以三十仙土 食物抽五日本 無稅 沙金及金抽五日本無稅 出口貨也 洋綿貨中 或抽七五 或抽十日本 抽八 錦種及材木抽五 大抵自五·七五·十·二十免稅 禁條六等云

【관련문서】

是夜七時 美使設晚饌 請督辦及英使·日使共卓 盡歡而散 是夕 督辦言于美使曰 凡於英約 有迷訝之條 當與閣下議之也 美使多謝謝 督辦又告曰 前外衙門所議英約幾條與昨日日記 所載同條 美使曰 余不意英使許洋綿貨抽七五也 若果然則實爲貴國賀之 又曰 閣下勿以三十·二十五爭之 何則 凡稅則中 抽三十·二十五之條 不過二三 而又不過洋人所用酒及草也 其入額不多 其征稅何足掛數 第一擇入額之多者 而定高稅 然後可有所益也 請閣下記之 督辦稱謝 是夜 余發明日前美使之言 由李狐之反覆事 罷漏入侍 奏此日遊宴事

尹致昊(1883. 11. 16/高宗二十年十月十七日)

Parkes와 협상 결렬 기록

관련문서 Foote의 논평

是夜入侍 聞英使罷條約事歸去云云 以我國不許其所願三條 一 英人來朝鮮旅行 用自己官員憑文 二 雖朝鮮人犯法 悉聽英官裁判 三 英人來朝鮮內地 販貨到處開市事 此是英使所願而我國之不許者也 故也

【관련문서】

是早 言英使將去緣由於美使 美使曰 樸氏頭鬢蒼白 余以爲彼必有慈心矣 以此幾件 觀其狼心不老 然而貴國何可許此幾條耶 且余想樸斯 雖言如此 此是試貴國之聽耶否 非其眞欲得行 亦必退去也 何則 英國爭此條於日本及淸國而不得 彼豈以爲貴國許之耶 蔽一言 貴國不可許也 是日入侍奏美使之言 聞是日外務督辦 贈書于英使 言閣下將不議條約而去 甚實悵歎云云矣 英使答以再議云云

H.S. Parkes(1883. 11. 17) ➜ 閔泳穆

영사재판권 조항의 재고를 청하는 자문

관련문서 Parkes의 회신(1883. 11. 17)

十月十八日抵英使書 英民管轄事
逕啓者 昨日貴大臣 將日後云云一段 不肯於條約內載明 這一段已在於去年各國條約內 因爲往來交涉緊要不可已者 本國久願與貴國立約 必有兩面利益者 所以通商章程稅則 已多照貴大臣旨議降心相從 克底于成 只緣這一段未能妥協 甚用悵惜 貴大臣所奉訓諭 乃若堅重 竊望貴國政府之更加深量焉 肅此 敬頌日祺
癸未十月十八日 名另具 督辦

【관련문서】

巴公使答書
逕覆者 頃准來函 以日後云云一段 已在於去年各國條約內 因爲緊要不可已者 只緣未能妥協 甚用悵惜等語 查日後各國官員在貴國審理各本國民人之權酌爲收回一條 雖去年載入 英·美·德 三國約內 然貴國與東洋議定條約 暨中國客歲所定章程 並本年貴國與奧斯馬加國擬立約稿內 均無此議 何獨必以此節載入 英·美·德 三國約內爲重 而他國之約竟不其然哉 惟閱來函內 有只這一段未能妥協之語 誠如斯言 則因此意見不合之一端 致誤議約成局 本大臣暨德國大臣亦同悵惜 再四思惟 尚有一策似可解釋前紛 玆擬於明日九點鐘前赴貴署面達一切是否何如 希即示覆爲荷 此頌日祉
十月十八日 名另具 巴夏禮

184

閔泳穆(1883. 11. 24/高宗二十年十月二十五日) ➡ H.S. Parkes

세칙(稅則) 관련 문제발생시 재협상을 확인하는 조회

관련문서 Parkes의 회신(1883. 11. 27)

大朝鮮督辦交涉通商事務閔 爲照會事 照得 本大臣與貴大臣今日畫押之條約稅則一事 現遵政令言明 倘若日後邊境所征陸路稅則有碍於通商各口貿易 本國政府願將各項稅則酌爲整頓 庶將一切歧輕歧重之處刪除淨盡 爲此照會 須至照會者
右照會
大英欽差駐劄中華便宜行事大臣 巴
癸未十月二十五日 照會

【관련문서】

大英欽差駐劄中華便宜行事大臣巴 爲照覆事 本年十月二十五日 接准貴大臣來文內開 今日畫押之條約稅則一事 現遵政令言明 倘若日後邊境所征陸路稅則有碍於通商各口貿易 本國政府願將各項稅則酌行整頓 改爲均一 俾得其平等因 准此 俟本大臣將彼此畫押約條咨送本國政府查閱時 亦必譯錄此文 幷行附呈 諒我國政府披覽之下 無不視爲恰當也 爲此照覆 須至照會者
右照會
大朝鮮國督辦交涉通商事務 閔
一千八百八十三年十一月二十七日 癸未年十月二十八日

閔泳穆(1883. 11. 24/高宗二十年 十月二十五日) ➡ H.S. Parkes

비준서 교환시 高宗의 조회에 대한 국서 교부를 청하는 조회

관련문서 Parkes의 회신(1883. 11. 27)

大朝鮮督辦交涉通商事務閔 爲照會事 上年條約畵押之後 本國大君主照會貴國大君主國書 曾經本國大臣面交貴國大臣賫往 這照會尚未有照覆 今年新約商酌之時 本大臣已詢此由 貴大臣答以條約批准互換以前 未有兩國君主照會往來之例 本大臣據此奏明 既蒙我大君主俞允 而因勅本大臣 俟議約事完 將上年照會事情照會貴大臣 請煩奏明貴國大君主 以便此次條約互換批准之時 貴國全權大臣賫來貴國大君主照覆 以昭憑信爲要 爲此照會 須至照會者
右照會
大英欽差駐劄中華便宜行事大臣 巴
癸未十月二十五日 照會

【관련문서】

大英欽差駐劄中華便宜行事大臣巴 爲照覆事 本年十月二十五日 接准貴大臣照會 以上年條約畵押之後 貴國大君主照會本國大君主國書一事 查來文所開各節 本大臣自必逐一詳咨我國政府 以便轉行入奏可也 爲此照覆 須至照會者
右照會
大朝鮮督辦交涉通商事務 閔
一千八百八十三年十一月二十七日 癸未年十月二十八日

186

閔泳穆(1883. 11. 26/高宗二十年十月二十七日) ➜ H.S. Parkes

보호선척장정(保護船隻章程) 발송 조회

관련문서 Parkes의 회신(1883. 11)

大朝鮮督辦交涉通商事務閔 爲照會事 玆有本國船隻保險章程 照錄一本呈閱
請煩貴大臣查照施行可也 爲此照會 須至照會者
右照會
大英欽差駐劄中華便宜行事大臣 巴
癸未十月二十七日 照會

督辦交涉通商事務閔爲示諭事本衙門議定保護本國及各國船隻遭風遇險章程
五條已經稟旨關飭沿海各地方出示曉諭仍將此項章程分給各船收執查本國及
各國兵商船隻在於本國沿海水面如有遭風遇險等事該地方營邑鎭堡各官及諸
民人等一經得知自應照章妥爲救護以拯危難合行查照章程開單爲此曉示仰該
處地方各官及諸民人等並船主一體知悉毋違特示計開單

一 定地段以專責成也
　查沿海島嶼交錯非明定界址必致彼此推諉應由沿海營邑鎭堡各官首先明
　定所轄界限每以十里爲一段仍飭各島各浦保擧頭目一人列名冊報以專責
　成無論何國船隻遇有漂撞礁淺一切危險該船晝則高掛白旗夜則接懸兩燈
　以示求救之意該地居民漁戶人等見有此樣旗燈即報頭目一面飛報就近地
　方官一面聚集船夫居民合力助救該地方官聞報後亦即督率兵役親往救護
　不得稍有遲訣其往來報信之人一切費用均由失事船主給還但官役不得向
　船主勒索使費
一 明賞罰以免推諉也
　查沿海地方官如有救護人命十名以上及船貨一萬兩以上者一經該管上司
　查明申報或領事官照會海關監理本衙門立即註冊紀功論獎其頭目居民等
　出力助救者亦分別上次功勞隨時賞資以昭激勸倘各官不肯認真辦理頭目
　居民亦或救護不力甚至希冀分肥者當分輕重嚴究決不饒恕至於望見船隻

危險報知頭目與就近各官者以初報之人爲首功由失事船主酌給勞費銀大船多至三十兩中小船以十兩爲限
一 定章程以免混亂也
凡遇險船隻其力尙可自存船主並不願他人上船者救援之人自不得混行上船倘船主須人救援或係應先救人或係應先救船或係應救貨均聽船主情願不得自行動手其所救起貨物寄頓處所亦由船主作主其有擅行搬取或私自藏匿者一經船主及頭目指明有確據者自官卽行追究
一 定酬勞以資鼓勵也
凡救起之貨須候地方官驗報如係外國船貨則並報明附近領事官會同查核將貨估價按照出入多寡難易抽撥充賞多至三分之一以賞救援之人若有貨無人則須稟明就近地方官及領事官秉公將貨酌賞倘無貨有人則無論何國人給以衣食送交就近領事官分別資送倘外國人無領事可交者一面報明本衙門一面由地方官資給盤纏俾令自行回國其小船無力可以酬謝者卽就近稟報地方官小船每救人一名賞給銅錢五十兩由地方官先行核給按月彙報就近海關監理撥還虛捏者嚴究倘遇風濤汹湧人力難施或在大洋救援所不及者均宜各安天命不得移怒他人惹端滋擾
一 廣曉諭以昭勸戒也
凡海濱愚民皆緣不知救援之有賞不救之有罰是以堅視不救或乘機搶奪嗣後沿海營邑鎭堡各官均宜將以上告示眞諺翻謄書寫木牌遍處懸掛使海濱居民漁戶人等皆知遇險之船救護爲有功不救爲有罪庶人人競勸危難有濟矣

【관련문서】

大英欽差駐劄中華便宜行事大臣巴 爲照覆事 本年十月二十七日 接准貴大臣來文 以貴國保護船隻章程錄送前來 本大臣俱已收閱 合卽備文照覆 請爲查照可也 爲此照覆 須至照會者

187

H.S. Parkes (1883. 12. 1) ➡ G.L.G. Granville (1884. 1. 16)

2차 조영조약 체결 보고

Sir H.S. Parkes to Earl Granville.-(Received January 16, 1884)

(No. 39. Ext. 9)

Chefoo, December 1, 1883

My Lord,

I HAVE the honour to report to your Lordship that I reached the capital of Söul on the 27th ultimo, on the same day with Herr Zappe, the German Plenipotentiary.

A draft of the Treaty was presented to the Corean Foreign Office on the 3rd instant. The negotiations lasted without intermission until the 26th November, when Treaties were signed by my German colleague and myself which included all the conditions we were instructed to obtain. The King of Corea received Herr Zappe and myself in audience on the following day, and I was able to embark on board Her Majesty's ship "Sapphire" on the evening of the 29th ultimo.

I have already reported the substance of the above to your Lordship by telegraph.

I have, &c.
(Signed)　　HARRY S. PARKES

H.S. Parkes (1883. 12. 1) ➡ G.L.G. Granville (1884. 1. 16)

2차 조영조약 관련 청국·일본 상공회의소에 보낼 서신 발송

Sir H.S. Parkes to Earl Granville.-(Received January 16, 1884)

(No. 40)

Chefoo, December 1, 1883

My Lord,

WITH reference to my previous despatch No. 39 of this date, I have the honour to report that on arriving here this morning I find a vessel on the point of leaving for Shanghae, and I therefore forward to your Lordship by this opportunity, in the Treaty series of my despatches, the Treaty which I signed at Söul on the 26th ultimo.

Time, however, will not permit me to offer to your Lordship on this occasion any observations. Owing to the protracted character of the negotiations in which I and my German colleague were obliged to engage with the Corean Government, my proceedings must form the subject of a lengthy Report which I shall forward as soon as possible. For the moment I have to secure my return to Tien-tsin before the river becomes closed by ice, and I shall therefore proceed there in Her Majesty's gunvessel "Kestre" at daybreak to-morrow morning.

Prompted by the belief that your Lordship may wish to receive the opinions of the Chambers of Commerce in China and Japan on this Treaty, I have arranged that copies shall be confidentially communicated to them in the letter of which I inclose a copy; and I also inclose a copy of a letter in which I have requested to Crown Advocate at Shanghae to submit an opinion to your Lordship on the nature of the Order in Council which will be required to enable Her Majesty's officers who may be appointed to Corea to exercise in that country the jurisdiction over British subjects granted by this Treaty.

I have, &c.

(Signed)   HARRY S. PARKES

Sir H.S. Parkes to the Chairman of the Chamber of Commerce, Shanghae*

(Confidential) Chefoo, December 1, 1883

Sir,

BEING aware that Her Majesty's Principal Secretary of State for Foreign Affairs consulted your Chamber on the Treaty with Corea concluded last year by Vice-Admiral Willes, I think it probable that his Lordship would also wish to receive your opinion on a Treaty with the same Power which I signed on the 26th ultimo, and which is intended to replace the Treaty first named.

I therefore inclose you a copy of the Treaty signed by myself, and request you to be so good as to forward direct to Earl Granville as soon as convenient any representations thereon which you may think fit to make. I should add, however, that in taking the unusual step of communicating to you a Treaty which has not yet been received by Her Majesty's Government, I am acting on my own responsibility, and that I undertake this step in the confident reliance that you will treat this communication as strictly confidential, and that neither you nor any member of the Committee of your Chamber whom you may have to consult on the subject will give publicity to the Treaty which I inclose.

I have, &c.
(Signed)　　HARRY S. PARKES

Inclosure 2

Sir H.S. Parkes to Mr. Wilkinson.

Sir, *Chefoo, December* 1, 1883

I HAVE requested Her Majesty's Consul at Shanghae to place in your hands a copy of the Treaty with Corea (with Regulations of Trade, Tariff, and Protocol annexed) which I signed at Söul on the 26th ultimo, in order that you may be so good as to furnish an opinion to Her Majesty's Secretary of State for Foreign Affairs on the nature of the Order in Council which will be required to enable Her Majesty's authorities who may be appointed to Corea to exercise the jurisdiction over British subjects granted by this Treaty.

It appears to me that a short Order extending the provisions of the existing China and Japan Orders in Council is all that would be requisite, in the first instance at least, and as it is advisable that such an Order should come into operation at the date on which the ratifications of the Treaty shall be exchanged, I have to request you, with the view of preventing delay, to prepare and forward to Earl Granville a draft of the Order which you would advise.

I have, &c.

(Signed)　　HARRY S. PARKES

189

H.S. Parkes (1883. 12. 6) ➡ G.L.G. Granville (1884. 2. 1)

2차 조영조약 협상 전말 보고

Sir H.S. Parkes to Earl Granville.-(Received February 1, 1884)

(No. 42)

Tien-tsin, December 6, 1883

My Lord,

I PROPOSE to furnish in this despatch some account of my negotiations at Söul.

I reported the commencement of those negotiations in my despatch No. 38 of the 7th ultimo. I then mentioned that on the 3rd ultimo the German Minister and myself took the initiatory step of delivering our proposals to the Corean Plenipotentiary in the form of a draft Tariff, with Regulations of Trade annexed, and a statement of the principles on which we desire to construct the Tariff, and that these proposals were read through clause by clause on that day by our Secretaries with the Ministers of the Foreign Office. The observations made by the latter, as the reading proceeded, afforded an insight into the objections we should have to encounter, and enabled us to perceive that, though the Corean Government were willing to amend the Treaties of last year, they were strongly opposed to their rejection. They also complained of delay on the part of both our Governments, as eighteen months had nearly elapsed since those Treaties were concluded, and they expressed considerable disappointment at finding that neither I nor Herr Zappe had brought a reply to the letter addressed last year by the King of Corea both to Her Majesty and the Emperor of Germany.

Herr Zappe and myself therefore thought it desirable to take up these points ourselves at the opening conference with the Corean Plenipotentiary, which took place on the 5th. His Excellency was assisted at this and at all the subsequent conferences by Kim Hong-jip and Li Tso-yöu, Vice-Ministers of the Foreign Office, and Herr von Möllendorff, who holds similar rank in the service of the Corean Government.

Speaking for Herr Zappe and myself, I at once entered on a review of the antecedents which had led to our present mission. I observed that the Treaties of last year were, in fact, a proposal on the part of the Corean Government to the Governments of Great Britain and Germany. They were drawn up by the Corean Governments, with the assistance of that of China, and the contents of them were not known to our Governments until they reached home. They were accompanied in each instance by a letter from the King of Corea to our respective Sovereigns, which was appreciated as a friendly act on His Majesty's part. Our Governments had scarcely received the Treaties when they heard that disastrous events had occurred in Corea; that a serious revolt had broken out in the capital, which appeared to overthrow the King's authority; that the Queen and many of His Majesty's Ministers had been killed; that the Japanese Legation in Söul had been attacked and destroyed; and that the Japanese Minister, who had received no protection from the Government, had escaped with great difficulty, and that several of his retinue had been killed in the struggle. Later on they heard that the capital had been occupied by Chinese troops, and that the King's father, who was charged with having instigated the revolt, had been taken as a prisoner to China. These deplorable events obliged our Governments to pause before they proceeded with the consideration of the Treaties, as they naturally felt that while the country was disturbed the lives and property of their subjects would not be safe in Corea. Owing to the distance of the latter country from Europe, and in particular to the very scant means of communication, it was not until the beginning of this year that our Governments heard of the settlement of the difficulty with Japan, and were assured that order had been restored. They then entered on the consideration of the Treaties, but as it was found that these contained various objectionable provisions, for the removal of which fresh negotiation would be required, and as the time named for the exchange of the ratifications was close at hand, they proposed to the Corean Government to extend that date until the close of the year, in order to obtain time for the due consideration of the questions concerned. The Corean Government having agreed to this proposal, our Governments then proceeded to frame their counter-proposals, and, as a mark of respect and consideration for the former, they appointed special Plenipotentiaries of rank to conduct the necessary negotiation. Her Majesty's Government, in accrediting Her Majesty's Minister to China to the Court of Corea, had given the latter a proof of friendly and considerate estimation, while the German Government had paid the Corean Government a similar compliment by sending out a Minister Plenipotentiary from Europe, and he had made the long voyage to Corea with unexampled celerity. This statement, I observed, must satisfy the Corean Government that our Government could not be justly charged with delay.

I felt that I should also explain why the circumstances of the case did not permit of Herr Zappe and myself having the honour, in addition to that of being appointed Ministers Plenipotentiary to Corea, of being the bearers of replies from our respective Sovereigns to the letters of the King. We had to inform the Corean Government that the Treaties of last year could not be ratified, and to propose, in place of them, new Treaties. It remained to be seen whether the Corean Government would accept our proposals, and, therefore, whether Treaty relations would be established between our respective countries; but it was obvious that until such relations were established, it would be premature for the various Sovereigns to enter into personal communications with each other. If the result of the present negotiations should prove satisfactory, we felt confident that the King of Corea would not experience any want of cordiality on the part of our Sovereigns in this respect.

Proceeding then to the subject of our proposals, I pointed out that it would be impossible to retain the old Treaty, and to negotiate, as I understood the Corean Government desired, a Supplementary Treaty containing the various changes and additions which would have to be introduced. Two such Treaties would conflict with each other, and could not work harmoniously. The concessions made last year by Corea to China, also those which had been more recently made to Japan, and those which the Corean Government had proposed this year to that of Austria-Hungary, would have to be included, together with the amendments proposed by our Governments. And although many of the provisions of the Treaties of last year, with some modifications as to wording might be retained, it would be far better, in order to prevent trouble in the future, to recast them afresh and replace them with new ones. The draft Treaties which we had placed in the hands of the Corean Plenipotentiary were the result of a long experience in China and Japan, and terms which had been accepted by those Powers could not be considered disadvantageous to Corea. The object in view was to establish friendly and satisfactory relations between Corea and two of the leading States of Europe, such as would enable Corea to develop her dormant commercial resources, and open out to her people a wide field of industrial activity. The Treaties of last year, however well meant by the Corean Government, would not have secured that object, and would not have afforded satisfaction to any of the parties concerned. Those which we now proposed would, on the contrary, enable the wishes of the Corean Government to be fulfilled, they would secure great and permanent advantage to Corea, both political and commercial; and, if concluded, would not fail to be highly serviceable to Corea in her negotiations with other European Powers. Having made the above statement, which was entirely endorsed by Herr Zappe, I then invited the Corean Plenipotentiary to enter on the consideration of our proposals.

His Excellency thanked me for this full explanation of the position. He observed that he could now perceive that there had been no avoidable delay on the part of the British and German Governments, and could understand why the letters of the King had not been replied to. His Government attached great importance to the acknowledgment of those letters, as they considered that such correspondence denoted the independence of Corea, but he saw in the appointment of Ministers of the rank of Herr Zappe and myself a recognition of Corea's position which would be appreciated by his Government. The latter had thought that as the American Government had ratified their Treaty, the Governments of Great Britain and Germany might have done the same, and that if, after trial, the Treaties had been found defective, they might have been modified. But as those Governments took a different view, he was prepared to discuss their counter-proposals on their merits.

To this I replied that it was much easier to correct a defective measure before than after it had come into operation, and that, as the British and German Governments knew from their long experience of Oriental intercourse that the Treaties of last year would not work well, and would certainly occasion trouble and difficulties, it would have been both useless and unwise on their part to give a trial to arrangements which they knew would fail.

The consideration of our draft Treaty was then entered on. I need not detail the various objections which were at first raised by Corean Plenipotentiary, as these embraced nearly all the points of difference between the Treaties of last year and those which we proposed. Some of these objections were soon withdrawn, but we perceived that the points on which we should have to meet with most opposition were those which related to the formation and administration of the foreign Settlements at the ports, the Regulations relating to customs or other matters to which British and German subjects would be amenable in Corea, trade in the interior of the country, the interport or carrying trade between the open ports, the erection by foreigners of places of worship, and the text of the Treaty that was to determine disputes. Admiral Willes' Treaty had provided (by Articles V and VI) that the authorities of Corea were to make (or "fix") all Regulations, and simply "communicate them to the proper officials of the British Government to be by the latter notified to their subjects and duly observed;" that "all rights of jurisdiction over persons and property within the foreign Settlements remain vested in the authorities of Chosen," that "British subjects are not permitted either to transport foreign imports to the interior, or to proceed thither to purchase native produce, nor are they permitted to transport native produce from one open port to another open port." British subjects are not protected by that Treaty in the observance of their religion, nor is provision made therein as to which of the two languages, English or Chinese, shall be accepted as the original text. On all these points we had to maintain that the British and German authorities should have a voice in all arrangements respecting the laying out and government of the Settlements within which their people were to reside; that all Regulations to which they were to be subject should be jointly made by the said authorities and those of Corea; that British and German subjects should be allowed the free exercise of their religion; that trade in the interior and the transport of all kinds of merchandize, whether foreign or native, between the open ports should be allowed; and that the English version of the Treaties, in the case of Germany as well as of Great Britain, should be regarded as the original text.

We also found that the Corean Ministers were strongly inclined to oppose the Trade Regulations and the Customs Tariff which we proposed to annex to the Treaty. They had only recently concluded a long negotiation with the Japanese Government on these subjects, resulting in a Convention which came into operation on the 3rd ultimo, but which I had not seen before I arrived in Corea. It comprises a long Code of forty-two Trade regulations, which contain much redundant and defective wording, besides various objectionable stipulations, while the Tariff is arranged on a cumbersome and complicated method, and the rates of duty are too high in many instances. The Corean Ministers represented to us that these Regulations and Tariff had been established by the Corean Government as a general national statute which they were willing to extend to all foreign nations seeking Treaty relations with them. We had to point out that as a statute they greatly needed amendment, while as they had been incorporated in a Treaty with Japan we considered that we could claim such of their provisions as we thought it desirable to adopt; that the Regulations we proposed were far simpler in character, and would be found more effective in practice, as they provided severer penalties for offences against the revenue, and that our Tariff, although lower than that concluded with Japan, was based upon well-recognized principles of taxation, and was better calculated to encourage trade.

In my despatch No. 38 of the 7th ultimo I reported that after discussion on these various points had been continued for three days we arrived at a general agreement with the Corean Plenipotentiary on the provisions of the Treaty, and also that his Excellency had accepted our Regulations and Tariff as a basis of negotiation on those subjects. We afterwards found that this understanding was by no means so complete as we could have desired, and that the negotiations which followed involved a tedious repetition of discussion which were continued incessantly from the 7th to the 24th ultimo.

Thus the Tariff, which we proceeded to consider in detail on the 7th, closely occupied our attention for a whole week. The Import Tariff which had been arranged with Japan, or, as the Corean Ministers preferred to style it, "the Corean Tariff," comprised seven rates of *ad valorem* duty, namely, 5, 8, 10, 15, 20, 25, and 30 per cent., and was specially favourable to articles of Japanese production. The Tariff proposed by Herr Zappe and myself was based upon four rates only, namely, 5, 7½, 10, and 20 per cent., and secured due consideration for articles of European growth and manufacture.

In the 5 per cent. class we placed raw productions, some manufactured articles of common quality and ordinary use, oils, mineral or vegetable, and partially manufactured articles, as "unmanufactured" metals and yarns of all kinds. The 7½ per cent. class formed the most important section, as it included manufactures of all kinds in cotton, wool, or linen, and mixtures of these materials and of silk, carpeting, chemicals, dyes, leather, manufactured metals, hardware, cutlery, &c. The 10 per cent. class comprised manufactures wholly of silk, beer and wines, plated ware, glass ware, pictures, clocks and watches, and manufactured articles of similar finish and value. The 20 per cent. class was limited to costly articles of luxury, as amber, coral, jade, ivory, jewellery, precious stones, old and silver plate, furs, scents, and spirits.

About 200 articles were named in our Tariff, and the merits of each article was discussed by the Corean Ministers with remarkable minuteness and tenacity. In order to effect an agreement we had eventually to yield to them on some points of minor importance, which we chiefly regretted because they interfered with the symmetry of our arrangement. Thus we had to move timber, salt, vegetable oils, chemicals, &c., from the 5 per cent. to the 7½ per cent. class, to advance furniture, leather manufactures, hard woods, and a few other articles from the 7½ to the 10 per cent. class, and to place tobacco and spices under the 20 per cent. rate. But we used these concessions in regard to commodities in which we have but little concern, as a shield for the important interests of our European trade. Cotton and woolen manufactures and dyes, which will probably form six-tenths of the foreign trade with Corea, will pay a 7½ per cent. rate of duty, cotton yarns, metals, sugar, drugs, medicines, and kerosene, which may comprise three-tenths of that trade, will pay 5 per cent., and the remaining tenth of the trade will certainly not pay more than a 10 per cent. rate. The result, therefore, is an average rate of 7 per cent. I felt that 7½ per cent. must be the limit of that average, as it is the amount of the import and transit duties of China combined, and was recommended by the Hong Kong Chamber of Commerce in their letter to your Lordship of the 20th January last. The payment of the Tariff duty will frank goods throughout the country, as it is provided by section 4 of Article V of the Treaty that all imports, when conveyed into the interior, shall not be subject to any additional tax, excise, or transit duty whatsover.

The only allusion made to opium in the Treaty appears in the Tariff in the list of prohibited goods, which is confined to adulterated drugs and medicines, arms and munitions of war, counterfeit coins, and "opium, except medicinal opium."

The Export Tariff is very simple, as it consists of one uniform rate of 5 per cent. on all Corean productions.

Pressure of time obliges me to pass without comment our discussions on the Trade Regulations attached to the Treaty. These, like the Tariff, occupied considerable attention, but in the end the Corean Plenipotentiary agreed to set aside the so-called Corean Regulations, and to adopt those which we proposed in their place.

We had hoped by the 15th November that our discussions were drawing to a close, but on meeting the Corean Plenipotentiary on that day to read over the final drafts, his Excellency renewed various objections which we thought had been disposed of, and strenuously opposed in particular the omission of the following clause of the British and German Treaties of last year (Article VI): "It is, however, mutually agreed and understood between the High Contracting Powers that whenever the King of Chosen shall have so far modified and reformed the statutes and judicial procedure of his kingdom that in the judgement of the British Government they conform to the laws and course of justice in England [Germany] the right of extra-territorial jurisdiction shall be abandoned, and thereafter British subjects, when within the limits of the Kingdom of Chosen, shall be subject to the jurisdiction of the native authorities."

I had inserted this clause in the draft Treaty which I submitted to your Lordship in my despatch No. 108 (Tôkiô) of the 22nd June, because I thought that in principle it was unobjectionable, and that it formed a convenient declaration of the grounds upon which extra-territorial jurisdiction in Oriental countries is based, and further that it attests the necessity of maintaining that jurisdiction until the "laws and course of Justice" in those countries become similar to our own. But Herr Zappe had received positive instructions to omit this clause, and I therefore supported him in insisting that it could not be inserted in the Treaty. The Corean Plenipotentiary was equally persistent in demanding that it should be inserted, and, on the question being referred to the Council of the Government, he was supported by the latter in his resistance, and even went so far as to announce to us that unless we yielded the point negotiations must be broken off. I am not satisfied that this threat would have been carried out, but it caused our business to come to a stand for several days, and occasioned Herr Zappe and myself no small amount of trouble and anxiety. A written expression of regret from the Corean Plenipotentiary that the negotiations should fail on this single question, which he at the same time declared was the sole point of difference between us, and on which he recommended us to apply to our Governments for fresh instructions, enabled us to propose that a Declaration framed in the following words shall be attached to the Treaty;-

"It is hereby declared that the right of extra-territorial jurisdiction over British subjects in Corea granted by this Treaty shall be relinquished when, in the judgment of the British Government, the laws and legal procedure of Corea shall have been so far modified and reformed as to remove the objections which now exist to British subjects being placed under Corean jurisdiction, and Corean Judges shall have attained similar legal qualifications and a similar independent position to those of British Judges."

This proposal was eventually accepted by the Corean Plenipotentiary, and I need not point out to your Lordship that the contention resulted in the gain of advantage to ourselves. We have seen in the case of Japan that an oriental country may think itself justified in claiming the abolition of extra-territoriality on the ground of the compilation, made by foreigners in its employ, of a Code of laws based on Western principles of legislation. But such a Code is of limited value, and is insufficient in itself to insure adequate protection of rights and liberties unless it is applied under a sound system of procedure, and administered by properly qualified judges, invested with a position which gives them complete independence in the discharge of their highly important duties. With good laws, efficient procedure, and properly qualified and independent Judges, extra-territorial jurisdiction in Oriental countries would naturally cease and determine, and I am gratified to have been the means of appending to a Treaty with one of those States a statement, which may not be limited in its application to Corea alone, declaring that we shall be willing to relinquish that jurisdiction whenever the above-mentioned conditions shall have been fulfilled.

Another discussion, which involved an inconvenient loss time, arose in the course of the preparation of the Chinese version of the Treaty on the first section of Article V, which provides that "at each of the ports or places open to foreign trade, British subjects shall be at full liberty to import from any foreign port, or from any Corean open port, to sell to or to buy from any Corean subject or others, and to export to any foreign or Corean open port, all kinds of merchandize not prohibited by this Treaty, on paying the duties of the Tariff annexed Thereto." This provision clearly secures to British subjects the right to engage in the trade between the open ports of Corea, by whatever name that trade may be called-"interport," "carrying," or "coasting" trade-though I hold that the latter is an inappropriate term, as it covers a far wider field than a trade which is expressly limited to the open or Treaty ports.

The Chamber of Commerce of Hong Kong observed in their letter to your Lordship that they regarded the prohibition against the transportation by British traders of native produce between the open ports "as one of the most objectionable provisions in the Treaty" (signed by Admiral Willes). Herr Zappe was specially instructed to secure the interport trade, and I considered that my own instructions (as I had inserted the above provision in my draft Treaty) were to the same effect. I therefore repeatedly told the Corean Plenipotentiary in our discussions on the interport trade question that this Article was intended to secure, and, if agreed to, would secure, that right, and I pointed out that the same provision appeared in the British Treaty with Japan (Article XIV, Treaty of 1858), and in the Austro-Hungarian Treaty with that country (Article XI, Treaty of 1869), and that, under those Treaties we had always exercised that right. The section in question was eventually agreed to, but in the Chinese version of that section the Corean Plenipotentiary objected to the use of a Chinese character ("yun") which means "carrying," or "conveying," and desired to substitute another ("tsai") which means "to load," and also "to carry as ship's freight," in the passages where in the English version the words "to import" and "to export" occur. I should have attached little importance to this objection if it had not appeared to indicate a desire on the part of the Corean Plenipotentiary-which appeared to me to be attributable to certain foreign influence-to create a divergence of meaning between the English and the Chinese versions of the Treaty, as the weight which has Excellency seemed to attach to the selection of one of two terms of almost, if not quite, identical meaning was otherwise unaccountable, particularly in the face of his repeated assurances that whichever character might be adopted the question must be governed by the wording of the English text as provided by Article XII. In the end the character "tsai" was substituted for "yun" in the section in question, but the latter character was retained in numerous other passages of the Treaty and Regulations, which clearly showed that the two were used in an identical sense. In order, however, to prevent any possible misconstruction in future, I thought it prudent to hand to his Excellency the *note verbale* of which I inclose a copy, stating that I agreed to the insertion of the character "tsai" instead of "yun" in the section in question on the faith of his Excellency's assurances that the change which he desired related solely to a point of style, and affected in no degree the stipulations contained in the English text of that section. His Excellency expressed himself perfectly satisfied with this note, which became part of the record of our proceedings, and I should not trouble your Lordship with this detail if I had not to account for the time occupied by our negotiations, which were interrupted by this incident throughout two valuable days.

The right to travel and trade in the interior of Corea, secured by section 6 of Article IV of the present Treaty, formed also an important subject of consideration. The Corean Plenipotentiary at first represented that, although his Government were disposed to concede this right when it could be safely exercised, they considered that it would be premature to agree to it before the people in the interior had become better acquainted with foreigners. Herr Zappe and myself were not unwilling to admit the apparent force of this argument, and therefore proposed that the right should not be exercised for a term of three years from the date of the Treaties coming into effect; but while engaged in this discussion it came to our knowledge that a mining concession had been granted by the Corean Government to a well-known British firm in the East, and that the agents of that firm were then on the point of going into the interior to work the mineral deposits thus assigned to them. In the face of this fact it became impossible for me to conclude an arrangement which would have had the appearance of securing an exclusive privilege, namely, that of doing business in the interior, for a period of three years, to a particular British firm, nor could Herr Zappe consent to exclude German subjects from participating, whenever they might meet with the opportunity of doing so, in a right which had already been granted to the subjects of another nation. We were therefore obliged to fall back upon our original proposal, in which, under the force or circumstances created by the act of the Corean Government, the Corean Plenipotentiary felt bound to acquiesce. The liberty to travel and trade in the interior is therefore at once secured by this Treaty, although, as your Lordship is aware, it continues to be withheld in Japan.

In consequence of Chinese subjects being allowed, under Regulations made last year between Corea and China, to open commercial establishments at Hanyang (or Sŏul, the capital of Corea), I had named that city in the draft Treaty I submitted to your Lordship as one of the places which should be open to British trade; and as my German colleague and myself were both authorized to demand any privileges that had been accorded by Corea to China or Japan, we inserted Hanyang among the ports and places named in section I of Article IV of the present Treaty. The Corean Plenipotentiary contended for its omission on the ground that his Government were negotiating with the Chinese Government for the surrender by the latter of commercial access to Hanyang. As Yanghwa Chin, which is also to be opened under the same section, is within 5 miles of the capital, the right of residence for purposes of trade in the latter city is not of essential importance, so long as all foreigners are equally excluded from it, and we therefore arranged this question by appending a Declaration to the Treaty stating that if the Chinese Government should hereafter surrender the right of opening commercial establishments in Hanyang, the same right shall not be claimed for British (or German) subjects, provided that it be not granted by the Corean Government to the subjects of any other Power.

The Grand Secretary Li Hung-chang has informed me, since my arrival here, that the question has not come before his Government, and that he did not see why a proposal to exclude Chinese traders from Hanyang, if made by the Corean Government, should be entertained by that of China.

Freedom in respect to religious rights is secured to British subjects resident in Corea by section 2 of Article IV, which provides that "they shall be allowed the free exercise of their religion." Following my original draft Treaty, we had at first claimed that British and German subjects should have the right of erecting "places of worship" at the ports or places open to foreign trade. This phrase was considered obnoxious by his Excellency, and after we had firmly maintained in our argument that our people could not be required by the Corean Government to ignore their religion, we proposed to substitute for it the words above mentioned, and to this his Excellency agreed. The stipulation as it now stands is more comprehensive than our original proposal, and clearly includes the right to erect places of worship whenever these may be needed.

The Treaty, in the form in which it now appears, with the Regulations, Tariff, and Protocol annexed, was finally agreed to by the Corean Plenipotentiary on the evening of the 24th ultimo. In order to state in brief the advantages which it contains, I may observe that it contains every condition named in the draft Treaty which I submitted last June to your Lordship's consideration, and which your Lordship and the German Government approved as a basis of negotiation. A comparison of that draft with the Treaty as signed will show that in the main it has been closely adhered to, although improvements have been introduced in wording and arrangement; and here I should not omit to acknowledge that for many of these amendments, especially those which appear in the Trade Regulations as well as in the Tariff, which was only roughly sketched in my original draft, I am greatly indebted to the able suggestions and efficient co-operation of my collegue, the Minister Plenipotentiary of Germany.

I should also point out that all the additional conditions which Herr Zappe and myself were instructed to propose have been secured. In my case, those conditions, as made known to me in your Lordship's telegrams of the 3rd and 17th October, were the following:-

1. The omission of opium from the body of the Treaty, and its entry as contraband in the Tariff Schedule. This has been done, and I am bound to say

that, although it involved the omission of the Article (VII) on this subject of the Treaties of last year, the Corean Plenipotentiary offered no objection to that Article being thus expunged.

2. The insertion in the favoured-nation Article (after the sentence, "shall participate in all privileges, immunities, and advantages") of the words especially in relation to import and export duties on goods and manufactures, and also the words, "this Article shall be interpreted in the most liberal sense."

I secured the insertion of the first of these two sentences (see Article X of the Treaty), but the Corean Plenipotentiary was unwilling to accept the latter one. I should observe that the consideration of this Article involved considerable discussion, as his Excellency contended strongly that it should contain the conditional clause which appears in the British and German Treaties of last year, but to this neither Herr Zappe nor myself could agree. The former was also instructed to omit the reciprocal clause in favour of Corea which forms the second paragraph of Article XII of my draft Treaty, and he was not instructed to make either of the two stipulations which your Lordship had instructed me to insert. We eventually carried our point in regard to the omission both of the conditional clause of last year's Treaties and also of the reciprocal clause in favour of Corea of my draft Treaty, whilst, as already mentioned, I secured the insertion of the words, "especially in relation to import and export duties on goods and manufactures." But I was obliged to yield in regard to the words, "this Article shall be interpreted in the most liberal sense," as the Corean Plenipotentiary was evidently distrustful of their meaning and object, and my German colleague attached no value to their insertion. If the reciprocal clause in favour of Corea had been retained, I might then have satisfied the Corean Plenipotentiary that these words involved no reflection on the liberal disposition of the Corean Government, as it would have been applicable to both of the High Contracting Powers; but I was deprived of this argument by the omission of that clause. Having with great difficulty prevailed on his Excellency to surrender the conditional clause of the Treaties of last year, it became evident that an important advantage should not be risked by prolonging the discussion on a minor point, and I trust, therefore, that your Lordship will approve of my having agreed, under the pressure of the circumstances above stated, to omit the sentence in question.

3. Your Lordship instructed me to insert a clause in the Treaty making it apply to all British Colonies, unless any exception is notified by Her Majesty's

Government within one year of the exchange of ratifications.

This instruction has been observed but as the German Plenipotentiary could not insert such a provision in his Treaty, and as it was desirable that the two Treaties should be, as far as possible, identical, I trust that your Lordship will approve of my having placed it in the form of a Declaration in the Protocol which is attached to the Treaty.

The additional conditions which Herr Zappe was instructed to secure were:-

1. To withdraw disputes between the subjects of two different Treaty Powers from the jurisdiction of the native Tribunals.

I had considered that this condition was secured by the wording of section I of Article III of my draft Treaty, as it provided that "jurisdiction over the persons and property of British subjects shall be vested exclusively in the duly authorized British authorities," and that therefore any foreigner having to prosecute a complaint against a British subject must bring his case into the British Court. But, in order to meet the wishes of the German Government on this point, we added the words, "The British [German] authorities shall hear and determine all cases brought against British [German] subjects by any British [German] or other foreign subject or citizen without the intervention of the Corean authorities" (see Article III, section I).

2. The acceptance by the Corean Government of the "Strand or Salvage Regulations" which were promulgated by the Chinese Government in 1876.

The Corean Plenipotentiary informed us that his Government had already adopted these Regulations, and his Excellency communicated to us officially a copy of the Decree making them law in Corea.

3. The issue of drawback certificates and the application of tonnage dues to lighting the sea-coast and facilitating navigation.

Both these provisions were inserted in my draft Treaty (see sections 2 and 7 of Article V), and they appear in the same position in the Treaties which we signed.

4. The permission to foreign merchants to accompany and sell their goods in the interior of the country and the opening of the coasting trade.

These two provisions are likewise contained in my draft Treaty (see Article IV, section 4, and Article V, section 1), and they are inserted in the same Articles in the Treaties now concluded.

The German Government, as your Lordship informed me, claimed these concessions on the ground that they appear in the draft of a Treaty proposed by the Corean Government to that of Austria-Hungary. The Corean Plenipotentiary, however, denied all knowledge of this draft Treaty, and Herr von Möllendorff, who is named therein as one of the Corean Plenipotentiaries, explained an occurrence with which the Corean Government appeared to be entirely unacquainted. During a visit which he had paid to Shanghae last spring, he conversed with M. Haas, the Acting Consul-General for Austria-Hungary at that port, on the desirability of a Treaty being concluded between that Power and Corea, and stated the terms which he believed the Corean Government would be disposed to grant. He denied having compiled the draft Treaty with M. Hass, and declared his surprise at hearing that his suggestions had assumed that shape. They could not, he asserted, be called proposals on the part of the Corean Government, and he disclaimed having named himself as one of the Corean Plenipotentiaries. M. Haas is now in the service of the Corean Government as Secretary to Herr von Möllendorff.

Our discussions having terminated, as I have already stated, on the evening of the 24th ultimo, both Treaties, British and German, were signed in triplicate on the 26th. One the 27th Herr Zappe and myself were received by the King in a very gracious manner at separate audiences, upon which I propose to report in another despatch. On the 28th paid official visits of leave to the Corean Ministers, and was called on by them and other Corean dignitaries. On the 29th I left Sŏul for Chemulpo in advance of Herr Zappe, as he was not equally pressed for time, and as he was proceeding to Japan he kindly provided Mr. Aston with a direct passage to his post. I embarked the same evening in Her Majesty's ship "Sapphire," as I have already reported to your Lordship.

Your Lordship having instructed me to act throughout this negotiation in concert with the German Plenipotentiary, I should not omit to state that all our proceedings were conjointly conducted in perfect harmony and with the most cordial understanding, and we moreover had the satisfaction of knowing that each rendered the other material assistance.

I beg to offer my grateful appreciation of the large discretionary powers in this negotiation which your Lordship was pleased to intrust to me, and to express the hope that the confidence with which I have thus been honoured has been exercised in a manner that will meet with the approval of Her Majesty's Government.

It remains for me to endeavour to duly acknowledge the services which

I have received from my staff. In regard to Mr. Aston, I can only say that his assistance was invaluable, whether in regard to the soundness of his counsel, his proficiency in the Corean, language or the position he has attained as *Persona grata* with the Corean Ministers.

Mr. Maude, Second Secretary of this Legation, and Mr. Hillier, the Acting Chinese Secretary, rendered me in their respective capacities most zealous and efficient support, and greatly contributed to the dispatch which I venture to believe-when the nature of the difficulties encountered and the character of the work accomplished is considered-will be seen to have marked this negotiation. I may say that the excellent translation of the Chinese version of the Treaty is Mr. Hillier's labour, and also that his mastery of that language and his possession of other qualities which insure influence and advantage in dealings with Orientals have proved of great service to me on this occasion.

I have, &c.

(Signed)　HARRY S. PARKES

Inclosure 1

Note Verbale

SOME discussion having arisen between the British and the Corean Plenipotentiary in consequence of the latter having proposed to substitute the character "tsai" for "yün" in several places in the Chinese version of Article V of the Treaty, the British Plenipotentiary thinks it desirable to state, in order to prevent future misconception, that he has acquiesced in this proposal on the faith of the assurance of the Corean Plenipotentiary that the change which the latter proposed relates solely to a point of style, and affects in no degree the stipulations contained in the English text of that Article.

(Signed)　HARRY S. PARKER

Hanyang, November 24, 1883

190

H.S. Parkes (1883. 12. 7) ➜ G.L.G. Granville (1884. 2. 1)

속방조회문에 대한 회답 국서 요청 보고

Sir H.S. Parkes to Earl Granville.—(Received February 1, 1884)

(No. 45)
My Lord,

Tien-tsin, December 7, 1883

I HAVE the honour to inclose a translation of a note which I received from the President of the Corean Foreign Office on the subject of the letter addressed last year by the King of Corea to the Queen.

The Corean Government are particularly anxious that this letter should be acknowledged by Her Majesty, and in my despatch No. 42 of yesterday's date, reporting the particulars of my recent negotiations, I showed that his subject had to be considered as soon as those negotiations commenced.

If it should please Her Majesty to ratify the Treaty which I have concluded with Corea as her Plenipotentiary, I am certainly of opinion that the Representative who shall be commissioned to exchange the ratifications should be the bearer of a reply from the Queen to the letter of the King.

I add a copy of my answer to the President of the Foreign Office, in which I stated that I should report to my Government the receipt of his Excellency's communications.

The German Minister received a similar note, and returned a similar reply.

I have, &c.
(Signed)　　HARRY S. PARKES

Inclosure 1

Min Yŏng-mok to Sir H.S. Parkes.

(Translation)

Kuei Wei, 10*th moon,* 25*th day* (*November* 24, 1883)

MIN, President of the Corean Foreign Office, makes a communication to the British Plenipotentiary.

After the signature of the Treaty last year, the Sovereign of the President's country made an official communication to Her Majesty the Queen, which was handed in person by a high officer of the Corean Government to the high officer of the British Government for transmission to its destination.

As yet there has been no reply to this official communication, and on the occasion of the negotiations for a fresh Treaty during the present year, the President, on inquiring into the cause, was informed by his Excellency the British Plenipotentiary, in reply, that it was not customary for the Sovereigns of two countries to enter into personal correspondence previous to the exchange of ratified Treaties.

The President, on the faith of this assurance, reported the circumstances to his Sovereign, who was graciously pleased to acquiesce, and has accordingly commanded the President, upon the conclusion of the Treaty negotiations, to write officially to his Excellency the British Plenipotentiary upon the subject of the communication of last year, and to request him to submit it to the notice of Her Majesty his Sovereign, in order that, when the ratifications of the present Treaty shall be exchanged, the British Plenipotentiary may bring with him a reply from Her Britannic Majesty the Queen to the official communication of His Majesty the King of Corea.

It is important that this should be done as a manifestation of good faith.

Inclosure 2

Sir H.S. Parkes to Min Yŏng-mok.

Sŏul, November 27, 1883

Sir,

I HAVE the honour to acknowledge the receipt of your Excellency's note of the 24th instant, on the subject of the letter addressed by His Majesty the King of Corea to Her Majesty the Queen when the Treaty of last year was signed.

　In reply, I beg to inform your Excellency that I shall not fail to report to my Government the receipt of this communication in order that its contents may be duly submitted to the notice of my august Sovereign.

I have, &c.

(Signed)　　HARRY S. PARKES

H.S. Parkes (1883. 12. 7) ➜ G.L.G. Granville (1884. 2. 1)

조청무역에 비해 상대적 불이익 발생시 재협상 약속 보고

Sir H.S. Parkes to Earl Granville.—(Received February 1, 1884)

(No. 44) *Tien-tsin, December* 7, 1883

My Lord,

BY the Regulations made last year between China and Corea, the frontier trade of the two countries is conducted under *ad valorem* duties of 5 per cent. As the Tariff which is attached to the Treaty which I signed at Söul on the 26th ultimo is based on *ad valorem* rates of 5, 7½, 10, and 20 per cent., the German Minister and myself considered it necessary to receive an assurance from the Corean Plenipotentiary that if that Tariff should place British and German trade in Corea at any disadvantage in its competition with the Chinese frontier trade, its rates should be readjusted so as to remove that disadvantage.

This understanding is recorded in a note which we received from the President of the Corean Foreign Office (who was also the Corean Plenipotentiary for the negotiation of the Treaty), and of which I inclose a translation. I also forward a copy of my reply, in which I observed that I had no doubt that his Excellency's note on this subject would be received with satisfaction by Her Majesty's Government.

I may add, however, that as eight or nine tenths of the British trade with Corea will enter under the 5 and 7½ per cent. rates of the Tariff attached to our Treaty, I have little doubt that it will be able to compete successfully with the Chinese frontier trade, which will be burdened by the heavy charges of land transit.

I have, &c.
(Signed)   HARRY S. PARKES

Inclosure 1

Min Yŏng-mok to Sir H.S. Parkes

(Translations)   *Kuei Wei, 10th moon, 25th day* (*November* 24, 1883)

MIN, President of the Corean Foreign Office, makes a communications to the British Plenipotentiary.

With reference to the Tariff attached to the Treaty signed this day by the President and his Excellency, the President is authorized by his Government to state that if the duties levied at their land frontier should hereafter become prejudicial to the trade at the open ports of Corea, the Corean Government will be willing to take into consideration the readjustment of their Tariffs, with the object of placing them on an uniform and equal basis, &c.

Inclosure 2

Sir H.S. Parkes to Min Yŏng-mok.

Söul, November 27, 1883

Sir,

I HAVE the honour to acknowledge the receipt of your Excellency's note dated the 24th instant, stating that, with reference to the Treaty signed by your Excellency and myself, you are authorized by your Government to state that if the duties levied at their land frontier should hereafter become prejudicial to the trade of the open ports of Corea, the Corean Government will be willing to take into consideration the readjustment of their Tariffs, with the object of placing them on an uniform and equal basis.

In forwarding to my Government the Treaty which has been signed by your Excellency and myself, I shall at the same time transmit a translation of the note under acknowledgment, which I have no doubt will be received with satisfaction by my Government.

I take, &c.

(Signed)   HARRY S. PARKES

(5) 후속 조치 및 비준

H.S. Parkes (1883. 12. 7) ➡ G.L.G. Granville (1884. 2. 1)

李鴻章과 회담 보고

Sir H.S. Parkes to Earl Granville. (Received February 1, 1884)

(No. 43)

Tien-tsin, December 7, 1883

My Lord,

I ARRIVED here from Chefoo in the afternoon of the 4th instant, and was immediately visited by an officer of the staff of the Grand Secretary Li Hung-chang, who informed me that his Excellency desired to see me as soon as convenient.

I therefore called on his Excellency the next day. I found that he was anxious to know what I had done in Corea, and I thought it would be polite to be frank with him on the subject, and to give him a full recital. This led, as I anticipated, to a request that I would show him the Treaty, and I observed that, although I should be transgressing rules in doing so, I would communicate it to him in strict confidence, which I felt assured would not be misused.

I adopted this course because I perceived that if I had refused to show his Excellency the Treaty I should have given him offence, and have awakened distrust on his part, and possibly opposition also, without any corresponding gain, as the text of the Treaty would probably soon be communicated to him by the Agent of the Chinese Government in Corea. And, on the other hand, I considered that if his Excellency approved the Treaty, I should derive some advantage from that circumstance.

His Excellency observed to me that the French Minister had told him, shortly after I left for Corea, that my negotiations would create a false position for China in respect to that country, but that he had replied that he did not apprehend any result of that nature. I replied that when his Excellency read the Treaty he would see that his confidence had been fully justified.

I accordingly gave his Excellency a copy of the Treaty and Trade Regulations when he returned my visit on the following day. His Excellency read these documents through from beginning to end, and then spontaneously expressed a hearty approval of them. There was nothing in them, he said, which concerned China in the least degree, and he would adopt the Tariff in the case of Chinese subjects. I profited by the opportunity to inquire whether the Chinese Government contemplated giving up the right of their subjects to trade in Hanyang (or Söul), which forms the subject of the second Declaration in the Protocol attached to the Treaty, and his Excellency replied that they entertained no such intention.

Mr. Hillier has prepared a careful Memorandum of the conversation which passed at both these interviews, and I inclose a copy, as I think it of sufficient importance to merit your Lordship's notice. Your Lordship will observe that the Grand Secretary pointedly inquired how Great Britain would be diplomatically represented in Corea, and urged that Her Majesty's Minister in Peking should be intrusted with that representation. I have reasons for concurring in his Excellency's views, which I shall submit to your Lordship in another despatch.

His Excellency also asserted that the Russian frontier was not conterminous to that of Corea at the *embouchure* of the T'umên River, but as far as I am aware this view is not shared either by the Russian Government or that of Corea, nor does it seem to be borne out by the terms of the Ist Article of the Treaty between Russia and China of the 2nd (14th) November, 1860, although those terms are somewhat dubiously worded. His Excellency, however, insisted that the Map which was attached to that Treaty left this question beyond doubt; but he at the same time observed that it was to be made the subject of a joint Commission of Inquiry on the part of Russia and China.

I have, &c.
(Signed)　HARRY S. PARKES

Inclosure

Memorandum of Interview with the Grand Secretary Li.

SIR H.S. Parkes, accompanied by Mr. Hillier, called on the Grand

Secretary Li by the invitation of his Excellency, who had sent an officer to wait on Sir H.S. Parkes on his arrival at Tien-tsin the previous afternoon, and to beg him to favour the Viceroy with an early call.

The conversation was first directed to Sir H.S. Parkes' recent visit to Corea, the Grand Secretary asking many questions as to the nature of the Treaty, the alterations in the Tariff arranged with the Japanese, the ability of the Corean officials to comprehend the principles of foreign intercourse, and the position and attitude of M. von Möllendorff, the foreign adviser to the Corean Government. His Excellency said that he had been blamed by the Tsung-li Yamên for having neglected to send a Chinese official over with Sir H.S. Parkes, and described a conversation he had with M. Tricou, in which the French Minister had predicted that the arrangements which the British and German Representatives would make in Corea would place China in a false position as regarded her tributary, but to which he had replied that he could trust Sir H.S. Parkes to do nothing of the kind.

Sir H.S. Parkes was glad to hear that the Grand Secretary had done him this justice. The Treaty contained nothing that in his opinion, China could possibly object to, and he was certain that it would prove very beneficial to Corea. The negotiations had been protracted, as it required time and patience to instill modern ideas into the minds of Corean Officials, whose conceptions of foreign intercourse were necessarily limited. Though protracted, they had been amicable throughout, and nothing had been forced upon the Corean nation. The Treaty was a new one, it having been found impracticable to retain the Treaty of last year, which was too restrictive to be feasible. That this was the case was proved by the fact that ever since his arrival in the country the United States' Minister had been vainly striving to modify the instrument that his Government had seen fit to ratify.

The Tariff agreed to between Corea and Japan had been altered in some respects in order to secure more conformity with the principles upon which customs dues should be levied. Four rates of duty had been laid down, and article had been classified under these different rates on an intelligible system, instead of, as in the Japanese Tariff, being inserted more or less at random. Some reductions had been made in the latter Tariff, as, in deference to China, it would not have been right that the average rate of this Tariff should have exceeded $7\frac{1}{2}$ per cent. His Excellency laughingly acknowledged the compliment, and observed that $7\frac{1}{2}$ per cent. was the amount of the import duties and transit duties of China combined.

Sir H.S. Parkes went on to say that a 10 and a 20 per cent. rate had also been somewhat reluctantly added at the insistence of the Corean Government, who seemed to be greatly in want of revenue, but these rates had been confined to costly commodities. The Trade Regulations were an improvement on the cumbrous Rules promulgated by the Corean Foreign Office with the aid of M. von Möllendorff, but it had naturally been a work of some time to convince them of the inferiority of their own production to the shorter document that they finally agreed to accept.

The Grand Secretary having remarked that the commercial capacities of Corea were exceedingly limited, Sir H.S. Parkes remarked that he hoped Corea would now bestir herself, and take advantage of the opportunity afforded her of improving her present backward condition by the development of resources which had hitherto lain dormant in the absence of any but purely local demands. In any case, he feared some years must elapse before the trade of the country would become of consequence to British merchants.

His Excellency then asked what was to be the arrangement with regard to the appointment of British officials in Corea. It seemed to him, both on the score of economy and propriety, that the British Minister in China should combine Corea with his diplomatic duties. Local matters could be settled between the Consul and the Corean authorities, but important questions should be referred to the sovereign country, and discussed by the Chinese Government and the British Representative. Corea was actually nearer to Peking and more accessible than many Chinese provinces, and it was eminently fitting that the British Representative in China should also control British interests in the tributary country. His Excellency hoped that Sir H.S. Parkes would urge the expediency of this arrangement upon Her Majesty's Secretary of State for Foreign Affairs.

Sir H.S. Parkes concurred in the reasonableness of his Excellency's suggestion, and said that he would bring it to the notice of Her Majesty's Government. In reply to a request from the Grand Secretary to be furnished with a copy of the Treaty and Tariff, he said he would endeavour to let him have one, but as it was unusual to communicate documents of this nature before they had been received by the Home Government, he must request his Excellency to consider the communication as strictly confidential.

The Grand Secretary called at Her Majesty's Consulate on the following afternoon (6th December), to return the visit of Sir H.S. Parkes, and at the same time to bid farewell to Mr. Grosvenor.

His Excellency's first question was whether the copy of the Treaty with Corea which had been promised him was ready, and after reading it from beginning to end, he agreed, in answer to a question from Sir H.S. Parkes, that it contained nothing that was calculated to place China in a false position with regard to Corea, and spontaneously expressed his high approval of the tact and intelligence that its preparation evinced. He observed that, as its provisions were wholly commercial, China was in no degree concerned in them. He only commented on one point during the perusal of the Treaty, remarking, on coming to the clause securing the free exercise of their religion to British subjects, that it gave missionaries the right to exercise their calling as well. The Trade Regulations his Excellency warmly approved of, and pronounced them to be concise and clear. He was promised a copy of the Tariff as soon as it could be conveniently prepared. He should, his Excellency said, like to see it, as he proposed to make it binding on Chinese subjects as well, for though Corea was her tributary, China did not interfere in the fiscal administration of the country, and Corea was at liberty to make her own Tariff.

A short conversation followed on the subject of the prohibition of the export of red ginseng, which Sir H.S. Parkes thought the Corean Government would do well to remove in their own interests. The Grand Secretary explained that the sale of red ginseng was a monopoly of the King's, and the income which he derived from it was all that he had to depend upon for subsistence. The monopoly exercised was in some respects similar to that maintained in the case of opium in India. All the places in which red ginseng was grown were under official supervision, and yearly Returns of the crops were furnished to the King, who levied a royalty upon the sales of about 40 per cent. Tong King-sing, the well-known Chinese financial agent, had endeavoured last year to purchase this monopoly from the King at a fixed annual sum, but the King had declined the offer. It might be possible in time, when Corea was better acquainted with the principles of trade, to allow the export of red ginseng at a special rate of duty in advance of those laid down in the Tariff, but at present nothing but an *ad valorem* duty of 40 or 50 per cent. would secure the King his usual income, and that rate was more than foreign Governments would be disposed to agree to.

On being asked what was the truth of the rumoured intention of the

Chinese Government to waive the right granted to Chinese merchants to open commercial establishments in Sŏul, the Grand Secretary replied that he knew of no such intention. Practically, Chinese merchants found no inducement to settle there, but in any case, as the right was granted in the British Treaty, it need not be withdrawn from Chinese.

Sir H.S. Parkes explained that at the solicitation of the Corean Government, who had informed him that the question was under the consideration of the Chinese Government, he had consented to waive this right if the Chinese did so, being anxious, as he had explained yesterday, not to coerce Corea in any way. At the same time, he was glad to find that the rumour had no foundation, as the withdrawal of commercial privileges from the most important of the few trading centres that the country possessed would be manifestly undesirable in the interests of Corea herself. His Excellency repeated that there was no such intention under consideration.

Reference being made to the land trade with China across the Corean frontier, which pays only a 5 per cent. rate of duty, his Excellency contended that in this respect the situation and peculiar relations of the two countries presented conditions which could not be shared by other nations.

He was reminded that another nation, namely, Russia, had a frontier conterminous with that of Corea, but this his Excellency denied. It was true, he said, that the T'umên River was the frontier of Corea, and the Russian Treaty with China of 1860 denoted the T'umên River as the Russian boundary-line in that direction, but the same Article declared that the limitations as laid down in a Map to be drawn up were to form the actual boundary, and on this Map the frontier-line was placed some 20 li away from the T'umên River. There intervened, therefore, between the Corean and the Russian limits a strip of waste ground belonging to China. His Excellency went on to say that when the question of a Treaty between Russia and Corea was under consideration last year, the Russian Minister, M. de Butzow, had raised this very point. On reference being made to the Corean Government, they had replied that as their own and the Russian frontier were not contiguous, there was no occasion to discuss the question of frontier trade at all.

Sir H.S. Parkes suggested that the Corean Government were not in a position to say more than that their frontier stopped at the T'umên River. He spoke of course under correction, but he had always understood, and it was popularly believed, that the Russian frontier was contiguous with that of Corea at a certain point on that river.

The Grand Secretary said he would tell Sir H.S. Parkes in confidence what was the actual state of the case at present. The Russians had crossed their frontierline and advanced to the T'umên River, but on the fact of this encroachment coming to the notice of the Chinese authorities last year, a protest was sent by the Tsung-li Yamên to the Russian Minister. The Russian Minister replied that he had received no information on the subject, but if there had been any encroachment, the matter must be settled by special Commissioners. The attention of the Russian Minister was again drawn to the matter in the spring of this year, when he once more suggested the appointment of a Commission of Inquiry, which the Grand Secretary thought might possibly be arranged for next spring.

Tien-tsin, December 5, 1883

李鴻章 ➡ 總署(1883.12.8/光緒九年十一月九日)

Parkes와 회담 및 조영조약 관련 보고

十一月初九日 署北洋大臣李鴻章函稱 英國巴使在朝鮮議約情形 業於十月二十八日馳報在案 十一月初五日巴使回津 初六來謁 所有問答各事節略 錄呈鑒核 初七下午往彼答拜 索觀新訂約稿共十三款 續通商章程三款 續稅則一本 較上年原約頗有增損 第皆係通商稅則等事 朝鮮可自專政 與中國無所關礙 約尾仍例明朝鮮開國某年卽中國光緖九年十月字樣 與前約無異 據稱英德一律 美約亦將照此續改 聞朝鮮自上年訂約後 各國商船鮮至者 自因地瘠貨少 稅章過嚴 該國君臣或有意招徠 稍從遷就耶 巴使面稱匆匆赴京 鈔手難覓 稍遲必爲錄寄 然計朝鮮國王不日亦當循例咨呈鈞署也 格維訥日前來晤 據云 各使擬派作沙面案中人 玆聞卽日回國 調充比利時參贊矣 專肅奉布 祗頌大人王爺中堂鈞福

194

H.S. Parkes (1883. 12. 16) ➡ G.L.G. Granville (1884. 2. 14)

영사재판권의 조속한 시행 건의

Sir H.S. Parkes to Earl Granville.—(Received February 14, 1884)

(No. 53)
My Lord,

Peking, December 16, 1883

I HAVE the honour to inclose copy of a despatch which I have received from Mr. Hall, Her Majesty's Acting Consul at Nagasaki, forwarding to me a claim for debt brought by a Japanese subject in Corea, and communicated to MR.Hall by the Acting Japanese Consul-General at Pusan.

Mr. Hall having suggested that some provisional arrangement should be made for dealing with such cases, I have pointed out in my reply, of which I beg to inclose a copy, that until the Queen shall have acquired, as she would acquire by the ratification of the Treaty signed at Söul on the 26th ultimo, jurisdiction over British subjects in Corea, her officers can provide no legal remedy for any civil or criminal wrong that her subjects may commit in that country, and that although the latter are doubtless at present amenable to Corean law, it would not be politic on our part to suggest its application in the case at least of civil suits occurring between foreigners in Corea.

The case in question is important only in its indications. As Mr. Hall observes, there are already several British subjects stationed at the Corean ports, and it is probable that others will be resorting thither very shortly. Not only that, but I fear that many of the first comers may belong to that class of needy and questionable adventures, known under the appellation of "roughs," who suddenly turn up in every new field, however remote, in which law is preceded by enterprise. We had prejudicial experience of this contingency in the earliest days of our intercourse with Japan, and I should regret to see that experience repeated in Corea. The man Harrison of the present case, who appears to have refused to pay the Japanese complainant for his board and lodging, belongs probably to that class, and I believe I am not doing an injustice to several loungers whom I noticed during the few hours I spent at Chemulpho on the

29th instant in including them in the same fraternity.

The conclusion to which these remarks point is the urgent desirability of giving effect to the Queen's jurisdiction over British subjects in Corea as soon as this can be done, if Her Majesty should be pleased to ratify the Treaty signed on the 26th ultimo. As British subjects would be withdrawn by that Treaty from Corean control, and in view of the possibility of that freedom being abused by the class to which I have referred, I think it to be due to the friendly Government of Corea, as well as to our own reputation and the interests of the orderly British subjects who may repair to Corea, that that jurisdiction should be promptly established and effectively exercised.

I have, &c.

(Signed)　　HARRY S. PARKES

H.S. Parkes (1883. 12. 16) ➡ G.L.G. Granville (1884. 2. 14)

조선 총영사직 설치 건의

Sir H.S. Parkes to Earl Granville.—(Received February 14, 1884)

(No. 54 Confidential)

Peking, December 16, 1883

My Lord,

  THE Treaty signed at Söul on the 26th ultimo provides in Article 11 that "the High Contracting Parties may each appoint a Diplomatic Representative to reside permanently or temporarily at the capital of the other, and may appoint a Consul-General, Consuls, or Vice-Consuls to reside at any or all of the ports or places of the other which are open to foreign commerce."

  Those ports and places are named in Article IV by their Corean names of Chemulpho [or Jenchuan], Wönsan [or Gensan], Pusan [or Fusan], and the town of Yanghwachin-the words in brackets being the Chinese or Japanese names for those places, which should be replaced by the correct Corean appellations now that the latter have become known to us. Article III further provides that; "Jurisdiction over the persons and property of British subjects in Corea shall be vested exclusively in the duly authorized British judicial authorities."

  In order to carry out the above-mentioned stipulations, it will be necessary to provide that a Diplomatic Representative of Her Majesty shall be accredited to the Court of Söul, and that Consular officers invested with magisterial and judicial powers, as in China, Japan, and elsewhere, shall be appointed to the various ports above named.

  Presuming that your Lordship will expect to receive from me some statement of opinion relative to these appointments, I venture to submit the following recommendations to your Lordship's consideration.

  I consider that it would be unnecessary, at the outset at least of our intercourse with Corea, to incur the expense of appointing to that country a special Legation. The United States of America, it is true, have seen fit to accredit to Corea a Diplomatic Representative, with the rank of Envoy

Extraordinary and Minister Plenipotentiary, but I did not find that that appointment gave to that Power in Corea a degree of influence which could not be acquired by other means. I could, indeed, perceive that General Foote was disappointed in the results of his appointment as a Minister of that rank, which it was supposed would have weight with the Coreans. He had endeavoured in vain, he told me, to obtain, during the six months of his residence, some modifications of the objectionable provisions of the American Treaty of last year, a circumstance which shows the inadvisability of commencing relations with an Oriental country on an imperfect basis, in the hope that fuller concessions may subsequently be obtained. My experience in China and Japan is that those Powers invariably insist on interpreting a Treaty in the letter, and not in the spirit, and this also appears to have been General Foote's experience in Corea. The insertion of the thin end of the wedge, as it is called, is a futile step in such relations, unless the Power who inserts the wedge is prepared to drive it home whenever further advance is required.

I should at the same time observe, however, that the Corean Ministers impressed upon me their desire that the Powers with whom they might conclude Treaties should be diplomatically represented in Corea, and they expressly stated that they trusted that Great Britain would not disappoint them in that hope. Their interest in such appointments is obvious in the importance which Corea would thereby acquire in the eyes of the world, and in the recognition of sovereignty which such appointments would convey. But whilst urging the appointment of a British Minister to Corea, the Corean Ministers also gave me to understand that it would not only be satisfactory, but even preferable, to their Government if the British Minister to China should be intrusted with that appointment. This suggestion has also its interested side, as, if it should be adopted by Her Majesty's Government, the Corean Government would secure the compliment of a Minister of the same rank as the Representative accredited by Her Majesty to China.

The application, however, which this proposal bears to myself would naturally make me hesitate to do more than report it to your Lordship, were it not apparent that Her Majesty's Minister to China would gain nothing in dignity or importance by being also accredited as Her Majesty's Minister to Corea. But I am sensible that some advantage might accrue to our interests, not only in Corea, but also in its neighbourhood, from the first Diplomatic Representative in that country being one who is already well known to its Government, and who, from having conducted the recent negotiations, is fitted for the charge of putting a Treaty into operation, which in Oriental countries is often a more arduous task than negotiating the Treaty itself. The peculiarity of the relations between China and Corea, and the possible influence which the Treaty of the 26th ultimo may have upon Treaty questions in China and Japan, serve also as a further recommendation for the combined appointment, which, as I have already reported in my despatch No. 43 of the 7th instant, was moreover specially commended by the Grand Secretary Li Hung-chang. I do not participate in the reasons which his Excellency assigned for that appointment, namely, that "important questions should be referred to the sovereign country, and discussed by the Chinese Government and the British Representative," as I presume that Her Majesty's Government would only be willing that any interference on the part of China in such questions should be limited to the exercise of good offices, to be availed of or not at their option. Assuming, however, that His Excellency expresses the views of his Government in approving the combined appointment, there is an apparent value in the fact that it is expressly desired by the Government of China, as well as by that of Corea.

It remains for me to add that I am willing to undertake this additional duty if Her Majesty's Government consider that I may be properly charged with it. I could visit Corea, when occasion should arise for my doing so, with greater case than I could visit many of the Chinese ports, but I am not unmindful that, in the earlier years of our intercourse with Corea, Her Majesty's Diplomatic Representative in that country must be prepared to give attention to many matters of detail, such as those which relate to the formation and administration of the future foreign Settlements, and similar questions, until these shall have been guided into a regular course. But it would be necessary that the immediate supervision of these measures should be intrusted to a Consular officer of position and of local experience, as otherwise the general superintendence of a Minister Resident at Peking might prove inadequate, and also unduly burdensome to the latter. I therefore recommend as an essential arrangement the appointment of a Consul-General to Corea, and I have no hesitation in adding that it is most desirable in the public interest that this appointment should be conferred upon Mr. Aston.

I need not point out to your Lordship, who is familiar with the excellent service which that officer has rendered in connection with Corean matters during the last two years, his special qualifications for this post. His intimate knowledge of the state of the country and of its language, his friendly personal acquaintance with the Corean Ministers, his familiarity with all the antecedents of our intercourse with its Government which have led to the conclusion of the recent Treaty, and the prominent part which he took under my direction in the negotiation of that Treaty, enable me to say, without disparagement to any other officer in Her Majesty's Consular Service, that he is the man best fitted for the appointment, and therefore the man who would best enable me to discharge with the desired degree of promptness and efficiency the duties of Her Majesty's Diplomatic Representative in Corea.

I have also to recommend the appointment of a Consul at Pusan, or, in the words of Article IV of the Treaty, "at such other port as may be selected in its neighbourhood." The reasons for providing for such a selection may be more appropriately considered in another despatch.

The affairs of the port of Chemulpho, which will probably prove the principal Treaty port of Corea, as also those of Yanghwachin, which is a town on the river within five miles of the capital, would come under the direction of the Consul-General; but as he would probably find it necessary to reside chiefly at the capital, it would be indispensable that he should be assisted by a Vice-Consul at Chemulpho. A similar appointment will doubtless also eventually become necessary at Wŏnsan, on the east coast, but the establishment of a Consular officer at that distant port does not possess the same immediate importance as that of Consular officers at Chemulpho and Pusan.

The most convenient course which I can suggest in respect to all these Consular appointments, with the exception of that of Consul-General, which I submit should be made by Her Majesty's Government without any delay, is to permit me, in case I should be accredited as Her Majesty's Minister to Corea, to make such acting appointments as I should find necessary, and to select the officers for those appointments from the Chinese Consular Staff. After a year's experience of the requirements of Her Majesty's service in Corea, those appointments could be either changed or confirmed as your Lordship might see fit. If the provisions of the China and Japan Order in Council, 1865, should be extended to Corea, then under the 25th clause of that Order any officer appointed by me (in the capacity of Minister to Corea) to act temporarily as Consul or Vice-Consul at any Corean open port would be duly authorized to hold and form at such a port a Provincial Court, and could thus be vested at once with those magisterial and judicial powers which, as I have shown in my despatch No. 53 of this date, it is of the first importance that the British Consular officers in Corea should be able to exercise at the earliest stage of our Treaty relations with that country.

I trust I have not gone beyond the limits of my duty in submitting these recommendations to your Lordship's consideration, but I confess that I feel some solicitude, if not responsibility, for the future effective working of the Treaty which I have been honoured with the charge of concluding; and I may add that I have also become sensible that although the present commercial position of Corea is comparatively insignificant, her geographical position, and the influence she may exercise when she enters, as I believe she shortly will, on a progressive course, will render this state, small as it is, a not unimportant factor in the development of our intercourse with the nations of the far East.

I have, &c.
(Signed)　HARRY S. PARKES

H.S. Parkes (1883. 12. 17) ➜ G.L.G. Granville (1884. 2. 14)

高宗 알현시 교지(敎旨)와 답사(答辭) 보고

Sir H.S. Parkes to Earl Granville.—(Received February 14, 1884)

(No. 55)
My Lord,

Peking, December 17, 1883

I HAD intended to report by this courrier particulars of my audience with the King of Corea on the 27th ultimo, but as I find I am unable to do so I think I should forward in advance the inclosed translation of the remarks which His Majesty was pleased to make to me on that occasion, and also a note of the short speech which I addressed to His Majesty, as these papers will alone suffice to show the cordial and gratifying character of my reception.

I should observe that the note of His Majesty's remarks was furnished to me by the Corean Ministers immediately after the audience, and is, therefore, their own version of His Majesty's observations. It is remarkable that His Majesty should have noticed as a service rendered to himself the part taken last year by Her Majesty's ship "Flying Fish" in rescuing the Japanese Minister and his suite when they were attacked and driven from Söul. I was particularly impressed by the graciousness of His Majesty's manners, the polish and attractiveness of his appearance, and the earnestness and intelligence with which he delivered all his observations.

I feel that I should also not defer to report that throughout the period of my stay in Corea, neither I myself nor any member of my suite experienced any incivility on the part of the Coreans, and that Captain Fullerton and the officers of Her Majesty's ships, who constantly made shooting excursions to a considerable distance from the anchorage of Chemulpho, were invariably received with kindness and good-feeling by all the people whom they met.

I have, &c.
(Signed)   HARRY S. PARKES

Note of the Remarks of His Majesty the King of Corea on the occasion of the Audience granted to Sir H.S. Parkes on the 27th November, 1883—(Supplied by the Corean foreign Office)

(Translation)

HIS Majesty having inquired after the welfare of Her Majesty the Queen, the British Plenipotentiary replied.

His Majesty then expressed his gratification at the fact of the British Representative having satisfactorily accomplished so long a journey at an inclement season of the year, and the British Representative having made a suitable reply, His Majesty went on to remark that the British Representative having been sent by Her Majesty's commands to negotiate a Treaty with His Majesty's Plenipotentiary, had succeeded in concluding a good and thoroughly satisfactory arrangement. The two countries would thenceforward be in perpetual peace and friendship one with the other, and the advantages which their respective subjects would derive from this Treaty would be entirely due to the exertions of the British Representative, to which His Majesty alluded in the most laudatory terms. After the British Representative had replied to these remarks, His Majesty asked after the welfare of the Captain of Her Majesty's ship-of-war, and then addressed similar inquiries to the Consul and Secretaries in the suite of the British Representative. His Majesty further expressed his gratitude for the dispatch of a British ship-of-war by Her Majesty's Government to Corea to make inquiries during the troubles that occurred in the country during the summer of the previous year, and added after the British Representative had replied, that he earnestly hoped for the active assistance and protection of England in the event of any occasion arising hereafter when such aid could be given. His Majesty finally expressed a hope that the British Representative would pray his Sovereign to ratify this Treaty with all dispatch, adding that the constant presence of the British Representative in Corea would, it was to be hoped, afford opportunities for closer intercourse. In asking whether the British Representative was about to return to Peking, His Majesty wished him a prosperous voyage.

Inclosure 2

Reply of Sir. H.S. Parkes to the first part of the Remarks made by His Majesty the King of Corea at the Audience of the 27th November, 1883.

I BEG to thank your Majesty for your gracious inquiries respecting myself. I feel confident that the Treaty which I had the honour to sign yesterday with your Majesty's Plenipotentiary will bring our two nations into close and friendly relations, and that the commerce it secures will prove mutually beneficial. I feel that I should express my appreciation of the hospitality I have received throughout my stay in Corea, and I assure your Majesty that I shall use my best efforts to promote a cordial understanding between your Majesty's Government and that of my august Sovereign.

197

H.S. Parkes (1883. 12. 31) ➜ G.L.G. Granville (1884. 2. 28)

2차 조영조약의 조항별 분석 보고

Sir H.S. Parkes to Earl Granville.—(Received February 28, 1884)

(No. 70) *Peking, December* 31, 1883

My Lord,

I HAVE the honour to enclose some observations on each Article of the Treaty signed at Söul on the 26th ultimo, which are intended to supplement my General Report on this subject of the 6th instant. (despatch No. 42)

I could have wished to have extended these observations to the Regulations of Trade and Tariff, but I am obliged, at present, to defer doing so.

I have, &c.

(Signed)　　HARRY S. PARKES

Treaty between Great Britain and Corea, signed at Söul, November 26, 1883; with Observations by Sir H.S. Parkes.

ARTICLE I

1. There shall be perpetual peace and friendship between Her Majesty the Queen of the United Kingdom of Great Britain and Ireland, Empress of India, her heirs and successors, and His Majesty the King of Corea, his heirs and successors, and between their respective dominions and subjects, who shall enjoy full security and protection for their persons and property within the dominions of the other.

2. In case of differences arising between one of the High Contracting Parties and a third Power, the other High Contracting Party, if requested to do so, shall exert its good offices to bring about an amicable arrangement.

Section 1. The Queen's title of "Empress of India" is inserted.

The King is termed "the King of Corea," instead of "King of Chosen" as in Admiral Willes' Treaty, and the word "Corea" is substituted for "Chosen" throughout this Treaty with the full approval of the Corean Plenipotentiary.

Section 2. This section is differently worded to the corresponding passage in Article I of Admiral Willes' Treaty, but it satisfied the Corean Plenipotentiary, who attached great importance to its insertion. It was especially alluded to by the King, when His Majesty received both Herr Zappe and myself, as a provision which had afforded His Majesty much gratification.

ARTICLE II

1. The High Contracting Parties may each appoint a Diplomatic Representative to reside permanently or temporarily at the capital of the other, and may appoint a Consul-General, Consuls, or Vice-Consuls to reside at any or all of the ports or places of the other which are open to foreign commerce. The Diplomatic Representative and Consular functionaries of both countries shall freely enjoy the same facilities for communication, personally or in writing, with the authorities of the country where they respectively reside, together with all other privileges and immunities as are enjoyed by Diplomatic or Consular functionaries in other countries.

2. The Diplomatic Representative and the Consular functionaries of each Power, and the members of their official establishments, shall have the right to travel freely in any part of the dominions of the other, and the Corean authorities shall furnish passport to such British officers travelling in Corea, and shall provide such escort for their protection as may be necessary.

3. The Consular officers of both countries shall exercise their functions on receipt of due authorization from the Sovereign or Government of the country in which they respectively reside, and shall not be permitted to engage in trade.

Section 1. Under this section it will not be necessary to appoint a permanent Diplomatic Representative to Corea unless this should be desired by Her Majesty's Government. The British

Consular functionaries will enjoy the same facilities of communication, personally or in writing, with the Corean authorities as they enjoy in any other country. This provision will prevent questions arising on the point of relative rank, such as those alluded to in the letter of the Hong Kong Chamber of Commerce of the 20th January, 1883.

Section 2 may appear superfluous in view of section 6 of Article IV, which gives the right to all British subjects to travel under passport in Corea, but considering the difficulties which have occurred in China, it may be well in an unknown country like Corea that the Corean authorities should be made directly responsible for the security of British functionaries.

Section 3. This wording will enable the special form of Exequatur to be dispensed with, if it should not be required, and will facilitate the authorization of provisional Consular appointments.

ARTICLE III

1. Jurisdiction over the persons and property of British subjects in Corea shall be vested exclusively in the duly authorized British judicial authorities, who shall hear and determine all cases brought against British subjects by any British or other foreign subject or citizen without the intervention of the Corean authorities.

2. If the Corean authorities or a Corean subject make any charge or complaint against a British subject in Corea, the case shall be heard and decided by the British judicial authorities.

3. If the British authorities or a British subject make any charge or complaint against a Corean subject in Corea, the case shall be heard and decided by the Corean authorities.

4. A British subject who commits any offence in Corea shall be tried and punished by the British judicial authorities, according to the laws of Great Britain.

5. A Corean subject who commits any offence against a British subject shall be tried and punished by the Corean authorities, according to the laws of Corea.

6. Any complaint against a British subject involving a penalty or confiscation by reason of any breach either of this Treaty or of any Regulation annexed thereto, or of any Regulation that may hereafter be made in virtue of its provisions, shall be brought before the British judicial authorities for decision, and any penalty imposed, and all property confiscated in such cases,

shall belong to the Corean Government.

7. British goods, when seized by the Corean authorities at an open port, shall be put under the seals of the Corean and the British Consular authorities, and shall be detained by the former until the British judicial authorities shall have given their decision. If this decision is in favour of the owner of the goods, they shall be immediately placed at the Consul's disposal. But the owner shall be allowed to receive them at once on deposition of their value with the Corean authorities pending the decision of the British judicial authorities.

8. In all cases, whether civil or criminal, tried either in Corean or British Courts in Corea, a properly authorized official of the nationality of the plaintiff or prosecutor shall be allowed to attend the hearing, and shall be treated with the courtesy due to his position. He shall be allowed, whenever he thinks it necessary, to call, examine, and cross-examine witnesses, and to protest against the proceedings or decision.

9. If a Corean subject who is charged with an offence against the laws of his country takes refuge on premises occupied by a British subject, or on board a British merchant-vessel, the British Consular authorities, on receiving an application from the Corean authorities, shall take steps to have such person arrested and handed over to the latter for trial. But without the consent of the proper British Consular authority, no Corean officer shall enter the premises of any British subject without his consent, or go on board any British ship without the consent of the officer in charge.

10. On the demand of any competent British Consular authority, the Corean authorities shall arrest and deliver to the former any British subject charged with a criminal offence, and any deserter from a British ship of war or merchant-vessel.

Section 1. The first sentence of this section really covers the remainder, which was added by the wish of the German Government, and it may be said that it also covers section 2, 3, 4, and 5. The details of those clauses, however, add distinctness to the absolute nature of the jurisdiction over British subjects in Corea, which is thus conceded to the Queen in far clearer terms than those of the Chinese and Japanese Treaties. The provision in section 2 that the Corean authorities must also sue or prosecute British subjects in a British Court is useful in view of the contention still maintained in China, and at one time in Japan, that the authorities of those countries need not proceed against British subjects in a British Court.

Sections 6 and 7 also give complete jurisdiction to British Courts in all cases of confiscation or penalty for any breach of Treaty or Regulations, or of seizure of goods by the Corean Customs. The value of this provision is obvious when the arbitrary practice of the Chinese Government in such cases is considered, and also the imperfect nature of the procedure which has consequently to be adopted in China.

Section 8 secures efficiency and fairness in the trial of all cases in Corean Courts in which a British subject is concerned.

Section 9 clearly provides for the inviolability both of the premises of British subjects in Corea and of British vessels in Corean waters. This and section 10 are useful additions to my draft Treaty. The sentence relative to deserters from ships of war was suggested by the German Government, and I added to it deserters from merchant-vessels also.

Herr Zappe and myself having thus stipulated that German and British offenders or deserters should be surrendered unconditionally, we felt that we could not demand, as suggested by the Hong Kong Chamber of Commerce, that Coreans charged with offences, and taking refuge in the premises or vessels of our people, should only be surrendered by our Consular authorities on the latter "being satisfied as to the justice of the charge made." This condition might involve much contention and even judicial investigation, which those authorities would have no right to demand or power to conduct.

ARTICLE IV

1. The ports of Chemulpho (Jenchuan), Wŏnsan (Gensan), and Pusan (Fusan), or, if the latter port should not be approved, then such other port as may be selected in its neighbourhood, together with the city of Hanyang and the town of Yanghwachin, or such other place in that neighbourhood as may be deemed desirable, shall, from the day on which this Treaty comes into operation, be opened to British commerce.

2. At the above-named places British subjects shall have the right to rent or to purchase land or house, and to erect dwellings, warehouses, and factories. They shall be allowed the free exercise of their religion. All arrangements for the selection, determination of the limits, and laying out of the sites of the foreign settlements, and for the sale of land at the various ports and places

in Corea open to foreign trade, shall be made by the Corean authorities in conjunction with the competent foreign authorities.

3. These sites shall be purchased from the owners, and prepared for occupation by the Corean Government, and the expense thus incurred shall be a first charge on the proceeds of the sale of the land. The yearly rental agreed upon by the Corean authorities in conjunction with the foreign authorities shall be paid to the former, who shall retain a fixed amount thereof as a fair equivalent for the land tax, and the remainder, together with any balance left from the proceeds of land sales, shall belong to a municipal fund to be administered by a Council, the constitution of which shall be determined hereafter by the Corean authorities in conjunction with the competent foreign authorities.

4. British subjects may rent or purchase land or houses beyond the limits of the foreign settlements, and within a distance of 10 Corean *li* from the same. But all land so occupied shall be subject to such conditions as to the observance of Corean local regulations and payment of land tax as the Corean authorities may see fit to impose.

5. The Corean authorities will set apart, free of cost, at each of the places open to trade, a suitable piece of ground as a foreign cemetery, upon which no rent, land tax, or other charges shall be payable, and the management of which shall be left to the Municipal Council above mentioned.

6. British subjects shall be allowed to go where they please without passports within a distance of 100 Corean *li* from any of the ports and places open to trade, or within such limits as may be agreed upon between the competent authorities of both countries. British subjects are also authorized to travel in Corea for pleasure or for purposes of trade, to transport and sell goods of all kinds, except books and other printed matter disapproved of by the Corean Government, and to purchase native produce in all parts of the country, under passports which will be issued by their Consuls and countersigned or sealed by the Corean local authorities. These passports, if demanded, must be produced for examination in the districts passed through. If the passport be not irregular, the bearer will be allowed to proceed, and he shall be at liberty to procure such means of transport as he may require. Any British subject travelling beyond the limits above named without a passport, or committing when in the interior any offence, shall be arrested and handed over to the nearest British Consul for punishment. Travelling without a passport beyond the said limits will render

the offender liable to a fine not exceeding 100 Mexican dollars, with or without imprisonment for a term not exceeding one month.

7. British subjects in Corea shall be amenable to such municipal, police, and other regulations for the maintenance of peace, order, and good government, as may be agreed upon by the competent authorities of the two countries.

Section 1 opens to British trade the three ports named, the town of Yanghwachin, which is situated on the Han River within 5 miles of the capital, and also the capital itself, known to foreigners as Söul (or "capital"), but the proper Corean name of which is Hanyang. Choice, however, may be made of another town in the neigbourhood of Yanghwachin, and of another port in the neighbourhood of Pusan, if that port should not be approved. Reserve in these two cases was rendered necessary by imperfect information. Yanghwachin had been named both by the Japanese and Chinese in their arrangements with the Corean Government; but I learned that Mapu, which is in the immediate vicinity of the former, may prove a more desirable location. This is a point of small importance, but the option which may be exercised in the case of the port of Pusan is more material. Pusan has the advantage of a good harbour and of being the port at which the Japanese have traded for centuries with Corea. But it has no water communication with the interior, while Masanpo, situated at the mouth of the Naktong River, and distant only about 30 miles from Pusan, possesses accessibility to inland navigation, and also a harbour which is believed to be superior to that of Pusan. Much of the produce which is exported from Pusan is brought down that river and passes Masanpo on its way to Pusan. It could, therefore, be shipped with greater ease at the former port, as, in order to get to Pusan, the native boats have to go our into the open sea and to contend with strong coast gales, for which they are unfitted. Trade doubtless follows beaten tracks, but not when better ones can be chosen. It is scarcely desirable that British commerce should be bound to run in an antiquated Japanese groove, in which the new-comers would be placed at a disadvantage, for the natural reason that at Pusan the Japanese have long occupied the best position for a settlement, and have attained a present ascendency with the people of the neighbourhood. I am inclined to think, therefore, that, looking to the future rather than to the past, Masanpo is better adapted than Pusan to meet the greater stimulus to commercial activity which our advent may be expected to create in Corea. The question, however, is one which obviously requires further consideration, and also a careful inspection of the respective localities, before it is finally determined.

Section 2 and 3 contain several pregnant provisions. They provide for the purchase of land by British subjects at the open ports, and for the inclusion of manufacturing establishments in the constructions which they may erect upon such property. In making this provision I had in view the difficulties on this point which have lately been experienced in China. I also trust that the stipulations respecting the formation and government of the future foreign settlements in Corea will obviate the troubles which have arisen in regard to the management of such settlements both in China and Japan. By section 4 British subjects may occupy land and houses beyond th limits of those settlements if they please, but in that case they will become subject to Corean Regulations. Free cemeteries, under the management of the foreigners themselves, provided by section 5, secures a right on which the Japanese Government have lately raised vexatious contention.

Section 6 opens the interior of Corea to travel or trade on similar terms to those which exist in China, but which ar still withheld in Japan. I need not observe that the sentence, "except books and other printed matter disapproved of by the Corean Government," is attributable to the insistance of the Corean Plenipotentiary. The phrase is a compromise of much more objectionable wording, which the Corean Government desired to direct against missionary enterprise. As it stands it may be held to apply to seditious or obscene literature, to which the Corean Government have an undoubted right to object, but which I could not consent to be named in the same category as religious publications. I did not consider it desirable to seek for special privileges for missionaries, as I saw, from the present apprehensive feeling of the Corean Government on this point, that I might have wrecked the Treaty by raising the question; but the same rights are secured to that class as to other British subjects, and the judicious exercise of those rights will afford ample opportunities for the fulfillment of a zealous and sacred vocation without occasioning offence to the powers that be.

By section 7 British subjects resident in Corea are amenable only to such municipal, police, or other regulations affecting their government as may be agreed upon by the competent authorities of the two countries. On the value of this provision, or on the kindred condition contained in section 8 of Article

V, I need not remark. I regard them as two of the most important clauses of the Treaty, as they secure to Her Majesty's Government a controlling voice in any arrangements that may be needed either for the trade, the comfort, or the well-being of Her Majesty's subjects who may choose to settle in Corea.

ARTICLE V

1. At each of the ports or place open to foreign trade, British subjects shall be at full liberty to import from any foreign port or from any Corean open port, to sell to or to buy from any Corean subjects or others, and to export to any foreign or Corean open port, all kinds of merchandize not prohibited by this Treaty, on paying the duties of the Tariff annexed thereto. They may freely transact their business with Corean subjects or others without the intervention of Corean officials or other persons, and they may freely engage in any industrial occupation.

2. The owners or consignees of all goods imported from any foreign port upon which the duty of the aforesaid Tariff shall have been paid shall be entitled, on re-exporting the same to any foreign port at any time within thirteen Corean months of the date of importation, to receive a drawback certificate for the amount of such import duty, provided that the original packages containing such goods remain intact. These drawback certificates shall either be redeemed by the Corean Customs on demand, or they shall be received in payment of duty at any Corean open port.

3. The duty paid on Corean goods, when carried from one Corean open port to another, shall be refunded at the port of shipment on production of a Customs certificate showing that the goods have arrived at the port of destination, or on satisfactory proof being produced of the loss of the goods by shipwreck.

4. All goods imported into Corea by British subjects, and on which the duty of the Tariff annexed to this Treaty shall have been paid, may be conveyed to any Corean open port free of duty, and when transported into interior shall not be subject to any additional tax, excise or transit duty whatsoever in any part of the country. In like manner full freedom shall be allowed for the transport to the open ports of all Corean commodities intended for exportation, and such commodities shall not, either at the place of production or when being conveyed from any part of Corea to any of the open ports, be subject to the

payment of any tax, excise or transit duty whatsoever.

5. The Corean Government may charter British merchant-vessels for the conveyance of goods or passengers to unopened ports in Corea, and Corean subjects shall have the same right, subject to the approval of their own authorities.

6. Whenever the Government of Corea shall have reason to apprehend a scarcity of food within the kingdom, His Majesty the King of Corea may, by Decree, temporarily prohibit the export of grain to foreign countries from any or all of the Corean open ports, and such prohibition shall become binding on British Subjects in Corea on the expiration of one month from the date on which it shall have been officially communicated by the Corean authorities to the British Consul at the port concerned, but shall not remain longer in force than is absolutely necessary.

7. All British ships shall pay tonnage dues at the rate of 30 cents (Mexican) per register ton. One such payment will entitle a vessel to visit any or all of the open ports in Corea during a period of four months without further charge. All tonnage dues shall be appropriated for the purpose of erecting lighthouses and beacons and placing buoys on the Corean coasts, more especially at the approaches to the open ports, and in deepening or otherwise improving the anchorages. No tonnage dues shall be charged on boats employed at the open ports in landing or shipping cargo.

8. In order to carry into effect and secure the observance of the provisions of this Treaty, it is hereby agreed that the Tariff and Trade Regulations hereto annexed shall come into operation simultaneously with this Treaty. The competent authorities of the two countries may from time to time revise the said Regulations with a view to the insertion therein, by mutual consent, of such modifications or additions as experience shall prove to be expedient.

Section 1 secures trade to British subjects both from and to foreign ports and from or to any Corean open port; it also provides that they may conduct their business free of any interference, and also that they may freely engage at the open ports in any industrial occupation.

Section 2 provides for drawback of duty being paid on goods re-exported within thirteen Corean months, which cover a year of the foreign calendar. I think this term is sufficient in the case of the Corean trade, which, for some time at least, is likely to he an offshoot of the trade with China and Japan.

Section 3 provides that Corean goods or produce may be carried practically free of duty between one open port of Corea and another, instead of paying a duty of 2½ per cent., as is the case in China.

Section 4 provides that goods that have once paid the duty of the Import Tariff may be conveyed to any other open port, and also to any part of the interior, free of any tax, excise or transit duty whatsoever; and it also secures the same freedom from charges of any kind to Corean commodities in transitu intended for exportation. In China all goods in which foreigners are interested are liable, when conveyed from the Treaty ports to the interior, or when brought down from the interior to the same ports, to a transit duty of 2½ per cent.; but this payment does not free those goods from any additional charges that the Chinese local authorities may choose to impose, either, in the case of foreign imports, after they have been disposed of by the person who paid the transit duty, or, in the case of native exports, before they pass into the hands of the person who has to pay that duty. By this section trade in Corea, whether in imports or exports, will be freed both from transit duty and from all burdens of the nature named, and the single payment of the duty of the Tariff will frank all commodities in transitu throughout the country, whether these are being conveyed from the open ports to the interior, or from the interior to the open ports for exportation.

Section 5 enables British vessels to run between other than the open ports for the conveyance of goods or passengers, subject to the approval of the Corean Government.

Section 6 provides for the export of grain from the Corean ports being prohibited in times of scarcity. This condition was desired by the Corean Government, but is of no importance to ourselves. Scarcity of grain in Corea will stimulate importation by foreigners rather that its export.

Section 7 provides for tonnage dues at the rate of 30 cents per register ton, one payment to enable a vessel to run between Corean ports for a period of four months. This rate is less than half of that named in Admiral Willes' Treaty, and is about half the rate which is levied in China, but I think it is as high as the trade will bear. It is, however, also provided that the trade shall have the whole benefit of the charges, as these hues are to be appropriated to lighting the harbours and coasts, and to the improvement of the anchorages. Cargo lighters will be free from payment of tonnage dues, a condition which was suggested by the attempt recently made in China to subject these boats to that charge.

ARTICLE VI

Any British subject who smuggles, or attempts to smuggle, goods into any Corean port or place not open to foreign trade, shall forfeit twice the value of such goods, and the goods shall be confiscated. The Corean local authorities may seize such goods, and may arrest any British subject concerned in such smuggling or attempt to smuggle. They shall immediately forward any person so arrested to the nearest British Consul for trial by the proper British judicial authority, and may detain such goods until the case shall have been finally adjudicated.

This Article gives sole jurisdiction to the British Courts in all cases of smuggling at Corean ports not opened to trade. The penalty for the offence is confiscation of the condemned goods and forfeiture of twice their value. Admiral Willes' Treaty provided (Article III) in imitation of that in force in China, that a vessel concerned in such smuggling, together with her cargo, should be seized and confiscated, and as no provision was made to the contrary, this heavy penalty could be inflicted, as the Hong Kong Chamber of Commerce pointed out, "by the Corean authorities of their own motion, and with or without trial, subject to no investigation by, or appeal to, British officials." The injustice of such a condition is obvious, as any individual on board a ship might, by attempting to smuggle a small venture of his own, expose the innocent owners of the ship and cargo to overwhelming loss. By this Article the penalty will be inflicted on the offending party, it will bear a just proportion to the extent of the offence, and it will be determined by the sentence of a British Court. The Corean Plenipotentiary was perfectly satisfied with this arrangement.

ARTICLE VII

1. If a British ship be wrecked or stranded on the coast of Corea, the local authorities shall immediately take steps to protect the ship and her cargo from plunder, and all the persons belonging to her from ill-treatment, and to render such other assistance as may be required. They shall at once inform the nearest British Consul of the occurrence, and shall furnish the shipwrecked persons, if necessary, with means of conveyance to the nearest open port.

2. All expenses incurred by the Government of Corea for the rescue, clothing, maintenance, and travelling of shipwrecked British subjects, for the recovery of the bodies of the drowned, for the medical treatment of the sick and injured, and for the burial of the dead, shall be repaid by the British Government to that of Corea.

3. The British Government shall not be responsible for the repayment of the expenses incurred in the recovery or preservation of a wrecked vessel or the property belonging to her. All such expenses shall be a charge upon the property saved, and shall be paid by the parties interested therein upon receiving delivery of the same.

4. No charge shall be made by the Government of Corea for the expenses of the Government officers, local functionaries, or police who shall proceed to the wreck, for the travelling expenses of officers escorting the shipwrecked men, nor for the expenses of official correspondence. Such expenses shall be borne by the Corean Government.

5. Any British merchant-ship compelled by stress of weather, or by want of fuel or provisions, to enter an unopened port in Corea shall be allowed to execute repairs and to obtain necessary supplies. All such expenses shall be defrayed by the master of the vessel.

This Article contains the conditions of the Agreement relating to shipwrecks made by Great Britain with Japan in 1879, which was based on Conventions concluded with other Powers on the same subject. The German Government having attached importance to the acceptance by the Corean Government of the Salvage Rules of the Chinese Government of 1876, I was prepared with Herr Zappe to add a clause stipulating for the adoption and promulgation of these Rules in Corea, when we were met by the assurance of the Corean Plenipotentiary that they had already been published, and he subsequently furnished is with an official copy of the Decree. I can only hope that they will prove of more value in Corea than in China, where they have not been observed. The execution of their conditions, however, will be secured by the faithful fulfilment of the provisions of this Article.

ARTICLE VIII

1. The ships of war of each country shall be at liberty to visit all the ports

of the other. They shall enjoy every facility for procuring supplies of all kinds or for making repairs, and shall not be subject to Trade or Harbour Regulations, nor be liable to the payment of duties or port charges of any kind.

2. When British ships of war visit unopened ports in Corea, the officers and men may land, but shall not proceed in the interior unless they are provided with passports.

3. Supplies of all kinds for the use of the British navy may be landed at the open ports of Corea, and stored in the custody of a British officer, without the payment of any duty. But if any such supplies are sold the purchaser shall pay the proper duty to the Corean authorities.

4. The Corean Government will afford all the facilities in their power to ships belonging to the British Government which may be engaged in making surveys in Corean waters.

Secures, I think, to British ships of war and to their officers and crews every privilege or right that they enjoy elsewhere. It also provides that naval stores may be established at any of the open ports of Corea, and that the Corean Government shall facilitate, as far as lies in their power, the much-needed work of surveying in Corean waters.

ARTICLE IX

1. The British authorities and British subjects in Corea shall be allowed to employ Corean subjects as teachers, interpreters, servants, or in any other lawful capacity, without any restriction on the part of the Corean authorities; and, in like manner, no restrictions shall be placed upon the employment of British subjects by Corean authorities and subjects in any lawful capacity.

2. Subjects of either nationality who may proceed to the country of the other to study its language, literature, laws, arts, or industries, or for the purpose of scientific research, shall be afforded every reasonable facility for doing so.

Was thought by the Corean Plenipotentiary to be unnecessary, and it is open to the Corean Government to prove it to be so by loyal and liberal action. In view, however, of our limited experience of their disposition, Herr Zappe and myself considered it desirable to insert its provisions. The Article would possess material value in China even at the present date.

ARTICLE X

It is herby stipulated that the Government, public officers, and subjects of Her Britannic Majesty shall, from the day on which this Treaty comes into operation, participate in all privileges, immunities, and advantages, especially in relation to import or export duties on goods and manufactures, which shall then have been granted, or may thereafter be granted, by His Majesty the King of Corea to the Government, public officers, or subjects of any other Power.

I have already fully considered the terms of this Article in my despatches No. 42 of the 6th and No. 46 of the 8th instant. It is an unconditional favoured-nation clause.

ARTICLE XI

Ten years from the date on which this Treaty shall come into operation, either of the High Contracting Parties may, on giving one year's previous notice to the other demand a revision of the Treaty or of the Tariff annexed thereto, with a view to the insertion therein, by mutual consent, of such modifications as experience shall prove to be desirable.

Provides that the Treaty and Tariff shall continue in operation for a term of ten years, when either or both may be modified, but only with the mutual consent of the Contracting Parties.

ARTICLE XII

1. This Treaty is drawn up in the English and Chinese languages, both of which versions have the same meaning, but it is hereby agreed that any difference which may arise as to interpretation shall be determined by reference to the English text.
2. For the present, all official communications addressed by the British authorities to those of Corea shall be accompanied by a translation into Chinese.

Secures the important provision, which was not conceded without difficulty, that the English version of this Treaty shall be the ruling text. The same condition is inserted in the German Treaty, which is drawn up in three languages, German, English, and Chinese.

HARRY S. PARKES

ARTICLE XIII

The present Treaty shall be ratified by Her Majesty the Queen of the United Kingdom of Great Britain and Ireland, Empress of India, and by His Majesty the King of Corea, under their hands and seals. The ratifications shall be exchanged at Hanyang (Sŏul) as soon as possible, or at latest within one year from the date of signature; and the Treaty, which shall be published by both Governments, shall come into operation on the day on which the ratifications are exchanged.

In witness whereof the respective Plenipotentiaries above named have signed the present Treaty, and have thereto affixed their seals.

H.S. Parkes (1883. 12. 31) ➔ G.L.G. Granville (1884. 2. 28)

청국의 종주권에 관한 陳樹棠 포고문 보고

Sir H.S. Parkes to Earl Granville.—(Received February 28, 1884)

(No. 73)   *Peking, December* 31, 1883

My Lord,

THE inclosed Proclamation, which was issued by the Chinese Commissioner at Söul shortly before I arrived there, will serve to illustrate the way in which the Chinese Government exercise suzerain rights over their so-called tributary States. The display of authority in this form appears to have a greater importance in their eyes than the question of Treaty relations between those States and European Powers. It did not appear to me that the Chinese Commissioner was much consulted by the Corean Government on the provisions of the Treaty which I negotiated, and if the difficulty I at one time encountered in settling the question of interport trade was not attributable to his influence, or to the reputed desire of the Grand Secretary Li Hung-chang to secure a monopoly of the Corean carrying trade to a Chinese side in concluding that Treaty.

I have, &c.
(Signed)   HARRY S. PARKES

Inclosure

Proclamation issued by the Chinese Trade Commissioner at Söul.

(Translation)

CH'EN, by Imperial command General Director of Foreign Trade at the ports of Corea, with a brevet rank of the second grade, a Taotai on the list for immediate promotion in any province, who holds two steps of commutative rank, and has shown records of merit against his name:

    In the matter of a Proclamation,

 Be it known that I, having reverently received His Majesty's commands to assume the general management of international trade at the various ports of Corea, arrived by ship at the port of Jên-Ch'uan on the 14th day of the present moon, and disembarked. On the 16th I reached the city of Han, and on the 20th I entered upon the duties of my office.

 I would observe that Corea is a tributary of China, and ever since the time that Chi-Tzŭ was invested with the sovereignty of the kingdom up to the present day, a period of several thousand years, this nation has given special prominence to the civilizing influences of poetry, literature, and the requirements of propriety and decorum, thereby having long been held in respect and esteem by the world in general. It may be truly said of her that she is a country whose people deservedly bear the reputation of maintaining a well-balanced equilibrium of elegance and simplicity, and in which culture and refinement prevail.

 Since the existence of the present dynasty, now some 200 years and more, she has been reverent and submissive to her Suzerain in a marked and special degree. Her officials, people, gentry, and merchants have never failed to be courteous and jest in their relations with the subjects of the Emperor their Suzerain, nor has there ever been an expression of differences of opinion between them. Such a state of things is most commendable.

 The world has now become one family, and the carious nations therof trade one with another, exchanging each other's resources for their respective needs, and mutually enjoying the hospitality of each other's States. The prohibitions against external intercourse having been universally removed, the Court of China has now granted special permission to Corea to engage in foreign trade, that she may reap the advantages therof, and hold the profits to be gained by this commerce in her own hands. A Code of Trade Regulations in eight Articles has been promulgated, authorizing the people of the parent and the subject country to engage in trade with each other, respectively giving each other's products in exchange for their mutual wants, thereby stimulating the increase of the natural resources of either country, and developing their wealth and power.

 His Majesty the Emperor has further specially selected me and sent me to reside in the city of Han, in order to assume the general management of all matters affecting commercial relations at the different ports, to exercise supervision over the interests of the merchants and subjects of the mother-country, and to promote the general advance of trade, in such wise that both countries may reap the advantages therof. In due course officers will be sent to reside at Jên-Ch'uan, Fu-shan, and Yuan-shan.

Having now entered on the duties of my office, it is my duty to issue a Proclamation for general information. In addition to exhibiting at my official residence the Trade Regulations promulgated by the Imperial Court, I hereby inform all Chinese merchants, gentry, and people that all who come to this country to trade, whether travellers or residents, must give prominence to the requirements of honesty and good faith, and pay special obedience to the aforesaid Rules. In their relations with the people of this country they must positively cultivate friendship and harmony, in order to manifest the principles of integrity and good faith, by which the subject race are actuated, and pay special heed to the maintenance of that family relationship under one common head which it is the earnest wish of both countries to preserve.

Those Chinese merchants who come here from distant places across the sea to engage in trade are actuated by motives of personal advantage, and they should therefore thoroughly appreciate the principle that harmony is the high road to wealth. In their relations with the people of Corea or of any foreign country they must on no account show unfriendliness, even in the slightest degree, thereby causing adverse comments on their behaviour.

Commercial matters are under my charge, and it is my special duty to attend to the interests of the merchants of my country. Should any of them, therefore, whether residents of travellers, encounter anything of an unsatisfactory nature, whether grave of slight, in their relations with others, they must come to my official residence to report the same, and await my instructions and action thereon. Let them take heed lest, in their impatience, they are guilty of any wrong action, whereby they are led in a momentary fit of anger to commit an offence against the law, as the consequences of such action may be most inconvenient to themselves.

A special Proclamation.

Kung Hsü, 9th year, 9th moon, 24th day (October 24, 1883)

邵友濂 ➡ 總署(1884. 1. 2/光緒九年十二月五日)

2차 조영조약문에 속방 관계조항 누락 보고

十二月初五日 江海關道邵友濂函稱 頃閱字林西字報所載 本年十月二十七日 高麗與英國新立合約十二款 業已簽名 並無認高麗爲中國所屬之語 查去年西字報載 高麗與美國立約 第一款卽註明向來高麗入貢歸附中國 美國亦以爲是 玆與英國立約不載此條 深恐將來又成法越故事 多費脣舌 應否乘其合約未定時卽今更正之處 玆將譯出西報所載高麗與英國所立新約十二款 並美高合約第一款 一並照抄 送祈察閱 應否轉呈堂憲核辦之處 並乞卓裁是幸 專泐 敬請 台安

200

總署(1884. 1. 8/光緒九年十二月十一日) ➡ 李鴻章

조영조약문 내 속방 관계 명문화에 관한 조회

관련문서 李鴻章의 회신(1884. 1. 10)

十二月十一日 致署北洋大臣李鴻章函 詳見密啓
浮籤籤 函述朝鮮與英德兩國換約內有漏敍之處 應行更正 並抄邵道來函附
閱由

【관련문서】

覆總署 論朝鮮新約附有照會
光緒九年十二月十三日
敬復者 昨奉十二月十二日公函 以朝鮮咨送英德兩國商訂新約十三款未聲明 中國屬藩 上海邵道頗以爲疑 應如何更正添載明白等因 查上年美高議約之先 卽經敝處與鈞署往復函商 約稿內首須聲明中國屬邦 迨美署使何天爵來津 與 美總兵薛孚爾在敝署會議此事 斷斷辨爭 謂旣與朝鮮立約 彼此均是與國 平 行相待 美約內首言中國屬邦 有失美國之體 電詢美廷萬不能允 而朝爲中屬 則各國皆知 只可於訂約時另給照會 聲明朝鮮於中國分內一切應行各節 於美 國毫無干涉等語 嗣後派員赴朝襄同薛孚爾與朝鮮訂約 卽照此議另作照會附 於約後 卽來函抄件是也 並無美約第一款注明高麗入貢 歸附中國之文 西字 報不得其詳 邵道未親其事 故有是疑 似於當日事實不符 英德隨赴朝議約 亦 卽照美約一律繕寫照會 申明其義 今冬英國巴使往朝改約 不欲中國派員攙預 鴻章恐其擅改上年成議 先咨明朝王 以通商稅則如有變通伊可專主 或於通商 外更有所議 與上年照會之意相左 斷不可許 致貽後悔等語 旋經吳提督長慶 抄寄朝鮮 與英德議略內有本國去年另行聲明照會於英德兩國者 尙未有復 英 德使答俟立約后當有照復云云 業於本年十月二十八日函抄呈覽在案 此次朝 王咨照敝處文內亦稱 先將上年照會聲明一節申行言明 凡於通商事宜之外一 切旨意無甚差爽 未知咨鈞署文內亦有此語否 謹照抄原咨以憑印証 盖西洋屬

邦有所謂半主之國 通商稅則可自訂立 朝鮮自與英德美等商訂稅則 設埠等事 隨時變通 按之西例半主屬邦尙無不合 若必令將中華屬國載在約內第一款 朝鮮卽可遵行 美爲合衆\聯邦尙不肯允 英德龐然自大 更無允行之理 彼與中國朝鮮皆系立約平行 若朝約內明載中屬 自覺有碍體面 我亦未便强令更正 但旣有照會另行聲明 載在盟府 日後各國設相侵陵或朝鮮有背叛之處 中國盡可執義責言 不至竟成法越覆轍 是否有當 仍候卓裁 專肅復頌中堂 王爺 大人鈞福 制李鴻章謹上 直字三百八十八號

201

H.S. Parkes (1884. 1. 19) ➜ G.L.G. Granville (1884. 3. 26)

회답 국서의 의장(意匠)에 관한 건의

Sir H.S. Parkes to Earl Granville.—(Received March 26)

(No. 2 Treaty) *Peking, January* 19, 1884.

My Lord,

WITH reference to my despatch No. 45 of the 7th ultimo, I have suggested, in a telegram of this date, that the Queen's letter to the King of Corea, if one should be sent, should be inclosed in a suitable case, such as a silver-gilt box, embossed or engraved with the Royal Arms. The absence of a covering suited to the dignity of the communication would be liable to be misconstrued by the Ministers of the Corean Court, who treat with great reverence a missive from the Court of China, and they might think that it denoted on our part a limited degree of respect to our own Sovereign, which might affect their estimation of the value of the compliment which such a letter would confer upon their King.

I have, &c.
(Signed)　　HARRY S. PARKES

G.L.G. Granville (1884. 2. 15) ➡ H.S. Parkes

여왕의 비준서 및 국서 발송 예정 통보

Earl Granville to Sir H.S. Parkes.

(No. 37)

Foreign Office, February 15, 1884

Sir,

I HAVE received and have laid before the Queen your despatch No. 1, Treaty, of the 1st December last, forwarding the Treaty which you signed on the 26th November with the Representative of the King of Chosen.

The provisions of this Treaty are entirely approved by Her Majesty's Government, and I have much pleasure in conveying to you their high appreciation of the manner in which you conducted the negotiations with the Corean Government to a successful issue.

It is mainly due to your able and energetic efforts that results have been obtained which cannot fail to be highly beneficial to British commercial interests in the far East.

The Queen's ratification is being prepared, and will be sent to you at an early date, with a letter from Her Majesty to the King.

The Order in Council giving the necessary powers to Her Majesty's Consular authorities in Corea will also be issued forthwith.

I am, &c.

(Signed)　　GRANVILLE

Münster(1884. 2. 23) ➜ G.L.G. Granville (1884. 2. 28)

조청무역에서 관세율 특혜가 있을 경우 독일 정부의 방침 전달

관련문서 Granville의 회신(1884. 3. 8)

Count Münster to Earl Granville.—(Received February 28)

(Translation)

My Lord,   *German Embassy, February* 23, 1884

YOUR Lordship has been good enough to communicate to the Imperial Government the Treaty signed at Söul on the 26th November of last year between Great Britain and Corea, as also the Reports upon the progress of the negotiations sent in by Sir Harry Parkes up to the 8th November.

For this I have the honour, in pursuance of my instructions, most respectfully to express the thanks of my Government to your Lordship, and, at the same time, to transmit your Lordship an English version of the German-Corean Treaty, with an Annex.

I permit myself further to forward your Lordship, confidentially, the copy of a note from the Corean Secretary of State for Foreign Affairs, Min, under date 24th November, 1883, with the answer of the Imperial Consul-General Zappe thereto, dated the 29th of the same month.

The Imperial Government would be glad to learn whether a similar correspondence has taken place between the Corean Government and the Plenipotentiary of Great Britain, and what attitude the British Government is disposed to assume towards the question which has been thus raised respecting the possible assimilation of the Customs Tariffs for inland and maritime commerce.

Although there can be no doubt that the right of the most favoured nation has been conceded to the German and English Governments in the new Treaties with Corea, still the note of the Corean Foreign Office of the 24th November prompts the apprehension that the Corean Government wishes to reserve to itself the right to allow the introduction of lower customs rates for overland frontier trade with China. This apprehension is increased by "The Practical Regulations, in twenty-four paragraphs, for the Trade on the Frontier between

Manchuria and Corea," elaborated by Li Hung-chang, and also inclosed herewith.

Should this Chinese project, the object of which is to secure for China, as Suzerain, special commercial advantages in Corea, be accepted by the Corean Government, the commercial advantages which should accrue to Germany and England from the new Treaties would at once be jeopardized.

The Imperial Government wishes at the outset to prevent all misunderstandings, and purposes, accordingly, at once to apprise the Corean Government that Germany cannot assent to a differential treatment of German and Chinese subjects with reference to import and export duties. The German Representative, Consul-General Zappe, is therefore to be instructed to convey by a note the declaration that the Imperial Government, in case lower customs rate than those stipulated in the German-Corean Treaty should be accorded to the Chinese, would at once, in virtue of section 10 of the Treaty, claim these lower customs rates for its own trade. The Imperial Government would eventually renew this declaration in the Protocol respecting the exchange of ratifications.

In order to be able to act further in this matter *pari passu* with the Government of Great Britain, my Government would be glad to know, as early as possible, how your Lordship is disposed to treat the question.

I beg, therefore, most respectfully to inquire of your Lordship whether a note of similar tenour with that of the 24th of last November has been sent from the Corean Foreign Office to the English Representative, and, if so, what answer the British Government is minded to give thereto.

With, &c.

(Signed)　　MÜNSTER

【관련문서】

Earl Granville to Count Münster.

M. l'Ambassadeur,　　　　　　　　　　*Foreign Office, March* 8, 1884

I HAVE the honour to acknowledge the receipt of your Excellency's letter of the 23rd ultimo, transmitting an English version of the Treaty concluded between Germany and Corea on the 26th November last, and I have to tender you my thanks for this communication.

Your Excellency will have learned from my letter of the 28th ultimo, and the papers which accompanied it that a note, similar to that of which you inclose a copy, was addressed to Her Majesty's Minister Plenipotentiary by the Corean Minister for Foreign Affairs. Sir H.S. Parkes' reply, in which he stated that he would forward a translation of it to his Government, and that he had no doubt that it would be received by them with satisfaction, has been approved.

A reference to Sir H.S. Parkes' despatch will show that he is of opinion that as by far the greater part of the British imports would enter Corea under the 5 and 7½ per cent. rates of the Tariff attached to the Treaty, our trade will be able to compete successfully with the Chinese frontier trade, which is burdened by the heavy charges of land transit. But in the event of any injury being done to the trade by the lower rate of duties on the Chinese land frontier, Sir H.S. Parkes appears to have considered that Min's note of the 24th November would sufficiently provide for a readjustment of the Corean Tariff in our favour.

This seems to Her Majesty's Government to be a fair and reasonable view, and it is not their intention to make any declaration in regard to the Chinese Regulations, which were no doubt fully considered by the English and German Plenipotentiaries at the time that they accepted the Corean note of the 24th November.

Her Majesty's Government would, however, be glad to learn from the German Government further particulars as to the grounds on which they consider that the 5 per cent. land frontier duty would act injuriously on the trade at the open ports under the Tariffs agreed to by the English and German Plenipotentiaries.

I have, &c.
(Signed)   GRANVILLE

Queen Victoria (1884. 2. 27)
Parkes의 비준서 교환 전권위임장

英國國書四月初七日呈

大英國大君主大護教兼膺五印度大后帝費格多利雅 問大朝鮮國大君主好 朕寅承天命 統綏大英等國疆域 玆因切欲兩國和好永敦弗替 彼此人民往來貿易 亦欲致其日興 我忠勤明敏愛臣頭等邁吉利寶星兼二等拔德寶星欽差駐劄中華便宜行事大臣巴夏禮 朕所素信 命爲駐劄貴國京都欽差便宜行事全權大臣 遵即任事 朕知此臣忠勤謹智 自能一切辦理妥協 用備書 由該大臣親呈大君主展閱 幷屬該大臣代達朕誼重友邦 敬祝大君主福壽無疆之至意 該大臣洞悉本國人民懇遷及僑寓朝土各情 必能極力仰體朕意 將兩國和好永加敦睦 尙望大君主從優接待 准其隨時入覲 所有該大臣代達朕言 亦希逐一誠信 順祝大君主永享天賜成全之福不盡 朕御極之四十七年 玆於降生一千八百八十四年二月二十七日即甲申二月初一日 在溫所爾御宇親筆書押 用伸親誼
降生一千八百八十四年二月二十七日即臨御四十七年在溫所爾本宮親筆書押
　　　　　　　　　　　　總理各國事務丞相歌蘭非勒恭隨押訖

205

Queen Victoria (1884. 2. 28)

영국 비준서

大英國大君主大護敎兼膺五印度大后帝費格多利雅 問大朝鮮國大君主好 前年接准大君主惠書 展閱之餘 實深怡悅 玆聞我兩國簡派全權大臣 業經會議條約 以期兩國和好通商 永敦弗替 尤爲欣慰 此約已據奏明呈覽 用將朕經批准約文 授與全權大臣 親呈鑒收 換回大君主批准約文 如此立意修睦 定能誠使兩國和好及彼此人民已成交誼益臻固密 此後朕所派領事等官分別駐劄貴國地方 及朕屬寓朝人民 尙望大君主時行優待保護 順祝大君主永享遐齡 幷受天賜成全之福不盡 朕御極之四十七年 玆於降生一千八百八十四年二月二十八日卽甲申二月初二日 在溫所爾御宇親筆書押 用伸親誼

降生一千八百八十四年二月二十八日卽臨御四十七年在溫所爾本宮親筆書押
　　　　　總理各國事務丞相 歌蘭非勒 恭隨押訖

G.L.G. Granville (1884. 3. 17) ➜ W.G. Aston

조선 총영사 임명장

Earl Granville to Mr. Aston.

Sir,   *Foreign Office, March* 17, 1884

THE Queen having been graciously pleased to approve of your selection for the provisional appointment of Her Majesty's Consul-General for Corea, I inclose Her Majesty's Commission to that effect. Your duties whilst so employed will consist in visiting the Corean ports opened to British trade by the Treaty of the 26th November last, and you will report on the Consular arrangements required for the future. In the meanwhile you will act as Consul-General for the country generally, and will exercise judicial powers over British subjects under the Orders in Council which are being prepared for the purpose.

You will continue to draw the salary of your post as Her Majesty's Consul at Nagasaki, and a further allowance of 1ℓ. a day has been assigned to you, with house rent, office, and travelling expenses.

You will acknowledge to me the receipt of your Commission.

I am, &c.
(Signed)   GRANVILLE

G.L.G. Granville (1884. 3. 17) ➜ W. R. Carles

조선 부영사 임명장

Earl Granville to Mr. Carles.

Sir, *Foreign Office, March* 17, 1884

THE Queen having been graciously pleased to approve of your selection for the provisional appointment of Her Majesty's Vice-Consul for service in Corea, I inclose Her Majesty's Commission to that effect.

You will place yourself under the orders of Mr. W. S. Aston, who has received the provisional appointment of Her Majesty's Consul-General for Corea, and you will obey such instructions as he may from time to time issue to you.

You will continue to draw the present pay of your rank, and a further allowance of 15*s.* a-day has been assigned to you, with house rent, office, and travelling expenses.

You will acknowledge to me the receipt of your Commission.

I am, &c.
(Signed)   GRANVILLE

H.S. Parkes(1884. 3. 27) ➜ 閔泳穆

2차 조영조약의 비준을 알리는 조회

大英欽差駐劄中華全權便宜行事大臣巴 爲照會事 照得 上年十月二十七日 本大臣與貴大臣彼此議定條約 現已恭奉我國大君主大后帝逐一批准 并蒙特派本大臣做爲欽使與貴國 查我國如此速辦 足見有懷益敦兩國和好 并期開廣彼此商民利源之至意 諒必貴大臣亦可洞悉矣 本大臣現擬不日親赴貴國京都 以將批准約文互相奉換 理應早日布知 是以仍派禧正使先赴貴國 轉將此文面爲呈遞 因思約條即蒙我國大君主大后帝已然批准 務期貴大臣亦可將大朝鮮大君主業已批准約文之處 即行示覆 一俟覆文由禧正使帶回呈閱後 本大臣便可急赴貴國 以便將批准和約各文互相奉換 幷將欽奉出使勅書照列[sic]呈閱 須至照會者
右照會
大朝鮮督辦交涉通商事務大臣 閔
西曆一千八百八十四年四(*sic.*)月二十七日 光緒十年三月初一日

H.S. Parkes (1884. 3. 31) ➡ G.L.G. Granville (1884. 5. 20)

대원군 귀국설 및 조선의 비준서 교환 거부설 보고

Sir H.S. Parkes to Earl Granville.—(Received May 20)

(No. 66 Confidential) *Peking, March* 31, 1884

My Lord,

    IT is unsatisfactory to me to have to inform your Lordship that I have received some indications, which appear to denote that the exchange of the ratifications of the Treaty with Corea may not be effected as smoothly as could be desired. Japanese newspapers have several times declared that the Corean Government do not intend to carry out the Treaties they have concluded with Great Britain and Germany, but I should not attach much significance to such statements coming from that quarter, were it not that the Grand Secretary Li Hung-chang spoke strongly against those Treaties in a conversation which he held with Mr. Davenport, Her Majesty's Consul at Tien-tsin on the 11th instant.

    I had instructed Mr. Davenport to endeavour to learn from his Excellency whether there was any truth in a report which had become prevalent, that the Chinese Government intended to send back to Corea the Tai-Yun-kun, or ex-Regent, with a additional force of Chinese troops. This Prince—the father of the King of Corea—was carried away as a prisoner to China, as your Lordship is aware, in consequence of having instigated the revolt and massacres, and the attack on the Japanese Legation, which occurred in July 1882. He has since remained in exile at Pau-ting-fu, the capital of this province, in the charge of Li Hung-chang. Being the head of the Conservative party in Corea which is opposed to foreign relations, and intolerant of any other ideas than those which Corea has for centuries past derived from China, that party naturally desires the restoration of the Prince, and his adherents are constantly intriguing to effect that end.

    Li Hung-chang observed to Mr. Davenport that the Prince had committed no offence, which, if true, would utterly condemn the course taken by the Chinese Government in making him a prisoner, and his Excellency added that it would not be right to keep him in confinement for ever, which was a more reasonable observation. He admitted that there was some trouble in Corea which he was taking measures to pacify, but he declared that the recent British and German Treaties were the cause of that trouble, and that the Coreans were greatly dissatisfied with them. That although Corea was a subject state of China, I had not consulted him as I should have done before negotiating the British Treaty; that I had secured all sorts of advantages to foreigners without corresponding benefit to the Coreans, and had acted altogether too precipitately, swallowing, as he expressed it, the whole cupful at one draught. The Coreans would have been quite content with Admiral Willes' Treaty, but they were opposed to mine, and wanted the ex-Regent to return in order to extricate them from the difficulty which I had created.

This adverse criticism of that Treaty is wholly at variance with the favourable opinion of it which his Excellency expressed on my return from Corea, and which I reported to your Lordship in my despatch No. 43 of the 7th December.

The Japanese Chargé d'Affaires has also informed me that the Japanese Legation at Söul had reported to Tôkiô that endeavours were being made by the opposition party in Corea to obtain the release of the ex-Regent, and that the Legation had been warned that if these endeavours should succeed civil commotion might ensue, which would probably be directed against the Japanese as well as against the authority of the King.

These circumstances determined me on receipt of your Lordship's telegrams Nos. 8 and 10 to proceed to Shanghae, in order to meet there the ratifications and my credentials as Minister, and thus be able to go on at once to Corea, if it should be desirable to do so. It appeared to me important, however, that before proceeding there myself I should endeavour to obtain information as to the state of affairs in Corea, and also some assurance that the Corean Government would not offer objections to the exchange of the ratifications.

I have therefore sent Mr. Hillier to Söul with this purpose. I furnished him with the inclosed letter to the President of the Foreign Board who negotiated the Treaty, informing him that it had been ratified by Her Majesty, and that I trusted it had also been ratified by the King. That I had been appointed Her Majesty's Minister to Corea, and should be prepared to proceed there to exchange the ratifications and deliver my credentials on hearing from his Excellency that his Government were prepared to receive me for this purpose.

I also add a copy of the instructions I gave to Mr. Hillier. He will be conveyed from Chefoo to Söul and back to Chefoo in a gun-vessel which the naval Commander-in-chief, Sir William Dowell, had been so good as to send on this service. The reply which he will bring me from the President or the information he will obtain will enable me to judge whether the Corean Government are ready to adhere to their engagements. They may perhaps have been told that as Her Majesty's Government declined to ratify Admiral Willes' Treaty, they may exercise similar liberty in regard to the Treaty concluded by myself. If they are disposed to act upon such unwise counsel it is obviously desirable that I should be warned of their intention, and that I should seek the instructions of your Lordship before attempting to deal with the very unpleasant position which would thus be created.

I have, &c.

(Signed) HARRY S. PARKES

Inclosure 1

Sir H.S. Parkes to Mr. Hillier

Sir, *Peking, March 27, 1884*

AS it is necessary that I should communicate with the Government of Corea for the objects with which you are acquainted, I have to instruct you to proceed to Söul for that purpose.

I conclude that you will find on your arrival at Chefoo that the Commander of Her Majesty's gun-boat stationed at that port is in readiness to embark you on your arrival there, as the naval Commander-in-chief informed me by telegraph on the 24th instant that he had ordered that officer to take you from that port to Corea, and to bring you back to Chefoo.

On reaching Chemulpo you will at once proceed to Söul, and apply for and interview with the President of the Foreign Board, to whom you will deliver the despatch which I have addressed to his Excellency. You are at liberty to use your own discretion as to whether this despatch should be delivered at or prior to the interview.

You will request his Excellency to set on foot at once the arrangements which should be made for my reception, and you will endeavour to secure for the accommodation of myself and suite the buildings we occupied on our former visit. You will charge Mr. Scott, who accompanies you, with the supervision of the details of these arrangements, and he will remain at Söul to carry out your directions.

You will use your best efforts to obtain from the President, as early as possible, a reply to my despatch of the character I have requested, and as soon as you have received it you will return to Chefoo, where I expect to arrive about the 10th proximo. In case I should have left Chefoo before you return there, you will follow me to Shanghae by the first opportunity.

I inclose a letter to the Commander of Her Majesty's ship "Cockchafer," requesting him to embark yourself, Mr. Scott, and servants.

I am, &c.

(Signed)   HARRY S. PARKES

Inclosure 2

Sir H.S. Parkes to Min Yŏng-nok.

Sir,   *Peking, March* 27, 1884

I HAVE the honour to inform Your Excellency that I shall shortly proceed to Corea in order to exchange the ratifications of the Treaty which I concluded with Your Excellency on the 26th November last.

I have also the satisfaction of informing your Excellency that my Sovereign the Queen and Empress has been graciously pleased to appoint me to be Her Majesty's Minister to Corea.

I feel confident that your Excellency will see in these acts of Her Majesty's Government, a distinguished proof of their desire to cultivate the most friendly relations with the Government of His Majesty the King, and to promote the development of mutually advantageous intercourse between the people of both countries.

I consider it to be due to your Excellency to give you the earliest intimation in my power of my approaching visit, and I accordingly depute my secretary, Mr. Hillier, who is already well-known to your Excellency, to proceed to Söul for the purpose of delivering to you this note.

As Her Majesty the Queen and Empress has already ratified the Treaty, I trust that your Excellency will inform me, in reply, that it has already been ratified by His Majesty the King. Mr. Hillier will wait for this reply, and as soon as I receive it I shall proceed to Söul to exchange the ratifications, and deliver my credentials as Minister.

I gladly take advantage of this opportunity to renew to your Excellency the assurance of my highest consideration.

I have, &c.
(Signed)   HARRY S. PARKES

閔泳穆(1884. 4. 7/高宗二十一年三月十二日) ➜ H.S. Parkes

2차 조영조약의 비준 의사를 확인하는 조회

大朝鮮國督辦交涉通商事務閔 爲照覆事 照得 本年三月初一日 接准貴大臣 照會內開云云等因前來 本大臣准此均已閱悉 不勝欣慰 我國大君主聞知貴國 大君主大后帝業將條約批准 深爲懽喜 幷我大君主勅下本大臣 轉行告爲貴大 臣 以貴大臣作爲欽差大臣 是尤本國所素爲信重者 惟本大臣旣知貴大臣做爲 欽使與本國 則兩國克敦和好 曁永久利益商民之處 均於是乎在 是以我國大 君主以貴國大君主大后帝批准如是之速 益加慶幸 我國大君主業經批准 本大 臣祗冀貴大臣早日茲止 以便互換 玆准禧正使遞到貴大臣來文 本大臣備玆覆 文 仍仰禧正使代呈 須至照覆者
右照覆
大英欽差駐劄中華全權便宜行事大臣 巴
甲申三月十二日

H.S. Parkes (1884. 4. 16) ➜ G.L.G. Granville (1884. 5. 26)

조선의 비준 의지 보고

Sir H.S. Parkes to Earl Granville.—(Received May 26)

(No. 78) *Shanghae, April* 16, 1884

My Lord,

IN my despatch No. 66, Confidential, of the 31st ultimo, I reported the circumstances which rendered it advisable that I should take the precautionary measure of sending Mr. Hillier to Corea; and I have now the satisfaction of reporting that the object of his mission has been completely gained, and that he has returned with an official declaration from the Corean Government that the Treaty has been ratified by the King, and that they are prepared to exchange the ratifications as soon as I can proceed there.

Mr. Hillier obtained this declaration during a stay of only one clear day at Söul, and the readiness with which it was given and the cordiality of his reception satisfied him that the Corean Government are looking forward with eagerness to the Treaty being brought into operation as soon as possible.

The quickness of Mr. Hillier's proceedings enabled him to join me at Chefoo during the few hours I spent at that port on the 10th instant, and your Lordship will understand that it was very gratifying to me to learn from his Report that the designs which had occasioned me the solicitude I had expressed in the abovementioned despatch had not been allowed to influence the friendly action of the Corean Government.

In another despatch I shall have occasion to refer to a conversation which I held on the subject of the Corean Treaty with the Grand Secretary Li Hung-chang when I passed through Tien-tsin on the 8th instant, as his remarks confirmed my previous belief that that Treaty is regarded with disfavour, both at Peking and at Söul, by the parties at those capitals who are opposed to all progress.

I inclose Mr. Hillier's Report, and beg to recommend to your Lordship's notice the interesting information it contains, and the ability he showed in obtaining so promptly the declaration that the Treaty had been ratified, which was the object I had in view in sending him to Corea. I can now not only feel confident that I shall encounter no difficulty in exchanging the ratifications, but that I shall also be received as a welcome friend.

I also inclose a translation of the reply of the President of the Foreign Board to the note from myself which Mr. Hillier delivered. His Excellency observes in very gratifying terms that the news of the Treaty having been ratified by the Queen has afforded the King the highest satisfaction, and that my appointment as Minister is most acceptable to His Majesty and the Corean Government. He then adds that the Treaty has been ratified by the King, and he trusts that I shall shortly proceed to Corea to exchange the ratifications.

I have, &c.

(Signed) HARRY S. PARKES

Inclosure 1

Mr. Hillier to Sir H.S. Parkes.

Shanghae, April 14, 1884

Sir,

I HAVE the honour to report that, in obedience to the instructions furnished me in your despatch of the 27th March, I left Chefoo for Corea on the afternoon of the 3rd April in Her Majesty's ship "Cockchafer," and reached Chemulpo at noon on the 5th.

The remainder of the day was occupied in procuring baggage animals for the conveyance of Mr. Scott and myself to Söul on the following morning.

While waiting for the arrival of these baggage animals we occupied ourselves in walking about the Settlement, and as it may interest you to know what changes have occurred in the place since your visit in November last, I venture to record some of the impressions I gathered in the course of my walk.

I noticed a considerable increase in the number of houses in the Japanese Settlement, particularly on the lower road near the beach, where a regular street has been formed with shops on both sides, at the upper end of which fairly extensive warehouses have been erected by the Mitsu Bishi Steam Navigation Company, a Japanese syndicate which is now running a steamer regularly between Nagasaki, Fusan, and Chemulpo. These were shortly to be supplemented, I was informed, by Government godowns in charge of the Corean Customs, where cargo would be stored for owners or consignees at a certain fixed scale of charges. An establishment of the kind will, I understand, supply a want that is already beginning to be felt, as there is at present no place of storage other than the private godowns of the Mitsu Bishi Company for cargo awaiting shipment or transport into the interior, which at present has to lie on the beach for days exposed to the action of the weather.

A portion of the ground which you had selected as the probable site of the future British Settlement has been assigned to the Chinese, in whose concession is included the rough jetty that was in process of construction last November, but the most desirable portion of the ground you had fixed upon is still unoccupied, and is, I understand, being reserved for the British Government.

Upon inquiry amongst the Customs officials and others I learnt that the trade of the port had developed considerably during the past few months, and though it was not yet on a sufficiently large scale to prove remunerative to vessels that visited the port, the monthly revenue already showed a fair surplus after paying the salaries of the Customs staff. This statement, I may add, was subsequently corroborated by M. von Möllendorff, the Foreign Adviser to the Corean Government. The overbearing conduct of the Japanese settlers was a general subject of comment and complaint, and the arrival of a British authority was looked forward to with some eagerness, as it was hoped that the presence of the official of another Power might be a support to the local authorities in their attempts to prevent the not unfrequent collisions that occur between the natives and the Japanese.

Starting on the morning of the 6th instant, we reached Söul in the afternoon, and I was glad to notice a considerable improvement in the condition of the road to the capital since my last visit. A new road is in process of construction for a portion of the way to Söul, which will lessen the distance, and is eventually intended to be made available for carriage traffic.

On arrival at Söul I called on M. von Möllendorff and informed him that I was the bearer of a note from yourself to the President of the Foreign Office which I was ordered to deliver in person, and as your instructions allowed me to exercise a certain discretion in the manner of delivering this note, I thought it advisable to show M. Möllendorff a copy of it, with a translation into Chinese which I had prepared for presentation to the President.

M. von Möllendorff proceeded then and there to draft a reply in English, and he undertook to have it translated in the course of the evening in order to avoid any unnecessary delay in furnishing me with an answer on the following day. This answer I have little doubt was considered by the Foreign Office that night.

An interview having been arranged for the following morning, the 7th, I called at the Foreign Office at 11 A.M., and was most cordially received by the President and Assistant Ministers, to whom I delivered your note.

They appeared astonished when I informed them that I wished to return on the following morning, and asked me to remain a few days, but I replied that I was under instructions to return with all possible dispatch, and said that I felt sure you would appreciate a recognition on their part of the promptitude with which you had announced the ratification of the Treaty. This recognition would best be shown by a similar announcement on the part of the President, which I should be glad to be able to report had been supplied without any delay.

After some discussion it was arranged that the President should go at once to the Palace, and should furnish me with an answer in the terms of M. von Möllendorff's draft in the course of the afternoon. His Excellency added that he would do me the honour to bring me the letter in person.

I then proceeded to ask his Excellency what accommodation the Government could provide for you on your approaching visit to Sŏul. I should first mention that I had discussed this matter privately with M. von Möllendorff on the previous evening. He told me that he felt sure that the King and Queen would consider it a high compliment if you could arrange to bring any ladies of your family with you when you came to Sŏul, to which I replied that you might possibly be disposed to do so provided that suitable accommodation for the reception of ladies was provided. When I called at the Foreign Office he informed me that the Ministers were much pleased to hear that there was a probability of your bringing a lady member of your family with you, and that they would make every possible arrangement in their power to suit your convenience.

Upon broaching the subject of your accommodation to the President, his Excellency said that the quarters assigned to Herr Zappe, the German

Plenipotentiary, last year, had been prepared for your reception, but that if I considered the accommodation was insufficient he would be happy to get more rooms ready for you in the immediate vicinity of the other buildings. A Secretary of the Foreign Office would show me the additional rooms which could be placed at your disposal. I visited the premises in the afternoon, and as I have already verbally reported to you, I considered the accommodation that these extra rooms provided would be sufficient for your wants.

I thought it advisable to ask the President what form of ratification the Corean Government proposed to adopt. His Excellency replied that the King would sign and seal the Treaty, and that, subject to your approval, it was proposed to adopt the form of ratification attached to the United States' Treaty. A copy of this form of ratification was given me, which I append to this Report.

In your verbal instructions to me I was ordered to ask whether accommodation could be provided for Her Majesty's Vice-Consul at Chemulpo. M. von Möllendorff, speaking for the President, said that he was prepared to buy a Japanese house and have it erected on the British Concession. He would let this house, he said, to the British Government for as long a time as it was wanted, using it as a residence for one of the Officers of the Customs staff when it was no longer required by the Vice-Consul.

In fulfilment of his promise, the President called on me in the evening with his answer to your note. A translation is appended.

The extremely cordial tone of the President and Assistant Ministers led me to the conclusion that they are eager to see the ratifications of the Treaty exchanged. This impression was confirmed by several remarks let fall from M. von Möllendorff, who seems to have had great difficulty in combating the demands of the Chinese and Japanese, whose interests appear to be in some respects conflicting. He was especially earnest in his expressions of a hope that the British Representative in Söul would support him in the carrying out of measures that were absolutely necessary for the maintenance of order in the foreign Settlements, and uniformity in the carrying out of the numerous Customs and other Regulations, the adoption of which requires the joint consent of the Consular and local authorities.

I [left] Söul on the morning of the 8th instant, Mr. Scott remaining there to superintend the preparations for your accommodation, and reached Chefoo at noon on the 10th. I informed the President before I left that you would probably be in Chemulpo in about a fortnight's time.

                                                                    I have, &c.
                                            (Signed)   W.C. HILLIER

Inclosure 2

Form of Ratification appended to the United States' Treaty with Corea.

(Translation)

WE have carefully perused this Treaty with the United States, and we find that each and every Article and section can be given effect to.

We do accordingly ratify the same, affixing thereto the national seal, and signing it with our own hand in token of good faith.

Dated this 14th day of the 4th moon of the 492nd year of the Corean era.

                                            (L.S)   (Royal Signature)

Inclosure 3

Min Yŏng-mok to Sir H.S. Parkes.

                                                            April 7, 1884

(Translation)

MIN, President of the Corean Foreign Office, makes a communication in reply to Sir Harry Parkes.

The President has the honour to acknowledge the receipt, on the 21st ultimo, of Sir Harry Parkes' note, in which his Excellency states that Her Majesty the Queen and Empress had ratified the Treaty concluded with the President on the 26th November last, and had been pleased to appoint Sir Harry Parkes to be Her Majesty's Minister to Corea. Sir Harry Parkes felt confident that the President would see in this prompt action on the part of Her Majesty's Government a distinguished proof of their desire to cultivate the most friendly relations with the Government of His Majesty the King, and to promote the development of mutually advantageous intercourse between the people of both countries. His Excellency considered it to be due to the President to give him the earliest intimation of his approaching visit to the capital to exchange the ratifications of the Treaty, and had accordingly deputed Mr. Hillier, the Chinese Secretary, to proceed to Sŏul for the purpose of delivering this note.

As Her Majesty the Queen and Empress, Sir Harry Parkes continued, had already ratified the Treaty, he trusted that the President would inform him, in reply, that it had also been ratified by His Majesty the King. Mr. Hillier would wait for this reply, and as soon as Sir Harry Parkes received it he would proceed to Sŏul to exchange the ratifications and deliver his credentials as Minister.

The perusal of this note has been a source of unbounded pleasure to the President, whose august Sovereign was deeply gratified to hear that Her Majesty the Queen and Empress had already ratified the Treaty. He is commanded by His Majesty to inform Sir Harry Parkes that the appointment of His Excellency as Her Majesty's Representative in Corea is most acceptable to the Government of that country, and the President begs to express, on his own part, his conviction that this appointment cannot fail eminently to conduce to the lasting maintenance of friendly relations between the two Governments, as well as to the mutual advantage of their respective subjects.

His Majesty is specially gratified at the promptitude with which Her Majesty the Queen and Empress has ratified the Treaty, which has also been ratified by himself, and it only remains for the President to express a hope that Sir Harry Parkes will shortly arrive, in order that these ratifications may be duly exchanged.

Mr. Hillier has been asked to be good enough to be the bearer of this reply.

金炳始(1884. 4. 21/高宗二十一年三月二十六日) ➜ H.S. Parkes

영접관 파견을 알리는 조회

大朝鮮督辦交涉通商事務金 爲照會事 照得 貴大臣現因批准約文互相奉換
銜命遠涉 重到本國地方 曷任忻喜 玆派本衙門協辦金晩植 主事鄭憲時 前往
仁川口岸迎接 卽同貴大臣到京 惟祈遄臨 爲此備文照會 須至照會者
右照會
大英國欽差駐劄中華全權便宜行事大臣 巴
甲申三月二十六日

尹致昊(1884. 4. 24/高宗二十一年三月二十九日)

내지여행권 조항에 관한 高宗과 Foote의 대화

是日午後一點鍾 上引見美使于後苑便殿 辟坐[sic]右而賜座 有件下詢事如左 其一 英使巴氏 今到濟浦 入閫在邇 或云若我政府請改定條約內一二件 則英使有可從之意云云 卿以爲此事可成乎 美使對曰 何件是聖意所欲改定耶 上曰 旅行護照一件尤緊此是十餘日前 余之奏達事也 美使對曰 英使初定條約之時 外臣 曾勸貴政府能不讓此權 故以此言于美政府矣 美政府大加襃賞于外臣 以外臣之能勸此事于貴政府也 豈料那時 執事懦弱 竟讓此權利于彼 實無任恨歎 而凡一有所得 固執不讓利自己之事 英國素習也 如貴國欲改此件 必須巨大勞力 而猶恐彼不從也 當英使之定約也 勿讓此權理之事 非啻美使之所勸 余之幾十次奏達事 而因爲諸狐所欺 竟被奪此權于彼 日前余奏此事之大失措 上似有採納之意 今日此敎 其來有原 然而事已遲矣 後悔 何及 竟容那時執事外務官人 罪當罰 而反見幸寵 爲萬民可歎

H.S. Parkes(1884. 4. 28) ➜ 金炳始

Aston 일행 파견 통보

관련문서 金炳始의 회신(1884. 4. 29)

大英國駐劄朝鮮欽差大臣巴 爲照會事 照得 本國外務大臣 委派阿士噸 在朝鮮國辦本國總領事官之事 及加里士在濟物浦辦本國副領事官之事 本大臣相應請貴大臣 照條約第二款 貴國政府迅速給與該官允文 以便躬親任事 爲此照會 請煩查照施行 須至照會者
右照會
大朝鮮國督辦交涉通商事務 金
西曆一千八百八十四年四月二十八日 甲申四月初四日

【관련문서】

大朝鮮督辦交涉通商事務金 爲照覆事 照得 四月初四日 接准貴大臣照會內開云云等因前來 本大臣查爲阿總領事及加副領事 已得我政政[sic]府准行文憑 幷諭令三口監理事務及地方官遇事通辦 至阿總領事 聲名素著 本大臣實深欽仰 亦旣長駐本國 尤爲忻慰 爲此照覆 請煩查照施行 須至照覆者
右照覆
大英國駐劄朝鮮欽差大臣 巴
甲申四月初五日

H.S. Parkes (1884. 4. 28) ➜ G.L.G. Granville (1884. 5. 2)

비준 완료 보고

Sir H.S. Parkes to Earl Granville.—(Received May 2)

(Telegraphic) *Corea, April* 28, 1884

RATIFICATIONS exchanged to-day.

H.S. Parkes (1884. 4. 28) ➜ G.L.G. Granville (1884. 6. 27)

2차 조영조약 비준서 교환 보고

Sir H.S. Parkes to Earl Granville.—(Received June 27)

(No. 1. Corean Mission)
My Lord,   *Hanyang, April* 28, 1884

I HAVE the honour to report that early on the morning of the 21st instant I embarked with Messrs. Aston and Hillier at Shanghae on board Her Majesty's ship "Albatross," in order to join at Woosung Her Majesty's ship "Cleopatra," which had been appointed by the Commander-in-chief to convey me to Corea. Leaving Woosung at noon on the same day, we arrived at Chemulpo on the afternoon of the 23rd instant.

I was at once visited by one of the Vice-Ministers of the Foreign Office and several other Corean functionaries, who delivered a letter from the President of that Department, of which I inclose a translation, expressing the pleasure of his Government on my returning to Corea with the ratification of the Treaty. I learned from this letter that the Minister Min Yong-mok, with whom I had negotiated the Treaty, had been replaced in the office of President by the writer, Kim Pyöng-si, and that this and other changes in the Government had very recently occurred. I shall have to report on this subject in a later despatch.

The following day, the 24th, was engaged in disembarking baggage, preparing for the journey to the capital, and in returning on shore the call of the Vice-President.

I arrived here at 5 P.M. on the 25th, and was at once visited by the new President and four of the Vice-Ministers of the Foreign Office. After expressing their personal congratulations, the President inquired after the health of Her Majesty, and I should not omit to report that His Excellency rose to his feet as he named the Queen, and that all the Vice-Ministers simultaneously observed the same mark of deep respect for Her Majesty. I, of course, returned a similar compliment on alluding, in reply, to the health of His Majesty the King. I also arranged at this interview that the ratifications of the Treaty should be exchanged on the morning of the 28th.

The interviewing two days' were fully occupied in preparing the papers for that ceremony in arranging for temporary quarters, and in necessary official visits.

This morning I proceeded to the Foreign Office at 11 o'clock, and exchanged in due form the ratifications of the Treaty concluded here on the 26th November last. As soon as the seals and signatures had been affixed to the certificate of exchange, the President stated that he was charged to express on the part of the King the great pleasure which was felt by His Majesty on the Treaty having thus come into operation, and also the hope that the event afforded similar gratification to the Queen. In reply, I alluded to the terms of Her Majesty's letter to the King, a copy of which I then delivered to his Excellency, in order to show that the establishment of Treaty relations with Corea had afforded Her Majesty the same cordial satisfaction.

The President also informed me that the King would grant me an audience on the 1st proximo for the purpose of receiving from me the letter of the Queen and my credentials as Her Majesty's Envoy Extraordinary and Minister Plenipotentiary to this Court.

I inclose a copy of a notification which I have now issued, informing Her Majesty's subjects that the ratifications of the Treaty have been exchanged, and that it accordingly comes into operation on this date. If the arrangements made for this purpose have been successfully carried out, the event will have been made known at the port of Chemulpo at noon this day by a salute of twenty-one guns fired by Her Majesty's ship "Cleopatra" in honour of the occasion, and also of the Corean flag, which will thus have been saluted by us for the first time. His Excellency Min Yŏng-mok, the Minister who negotiated the Treaty, together with one of the Vice-Ministers of the Foreign Office, were instructed to proceed to Chemulpo in order to receive this compliment from Her Majesty's ship.

I have, &c.
(Signed)   HARRY S. PARKES

H.S. Parkes (1884. 4. 30) ➜ 金炳始
高宗 알현시 수행원 명단

敬啓者 昨蒙見約 本大臣等於明日覲見貴國大君主 但大君主命於明日何時著
本大臣等趍廷覲見 敢祈貴大臣先行示知 不勝盼望之至 所有本大臣隨帶屬員
之官階及姓名 理合開明佈知 謹此幷頌日祉
四月初六日 名另具 巴夏禮

計附呈各官銜名一紙幷附送英文文稿一紙
大英欽差駐劄朝鮮全權便宜行事大臣 巴夏禮
大英欽命駐劄朝鮮管理本國通商事務總領事官 阿須頓
大英駐劄朝鮮副領事官 賈禮士
大英駐劄朝鮮漢陽漢文繙繹官 薩允格
大英欽命統帶本國水師總兵官 赫泊士
大英管帶水師都司 師多福
　　管帶水師都司 柏勒德
　　水師隨營總醫官 吳鐸
　　水師隨員 許士
　　水師隨員 波得利

金炳始(1884. 4. 30/高宗二十一年四月六日) ➜ H.S. Parkes

高宗 알현 일시 통보

敬覆者 頃承雅意 以明日覲見時刻見詢 并示貴各官銜名一紙 均已領悉 玆爲此事 已由軍國衙門函告貴大臣 明日上午十一點鍾進宮爲盼 肅此佈覆 順頌日祉

四月初六日 名另具 金炳始

金炳始(1884. 5. 1/高宗二十一年四月七日) ➜ H.S. Parkes

비준서 교환시 축사

관련문서 Parkes의 답사(答辭)(1884. 5. 1)

祝宴致詞 四月初七日
今大英國欽差大臣 奉大英國大君主欽命 前來本國京城 互換批准條約 親呈國書 陛見禮成 我大君主深用嘉悅 俺等亦慶祝無比 且以巴大臣信義之重迅辦再苞 將見交際日篤 情好益密 而大美國欽差大臣·大日本署理公使亦在此座 與共欣賀 實與國同有之慶 萬世無窮之休 本大臣不勝懽忭 敬祝大朝鮮國大君主 大英國大君主 大美國伯理璽天德 大日本國皇帝共享萬壽 暨子孫人民永受遐福

【관련문서】

英使答祝詞 同日
兹聞貴大臣以詩篇之句 頌祝我國大君主 語意盹誠 本大臣耳聆心篆 忻忭弗勝 況今大朝鮮國與我國既已互換條約 幷同萬國一體親和 正足以使萬國同深敬佩 本大臣深知我國大君主定然怡懌 心悅靡渥 伏思本大臣所賫呈我國大君主之國書意照於辭 要在兩國共敦友誼 以至於永遠而無更 亦足見我國大君主與大朝鮮國大君主誼重友邦 情深親睦 定堪永保修和之道 而至於萬斯年也 且思大朝鮮國自開國至今祚永年長 大君主保赤爲懷 率作興事 固足以令擧國服疇食德之倫共深感戴矣 維大君主與我國大君主 篤深交友之情 批准條約 永敦和好 以本大臣之愚見視之 百度惟貞 善有莫喻 本大臣惟仰祈於天錫大朝鮮國大君主多福多壽 純嘏無疆 俾人民共霑恩澤 永享和平 則美善全歸 有莫加乎此者 是所欣願之至
　　附送英文辭稿一紙

高宗 ➡ 總署(1884. 6. 5/光緒十年五月十二日)

2차 조영조약 비준서 교환 통보

五月初十日 朝鮮國王文稱 照得光緒九年九月二十七日 敝邦與英國全權大臣 巴夏禮重訂條約 通商章程 稅則及善後續條各件 畫押鈐印 互相憑據之由 已經咨明 而本年四月初四日 英國公使巴夏禮賫其國書來到敝邦京城 與督辦交涉通商事務金炳始將上年所訂條約批准互換 再行照會聲明 內地游歷通商一事 該公使仍駐紮京城 交際事件 幸臻妥完 實由 皇上綏靖之恩 亦荷貴王公諸大人曁北洋大臣經畫遠謨 維持局面 謹與一國臣庶北望攢頌 無任感紉 請煩轉奏 天陛 以表小邦無事不達之忱 除將鈔錄該國國書及往復照會 庸備轉奏外 理合具交咨明 爲此咨會

【關係資料】

1.

(1882. 6. 6/高宗十九年 四月二十一日)

1차 조영수호통상조약

大朝鮮國與大英國均願敦崇和好惠顧彼此人民是以大朝鮮國大君主特派大官經理統理機務衙門事趙寗夏副官經理統理機務衙門金宏集大英國大君主特派水師提督駐紮中國各兵船統領勳錫佩帶三等寶星韋力士彼此皆係特派議約大員互訂條款臚列於左

　第一款
嗣後大朝鮮國大君主大英國大君主並其人民各皆永遠和平友邦若他國有何不公輕藐之事一經照知必須相助從中善爲調處以示友誼關切

　第二款
此次立約通商和好後兩國可交派秉權大臣駐紮彼此都城並於彼此通商口岸設立領事等官均聽其便此等官員與本地官交涉往來均應用品級相當之理兩國秉權大臣與領事等官享獲種種恩施與彼此所待最優之國官員無異領事官必須奉到駐紮之國批准文憑方可視事所派領事等官必須眞正官員不得以商人兼充亦不得兼作貿易儻各口未設領事官或請別國領事兼代亦不得以商人兼充或卽由地方官照現定條約代辦若駐紮朝鮮之英國領事等官辦事不合須知照英國公使彼此意見相同可將批准文憑追回

　第三款
英國船隻在朝鮮左近海面如遇颶風或缺糧食煤水距通商岸口太遠應許其隨處收泊以避颶風購買食量修理船隻所有經費係由船主自備地方官民應加憐恤援助供其所需如該船在不通商之口潛往貿易拿獲船貨入官如英國船隻在朝鮮海岸破壞朝鮮地方官一經聞知卽應飭令將水手先行救護供其糧食等項一面設法

保護隻船貨物竝行知照領事官俾將水手送回本國並將船貨撈起一切費用或由船主或由英國認還

　第四款
英國民人在朝鮮居主安分守法其性命財產朝鮮地方官應當代爲保護勿許稍有欺陵損壞如有不法之徒欲將英國房屋產業搶劫燒毀者地方官一經領事告知卽應派兵彈壓並查拿罪犯按律重辦朝鮮民人如有欺陵英國民人應歸朝鮮官按朝鮮律例懲辦英國民人無論在商船在岸上如有欺陵騷擾損傷朝鮮民人性命財產等事應歸英國領事官或英國所派官員按照英國律例查拿懲辦其在朝鮮英國民人如有涉訟應由被告所屬之官員以本國律例審斷原告所屬之國可以派員聽審審官當以禮相待聽審官如欲傳訊查訊分訊訂見亦聽其便如以審官所斷爲不公亦許其詳細駁辯大英國與大朝鮮國彼此明定如朝鮮日後改定律例及審案辦法在英國視與本國律例辦法相符卽將英國官員在朝鮮審案之權收回以後朝鮮境內英國人民卽歸地方官管轄

　第五款
朝鮮國商民並其商船前往英國貿易凡納稅船鈔並一切各費應遵照英國海關章程辦理與徵收本國人民及相待最優之國稅鈔不得額外加增英國商民並其商船前往朝鮮貿易進出口貨物均應納稅其收稅之權應由朝鮮自主所有進出口稅項及海關禁防偸漏諸弊悉聽朝鮮政府設立規則先期知會英國官布示商民遵行現擬先訂稅則大略各色進口貨有關民生日用者照估價值百抽稅不得過一十其奢靡玩耍等物如洋酒呂宋煙鐘錶之類照估價值百抽稅不得過三十至出口土貨槪照值百抽稅不得過五凡進口洋貨除在口岸完納正稅外該項貨物或入內地或在口岸永遠不納別項稅費英國商船進朝鮮口岸須納船鈔每噸銀五錢每船按中歷一季抽一次

　第六款
朝鮮國商民前往英國各處准其在該處居住賃房買地起蓋棧房任其自便其貿易工作一切所有土產以及製造之物與不違禁之貨均許買賣英國商船商民前往朝鮮已開口岸准其在該處所定界內居住賃房租地建屋任其自便其貿易工作一切所有土產以及製造之物與不違禁之物均許買賣惟租地時不得稍有勒逼該地租價悉照朝鮮所定等則完納其出租之地仍歸朝鮮版圖除按此約內所指明歸英國

官員應管商民外皆仍歸朝鮮地方官管轄英國商民不得以洋貨運入內地售賣亦不得自入內地采買土貨併不得以土貨由此口販運彼口違者將貨物入官並將該商交領事官懲辦

　　第七款
朝鮮國與英國彼此商定朝鮮商民不准販運洋藥入英國通商口岸英國商民亦不准販運洋藥入朝鮮通商口岸並由此口運往彼口亦不准作一切買賣洋藥之貿易所有兩國商民無論僱用本國船別國船及本國船爲別國商民僱用販運洋藥者均由各本國自行永遠禁止查出從重懲罰

　　第八款
如朝鮮國因有事故恐致境內缺食大朝鮮國大君主得暫禁米糧出口經地方官照知後由英國官員轉飭在各口英國商民一體遵辦惟於已開仁川一港各色米糧概行禁止運出紅蔘一項朝鮮舊禁出口英國人如有潛買出洋者均查拿入官仍分別懲罰

　　第九款
凡礮位鎗刀火藥鉛丸一切軍器應由朝鮮官自行采辦或英國人奉朝鮮官准買明文方准進口如有私販查貨入官仍分別懲罰

　　第十款
凡兩國官員商民在彼此通商地方居住均可僱請各色人等勷執分內工作惟朝鮮人遇犯本國例禁或牽涉被控凡在英國商民寓所行棧及商船隱匿者由地方官照知領事官或准差役自行往拿或由領事派人拿交朝鮮差役英國官民不得稍有庇縱捐留

　　第十一款
兩國生徒往來學習語言文字律例藝業等事彼此均宜勷助以敦睦誼

　　第十二款
玆朝鮮國初次立約所訂條款姑從簡略應遵條約已載者先行辦理其未載者俟五年後兩國官民彼此言語稍通再行議定至通商詳細章程須酌照萬國公法通例公

平商訂無有輕重大小之別

　第十三款
此次兩國訂立條約與夫日後往來公牘專用華文英國亦用華文或用英文必須以華文註明以免歧誤

　第十四款
現經兩國議定嗣後大朝鮮國大君主有何惠政恩典利益施及他國或其商民無論關涉海面行船通商貿易交往事爲該國並其商民從來未霑抑爲此條約所無者亦准英國官民一體均霑惟此種優待他國之利益若立有專條互相酬報者英國官民必將互訂酬報之專條一體遵守方准同霑優待之利益

以上各款現經大朝鮮國大英國大臣同在朝鮮仁川府議定繕寫華洋文三分句法相同先行畫押蓋印以昭憑信仍俟兩國御筆批准總以一年爲期在朝鮮仁川府互換然後將此約各款彼此通諭本國官員商民俾得咸知遵守

大朝鮮國開國四百九十一年 即中國光緒八年四月二十一日
西曆一千八百八十二年六月初六日

Treaty

The United Kingdom of Great Britain and Ireland, and the Kingdom of Chosen, being sincerely desirous of establishing permanent relations of amity and friendship between their respective peoples, have, to this end, appointed, that is to say, Her Majesty, the Queen of Great Britain and Ireland, Vice Admiral George Ommanney Willes, a Companion of the Most Honourable Order of the Bath and Commander-in-Chief of Her Majesty's Ships employed on the China Station as Her Representative, and His Majesty, the King of Chosen, Isas Ling Hsia, a Member of the Royal Council, and Ching Hung Kie, a Member of the Royal Council, as His Representatives, who, being duly powered, have agreed upon the several following Articles: -

ARTICLE I – There shall be perpetual peace and friendship between the Queen of Great Britain and Ireland and the King of Chosen, and the subjects of their respective Governments. If other Powers deal unjustly or oppressively with either Government, the other will exert its good offices, on being informed of the case, to bring about an amicable arrangement, thus showing friendly feelings.

ARTICLE II – After the conclusion of this Treaty of Amity and Commerce, the High Contracting Powers may each appoint Diplomatic Representatives to reside at the Court of the other, and may each appoint Consular Representatives at the Ports of the other, which are open to foreign commerce, at their own convenience. These officials shall have relations with the corresponding local authorities of equal rank, upon a basis of mutual equality.

 The Diplomatic and Consular Representatives of the two Governments shall receive, mutually, all the privileges, rights, and immunities, without discrimination, which are accorded to the same class of representatives from the most favoured nation.

 Consuls shall exercise their functions only on receipt of an exequatur from the Government to which they are accredited. Consular authorities shall be bona fide officials. No merchants shall be permitted to exercise the duties of the office, nor shall Consular Officers be allowed to engage in trade. At Ports to which no Consular Representatives have been appointed, the Consuls of other powers may be invited to act, provided that no merchant shall be allowed to assume Consular functions, or the provisions of this Treaty may, in such case, be enforced by the local authority.

If Consular Representatives of the British Government in Chosen conduct their business in an improper manner, their exequaturs may be revoked, subject to the approval, previously obtained, of the Diplomatic Representative of the British Government.

ARTICLE III – Whenever British vessels, either because of stress of weather, or by want of fuel or provisions, cannot reach the nearest open port in Chosen, they may enter any port or harbour, either to take refuge therein, or to get supplies of wood, coal or other necessaries, or to make repairs, the expenses incurred thereby being defrayed by the ship's master. In such event the Officers and people of the locality shall display their sympathy by rendering full assistance and their liberality by furnishing the necessaries (see) required. If a British vessel carries on a clandestine trade at a port not open to foreign commerce such vessel with her cargo shall be seized and confiscated.

If a British vessel be wrecked on the Coast of Chosen, the local authorities on being informed of the occurrence shall immediately render assistance to the crew, provide for their present necessities, and take measure necessary for the salvage of the ship and the preservation of her cargo. They shall also bring the matter to the knowledge of the nearest Consular Representative of the British Government in order that steps may be taken to send the crew home and to save the ship and her cargo. The necessary expenses shall be defrayed either by the ship's master or by the British Government.

ARTICLE IV – All British subjects in Chosen peaceably attending to their own affairs shall receive and enjoy for themselves and everything appertaining to them the protection of the local authorities of the Government of Chosen, who shall defend them from all insult and injury of any sort.

If their dwellings or property be threatened or attacked by mobs, incendiaries or other violent or lawless persons the local officers on requisition of the Consul shall immediately dispatch a military force to disperse the rioters, apprehend the guilty individuals and punish them with the utmost rigour of the law. Subjects of Chosen guilty of any criminal act towards British subjects shall be punished by the Authorities of Chosen according to the laws of Chosen; and British subjects, either on shore or in any merchant vessel who may insult, trouble or wound the persons or injure the property of the people of Chosen shall be arrested and punished only by the Consul or other public British functionary thereto authorized according to the laws of the British Government. When controversies arise with the Kingdom of Chosen between subjects of Her Majesty the Queen of Great Britain and Ireland, and subjects of His Majesty the King of Chosen, which need to be examined and decided by the public officers of the two nations, it is agreed between the two Governments of England and Chosen that such cases shall be tried by the proper official of the nationality of the defendant, according to the laws of that nation.

The properly authorized official of the plaintiff's nationality, shall be fully permitted to attend the trial, and shall be treated with the courtesy due to his position. He shall be granted all proper facilities for watching the proceedings in the interests of justice. If he so desires, he shall have the right to present and to examine and cross-examine witnesses. If he is dissatisfied with the proceedings, he shall be permitted to protest against them in detail.

It is however mutually agreed and understood between the High Contracting Powers, that whenever the King of Chosen shall have so far modified and reformed the statutes and judicial procedure of his kingdom, that in the judgment of the British Government, they conform to the laws and course of justice in England, the right of exterritorial jurisdiction over British subjects in Chosen shall be abandoned, and thereafter British subjects when within the limits of the Kingdom of Chosen, shall be subject to the jurisdiction of the native authorities.

ARTICLE V – Merchants and merchant vessels of Chosen visiting the United Kingdom of Great Britain and Ireland, and its colonies and possessions for the purpose of traffic, shall pay duties and tonnage dues, and all fees, according to the Custom Regulations of the British Government, but no higher or other rates of duties and tonnage dues shall be exacted of them than are levied upon British subjects, or upon citizens or subjects of the most favored nation.

British merchants and merchant vessels visiting Chosen for the purpose of traffic shall pay duties upon all merchandise imported and exported.

The authority to levy duties is of right vested in the Government of Chosen. The tariff of duties upon exports and imports, together with the Customs Regulations for the prevention of smuggling and other irregularities, will be fixed by the Authorities of Chosen and communicated to the proper officials of the British Government, to be by the latter notified to their subjects and duly observed.

It is however agreed in the first instance as a general measure that the tariff upon such imports as are articles of daily use shall not exceed an *ad valorem* duty of ten per centum; that the tariff upon such imports as are luxuries, as, for instance, foreign wines, foreign tobacco, clocks and watches shall not exceed an *ad valorem* duty of thirty per centum; and that native produce exported shall pay a duty not to exceed five per centum *ad valorem*; and it is further agreed that the duty upon foreign imports shall be paid once for all at the port of entry, and that no other dues, duties, fees, taxes or charges of any sort shall be levied upon such imports either in the interior of Chosen or at the Ports.

British merchant vessels entering the ports of Chosen shall pay tonnage dues at the rate of five mace per ton, payable once in three months on each vessel, according to the Chinese Calendar.

ARTICLE VI – Subjects of Chosen who may visit Great Britain, its colonies and possessions, shall be permitted to reside, and to rent premises, purchase land, or to construct residences or warehouses in all parts of the country. They shall be freely permitted to pursue their various callings and avocations, and to traffic in all merchandise, raw and manufactured, that is not declared contraband by law.

British subjects who may resort to the ports of Chosen which are open to foreign commerce, shall be permitted to reside at such open ports within the limits of the concession, and to lease buildings or land, or to construct residences or warehouses therein. They shall be fully permitted to pursue their various callings and avocations within the limits of the port, and to traffic in all merchandise, raw and manufactured, that is not declared contraband by law. No coercion or intimidation in the acquisition of land or building shall be permitted, and the land rent as fixed by the Authorities of Chosen shall be paid.

And it is expressly agreed that land so acquired in the open ports of Chosen still remains as integral part of the Kingdom, and that all rights of jurisdiction over persons and property within such areas remain vested in the Authorities of Chosen, except in so far as such rights have been expressly relinquished by this Treaty.

British subjects are not permitted either to transport foreign imports to the interior, or to proceed thitherto purchase native produce; nor are they permitted to transport native produce from one open port to another open port. Violations of this rule will subject such merchandise to confiscation, and the merchant offending will be handed over to the Consular Authorities to be dealt with.

ARTICLE VII – The British Government and the Government of Chosen mutually agree and undertake that subjects of Chosen shall not be permitted to import opium into any British port, and British subjects shall not be permitted to import opium into any of the open ports of Chosen, to transport it from one open port to another open port, or to traffic it in Chosen.

This absolute prohibition, which extend to vessels owned by subjects of either power, to foreign vessels employed by them, and to vessels owned by the subjects of either power and employed by other persons for the transportation of opium, shall be enforced by appropriate legislation on the part of the British Government and of Chosen, and offenders against it shall be severely punished.

ARTICLE VIII – Whenever the Government of Chosen shall have reason to apprehend a scarcity of food within the limits of the kingdom, His Majesty may, by decree, temporarily prohibit the export of all breadstuffs, and such decree shall be binding on all British subjects in Chosen, upon due notice having been given thus by the Authorities of Chosen, through the proper officers of the British Government; but it is to be understood that the exportation of rice and breadstuffs of every description is prohibited from the open port of Jin Chuen.

Chosen having of old prohibited the exportation of red ginseng, if British subjects clandestinely purchase it for export, it shall be confiscated and the offenders punished.

ARTICLE IX – The purchase of cannon, small arrows, swords, gunpowder, shot and all munitions of war, is permitted only to officials of the Government of Chosen, and they may be imported by British subjects only under a written permit from the Authorities of Chosen.

If these articles are clandestinely imported, they shall be confiscated and the offending parties shall be punished.

ARTICLE X – The officers and people of either nation residing in the other shall have the right to employ natives for all kinds of lawful work.

Should, however, subjects of Chosen, guilty of violation of the laws of the kingdom, or against whom any action has been brought, conceal themselves in the residences or warehouses of British subjects or on board British merchant vessels, the Consular Authorities of the British Government, on being notified of the fact by the local authorities, will either permit the latter to despatch constables to make the arrests or the persons will be arrested by the Consular Authorities and handed over to the local constables. British officials or subjects shall not harbour such persons.

ARTICLE. XI – Students of either nationality who may proceed to the country of the other in order to study the language, literature, laws or arts, shall be given all possible protection and assistance in evidence of cordial good will.

ARTICLE XII – This being the First Treaty negotiated by Chosen, and hence being general and incomplete in its provisions, shall in the first instance, be put into operation in all things stipulated herein.

As to stipulations not contained herein, after an interval of five years when the officers and people of the two Powers shall have become more familiar with each others language, a further negotiation of commercial provisions and regulations in detail, in conformity with international law and without unequal discriminations on either part, shall be had.

ARTICLE XIII – This Treaty and future official correspondence shall be made on the part of Chosen in the Chinese language. The British Government shall either use the Chinese language or, if English be used, it shall be accompanied with a Chinese version in order to avoid misunderstanding.

ARTICLE – XIV The High Contracting Powers hereby agree that, should at any time the King of Chosen grant to any nation, or to the merchants or citizens of any nation any right, privilege, or favour, connected either with the navigation, commerce, political, or other intercourse which is not conferred by this Treaty, such right, privilege, and favour, shall freely inure to the benefit of the Kingdom of Great Britain and Ireland, its public officers, merchants, and citizens; provided always that whenever such right, privilege, or favour, is accompanied by any condition or equivalent concession granted by the other nation interested, the British Government, its officers, and people, shall only be entitled to the benefit of such right, privilege, or favour, upon complying with the conditions or concessions connected therewith.

In faith whereof the respective representatives have signed and sealed the foregoing at Jin Chuen in English and Chinese, being three originals of each text of even tenor and date, the ratifications of which shall be exchanged at Jin Chuen within one year from the date of its execution, and immediately thereafter this Treaty shall be in all its provisions publicly proclaimed, and made known by both Governments in their respective countries, in order that it may be obeyed by their subjects respectively.

Dated this sixth day of June, one thousand eight hundred and eighty two.

(Signed) GEORGE O. WILLES (I.S)
Vice-Admiral, Commander-in-Chief

Signatures of [　] Plenipotentiaries

2.

(1883. 11. 26 /高宗二十年 十月二十七日)

2차 조영수호통상조약

朝英通商條約

大朝鮮國大君主大英國大君主兼膺五印度大后帝 切願永敦兩國和好 議定彼此往來久遠通商事宜 是以大朝鮮國大君主 特簡督辦交涉通商事務一品崇祿大夫行議政府左參贊兼奎章閣提學世子左副賓客閔泳穆 大英國大君主五印度大后帝 特簡頭等邁吉利寶星兼二等拔德寶星駐箚中華便宜行事大臣巴夏禮 均作爲便宜行事全權大臣 各將所奉全權大臣便宜行事之上諭 互相較閱畢 俱屬妥宜 卽將會議 各款臚列於左

第一款
一 大朝鮮國大君主大英國大君主兼膺五印度大后帝及兩國後代嗣君與其人民 彼此皆各永遠和平友睦 此國人民住彼國者 必受該國妥行保護身家財産之益
二 彼國日後 倘有與別國相歧之處 此國一經彼國相約 應卽設法 從中善爲調處

第二款
一 大朝鮮·大英君主 均可互相簡派使臣 駐箚大朝鮮·大英國京師 或隨時往來 亦可彼此酌設總領事官 領事官或副領事官 在各通商口岸處所駐箚 所有以上使臣總領事官等 與彼此駐箚之國官員 會晤及往來文件 必須享獲他國互相款待使臣領事最優之禮及一切種種利益之處
二 兩國所派使臣總領事官等及一切隨員 均可聽其互相前往各處游歷勿阻 在朝鮮國者 由大朝鮮國官員 發給護照 並行斟酌派人護送 以重妥爲保護之義

三 兩國總領事等官 必須奉到駐箚之國勅准或政府允文 方可躬親任事 其所派總領事等官 不得兼行貿易

第三款
一 英國民人及其財産在朝鮮者 應歸英國所派辦理刑名詞訟之員 專行管轄 凡英國民人 互相涉訟 或別國人控告英民之案 均由英國刑訟之員審理 與朝鮮官員無涉
二 朝鮮官貟及民人等 若有控告居住朝鮮英民之案 應歸英國刑訟之貟審斷
三 英國官貟及民人等 若在朝鮮 遇有控告朝鮮民人案件 應歸朝鮮官員審斷
四 英國民人 在朝鮮者 如有犯法之事 應由英國刑訟之員 按照英國律例審辦
五 朝鮮民人 在朝鮮境內 如有欺凌擾害損傷英國民人身家性命財産等事 應由朝鮮官貟 按照朝鮮律例 查拏審辦
六 凡有控告英國民人 因違背此約及附立章程 並將來按約續立各章有涉 罰款入官及一切罪名 應歸英國刑訟之員 自行審斷 其所罰之款以及入官財貨 全歸朝鮮國充公
七 凡有朝鮮國官員 在通商口岸 因事扣留英民貨物 應由朝鮮官員 會同英國領事官 先行查封 暫由朝鮮官員看管 俟英國刑訟之員審定 以後發落 如審明貨主 並無非是 卽應將所封貨物全數 送交領事官發還 惟所封貨物 應聽貨主 將貨物估價 折銀若干 暫存朝鮮官員處所 立卽將貨領出 俟英國刑訟之員審定後 其折價存款分別充公發還
八 在朝鮮境內 所有兩國民人 一應詞訟刑名交涉之案 如應在英署審訊者 朝鮮國卽可遴派妥員聽審 如應在朝鮮署內審訊者 英國亦可遴派妥員聽審 其奉派聽審之員彼此承審各官 皆應優禮如儀相待 聽審官如欲轉請傳訊人証 以便自行駁詰 亦聽其便 如以承審官 審斷爲不符 猶許聽審官逐一駁辯
九 凡有首告朝鮮民人 有犯本國律禁 在英國商民開設行棧居住寓所等處及英國商船隱匿者 由地方官照知英國領事官 應由領事官設法 將隱匿之人 查拏交出審辦 領事官尙未照諾 除寓主自行依允外 朝鮮官役 槪不得擅入英國商民行棧寓所等處 其在船上者 應由船主相許 始可登船搜緝
十 凡有英國民人 被人控告違犯法律 或師商各船 在逃人犯 一經英國領事等官 照知朝鮮官員 卽應設法 查緝交出

第四款

一 兩國所立條約 從施行之日起 朝鮮國仁川府之濟物浦元山釜山各口釜山一口設有不宜之處 則可另揀附近別口 並漢陽京城楊花津或附近便宜別處 皆作爲通商之處 任聽英民來往貿易

二 英國商民 前往以上指定處所 或欲永租地段 或欲賃購房屋起蓋房室設立棧房作房等工 均聽其便 至於本教典禮各儀 均聽隨意自行 在朝鮮通商口岸處所 所有揀擇地畝 立定界限 經營基址 作爲洋人居住之處 及轉行永租地段 各事宜應由朝鮮官員 會同各國所派官員 妥行商辦

三 以上地段 應由朝鮮政府 先向該地業主價買 加以經營用費選擇 俟永租有人 將原出地價及經營之費 由所得永租價內 先行扣除 該地年稅 應由朝鮮及各國官員 會同議定 其年稅 應納於朝鮮政府 由朝鮮政府 公平酌留若干 其餘年稅及所得永租地段餘價 一並歸入充公存備金內 至充公存備金 何人取用 應由管理租界事務紳董公司 支取 應如何設立公司之處 日後由朝鮮官員 會同各國所派官員 酌商

四 如英人欲行永租 或暫租地段 賃購房屋 在租界以外者聽 惟相離租界 不得逾十里朝鮮里 而租住此項地段之人 於居住納稅各事 應行一律遵守 朝鮮國自定地方稅課章程

五 朝鮮官員 應在各通商處所 讓出妥善之地 作爲外國營葬之區 其地價及一應年租課稅等項 一律蠲免 所有管理塋地章程 統由以上紳董公司 自行定奪擧辦

六 離通商各處百里內者朝鮮里 或將來兩國所派官員 彼此議定界內 英民均可任便游歷 勿庸請領執照 惟英國民人 亦准持照 前往朝鮮各處 游歷通商 並將各貨 運進出售惟朝鮮政府不允之書籍印板字帖等 不准在內地銷售 及購買一切土貨 所持執照 應由英國領事官繕發 朝鮮地方官 或加蓋印信 或秉筆書押 所有經過之處 如地方官 飭交驗照 卽應隨時呈驗 無訛放行 至雇覓所需車船人夫等 裝運行李貨物 亦聽其便 如英民逾越以上界限 並無執照 或在內地 有不法情事 應行挐交就近領事官 懲辦 其逾界無照英民 卽可酌罰 並行監禁 或只罰不禁 惟罰款 不得逾墨洋百元 禁期不得逾一月

七 英國民人 居住朝鮮 應遵兩國所派官員 會同議定 租界以內街道規則巡查匪類及一切除莠安良之章

第五款

一 英國商民 由別國口岸 或由朝鮮各通商口岸 欲將貨物 載入朝鮮某通商口

岸 均聽其便 其一切進出貨物 除條約明禁之物不計外 應准英國民人與朝
鮮國人及在朝鮮之他國人等 槪行賣買交易 並所交易貨物 任便載徃朝鮮
通商各口及他國口岸 朝鮮官員等 槪勿阻止 惟進出口貨 先應按照 後開稅
則完納稅項 始可聽其出入 凡英國商民 一切工作改造洋土各貨之事 朝鮮
官員等 亦可任聽其便

二 凡由他國口岸 販來一切貨物 進入朝鮮口岸 旣經貨主或寄交之人 納淸以
上稅課 復欲載徃他國口岸者 由進口之日起 期在十三個月內 如係原貨原
包 應行發給 該貨物已經完稅存票一紙 以抵該貨已納之稅 此項存票 該商
或持徃朝鮮海關 領價 卽應照付 或持徃朝鮮通商各口 抵作貨物納稅之款
均聽商便

三 朝鮮土貨 如由朝鮮此通商口岸 載徃朝鮮彼通商口岸 所已納出口稅項 應
於原出之口 全行給還 惟載貨之人 先宜呈交所進口之海關給發進口憑單
始可發還 倘該貨中途有失 亦應呈出失物確據 方能將稅發還

四 英國商民 將貨物 載入朝鮮國 旣經按照 後開稅則 完納稅項 該貨或轉徃
朝鮮通商別口 或轉徃內地 無論何處 所有一切抽收稅釐規費等項 永勿再
事征收 凡朝鮮一切土貨 由內地無論何處 意欲運出朝鮮各通商口岸 聽便
勿阻 其貨在出產之地 或在沿途 所有一切稅釐及各項規費 亦槪免其征收

五 朝鮮政府 如欲雇賃英國商船 裝載客貨 前赴朝鮮境內未通商口岸 亦聽其
便 朝鮮商民 如欲雇賃英國商船 裝載客貨 赴朝鮮未通商口岸者 應行一體
酌准 惟宜先蒙本國官員允許 方可施行

六 如朝鮮政府 因有事故 恐致境內缺食 大朝鮮國大君主降旨 暫禁米粮出某
通商口岸 或各通商口岸 經朝鮮官員照知某口領事官一月之後 則該口英
國商民 卽應一體遵守 惟此禁旣係因時制宜 自當設法 酌爲早弛

七 英國商船 駛進朝鮮各通商口岸 應納船鈔 每噸墨洋三十先時卽洋元百分之
三十 各船所完鈔項 每四個月 征納一次 其已完鈔項之船 在四個月內 准其
前徃朝鮮各通商口岸 無須再納 所征船鈔 皆須用爲建立燈樓浮樁塔表望
樓等項 在於進朝鮮通商各口門次及沿海各處 並備辦船隻停泊處所 淘挖
整頓各工之費 其在通商口岸 撥貨船隻 不得完納船鈔

八 所有約後 附續稅則及通商章程 兩國議定 應由此約施行之日 一並飭遵 以
便條約內所指各節 統歸畫一遵守 以上各章 均可由兩國所派官員 隨時隨
事 一並會同酌議增改

第六款

英國商民 如將貨物 偸運非通商口岸及禁往處所 不論已行未行 均應將貨物入官 違犯之人 按入官貨物之價 加倍示罰 以上違禁貨物 可由朝鮮地方官 酌量扣留 其希圖違禁之英民 無論事成與否 竝可查拿 隨卽轉送就近英國領事官 由英國所派刑訟之員 審讞 貨物扣留 俟定案後 再行分別辦理

第七款

一 英國船隻 在朝鮮海面 如遇颶風失事及擱淺不測之虞 朝鮮地方官 應卽一面速行設法 妥行往救 並保護被難人船貨物 免致本地莠民肆行搶掠欺凌 一面速卽知照附近英國領事官 並將救護被難英民 分別資送附近通商口岸
二 凡朝鮮政府 所出救護英國難民衣食解送及一切打撈葬埋屍身醫治傷病各資 應由英國政府 照數付還
三 撈救保護被難船隻及打撈該船貨物之費 應將船貨交還原主時 由原主照數付還 不得向英國政府索償
四 朝鮮國所派官員及地方委弁巡役人等 前赴英國難船失事處所及護送被難英民之員弁人等 所用資費 以及文函往來脚力 均由朝鮮政府 自行辦理 不得向英國政府取償
五 英國商船 在朝鮮左近海面 如遇颶風 或缺粮食煤水等需用之物 無論是否通商口岸 應許其隨處收泊 以避狂颶 兼修船隻 購買一切缺少之物 所有花費 全由船主 自行備辦

第八款

一 兩國師船 無論是否通商口岸 彼此均許駛往 其所需一切修船材料及食用各等物件 均應彼此互相幇同購取 以上船隻 勿庸遵守通商及口岸章程 其購取勿料 一應鈔稅各等規費 均應豁免
二 英國師船 駛往朝鮮非通商口岸 其船上員弁兵役 槪准登岸 惟未曾執領護照者 不准前往內地
三 英國師船所用軍裝物料及一切餉需各件 可在朝鮮通商各口 存寄交英國委派之員看管 此項軍裝物料 槪行免征稅項 倘有因事轉售者 則由買客 將應完稅課 照例補交
四 英國師船 在朝鮮沿海處所 踏看水路形勢 朝鮮政府 亦應竭力相助

第九款

一 英國官民人等在朝鮮者 均可約雇朝鮮民人 作爲幕友通事及服役人等 勤執分內一切事業工作之端 朝鮮官民人等 亦可分別 約請雇用英國民人 幫同辦理一切未干例禁之事 朝鮮官員 概應聽准

二 兩國民人 均許互相前赴各國境內 學習語言文字律例及織造格致肄業等事 彼此皆宜妥行相助 以敦睦誼

第十款

現經兩國議定 自以上條約施行日期之後 大朝鮮國大君主 於各項進出口貨稅則及一切事宜 今後有何惠政利權 施及他國 並他國臣民人等之處 英國及英國臣民人等 亦可一體均霑

第十一款

兩國議立此約 自施行之日起 十年爲限 所有條約及附約通商稅則 如有應行更改之處 均可互相請爲會同重修 庶將彼此交接日久 所識因革損益之處 酌量增刪 惟應一年之先 豫爲聲明

第十二款

一 兩國議立此約 原係漢·英兩國文字 均經詳細校對 詞意相同 嗣後 倘有文辭分歧之處 應歸英文講解 以免彼此辯論之端

二 凡由英國官員 照會朝鮮官員文件 暫可譯成漢文 與英文配送

第十三款

本約立定後 俟兩國御筆批准 自畫押之日起 速行遲則一年爲限 各派大臣於漢陽京城 互相交換 卽以交換之日 作爲此約施行之期 彼時兩國 均應刊刻約文 通行曉諭 玆由前列兩國欽派全權大臣 在漢陽京城 將約文漢·英各三分 先行畫押 蓋用印章 以昭信守

大朝鮮國開國四百九十二年 卽中國光緒九年十月二十七日
　特簡全權大臣 督辦交涉通商事務從一品崇祿大夫行議政府左參贊兼奎章閣提學世子左副賓客 閔泳穆

西曆一千八百八十三年十一月二十六日

　　　　　　　　　　　　　　　Harry S. Parkes

英約附續通商章程

第一款 船隻進出海口
一 凡英國船隻 進入朝鮮通商口岸 應由船主 在二十四個時辰內禮拜及停公日不計 將該船所持領事官發給船牌收據 呈交該口海關驗收 一面將船名由何口駛至及船主姓名搭客人數如海關欲知搭客姓名亦應逐一開列并將該船噸數若干水手幾名列單 由船主押結爲據 一面按照運單 將該船所載貨物 復繕清摺 摺內詳細註明箱包數目貨色記號及寄交何人姓名 亦由船主 畫押爲據 同時并呈 此卽報船之法也 船隻一經如法報到 卽由海關 發給開艙准單 令押船巡役寓目 始可開艙起貨 如未領准單 擅行開艙起貨者 船主可以酌罰 惟罰款不得逾墨洋百元
二 進口總單內 倘查有錯誤者 從遞單之時起 在十二個時辰內禮拜及停公日不計 卽可改正 勿庸納費 如在十二個時辰之外 遇有增刪更改 應納規費墨洋五元
三 凡船隻進口 已逾前定限期 該船主尙未如法報到者 每逾十二個時辰 卽罰墨洋不得逾五十元
四 凡英國船隻 停泊通商口岸時 在二十四個時辰內禮拜及停公日不計未曾開艙起貨及遇颶進口躱避 或專欲購買食用等物 未經貿易者 概無須到關呈報 亦不得征收船鈔
五 凡船隻欲行出口 應由船主 將出口總單卽如進口所繕淸摺呈報 由海關 發給准行出口單票 并將前呈領事官船牌收據 附還 該船主卽將以上票據 呈交領事官 領事官始可將前收船牌 飭還放行
六 凡船隻不遵以上章程報明海關 擅行出口者 卽可將該船船主 分別示罰 其罰款不得逾墨洋二百元
七 英國輪船 進出各口 均可同日報明出入 其貨物總單 除在本口起卸幷撥載他船外 其餘貨物 勿庸報明

第二款 上下貨物納稅
一 凡商賈運貨進口 欲行起卸者 應赴海關 呈遞報單 單內載明本商姓名船名及運進貨色數目記號價值各節 畫押以爲實據 如海關欲驗各貨原處發票 應卽呈驗 若無發票 亦不言明未能呈票之故 應由該貨主 加倍納稅 始可聽

其起卸 俟發票呈驗時 應將多納之稅 卽行筋還

二 凡照以上規例報明 准行起卸之貨 可由海關 在於定准驗貨處所 委員查驗 惟查驗各貨 勿致損傷 亦不得耽誤遲延 貨物查驗畢 卽宜勉照前式 歸裝原箱原包

三 進出口貨 如貨主所報照估價納稅之貨價値 似有不符 應許海關專派估價之人 另行重估 卽令貨主照納稅項 如貨主以海關專派估價之人所估爲不符 應在十二個時辰內禮拜及停公日不計報明海關稅務司 幷聲明所以不符之故 隨卽自行倩人 再爲復估 海關或照所報復估之價征稅 或照復估之價値 百加五 由稅務司價買 其價銀 無論進出口貨 統自所報復估之日起 限五日內付淸

四 各項進口貨物 如在中途受有損壞者 應行酌量 分別持平 減免稅課 如所減之稅 貨主以爲不足 應照前條辦理

五 凡欲運出貨物 應行預向海關報明 始可裝載上船出口 其報單上 應將船名貨色數目記號及件數幾何 幷價値若干 逐一開列 由運貨者 押詰爲據

六 凡進出貨 除朝鮮海關指定處所 不能起卸裝載 其時在日出之前日沒之後幷禮拜日及停公之期 須由海關特允 方能起卸裝載 然應公平酌納酬勞規費

七 凡進出口貨主 如欲追回多納之稅 或海關欲行追取未足之稅 均應自原收納之日起 在三十日內 卽行聲明 倘逾限期 槪不得追取

八 英國船隻水手搭客人等食用物件及搭客行李箱隻 勿庸專開報單 惟俟海關查驗畢 卽可隨時聽其上下

九 凡船隻應行修理者 所載貨物 均可起卸上岸存放 勿庸納稅 此項上岸貨物 全由朝鮮官員 自行看管 其一切運物脚力存棧租銀及看守辛工 統由該船船主楚付 惟各價均需核實取索 不得浮冒 倘上岸之貨 間有出售者 其出售之貨 自必照例納稅

十 凡欲將貨物 由此船起運彼船者 先應呈領海關發給撥貨准單 方可照數分撥

第三款 防守偸漏逭越

一 英國商船 一經進口 卽可由海關 筋派巡役 隨船管押 所有裝貨各處 聽其省視 該巡役到船時 應行禮待 幷妥爲安置起坐之處

二 船隻裝貨艙口各處 可由海關巡役 於日出之前日沒之後幷禮拜日及停公之

期 設法鎖封 如不候海關明示 擅行揭啓封鎖者 除擅爲者示罰外 該船主亦可一體酌罰 惟罰款均不得逾墨洋百元
三 凡英國商民 進出各貨 未經遵照前法預向海關報明 擅行裝卸及單貨不符 幷違禁者 無論事成與否 貨物均應入官 違犯之人 按入官貨物之價 加倍示罰
四 凡押結報單不實 希圖偸漏朝鮮稅課者 卽可酌罰 惟罰款不得逾墨洋二百元
五 以上章程內所開各節 如有違犯 未經載明如何懲治者 均應隨時隨勢 酌擬示罰 惟款槪不得逾墨洋百元

以上章程內所列報單淸摺等件 均可以英文書寫

閔泳穆

Harry S. Parkes

善後續條

前列兩國全權大臣 將後開三條 附錄於左

一 本約第三款內 所指各節 現經兩國 彼此言明 此條約內 朝鮮准以英民服英國官員管轄 如日後朝鮮 整頓改變律例及審案辦法 在英國政府視之 以爲英民現在難服朝鮮官員管轄之處 俱已革除 並朝鮮審案官員 與英國審案官員 同一明晰律例之能及同一承受獨斷權位 則卽可將英國官員 在朝鮮審理本國民人之權 收回
二 本約第四款內所載各節 現經彼此明訂 中國政府 日後 倘將去年所議中國商民 准入漢城開設行棧之益 允爲撤消 英國商民 則不得援引此款之例 惟朝鮮政府 若將此益利 濟他國商民 則英國商民 亦應一體均沾
三 本約內載各節 彼此言明 所有英國屬下各邦 皆當一律遵守 惟日後 倘查有某邦宜行變通之處 應由英國政府 於此約互換日起 一年爲限 將應行變通者 向朝鮮政府 逐一聲明 方可議更

以上善後各條 均應彼此並同約文 具奏呈覽 與約文齊蒙批准 勿勞專邀特旨允行 玆由前列兩國欽派全權大臣 在漢陽京城 先行畫押蓋用印章 以昭信守

大朝鮮國開國四百九十二年卽中國光緒九年十月二十七日
　　特簡全權大臣督辦交涉通商事務一品崇祿大夫行議政府左參贊兼奎章閣提學世子左副賓客
　　　　　　　　　　　　　　　　　　　　　　　　　閔泳穆
西曆一千八百八十三年十一月二十六日
　　　　　　　　　　　　　　　　　　　　　　　Harry S. Parkes

Treaty

Her Majesty the Queen of Great Britain and Ireland Empress of India, and His Majesty the King of Corea being sincerely desirous of establishing permanent relations of Friendship and commerce between Their respective dominions have resolved to conclude a Treaty for that purpose and have therefore named as Their Plenipotentiaries that is to say:

H. M. the Queen of the United Kingdom of Great Britain and Ireland Empress of india, Sir Harry Smith Parkes, Knight Grand Cross of the most distinguished order of St. Michael and St. George Knight Commander of the most Honourable order of the Bath, H. M's Envoy Extraordinary and Minister Plenipotentiary to H.M. the Emperor of China

H.M the King of Corea, Min Yong Mok, President of H.M Foreign Office, a Dignitary of the first Rank Senior Vice President of the Council of State, Member of H.M. Privy Council and Junior Guardian of the Crown Prince, who, after having communicated to each other their respective Full Powers, found in good and due form, have agreed upon and concluded the following Arts.

Art I

1. There shall be perpetual Peace and Friendship between H.M. the Queen of the
United Kingdom of Great Britain and Ireland, Empress of India, her heirs and successors and between Their respective dominions and subjects, who shall enjoy full security and protection for their persons and property within the Dominions of the other.

2. In case of differences arising between one of the High Contracting Parties and
a third Power, the other High contracting Party, if requested to do so shall exert its good offices to bring about an amicable arrangement.

Art II

1. The High Contracting Parties may each appoint a Diplomatic Representative, to reside permanently or temporarily, at the Capital of the other and may appoint a Consul General, Consuls or Vice Consuls to reside at any or

all of the Ports or places of the other which are open to Foreign Commerce. The Diplomatic Representatives and Consulars functionaries of both countries shall freely enjoy the same facilities for communication personally, or in writing, with the Authorities of the Country where they respectively reside, together with the other privileges and immunities as are enjoyed by Diplomatic or Consular functionaries in other Countries.

2. The Diplomatic Representative and the Consular functionaries of each Power are the members of their official establishment shall have the right to travel freely in any part of the Dominions of the other and the Corean Authorities shall furnish Passports to such British officers travelling in Corea, and shall provide such escort for their protection as may be necessary.

3. The Consular Officers of both countries shall exercise their functions on receipt of due authorization from the Sovereign or Government of the Country in which they respectively reside and shall not be permitted to engage in trade.

Art III

1. Jurisdiction over the persons and property of British Subjects in Corea shall be vested exclusively in the duly authorized British judicial Authorities, who shall hear and determine all cases brought against British Subjects by any British or other foreign subject or citizen without the intervention of the Corean authorities.

2. Of the Corean authorities or a Corean subject make any charge or complaint against a British Subject in Corea, the case shall be heard and decided by the British Judicial Authorities.

3. If the British Authorities or a British subject make any charge or complaint against a Corean subject in Corea, the case shall be heard and decided by the Corean Authorities.

4. A British subject who commits any offence in Corea shall be tried and punished by the British Judicial Authorities according to the laws of Great Britain.

5. A Corean subject who commits in Corea any offence against a British subject shall be tried and punished by the Corean Authorities according to the laws of Corea.

6. Any complaint against a British subject involving a penalty or

confiscation by reason of any breach either of this Treaty or of any Regulation annexed thereto, or of any Regulation that may hereafter be made in virtue of its provisions shall be brought before the British Judicial Authorities for decision and any penalty imposed and all property confiscated in such cases shall belong to the Corean Government.

7. British goods when seized by the Corean Authorities at any open port shall be put under the seals of the Corean and the British Consular Authorities, and shall be detained by the former until the British Judicial Authorities, shall have given their decision. If this decision is in favour of the owner of the goods, they shall be immediately placed at the Consul's disposal. But the owner shall be allowed to receive them at once on depositing their value with the Corean Authorities pending the decision of the British Judicial Authorities.

8. In all cases whether civil or criminal, tried either in Corean or British Courts in Corea, a properly authorized official of the nationality of the plaintiff or prosecutor shall be allowed to attend the hearing and shall be treated with the courtesy due to his position. He shall be allowed, whenever he thinks it necessary to call, examine and cross examine witnesses and to protest against the proceedings or decision.

9. If a Corean subject who is charged with an offence against the laws of his country takes refuge on premises occupied by a British Subject, or on board a British Merchant vessel, the British Consular Authorities on receiving an application from the Corean Authorities, shall take steps to have such person arrested and handed over to the latter for trial. But without the consent of the proper British Consular Authority, no Corean officer shall enter the premises of any British subject without his consent or go on board any British ship without the consent of the officer in charge.

10. On the demand of any competent British Consular Authority, the Corean Authorities shall arrest and deliver to the former any British subject charged with a criminal offence and any deserter from a British ship of war or merchant vessel.

Art IV

1. The Ports of Chemulpo (Jinchuan), Wonsan (Gensan), and Pusan (Fusan) or if the latter port should not be approved, then such other port as may be selected in its neighbourhood, together with the city of Hanyang and the

town of Yang Hwa Chin, or such other place in that neighbourhood as may be deemed desirable, shall from the day on which this Treaty comes into operation, be opened to British Commerce.

2. At the above named places, British subjects shall have the right to rent or to purchase land or houses, and to erect dwellings, warehouses and factories. They shall be allowed the free exercise of their religion. All arrangements for the selection, determination of the limits and laying out of the sites of the foreign settlements, and for the sale of land at the various ports and places in Corea open to foreign trade, shall be made by the Corean Authorities in conjunctions with the competent foreign Authorities.

3. These sites shall be purchased from the owners and prepared for occupation by the Corean Government, and the expense thus incurred shall be a first charge on the proceeds of the sale of the land. The yearly rental agreed upon by the Corean Authorities in conjunction with the foreign Authorities shall be paid to the former, who shall retain a fixed amount thereof as a fair equivalent for the land tax, and the remainder together with any balance left from the proceeds of land sales, shall belong to a Municipal fund to be administered by a Council, the constitution of which shall be determined hereafter by the Corean Authorities in conjunction with the competent foreign Authorities.

4. British subjects may rent or purchase land or houses beyond the limits of the foreign settlements and within a distance of ten Corean li from the same. But all land so occupied shall be subject to such conditions as to the observance of Corean local regulations and payment of land tax as the Corean Authorities may see fit to impose.

5. The Corean Authorities will set apart free of cost, at each of the places open to trade, a suitable piece of ground as a foreign cemetery, upon which no rent land tax or other charge shall be payable, and the management of which shall be left to the Municipal Council above mentioned.

6. British subjects shall be allowed to go where they please without passports within a distance of 100 Corean li from any of the ports and places open to trade or within such limits as may be agreed upon between the competent Authorities of both Countries. British subjects are also authorized to travel in Corea for pleasure or for purposes of trade, to transport and sell goods of all kinds except books and other printed matter disapproved of by the Corean Government, and to purchase native produce in all parts of the country under

passports which will be issued by their Consuls and countersigned orsealed by the Corean local Authorities. These passports, if demanded, must be produced for examination in the districts passed through. If the passport be not irregular, the bearer will be allowed to proceed, and he shall be at liberty to procure such means of transport as he shall require. Any British subject travelling beyond the limits above named without a passport, or committing when in the interior any offence, shall be arrested and handed over to the nearest British Consul for punishment. Travelling without a passport beyond the said limits will render the offender liable to a fine not exceeding one hundred Mexican dollars with or without imprisonment for a term not exceeding one month.

7. British subjects in Corea shall be amenable to such Municipal Policies and other Regulations for the maintenance of peace order and good government as may be agreed upon by the competent Authorities of the two countries.

Art V

1. At each of the ports or places open to foreign trade British subjects shall be at full liberty to import from any foreign port, or from any Corean open port, to sell to, or to buy from, any Corean subject or others, and to export to any foreign or Corean open ports, all kinds of merchandise not prohibited by this Treaty, on paying the duties of the Tariff annexed thereto. They may freely transact their business with Corean subjects or others without the intervention of Corean officials or other persons, and they may freely engage in any industrial occupation.

2. The owners or consignees of all goods imported from any foreign port upon which the duty of the aforesaid Tariff shall have been paid shall be entitled on re exporting the same to any foreign port at any time within 13 Corean months of the date of importation to receive a drawback certificate for the amount of such import duty, provided that the original packages containing such goods remain intact. These drawback certificates shall either be redeemed by the Corean Customs on demand, or they shall be received in payment of duty at any Corean open port.

3. The duty paid on Corean goods when carried from the Corean open port to another, shall be refunded at the port of shipment on production of a Customs Certificate showing that the goods have arrived at the port of destination, or on satisfactory proof being produced of the loss of the goods by

shipwreck.

4. All goods imported into Corea by British subjects, and on which the duty of the Tariff annexed to this Treaty shall have been paid may be conveyed to any Corean open port free of duty, and, when transported into the interior shall not be subject to any additional tax, excise or transit duty whatsoever in any part of the Country. In like manner, full freedom shall be allowed for the transport to the open ports of all Corean Commodities intended for exportation, and such commodities shall not, either at the place of production or when being conveyed from any part of Corea to any of the open ports, be subject to the payment of any tax, excise or transit duty whatsoever.

5. The Corean Government may charter British merchant vessels for the conveyance of goods or passengers to unopened ports in Corea, and Corean subjects shall have the same right subject to the approval of their own authorities.

6. Whenever the Government of Corea shall have reason to apprehend scarcity of food within the Kingdom, H.M. the King of Corea may, by decree, temporarily, prohibit the export of grain to foreign countries from any or all of the Corean open ports, and such prohibition shall become binding on British subjects in Corea on the expiration of one month from the date on which it shall have been officially communicated by the Corean Authorities to the British Consul at the port concerned but shall not remain longer in force than is absolutely necessary.

7. All British ships shall pay tonnage dues at the rate of thirty cents (Mexican) per register ton. One such payment will entitle a vessel to visit any or all of the open ports in Corea during a period of four month without further charge. All tonnage dues shall be appropriated for the purposes of erecting lighthouses and beacons and placing buoys on the Corean Coast, more especially at the approaches to the open ports, and in deepening or otherwise improving the anchorages. No tonnage dues shall be charged on boats employed at the open ports in landing or shipping cargo.

8. In order to carry into effect and secure the observance of the provisions of this Treaty it is hereby agreed that the Tariff and Trade Regulations thereto annexed shall come into operation simultaneously with this Treaty. The competent Authorities of the two Countries may from time to time revise the said Regulations with a view to the insertion therein by mutual consent of such modification or additions as experience shall prove to be expedient.

Art VI

Any British subject who smuggles, or attempts to smuggle, goods into any Corean port or place not open to foreign trade shall forfeit twice the value of such goods, and the goods shall be confiscated. The Corean local Authorities may seize such goods, and may arrest any British subjects concerned in such smuggling or attempt to smuggle. They shall immediately forward any person so arrested to the nearest British Consul for trial by the proper British judicial Authority, and may detain such goods until the case shall have been finally adjudicated.

Art VII

1. If a British ship be wrecked or stranded on the Coast of Corea, the local authorities shall immediately take steps to protect the sp and her cargo from plunder and all the persons belonging to her from ill treatment, and to render such other assistance as may be required. They shall at once inform the nearest British Consul of the recurrence, and shall furnish the shipwrecked persons, if necessary, with means of conveyance to the nearest open port.

2. All expenses incurred by the Government of Corea for the rescue, clothing, maintenance, and travelling of shipwrecked British subjects, for the recovery of the bodies of the drowned, for the medicinal treatment of the sick and injured, and for the burial of the dead, shall be repaid by the British Government to that of Corea.

3. The British Government shall not be responsible for the repayment of the expenses incurred in the recovery or preservation of a wrecked vessel or the property belonging to her. All such expenses shall be a charge upon the property saved and shall be paid by the parties interested therein upon receiving delivery of the same.

4. No charge shall be made by the Government of Corea for the expenses of the Government officers, local functionaries or police, who shall proceed to the wreck for the travelling expenses of officers escorting the shipwrecked men, nor for the expenses of official correspondence. Such expenses shall be borne by the Corean Government.

5. Any British merchant ship compelled by stress of weather or want

of fuel or provisions to enter an unopened port in Corea shall be allowed to execute repairs and obtain necessary supplies. All such expenses shall be defrayed by the master of the vessel.

Art VIII

1. The ships of war of each country shall be at liberty to visit all the ports of the other. They shall enjoy every facility for procuring supplies of all kinds, or for making repairs, and shall not be subject to trade or harbour Regulations, not be liable to the payment of duties or port charges of any kind.

2. When British ships of war visit unopened ports in Corea, the officers and men may land, but shall not proceed into the interior unless they are provided with passports.

3. Supplies of all kinds for the use of the British navy may be landed at the open ports of Corea and stored in the custody of a British officer without the payment of any duty. But if any such supplies are sold, the purchaser shall pay the proper duty to the Corean Authorities.

4. The Corean Government will afford all the facilities in their power to ships belonging to the British Government which may be engaged in marking surveys in Corean waters.

Art IX

1. British Authorities and British subjects in Corea shall be allowed to employ Corean subjects as teachers, interpreters, servants or in any other lawful capacity, without any restriction on the part of the Corean Authorities, and in like manners, no restrictions shall be placed upon the employment of British subjects by Corean Authorities and subjects in any lawful capacity.

2. Subjects of either nationality who may proceed to the country of the other to study its language, literature, laws, arts or industries, or for the purpose of scientific research, shall to afforced every reasonable facility for doing so.

Art X

It is hereby stipulated that the Government, public offices and subjects of Her Britannic Majesty shall, from the day on which this Treaty comes into operation, participate in all privileges, immunities and advantages, especially in relation to import or export duties on goods and manufacturer, which shall thus have been granted or may thereafter be granted, by His Majesty, the King of Corea to the Government public officers or subjects of any other power.

Art XI

Ten years from the date on which this Treaty shall come into operation either of the High Contracting Parties may, on giving one year's previous notice to the other, demand a revision of the Treaty or of the Tariff annexed thereto, with a view to the insertion therein, by mutual consent, of such modifications as experience shall prove to be desirable.

Art XII

This Treaty is drawn up in the English and Chinese languages, both of which versions have the same meaning, but it is hereby agreed that any difference which may arise as to interpretation shall be determined by reference to the English text.
2. For the present all official communications addressed by the British Authorities to those of Corea shall be accompanied by a translation into Chinese.

Art XIII

The present Treaty shall be ratified by Her Majesty the Queen of the United Kingdom of Great Britain and Ireland, Empress of India, and by His Majesty the King of Corea under their hands and seals; the Ratifications shall be exchanged at Hanyang(Soul) as soon as possible or at latest within one year from the date of signature, and the Treaty which shall be published by both Governments, shall come into operation on the day on which the Ratifications are exchanged.
In witness whereof the respective Plenipotentiaries above named have signed the present Treaty and have thereto affixed their seals.
Done in triplicate at Hanyang this 26th day of November in the Year Eighteen hundred and eighty three, corresponding to the Twenty seventh day of

the tenth month of the Four hundred and ninety second year of the Corean Era, being the ninth year of the Chinese reign Kwang Hsu.

Signed
Harry S. Parkes
Min Yongmok

Regulations under which British Trade is to be conducted in Corea

I. Entrance and Clearance of vessels

1. Within forty-eight hours (exclusive of Sundays and holidays) after the arrival of a British ship in a Corean port, the Master shall deliver to the Corean Customs Authorities the receipt of the British Consul stating that he has deposited the Ship's papers at the British Consulate and he shall then make an entry of his ship by handing in a written paper stating the name of the ship, of the port from which she comes, of her master, the number and if required, the names of her passengers, her tonnage and the number of her crew, which paper shall be certified by the Master to be a true statement and shall be signed by him. He shall at the same time deposit a written manifest of his cargo, setting forth the marks and numbers of the packages and their contents as they are described in the Bills of Lading, with the names of the persons to whom they are consigned. The Master shall certify that this description is correct, and shall sign his name to the same. When a vessel has been duly entered, the Customs Authorities will issue a permit to open hatches which shall be exhibited to the Customs Officer on board. Breaking bulk without having obtained such permission will render the Master liable to a fine not exceeding one hundred Mexican dollars.

2. If any error is discovered in the manifest it may be corrected within twenty four hours (exclusive of Sundays and holidays) of its being handed in, without the payment of any fee, but for any alteration or port entry after that time, a fee of five Mexican dollars shall be paid.

3. Any Master who shall neglect to enter his vessel at the Corean Custom house within the time fixed by this regulation shall pay a penalty not exceeding

fifty Mexican dollars for every twenty four hours that he shall so neglect to enter his ship.

4. Any British vessel which remains in port for less than forty-eight hours (exclusive of Sundays and holidays) and does not open her hatches, also any vessel driven into port by stress of weather, or only in want of supplies, shall not be required to enter or to pay tonnage dues so long as such vessels does not engage in trade.

5. When the Master of a vessel wishes to cleared, he shall hand into the Customs Authorities an Export Manifest containing similar particulars to those given in the Import Manifest. The Customs Authorities will then issue a clearance certificate and return the Consul's receipt for the ships papers. These documents must be handed into the Consulate before the ship's papers are returned to the Master.

6. Should any ship leave the port without clearing outwards in the manner above prescribed, the Master shall be liable to a penalty not exceeding two hundred Mexican dollars.

7. British steamers may enter and clear on the same day, and they shall not be required to hand in a manifest except for such goods as are to be landed or transshipped at the port of entry.

II. Landing and Shipping of Cargo and payment of duties

1. The importer of any goods who desires to land them shall make and sign an application to that offset at the Customs house, stating his own name, the name of the ship in which the goods have been imported, the marks, numbers and contents of the packages and their values, and declaring that this statement is correct. The Customs Authorities may demand the production of the invoice of such consignment of merchandise. If it is not produced, or if its absence is not satisfactorily accounted for, the owner shall be allowed to land his goods on payment of double the Tariff duty but the surplus duty so levied shall refunded on the production of the invoice.

2. All goods so entered may be examined by the Customs officers at the places appointed for the purpose. Such examination shall be made without delay or injury to the merchandise, and the packages shall be at once restored by the Customs Authorities to their original conditions in so far as may be practicable.

3. Should the Customs Authorities consider the value of any goods paying an *ad valorem* duty as declared by the importer or exporter insufficient, they shall call upon him to pay duty on the value determined by an appraisement to be made by the Customs appraiser. But should the importer or exporter be dissatisfied with that appraisement, he shall within twenty four hours (exclusive of Sundays and holidays) state his reasons for such dissatisfaction to the Commissioner of Customs and shall appoint an appraiser of his own to make a re-appraisement. He shall then declare the value of the goods as determined by such re-appraisement. The Commissioner of Customs will thereupon at his option either assess the duty on the value determined by this re-appraisement, or will purchase the goods from the importer or exporter at the price thus determined with the addition of five per unit. In the latter case, the purchase money shall be paid to the importer or exporter within five days from the date on which he has declared the value determined by his own appraiser.

4. Upon all goods damaged on the voyage of importation a fair reduction of duty shall be allowed proportionate to their deterioration. If any disputes arise as to the amount of such reduction, they shall be settled in the manner pointed out in the preceding clause.

5. All goods intended to be imported shall be entered at the Corean Custom house before they are shipped. The application to ship shall be made in writing, and shall state the name of the vessel by which the goods are to be exported, the marks and number of packages, and the quantity, description, and value of the contents. The exporter shall certify in writing that the application gives a true account of all the goods contained therein and shall sign his name thereto.

6. No goods shall be landed or shipped at other places than those fixed by the Corean Customs Authorities, or between the hours of sunset and sunrise, or on Sundays or holidays without the special permission of the Customs Authorities, who will be entitled to reasonable fees for the extra duty thus performed.

7. Claims by importers or exporters for duties paid in excess; or by the Customs Authorities for duties which have not been fully paid, shall be entertained when made within thirty days from the date of payment.

8. No entry will be required in the case of provisions for the use of British ships, their crews and passengers, nor for the baggage of the latter which may be landed or shipped at any time after examination by the Customs officers.

9. Vessels needing repairs may land their cargo for that purpose without the payment of any duty. All goods so landed shall remain in charge of the Corean Authorities, and all just charges for storage, labour, and supervision, shall be paid by the Master. But if any portion of such cargo be sold the duties of the Tariff shall be paid on the portion so disposed of.

10. Any person desiring to transship cargo shall obtain a permit from the Customs Authorities before doing so.

III. Protection of the Revenue

1. The Customs Authorities shall have the right to place Customs officers on Board any British merchant vessel in their ports. All such Customs officers shall have access to all parts of the ship in which cargo is stowed. They shall be treated with civility, and such reasonable accommodation shall be allotted to them as the ship affords.

2. The hatches and all other places of entrance into that part of the ship where cargo is stowed may be secured by the Corean Customs officers between the hours of sunset and sunrise, and on Sundays and holidays, by affixing seals, locks, or other fastenings, and if any person shall, without due permission, willfully open any entrance that has been so secured, or break any seal, lock, or other fastening that has been affixed by the Corean Customs officers, not only the person so offending, but the master of the ship also, shall be liable to a penalty not exceeding one hundred Mexican dollars.

3. Any British subject who ships or attempts to ship, or discharges or attempts to discharge goods which have not been duly entered at the Custom house in the manner above provided, or packages containing goods different from those described in the import or export permit application, or prohibited goods, shall forfeit twice the value of such goods, and the goods shall be confiscated.

4. Any person signing a fake declaration or certificate with the intent to defraud the revenue of Corea shall be liable to a fine not exceeding two hundred Mexican dollars.

5. Any violation of any provision of these Regulations to which no penalty is especially attached herein may be punished by a fine not exceeding one hundred Mexican dollars.

Note. All documents required by these Regulations and all other communications addressed to the Corean Customs Authorities may be written in the English language.

Signed
Harry S. Parkes
Min Yongmok

Import Tariff
Classified according to rate of duty

Class I. Duty Free Goods

Agricultural Implements
Books, Maps and Charts
Bullion being gold and silver refined
Coins gold and silver
Fire Engines
Models of Inventions
Packing bags, Packing matting, tea lead and ropes for packing goods
Plants, Trees and shrubs of all kinds
Samples in reasonable quantities
Scientific Instruments, as physical, mathematical, meteorological and surgical instruments and their appliances.
Travellers baggage
Types, new and old.

Class II. Import Goods subject to an *ad valorem* duty of 5 per cent

Alum
Anchors and Chains
Bark for tanning
Bamboo, Split or not
Beans, peas, and pulse, all kinds

Bones

Bricks and Tiles

Camphor, crude

Cotton, raw

Drugs and medicines, all kinds

Fish, fresh

Flax, hemp and jute

Flints

Flour and meal, all kinds

Fruit, fresh, all kinds

Glue

Grain and corn, all kinds

Grains and manures, all kinds

Hides and skins, raw and undressed

Horns and hoofs, all kinds not otherwise provided for

Kerosene and petroleum, and other mineral oils

Lanterns, paper

Lime

Matches

Matting, Floor, Chinese and Japanese, [____] and common qualities

Meat, fresh

Metals, all kinds in pig, block, ingot, slab, bar, rod, plates, sheet, hoop, strip, bond and flat

T end angle iron, old and scrap iron

Oil can

Oil, wood (Sung gu)

Paper, common qualities

Pepper, unground

Pitch end tar

Ratans, slit or not

Seales and balances

Seeds, all kinds

Soap, common qualities Soy, Chinese and Japanese

Twine and Thread, all kinds except in silk

Umbrella, Paper

Vegetables, fresh, dried and salted

Wool, Sheeps, raw

Yarns, all kinds, in cotton, wool hemp

All unenumerated articles raw or unmanufactured.

Class III. Import goods subject to an *ad valorem* duty of 71/2 percent

Beverages, such as lemonade, ginger beer, soda and mineral waters

Blankets and rugs

Buttons, Buckles, books and eyes

Candles

Canvas

Carpets of Jute, hemp or felt patent tapestry

Charcoal

Chemicals, all kinds

Creams

Cement, as Portland and other kinds

Cordage and rope, all kinds and sizes

Clothing and wearing apparel of all kinds, hats, boots, shoes,

Cotton manufacturers, all kinds

Cotton and woolen mixtures, all kinds

Cotton and silk mixtures all kinds

Dyes, Colours, and paints, paint oils and materials used for mixing apints

Earthenware

Fans

Feathers Felt

Fish, dried and salted

Floor rugs, all kinds

Foil, tin, copper, and all other kinds except gold and silver

Fruits, dried, salted or preserved

Gem bages

Glass, window, plain and colored, all qualities

Grass cloth and all textiles in hemp, jute

Hair, all kinds except human

Hides and skins tanned and dressed

Isinglass, all kinds

Lamps, all kinds

Leather, all ordinary kinds, plain

Linen, linen and cotton, linen and woolen, linen and silk mixtures, grey, white or pointed

Matting, superior quality, Japanese tatamis

Meat, dried and salted

Metals, all kinds in pipe and tube, corrugated or galvanized, wire steel, implates, nickel, platinum, quicksilver, german silver, tutenegue or white copper, yellow metal, unrefined gold and silver

Metal manufactures, all kinds as nails, screws, tools, machinery, railway plant and hardware

Mosquito netting not made of silk

Needles and pins

Oils, vegetable all kinds

Oil and floor cloth, all kinds

Paper, all kinds not otherwise provided for

Planks, soft wood

Porcelain, common quality

Rosin

Salt

Sapan wood

Sea products as seaweed, beche le mer etc.

Silk, raw, reeled, thown, flors or waste

Silk manufactures not otherwise provided for

Spectacles

Spirits in jars

Stationary and writing materials of all kinds, blank books etc.

Stones and slate cut and dressed

Sugar, Brown and white, all qualities, molasses and syrups

Sulphur

Table stores, all kinds, and preserved provisions

Tullow

Tea

Umbrellas, cotton

Umbrella frames

Varnish

Vermiculite

Wax, bees or vegetable

Wax cloth

Woods and time, soft

Woollen manufactures, all kinds

Woollen and silk mixtures, all kinds

All unenumerated articles partly manufactured

    Class IV. Import goods subject to an *ad valorem* duty of ten percent

Beer, Portes, and cider

Camphor refined

Carmine

Carpets, superior qualities, as Brussells, Kiddermiester, and other kinds not enumerated

Clocks and parts thereof

Clothing made wholly of silk

Confectioneries and sweetments, all kinds

Explosives used for mixing and etc (imported under special permit)

Foil, gold and silver

Furniture of all kinds

Glass, plate, silvered or unsilvered, framed or unframed

Glass ware all kinds

Hair, human

India rubber manufactured or not

Leather, superior kinds, or stamped, figured or coloured

Leather manufactures, all kinds

Lacquered ware, common

Materials for seals etc.

Musical boxes

Musical instruments, all kinds

Mosquito netting made of silk

Paper, coloured, fancy, wall and hanging

Photographic apparatus

Planks hardwood

Plated ware, all kinds

Pictures, Prints, Photographs, Engravings, all kinds, framed or unframed

Porcelain, superior quality

Saddlery and harness

Silk thread and floss silk in skin

Silk manufactures, as graze, crape, Japanese amber lustering, satins, satin damasks, figured satins, Japanese white silk (hibutee)

Soap, superior qualities

Sugar candy

Telescopes and binocular glasses

Tooth powder

Trunks and portnenteaux

Umbrellas, silk

Vermilion

Watches and parts thereof in common metal, nickel or silver

Wines in wood or bottles, all kinds

Wood or timber, herd and all unenumerated Articles completely manufactured.

Class V. Import Goods subject to an *ad valorem* duty of 20 percent

Amber

Arms, firearms, fowling pieces etc imported under special permit

Artificial flowers

Birds nests

Carpets, velvet

Carriages

Cochineal

Coral, manufactured or not

Embroideries in gold, silver or silk

Enamel ware

Fireworks

Furs superior, as sible, sea otter, seal, otter, beaver etc

Ginseng, red white crude and clarified

Hair ornaments, gold and silver

Incense sticks

Ivory, manufactured or not

Jade ware

Jewelry, real or imitation

Incapered ware, superior
Musk
Pearls
Perfumes and scents
Plate, gold and silver
Precious stones
Rhinoceros horns
Scented woods, all kinds
Spices, all kinds
Spirits and liquers in wood or bottle, all kinds
Tobacco, all forms and kinds
Tortoise shell, manufactured or not
Velvet silk
Watches and parts thereof, in gold or gilt
Works of art

Class VI. Prohibited Goods

Adulterated drugs or medicines
Arms, munitions and implements of war, as ordinance or cannon, shot and shell, firearms of all kinds, cartridges, side arms, spears, or pikes, salt petre, gunpowder, gunchothon, dynamite, and other explosive substances. The Corean Authorities will grant special permits for the importation of arms firearms and ammunition for purposes of sport or self defence, on satisfactory proof being furnished to them of the bonifide character of the application.
Counterfeit coins, all kinds
Opium, except medicinal opium

Foreign ships when sold in Corea will pay a duty of twenty five cents per ton on sailing vessels and fifty cents per ton on steamers.

Export Tariff

Class I. Duty Free export Goods

Bullion being gold and silver refined
Coins, gold and silver, all kinds
Plants, trees and shrubs, all kinds
Samples in reasonable quantity
Travellers baggage

Class II

All other native good or productions, not commented in Class I, will pay an *ad valorem* duty of five per cent. The exportation of Red Ginseng is prohibited.

Rules

In the case of imported articles the *ad valorem* duties of this Tariff will be calculated on the actual cost of the goods at the place of production or fabrication, with the additions of freight, insurance etc. In the case of export articles the *ad valorem* duties will be calculated on market values in Corea.

Duties may be paid in Mexican dollars or Japanese silver yen.

The above Tariff of Import and Export Duties shall be converted as soon as possible, and as far as may be deemed desirable, into specific rates by agreement between the competent authorities of the two countries.

Signed
Harry S. Parkes
Min Yongmok

3. Hertslet Memorandum (1882. 12. 19)

Memorandum respecting Corea

THE question of establishing political and commercial relations with Corea first arose in 1854.

In August of that year Sir John Bowring, who was at that time Superintendent of British Trade in China and Governor of Hong Kong, addressed a despatch to Lord Clarendon upon the subject of Corea, in which he said -

"My attention has for some time been called to the Kingdom of Corea, as one of those hitherto in accessible regions, which, by the force of present circumstances and the irresistible pressure of future events, must ere long be opened to the commercial enterprise of Western nations, and I hope to induce your Lordship to move Her Majesty to honor me with Plenipotentiary powers, which may enable me, should a favourable opportunity present itself, to establish commercial relations with the Corean people.

"The country is in a state of great degradation and misery, and I cannot convey to your Lordship a more lively picture of the condition of Corea than will be found in an extract from a Latin letter(which was inclosed) written by a native Corean, who has visited Europe under the protection of the Propaganda, and who has returned to his country, in which the Catholic missionaries have again reestablished themselves, after an exclusion of nearly thirteen years.

"There is reason to believe that the Russian Government has been long looking with an ambitious and covetous eye upon the Corean territory, and that the presence of the Russian fleet in these seas, the movement down the River Amoor, and the depôt lately established in Saga-lien, have been co-operative to view upon Corea.

"The population is believed to amount to about 10,000,000 souls, of which 200,000 inhabit Seoul, the capital city.

"There is a nominal dependence upon China, very similar to that recognized by Siam and Cochin China. Tribute is regularly sent. Acts of submission are from time to time recorded: but the Chinese Government exercise no real authority, and seems never to interfere with the jurisdiction of Corean functionaries. The authority of the King is absolute, so absolute that high officers of the Crown destroy themselves on receiving the Royal Order to commit suicide, even by slow process of starvation.

"I am informed there would be a considerable demand for white cotton goods were their importation allowed, but all communication with foreigners is most strictly prohibited. The ordinary dresses of the people are made of home-manufactured silk, cotton, and flax. Woollen garments unknown. Corea is celebrated for the production of a paper strong enough for garments, which I have seen exposed for sale in China.

"Two principal factions are said to divide all authority and influence beyond the Court circle. The Nobles are oppressive, and the people trodden down. Communication are difficult: bad roads and few navigable rivers.

"The precious metals are rarely seen, and all payments are made in Chinese cash. The rate of interest inordinately high, 30 per cent. per annum being the minimum value of money."

In compliance with the request contained in this despatch, full powers were forwarded to Sir J. Bowring to enable him to conclude a Treaty with Corea, but he was at the same time informed by Lord Clarendon that "so little was known concerning that country, its produce and inhabitants, that it was difficult to form any opinion as to the advantages to be derived from such a Treaty as he contemplated, but that it could scarcely be anticipated that it would lead to any very important results."

On receipt of these full powers, Sir J. Bowring admitted that he did not see any probability at that moment of his being able to employ them for the protection and advancement of British interests unless Corea should become a field where Russian ambition might seek development: and a few months afterwards he reported that he had been informed by Catholic missionaries that the Russian Government had opened communications with the Corean authorities, with a view to the obtaining a Treaty of Amity and Commerce; but he added that he had heard, generally, that the negotiations had led to no result.

It may here be mentioned incidentally that in 1855 the French frigate "Virginie" surveyed a part of the Corean Coast in the neighbourhood of the Seoul River.

In October 1865 Mr. Morrison visited the west coast of Corea, He found the people nowhere hostile, and at one place, where most of the smuggling trade with China was carried on, very friendly. The English gun-boat was, however, refused supplies all along the coast.

Mr. Morrison reported that the smugglers imported into Corea shirtings, drills (a favorite article with the Coreans), camlets, opium, sugar, satin, and tortoise-shell; and exported ginseng, salt, fish, gold, iron and steel, timber, leather, paper, cotton, and rice.

He also said that resin abounded in the Corea in a crude state, but was not an article of trade, and that the cotton was very favourably spoken of by the Chinese.

In sending home a copy of Mr. Morrison's Report, Mr. Wade said that, on reading it, it had occurred to him that it might be of advantage to British trade to establish commercial relations with Corea.

The French Roman Catholic missionaries were at this time very jealous of the Russian proceedings on the north-east coast of Corea, but Mr. Wade remarked that if there were on foot any designs worth frustration, they would be most surely frustrated by the opening of the coast, and that, as a survey of the coast would, in his opinion, be the best means of familiarizing the people with the presence of Englishmen, and of obtaining the preliminary knowledge essential to any further advances, he had addressed a letter to the Prince of Kung with reference to the refusal of the Corean people to supply provisions to one of Her Majesty's gun-boats.

In this letter he said: -

"I have just been informed that one of Her Majesty's gun-boats, while cruizing a short time since along the west coast of Corea, was refused provisions, the people alleging that they could not sell any without incurring the displeasure of their authorities.

"I trust that the Imperial Government may be enabled to prevent the recurrence of such acts of discourtesy. There is no European who desires to see Eastern nations preserve their independence that does not deplore their adherence to a system of non-intercourse, commercial or political, which it rests with any Western Power that may find a pretext for resorting to force to subvert, and the subversion of which by any single Power would probably be followed, as we have seen in Cochin China, by the subjugation or repartition of the offending State. If the Kingdom of Corea understood its own interests, it would at once invite all foreign nations to trade with it. But ever if it be so ill-advised as still to entertain its interdict on foreign commerce, it should at least be careful not to affront a Naval Power by conduct such as that to which I have requested your Imperial Highness' attention."

Mr. Wade said, however, that" he had not come straight to the point with His Highness, because, although the vassalage of the King or Corea was complete, the Emperor of China had no resident at his Court, and Chinese Ministers were always careful to proclaim, when Corea was alluded to, that she governed herself, and that China did [not?] interfere in her internal economy."

Sir R. Alcock was then instructed, at the request of the Admiralty, to use his influence in order to obtain for Her Majesty's surveying vessel, which was about to proceed to the northern portion of the Chinese Seas, facilities for the examination of the coasts of the Corea.

Sir R. Alcock accordingly address a note to the Prince of Kung, in which he reminded him of what had occurred n October 1865, when one of Her Majesty's gun-boats was refused provisions, and expressed a hope that the influence of His Imperial Highness would be exerted to prevent the recurrence of a proceeding so inhospitable in itself, and so calculated to imperil the interests of peace.

To this note the Prince of Kung replied that the French were about to commence hostilities against Corea, and that when, in the previous year, the Yamên of foreign Affairs was applied to by the French Minister, M. Barthémy, to inform Corea that missionaries wanted to enter that country, it became the Prince's duty to tell him that, "although Corea was a dependence [of China], she had never been so otherwise that as a nation accepting the Calendar of China, and periodically bringing tribute; "that her adoption of Christianity being a question in which China, consequently, could not constrain her, it would not be possible for China to take on herself to write officially to the Corea respecting the missionaries, and the Prince added that "it would at that moment be more difficult than ever for the Yamên of Foreign Affairs to write to Corea regarding the intention of the British Government to send a surveying vessel to her coasts."

In May 1866 Mr. C. Alabaster sent home a Private and Confidential Memorandum, in which he reported that certain agents of the house of Jardine, Mathison, and Co. had gone in a steam-vessel, the "Glengyle," to a port in Corea, with a view to opening direct trade with that country.

Mr. Alabaster said these agents were provided with presents for the King of Corea, "and that they had succeeded in opening communications with the authorities, whom they interested with a list of musical boxes, China silks, &c., intended for the King, but that they did not wait for an answer from the Court, as it would take twenty days to procure it, but that they purposed returning.

The Mandarins, it appears, expressed great alarm on the arrival of the "Glengyle," which they at first imagined to be a vessel of war, and made great objections to the receipt of the letter for the Court, but at once offered supplies: and that the chief local authority, described as equal in rank to a Taotai, was eventually induced to visit the vessel.

The people were said to be very well disposed, but to live in great dread of the Mandarins, who, in their turn, appeared to stand in great awe of the Supreme Government.

Mr. Alabaster then gave a description of the trade which it was proposed to open.

On receipt of this Memorandum, Sir R. Alcock was instructed to consider and report whether it would be advisable or practicable to make a Treaty with Corea, and if so, how it had better be done. To this he replied, in October following, that, under the existing circumstances, it was undesirable to attempt to enter into any negotiations with a view to making a Treaty with the King of Corea. Her Majesty's Government entirely concurred with Sir R. Alcock in this view, but full powers were shortly afterwards sent to him, constituting and appointing him Her Majesty's Plenipotentiary for negotiating with the King of Corea in the event of an opportunity offering itself.

It may here be mentioned that the following were the views entertained at this time by Dr. Winchester, Her Majesty's Consul at Shanghae, with regard to Corea: -

In a letter to Mr. Hammond he said: -

"Corea is of more geographical and political importance than commercial. Still, even in a trading point of view, its relations may ultimately prove considerable.

"Corea, like Loo Chew, oscillates between the two Great Powers who are its nearest neighbours, China and Japan, and manages, by a few compliances, to maintain a tolerably effective independence. On the north-west coast the Chinese influence is felt, on the south-west that of Japan.

"I suppose the Shetlanders of the 15th and 16th centuries were as much Canes as Scotch.

"The conditions of Government in a country so peculiarly situated must be an interesting study."

It was in this year (1866) that certain events occurred which brought the question of Corea more prominently forward.

In February the King of Corea received intelligence that the Russians had crossed his frontier, and were holding intercourse with his subjects.

At the same time, a Corean Embassy which had been sent to China informed their Sovereign that the Chinese had murdered two Catholic missionaries, and that it would be well to imitate their example. Upon this a general order was given to carry out a persecution against the Christian Churches.

Two French Bishops and seven priests were accordingly arrested, and, after having been cruelly tortured, were beheaded. Many other Christians were murdered, others were ordered to renounce their faith, some (including three French missionaries) succeeded in making their escape; bit the property of the Christians and of their Churches was utterly destroyed.

The Chinese Government at once declined all responsibility for these outranges, and expressed their intention to remain neutral in the event of steps being taken to obtain redress and enforce the punishment of those concerned in them.

As soon as the news of the outrages reached the French authorities, a naval force was ordered to be fitted out for the Corea.

This expedition left Chefoo in September of October 1866. A landing was effected at Kanghoa, a town, capable of holding from 20,000 to 30,000 inhabitants, which was captured without resistance. After a few day's unsuccessful negotiations with the Coreans, the French advanced towards Seoul, the capital, but they were opposed at a certain point on the river, and, although they drove the Coreans from their positions, still, as the whole country rose to oppose them, and a Siberian winter was setting in, the pursuit was abandoned, and the French troops make their way back to the place where they had landed, burning villages and destroying Government property on the way to the extent of some millions of dollars. All the French vessels of war then returned to Chefoo.

On the 2nd September of the same year an American schooner, the "General Sherman," was wrecked on the Corean coast, when all the crew and passengers, among whom were two British subject, were murdered, with the exception of a missionary (Mr. Thomas) who had previously visited the country, and who was reported to have escaped.

In sending home a report of this massacre, Sir R. Alcock said that there was little doubt that this vessel, which nominally cleared from Tien-tsin with a cargo for Papiette, the nearest Russian port, and freighted with sundries by an English merchant, was in reality destined for the Corean coast, where it was lost, and that it went there for the purpose of trading in a country where all trade of intercourse with foreigners was strictly prohibited under penalty of death.

In fact, Mr. Seward admitted that the vessel was engaged in carrying munitions of war, with the intention of aiding the Coreans in resisting the attempt of the French to obtain satisfaction for the murder of their missionaries; and in a conversation which passed between Mr. Seward and the British, French, and German Ministers at Washington on the subject, the view generally entertained was in favour of the Americans attempting, in the first instance, to come to an understanding with the Coreans through the good offices of the Chinese Government.

Sir R. Alcock subsequently addressed a note to the (Chinese) Tsung-li Yamê-n in which he expressed a hope that in the event of the two Englishmen who were on board the "General Sherman" being still alive and detained in prison by the Coreans, they might be released and forwarded to Pecking; to which the Tsung-li Yamên replied that there were no English captives in Corea; that it was the custom of the Coreans to succour and relieve shipwrecked sailors; but he added that, "although Corea was tributary to China, yet it was independent in its Government and entire master of its own actions, with which China never interfered."

In March 1868 Mr. Aston made a Report to Sir H.S. Parkes upon the subject of Corea, in which he said that the Japanese asserted that they possessed great influence in Corea. That this influence, they said, rested on the two conquests of Corea by Japan, since the latter of which, three hundred years ago, their relations with that country had been maintained without interruption, and also on the acknowledged superiority of the Japanese civilization; and that they maintained that Corea was still, in a certain sense, under Japanese protection.

Upon this assertion, Mr. Aston remarked that the Japanese trade with Corea was under the control for the Japanese officials, who treated the Corean merchants with great indignity, driving them out of their settlements as soon as the market was over; although, he added, a precisely similar course was pursued by the Corean officials towards Chinese merchants at the fairs on the Chinese frontier.

In May 1868 another incident occurred, which it may be as well to place on record.

A subject of the North German Confederation, named Ernest Oppert, hired a Prussian vessel, the "China," at Shanghae, shipped on boared of her 21 Manilamen, 7 English sailors, 1 American, and over 100 Chinese, with arms and digging tools. The vessel then went to Nagasaki, where she also took on boared a French priest, and then proceeded under the guidance of this so-called French missionary to the coast of Corea, and there made an armed descent with intent to rifle a King's tomb in which it was reported great treasure lay buried. Fortunately this nefarious and buccaneering expedition ended in disaster rater than booty. Attacking without scruple the Coreans whom they found in their path, and being attacked in return by a larger body, they had to throw away their arms and escape as best they could.

The Prussian Representatives at Peking would appear not to have acted with adequate energy in the affair, and a correspondence passed between Sir R. Alcock and Baron Rehfues upon the subject. Sir R. Alcock informed Baron Rehfues, in one of his letters, that the violation of the Corean territory by subjects of ships under the Prussian flag, was calculated to inflict discredit on European nationalities in general, and was not free from danger to all. He alluded to the hostilities which had shortly before taken place between the French and the Coreans, as well as to the case of the American vessel "General Sherman," and he then remarked to Baron Rehfues that if proceedings such as those undertaken by Oppert were allowed to pass without steps being publicly taken to vindicate the laws so signally outraged, the crew of no European ship that might thereafter be wrecked on the Corean coast could have any hope of escaping ill-treatment or death; whereas before, a shipwrecked drew had been most humanely treated and sent back to China by the Corean authorities.

An American citizen who took part in the expedition was tried before the United States' Consul-General and Assessors at Shanghae, but in sending home a Report of the trial, Sir R. Alcock expressed his regret that justice should have again failed to overtake evident and notorious guilt.

In September 1868 a copy of a Report which had been addressed to the Admiralty by Vice-Admiral Sir Henry Keppel, giving an account of a visit which he had recently made to Russian Tartary was received at this Office from

Sir R. Alcock, and in his despatch forwarding it, he observed that the general drift of all Sir Henry Keppel's observations tended to confirm the very common belief that Russia contemplated, as time and opportunity might serve, to absorb Corea and obtain a port or ports further south than Papiette, which was liable to be frozen over in serve winter.

Shortly after this it was reported that the French expedition had excited a strong feeling in Corea against foreigners generally, one result of which had been the expulsion of the Russians from the Broughton Bay Settlement and the destruction of their settlement boats and other property; that a collision had taken place between the Russian gun-boat "Loble" and Corean soldiers in the neighborhood of the Seoul River, resulting in the bombardment of a Corean town.

In July 1869 a letter was received from the Admiralty inclosing a Report from Vice-Admiral Sir Henry Keppel stating that he had been credibly although unofficially informed that on the 18th May an American expedition consisting of nine vessels had left Shanghae for the Corea, ostensibly to demand satisfaction for the murder of the crew of the "General Sherman," but with the supposed object of opening the country and of obtaining a port.

Nothing further was reported respecting this expedition; but on the 16th May, 1871, an expedition to the Corea was undertaken by the United States' squadron in the Chinese Seas commanded by Admiral Rogers, and accompanied by Mr. Low, the United states' Minister to China.

Before leaving Pecking, Mr. Low have full information to the Chinese Government on the subject of his proposed expedition.

About the 28th May it reached the outlet of the river on which Seoul, the capital, is situated.

On the 1st June two of the vessels composing the expedition proceeded up the river accompanied by four steam-launches, passing forts on either side, and not anticipating any opposition, but on reaching a sharp and narrow bend in the river which was commanded by guns on both sides, a heavy fire was suddenly opened upon them by the Americans and with such precision that the Corean forts were silenced after a few rounds; but not deeming it advisable to proceed further without reinforcements the American vessels descended the river.

In July 1875 it was reported that difficulties were arising between Japan and Corea; that Russia and Japan had come to an understanding with regard to an attack on Corea; and that Japanese and German vessels were surveying the west coast; and, in view of the important events which it was thought would be likely to take place in those seas, it was suggested by Sir H.S. Parkes and Admiral Ryder that Port Hamilton should be occupied by a British force.

Port Hamilton is a spacious and well-sheltered harbour, formed by a group of three small islands off the south end of Corea, and its position is considered to be the key to the Corean Strait. It was first visited by Europeans in 1845, when Sir E. Belcher surveyed it, and gave it the name of the then Secretary of the Admiralty. At this time (1875) it was occupied by a few Coreans.

Lord The Earl of Derby was, however, of opinion that it was not desirable to set to other nations the example of occupying places to which Great Britain had no title, and Sir H.S. Parkes was so informed.

In September following, the Japanese gun-boat "Unyokan" was fired upon by the Coreans. This led to negotiations for the conclusion of a Treaty for the opening of one or more of the Corean ports to Japanese, as well as of vessels driven into port by stress of weather; and for explanation of the attack upon the "Unyokan."

The Tsung-li Yamên informed Sir Thomas Wade that China would not interfere in the Corean question, and on the 27th February, 1876, a Treaty was concluded between Japan and Corea, which was published by the Japanese on the 25th of the same mouth; the 1st Article ran as follows; —

"Chôsen, being an independent State, enjoys the same sovereign right as does Japan."

In alluding to this Article Sir H.S. Parkes observed; " I learn that this Article, which was naturally acceptable to the Coreans, is also valued by the Japanese (by whom it was suggested), as denoting the Corea in independent of China.

In October 1876 a Supplementary Treaty to the "Treaty of Friendship and Trade Regulations" of the 26th February, 1876, was concluded between Japan and Corea.

These "Additional Article" as they were also called, related to a variety of subjects, and contained this clause relating to foreign vessels stranded on the coast or driven into Corean ports by stress of weather; —

"Article X

"Although no relations as yet exist between Corea and Foreign countries, yet Japan has, for many years back, maintained friendly relations with them; it is therefore natural that in case a vessel of any of the countries of which Japan thus cultivates the friendship, should be stranded by stress of weather or otherwise on the coast of Corea, those on board shall be treated with kindness by Corean subjects; and should such persons ask to be sent back to their homes, they shall be delivered over by the Corean Government to an Agent of the Japanese Government residing at one of the open ports of Corea, requesting him to send them back to their native countries, which request the Agent shall never fail to comply with."

In May of the present year the United States entered into negotiation with the Corean Government for the conclusion of a Treaty of Amity and Commerce, and although a Treaty was eventually signed, it would appear that it is not likely to be ratified by the United States' Congress.

The first Article, as it appeared in the draft of the Treaty, ran as follows;

"Corea is a dependency of China, but has always been autonomous as regards both internal government and foreign relation. Corea and America having mutually agreed that the King of Corea enters into this Treaty in accordance with international law relating to autonomy, the latter undertakes to carry it out faithfully, while the President of th United States will not interfere with Corea's relationship of dependency on China."

But as this Article gave considerable umbrage to the Japanese, it was omitted from the Treaty signed by Commodore Shufeldt, and transferred to a letter from the King of Corea to the President of the United States. In this letter (dated the 24th May, 1882) the King said; —

"Although it is the case that Corea has been so far a vassal of China, the entire conduct of her internal affairs and of her foreign relations remains in her own hands, as an independent Sovereign State.

Corea is now concluding a Treaty of Amity and Commerce with the United States, and commission has been given to the States Councillor Shên Hsien, as Minister Plenipotentiary, and to the States Councillor Chin Hung-chi, as his Deputy, to proceed to Jên Shan and conclude the matter.

His Corean Majesty distinctly pledges himself to accept and observe the provisions of the Treaty, in accordance with international law, as binding upon independent Sovereign States.

"With regard to Corea's being vassal to China, America has absolutely no concern with whatever obligations Corea may be under in this respect."

On the 6th, June Vice-Admiral Willes, acting under instructions which he had received from the Admiralty to watch the proceedings of the Americans at Corea and to secure the advantages of the most-favoured nation for this country, in the event of the Americans concluding a Treaty with the Coreans, succeeded in concluding a Treaty to that effect with the Representatives of the King — (but which has not yet been ratified)

As in the case of the American Treaty, no reference was made to the dependency of Corea on China, but the King addressed a letter to the Queen (dated the 30th May, 1882), in which His Majesty said: —

"The King of Great Chôsen makes a communication.

"He begs to say, as regards Chôsen, that it is simply a dependency of China, but that its internal administration and its external intercourse are entirely and in all respects within his discretion and control as an independent King. In now making a Treaty with each other, the States of Great Chôsen and Great England shall conduct their intercourse in every respect on the footing of equality. The King of Great Chôsen expresses his willingness that all the stipulations of the proposed Treaty shall be arranged in strict accordance with the international usage of independent States. On the other hand, Great Chôsen, being a dependency of China, shall fully discharge in all particulars the duties of that relation, but this shall in no wise affect of concern Great England. Moreover, before Deputies are appointed to negotiate the Treaty (he) has deemed it incumbent to set forth clearly, as above, his position, and he begs the Queen of Great England that the matter may be arranged on the understanding herein above set forth."

In forwarding home this Treaty, Admiral Willes said; —

"The Government [of Corea] is vested in the King as an absolute monarch. He calls to his assistance a Board of Councillors. At the present moment there are two parties in the state, of almost equal strength; The one is Progressist, headed by the King and ready and anxious to admit foreign intercourse, the other entirely opposed to any such policy.

In a private letter to Lord Tenterden Sir H.S. Parkes made the following remarks on this Treaty. He said; —

"This and the American Treaty are believed here to be Li Hung Chang's work. Besides opening Corea to the Western Powers, which has become essential to the security of China, there is, I fancy, much in these Treaties which is intended to the address of Western Powers in China, as well as to that of Japan. The declaration of dependency on China is a *tu quoque* to Japan for having persuaded Corea to declare herself independent in the Japan Treaty, and for Japan's action in Loochoo. It may also be intended to guard against Corea acting wholly independently of China, as Siam has done. How we are to recognize this quasi-de-pendent condition, and at the same time to treat Corea as an equal, the King being placed on the same footing as the Queen, appears to me rather a puzzling problem. This declared suzerainty will be annoying to Russia and Japan, and will promote the aim of the former to attach the latter to her interests."

In a later despatch Sir H.S. Parkes sent home another translation of the letter said to have been addressed by the King of the Corea to the president of the United States, and in doing so he observed that it was noteworthy that it appeared in the Chinese vernacular press at a date which afforded good ground for the conclusion that it was drafted at Tien-tsin and taken by Commodore Shufeldt to Corea, in order that the King might be allowed the option of acknowledging his dependency on China, either in the Treaty or in the form of a letter to the Sovereigns with whom he was treating.

The following is the translation of the letter from the King, which was went home by Sir H.S. Parkes; –

"The King of Corea acknowledges that Corea is a tributary to China, but, in regard to both foreign policy and domestic legislation, it enjoys full independence. Now, as we wish to establish Treaty relations between Corea and the United States, we hereby appoint his Excellency Shên and the Assistant Chin, as above described, to repair to Jen-shan, to confer upon the matter with due caution; and the King of Corea distinctly undertakes, on his own responsibility, to carry out the Articles contained in the Treaty that shall be made, to which both parties must conform. As regards the tributary relations subsisting between Corea and China, these have nothing to do with the United States."

It will be observed that in one of these letters Corea is spoken of as being a vassal of China; in another of its being a "dependency;" and in another of its being a tributary to China.

On the 8th July a Treaty was concluded between Germany and Corea containing stipulations similar to those which were embodied in the American and English Treaties; but it has not yet been ratified, so far as I am aware.

Shortly after these Treaties and letters, above referred to, were signed, an event occurred which brought the question of the Corea still more prominently to public notice.

On the 23rd July last an attack was made on the Japanese Legation in Corea. Several of the members of the Japanese Legation were wounded, and of the police escort two were killed and three were wounded; and the Minister and twenty-six of his staff escaped on board the British surveying ship, and were landed at Nagasaki. The Japanese Minister for Foreign Affairs expressed to Sir H.S. Parkes his belief that the anti-foreigner party had risen against the King for concluding foreign Treaties.

This was followed by the news that the Government of Corea had been overthrown, that the Queen and many leading statesmen and Japanese officers in Corean service had been murdered, and that the father of the King who was hostile to foreigners had seized the Government.

In commenting upon these events, Sir H.S. Parkes said the Japanese Government feared that disorder in Corea might attract intervention either from a powerful Western nation, whose frontier was conterminous to Corea, or from China, who had just then given evidence of a readiness to interfere by sending to that country a force of ten gun-boats and 1,000 troops (which was afterwards increased to 2,000 and then to 30,000), together with a Chinese Commissioner escorted by three vessels; but that the principal desire of the Japanese Government was to be allowed to obtain themselves from Corea, and without recourse to force, reparation for the injuries which had been caused to Japan by the uncontrollable enmity for each other of the rival Corean factions.

On the arrival of the Chinese troops they at once entered the capital (23rd August), and a Proclamation having been issued by the Chinese Commissioners declaring that, as "Corea was a dependency of China, the Emperor had determined to put a stop to the terrible disorders and unheard-of scenes of butchery which had occurred there,' they proceeded to arrest the chief ringleader, the King's father and ex-Regent, Tai-wŏn-Kun, and to send him to Tien-tsin, at which place he was sentenced by the Chinese to remain for ever, and never to be allowed to return to his native country.

The Chinese Minister at Tôkiô, however, informed the Japanese Minister for Foreign Affairs, under instructions from his Government, that as China regarded Corea as a dependency, they considered it their duty to require the Corean Government to afford satisfaction to that of Japan, and also to see that the Japanese Legation at Seoul was adequately protected.

Sir H.S. Parkes then went on to recount the conversation which he had had with the Japanese Minister for Foreign Affairs upon the general question. He said;

"Japan only knew Corea as an independent State, which she was declared to be in the 1st Article of her Treaty with Japan. China had never objected to that declaration, she had never attempted to intervene in the differences which had occurred between Japan and Corea before that Treaty was signed in 1876, and, until this moment, she had never conveyed any intimation to Japan that relations of dependency existed between her and Corea. China had also ignored all responsibility for Corea when difficulties arose between that country and France in 1866, and again with the United States in 1871. Although Japan might not be disposed to insist that the complete independency of Corea, as declared by Treaty, should be maintained, if the Corean nation desired to exchange that position for one of dependency on China, still, the Japanese Government could not admit the right of China to interfere at this juncture. They would, therefore, claim to be allowed to settle pending questions by themselves alone, but would be willing to enter subsequently on the consideration of the relations between China and Corea, if the Chinese government so desired. The latter question, the Foreign Minister added, was one which, if it were raised by China, would not only concern Japan, but also the European Powers who had recently concluded Treaties with Corea, and China would have to reconcile any position she might assume with the declarations which the Foreign Minister understood had been made to those Powers by Corea that she possessed independent autonomy in all her external as well as internal affairs. Japan would, therefore, seek the opinions for those Powers, and would endeavour to conform her action to the course they deemed it expedient to adopt after full investigation had been made into the subject, and the respective responsibilities of China and Corea had been clearly ascertained and defined."

The Japanese also sent a force consisting of 10,000 men to Corea, accompanied by a Japanese Minister (Mr. Hanabusa), who arrived at Seoul on the 16th August, and was received by the King on the 20th. Negotiations ensued, and on the 30th August a Convention was concluded between Japan and Corea, whereby it was agreed that the ringleaders of the attack on the Japanese Legation should be severely punished; that a public funeral should take place of the Japanese who fell victims to that attack, as well as those who were otherwise murdered Japanese; that Japanese troops should be stationed at the capital for the protection of the Legation, to be withdrawn at the end of a year at the discretion of the Japanese Minister; that a special Envoy should be sent to Japan with a Royal letter of apology; that the Treaty limits of the three open ports should be extended; that Yokachin (a town in the immediate vicinity of the capital) should be opened to trade in one year; and that Japanese Diplomatic and Consular officers, with their families and servants, should be free to travel throughout the interior on passports issued by the local authorities and to be properly escorted. In consequence of these proceedings on the part of the Chinese, the question is now asked whether Corea is regarded by Her Majesty's Government as an independent State or as a dependency of China.

The Japanese view of the question is fully discussed in extracts from Japanese newspapers sent home by Sir H.S. Parkes, whilst the Chinese view is given in the "Peking Gazette" sent home by Mr. Grosvenor, but to attempt to epistomise these documents would extend this paper to an inconvenient length, and it has been thought sufficient, therefore, to summarize the facts recorded in the preceding pages of this Memorandum.

SUMMARY

Corean View of the Question.

There is no doubt that the Coreans pay tribute periodically to China, and comply with certain ceremonial observances.

On the 27th February, 1876, they concluded a Treaty with Japan, and recorded therein that they were an independent State.

In May 1882 they concluded a Treaty with the United States, and on the 24th of the same month the King of Corea wrote a letter to the president of the United States, in which he said; "Although it is the case that Corea has been so far a vassal of China, the entire conduct of her internal affairs, and of her foreign relations, remains in her own hands as an independent Sovereign State," and His Majesty added that with regard to Corea being a vassal to China, America had absolutely no concern with whatever obligation Corea might be under in this respect.

On the 6th June last Corea concluded a Treaty with the English Admiral Willes, and in a letter written by the King to Her Majesty at the time of its conclusion, the King said, "As regards Chôsen, it is simply a dependency of China, but its internal administration and its external intercourse are entirely, and in all respects, within his discretion and control as an independent King;" and His Majesty added that although Great Chôsen, being a dependency of China, would fully discharge, in all particulars, the duties of those relations, they would in no wise affect Great Britain.

On the 30th August, 1882 Corea concluded a Treaty with Germany.

And so recently as October last the leader of the Liberal party in Corea, who accompanied the Corean Mission to Japan, informed Sir H.S. Parkes that they were an independent nation; they denied the right of China to interfere in the way in which they had recently done in the internal affairs of their country, and declared that the tributary relations of Corea to China were confined to certain ceremonial observances; although these statements scarcely harmonize with the recent attitude of the King towards the Chinese Emperor.

Japanese View of the Question.

The Japanese have at times declared that they possessed great influence in Corea; and so recently as 1868 they asserted that Corea had for a very long period been, in a certain sense, under their protection. It is a fact that there has existed a Japanese official settlement or establishment at Sorio, in Fusan; but, on the 27th February, 1876, a Treaty was concluded between Japan and Corea, in which Corea was recognized as an independent State, and as enjoying the same sovereign right as Japan herself; and in August last the Japanese Minister for Foreign Affairs informed Sir H.S. Parkes that "Japan only recognized Corea as an independent State;" and on the 30th of the same month another Treaty was concluded between Japan and Corea.

Chinese View of the Question.

The Chinese also have generally been believed to possess great influence over Corea; but they have declared (until this year) that Corean governed herself, and that China did not interfere in her internal economy.

In 1865 they informed the French that, although Corea was a dependency of China, she had never been so otherwise than as a nation accepting the calendar of China, and periodically bringing tribute.

In the same year they refused to write to Corea regarding the intention of the British Government to send a surveying ship to their coasts.

In the same year they declined all responsibility with regard to the murder, by the Coreans, of the French missionaries and the destruction of the property of the Christians, and expressed their intention to remain neutral in the event of steps being taken to obtain redress and enforce the punishment of those concerned in those outrages.

In 1868, when the American schooner General Sherman was wrecked on the Corean coast, and the passengers and crew murdered, the Chinese declared that "although Corea was tributary to China, yet that it was independent in its government and entire master of its own actions, with which China never interfered."

In 1875, when differences arose between Japan and Corea, and a Japanese gun-boat was fired upon by the Coreans, the Chinese Government declared that it would not interfere in the Corean question.

But on the occasion of the attack made in July last on the Japanese Legation in Corea, the Chinese Government, contrary to the policy which she had pursued during recent years, at once interfered and sent a naval and military expedition to Corea to restore order, and they informed the Japanese Minister for Foreign affairs that they had done so because "China regarded Corea as a dependency."

Views of British Authorities and others on the Question.

The following are the view entertained by others with regard to the independence of Corea:

In 1854 Sir John Bowring said that there was a nominal dependence of Corea upon China; that tribute was regularly sent; that acts of submission were from time to time accorded, but that the Chinese Government exercised no real authority.

In 1865 Mr. Wade said that although the vassalage of the King of Corea was complete, yet that the Chinese Ministers always proclaimed, when Corea was alluded to, that she governed herself, and that China did not interfere in her internal economy.

In 1866 Dr. Winchester, then Her Majesty's Consul at Shanghae, said that Corea managed, by a few compliances, to maintain a tolerably effective independence; and in June last Admiral Willes said, "The Government of Corea was vested in the King as an absolute Monarch."

Grosier, in his description of China, and Rees, in his "Cyclopaedia," both say the Sovereign of Corea exercises an absolute sovereignty over his subjects, although he himself is a vassal and tributary of the Emperor of China.

Ellis, in his narrative of Lord Amhurst's Embassy to China, ways the Corean Sovereign is entirely independent in the internal administration of his country; although he adds that ambassadors are dispatched at stated periods by the King to pay, in his name, homage to his Paramount, and to convey the regular tribute.

Gutzlaff says although the Kingdom of Corea is powerful enough to maintain itself independent, the King has long submitted to pay tribute to the Celestial Empire four times a-year; that the King cannot reign without the Imperial sanction, nor can he himself confirm the choice of a colleague of successor; that all these must be sanctioned by the Court of Peking; but that in all other respects, it is an independent Kingdom.

Malte-Brun says, "Le pays est gouverné par un Monarque heréréditaire, tributaire de la Chine."

* * * * *

"Chez lui, le Roi est despote absolu."

The "Encyclopaedia Britanica" says, "the King of Corea, though a vassal of the Chinese Empire, is, within his own country, an absolute Monarch."

In the Appendix will be founded further extracts from the above and other works, bearing on the subject of the independence of Corea.

E. HERTSLET

Foreign Office
December 19, 1882

Appendix

Grosier, in his work on the general description of China and its tributary countries, published in 1788, says :—

"This kingdom is governed by a Sovereign, who exercises an absolute authority over his subject, although he himself is a vassal and tributary of the Emperor of China. As soon as this Prince dies, the Emperor deputes to his son two of the nobility of his Court, to confer upon him the title of Kouévang; that is to say, of King. When the King of Corea is afraid that the succession may occasion disturbance after his death, he appoints some Prince his heir and begs the Emperor to confirm his nomination. The prince receives on his knees the investitute of his State, and distributes among the Emperor's Envoys the sum of 800 taels, and several other customary presents. The Minister of Corea repairs afterwards to Pecking, to prostrate himself before the Emperor, and present him the tribute. The Princess who has espoused the King cannot assume the title of Queen until she has received it from the Court of Pecking.

"The Japanese conquered this kingdom about the end of the sixteenth century; but the Coreans, assisted by the Tartars, who had subdued China, drove them from their country. The Mantchews, thus masters of Corea, endeavoured to compel their new subjects to shave their heads, after their manner, and to adopt the Tartar dress. This innovation irritated their minds, and occasioned a general revolt throughout all Corea, which was at length appeased by the prudent care of the reigning family.

"This Prince is absolute master of all the wealth of his subjects, which he inherits after their death.

"Every seventh year all the freemen of the different provinces are obliged to go Court in rotation, and to keep guard round his person for two months; so that, during this year, all Corea is in motion and under arms.

"China imports every year a considerable quantity of the paper of Corea. It is made of cotton, is as strong as cloth, and those who write on it make use of a small hair-brush or pencil; before it can be written on with our European pens it must be done over gently with a little alum-water; without this precaution it would not bear the ink. With this paper the Coreans partly pay the tribute due to the Emperor; they supply the Palace every year with it. The Chinese do not purchase it for writing, but for filling up the squares of their sash-windows, because, when oiled, it resists the sand and rain much better than theirs; they also use it as wrapping-paper; it is likewise serviceable to their tailors, who rub it between their hands until it becomes as soft and flexible as the finest cotton cloth, instead of which they often employ it in lining clothes. What is most singular in this paper is, that if it be too thick for the purpose intended, it may be easily split into two or three leaves; and these leaves are even stronger, and less liable to be broken, than the best paper of China.

"We have said that the King of Corea is not only obliged to receive from the Emperor of China the investiture of his States, but that his Princess cannot assume the title of Queen without the consent of the Court of Pecking. This usage and the rights of the Emperor of China seem to be fully established in the following petition, which was presented to the Emperor Rang-hi in 1694 by the

King of Corea; –

"I, who am your subject, am a man whose destiny has been unfortunate; I have been a long time without having a successor; but at length one of my concubines has brought me a male child. His birth filled me with inexpressible joy; and immediately formed the resolution of exalting the mother who thus increased my happiness; but in this I committed an error, which has been the source of much uneasiness and suspicion; I obliged the Queen, my spouse, to retire to a private house, and I made my second wife Queen in her stead. I shall give your Majesty a particular detail of the whole affair. When I at present reflect that my spouse received the patent of her creation from your Majesty, that she has managed my family, assisted me in sacrifices, served the Queen my great-grand-mother, and the Queen my mother, and that she wore mourning with me for the space of three years, I am sensible that I ought to treat her with honour and respect; but I have allowed myself to be carried away by imprudence. After this rash action I was exceedingly sorry; and now, that I may gratify the desires of the people of my kingdom, I am resolved to restore my spouse to her Royal dignity, and send back my concubine to her former condition. By these means order will be established in my family, and a foundation laid for good morals and for the reformation of the whole State.

"I, who am your subject, though I have disgraced, by my ignorance and stupidity, the title which I inherited from my ancestors, have however served your Supreme Majesty these twenty years, and I owe what I am to your beneficence- which covers and protects me like heaven. There is no affair, whether public or domestic, of whatever nature it may be, that I dare to conceal from you; I have therefore been emboldened to importune your Majesty so often on this subject; indeed, I am ashamed thus to transgress the bounds of decency; but as this affair nearly concerns that good order and regularity which should be observed in my family, and as it is my duty to declare the wishes of the people, justice impels me to make them known to your Majesty with all due respect.'

"To this petition the Emperor replied by the following Edict; 'Let the Court to which it belongs deliberate, and let the result be laid before me.'

"The examination of this affair belonged to the Court of Ceremonies, which determined that the request of the King of Corea ought to be granted; and this Judgement was ratified by the Emperor. In consequence of this, several of his officers carried magnificent vestments to the Queen, letters of re-establishment, and every thing necessary to restore her to her former rank, with the usual formalities.

"The following year the same King of Corea sent another Memorial to Kang-hi, who, after having read it, issued the following Edict;

"I have seen the compliment of the King; I know it; let the Court to which it belongs take cognizance of it. The style of his petition is improper; it is wanting in respect. I command that it may be examined, and that the Court, after deliberation, will inform me."

"After this order the Li-pou, or Court of Ceremonies, condemned the King of Corea to pay a fine of ten thousand Chinese ounces of silver, and to be deprived, for three years, of the presents annually given him when he sends a deputation to pay his tribute.

Ellis in his narrative of Lord Amherst's Embassy to China in 1816, says;–

"Corea, called Kao-li by the Chinese, is bounded on the north by Man-tehoo Tartary, on the west by Leo-tong; the line of separation on this side is marked by a palisade of wood, and it has not been unusual to leave a portion of land on the frontiers unclaimed by either nation. Other accounts describe the River Ya-lon- as the boundary.

"This country was brought under subjection by the Chinese in the year 1120 before the Christian era, from which period it has continued a connection more or less intimate, according to the political situation of the superior State.

"It has been the object of the Emperors of China to reduce Corea to the situation of a province; in this they have never succeeded for any length of time; and the present has most generally been the state of the relation between the two countries—that of a state governed by native hereditary monarchs, holding under a Lord paramount, on condition of the ceremony of homage, and the payment of a small tribute. The Japanese, for a time, established themselves in some provinces of Corea, but seem to have abandoned their conquest, from the difficulty of maintaining a possession so distant from their resources.

"Corea was subdued by the Man-tehoo Tartars before the conquest of China was attempted, and their tributary connection has suffered no interruption since the establishment of the Ta-tsing dynasty. On the death of the King of Corea, his successor does not assume the title until an application for investiture has been made, and granted by the Court of Peking. A Mandarin of rank is deputed as the Emperor's representative, and the regal dignity is conferred on the candidate kneeling; the ceremony altogether nearly resemble the feudal homage of ancient Europe. Several articles, the production of the country, and 800 taels, or ounces of silver, are immediately offered by the King, either as a fee of investiture of as the commencement of the tribute. The name of the regning family is Li, and the title is Kou-i-wang. The Corean Sovereign is entirely independent in the internal administration of his country. In regard to foreign policy, the active interference of China may be inferred from the opposition made by the Coreans, in the instance of Captain Maxwell, to any communication with the interior of the country; an opposition, as has already been remarked, evidently arising from the positive laws of the kingdom. Corea is divided into eight provinces, and these into minor jurisdictions. The capital, King-ki-tao, is situated in the centre of the kingdom. The principal rivers are the Ya-lou and the Tamen-oula.

"Ambassadors are dispatched at stated periods by King of Corea to pay, in his name, homage to his Paramount, and to convey the regular tribute. This consists of ginseng, zibelines, paper made from cotton, much preferred, from its strength, for windows and a few other articles the produces of the country. There is reason to believe that the tribute is rather sought for as a mark of subjection than a branch of revenue. The Corean Ambassadors do not take precedence of Mandarins of the second rank, and are most strictly watched during their stay in China. It is somewhat singular that equal restrictions are imposed in Corea upon the Representative of the Emperor."

Rees' Cyclopaedia, published in 1819, says:—
"Corea, in geography, called by the a Chinese Kao-li, and by the Mantchu Tartars Sol-go, a Kingdom of Asia, in the form of a peninsula, extended between China and Japan, and everywhere surrounded by the sea, except towards the north, where it is connected with Chinese Tartary, which bounds it on the north; it is bounded on the east by the sea and isles of Japan; on the south by the Straits of Corea, separating it from Japan, and by the ocean: and on the west by the Yellow Sea, which parts it from China. This kingdom is commonly reckoned to be 200 leagues in length from north to south, and 100 leagues in breadth from east to west. The great number of shoals and sandbanks which surround the coasts of this peninsula render access to it by sea equally dangerous and difficult. Its least distance from Japan in only 25 leagues. The origin of the Coreans is very obscure. It appears, however, that this peninsula was at first inhabited by different tribes, which composed several States; and

that, in process of time, they united under the same Government, and formed one kingdom, which was called Kao-li. The Coreans were most probably of Tartarian extraction.

This kingdom is governed by a Sovereign, who exercises absolute authority over his subject, although he himself is a vassal and tributary of the Emperor of China."

[But this passage, as well as the remainder of the article, is evidently copied from Grosier. See P.24.]

Gutzlaff, in his "Journal of Three Voyages along the Coast of China in 1831, 1832, and 1833," says: -

"The king of Corea may well be styled' the Sovereign of then thousand Isles, for the whole coast is studded with islands of every shape. Though his kingdom is powerful enough to maintain itself independent, he has long submitted to pay tribute to the Celestial Empire four times a-year.

The kingdom was known to the Chinese as early as the times of Yaou. At different periods they attacked the 'middle kingdom' and often proved victorious. It was natural that they should early adopt the Chinese writing character, the use of which prevails among them to this time. Several domestic broils, which seem to have been fomented by Chinese policy, together with the variety of tribes inhabiting the country, seem to have kept this kingdom in barbarism, from which it did not emerge; while their neighbours, the Chinese as well as the Japanese, made rapid advances in civilization. As soon as the Ming dynasty ascended the Chinese throne (A.D. 1368), the Coreans sent an Ambassador to Hungwoo, the Emperor desiring the inauguration of their King with the Imperial Seal. This was readily granted, and Corea was henceforth considered a tributary kingdom. During the reign of Tai-kosama, the warlike Emperor of Japan, Corea was repeatedly invaded by the Japanese, and finally conquered. The Chinese tried in vain to expel the Japanese, for they maintained themselves with the utmost bravery; and so far from yielding up Corea, they disquieted all the Chinese coast with their fleet. It was at this time that Christianity, or rather Popery, was first promulgated in Corea: for the Generals for the Japanese, and many of the soldiery, were Christians. When Tai-Kosama died the Japanese General-in-chief withdrew to his own country (1598) after the war had raged seven victories lost to the Japanese. The Chinese did not fail to establish their authority as supreme masters, to whom all the earth should bow. Since that time the country has undergone little change. The King cannot reign without the Imperial sanction, nor can he himself confirm the choice of a colleague of successor; all these must be sanctioned by the Court of Peking. In other respects it is an independent kingdom, and the Chinese meddle very little with their internal administration. Its subjects are not allowed to visit other countries, nor are even Chinese admitted to settle among them. They trade with the frontiers of Japan at Tuymataou, which is opposite to the Corean Island of Kin-shang. Their trade with Chinese and Tartars is carried on at Fung-hwang-ching, the frontier town of Mantehou Tartary. This traffic is conducted with great secresy and circumspection, lest one nation should spoil the other, and thus tend to subvert their ancient regulation. Nothing is more ridiculous than to see the people so tenacious ancient and useless forms, rather than desirous to keep pace with the match of improvement."

The King of Corea, though a vassal of the Chinese Empire, is within his own country an absolute monarch, with power of life and death over the noblest in the land. He is the object of almost Divine honours; it is sacrilege to utter the name which he receives from his Suzerain, and that by which he is known in history is only bestowed upon him after his death by his successor. To touch his person with a weapon of iron is high treason; and so rigidly is this rule enforced that Tieng-tsong-tai-oang suffered and abscess to put an end to his life in 1800 rather than submit to the contact of the lancet. Every horseman must dismount as he passes the Palace, and whoever enters the presence-chamber must fall prostrate before the throne. Should the ignoble body of a subject be touched by the Royal hands, the honour thus conferred must be over after commemorated by a badge. In consequence of such punctilious etiquette, personal access to the King is exceedingly difficult; but as, according to theory, his ear ought always to be open to the complaints of his people, an appeal to his authority is nominally permitted. He is expected to provide for the poor of his realm, and there are always a large number of pensioners on the Royal bounty. The Princes of the blood are most jealously excluded from power, and their interference in the slightest degree in a matter of politics is regarded as treason. The Nobles, however, have within the present century extended their influence, and infringed on the Royal prerogatives."

부록 문서 목록

번호	발신일/수신일*(음력)	문서제목	발신	수신	문서출처	번역문 출처	관련문서 제목	관련문서 출처
(1) 조약 체결 이전 영국의 조선 관련 보고							
1	1875. 5. 25	조선에 파견할 일본군함의 동정 보고	H. S. Parkes	Derby	FO 46/191.			
2	1875. 7. 17/ 1875. 8. 24*	玄昔運·森山茂 교섭 결렬 보고	H. S. Parkes	Derby	FO 881/2700; BDFA pp. 41-2.			
3	1875. 7. 24/ 1875. 9. 5*	조일 갈등과 러시아 개입 가능성 보고	H. S. Parkes	Derby	FO 881/2700; BDFA pp. 46-7.			
4	1875. 12. 6/ 1876. 1. 21*	영국 선박의 난파 조선인 구출 보고	H. S. Parkes	Derby	FO 46/195.			
5	1875. 12. 6/ 1876. 1. 21*	木戸孝允의 조선정책 각서 보고	H. S. Parkes	Derby	FO 46/195.			
6	1875. 12. 9	조일 교섭 가능성과 黑田淸隆 조선 파견 계획 보고	F. R. Plunkett	Derby	FO 410/15; AADM pp. 5-6.			
7	1875. 12. 13	일본의 조선교섭 준비 보고	F. R. Plunkett	Derby	FO 410/15; AADM pp. 7-10.			
8	1875. 12. 31/ 1976. 2. 12*	黑田淸隆의 강화도 파견 및 러시아 개입 가능성 보고	H. S. Parkes	Derby	FO 410/15; AADM pp. 13-20.			
9	1876. 01. 10/ 1876. 02. 21*	黑田淸隆 파견 관련 森山茂의 내방 및 회견 보고	H. S. Parkes	Derby	F. O. 46/202; FO 410/15			
10	1876. 2. 16	조일 교섭에 대한 주변국 반응 보고	T. F. Wade	Derby	FO 17/720.			
11	1876. 3. 3/ 1876. 4. 4*	조일수호조규 체결을 알리는 鮫島尙信 등 메모 보고	F. R. Plunkett	Derby	FO 410/15; AADM p. 37.			
12	1876. 3. 25/ 1876. 5. 7	조일수호조규 영역본 보고	H. S. Parkes	Derby	FO 410/15; AADM pp. 42-5.			
13	1876. 3. 27/ 1876. 5. 11*	강화도 협상 관련 森山茂와 회담 보고	H. S. Parkes	Derby	FO 410/15; AADM pp. 45~8.			
14	1876. 3. 27/ 1876. 5. 11*	조일수호조규 분석	H. S. Parkes	Derby	FO 410/15; AADM pp. 52-3.			
15	1876. 4. 15	프랑스의 협조 의사 보고	Adams	Derby	FO 27/2162.			
16	1876. 4. 22	독일의 협조 의사 보고	B.O. Russell	Derby	FO 64/851.			
17	1876. 5. 12	조선 교섭 방식에 관한 전보	H. S. Parkes	Derby	FO 46/206.			
18	1876. 5. 12	조선의 배외정책 보고 및 교섭시 무력 동원 건의	Adams	Derby	FO 27/2163.			
19	1876. 5. 12	청국에 중개 요청 건의	Adams	Derby	FO 27/2163.			

번호	발신일/수신일*(음력)	문서제목	발신	수신	문서출처	번역문 출처	관련문서 제목	관련문서 출처
20	1876. 5. 23	조선 교섭시 영·불·독의 연합함대 파견 건의	H. S. Parkes	Derby	FO 46/206.			
21	1876. 6. 2	Parkes의 보고에 대한 프랑스 정부 입장 보고	Adams	Derby	FO 27/2164.			
22	1876. 6. 9/ 1876. 7. 16*	일본의 중개에 관한 寺島宗則와 회담 보고	H. S. Parkes	Derby	FO 46/206.			
23	1876. 6. 9	수신사 金綺秀의 동정 및 森山茂 회견 보고	H. S. Parkes	Derby	FO 46/206.			
24	1876. 8. 11	宮本小一의 조선 교섭 및 Sylvia의 조선 해안 탐사에 관한 보고	H. S. Parkes	Derby	FO 46/207.			
25	1876. 8. 11	조선 연해 탐사에 대한 조선 정부의 태도 변화 보고	H. S. Parkes	Derby	FO 46/207.			
26	1876. 8. 15	일본의 중개에 관한 岩倉具視와 회견 보고	H. S. Parkes	Derby	FO 46/207.			
27	1876. 9. 26	서양선박 보호에 관한 宮本小一의 제안 보고	H. S. Parkes	Derby	FO 46/208.			
28	1876. 10. 11	조선의 배외주의와 수교 가능성에 관한 嚴倉와 회견 보고	H. S. Parkes	Derby	FO 46/208.			
29	1876. 11. 30	조선 교섭 연기 지령	FO	H. S. Parkes	FO 46/201.			
30	1878. 11. 11	Barbara Taylor 조난시 조선 정부의 원조 보고	H. S. Parkes	Salisbury	FO 46/231.			
31	1878. 11. 25	E. Satow의 제주도 파견 보고	H. S. Parkes	Salisbury	FO 46/231.			
32	1878. 12. 2/ 1879. 1. 18*	관세 협상을 위한 花房義質의 조선 파견 보고	H. S. Parkes	Salisbury	FO 46/231.			
33	1878. 12. 2/ 1879. 1. 18*	Satow가 지참한 감사 서한의 접수 거절 보고	H. S. Parkes	Salisbury	FO 46/231.			
34	1878. 12. 18	Satow의 제주도 방문시 조선인의 우호적 태도 보고	H. S. Parkes	Salisbury	FO 46/231.			
35	1878. 12. 30/ *1879. 2. 15	일본 정부 중개의 한계 보고	H. S. Parkes	Salisbury	FO 46/231.			
36	1879. 5. 15/ 1879. 6. 21*	개항장 추가를 위한 花房義質의 조선 파견 보고	H. S. Parkes	Salisbury	FO 46/246.			

번호	발신일/수신일* (음력)	문서제목	발신	수신	문서출처	번역문 출처	관련문서 제목	관련문서 출처
37	1879. 5. 15/1879. 6. 21*	Shufeldt의 조선행 관련 花房義質와 면담 내용 보고	H. S. Parkes	Salisbury	FO 46/246.			
38	1879. 5. 15/1879. 6. 21*	Satow의 제주도 파견 경과 보고	H. S. Parkes	Salisbury	FO 46/246.			
(2) 제1차 조약 체결 과정								
39	1879. 7. 3	조선과 서구 열강의 수교를 總罰에 건의한 사실 보고	Braus	H. S. Parkes	Parkes Papers 1/B114.			
40	1880. 3. 14/1880. 5. 2*	井上馨와 회견 보고 (1)	J. G. Kennedy	Salisbury	FO 46/256; FO 881/4718; BDFA p. 75.			
41	1880. 3. 25/1880. 5. 8*	청-러 개전 가능성 및 일본, 조선의 동향 보고	J. G. Kennedy	Salisbury	FO 46/256; FO 881/4718; BDFA p. 77. AADM pp. 55-6.			
42	1880. 5. 25/1880. 7. 14*	井上馨와 회견 보고 (2)	J. G. Kennedy	Salisbury	FO 46/257; FO 881/4718; AADM pp. 57-8.			
43	1880. 6. 29/1880. 8. 13*	청-러 개전 가능성 및 조선과 조약 체결 필요 상신	J. G. Kennedy	G. L. G. Granville	FO 46/257; FO 881/4521; AADM pp. 60-2.			
44	1880. 7. 27/1880. 9. 16*	李裕元-李鴻章 왕복 서한 및 조선관련 정보 보고	J. G. Kennedy	G. L. G. Granville	FO 46/257; FO 881/4521; AADM pp. 64-72.			
45	1880. 11. 21/1881. 1. 3*	조선의 개국 가능성 보고	J. G. Kennedy	G. L. G. Granville	FO 46/258; FO 881/4595; AADM pp. 77-8.			
46	1880. 11. 22/1881. 1. 3*	何如璋의 조약 체결 권고 보고	J. G. Kennedy	G. L. G. Granville	FO 46/258; FO 881/4595; AADM pp. 78-9.			
47	1881. 1. 7	러시아의 조선 영토 일부 점령 가능성 보고	T. F. Wade	G. L. G. Granville	FO 17/859			
48	1881. 1. 20	조영조약 체결을 위한 청국의 중재 가능성 확인 지령	F. O	T. F. Wade	FO 17/859			
49	1881. 1. 11	조영조약 체결 시기에 관한 Memorandum	H. S. Parkes		FO 881/4595; AADM pp. 79-80.			
50	1881. 1. 14/1881. 1. 27*	러시아 동향 보고	T. F. Wade	G. L. G. Granville	FO 881/4595; AADM pp. 81.			
51	1881. 1. 20	조약 체결에 대한 청국의 입장 확인 지시	G. L. G. Granville	T. F. Wade	FO 881/4595; AADM pp. 80-1.			
52	1881. 2. 9/1881. 2. 23*	청국의 중개를 통한 교섭 추진 보고	T. F. Wade	G. L. G. Granville	FO 881/4595; AADM pp. 81-2.			
53	1881. 2. 26	Wade의 기밀 보고서에 관한 Memorandum	H. S. Parkes		FO 881/4595; AADM p. 82			

번호	발신일/수신일* (음력)	문서제목	발신	수신	문서출처	번역문 출처	관련문서 제목	관련문서 출처
54	1881. 2. 18/ 1881. 4. 16*	Spence의 부산, 원산, 영흥만 조사 보고서	T. F. Wade	G. L. G. Granville	FO 17/857; FO 881/4595; AADM pp. 83-100			
55	1881. 3. 24/ 1881. 5. 9*	러시아 함대의 원산항 점령 가능성 보고	J. G. Kennedy	G. L. G. Granville	FO 881/4595; AADM pp. 100-1			
56	1881. 6. 8/ 1881. 8. 2*	조사시찰단(朝士視察團) 일본 파견 및 何如璋 문서 보고	J. G. Kennedy	G. L. G. Granville	FO 881/4595; AADM pp. 101-2.			
57	1881. 9. 28	조영조약 체결 관련 업무의 잠정 중단 보고	J. G. Kennedy	Tenterden	FO 363/1			
58	1881. 10. 22/ 1881. 11. 5*	러시아의 조선 점령 가능성 및 미국의 조선 교섭 계획 보고	V. Drummond	G. L. G. Granville	FO 881/4595; AADM p. 115.			
59	1882. 1. 10	Shufeldt의 교섭 시도 보고	J. G. Kennedy	G. L. G. Granville	FO 46/284.			
60	1882. 4. 17	최혜국대우 균점(均霑)을 위한 교섭 권한 부여	R. Hall	G. O. Willes	ADM 125/142/3.			
61	1882. 4. 18/ 1882. 6. 7*	Willes의 조선행을 지시한 외무부 전신 수령	H. S. Parkes	G. L. G. Granville	FO 46/285.			
62	1882. 4. 21/ 1882. 5. 29*	조선의 수입관 세율 전망 보고	H. S. Parkes	G. L. G. Granville	FO 46/285.			
63	1882. 5. 12/ 1882. 6. 19*	조미조약 체결 이후 일본의 조선정책 전망 보고	H. S. Parkes	G. L. G. Granville	FO 46/285.			
64	1882. 5. 11	조선에 제시할 소개 서한 요청	T. F. Wade	李鴻章	FO 17/895.			
65	1882. 5. 12	李鴻章의 일시 사직 보고	T. F. Wade	G. L. G. Granville	FO 17/895.			
66	1882. 5. 12	조선 문제 관련 李鴻章 및 總署와 교섭 보고	T. F. Wade	G. L. G. Granville	FO 17/895.			
67	1882. 5. 12/ 1882. 7. 22*	Shufeldt의 청국 해군 임용 실패와 조미조약에 대한 청국 태도 보고	T. F. Wade	G. L. G. Granville	FO 17/895.			
68	1882. 5. 12/ 1882. 7. 22*	조미수호통상 조약안 분석 보고	T. F. Wade	G. L. G. Granville	FO 17/895.			
69	1882. 5. 12	조미조약안의 조선 속방론 규정에 관한 보고	T. F. Wade	G. L. G. Granville	FO 17/895.			
70	1882. 5. 17	베트남, 조선 문제에 관한 李鴻章과 회견 보고	T. F. Wade	G. L. G. Granville	FO 17/895.			

번호	발신일/수신일* (음력)	문서제목	발신	수신	문서출처	번역문 출처	관련문서 제목	관련문서 출처
71	1882.5.22	조미조약초안의 한문본 전달 및 馬建忠 접촉 지시	T. F. Wade	C. T. Maude	FO 17/895.		Willes에게 보낸 Maude 파견시 지참 문서 내용	FO 17/895.
72	1882.5.22	Willes 통역 지시	T. F. Wade	D. Spence	FO 17/895.			
73	1882.5.22	Willes에 앞서 조선에 갈 것을 지시	T. F. Wade	Bridger	FO 17/895.			
74	1882.5.23	조미 교섭에 관한 李鴻章, 總署 王大臣과 면담 보고	T. F. Wade	G. L. G. Granville	FO 17/895.			
75	1882.5.23	Willes의 芝罘 출항 보고	T. F. Wade	G. L. G. Granville	FO 17/895.			
76	1882.5.27	Maude의 조선행 보고	T. F. Wade	G. L. G. Granville	FO 17/895.			
77	1882.5.27	조영조약에 조미조약 원용 건의	T. F. Wade	G. L. G. Granville	FO 17/895.			
78	1882.5.27(光緖八年四月十一日)	馬建忠·Willes 회담	馬建忠		『東行初錄』p. 370.			
79	1882.5.27(光緖八年四月十一日)	영국과 조약 체결 권고	馬建忠	申櫶 金弘集	『구한국』10(미안 1) pp. 14-5.			
80	1882.5.28(高宗十九年四月十二日)	趙寧夏·金弘集 협상 전권 부여	統理機務衙門		『일록』高宗 19년 4월 12일; 『일기』『실록』같은 날.			
81	1882.5.29(光緖八年四月十三日)	馬建忠·韓文奎·高永周 회담	馬建忠		『中日韓』2, 문서번호 420의 부건 37, pp. 660-2.			
82	1882.5.30(高宗十九年四月十四日)	속방조회문(屬邦照會文)	高宗	Queen Victoria	『구한국』13(영안 1) p. 1; FO 1080/6; 『中日韓』2, 문서번호 455의 부건 2, p. 724; 『淸外』27, p. 32.			
83	1882.5.30(光緖八年四月十四日)	馬建忠·趙寧夏 회담	馬建忠		『中日韓』2, 문서번호 420의 부건 38, 39, pp. 662-5.			
84	1882.6.2	Dillon 영사 내방과 조불조약에 관한 의견 보고	T. F. Wade	G. L. G. Granville	FO 17/895.			
85	1882.6.3/ 1882.7.22*	Hughes 영사의 Shufeldt 면담 보고	T. F. Wade	G. L. G. Granville	FO 17/890.			
86	1882.6.5 이전	조영조약안 결정 경위 보고	馬建忠	李鴻章	『中日韓』2, 문서번호 413의 부건 1, pp. 586-7; 『東行初錄』p. 374.			

번호	발신일/수신일*(음력)	문서제목	발신	수신	문서출처	번역문 출처	관련문서 제목	관련문서 출처
87	1882. 6. 5(高宗 十九年四月 二十日)*	조영조약 외 추가 3개조의 성명을 요구하는 조회	G. O. Willes	趙寧夏 金弘集	『구한국』13(영안 1) pp. 1-2; 『음청』 pp. 159-60; 『中日韓』2, 문서번호 455의 부건 3 p. 724; 『中日』3, 문서번호 109의 부건 4 p. 52; 『淸外』 卷27, pp. 32-3.		조선측 회신	『음청』pp. 160; 『구한국』13(영안 1)pp. 2.
88	1882. 6. 9	조영수호통상조약 체결 보고	G. O. Willes	Admiralty	ADM 125/142/5.			
89	1882. 6. 12/1882. 7. 17*	조선주재 외교관 임명에 관한 상신	H. S. Parkes	Hallell	FO 46/285.			
90	1882. 6. 21/1882. 7. 27*	조미조약 한문 초안의 번역문 보고	H. S. Parkes	G. L. G. Granville	FO 46/285.			
91	1882. 7. 5/1882. 8. 12*	Willes의 통역으로 Aston 파견 보고	H. S. Parkes	G. L. G. Granville	FO 46/285.			
(3) 제1차 조약 이후 청조(淸朝)의 대응								
92	1882. 6. 9(高宗 十九年四月 二十四日)	조영조약의 체결을 알리는 자문(咨文)	高宗	禮部	『자문』2 「與英使講定修好通商條規事北京禮部咨」; 『中日韓』2, 문서번호 456의 부건 1, pp. 726-7.			
93	1882. 6. 13(光緒八年四月 二十八日)*	조영조약 체결 통보	T. F. Wade	總署	『中日韓』2, 문서번호 425. p. 679.		總署의 회신	『中日韓』2, 문서번호 434, p. 686.
94	1882. 8. 6(光緒八年六月 二十三日)	조영, 조독 조약 체결 전말 상주	張樹聲		『中日』3, 문서번호 112, p. 24; 『淸外』28, p. 10-2; 『張靖公奏議』6, pp. 345-8.			
(4) 제2차 조약 체결 과정								
95	1882. 6. 21	1차 조영조약에 대한 비판 및 조선 영사관 설치 건의	H. S. Parkes	Tenterden	FO 46/285.			
96	1882. 7. 5/1882. 8. 12*	아산, 인천 등 서해안 개항장 후보지 조사 보고	H. S. Parkes	G. L. G. Granville	FO 46/285.			
97	1882. 7. 6/1882. 8. 31*	1차 조영조약 체결 과정에 관한 Maude Report	T. F. Wade	G. L. G. Granville	FO 17/897.			
98	1882. 7. 24/1882. 8. 25*	1차 조영조약에 따른 일본의 조약개정 요구 보고	H. S. Parkes	G. L. G. Granville	FO 46/285.			
99	1882. 8. 3/1882. 9. 26*	조선의 개항과 수출입 현황에 관한 Spence Report	T. F. Wade	G. L. G. Granville	FO 17/897.			

번호	발신일/수신일*(음력)	문서제목	발신	수신	문서출처	번역문 출처	관련문서 제목	관련문서 출처
100	1882. 9. 3	영국 군함의 조선 해안 측량 보고	前田獻吉	吉田淸成	『日外』15, 문서번호 151.			
101	1882. 9. 12	조선의 국제적 지위에 관한 井上馨와 회견 보고	H. S. Parkes	G. L. G. Granville	FO 46/288.			
102	1882. 9. 22.	조영조약 비준 요청에 대한 회신	N. R. O'Conor	趙寧夏 金弘集	『구한국』13(영안 1) pp. 2-3.			
103	1882. 9. 25	Aston의 조선 개항장 조사 보고	H. S. Parkes	G. L. G. Granville	FO 46/288; London Gazette(1882. 12. 22)			
104	1882. 10. 16/ 1882. 11. 20*	수신사 朴泳孝 일행 임무 보고	H. S. Parkes	G. L. G. Granville	FO 46/285.			
105	1882. 10. 24/ 1882. 11. 28*	金玉均과 면담 보고	H. S. Parkes	G. L. G. Granville	FO 46/288.			
106	1882. 11. 25/ 1883. 1. 8*	수신사 朴泳孝 일행의 내방 및 조선 정세 보고	H. S. Parkes	G. L. G. Granville	FO 405/33; BDFA p. 99; AADM p. 116.			
107	1882. 11. 25/ 1883. 1. 6*	Möllendorff의 외교고문 초빙 보고	T. G. Grosvenor	G. L. G. Granville	FO 405/33; AADM p. 117-8.			
108	1882. 12. 4/ 1883. 1. 22*	조청상민수륙무역장정 영역문 보고	T. G. Grosvenor	G. L. G. Granville	FO 17/900; FO 405/33; AADM pp. 119-122.			
109	1882. 12. 14/ 1883. 2. 14*	조러 육로교섭 보고	T. G. Grosvenor	G. L. G. Granville	FO 405/33; AADM pp. 139-140.			
110	1882. 12. 21/ 1883. 1. 29*	조청상민수륙무역장정 체결에 따른 1차 조영조약 개정 건의	H. S. Parkes	G. L. G. Granville	FO 405/33; BDFA pp. 104-6; AADM pp. 131-3.			
111	1882. 12. 29/ 1883. 2. 5*	朴泳孝와 1차 조영조약 개정 협상 보고	H. S. Parkes	G. L. G. Granville	FO 405/33; AADM pp. 134-8.			
112	1882. 12. 31	朴泳孝의 전권 소지여부에 관한 회신	H. S. Parkes	G. L. G. Granville	FO 46/290.			
113	1883. 1. 9/ 1883. 2. 20*	1차 조영조약에 대한 橫濱 상공회의소 의견 상신	J. P. Mollison	G. L. G. Granville	FO 405/33; AADM pp. 141-3.			
114	1883. 1. 12/ 1883. 2. 20*	조일 관세율 협정에 관한 朴泳孝·井上馨의 회담 보고	H. S. Parkes	G. L. G. Granville	FO 405/33; AADM pp. 143-4.			
115	1883. 1. 12/ 1883. 2. 20*	조약 개정에 관한 金玉均과 회담 보고	H. S. Parkes	G. L. G. Granville	FO 405/33; BDFA p. 112; AADM pp. 144-5.			
116	1883. 1. 17/ 1883. 2. 28*	1차 조영조약에 대한 上海 상공회의소 의견 상신	E. G. Low	G. L. G. Granville	FO 405/33; AADM pp. 157-9.			

번호	발신일/수신일* (음력)	문서제목	발신	수신	문서출처	번역문 출처	관련문서 제목	관련문서 출처
117	1883. 1. 20	1차 조영조약에 대한 香港 상공회의소 의견 상신	F. B. Johnson	G. L. G. Granville	FO 405/33; AADM pp. 163-9.			
118	1883. 1. 24	조청상민수륙무역장정과 1차 조영조약 비교	J. Saumarez		FO 405/33; BDFA p. 101-4; AADM pp. 125-8.			
119	1883. 1. 29	조영조약의 개정을 위해 독일과 공조 필요 상신	P. Currie		FO 17/900.			
120	1883. 2. 2	조청상민수륙무역장정에 대한 미국의 견해 확인	Pauncefote		FO 17/900.			
121	1883. 2. 16/ 1883. 2. 17*	1차 조영조약에 대한 London 상공회의소 의견 상신	K. B. Murray	G. L. G. Granville	FO 405/33; BDFA p. 110-1; AADM p. 140-1.			
122	1883. 2. 16	Aston의 조선행 보고	H. S. Parkes	G. L. G. Granville	FO 46/297.			
123	1883. 2. 17/ 1883. 3. 28*	김옥균 및 井上馨와 회담 보고	H. S. Parkes	G. L. G. Granville	FO 405/33; AADM pp. 170-1.			
124	1883. 2. 20	Aston의 조선행 승인	H. S. Parkes	G. L. G. Granville	FO 46/297.			
125	1883. 2. 28	조청상민수륙무역장정 이후 조선의 국제적 지위에 관한 보고	G. L. G. Granville	Ampthilll	FO 405/33; BDFA p. 120-1; AADM p. 159-60.			
126	1883. 3. 9/ 1883. 4. 14*	Aston의 조선행 및 지시내용 보고	H. S. Parkes	G. L. G. Granville	FO 405/33; BDFA pp. 126-30; AADM pp. 185-91.	[漢譯] 『구한국』13(영안 1) p. 3		
127	(1883/高宗二十年)	Parkes 조회에 대한 회신	洪淳穆	H. S. Parkes	『구한국』13(영안 1) p. 4.			
128	1883. 3. 10	조선 관세율에 관한 井上馨와 회견내용 통보	H. S. Parkes	W. G. Aston	FO 405/33; BDFA p. 139.			
129	1883. 3. 19/ 1883. 3. 20*	1차 조영조약에 대한 香港 상공회의소 의견 상신	R. G. W. Herbert	P. Currie	FO 405/33; AADM pp. 163-9.			
130	1883. 3. 24/ 1883. 5. 8*	Willes의 지시에 따른 Moorhen과 Darling의 임무 교대 보고	H. S. Parkes	G. L. G. Granville	FO 405/33; BDFA p. 131; AADM p. 197.			
131	1883. 4. 7/ 1883. 5. 23*	조선 광산 탐측 결과 보고	H. S. Parkes	G. L. G. Granville	FO 405/33; AADM pp. 199-206.			
132	1883. 4. 10/ 1883. 4. 12*	조독조약 비준 연기를 알리는 Bismarck의 통지 보고	Ampthill	G. L. G. Granville	FO 405/33; AADM pp. 180-1.			
133	1883. 4. 12(高宗二十年三月六日)	공관부지 선정 및 공법 준수요청에 대한 회신	閔永穆	H. S. Parkes	『구한국』13(영안 1) p. 4.			

번호	발신일/수신일*(음력)	문서제목	발신	수신	문서출처	번역문 출처	관련문서 제목	관련문서 출처
134	1883. 4. 20/ 1883. 6. 4*	Darling 함장 Eliott의 해임 경위 보고	H. S. Parkes	G. L. G. Granville	FO 405/33; AADM 210-15.			
135	1883. 4. 21/ 1883. 6. 4*	조선의 조약 개정 의도와 정세에 관한 Aston 전보 보고	H. S. Parkes	G. L. G. Granville	FO 405/33; AADM 215-6.			
136	1883. 4. 21/ 1883. 6. 4*	Aston의 조선 행 및 지시내용에 관한 추가 보고	H. S. Parkes	G. L. G. Granville	FO 405/33; BDFA pp. 143-4; AADM p. 216-8.			
137	1883. 4. 22	독일과 영국의 조약 비준 연기 통보	G. L. G. Granville	H. S. Parkes	FO 405/33; AADM p. 193-4.			
138	1883. 4. 28	Aston의 재파견을 알리는 조회	H. S. Parkes	閔泳穆	『구한국』13(영안 1) p. 5.		閔泳穆의 회신	『구한국』13(영안 1) p. 6.
139	1883. 4. 28	1차 조영조약의 비준서 교환 연기를 통보하는 조회	H. S. Parkes	閔泳穆	『구한국』13(영안 1) p. 5.		閔泳穆의 회신	『구한국』13(영안 1) pp. 5-6.
140	1883. 4. 28/ 1883. 6. 19	조선에서의 협상에 관한 Aston의 despatch 발송	H. S. Parkes	G. L. G. Granville	FO 405/33; BDFA pp. 144-9; AADM 221-5.			
141	1883. 4. 28/ 1883. 6. 19	조선 정세에 관한 Aston의 Memorandum 발송	H. S. Parkes	G. L. G. Granville	FO 405/33; BDFA pp. 149; AADM pp. 226-230.			
142	1883. 4. 28/ 1883. 6. 19	Aston의 영국 공관, 영사관 부지 선정 보고	H. S. Parkes	G. L. G. Granville	FO 405/33; AADM pp. 230-4.			
143	1883. 4. 28/ 1883. 6. 19	조영, 조독조약 비준서 교환 연기 통보를 위한 Aston의 재파견 보고	H. S. Parkes	G. L. G. Granville	FO 405/33; BDFA pp. 156-7; AADM pp. 235-9.			
144	1883. 4. 28/ 1883. 6. 19	Foote의 일본 도착 보고	H. S. Parkes	G. L. G. Granville	FO 405/33; AADM pp. 240.			
145	1883. 4. 29/ 1883. 4. 29*	상업 특권 양여에 대한 미국의 반대 보고	H. S. Parkes	G. L. G. Granville	FO 405/33; AADM p. 194.			
146	1883. 5. 14/ 1883. 6. 18*	Foote와 회견 및 Foote의 조선행 보고	H. S. Parkes	G. L. G. Granville	FO 405/33; AADM pp. 242-3.			
147	1883. 5. 15(高宗 二十年四月九日)	비준서 교환 연기 요청 수락	統署		『일록』高宗 20년 4월 10일; 『일기』『실록』같은 날.			
148	1883. 5. 15(高宗 二十年四月九日)	Aston과 협의한 3개조 조약안의 시행여부를 문의하는 조회	閔泳穆	H. S. Parkes	『구한국』13(영안 1) pp. 6-7.			
149	1883. 5. 30/ 1883. 7. 26*	조약 개정에 관한 李鴻章과 회견 내용 보고	G. O. Willes	Secretary to the Admiralty	FO 405/33; BDFA p. 186-7.			
150	1883. 5. 30/ 1883. 7. 23*	李鴻章・Willes 회담 보고	P. J. Hughes	T. G. Grosvenor	FO 405/33; BDFA p. 182; AADM P. 286.			

번호	발신일/수신일*(음력)	문서제목	발신	수신	문서출처	번역문 출처	관련문서 제목	관련문서 출처
151	1883. 5. 30/ 1883. 7. 7*	비준서 교환 연기협정 보고 (1)	H. S. Parkes	G. L. G. Granville	FO 405/33; BDFA pp. 171-2; AADM pp. 260-1.			
152	1883. 5. 30/ 1883. 7. 7*	비준서 교환 연기협정 보고 (2)	H. S. Parkes	G. L. G. Granville	FO 405/33; AADM P. 259.			
153	1883. 5. 31/ 1883. 7. 7*	비준서 교환 연기협정 보고 (3)	H. S. Parkes	G. L. G. Granville	FO 405/33; BDFA p. 173.			
154	1883. 5. 31/ 1883. 7. 7*	비준서 교환 연기협정 보고 (4)	H. S. Parkes	G. L. G. Granville	FO 405/33; BDFA p. 172-3; AADM P. 261-3.			
155	1883. 5. 31/ 1883. 7. 7*	조선의 정세에 관한 Aston의 Memorandum 발송	H. S. Parkes	G. L. G. Granville	FO 405/33; AADM P. 264-7.			
156	1883. 5. 31/ 1883. 7. 7*	조일무역규칙 초안 및 3개조 조약에 관한 Aston의 Memorandum 발송	H. S. Parkes	G. L. G. Granville	FO 405/33; BDFA pp. 176-7; AADM pp. 267-72.			
157	1883. 6. 10/ 1883. 7. 16*	1차 조영조약 개정에 관한 의견	H. S. Parkes	G. L. G. Granville	FO 405/33; BDFA pp. 178-81; AADM pp. 279-84.			
158	1883. 6. 11/ 1883. 7. 16*	Parkes 서신에 대한 洪秉韠과 閔泳穆의 회신 보고	H. S. Parkes	G. L. G. Granville	FO 405/33; AADM pp. 284-5.			
159	1883. 6. 11/ 1883. 7. 25*	조약 개정 교섭 시 해군 파견에 관한 훈령	G. L. G. Granville	H. S. Parkes	FO 405/33; AADM P. 219.			
160	1883. 6. 11/ 1883. 7. 25*	2차 조영조약 초안, 무역규칙안, 관세율안 보고	H. S. Parkes	G. L. G. Granville	FO 405/33; BDFA pp. 182-6; AADM pp. 287-303.			
161	1883. 7. 16/ 1883. 8. 25*	金玉均과 면담 보고	H. S. Parkes	G. L. G. Granville	FO 405/33; BDFA pp. 188-9; AADM pp. 319-20.			
162	1883. 8. 23	Parkes에게 조약개정 전권 부여 후 조선 파견 예정 통보	G. L. G. Granville	Baron von Plessen	FO 405/33; BDFA p. 187.			
163	1883. 8. 24.	Parkes 전권위임장	Queen Victoria		『구한국』13(영안1) p. 8.			
164	1883. 8. 31	조선 개항장 현황 보고	G. O. Willes	Secretary to the Admiralty	FO 405/33; BDFA p. 195.			
165	1883. 8. 31	아편 수입금지 조항에 대한 Granville경의 견해 문의	P. Currie	L. Mallet	FO 405/33; BDFA pp. 189-90; AADM pp. 321-2.			
166	1883. 9 1/ 1883. 9. 3*	Zappe의 조선 파견 통보	J. Walsham	G. L. G. Granville	FO 405/33; BDFA pp. 191-2; AADM pp. 323-4.			
167	1883. 9. 3	조선에 부임하는 Zappe 독일 공사와의 협조 지시	G. L. G. Granville	H. S. Parkes	FO 405/33; AADM pp. 324.			

번호	발신일/수신일* (음력)	문서제목	발신	수신	문서출처	번역문 출처	관련문서 제목	관련문서 출처
168	1883. 9. 25/ 1883. 9. 25*	아편 수입금지 조항에 대한 Kimberley경의 견해 전달	L. Mallet	P. Currie	FO 405/33; BDFA p. 192; AADM pp. 333-4.			
169	1883. 10. 3	아편 수입금지 조항 및 수정 조약안에 관한 훈령	G. L. G. Granville	H. S. Parkes	FO 405/33; BDFA p. 193; AADM 336-7.			
170	1883. 10. 8	조약 개정 협상을 위한 사전준비 및 전권 임명을 청하는 조회	H. S. Parkes	閔泳穆	FO 405/33; AADM pp. 355-8.	[漢譯]『구한국』13(영안 1) pp. 7-8; FO 1080/191	閔泳穆의 회신	『구한국』13(영안 1) p. 9; FO 1080/191
171	1883. 10. 18/ 1883. 12. 7*	조약 개정 협상을 위한 조선행 보고	H. S. Parkes	G. L. G. Granville	FO 405/33; AADM pp. 355-8.			
172	1883. 10. 18/ 1883. 10. 22*	天津 조약에 준하는 전교, 내지여행권 명문화 요구	Balfour of Burleigh	G. L. G. Granville	FO 405/33; BDFA p. 194; AADM P. 341.			
173	1883. 10. 21(光緖九年九月二十一日)	李鴻章·Parkes 회담	李鴻章		『中日韓』3, 문서번호 769의 부건 1, pp. 1208-9; 『李鴻章』33, 信函 5, p. 322.			
174	1883. 10. 31/ 1883. 11. 8*	아편 수입금지 명문화를 촉구하는 청원	The society FOr the Suppression of the Opium Trade	G. L. G. Granville	FO 405/33; BDFA p. 195; AADM 343.			
175	1883. 11. 1/ 1884. 1. 2*	조선 입국 보고	H. S. Parkes	G. L. G. Granville	FO 405/33; BDFA pp. 198-9; AADM pp. 374-5.			
176	1883. 11. 3/ 1884. 1. 2*	조선 입국 직전 李鴻章과 회견 보고	H. S. Parkes	G. L. G. Granville	FO 405/33; BDFA pp. 200-2; AADM pp. 375-8.			
177	1883. 11. 7/ 1884. 1. 2*	조선 입국 후 교섭경과 보고	H. S. Parkes	G. L. G. Granville	FO 405/33; BDFA pp. 202-3; AADM pp. 378-80.			
178	1883. 11. 13/ 1883. 11. 14*	선교사들의 전교, 내지여행권 명문화 청원	United Presbyterian Church of Scotland	G. L. G. Granville	FO 405/33; BDFA p. 196; AADM P. 344.		T. V. Lister 의 회신	FO 405/33; BDFA p. 197.
179	高宗二十年十月	閔泳穆 전권위임장	高宗		『구한국』13(영안 1) p. 10; FO 1080/190			
180	1883. 11. 7(高宗二十年十月八日)	Parkes와 협상에 관한 Foote의 자문	尹致昊		『윤치호』1, pp. 18-9.		Foote 자문에 대한 국왕, 왕비, 尹致昊의 대화	『윤치호』1, pp. 20-1.
181	1883. 11. 8(高宗二十年十月九日)	관세협상 결과	尹致昊		『윤치호』1, pp. 21-2.		Foote의 논평	『윤치호』1, p. 22.

번호	발신일/수신일*(음력)	문서제목	발신	수신	문서출처	번역문 출처	관련문서 제목	관련문서 출처
182	1883.11.16(高宗二十年十月十七日)	Parkes와 협상 결렬 기록	尹致昊		『윤치호』1, p. 23.		Foote의 논평	『윤치호』1, p. 23.
183	1883.11.17	영사재판권 조항의 재고를 청하는 자문	閔泳穆	H. S. Parkes	『구한국』13(영안 1) p. 9; FO 1080/191		Parkes의 회신	『구한국』13(영안 1) p. 10; FO 1080-191-4①
184	1883.11.24(高宗二十年十月二十五日)	세칙(稅則)관련 문제발생시 재협상을 확인하는 조회	閔泳穆	H. S. Parkes	『구한국』13(영안 1) p. 11; FO 1080/190		Parkes의 회신	『구한국』13(영안 1) p. 12; FO 1080-191-4④
185	1883.11.24(高宗二十年十月二十五日)	비준서 교환시 高宗의 조회에 대한 국서 교부를 청하는 조회	閔泳穆	H. S. Parkes	『구한국』13(영안 1) p. 11; FO 1080/190		Parkes의 회신	『구한국』13(영안 1) pp. 12-3; FO 1080-191-4③
186	1883.11.26(高宗二十年十月二十七日)	보호선척장정(保護船隻章程) 발송 조회	閔泳穆	H. S. Parkes	『구한국』13(영안 1) pp. 11-12		Parkes의 회신	『구한국』13(영안 1) p. 12; FO 1080-190-11~12; FO 1080-191-4⑤
187	1883.12.1/1884.1.16*	2차 조영조약 체결 보고	H. S. Parkes	G. L. G. Granville	FO 405/34.			
188	1883.12.1/1884.1.16*	2차 조영조약 관련 청국·일본 상공회의소에 보낼 서신 발송	H. S. Parkes	G. L. G. Granville	FO 405/34; AADM p. 381.			
189	1883.12.6/1884.2.1*	2차 조영조약 협상 전말 보고	H. S. Parkes	G. L. G. Granville	FO 405/34; BDFA pp. 204-11; AADM pp. 388-97.			
190	1883.12.7/1884.2.1*	속방조회문에 대한 회답 국서 요청 보고	H. S. Parkes	G. L. G. Granville	FO 405/34; BDFA pp. 215-6; AADM p. 403.			
191	1883.12.7/1884.2.1*	조청무역에 비해 상대적 불이익 발생시 재협상 약속 보고	H. S. Parkes	G. L. G. Granville	FO 405/34; AADM pp. 401-2.			
(5) 후속 조치 및 비준								
192	1883.12.7/1884.2.1*	李鴻章과 회담 보고	H. S. Parkes	G. L. G. Granville	FO 405/34; BDFA pp. 212-5; AADM pp. 397-401.			
193	1883.12.8(光緒九年十一月九日)*	Parkes와 회담 및 조영조약 관련 보고	李鴻章	總署	『中日韓』3, 문서번호 788, p. 1227; 『李鴻章』33, 信函 5, G9-11-014, p. 331.			
194	1883.12.16/1884.2.14*	영사재판권의 조속한 시행 건의	H. S. Parkes	G. L. G. Granville	FO 405/34; BDFA p. 216.			
195	1883.12.16/1884.2.14*	조선 총영사직 설치 건의	H. S. Parkes	G. L. G. Granville	FO 405/34; BDFA pp. 216-9; AADM pp. 410-2.			

번호	발신일/수신일*(음력)	문서제목	발신	수신	문서출처	번역문 출처	관련문서 제목	관련문서 출처
196	1883. 12. 17/ 1884. 2. 14*	高宗 알현시 교지(教旨)와 답사(答辭) 보고	H. S. Parkes	G. L. G. Granville	FO 405/34; BDFA p. 219.			
197	1883. 12. 31/ 1884. 2. 28*	2차 조영조약의 조항별 분석 보고	H. S. Parkes	G. L. G. Granville	FO 405/34; BDFA p. 219-28; AADM p. 419.			
198	1883. 12. 31/ 1884. 2. 28*	청국의 종주권에 관한 陳樹棠 포고문 보고	H. S. Parkes	G. L. G. Granville	FO 405/34; AADM pp. 432-3.			
199	1884. 1. 2(光緒九年十二月五日)*	2차 조영조약문에 속방 관계 조항 누락 보고	邵友濂	總署	『中日韓』3, 문서번호 798, p. 1311.			
200	1884. 1. 8(光緒九年十二月十一日)	조영조약문 내 속방 관계 명문화에 관한 조회	總署	李鴻章	『中日韓』3, 문서번호 801, p. 1317.		李鴻章의 회신	『李鴻章全集』33, 信函 5, G9-12-016, pp. 344-5.
201	1884. 1. 19	회답 국서의 의장(意匠)에 관한 건의	H. S. Parkes	G. L. G. Granville	FO 405/34; AADM p. 467.			
202	1884. 2. 15	여왕의 비준서 및 국서 발송 예정 통보	G. L. G. Granville	H. S. Parkes	FO 405/34; AADM p. 414.			
203	1884. 2. 23/ 1884. 2. 28*	조청무역에서 관세율 특혜가 있을 경우 독일 정부의 방침 전달	Münster	G. L. G. Granville	FO 405/34; AADM pp. 443-4.		Granville의 회신	FO 405/34; AADM p. 453
204	1884. 2. 27	Parkes의 비준서 교환 전권위임장		Queen Victoria	『구한국』13(영안 1) p. 14.			
205	1884. 2. 28	영국 비준서		Queen Victoria	『구한국』13(영안 1) p. 15.			
206	1884. 3. 17	조선 총영사 임명장	G. L. G. Granville	W. G. Aston	FO 405/34; AADM p. 462.			
207	1884. 3. 17	조선 부영사 임명장	G. L. G. Granville	W. R. Carles	FO 405/34; AADM p. 462.			
208	1884. 3. 27	2차 조영조약의 비준을 알리는 조회	H. S. Parkes	閔泳穆	『구한국』13(영안 1) pp. 15-6. [漢譯文]『구한국』13(영안 1) p. 16.			
209	1884. 3. 31/ 1884. 5. 20	대원군 귀국설 및 조선의 비준서 교환 거부설 보고	H. S. Parkes	G. L. G. Granville	FO 405/34; AADM pp. 474-6.			
210	1884. 4. 7(高宗二十一年三月十二日)	2차 조영조약의 비준 의사를 확인하는 조회	閔泳穆	H. S. Parkes	『구한국』13(영안 1) p. 16.			
211	1884. 4. 16/ 1884. 5. 26*	조선의 비준의지 보고	H. S. Parkes	G. L. G. Granville	FO 405/34; AADM pp. 476-9.			
212	1884. 4. 21(高宗二十一年三月二十六日)	영접관 파견을 알리는 조회	金炳始	H. S. Parkes	『구한국』13(영안 1) p. 17.			
213	1884. 4. 24(高宗二十一年三月二十九日)	내지여행권 조항에 관한 高宗과 Foote의 대화	尹致昊		『윤치호』1, p. 60.			

번호	발신일/수신일*(음력)	문서제목	발신	수신	문서출처	번역문 출처	관련문서 제목	관련문서 출처
214	1884. 4. 28.	Aston 일행 파견 통보	H. S. Parkes	金炳始	『구한국』13(영안 1) pp. 18.		金炳始의 회신	『구한국』13(영안 1) pp. 18-9.
215	1884. 4. 28/ 1884. 5. 2*	비준 완료 보고	H. S. Parkes	G. L. G. Granville	FO 405/34; AADM p. 472.			
216	1884. 4. 28/ 1884. 6. 27*	2차 조영조약 비준서 교환 보고	H. S. Parkes	G. L. G. Granville	FO 405/34; AADM pp. 41882-3.			
217	1884. 4. 30	高宗 알현시 수행원 명단	H. S. Parkes	金炳始	『구한국』13(영안 1) pp. 19-20.			
218	1884. 4. 30(高宗二十一年四月六日)	高宗 알현 일시 통보	金炳始	H. S. Parkes	『구한국』13(영안 1) p. 20.			
219	1884. 5. 1(高宗二十一年四月七日)	비준서 교환시 축사	金炳始	H. S. Parkes	『구한국』13(영안 1) p. 21.		Parkes의 답사	『구한국』13(영안 1) pp. 21-2.
220	1884. 6. 3(光緒十年五月十日)*	2차 조영조약 비준서 교환 통보	高宗	總署	『中日韓』3, 문서번호 849, p. 1364.			

			관계자료					
1	1882. 6. 6(高宗十九年四月二十一日)	1차 조영수호통상조약			『朝英通商章程』(奎 23358)			
2	1883. 11. 26(高宗二十年十月二十七日)	2차 조영수호통상조약			FO 94/697; 『朝英通商條約』(국립중앙도서관, B10234-2-10); 『朝英通商條約』(奎23364); 『실록』20년 10월 27일			
3	1882. 12. 19	Hertslet Memorandum (1882. 12. 19)	E. Hertlset		FO 881/4695; BDFA pp. 1-39			

동북아역사 자료총서 122
近代韓國外交文書 5

2012년 12월 10일 초판 1쇄 인쇄
2014년 11월 24일 초판 2쇄 발행

편 근대한국외교문서편찬위원회
펴낸이 김학준
펴낸곳 동북아역사재단

등록 제312-2004-050호(2004년 10월 18일)
주소 서울시 서대문구 통일로 81(미근동 267) 임광빌딩
전화 02-2012-6065
팩스 02-2012-6189
e-mail book@nahf.or.kr

ⓒ 동북아역사재단, 2014

ISBN 978-89-6187-288-1 94910
　　　978-89-6187-444-1 세트

*이 책의 출판권 및 저작권은 동북아역사재단이 가지고 있습니다.
　저작권법에 의해 보호를 받는 저작물이므로 어떤 형태나 어떤 방법으로도
　무단전재와 무단복제를 금합니다.
*책값은 뒤표지에 있습니다. 잘못된 책은 바꾸어 드립니다.